C000148054

TRIUMPH REGAINED

TRIUMPH REGAINED

The Vietnam War, 1965–1968

MARK MOYAR

Encounter
BOOKS

New York • London

First edition published in 2022 by Encounter Books,
an activity of Encounter for Culture and Education, Inc.,
a nonprofit, tax-exempt corporation.
Encounter Books website address: www.encounterbooks.com

The maps that appear in this volume are courtesy of Cambridge University Press.

Manufactured in the United States and printed on
acid-free paper. The paper used in this publication meets
the minimum requirements of ANSI/NISO Z39.48-1992
(R 1997) (*Permanence of Paper*).

FIRST EDITION

LIBRARY OF CONGRESS CATALOGING-IN-PUBLICATION DATA

Names: Moyar, Mark, 1971– author.
Title: Triumph Regained : the Vietnam War, 1965–1968 / Mark Moyar.
Description: First edition. | New York, NY : Encounter Books, 2022.
Includes bibliographical references and index. |
Identifiers: LCCN 2022008881 (print) | LCCN 2022008882 (ebook)
ISBN 9781641772976 (hardback) | ISBN 9781641772983 (ebook)
Subjects: LCSH: Vietnam War, 1961-1975. | Vietnam—History—1945-1975.
Classification: LCC DS557.7 .M773 2022 (print) | LCC DS557.7 (ebook)
DDC 959.704/3—dc23/eng/20220315
LC record available at https://lccn.loc.gov/2022008881
LC ebook record available at https://lccn.loc.gov/2022008882

1 2 3 4 5 6 7 8 9 20 22

For Trent

CONTENTS

PREFACE

Work on this history began at the end of the twentieth century, when it was conceived as a one-volume account of the Vietnam War derived from other, more narrowly focused histories. The initial research revealed a need for a much larger exploration of primary sources than originally anticipated, which turned into a quest so lengthy as to necessitate division of the history, with the first volume ending in July 1965. This book, the second volume of what will be a trilogy, picks up the story in August 1965 and continues to the end of 1968 with the conclusion of Lyndon B. Johnson's presidency.

Triumph Regained, like its predecessor *Triumph Forsaken*, is based on sources from all sides of the conflict. As before, Merle Pribbenow provided translations of hundreds of informative documents, memoirs, and histories from the North Vietnamese and South Vietnamese sides. This book rebuts the "orthodox" school of Vietnam War history, which views America's involvement in the war as wrongheaded and unjust. It largely supports the revisionist school, which deems the war a worthy but improperly executed enterprise, because the facts led it there. Many of the book's major points have been made by the war's participants or historians but with less supporting evidence and analysis; others are new.[1]

As in *Triumph Forsaken*, the Vietnamese are central actors in the story. Pribbenow's translations and the research of several American and Vietnamese historians have made it possible to understand North and South Vietnamese perspectives much more fully than was possible in decades past.[2] The Vietnamese on both sides of the conflict clash not only with each other but with their great-power allies and their own Vietnamese allies. Vietnamese actions often influence, guide, or override the actions of the United States, China, and the Soviet Union.

The political turmoil in South Vietnam that was central to the first volume is absent from the period covered in this book, except for a brief and spectacular return in the spring of 1966. Because the United States has now been committed fully to the war, Asia's geopolitics are less important in how they influence American strategy than in how they are influenced by it. That influence is felt early on, in Indonesia during the fall of 1965, and continues with the ongoing competition among the great powers, namely the United States, the Soviet Union, and China.

By barring the path to Communist expansion on the Southeast Asian mainland, the American stand in South Vietnam emboldened Indonesia's military leaders to thwart the Communist putsch of October 1, 1965, and obliterate the Indonesian Communist Party. This turn of events irrevocably changed the complexion of Southeast Asia and inoculated its most strategically valuable country against the influences of Communism and China.[3] The upheaval in Indonesia and the thwarting of North Vietnamese ambitions by America's intervention in South Vietnam caused China's Mao Zedong to turn inward in his search for enemies, leading to the Great Proletarian Cultural Revolution. Commencing in the summer of 1966, the Cultural Revolution was to kill several million Chinese citizens. It would sap China's enthusiasm for exporting revolution and diminish the economic, diplomatic, and military power it could project abroad.

During the period covered by this volume, both the Chinese and the Soviets continued to share the view of their North Vietnamese allies that the Vietnam War was a pivotal contest between Communism and capitalism. Both showered the North Vietnamese with aid to further the cause of Communism and to bolster their own claims to preeminence in the Communist world. Repeated North Vietnamese flirtation with both suitors exacerbated the jealousies and antagonisms among all three.[4]

Although these changes did serious damage to the prospects for Communism in Southeast Asia, the Communist threat to the region remained high. The Johnson administration still maintained that a rapid withdrawal from South Vietnam would cause a loss of confidence in the United States so severe that the region's other countries would bow to the Communist powers or succumb to them by political or military means. That judgment proved correct.[5]

On August 18, 1965, American and North Vietnamese forces fought their first major battle, at the village of Van Tuong. American air and artillery strikes decimated large North Vietnamese forces in this battle and several that followed soon after. Demonstrations of American superiority in firepower and mobility compelled Hanoi to cancel its plans to seize Saigon, and to pursue a strategy of protracted attrition aimed at breaking America's will. North Vietnam's most famous general, Vo Nguyen Giap, advocated reliance on guerrilla tactics to inflict the casualties, but the majority of the North Vietnamese committee in charge of military strategy sided with General Nguyen Chi Thanh, the general in command of the war in the South, who favored large conventional battles.

The top American commander, General William Westmoreland, also adopted a strategy that emphasized attrition of enemy forces through combat but for the purpose of eroding the enemy's capabilities rather than its will. By depleting North Vietnam's military forces, Westmoreland intended to buy time for the rejuvenation of the South Vietnamese government and the reassertion of governmental control over South Vietnam's villages. Westmoreland's primary tactical instrument was the "search and destroy" operation. American ground forces looked far and wide for enemy troops and exploited superior American firepower and mobility to annihilate any units they could find. While American forces hunted for large enemy troops, South Vietnamese forces focused on counterinsurgency—the security, governance, and development activities required to wrest control of South Vietnam's villages from the Viet Cong insurgents.[6]

Westmoreland ordered his commanders to conduct search-and-destroy operations in remote, unpopulated areas. His critics, at the time and long afterward, assailed such operations as a senseless misapplication of conventional warfare against an unconventional opponent. The criticism was undeserved. Attacking enemy forces in every corner of South Vietnam forestalled enemy attacks on vulnerable South Vietnamese targets and prevented the North Vietnamese from maintaining bases and staging areas close to the South Vietnamese towns and cities that were Hanoi's ultimate objectives. The absence of civilians freed American forces of the firepower restrictions that were in place near the civilian population. South Vietnamese civilians were spared the ravages of war, and American forces were spared the negative publicity and personal anguish caused by civilian casualties.[7]

Search-and-destroy operations also took place amid populous rural areas to prevent the North Vietnamese from taking the citizenry's rice and using these areas to stage attacks on cities or military installations. American forces seldom killed civilians deliberately, but the crossfire between powerful adversaries inflicted sizable casualties on the civilian population and compelled great numbers of people to flee their villages for safer areas. The North Vietnamese Army's practice of impressing civilians as laborers added to the toll of civilian deaths.

American search-and-destroy operations inflicted massive losses on the North Vietnamese during the period from August 1965 to December 1968. The North Vietnamese military histories cited herein, many of which have been unknown outside Vietnam until now, dispel longstanding allegations that General Westmoreland and other American leaders vastly overstated the successes of these operations in their statements and statistical representations. In addition to attaining high levels of attrition, American search-and-destroy operations wreaked havoc on North Vietnamese logistics, imposing much greater constraints on North Vietnamese military operations than historians have hitherto recognized.[8]

The only senior leaders who grossly overestimated their side's military successes were located in Hanoi. To maintain the good graces of superiors, North Vietnamese military commanders in the South exaggerated their battlefield achievements in reports to higher headquarters. The most influential North Vietnamese leaders, General Nguyen Chi Thanh and Communist Party First Secretary Le Duan, took these reports as evidence that their conventional military tactics were working and hence kept ordering commanders to fight large battles that resulted in additional large North Vietnamese defeats.[9]

Hanoi compensated for heavy combat losses by stepping up infiltration of North Vietnamese troops into the South. President Johnson responded by boosting American troop strength. Mutual upping of the ante and of casualties recurred. At times, the North Vietnamese held their losses down by hiding forces in remote South Vietnamese bases or in the sanctuaries of Cambodia, Laos, and North Vietnam. When it kept its forces out of combat, however, Hanoi could not make progress toward its strategic objectives of inflicting casualties on American and South Vietnamese forces and controlling South Vietnam's rural population.

The North Vietnamese Army's reliance on Laotian and Cambodian territory to evade battle and resupply its forces led Westmoreland and other senior American generals to urge President Johnson to send American ground forces into the sanctuaries. They wanted a strategic campaign against the North Vietnamese logistical system of the sort that the United States had conducted against the Confederacy in the Civil War and against Germany and Japan in World War II. Secretary of Defense Robert S. McNamara and Secretary of State Dean Rusk convinced Johnson to stay out of Laos and Cambodia by discounting the relevance of those countries and by raising the specter of Chinese retaliation. Enemy infiltration through those countries, they said, could be stopped through bombing and secret programs that used chemicals to stimulate rainfall and turn soil to mud.[10]

North Vietnamese sources that became available after the war have made clear that the American generals had been right about the importance of Laos and Cambodia. North Vietnamese leaders had feared that American intervention in Laos and Cambodia would devastate their war effort. Postwar disclosures also revealed that China was never interested in fighting the United States in Laos, Cambodia, or North Vietnam. American bombing and chemical programs failed to stop the infiltration.

The American bombing of North Vietnam, codenamed Operation Rolling Thunder, slowly increased in intensity and scope according to the Johnson administration's policy of gradual escalation. American generals, former President Dwight Eisenhower, and other hawks recommended intensifying the bombing and mining of North Vietnam's ports but to no more effect than in the preceding period. Robert McNamara and his "Whiz Kids" at the Pentagon repeatedly convinced Johnson to reject those recommendations, first by claiming that the actions would incite the enemy to escalate, and later, after the enemy escalated anyway, by arguing that the bombing did not impede North Vietnamese infiltration of supplies into the South. McNamara supported both of these erroneous arguments by misusing statistics and dismissing contrary intelligence estimates.

Despite its limitations, American bombing did at times cause great harm to North Vietnamese capabilities, especially after the loosening of self-imposed restrictions in the middle of 1967. North Vietnamese ground forces often avoided battle because of supply shortfalls resulting from the combination of Rolling Thunder, the bombing in Laos, and the ground war in the South. Deficits of food and ammunition increasingly caused North Vietnamese units to seek shelter in external sanctuaries. The escalation of bombing in 1967 disrupted North Vietnam's importation of food so thoroughly that the country approached starvation conditions by the late summer. President Johnson, not knowing the severity of North Vietnam's difficulties, allowed the North Vietnamese to recover from this blow when he curtailed the bombing at the end of August 1967.[11]

By alleviating North Vietnamese military pressure, American military operations gave the South Vietnamese government time and space to stabilize. In the spring of 1966, South Vietnam's leaders faced one more challenge from the militant Buddhists. As during the 1963 Buddhist crisis, much of the U.S. press corps gave unjustifiably positive coverage to the Buddhists, and U.S. officials urged the Saigon government to use more restraint and conciliation than the government preferred. Unlike 1966, however, top U.S. officials sided with the government against the Buddhists, having concluded that the Buddhists were abetting the Communist cause. A forceful response by the Ky government in June put an end to Buddhist machinations once and for all.[12]

In September 1967, Nguyen Van Thieu won South Vietnam's first truly democratic national election. Thieu, a man often underestimated by Americans both then and since, devoted great energy to the vital task of installing better leaders in the government and armed forces. Gradually he reduced restrictions on speech and political activity, accentuating the differences in personal freedom between the two Vietnams.

The North Vietnamese, who in subsequent accounts would often be depicted as supremely patient, had become intolerably impatient with the pace and results of the war by the middle of 1967.[13] They resolved to seek a rapid victory by attacking South Vietnam's cities in January 1968. In launching surprise attacks during the Tet holiday truce, they expected to catch their enemies off guard and induce the urban population to rise up against the South Vietnamese government. As it turned out, the people shunned the Communists during the Tet Offensive, leaving Communist troops to fend for themselves with only light weapons. Unable to scatter as they had in jungle fighting, the Communist forces were chewed to pieces in futile efforts to hold ground. The North Vietnamese leadership ordered large urban offensives in May and August 1968 over strenuous objections from field commanders and suffered even more calamitous defeats.[14]

The North Vietnamese siege of Khe Sanh was not a mere feint designed to divert American attention from the urban attacks of Tet, as it has almost invariably been described.[15] In actuality, it was a genuine offensive operation aimed at winning a military victory as magnificent as the Communist triumph at Dien Bien Phu in 1954. American forces frustrated the North Vietnamese ambitions at Khe Sanh by controlling the hills around Khe Sanh and directing massive air and artillery barrages onto North Vietnamese forces with the assistance of new sensor technologies. The siege force of forty thousand North Vietnamese soldiers sustained crippling casualties during the three-month contest while killing fewer than five hundred U.S. Marines.

By most accounts, President Lyndon Johnson's announcement of a bombing halt north of the twentieth parallel and his withdrawal from the presidential race after the Tet Offensive were the first steps toward American disengagement from South Vietnam. Johnson's tepid reaction to the Tet Offensive did, in fact, increase popular dissatisfaction with his leadership and may have helped convince him to forswear a run for reelection. The Tet Offensive did not, however, cause him to set the United States on course for withdrawal from Vietnam. After Tet, Johnson rejected recommendations from the liberal wing of his party to remove American troops from Vietnam and compel South Vietnam's leaders to form a coalition government with the Communists. Nor was the bombing halt that Johnson announced at the end of March 1968 a harbinger of retreat. Rather, it was temporary suspension in areas that could not be bombed effectively in subsequent months because of bad weather, and it was replaced by heavy bombing in other locations, where it damaged North Vietnamese logistics far more seriously than was known at the time.[16]

When General Creighton Abrams replaced General William Westmoreland as commander of U.S. forces in June 1968, he initially employed the same tactics as Westmoreland. The debilitation of the North Vietnamese Army that culminated in the August 1968 offensive compelled Hanoi to discontinue urban attacks and shift to guerrilla warfare, which then led Abrams to reorient American forces toward pacification. Search-and-destroy operations did not end, but they occurred less frequently because they had become less lucrative.[17]

The failed Communist offensives of 1968 and the ruthless massacre of South Vietnamese civilians in Hue in February and March of that year galvanized the South Vietnamese people into more vigorous action. During the latter part of 1968, the Saigon government prosecuted the war with a newfound intensity, enabling South Vietnam's armed forces to shoulder a much larger burden of the allied casualties than before. Broad counterinsurgency gains followed.[18]

By reducing Communist access to South Vietnam's villages, the counterinsurgency operations deprived the Communist armed forces of native Southerners. The idea that the war was fundamentally a South Vietnamese civil war had contained a degree of truth early in the war, when South Vietnamese peasants had fought as guerrillas under North Vietnamese leadership, but that truth had eroded as tens of thousands of North Vietnamese soldiers streamed into the South after the assassination of Ngo Dinh Diem, and now it had been stripped of any plausibility by the complete Northern domination of the war effort.

North Vietnam's attrition warfare was unable to break America's will by the end of 1968. America's attrition warfare failed to break North Vietnam's will but did accomplish other key strategic objectives: gaining time for strengthening the Saigon government and restoring governmental control over South Vietnam's villages. The bolstering of South Vietnam could eventually convince Hanoi to relent and would in any event permit a reduction in American participation in the war, which would alleviate antiwar sentiment in the United States and promote self-reliance in South Vietnam. The bloody attrition struggle of 1965 to 1968, therefore, was not the result of American lack of imagination or unfamiliarity with counterinsurgency, as has often been portrayed. Nor was the inability of attrition to break Hanoi's will the stunning revelation of the limits of American power depicted by critics, for the American leadership had not expected that outcome.[19]

Throughout the period covered in this book, the North Vietnamese regime faced pressure from the Soviet Union and other Communist and neutral countries to negotiate an end to the war. The Johnson administration, under pressure itself from allies and some of its own politicians, undertook several bombing pauses to entice the North Vietnamese into talks. From 1965 to 1967, Hanoi thwarted all diplomatic efforts by refusing to negotiate unless the United States first made huge unilateral concessions. While some pessimists in the North were becoming more interested in a realistic diplomatic compromise, they were overruled and in some cases arrested by North Vietnamese hardliners. Le Duan, the leading hardliner, saw no need for negotiations until North Vietnam had prevailed on the battlefield, at which point Hanoi would negotiate the withdrawal of American forces. In the eyes of the top Communist Party leaders, the American bombing pauses were indications of American weakness that ought to be exploited, not gestures of goodwill that ought to be answered with like-minded goodwill and earnest diplomatic dialogue.[20]

After the catastrophic failures of North Vietnam's three offensives of 1968, the Hanoi government became more amenable to negotiations. In October of that year, the North Vietnamese agreed to negotiate on terms much more favorable to the United States and South Vietnam than any offered previously. President Johnson agreed to suspend Rolling Thunder in exchange for Hanoi's concessions. Recent Rolling Thunder strikes in southern North Vietnam had inflicted severe damage on North Vietnamese logistics, but the approach of foul weather meant that the bombing effort would be more effective in the coming months if it were shifted to Laos, as it was in November. Whether the North Vietnamese were prepared to negotiate a peace settlement or were simply using the negotiations to obtain a reprieve from the American bombing of North Vietnam had yet to be seen.[21]

When American ground troops first entered the fray in the middle of 1965, the war was, by all measures, popular among the American people. Most retrospective accounts have asserted that public support declined sharply between 1965 and 1968 as the result of mounting American casualties, the shock of the Tet Offensive of 1968, and growing awareness that the war could not be won.[22] Opposition to the war did in fact increase during this period among highly vocal groups—particularly the elites of the media and academia—but support for the war actually rose among the American people as a whole. Although the curbing of draft exemptions in 1967 led to heightened antiwar activity and draft evasion among select segments of society, hundreds of thousands of young men continued to go into the armed forces each year as either volunteers or conscripts.

The persistence of support for the war reflected the nation's culture rather than its leadership. President Johnson deliberately avoided selling the war to the American people because he feared that arousing patriotic sentiment would drain energy from his domestic programs and hamstring his efforts to improve relations with the Soviet Union. The American people supported the war through the end of 1968 because they still viewed international Communism as an existential threat and believed that turning against the war would undermine the nation's credibility and harm the young Americans serving in Vietnam.[23] Hubert Humphrey's endorsement of Lyndon Johnson's Vietnam policy in August 1968 underscored the reality that even in the Democratic Party, the supporters of the war outnumbered the opponents.

The activities of the antiwar movement, well publicized though they were, failed to turn significant numbers of Americans against the war during this period. The movement alienated much of the American population through the bad behavior of its demonstrators, its collusion with Communists, its contempt for American culture and society, and its unrealistic proposals for achieving peace. Revulsion at the movement actually sustained support for the war among some of the Americans who were beginning to weary of the bloodshed. The extensive media coverage of the antiwar movement, however, encouraged the North Vietnamese to believe that American public support for the war was diminishing and hence encouraged them to believe that their persistence would eventually lead to American capitulation.[24]

A few days before the U.S. presidential election of 1968, Hubert Humphrey's sagging poll numbers received a boost from President Johnson's announcement that Hanoi had agreed to negotiate. South Vietnamese President Thieu promptly diminished Humphrey's bump by saying publicly that he would not participate in the upcoming talks. Thieu was motivated not by the conspiratorial whisperings of Anna Chennault, as has often been believed, but by his own calculation of South Vietnam's interests.[25] Whereas Humphrey had talked of reducing American involvement in Vietnam and making large diplomatic concessions to Hanoi, Nixon was a diehard anti-Communist whom most observers expected to take a harder line against North Vietnam if elected.

When Nixon won the presidential election, Thieu and most of his countrymen rejoiced, believing that they would have a strong supporter in the White House for the next four years. The North Vietnamese sulked, anticipating that Nixon would be more forceful and resolute than his predecessor. Nixon's vague and at times contradictory campaign rhetoric had left the world guessing as to his precise intentions, but he had privately formed strategic ideas that would guide his decisions. Having criticized Lyndon Johnson for failing to explain the war to the American people and for rejecting recommendations from American generals for bolder actions, Nixon would have ample opportunities to correct these and other errors of the past.

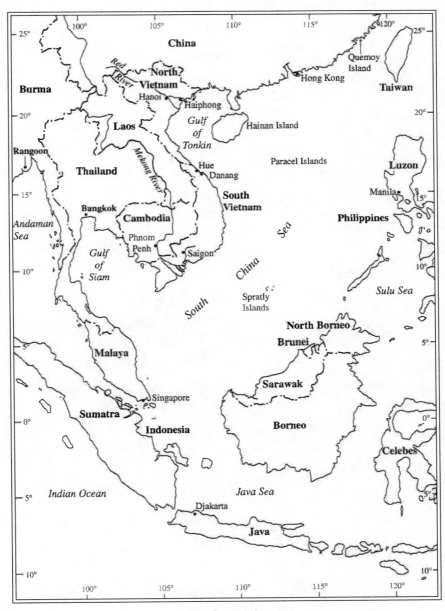

Southeast Asia

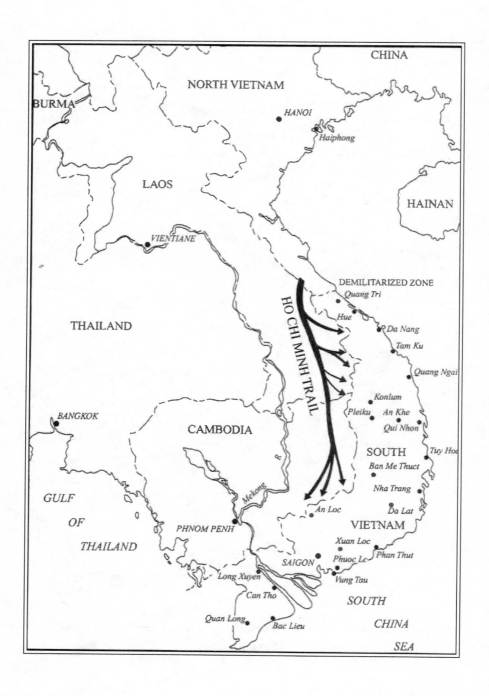

COMMUNIST (VIET CONG)

Demilitarized Zone

QUANG TRI

TRI-THIEN-HUE MR

Hue

THUA
THIEN

Da
Nang

QUANG DA

QUANG
NAM

QUANG
NGAI

MR 5

KONTUM

BINH
DINH

B 3
GIA LAI
FRONT

*Northern boundary
of COSVN area*

PHU
YEN

DAC LAC

KHANH
HOA

MR 10

QUANG
DUC

TUYEN

Da Lat

DUC

PHUOC
LONG

NINH
THUAN

TAY
NINH
(E10)

BINH
LONG

LAM
DONG

BINH
THUAN

E1

E5

BINH
TUY

MR 6

E2

U1

BA
LONG
(E9)

SAIGON

KIEN
PHONG

KIEN
TUONG

AN
GIANG

E3

E4

GO
CONG

MY THO

MR 7

DAO
PHU QUOC
(RACH GIA)

VINH
LONG

MEN
YHE

MR 2

NACH
GIA

CAN
THO

TRA
VINH

SOC TRANG

MR 3

CA MAU

CON SON

	Military region boundary
	Province boundary
Hue	Autonomous municipality

REPUBLIC OF VIETNAM

CHAPTER 1

. . .

FOREIGN ARMIES

August 1965

The village of Van Tuong lies on the seacoast of Quang Ngai Province, atop the narrow strip of rich soil that drew Vietnamese noblemen and rice farmers to the coastal plain one thousand years ago. Rice paddies stretch to the coastline, where sandy beaches alternate with sheer cliffs that plunge fifty feet into the lapping waves of the South China Sea. During the rainy season, the paddies flood to a depth of two feet or more, turning the soil into a thick mud that clings to shoes and hooves.

When thousands of soldiers from the other side of the planet arrived at Van Tuong in the middle of August 1965, the rice paddies were dry and hence easy to traverse by foot or vehicle. But interspersed among the paddies were hedgerows, earthen mounds, and marshes that presented formidable natural obstacles to any would-be conqueror. And, as the U.S. Marines were to discover when they disembarked from their helicopters and landing craft on August 18, North Vietnamese soldiers had turned Van Tuong into what they called a "combat village." By constructing fortified fighting positions and crisscrossing the area with trenches five feet deep and ten feet wide, the North

Vietnamese had ensured that the village could be taken from them only at heavy cost.

The population of Van Tuong had strong ties to the Vietnamese Communists. In 1954, many of its families had sent sons to North Vietnam, and a large number of those sons had returned to the South as trained insurgents in the early 1960s. The days of local men leading the opposition to the Saigon government in Van Tuong had, however, passed by well before the Americans paid their visit. In August 1965, the village was occupied by what the Americans dubbed the 1st Viet Cong (VC) Regiment. In American minds, the term Viet Cong implied that a unit was manned by natives of South Vietnam, in contrast to a unit designated as North Vietnamese Army (NVA), which was believed to be made up of native Northerners. But the 1st Viet Cong Regiment, like most of the other so-called Viet Cong units, was replete with North Vietnamese soldiers and fell within the same chain of command as the North Vietnamese Army units. To the North Vietnamese, it was simply the 1st Regiment.[1]

Although American engineers had begun constructing a large military base at Chu Lai, a mere seventeen kilometers from Van Tuong, the commander of the 1st Regiment was sure that the Americans would not find his unit. He was so sure that in early August he took all his battalion commanders with him to a conference of military leaders in the central highlands. When the Americans came to Van Tuong, therefore, the 1st Regiment and its four battalions would be under the command of their political officers, whose strengths lay in political indoctrination rather than combat leadership. As a further consequence, two of the 1st Regiment's battalions, the 45th and 90th, would at that time be collecting rice at a site fifteen kilometers to the south, leaving only the 40th and 60th battalions at the village.

The American assault on Van Tuong, like so many orchestrations of American military power that were to follow, originated with signals intelligence. Through the triangulation of enemy radio transmissions, American direction-finding equipment had pinpointed the 1st Regiment's headquarters at Van Tuong a few days earlier. Corroborating this intelligence was an enemy defector who told South Vietnamese soldiers that the 1st Regiment was massing near Van Tuong for an attack on the American base at Chu Lai.

Major General Lewis W. Walt, the senior U.S. Marine commander in South Vietnam, decided to attack the enemy at Van Tuong as soon as he learned of its presence. Although American combat forces had fought a few skirmishes with Communist soldiers since first coming ashore in March 1965, they had not previously engaged a large enemy unit, concentrating instead on defending expensive American aircraft and installations while their South Vietnamese allies undertook the major offensive operations. By the beginning of August, however, Communist offensive operations had depleted South Vietnam's armed forces to the point that the commander of the U.S. Military Assistance Command Vietnam, General William C. Westmoreland, had decided that American forces needed to go on offense. On August 6, he had notified General Walt that his orders had changed. Walt and his Marines were now authorized and encouraged to seek battle with large concentrations of the enemy.

General Walt assembled three battalions for the assault on Van Tuong, which was given the code name Operation Starlite. To lead the operation, he plucked the commander from the 7th Regimental Combat Team and put him in command of the three battalions. That officer was Colonel Oscar "Peat" Peatross, a twenty-five-year veteran who had earned Walt's respect as a battalion commander in the Korean War. Peatross developed a plan to converge on Van Tuong from all sides so as to trap and annihilate the North Vietnamese. One Marine battalion was to assault by helicopter, a second would land amphibiously on the beach, and a third would float in the USS *Talladega* and USS *Iwo Jima* offshore in reserve, ready to fly from helicopter pads to the shore at a moment's notice. Few of the Marines in these battalions had seen combat before, but they arrived with the confidence of well-trained and well-armed young men, certain that they could crush the armed forces of an impoverished Communist dictatorship, excited that they would escape the boredom of military routine to put years of preparation to real use.

At 5:00 a.m. on the morning of August 18, in a scene reminiscent of Tarawa, Saipan, and other epic struggles of World War II in the Pacific, ships of the U.S. Navy anchored off the coast near Van Tuong to disgorge amphibious Amtrac vehicles. Descendants of the tracked landing vehicles that had driven the Marines of World War II onto beaches studded with Japanese mines and machine guns, the Amtracs carried seven-hundred-horsepower engines that could propel their thirty-seven-ton hulks and thirty-seven passengers through the sea at a speed of eight miles per hour. The American destroyers *Orleck* and *Prichett* and the cruiser *Galveston* watched over the proceedings, their main guns pointing like eagle's talons at the shoreline as they awaited targeting data from the Amtracs.

The approach of the amphibious vehicles caught the eyes of North Vietnamese sentries on shore. The sentries rushed a report on the size and bearing of the Marine flotilla to the command post of the 1st Regiment, which was four kilometers from the coast. Based on this report, the staff at the regimental command post concluded that the axis of advance would bring the Marines directly to the command post's location. The acting regimental commander ordered 150 troops to conduct a delaying action while the command post and its staff relocated farther inland.

The small arms fire of the delaying force hit several Marines as they came ashore. One of them was Staff Sergeant Catfish Campbell, who suffered a wound in the scrotum. Evacuated to an American warship, Campbell was stitched up within a matter of hours and sent back into the fight later in the day. The amphibious battalion nonetheless had little difficulty in securing the beach. The Marines pressed forward for two kilometers in the Amtracs before encountering significant resistance, at which point the battalion slowed to a crawl while officers considered how best to press the attack.

The first American helicopters touched down at 7:00 a.m. One company of Marines was scheduled to land at each of three landing zones, dubbed Red, White, and Blue. Lacking enough helicopters to land an entire battalion at once, the Marines had to shuttle them in stages, which afforded the enemy time to move forces toward the landing zones while Marines were still arriving. At Red and White, successive clumps of Marines disembarked from UH-34D Seahorse helicopters without incident. At Blue, the first helicopters encountered no display of hostility, but the subsequent waves met heavy fire from the automatic and semiautomatic weapons of the 60th battalion, whose defensive perimeter was very close to LZ Blue. Camouflaging themselves to look like bushes, North Vietnamese troops advanced toward the landing zone unseen and then hit the Marines at close range. "We were taking fire from everywhere," remembered Lance Corporal Ernie Wallace.[2]

The Marine company at LZ Blue—Hotel Company of the 2nd Battalion, 4th Marines—sustained a considerable number of injuries and fatalities during the opening minutes of the engagement. Nevertheless, enough of its Marines reached the fringes of the landing zone to establish a solid perimeter. Helicopter gunships and fixed-wing A-4 Skyhawks and F-4 Phantoms hurried to the assistance of the Marines, loosing gushers of firepower that held the North Vietnamese battalion back.

At 9:00 a.m., the acting commander of the 1st Regiment concluded that the Americans were sending the preponderance of their troops to LZ Blue, owing to the amount of air support being marshaled in defense of Hotel company. He therefore decided to mass the 40th and 60th battalions, the entirety of his fighting strength at Van Tuong, to annihilate the Marines at LZ Blue before they could move into better defensive terrain and receive reinforcements. The 40th battalion marched toward LZ Blue in three columns to join the 60th battalion for a concerted onslaught.

While the 40th battalion was en route, the amphibious U.S. Marine battalion pushed toward the right flank of the 60th battalion. In response, a large detachment of the 60th battalion pulled back from LZ Blue to protect its flank. The movements of the American amphibious battalion spooked the North Vietnamese regimental commander, causing him to order all his units to shift from the offensive to the defensive.

The reduction in pressure on landing zone Blue convinced the commander of Hotel company, 1st Lieutenant Homer K. Jenkins, to send two of his platoons forward to the hamlet of Nam Yen 3, which he believed to be lightly guarded. Only when the two platoons reached the edge of the hamlet did they learn that scores of enemy soldiers had hidden themselves in trees and in fortified houses whose walls dropped down for firing. The North Vietnamese gunned down some of the Marines when they neared the hamlet. The remaining Marines laid poncho liners over the dead as best they could and withdrew to a berm that was dotted with trees.

Behind the berm, Sergeant Jerry Tharp gathered Marines from third platoon of Hotel company and barked out instructions for a renewal of the attack. One of the Marines listening to him was Private First Class Richard Boggia. "As we waited for Sergeant Tharp to give the command to assault, I saw him raise himself above the berm," Boggia recalled. "With a loud crack, he grabbed his chest and started pulling off his equipment to see what happened. Within a few seconds blood ran out of his mouth and he fell over."[3] Another Marine crawled to Tharp but found that he was already dead.

The loss of Sergeant Tharp did not slow the momentum of the Marines as another man was ready to step into his position. Employing tactics that had been drilled into them for months at bases in the United States, the Marines assaulted Nam Yen 3 from multiple directions. Although they suffered additional casualties in the approach, enough Marines penetrated the hamlet to give the enemy a good fight. Scattered groups of Americans and North Vietnamese engaged in close-quarter melees, with mortar rounds and grenades exploding among them in such a fashion that few could tell who was hitting whom.

If the North Vietnamese had hoped that the Americans would refrain from using heavy weapons in the presence of civilian noncombatants, they were sorely disappointed. When North Vietnamese soldiers fired at Americans from fortified positions in Nam Yen 3, American aircraft and tanks blasted the fortifications and their occupants into rubble. The Americans were not seeking to harm South Vietnamese civilians, but when forced to choose between risking civilian casualties by shooting their weapons and risking American casualties by not shooting, they chose to shoot. The same had been no less true of the Americans who had gone before them at Normandy, Okinawa, and Seoul. Like the civilians of France, Japan, and South Korea, the residents of Nam Yen 3 would subsequently be treated by American medical personnel in large numbers for wounds inflicted by American weapons that had been aimed at hostile combatants. The American firepower eventually broke the resistance of the North Vietnamese, enabling the Marines to take control of Nam Yen 3.

India company of 3rd Battalion, 3rd Marines, one of the companies that had driven ashore in the Amtracs, took the fortified hamlet of An Cuong 2 later in the morning. In this case, too, American tanks dislodged sizable numbers of North Vietnamese defenders from fortifications and trenches. After the firing subsided, one of the Marines began shooting enemy bodies strewn across the ground in case any were feigning death. One faker had already caused injury to two Americans. The company commander, Captain Bruce Webb, ordered the Marine to desist, on the grounds that firing bullets into the bodies was inhumane. A few minutes later, a North Vietnamese soldier who had been playing dead hurled a grenade at Captain Webb, killing him.

A column of five Amtracs and three M67 flame tanks motored from the south to resupply India company 3/3 with ammunition and water. In its haste, the column drove past India company, traveling another four hundred meters until it ran into the 3rd company of the enemy's 60th battalion, which had been hiding in hedgerows and thickets on the side of the road. The North Vietnamese opened fire with 57mm recoilless rifles, mortars, and rocket-propelled grenades. Their initial volleys missed. The American vehicles circled around to the northeast and assaulted the hedgerows and thickets, a bold move but one that underestimated the enemy's firepower.

As the Americans closed within one hundred meters, North Vietnamese recoilless rifles knocked several Amtracs out of action. The assault was halted so that the undamaged vehicles could come to the assistance of those that had been disabled. The officer commanding the rescue column, Lieutenant Robert F. Cochran Jr., dismounted and methodically organized the evacuation of the immobilized Amtracs and tanks, then positioned the other vehicles into a defensive formation. Once he had completed these tasks, he returned to one of the Amtracs. Rather than having the ramp lowered, which would have endangered the men inside, Cochran climbed up the side to crawl through the crew hatch. Hostile fire struck him while he was scaling the vehicle. Mortally wounded, he fell into the dust.

The remaining Amtracs and tanks stayed put, which made it easier for both them and their adversaries to score hits. North Vietnamese heavy weapons quickly disabled most of the vehicles, aside from one tank that fled the scene in what the battalion's executive officer subsequently adjudged an act of cowardice. Some of the surviving Marines disembarked, took up positions in the rice paddy, and used their assault rifles to pick off North Vietnamese infantrymen who attempted to close in on the smoking vehicles.

An Amtrac radio operator transmitted a message stating that the column was surrounded and about to be overrun. So panicked was he during his pleading that he held down the call button, which prevented him from hearing the operator on the other end asking questions about the unit's location. He kept his finger on the call button for over one hour.

Answers to those questions would have been of great assistance to the two infantry companies that Colonel Peatross had sent to rescue the supply column. Forging ahead based on vague estimates of the column's position, both companies stumbled into large enemy forces and were caught up in intense fighting that kept them from venturing any farther that afternoon. An American account noted that during these engagements, "The Marines discovered that some of the most macho among them in peacetime became very careful when real bullets were being fired, and that some of those most reticent around the barracks were tigers in combat."[4]

In the next few hours, as Marines were incapacitated and ammunition was expended, the bark of weapons from the beleaguered supply column became steadily softer. By the middle of the afternoon, only a dozen Marines remained alive in the vehicles, some of them seriously wounded, while another five were sprawled out in the rice paddies. They had only one machine gun that still worked. Lack of radio communications left them bereft of air or artillery support.

Perceiving that American firepower had dwindled, a North Vietnamese deputy company commander summoned additional soldiers to wipe out what was left of the Marines. Organized into three-man cells, the assault troops received instructions to climb onto the vehicles and kill the occupants. Although the North Vietnamese commander could have sent one hundred or more soldiers to attack at once, he instead opted to send them forward in small groups. No record of the battle explains this fateful decision; most likely it resulted from the cautiousness that typically induces commanders to probe the enemy with small units rather than commit large forces simultaneously.

Had the North Vietnamese attacked in strength from multiple directions, they undoubtedly would have overrun the Marines. By approaching piecemeal, they permitted the Americans to concentrate their limited fire. With the instinctive tenacity of men on the verge of extinction, the small band of Marine defenders unleashed well-aimed bursts of bullets at each three-man cell that came near the Marine Amtracs and tanks.

Some of the North Vietnamese soldiers reached the American vehicles, but none were able to overpower the Marines. According to a North Vietnamese history, "When 1st Cell charged, all of its men were killed. Then 2nd Cell charged, and all of its men were killed as well. 3rd Cell launched its assault and suffered heavy losses. The following cells continued to run up next to the vehicles, but they were unable to climb up onto the vehicles because the enemy vehicles were very tall and very slippery. When some of our men managed to climb up on an enemy vehicle, they were killed or wounded by fire from the other enemy vehicles."

When dusk came, the Marines were still alive. There was, however, no sign of the relief forces that should have arrived by now. After dark, the Marines kept their fingers on their triggers in expectation of a night assault by the North Vietnamese. It never came, for the North Vietnamese had decided to depart the area during the night. The next morning, an American aircraft would spot the isolated Marines and guide Marine ground forces to their rescue.[5]

The North Vietnamese forces on the other sections of the battlefield also disengaged at day's end. The regimental headquarters ordered the 40th and 60th battalions to leave Van Tuong because of the severe losses of life they had incurred during the day. As a result of the unexpected twists and turns in the fighting, some of the American units did not end the day in the places that had been planned, leaving gaps in the American cordon through which enemy soldiers could slip. Some of the survivors from the 40th and 60th battalions escaped from Van Tuong through these gaps, while others fled through an intricate tunnel system. The Americans spotted one group of a hundred men trying to flee by boat, and the main guns of the USS *Orleck* and USS *Galveston* riddled them with heavy shells. A similarly sized group was fleeing overland when the Americans sighted them in the open and summoned Marine aircraft to plaster them with napalm and rockets.

The headquarters of the North Vietnamese Army's 1st Regiment did not, however, intend to end the battle. Its 45th battalion, which had been informed of the fighting and was on its way to Van Tuong, received orders to attack the Marines upon reaching the village. At 0200, with all the soldiers of the 45th Battalion present at Van Tuong, the battalion's officers reported their men ready for combat. When regimental officers inspected the battalion, however, they determined that it was not yet ready. If the attack were delayed to complete the necessary preparations, the inspectors said, the battalion could get caught in open terrain by U.S. firepower after sunrise, to devastating effect. The acting regimental commander therefore decided to abort the attack and evacuate the entire regiment from the area.

During searches of the battlefield the next day, the Marines found the corpses of 614 enemy combatants. Interrogations of prisoners revealed that the 60th Battalion had been almost completely destroyed and the 40th Battalion had been badly damaged. From the stenches that persisted on the battlefield long afterward and from evidence that demolitions and air and artillery strikes had killed or trapped additional soldiers in bunkers and tunnels, the Marines estimated total enemy fatalities to be 1,430.

The North Vietnamese high command deemed the magnitude of its losses at Van Tuong to be nothing less than calamitous. Henceforth, it decreed, conventional North Vietnamese units were prohibited from maintaining bases on the coastal plain. They would instead set up camp in rougher terrain in the country's interior, where they could find better shelter from the boulder-crushing might of American air and artillery, and where they would be outside the range of American naval gunfire and amphibiously landed American battalions. From these base areas, they could march to the coast for offensive operations when the time was right.

U.S. Marine losses in Operation Starlite totaled 45 dead and 203 wounded. American officers who had witnessed previous battles as advisers to the South Vietnamese Army would not have been surprised that the Marines suffered this many casualties in such a battle. The price in blood was, however, higher than had been expected by newly arrived Marines, unfamiliar as they were with the enemy's tactical proficiency and tenacity.[6]

Operation Starlite had showcased most of the advantages that the U.S. military had brought with it to South Vietnam. Sophisticated intelligence equipment and techniques had pinpointed the forces of an elusive enemy. Helicopters, ships, amphibious vehicles, and ground vehicles had transported thousands of American troops to advantageous positions on the battlefield. Through radio communications and visual signals, American ground forces had rapidly directed the firepower of helicopter gunships, fixed-wing strike aircraft, and artillery tubes at enemy troops and fortifications.

The American strengths were not merely technological. The young American men who wielded weapons in Operation Starlite were products of a culture that had developed an aptitude for war over thousands of years. Western civilization had been carried to the American continent by the Englishmen who began settling there in the seventeenth century and was revised, nationalized, and institutionalized during the break from the English motherland. Protestantism had shaped every aspect of American culture, including those that the rest of the world deemed peculiarly American, such as rugged individualism and workaholism.

The giant hands of geography and climate had also helped sculpt the American nation and its approach to war as well as giving each of its regions unique cultural contours. Migrations across the harsh western frontier had fostered a spirit of pragmatic innovation, a readiness to use overwhelming force to resolve disputes, and a contempt for intellectuals and distant politicians and other would-be elites. The Americans who set down in the vast flatlands of the Midwest had developed, in the sedentary diligence of agricultural life, pronounced habits of moderation, agreeableness, and provincialism. Along the Atlantic and Pacific seaboards, the oceans had drawn Americans toward seafaring, trade, international travel, and foreign ideas. In the south, the need for agricultural labor capable of withstanding pestilence and heat had driven the importation of slaves from Africa, resulting ultimately in the region's devastation in the Civil War. That epochal event had ended slavery but had done little to change the white south's hostility to racial egalitarianism or its fondness for the use of force.

Only just now, one hundred years after the Civil War, was the white population of the United States beginning to integrate blacks into its society, and nowhere was that effort progressing as swiftly as in the military. In prior times of war, the U.S. armed forces had made cohesive fighting units from assorted young men of German, Irish, Italian, Jewish, Mexican, Chinese, and Polynesian ethnicities, relying upon the rigors and tribulations of military service to strengthen the bonds of common national identity. Now the U.S. armed forces were adding blacks into the military melting pot. Colin Powell, who served two tours in Vietnam and later became the first black to serve as chairman of the Joint Chiefs of Staff and secretary of state, recalled that the military appealed to him as a young man because its meritocracy and indifference to racial and ethnic identity provided blacks unparalleled opportunities for advancement and leadership. "You could not name, in those days, another profession where black men routinely told white men what to do and how to do it," Powell recounted.[7]

The Americans of the 1960s differed by region in their attitudes toward trade, diplomacy, government spending, and war, but they were unified by their faith in God and country. 97 percent of Americans surveyed in 1965 believed in God, and 93 percent identified themselves as Christian, while only 2 percent did not identify with a religion. Three in four Americans believed in life after death, an especially important belief for Americans preparing to wage war.[8] Polling companies did not produce surveys on patriotic sentiment in 1965, but by all accounts national pride was high. Americans young and old shared a common respect for the Founding Fathers, Paul Revere, the Constitution, the American flag, Davy Crockett, D-Day, and apple pie.

The young men of the 1960s had been reared on America's struggles, sacrifices, and triumphs in World War II. As boys, they had found role models in the movies of John Wayne and Robert Mitchum, the books of Audie Murphy and Richard Tregaskis, and the stories of fathers and uncles who had fought in Europe or the Pacific. They had spent holidays watching veterans parade down Main Street, wearing uniforms and medals that testified to patriotism and manliness. Many of them volunteered for the military because they considered it a duty and an honor for a man to risk his life for his country. That sentiment was particularly strong in the west and south, owing to the high esteem for the military among the descendants of frontiersmen and Confederates, though it could also be found in regions where martial culture was less in evidence. Among the young men who were not excited enough about automatic weapons and jungle combat to join the armed forces voluntarily, some entered the military through conscription, which had been introduced in 1940 and had continued at reduced levels during the periods of peace before and after the Korean War.

Americans were also united in their confidence that their political principles transcended ethnic and cultural boundaries and were worthy of adoption in every corner of the world. They differed on whether the United States should actively coerce others into adoption or only seek to persuade them, but that was mainly a detail for government officials to work out. Although the attention of the American people to international affairs had been known to wane in times of tranquility, Americans came together to launch overseas expeditions in the face of mortal threats. In the middle of the 1960s, international Communism was widely recognized as such a threat by liberals as well as conservatives, Democrats as well as Republicans. Few had voiced objections when Lyndon Johnson began deploying a massive expeditionary force to Vietnam in the first half of 1965.

National zeal made it possible to mobilize Americans for large military ventures on the other side of the world. During America's rise to global primacy in the first half of the twentieth century and the ensuing interventions in Korea and Vietnam, the United States had shown that it could project military power farther, faster, and in greater quantities than any nation or empire in history. The U.S. military did not always have as much finesse as its opponents, but it always had more weapons thanks to its gigantic industrial base. When faced with opponents of considerable willpower and capabilities, such as the Germans and Japanese in World War II, the United States could overpower them by weight of numbers and perseverance.[9]

The actions of the Americans at Van Tuong reflected the cultural norms of the U.S. military, many of which had been transposed from civilian society. American officers made sound decisions on the battlefield because they had been chosen based on merit rather than social status or personal connections. American troops heeded the orders of officers because military training had imbued them with respect for authority. The ability of American personnel to operate sophisticated equipment depended upon behaviors and skills that had been inculcated through education and training. It was prolonged training in tactics and weapons that enabled the American ground units at Van Tuong to fight effectively when air power and artillery could not be summoned.

Very few of the other nations of the day could assemble anything approaching the military capabilities of the United States. Only a handful had mastered the use of advanced technologies like the helicopter and the aircraft carrier. The military organizations of most countries outside the West trailed far behind the United States in leadership, discipline, and military professionalism, which explained why the United States had never faced a serious military challenge from those countries. In many societies, loyalty to family still trumped loyalty to the nation and its armed forces, with the result that powerful families influenced officer selection to their own advantages and soldiers ran away when confronted by dangerous foes. Cultures that did not value military service or technological innovation were unable to produce military organizations that deployed armed forces with state-of-the-art equipment and training.[10]

In recent decades, though, a small number of Asian countries had come close to Western standards in the human dimensions of military effectiveness by importing cultural ideas and military expertise from Western nations and the Soviet Union. These had been the countries with whom the United States had become enmeshed in prolonged warfare. Japan had been the first, its forces inflicting several spectacular defeats on the Americans in 1941 and 1942 before succumbing to America's military juggernaut and its nuclear weapons. China and North Korea had followed, battling the United States for three years over the Korean Peninsula. North Vietnam came next. In responding to these challenges, the United States had imparted elements of its own military culture to Asian allies.

The Vietnamese Communists had built formidable armed forces in North Vietnam, with extensive assistance from their Chinese and Soviet allies. Stern and industrious, the people of North Vietnam made soldiers of such high quality that European observers referred to them as "the Prussians of Asia." The North Vietnamese included the inhabitants of Tonkin, the northern region of the Vietnamese land mass, as well as those living in the northern half of Annam, the central region. Like all Vietnamese, they were the progeny of Chinese civilization, guided by Confucian precepts. Their Confucian heritage, however, had been beaten down by the North Vietnamese leadership, whose ideological convictions drove them to purge the culture of allegedly backward values like loyalty to family and concern for private property. North Vietnam's rulers nonetheless retained elements of tradition that could motivate the North Vietnamese population to sacrifice for the state and the world revolution. One such tradition was community solidarity, which was unusually strong among the Tonkinese and Annamese. Another was nationalism, a force that Marxist-Leninists had to handle gingerly because of its bourgeois origins and the willingness of Communist renegades like Yugoslavia's Tito to compromise revolutionary internationalism for nationalist reasons.

Intent on unifying greater Vietnam under Communist rule, Hanoi had for several decades sought to obtain the allegiance of people born south of the seventeenth parallel in what was now South Vietnam. The Vietnamese Communists had been most successful in the rural villages, where poorly educated peasants were easily swayed by political organizers who spoke well and killed their rivals from the South Vietnamese government. Communist recruiters had enjoyed far less success in South Vietnam's towns and cities, owing to the continuous presence of government security forces and the anti-Communist nationalism of much of the urban populace.[11]

The government of South Vietnam presided over Cochinchina, the southern third of Vietnam, as well as the southern half of Annam. For most of its history, the peoples of these lands had been ruled by a different government than the Vietnamese to their north, and geography and political developments had given them distinct regional cultures and identities. The Vietnamese of Cochinchina were more individualistic and more prone to infighting than their Tonkinese and Annamese counterparts, though they could be rallied to a common cause by perilous circumstances and strong leaders.

In 1965, South Vietnam's population possessed a common cause, anti-Communist nationalism. They faced a grave mutual peril in a radicalized North Vietnam that was infiltrating entire army divisions into their country. Generals Nguyen Van Thieu and Nguyen Cao Ky, who had just taken charge of the South Vietnamese government, were striving to supply leadership after the two years of political instability produced by the assassination of President Ngo Dinh Diem, but they had yet to repair the damage caused by repeated purges of military and civil leaders.

Although the war in Vietnam would ultimately be decided on land, it was made possible by naval power. The United States was the only nation in the world that had the naval strength to deploy and sustain several hundred thousand heavily armed troops on the other side of the planet. That it possessed such a navy was the result of an industrial base that could produce hundreds of sophisticated ships, a public that was supportive of seafaring and distant military expeditions, and political and military institutions that channeled national wealth and will into maritime operations.

The most powerful military asset that the Americans shipped across the Pacific was air power. Fleets of American helicopters and fixed-wing aircraft provided revolutionary capabilities in warfare's most fundamental dimensions: firepower and mobility. The small North Vietnamese Air Force was incapable of contesting American control over the skies of South Vietnam, and North Vietnamese employment of antiaircraft fire on South Vietnamese battlefields was severely constrained by the herculean labor required to transport antiaircraft weapons and ammunition without motor vehicles.

The North Vietnamese, however, had advantages that to some extent offset the advantages of American air power. Most notable was their excellence in moving undetected by foot, which allowed them to mass for the attack so quickly that even strike aircraft and airmobile infantry might struggle to respond in time. This asymmetry would do much to shape the strategies and tactics on both sides of the ground war into which the United States had just inserted its Army and Marine Corps.

The American victory at Van Tuong provided the first vindication of General Westmoreland's new strategy for the employment of U.S. ground forces in combat. That the Marine Corps had won the battle tinged the victory with irony, for senior Marine commanders harbored serious misgiving about Westmoreland's strategy and the tactics that went with it. At the time of Operation Starlite, in fact, Westmoreland was toiling strenuously to convince the Marine leadership of the virtues of his approach.

Westmoreland's strategy was often called a "strategy of attrition" because it emphasized the attrition of enemy forces through offensive military operations. The label, however, obscured the strategy's other major components, which included the bolstering of South Vietnamese capabilities and the reassertion of South Vietnamese control over the rural population. In Westmoreland's view, control of the rural population was essential to success, and it required the strengthening of the South Vietnamese government and its security forces, including militia and police forces that had been designed for rural pacification. "The ultimate aim," Westmoreland declared in a directive to commanders, "is to pacify the Republic of Vietnam by destroying the VC—his forces, organization, terrorists, agents, and propagandists—while at the same time reestablishing the government apparatus, strengthening GVN military forces, rebuilding the administrative machinery, and re-instituting the services of the government."[12]

Attrition assumed central importance at the beginning because it was required to stop the North Vietnamese Army's onslaught and would be required thereafter to provide protection for pacification and nation building. U.S. combat units and select South Vietnamese combat units would employ search-and-destroy tactics to achieve the attrition of enemy military forces, while the bulk of the South Vietnamese forces would use counterinsurgency tactics to secure and govern the rural population. Intent on preempting the enemy, Westmoreland directed his commanders to launch many of their search-and-destroy operations in unpopulated areas where the enemy prepared before combat and recuperated afterward. "Although a commander must observe caution," Westmoreland explained, "he wins no battles by sitting back waiting for the enemy to come to him."[13]

Search-and-destroy operations would allow U.S. forces to break up the big North Vietnamese units before they could concentrate for the attack at dispersed outposts and population centers. They would damage the North Vietnamese Army's logistical capabilities and force its soldiers to squander time and supplies by moving from place to place. In addition, Westmoreland argued, search-and-destroy operations would reduce the presence of North Vietnam's conventional forces near the rural population of South Vietnam, making it easier for South Vietnamese security forces and civilian officials to assert control over the villages.[14]

Because large South Vietnamese Army operations with entire battalions or brigades had seldom made contact with the enemy, Westmoreland advocated reliance on small-unit patrolling during the search phase. He also believed that much information could be obtained from local South Vietnamese security forces, signals intelligence, and aerial surveillance and reconnaissance. Recent technologies like side-looking airborne radar (SLAR), antipersonnel radar, and infrared devices promised unprecedented opportunities for locating unsuspecting enemy troops from afar. Once the enemy was found, the Americans were to attack quickly by inserting infantry with helicopters and supporting them with air and artillery strikes.[15]

Major General William E. DePuy, who as Westmoreland's assistant chief of staff for operations played a large role in crafting the initial strategy and tactics, believed that intensive attrition of North Vietnamese forces through search-and-destroy operations would cause the North Vietnamese to throw in the towel before long. DePuy later conceded that this view was mistaken. He attributed the mistake to his failure to anticipate massive North Vietnamese Army infiltration, his underestimation of the enemy's resolve, and the White House's toleration of enemy sanctuaries in Laos and Cambodia.[16]

Westmoreland did not share DePuy's confidence that attrition alone would break Hanoi's will. As Westmoreland saw the situation, a favorable outcome to the war would require a lengthy rebuilding of South Vietnam. Westmoreland's expectation of a prolonged conflict was shared by other leading figures in the Johnson administration, including President Johnson himself, who had foreseen high casualties for years to come when he had decided to insert American ground troops into the war.[17]

Westmoreland recognized that Hanoi could limit the effects of America's attrition warfare by changing its strategy and tactics. It could send more North Vietnamese troops to the South and disperse its forces among villages and uninhabited areas, where they would be difficult to find and destroy. In a protracted war,

Westmoreland perceived, attrition would be more valuable in damaging enemy capabilities than in damaging enemy will, as it would give the South Vietnamese government time and space to stabilize politically and revive militarily.[18]

Westmoreland directed his commanders to leave village security to South Vietnamese forces because they were better suited to the task than the Americans "by language, culture, and local knowledge."[19] The South Vietnamese national leadership wanted no American troops at all in populous regions of the country, believing that Americans would face inordinate difficulty in distinguishing insurgents from civilians and that their very presence might antagonize the ethnocentric South Vietnamese. Westmoreland, however, insisted that sizable American forces operate in certain populous areas to fend off large enemy units and galvanize the South Vietnamese.[20] "In order to be effective," Westmoreland wrote in August, "we cannot isolate U.S. troops from the population nor deploy them solely in jungle areas, where they can be bypassed and ignored by the VC." American forces had to be used in areas of importance to the government and the Communists, and "with few exceptions, important areas coincide with heavy population."[21]

In later years, Westmoreland's strategy and tactics would become the object of widespread derision, among both Americans who saw the war as utterly reprehensible and Americans who wanted the United States to win. In truth, Westmoreland's strategic and tactical formulations reflected a sound appreciation of Vietnam's recent events and present realities. Many of those events and realities were opaque to the outside world at the time and would remain so for many decades afterward.

Westmoreland's critics assailed his emphasis on attrition by contending that the tally of enemy casualties had little meaning in a war that was essentially a struggle for the loyalties of the civilian population. That claim would have had some validity in 1960 or 1963, when the enemy was waging a low-intensity guerrilla war in the countryside. Hanoi's shift to high-intensity conventional warfare in 1965 had rendered it obsolete, for troop numbers were paramount in such a war, as indeed they have been in most clashes of conventional armies since ancient times. The two military activities most vital to North Vietnam's ultimate objective of conquering South Vietnam, the destruction of opposing forces and the capture of cities, required great numbers of troops.

Search-and-destroy operations were essential to protecting South Vietnamese counterinsurgency personnel from the enemy's conventional forces. The freedom of movement enjoyed by Communist conventional units in 1964 and the first half of 1965 had permitted those units to obliterate the South Vietnamese village administrators and militia units that had competed with insurgent cadres and guerrillas for control of the population. A report from the U.S. Mission intelligence committee in July 1965 had concluded that counterinsurgency had made "steady if uneven progress" in areas where "the VC have not intervened with large main force elements." By contrast, "whenever and wherever the VC have the initiative and greater relative strength, particularly in main force elements, and are prepared to commit them, any local progress in [counterinsurgency] becomes virtually impossible."[22]

North Vietnamese military analysts generally viewed Westmoreland's strategy as an appropriate and effective answer to Hanoi's strategy. Search-and-destroy operations and counterinsurgency operations, they discerned, supported one another. One North Vietnamese observer explained that Westmoreland's strategy consisted of "large-scale operations attacking our bases, spring-board positions, and massed armed forces in order to create conditions that would allow the pacification program in the heavily populated areas to be carried out effectively, and on the other side of the coin, the successful implementation of the pacification program would create favorable conditions that would allow the enemy to mass large forces to mount attacks deep into our base areas."[23]

General Earle Wheeler, the chairman of the Joint Chiefs of Staff, as well as General Harold K. Johnson, the Army chief of staff, concurred with Westmoreland's strategy and tactics. General Wallace M. Greene, the Marine commandant, did not concur fully, nor did Major General Walt. As young officers, these Marines had learned about counterinsurgency from veterans of the "banana wars" the United States had fought in Nicaragua and Haiti during the 1920s and 1930s, who had taught that American forces could make effective counter-guerrillas in foreign lands. The American troops in Vietnam, Greene and Walt argued during the latter part of 1965, should spend most of their time on small-unit operations in the populous coastal regions to help protect American bases and rid the populous rice-growing regions of Communist soldiers and cadres. The South Vietnamese forces, they noted, could not fully accomplish these tasks on their own.[24]

At the outset, Walt and other senior Marines objected to prolonged search-and-destroy operations that were based only on speculation about the enemy's location. When solid intelligence pinpointed enemy forces, though, they were willing to mount search-and-destroy operations to rob the enemy of the initiative and preempt enemy attacks.[25] To those ends, Walt had authorized Operation Starlite.

During the late summer and fall, Westmoreland felt compelled to prod Walt to use his Marines more often in large, multi-battalion offensive operations in the inland jungles and mountains. Westmoreland did not confront Walt directly on the matter, but instead ordered him to undertake specific tasks that would require him to move Marines away from their beachheads.

Direct confrontation would have revived old and painful feuding between the Army and Marine Corps. Running afoul of General Walt would have been especially problematic because he was the golden boy of the Marine Corps and an American hero in his own right. During World War II, Walt had earned a Silver Star and a battlefield promotion to colonel at Guadalcanal and then a Navy Cross at Cape Gloucester and another at Peleliu. He had been selected to command the III Marine Amphibious Force, encompassing all the Marine combat units in Vietnam, ahead of all the two-star generals in the Marine Corps even though he was junior to every one of them.[26]

In Westmoreland's view, the need for search-and-destroy tactics was particularly acute in I Corps, the Marines' area of responsibility, because it was closest to North Vietnam and hence the easiest place for the enemy to infiltrate and supply big units. Unless hounded far from the coast, North Vietnamese regiments could exploit jungle-covered terrain to sneak up on the Americans and bring overwhelming numbers to bear on a military base or a city. Of greatest concern was the jungle mane of an Annamite mountain spur that came within ten kilometers of the coast at the Chu Lai plain, upon which the Marines were busily amassing men and materiel.[27]

In the late summer, Westmoreland acceded to Walt's request to use some Marines in population security, albeit under the conditions that the Marines always operate in tandem with South Vietnamese personnel and never stray far from their bases. In the heavily populated areas south and east of the Marine base at Da Nang, Walt's Marines patrolled alongside regulars of the South Vietnamese Army. At the Phu Bai base, in what became known as Combined Action Platoons, Marine squads were paired with platoons of South Vietnamese Popular Force militiamen. Although the South Vietnamese lieutenants in the militia platoons were ostensibly co-commanders with the Marine squad leaders, in practice the Marines commanded the units because Marine noncommissioned officers were generally more skilled and resolute in military leadership than the South Vietnamese officers. The Marines supplied the leadership, tactical prowess, and logistical wherewithal that the militiamen lacked, while the militiamen helped the Marines distinguish the Communists from innocent civilians and obtain information from the population. The initial successes of the Combined Action Platoons led General Walt to seek South Vietnamese concurrence in turning over more Popular Forces for the program in late 1965, which he quickly obtained.[28]

A small but vocal group of Marine officers advocated shifting most of the American combat forces from search-and-destroy operations to Combined Action Platoons, which they and a number of later counterinsurgency theorists believed would enable the United States to win the war in short order.[29] That hypothesis, however, rested on the fallacy that the Communists were still fighting a low-intensity guerrilla war. Without American combat troops constantly prowling the hinterlands to detect and disrupt the enemy, North Vietnamese Army battalions could sweep into villages with impunity and wipe out the little platoons. Large North Vietnamese units would, in fact, overrun a considerable number of the Combined Action Platoons in the coming years, and they would have overrun many more had relentless search-and-destroy operations not disrupted their marauding.[30] Because of the need to contend with the conventional forces of the North Vietnamese Army, the Marines would never allocate more than 3 percent of their manpower to the Combined Action Platoon program.[31]

American operations near the civilian population did not generate as much friction with the citizenry as South Vietnamese leaders had feared. Although some of the American troops took a disliking to South Vietnamese civilians out of suspicion that they were surreptitiously supporting the enemy, the presence of South Vietnamese personnel during most American operations and the discipline imposed by American officers prevented tensions from resulting in criminal violence against civilians in all but a few cases.[32] As Operation Starlite demonstrated, though, the South Vietnamese citizenry could and often did suffer horrific injury when American forces engaged North Vietnamese troops in the vicinity of villages.

The employment of U.S. forces in populated areas had other adverse consequences that had not been foreseen. Where American troops went, so too did members of the growing foreign press corps, and some of those journalists were willing, even eager, to produce accounts of Americans inflicting damage upon civilian property and person. The first incident occurred at the village of Cam Ne on August 3.

As a combined force of Marines and South Vietnamese militiamen approached Cam Ne, Communist machine guns and assault rifles poked out of hidden trenches and bunkers and spat bullets into the men at the front. The Marines returned fire with small arms, rockets, and flamethrowers, causing a number of huts to catch fire. In one hut, from which Communist soldiers were shooting, American projectiles killed a ten-year-old boy and wounded three other civilians. The Marines suffered three casualties before the hostile forces decided to withdraw.

After the enemy had departed, the South Vietnamese district chief directed the Marines to set ablaze any remaining huts that concealed trenches, bunkers, or tunnels. General Walt, who had flown to the scene himself, repeated this command to the Marines. Counting the structures burned during the fighting and afterward, fifty-one huts were destroyed in all.

Morley Safer, a Canadian correspondent working for CBS News, delivered a scathing and in many ways inaccurate report from Cam Ne. According to Safer, the Marines had destroyed 150 homes and had done so after receiving orders "to burn the village to the ground" if they "received even one round of enemy fire." The Americans had urged the villagers to leave their homes before they were destroyed, Safer reported, but the people did not heed them because they did not know English, a claim that gave CBS viewers the erroneous impression that civilians had been burned to death.[33]

American news organizations already had a long history of painting unduly bleak canvasses of the South Vietnamese armed forces and the senior U.S. military leaders in Vietnam, but they had not misrepresented or maligned American fighting men before. Cam Ne was the first rock through that window. For the time being, most other Western reporters took a favorable view toward the war and its combatants, much as they had in prior wars, but reporting like Safer's was to become more common as time went on.[34]

Although much of the debate over strategy and tactics in the summer and fall of 1965 was focused on the Marines in I Corps, the need for search-and-destroy operations was considerably greater in II Corps, owing to differences in terrain and enemy intentions. In the central highlands of II Corps, which fell under the purview of the U.S. Army, jungle-encrusted mountains and valleys cloaked the movement and enlargement of the North Vietnamese Army. At the beginning of August, several North Vietnamese Army divisions were preparing to lunge from the highlands to the coast on Route 19.

Westmoreland considered the North Vietnamese units in the highland province of Pleiku to pose the most immediate threat to South Vietnam's survival because he had correctly anticipated that they would attack down Route 19. If the North Vietnamese thrust reached the coast, it would cleave the country in two. For this reason, Westmoreland gave the highlands the highest priority in the allocation of newly arrived American combat forces during the summer. He sent his most mobile division, the 1st Cavalry, to An Khe, a town midway between Pleiku City and the coastal city of Qui Nhon.[35]

In western Pleiku Province, the South Vietnamese government had only one outpost left, at Duc Co. Garrisoned by militiamen, Duc Co had been surrounded by enemy forces in July. It received so much fire from North Vietnamese mortar and recoilless rifles at the beginning of August that helicopter resupply had to be discontinued.

On August 3, the South Vietnamese Army flew two of its elite Airborne battalions to Duc Co and drew up plans to open a supply artery on the ground. The paratroopers swept to the west of Duc Co to look for enemy forces and soon found them, engaging the better part of a North Vietnamese regiment for an afternoon before heading back to the outpost. Because of the enemy's numerical superiority and its possession of advantageous terrain, the airborne battalions made no further forays from the base.

One of the advisers to the South Vietnamese paratroopers was Major Norman Schwarzkopf, the man who would direct the American war effort in the Persian Gulf twenty-six years later as General Norman Schwarzkopf. "Each night we went to bed with the conviction that the camp would be overrun and we would be killed," recalled Schwarzkopf. He learned to listen for the nightly enemy mortar barrage in his sleep. "The thunk of rounds dropping into the mortar tubes was audible hundreds of yards away, and when I heard that sound I knew I had maybe eight seconds to make it in to a foxhole," Schwarzkopf attested. "Many nights I'd find myself sprinting for my foxhole without quite knowing why, but sure enough, explosions would erupt all around. In the morning we would wake up with relief and the realization that we might make it after all."[36]

In the opinion of the senior South Vietnamese leadership, reopening the section of Route 19 between Pleiku City and Duc Co required an armored task force of greater size than could be provided immediately by the South Vietnamese Army's mobile units. The South Vietnamese Joint General Staff asked Westmoreland to move U.S. forces to Pleiku City so that the city's South Vietnamese garrison could participate in an expedition to relieve Duc Co. Westmoreland obliged, sending the 173rd Airborne Brigade to the city by air.

The South Vietnamese commanders in charge of the relief mission had seen enough of the North Vietnamese to expect a large ambush of any force moving on Route 19 from Pleiku City toward Duc Co. Reviewing the terrain alongside their American advisers, they accurately predicted the place where the North Vietnamese would spring it. Preparation of effective countermeasures nonetheless remained a daunting task, for the North Vietnamese had chosen their spot in terrain that offered them huge advantages.

The South Vietnamese armored task force headed out of Pleiku City on August 8. When it reached the site of the anticipated ambush, North Vietnamese bugles and whistles pierced the air, signaling five North Vietnamese battalions to charge the column. Exploiting superior numbers, they penetrated the South Vietnamese column in several places and disabled a number of vehicles with recoilless rifles and rocket-propelled grenades. The South Vietnamese Marines and Rangers accompanying the column counterattacked with the support of American air power and pushed many of the North Vietnamese back. The lines seesawed back and forth during the afternoon.

Late in the day, the main body of the South Vietnamese task force attempted to pull back to better terrain for the night and consolidate its position. A North Vietnamese force blocked their advance, leaving them on low and very vulnerable ground. Major William G. Leftwich Jr., an American adviser serving with the South Vietnamese Marines, recounted, "Darkness descended on a confused and demoralized situation for the Government forces. They were jammed into a 200-by-800 meter perimeter with 50-odd vehicles lining the road within a tight ellipse of 1,400 men. The enemy looked down from ridge lines both east and west only 300 yards away. Heavy mortaring, if not all-out attack, appeared imminent."[37]

The North Vietnamese, however, had been hurt more grievously than the South Vietnamese and Americans knew. Heavy casualties during the day, compounded by punishing air strikes after dark, prevented the North Vietnamese from organizing a serious attack during the night. The North Vietnamese losses had become so severe by the early morning that the North Vietnamese command chose to withdraw not only the units at the ambush site but all other units in the vicinity of Duc Co.[38]

None of the available North Vietnamese sources addresses the strategic impact of this particular battle, but the slaughter at Duc Co appears to have rattled the North Vietnamese leadership. In late August, a few days after the costly defeats at Duc Co and Van Tuong, Hanoi decided to change its strategy. The rapid infusion of American forces, the North Vietnamese concluded, had put a swift conquest of South Vietnam out of reach. They therefore aborted the summer–fall offensive to capture Saigon and switched to a strategy similar to that of Westmoreland, combining attrition with efforts to control the population and build up locally recruited armed forces. The Communist forces would seek conventional battles in advantageous locations across South

Vietnam to inflict large numbers of casualties on their American and South Vietnamese enemies.[39] "Because of our lack of material strength," the Central Committee of the Vietnamese Communist Party concluded, "we are in a situation where we must use weakness to combat strength, and therefore we will require a process of protracted fighting in order to garner sufficient strength to completely defeat the enemy."

While the new strategy resembled Westmoreland's in its focus on destroying enemy military forces, it differed in that its ultimate objective was destroying the enemy's will rather than its capabilities. As the Central Committee explained, the new strategy would enable Hanoi "to exploit and exacerbate the political and military weaknesses of the American imperialists" and "crush the American will to commit aggression."[40] The Vietnamese Communists had driven out the French in 1954 by wearing down their will through attrition, and they intended to vanquish the Americans in the same way.

CHAPTER 2

. . .

DOMINO STANDING

September–October 1965

Because of Hanoi's strategic retrenchment, North Vietnamese commanders in the highlands canceled the planned thrust from Pleiku to the coast on Route 19. Forces originally assigned to that undertaking were instead to be used in a siege of the Plei Me CIDG camp. Located fifty kilometers south of Pleiku City, the Plei Me camp was surrounded by terrain ideally suited for the ambush of relief forces.

The North Vietnamese commanders predicted that the South Vietnamese Army would initially attempt to relieve the siege with one of its regiments, which they intended to destroy. Then, they prophesied, the Americans would send a battalion or more of their own combat forces, which they intended to engage in order to learn how the Americans fought. Some North Vietnamese officers argued that they should strive to annihilate several companies of American soldiers or an entire battalion. Others considered such goals unrealistic, noting that the Chinese had not destroyed an entire American battalion during the whole of the Korean War.

General Chu Huy Man, the North Vietnamese commander for the central highlands, bequeathed the Plei Me operation to the headquarters of the 304th Division. On orders from that headquarters, the 33rd Regiment of the North Vietnamese Army prepared to encircle and poke at the Plei Me camp. The 320th Regiment established ambush positions on the approaches to Plei Me.

The siege opened on October 19. Elements of the 33rd Regiment overran a tribal militia post guarding the southwestern flank of Plei Me, killing all twenty of its militiamen. Menacing attacks on the main camp followed, involving large numbers of troops who tried to show an intent to take the camp without actually taking it.

The Americans responded with air strikes, which the North Vietnamese must have expected, but the destructiveness of those strikes exceeded North Vietnamese expectations. The 33rd Regiment sustained fearsome personnel losses, and its communications systems were wrecked. Among some of the regiment's units, the devastation caused discipline to break down and troops to flee in panic. One company political officer, returning to the regimental command post with only four men left under his command, threw up his hands in a gesture of helplessness and exclaimed, "The battlefield has been turned into a wasteland!"[1]

The 320th Regiment, on the other hand, remained largely untouched in caves and mountainsides overlooking the road to Plei Me. Quietly it watched and listened for opponents to materialize from the direction of Pleiku City. Four days into the siege, the relief force appeared in the distance. As the North Vietnamese had hoped, it was a South Vietnamese force of regimental size.

A vanguard of sixteen tanks and fifteen armored personnel carriers rolled slowly down the road in front of South Vietnamese infantry until the column reached the exact spot where the South Vietnamese commander expected an ambush. The mountains erupted in fusillades of large projectiles, converging from a multitude of directions at the front of the South Vietnamese column. The South Vietnamese armor fired back in ferocious reply. American F-100 jet fighters and UH-1 Huey helicopter gunships, which had been waiting nearby, soared across the sky to shower the North Vietnamese with metal. Like a ram leading with its head, the South Vietnamese column kept the armor at the front, while the aircraft delivered their ordnance with deadly precision on confirmed and suspected North Vietnamese positions.

The North Vietnamese persisted in striking the head of the column for two hours, until they recognized the hopelessness of that tack. Rotating away from the initial ambush site, North Vietnamese infantrymen turned their fury on the supply trucks in the middle of the South Vietnamese column. Their initial assaults destroyed a considerable quantity of vehicles, including several ammunition trucks and gas tankers that caught fire and exploded. South Vietnamese Rangers and other South Vietnamese infantrymen, however, counterattacked with the support of American air strikes and threw them back. The North Vietnamese retreated as the sun set, the able-bodied bearing away great numbers of dead and wounded.

That night, the North Vietnamese mounted one last assault in the hope that the American aircraft that had mauled them in daylight would not find them in the dark. At three o'clock in the morning, a North Vietnamese battalion charged the head of the South Vietnamese column. American and South Vietnamese illumination flares quickly filled the sky with light, allowing the main guns of the South Vietnamese tanks to pepper the attackers with beehive rounds. The beehive round was an especially deadly munition, its twenty-pound cartridge containing ten thousand metal spikes that spread out in a shotgun pattern. American fighter-bombers and an AC-47 Spooky gunship fired rockets, cannons, machine guns, and cluster munitions into the assault force. The North Vietnamese attack was dead in a matter of minutes.[2]

At a temporary command post nearby, General Chu Huy Man was monitoring the tribulations of the 33rd and 320th regiments. These units had neither devastated a South Vietnamese regiment nor brought American forces to battle as he had intended, and both of those objectives now appeared hopelessly out of reach. He decided to withdraw his regiments to the Ia Drang Valley, a remote valley in western Pleiku Province ten miles from the Cambodian border. There, under thick jungle canopy, they would recuperate, reorganize, and receive reinforcements, then return to Plei Me to fight the Americans another day.

After collecting their casualties and packing their gear, the 33rd and 320th regiments headed toward Cambodia. Once the Americans realized that these regiments were leaving, General Westmoreland ordered a pursuit. He entrusted the mission to the 1st Cavalry Division, whose commander had been begging for an opportunity to hurl his forces at the enemy.

Formed in June 1965, the 1st Cavalry Division was an amalgam of the 2nd Infantry Division and the 11th Air Assault Division, the latter an experimental unit that had transported and supported itself almost entirely by helicopter. Army innovators had convinced Secretary of Defense McNamara to form the 11th Air Assault Division several years earlier by promising they could fly thousands of men over obstacles and into the enemy's rear. It was a truly revolutionary concept, and the Army succeeded in operationalizing it with the 11th Air Assault Division.

By the middle of 1965, the officers and enlisted men of the 11th Air Assault Division were thoroughly versed in helicopter warfare. Many of them, however, did not deploy with the 1st Cavalry Division to Vietnam because they either were rotating out or were scheduled to rotate out soon. Their replacements received only crash instruction on heliborne operations before heading into battle.[3]

The commanding officer of the 1st Cavalry Division at this time was Major General Harry W. O. Kinnard. During World War II, Kinnard's talents had vaulted him up the ranks at a rate unthinkable during a time of peace. He had held an officer's commission for just five years when he found himself the operations officer of the 101st Airborne Division at the pivotal Battle of Bastogne in December 1944. It was he who had suggested that Brigadier General Tony McAuliffe answer a German demand for surrender with the retort "Nuts!" Although the Germans did not understand the reply and had to request clarification, the American paratroopers relished the brazen riposte, which would come to symbolize the American grit that halted Germany's Ardennes offensive.

Upon receiving Westmoreland's pursuit order, Kinnard directed his 1st Brigade to insert infantry companies by helicopter into remote jungles outside Plei Me. He spread the infantrymen in a thin patina, which he intended to reinforce rapidly by air where his soldiers found large enemy forces. By exploiting signals intercepts, aerial surveillance, and captured documents and maps, the Americans would locate and engage the retreating North Vietnamese troop concentrations.

For the next twelve days, Air Cavalrymen landed on every side of the 33rd and 320th North Vietnamese Army regiments. North Vietnamese officers were bewildered by the ability of the Americans to find and attack their forces in the dense jungle. Unaware of the sophisticated targeting technologies available to the Americans, the North Vietnamese concluded that their units had been infiltrated by spies. Major General Hoang Phuong, whom the North Vietnamese sent to the area to analyze the fighting, recorded that the Americans "dropped troops close to our headquarters and very close to our units. Our units were broken up, dispersed." When the North Vietnamese pulled back from an engagement, the Americans "dropped troops to cut off our units."[4]

In several pitched battles, American companies encountered large North Vietnamese forces at close quarters and fought them off while the brigade dispatched reinforcements and delivered artillery and air strikes. Hundreds of North Vietnamese perished in each instance, while much smaller numbers of Americans were killed. By the time the 33rd NVA Regiment reached the Ia Drang Valley, more than two-thirds of the unit's men had become casualties. Rarely in the annals of warfare had a pursuit been so devastating in its effects.[5]

Operation Starlite and the pursuit out of Plei Me would become the most famous of the initial American search-and-destroy operations, but they were not the only ones to result in major American victories. In mid-September, during Operation Gibraltar, American soldiers in Binh Dinh Province found and engaged the training base of the North Vietnamese Army's 2nd Regiment. When half of that regiment formed up against them, the Americans established a defensive perimeter and called on strike aircraft to obliterate the North Vietnamese. American search parties located 226 enemy bodies after the battle, while the Americans suffered 13 dead and 28 wounded.[6]

By the end of October, the uninterrupted succession of American tactical victories put to rest South Vietnamese and American fears that the North Vietnamese would overrun Saigon and other major cities. They also ensured continuation of the reprieve from the political turmoil that had wracked Saigon between November 1963 and June 1965. Once the most immediate dangers had passed, attention began to shift to long-term problems, of which the most concerning was the ongoing North Vietnamese support for the war in South Vietnam via Laos and Cambodia.

The Joint Chiefs of Staff renewed their assertions that more force had to be employed outside South Vietnam's borders to curb North Vietnamese infiltration. They urged President Johnson to double Rolling Thunder strikes, from five hundred to a thousand per week, with particular emphasis on air defense sites, airfields, petroleum-oil-lubricants (POL) storage facilities, port facilities, and roads and railways connecting North Vietnam to China. Rolling Thunder had thus far done only modest damage to North Vietnamese capacity in many areas, the Joint Chiefs noted, and North Vietnam's dispersal and concealment of barracks and supply depots would decrease its vulnerability over time.[7]

The Joint Chiefs advocated the mining of North Vietnam's major harbors, where foreign ships were arriving heavily laden with Communist-bloc armaments. This escalation, the Chiefs asserted, would not provoke Chinese retaliation, because the Chinese would not want to risk a major conflict with the United States. Buttressing that claim was the continuation of Chinese public rhetoric intimating that China would fight the United States only if it invaded China.[8]

Prominent conservative congressmen of both parties and former President Dwight D. Eisenhower backed the prescriptions of the Joint Chiefs. Eisenhower told Lieutenant General Andrew J. Goodpaster, his main conduit to President Johnson, that it was "essential to go after the POL and the lines of communication" and "to go mine the harbors without delay." If the United States wanted to win, said the former supreme allied commander of World War II, then "we should not base our action on minimum needs, but should swamp the enemy with overwhelming force."[9]

Eisenhower's endorsement did nothing to persuade Johnson and McNamara to drop their objections to the military's recommendations. While the president and secretary of defense were willing to let Westmoreland decide how to run the war within South Vietnam, they believed that military actions beyond South Vietnam ran such a high risk of igniting a global conflagration that civilian authorities first had to weigh the international consequences themselves, which usually led to decisions against action. To support his case, McNamara cited intelligence estimates stating that the proposed actions "would not at this time significantly injure the VC ability to persevere in the South or persuade the Hanoi Government that the price of persisting was unacceptably high," and "may well lead to a more vigorous effort by the DRV in support of the VC in South Vietnam." He also warned that these actions could provoke Chinese air attacks.[10]

McNamara was at this time still under the influence of "limited war" theory, which had guided his thinking in 1964 and the first months of 1965. According to the theory, hostile nations could prevent local wars from escalating into global nuclear war by limiting their own use of force. If the United States refrained from hitting the North Vietnamese with massive force, then the North Vietnamese and their Chinese and Soviet backers would demonstrate restraint too. To McNamara, former CEO of the Ford Motor Company, it was not difficult to believe that the North Vietnamese leaders ran their country with the clinical rationality that limited war theory attributed to them, making decisions predictably based upon the data available. A technocrat in the mold of the Progressive movement, he was more taken by the theories of experts than by the events of human history, which had revealed recurring human tendencies for irrationality, misperception, and exploitation of weakness.

The North Vietnamese had done serious damage to limited war theory when they had escalated the ground war in early 1965, but they had not yet delivered the mortal blow. In the fall of 1965, it was not yet clear to the Americans whether the start of the bombing of North Vietnam in February 1965 had preceded the North Vietnamese offensive, and thus it was possible to believe that this offensive had been a reaction to the American bombing. McNamara seems to have accepted this interpretation, for he retained hope that by continuing to limit American military commitments and actions, the United States would convince North Vietnam to limit its commitments of North Vietnamese Army units to the South.[11]

President Johnson, being more skeptical than McNamara of academic theorists, never fully accepted limited war theory and its sunny predictions about mutual restraint. He did, however, share McNamara's wariness of escalation, based primarily on the lessons he had drawn from the Korean War, when American escalation had been followed by Chinese escalation. At this time, therefore, Johnson remained willing to let McNamara set limits on American military actions in Southeast Asia.

The intelligence community, for neither the first nor the last time, produced estimates that cast doubt on McNamara's preferred strategy. On September 22, the CIA, the Defense Intelligence Agency, the National Security Agency, and the U.S. Intelligence Board predicted in a unified estimate that intensified bombing in North Vietnam or Laos would cause Hanoi to de-escalate and negotiate and would not provoke Chinese intervention.[12] McNamara responded not by reconsidering his position but by commissioning a new estimate that would be certain to contradict the intelligence community's analysis and validate his own strategy. It was produced not by intelligence professionals but by policy experts, led by the political appointees John McNaughton and William Bundy, who shared McNamara's views on strategy and, it may be said, his very limited knowledge of Vietnam. This estimate concluded that intensified bombing and the mining of harbors would not cause favorable changes in North Vietnamese behavior and would dangerously arouse the Chinese and the Soviets.[13]

As Washington's leaves took on hues of crimson and amber and Hanoi's milk flower trees bloomed white, the first brush strokes were just appearing on the tapestry of battle between the United States and North Vietnam. Thousands more would be painted before the fates of the two Vietnams would be decided. Events in Vietnam were to affect millions of lives, in countries near and far, for decades to come. Some of the largest and most far-reaching consequences, though, arrived almost immediately, fifteen hundred miles to the south of Vietnam, in Indonesia.

During the late summer of what Indonesian President Sukarno would call the year of living dangerously, Sukarno and the Indonesian Communist Party had pulled the country further into the camp of international Communism. Speaking publicly on August 17 in the capital city of Jakarta, Sukarno proclaimed the inception of a "Jakarta-Peking-Pyongyang-Hanoi-Phnom Penh axis." The war in Vietnam, he said, was the fault of the "insane" United States. Sukarno vowed to block the Straits of Malacca in order to sever the east-west sea lanes that served the interests of "imperialism" so as to "make the lifeline of imperialism the deathline of imperialism." Turning to his own countrymen, he declared, "Those who are not revolutionary will not be permitted to exist in Indonesia."[14]

During August, Sukarno allowed Communist-inspired mobs to harass American diplomats and vandalize American consular facilities. He did not break off relations with the United States completely, although his motives in this regard appear to have been more personal than political. During his one meeting with the American ambassador, Sukarno avoided talk of Indonesia's relationship with the United States and instead requested that the Americans deliver copies of *Playboy* to him by covert means.

Sukarno explained that although he had himself banned publication of *Playboy* in Indonesia because of its indecent photographs, he enjoyed the magazine's fine movie and play reviews.[15]

Sukarno's swagger masked a rapid deterioration in his health. After several bouts of chest pain and vomiting in early August, he had asked D. N. Aidit, the head of the Indonesian Communist Party, to return immediately from a trip to China and to bring Chinese doctors with him. Aidit hurried back in a special Chinese military aircraft, Chinese physicians in tow. Upon inspecting the patient, the doctors pronounced that Sukarno "would die or become unable to rule within a short time."[16]

Fearing that Sukarno's incapacitation would incite anti-Communist Indonesian generals to seize control of the government and stifle the Communist Party, Aidit and his lieutenants devised a cunning plan to preempt the army leadership. Two army battalions and a presidential guard battalion, each commanded by officers with secret Communist sympathies, would serve as the hands of the surgeon, while a small group of covert Communist Party leaders would function as the brain. Aidit presented the plan to Sukarno, who gave it his blessing.[17]

The operation commenced at 2:00 a.m. on October 1, when the three battalions seized the palace, radio station, and telecommunications building. At 3:00 a.m., the battalions dispatched troops to raid the homes of the top seven anti-Communist generals. The plan was to arrest the generals and bring them before Sukarno with bogus accusations of treasonous plotting. According to Aidit's script, Sukarno would then relieve the generals on the spot and replace them with pro-Communist officers, ensuring permanent Communist control over the army and all Indonesia.

The kidnapping teams, however, had not been adequately prepared for the mission. As a consequence, only three of the seven generals were arrested. Three were killed, and the other, Defense

Minister Nasution, escaped his pursuers by climbing over a wall separating his yard from that of the Iraqi ambassador.[18]

Among the six who did not escape the early morning raids was the army's chief of staff, which meant that command of the army devolved to the officer immediately beneath him, General Suharto. The plotters had not targeted Suharto because they had pegged him as an opportunist who would sit back as the plot played out and embrace the new army leaders once Sukarno had installed them. Prior to this time, Suharto had demonstrated little interest in politics, aligning with neither the anti-Sukarno nor the pro-Sukarno factions within the military.[19] The conspirators, moreover, were confident that the army did not have enough troops near the city center to intervene before their work was done.

The morning's events reinforced the perception of Suharto as an opportunist. In his new role of acting army commander, Suharto had at his disposal two army paracommando units on the outskirts of Jakarta, which had escaped the attention of the conspirators because they were supposed to have deployed to North Borneo several days earlier. Pure chance, in the form of transportation snafus, had kept them in Jakarta. Suharto could have ordered the paracommandos to undertake immediate action against the battalions that had neutralized the military's top anti-Communists. Alternatively, he could have directed the para-commandos to join forces with the plotters and staked a claim to permanent leadership of the army now that his superiors had been neutralized. He did neither. Instead, he restricted his activities that morning to the gathering of more information.

The data points of greatest concern to Suharto were the allegiances of key military commanders in the Jakarta area. That information would show how many troops would be willing to take up arms for and against the three Communist-controlled battalions. Several of these commanders were maintaining a position of strict neutrality, intent on taking sides only after they were certain which side was going to prevail. Had enough of the commanders adopted this stance, Suharto likely would have held the army back, and the subsequent history of Indonesia would have been vastly different. A large number of other commanders, however, expressed a willingness to attack the three battalions. In the late morning, Suharto concluded that these commanders were sufficiently numerous to ensure a high probability of success for a counterstrike, and thereupon he resolved to crush the conspirators.[20]

The influence of events in Vietnam on Suharto's momentous decision was not readily apparent to the outside world. But the American intervention in the ground war a few months earlier loomed large in the minds of Suharto and the commanders whose anti-Communist convictions had caused Suharto to move against the putsch. If South Vietnam had fallen to the North Vietnamese by this time, numerous Indonesian military officers would have concluded that resisting Sukarno and his Communist backers was futile in an Asia where China rode the crest of a victorious wave and the United States wallowed in the trough of abandonment and defeat. The previous and subsequent statements of Indonesian military leaders concerning the relevance of Vietnam to Indonesia, as well as the later efforts of the Indonesian military to secure American assistance, lent strong support to this conclusion.[21] Although a few die-hard anti-Communists would have favored fighting the three battalions no matter the odds, they most likely would have been too few in number to rouse Suharto to mobilize large forces.[22]

One of the most important commanders who chose to side with Suharto, Brigadier General Kemal Idris of the Strategic Command, told Reuters correspondent Nick Turner a few weeks after the event that Johnson's intervention in Vietnam had been crucial in inspiring the Indonesian commanders to resist the Communists. It had shown, as General Idris put it, that President Johnson was "committed to preventing a Communist takeover in Southeast Asia."[23] Suharto himself spoke on the subject in 1970, informing U.S. government officials that the American stand in Vietnam had convinced the Indonesian generals to resist the Communists on October 1, 1965.[24]

When Sukarno learned that Suharto was moving the paracommandos toward the city center, he inserted himself more openly into the affair, in a desperate attempt to halt the wrecking ball that was now swinging in the direction of his Communist allies. Sukarno named himself the commander of the army and put a leftist general in charge of the army's day-to-day operations. He ordered Suharto to hold his troops back.

General Suharto and the commanders who had rallied to his side ignored the Indonesian president. At Suharto's direction, the paracommandos took up positions near the coup battalions. Suharto spent the afternoon and early evening employing a combination of persuasion and threats to encourage the officers of the three battalions to surrender.

In the evening, two of the three battalions yielded to Suharto. Once they gave in, the entire enterprise disintegrated. The head conspirators fled or took refuge behind Sukarno's pant legs.[25]

As news spread of Suharto's triumph over the men who had tried to decapitate the army, the armed forces and much of the Indonesian public rushed to embrace the general. President Sukarno summoned Suharto to Bogor and suggested that he relinquish control of the army, a suggestion that Suharto politely refused. Bestowing his personal protection on the plot's ringleaders, Sukarno convinced the army to refrain from immediate punishment of the Indonesian Communist Party, arguing that it had not taken part in the affair.[26]

The army, however, soon obtained a wealth of evidence implicating the Communists in the plot, and it was in no mood for lenience. Army units killed Indonesian Communists en masse, and they condoned killings of Communists by anti-Communist civilians. The deaths would eventually run into the hundreds of thousands.[27]

For several months to come, General Suharto would defer to President Sukarno on most political matters, because of Sukarno's longstanding popularity and prestige.[28] In the meantime, Suharto quietly put out feelers to the Americans to make sure they would side with him against Sukarno. The Americans responded with small covert deliveries of equipment and promises to provide additional aid once the country became overtly pro-American.[29] These assurances, and the successes of the American expeditionary forces in South Vietnam, removed any lingering doubts Suharto might have entertained about dumping Sukarno completely.

Sukarno would bring the contest to its climax a few months hence by attempting to insert Communist sympathizers into a new cabinet. Flying the cabinet members onto the palace grounds by helicopter to bypass anti-Communist protesters gathered outside, Sukarno proclaimed that the Indonesian revolution was reaching "the end of the national democratic stage and approaching the socialist stage." Anyone who failed to grasp this truth was, in Sukarno's words, a "stupid, headless chicken paralyzed by liberal thinking."[30]

The days of swaying Indonesians with extravagant socialist rhetoric, however, had passed. Suharto responded to Sukarno's effrontery by stripping him of his authority and purging Communist influences from the government once and for all.[31] The biggest domino of Southeast Asia was permanently rid of Communism.

CHAPTER 3

· · ·

WAR OF ATTRITION
November–December 1965

The soldiers of the 33rd North Vietnamese Army Regiment who survived the harrowing retreat from Plei Me staggered into the Ia Drang Valley in early November. So badly had the regiment been bludgeoned by the U.S. 1st Cavalry Division that its men were reorganized into a single battalion. Soon after their arrival, they were joined by the exhausted survivors of the 320th Regiment, which, although also heavily depleted by American firepower, still possessed enough troops to maintain multiple battalions. On November 10, the fresh 66th Regiment of the North Vietnamese Army showed up in the valley, having just trekked down the Ho Chi Minh Trail from North Vietnam.

These units began preparations for the next attack on Plei Me, scheduled for November 16. To coordinate the operation, General Chu Huy Man moved the headquarters for the North Vietnamese Army's B3 Front, the highlands command, to the Chu Pong massif. Abutting the southwestern corner of the Ia Drang Valley, the Chu Pong was a knotty conglomeration of limestone mountains, ridges, and ravines measuring roughly fifteen miles wide by ten miles long. Its highest peak overlooked the Ia Drang at a height of 2,400 feet.[1]

At this same time, General Kinnard withdrew his 1st Brigade from the hunt for the North Vietnamese in order to rest it, and in its stead slotted the 3rd Brigade, commanded by Colonel Tim Brown. On November 12, Brown received intelligence that put enemy forces in the vicinity of the Chu Pong massif and the Ia Drang Valley. He promptly ordered each of his three battalions to insert near these terrain features by helicopter. Brown assigned the area most likely to contain enemy forces, the Chu Pong massif and the adjacent valley floor, to the 1st Battalion, 7th Cavalry, because of his confidence in its commander, Lieutenant Colonel Harold G. Moore. "We believe there is a regiment of North Vietnamese Army soldiers in the area of the Chu Pong Massif," Brown told Moore. "Take your battalion in there and find and kill them."[2]

At 1030 on November 14, the first of Moore's helicopters touched down at Landing Zone X-Ray, a clearing on the edge of the Ia Drang Valley just below the massif. Shaped like a funnel, X-Ray was the length of a football field and ranged in width from forty-five yards at one end to ninety yards at the other. In its middle stood a patch of scrawny trees about as large as half a tennis court. Surrounding X-Ray were trees, five-foot-high elephant grass, and heavy brush, and mixed among the vegetation were ant hills up to eight feet in height, which offered excellent cover for infantrymen. To the west of X-Ray, trees and grass merged into the dense jungle that extended up the foothills and slopes of the Chu Pong massif.

Some of the cavalrymen in the initial landing took up positions behind trees or ant hills. Others patrolled the landing zone for hostile forces, firing their weapons at possible enemy positions. They received no return fire. Once the landing zone had been secured, Moore sent a detachment ahead toward the massif so that any enemy soldiers emerging from the mountainside could be engaged out of reach of X-Ray. Protecting the landing zone was his top priority for the day as vital men and supplies were scheduled to flow through it for hours to come. Because of demands for aircraft elsewhere, the battalion had been assigned only sixteen helicopters for transport, which could carry at most a total of eighty men and their equipment at one time. With the air base fifteen minutes away, ferrying all of Moore's men to the landing zone would take four hours, or longer if weather, mechanical problems, or the enemy disrupted flights.

The North Vietnamese Army's chances of severing the American aerial lifeline during those first four hours would have been considerably higher had the North Vietnamese commanders thought American intervention in the valley a real possibility. When the skids of the first American helicopters pressed into the dirt on X-Ray, all the commanders of the 66th Regiment were absent from their units, having gone off to survey terrain in preparation for the return to Plei Me. General Chu Huy Man was ten miles away, in Cambodia, as was the entire 320th Regiment.

The North Vietnamese commanding officer closest to the scene was Nguyen Huu An, the recently promoted deputy commander of the B3 Front. He was sitting in a command bunker one and a half miles from Landing Zone X-Ray. As soon as he learned of the American intrusion, he ordered the nearest unit, the 9th Battalion of the 66th Regiment, to attack at once. In the absence of the battalion commander, the battalion political officer was supposed to lead the unit into battle, but he proved to be a man of no mettle. Upon hearing that heavily armed Americans were disembarking from helicopters nearby, he fled the command post in a panic and lay down among the battalion's sick and wounded. With many other officers also away, a first lieutenant took charge of the 9th Battalion and organized the battalion's soldiers for the attack. Hustling down the mountain slopes, weapons in hand, the soldiers were pulsing with fear, anger, and excitement.

At 1120, an American reconnaissance squad captured a North Vietnamese soldier. Brought before Lieutenant Colonel Moore and an interpreter for questioning, the soldier told his captors, "There are three battalions on the mountain who want very much to kill Americans but have not been able to find any."[3] Three battalions likely meant at least 1,500 North Vietnamese troops. The number of Americans on the ground had by this point reached only 175, slightly less than half of Moore's battalion. To keep the North Vietnamese battalions out of reach of the landing zone, Moore sent additional men from his Bravo company toward the massif.

The forward elements of Bravo company had nearly reached the mountain slopes when, at 1220, they received the first hostile shots. After exchanging rifle fire sporadically for a few minutes, the front of Bravo company locked horns with the front of the cascading 9th Battalion of the 66th North Vietnamese Army Regiment. At 1315, second platoon of Bravo company, led by 2nd Lieutenant Henry T. Herrick, moved forward to outflank the North Vietnamese. The son of a UCLA astronomy professor, Herrick was known as an aggressive officer who drove his men hard, too hard in the opinion of some of his seniors. He had told his company commander that he aspired to win the Medal of Honor.

Herrick's platoon did not get far before it ran into the side of a North Vietnamese platoon that was rushing along a trail toward the fighting. Catching the North Vietnamese off guard, the Americans shot down numerous enemy soldiers at no cost to themselves. The rapid advance of Herrick's platoon had, however, separated it from the rest of Bravo company, and the space between them had since been filled by North Vietnamese reinforcements descending from the mountain.

Upon realizing that the American platoon was isolated, the North Vietnamese encircled it. Captain John Herren, the commander of Bravo company, ordered Herrick to take up defensive positions on favorable terrain, while the rest of the company prepared to fight their way to the platoon. Hunkering down on a knoll, Herrick's platoon fired outward in all directions at the North Vietnamese, who were congregating around the knoll at a frightening pace.

The first concerted North Vietnamese assault on the knoll involved simultaneous advances from three directions, with several platoons worth of soldiers charging each of Herrick's two machine guns. North Vietnamese soldiers killed the crew of one of the machine guns with grenades, then seized the weapon and turned it against the remaining American positions. On the other segments of the perimeter, the North Vietnamese were repulsed with help from 105mm howitzers that the 1st Cavalry Division had flown by helicopter to landing zones several kilometers away.

In the second North Vietnamese onslaught, 150 men stormed the knoll at multiple points. Herrick darted around the knoll, issuing orders, until hostile fire brought him to the ground. Bleeding from the hip, he radioed Captain Herren that he was turning the platoon over to Platoon Sergeant Carl Palmer. Herrick then told his men to destroy the signal codes, redistribute ammunition, call in artillery, and if possible attempt to break out. Although stricken with ghastly pain and on the verge of shock, Herrick told the platoon medic to help the other wounded first. To one of his sergeants, he remarked, "If I have to die, I'm glad to give my life for my country."[4] He died a few minutes later.

Sergeant Palmer had been in command of the platoon for only a few minutes when he was hit in the head and rendered unconscious. He awoke a short time later, only to be killed by an American grenade thrown by a North Vietnamese soldier. This soldier stood and laughed while the grenade did its work, but his merriment was cut short by an American onlooker who released a full magazine into the man's stomach.

By this time, most of Herrick's men had been killed or injured. All had been forced to lie flat on the ground to avoid the bullets leaping from North Vietnamese machine guns and assault rifles. With North Vietnamese soldiers still swarming around the knoll and stabbing at it from every direction, the platoon's doom appeared imminent. Yet the Americans succeeded, with considerable help from mortar and artillery fire, in frustrating the second round of attacks and then a third. Sergeant Robert L. Stokes, who took over the platoon after Palmer's death, was killed while crawling around to organize a breakout. Sergeant Ernie Savage, a twenty-one-year-old from McCalla, Alabama, assumed command, which he would retain to the end of the ordeal.

Although Herrick's aggressive pursuit of the enemy at the battle's start had cost him and many of his men their lives, it proved a blessing for the rest of the American battalion. The platoon became a magnet for hundreds of North Vietnamese soldiers who would otherwise have been drawn to the landing zone at X-Ray, where they could have thrown superior numbers against the American infantry and shot down the American helicopters. During the first hours of the fighting at the knoll, clumps of American soldiers continued to land unmolested every half hour at X-Ray, soldiers who would prove indispensable in combating the 9th Battalion of the 66th Regiment as well as two other North Vietnamese battalions that were heading to the battle from other locations, the 7th Battalion of the 66th Regiment and the battalion formerly known as the 33rd Regiment.

The deputy commander of the 66th Regiment, Pham Cong Cuu, had been at the 7th Battalion's headquarters when he received the news of the American arrival in the valley. He promptly dispatched the battalion's officers, reconnaissance personnel, and runners to survey the situation. Although X-Ray was only a few kilometers away, the reconnaissance party had trouble finding its way and did not reach anyone from the 9th Battalion or the 33rd Regiment until 1300, when it encountered wounded soldiers heading to a regimental medical aid station. The wounded men reported that behind them were numerous American troops, whom they characterized as "aggressive and over-confident." American air and artillery strikes, they said, were "vicious," and the 9th Battalion was in serious disarray.[5]

In the early afternoon, Lieutenant Colonel Moore ordered Alpha company to strengthen the flank of Bravo company and help it rescue Herrick's platoon. Alpha arrived next to Bravo just in time to block the advance of a North Vietnamese company that had maneuvered around Bravo and was heading into its rear. The opposing companies collided in a dry creek bed. American and North Vietnamese blood spilled into the creek bed as the adrenaline-charged men faced off with little cover. After the initial exchange, the Americans pulled back into more defensible terrain. The North Vietnamese pursued them, galloping across the creek bed, seeking to rout the Americans before they were ready to defend themselves. The Americans, however, were able to set up their weapons before the pursuers reached them. They scythed down the North Vietnamese in great numbers while incurring few casualties themselves.

Once the North Vietnamese company had been bled of its ability to take offensive action, Bravo company made a push toward Herrick's men. It was stopped seventy-five meters short of the knoll by a North Vietnamese force several times its size.

At 1442, the last part of Moore's Charlie company and the first part of his Delta company touched down at Landing Zone X-Ray. Anticipating a major enemy thrust against his thinly defended southern flank, Moore sent Charlie company to beef up the defenses on that side. Again, his timing was impeccable. Charlie company's commander, Captain Bob Edwards, organized his rifleman and machine gunners along 120 yards of the perimeter just in time to face two hundred North Vietnamese soldiers from the freshly arrived 7th Battalion of the 66th Regiment. Charlie company shot dozens of North Vietnamese before they could get within grenade range at a cost of only four American casualties. The North Vietnamese battalion continued to push men forward for ninety minutes, then pulled them all back.

After the threat on the southern edge of X-Ray had flamed out, Moore sent Alpha and Bravo companies ahead for another attempt to rescue Herrick's platoon. They ran into small arms fire from several hundred resolute North Vietnamese soldiers, who had rendered themselves virtually invisible by crawling inside spider holes or climbing into trees. The American companies advanced 150 meters before their casualties reached levels that convinced their officers to call a halt.

Moore pulled those two companies back near dusk under the cover of white phosphorous smoke and consolidated the perimeter at X-Ray. If the isolated platoon could not sneak out during the night, Moore would attack toward the platoon's position in the dark or early the next morning. His next relief mission would be larger than previous ones, thanks to the arrival of a company of reinforcements from another Air Cavalry battalion, 2/7, which had been flown into the landing zone late that afternoon at his request.

During the night, the North Vietnamese attacked the knoll thrice. Each time, American rifles, grenades, artillery rounds, and bombs stopped them just short of the thinly held perimeter. Herrick's platoon, which had been reduced from twenty-seven able-bodied men to twelve wounded and seven unwounded during the day, somehow sustained no further casualties overnight. Because the platoon was holding out so effectively, Moore put off the relief operation until dawn.

The landing zone faced no significant test of arms that night, although the North Vietnamese leadership had wanted to administer one. During the evening, General Nguyen Huu An had ordered a 3:00 a.m. attack on X-Ray by the 66th Regiment and the H-15 Battalion, the latter having just shown up after an eight-hour march. As the North Vietnamese units were moving toward their attack positions, the Americans detected their presence and raked them with air and artillery, causing extensive casualties and delaying the start of the attack. When the North Vietnamese belatedly reached the attack positions, they discovered that the Americans had drawn their perimeter back after nightfall, so the assault time had to be pushed back again, to daybreak.

At the first shimmers of sunlight, North Vietnamese soldiers were loading their weapons and receiving final instructions. Moments before they were to begin charging the landing zone, they saw small patrols of Americans coming toward them. Lieutenant Colonel Moore had sent these men out to reconnoiter the ground ahead of the large force that would retrieve the lost platoon. If the North Vietnamese proceeded with the attack on X-Ray, they would first have to fight these reconnaissance forces, which would tip off the Americans defending the landing zone. The North Vietnamese would then have to advance to the edge of the landing zone under fire. Weighing the risks, the North Vietnamese commander decided to go ahead with the attack.

Like a buffalo herd stampeding into a family of rabbits, masses of North Vietnamese soldiers rolled into the American reconnaissance forces. The Americans who were not killed outright scurried back inside the American perimeter. At the news of the North Vietnamese onslaught, Moore directed the Americans to switch from offensive preparations to defensive ones, and he ordered air and artillery strikes on the North Vietnamese positions.

The North Vietnamese took their first swing at X-Ray on the left side of Charlie company's sector. Bolting forward from elephant grass, North Vietnamese soldiers closed on the American perimeter so fast that air and artillery could not take them under fire. North Vietnamese officers guided their troops with whistles and hand and arm signals. They screamed at each other and at the Americans. Captain Edwards, who had orchestrated Charlie company's easy slaughter of North Vietnamese troops the previous day, requested reinforcements for what would be a much more difficult battle. Moore refused the request, believing that this North Vietnamese jab might be a feint.

Two of Edwards's machine guns inflicted a fearsome toll of carnage on the attackers. The North Vietnamese kept charging nonetheless, and by dint of sheer numbers they broke through the company's outer perimeter. The two American platoons in that sector became entangled in a gory close-quarters brawl with the onrushing North Vietnamese. At 0715, the enemy came within hand grenade distance of Charlie company's command post, prompting Edwards to make another request for reinforcements. This time, Moore gave Edwards a platoon from Alpha company, but he withheld the battalion reserve's platoon because the enemy's H-15 Battalion had just attacked Delta company's sector. That attack, though, would prove far less troublesome as Delta's six M-60 machine guns mowed down the attackers well short of the perimeter.

To capitalize on the penetration of Charlie company's perimeter, North Vietnamese soldiers withdrew from the other sectors and poured into the breach. At approximately 0730, they overran a line of Charlie company foxholes. Checking each foxhole, they shot the wounded Americans they found inside. During these executions, American witnesses saw the North Vietnamese laughing, which some Americans attributed to cruelty, others to the use of narcotics.

Twenty North Vietnamese soldiers advanced far enough to assault Charlie company's command post. The company command group was ready for them. From their foxholes, the command group gunned the assault force down with little difficulty. The North Vietnamese were to advance no farther.

Pounded unremittingly by overwhelming firepower, the mass of North Vietnamese troops in Charlie company's sector gradually lost its will and capability to fight. Two hours after the penetration of Charlie company's perimeter, they retreated in disorder, leaving hundreds of their dead behind. Charlie company, which had begun the day with 111 soldiers ready for duty, counted 42 of its men dead and 20 wounded.

The shrieks and roars of weaponry departed the valley, replaced by the gentle swooshes of helicopter blades as more American reinforcements flew into X-Ray and the wounded flew out. At 1330, the Americans pressed forward three hundred meters in all directions to rescue the lost platoon, recover casualties, and mop up remaining North Vietnamese elements. They found no enemy resistance, only enemy corpses and body parts and equipment strewn around in great quantities. A proliferation of blood trails and bandages testified to the removal of hundreds more North Vietnamese soldiers from the battlefield during the past twenty-four hours. The Americans stacked the North Vietnamese dead like firewood, the piles reaching six feet in height.

Later in the day, the B3 Front Forward Headquarters ordered another attack on LZ X-Ray by the same battalions that had been savaged in the morning. At 0422 the next morning, a few hundred North Vietnamese troops charged the sector held by Bravo company 2/7. An American flareship, which until now had been held in abeyance to avoid exposing Herrick's platoon to nocturnal attackers, shot flares over the open terrain in front of the perimeter. American machine guns and artillery made easy work of the illuminated North Vietnamese, obliterating two of their assault groups in the first half hour. Over the ensuing two hours, the North Vietnamese charged twice from the southwest, with no better result. American losses were remarkably light, consisting of just six casualties with minor wounds. The North Vietnamese retreated from X-Ray once more, and for the last time.

That afternoon, Moore's battalion flew back to Camp Holloway for two days of rest and refitting, leaving the landing zone in the hands of two other Air Cavalry battalions. During searches of the battlefield, the Americans turned up a total of 634 North Vietnamese bodies. American officers estimated that another 1,215 North Vietnamese casualties had been removed by their comrades. That estimate was plausible in light of the numerous failed assaults by large North Vietnamese units and the determination the North Vietnamese had demonstrated in recovering casualties during the battle. Total American casualties at X-Ray came to 79 killed and 121 wounded.[6]

U.S. officers looked on the ratio of enemy to friendly casualties with satisfaction. American air and artillery had proven capable of inflicting tremendous damage on enemy units, they noted, and had ensured that North Vietnamese forces could not overrun prepared American defenses. Through effective communication, analysis of terrain, and positioning of weapons, American infantrymen had been able to repulse large enemy forces when air and artillery were unavailable.

Other observations from the battle were less encouraging. Moore and other American witnesses reported that the North Vietnamese had shown themselves formidable and resilient opponents. North Vietnamese commanders had consistently displayed audacity and tactical acumen, and North Vietnamese soldiers had carried out their orders tenaciously, even in the face of near certain doom. The speed and skill with which North Vietnamese units conducted encircling movements against smaller numbers of American troops caught the attention of many.

Moore was impressed, in addition, by the enemy's marksmanship and use of camouflage. "He was a deadly shot," Moore said of the North Vietnamese soldier. "In caring for my men who had been killed and wounded, I was struck by the great number who had been shot in the head and upper part of the body—particularly in the head. He definitely aimed for the leaders—the men who were shouting, pointing, talking to radios."[7]

American intelligence personnel concluded that Chinese advisers had accompanied the North Vietnamese during the battle at X-Ray. A search party had discovered a body with a different uniform and larger physique than the Vietnamese, and prisoners captured near Plei Me had divulged that a Chinese adviser was accompanying each North Vietnamese regiment. Although the U.S. government could have made public the presence of Chinese advisers to drum up domestic and foreign support for the war, it chose to keep quiet on the subject. The disclosure would have elicited cries from American and Asian hawks for military action against China, at a time when the Johnson administration was intent on keeping the Chinese out of the conflict. The American officer who notified Westmoreland of the suspected Chinese body at X-Ray received an unusually caustic rebuke. "You will never mention anything about Chinese soldiers in South Vietnam!" Westmoreland barked. "Never!"[8]

The American battalions that remained at X-Ray could have been flown out from there safely, as Moore's battalion had been. Instead, they were ordered to move on foot to clearings several kilometers away for extraction. The next morning, the 2/5 Cavalry went to LZ Columbus without incident. The 2/7 Cavalry headed to LZ Albany, where it stumbled into one of the most vicious battles of the entire war.

Of all the American battalions in Vietnam in November 1965, the 2/7 Cavalry may have been the least fit for duty. The battalion had been assembled in great haste only weeks earlier by throwing together soldiers from other units. Its commander, Lieutenant Colonel Robert McDade, had commanded the battalion for fewer than three weeks, having taken over for an officer who had been deemed senile by his subordinates. Although a combat veteran of World War II and the Korean War, McDade had not led an infantry unit in nearly a decade. The battalion's Bravo company was absent on November 17, and in its place was a company from another battalion, Alpha company of 1/5. The headquarters of the 3rd Brigade had deliberately restricted the employment of 2/7 to locations believed to be devoid of enemy forces so that it could meld under low heat before subjection to the blast furnace of major combat. For reasons that were never clarified, the brigade's leadership had concluded that no enemy forces remained near X-Ray, Albany, or in between.

As McDade's battalion advanced toward Landing Zone Albany, its Alpha company marched in the lead, followed by Charlie company, Delta company, the battalion command group, and Alpha company of 1/5. Near midday, two hundred meters shy of the clearing, the battalion's vanguard encountered two North Vietnamese soldiers and took them prisoner at gunpoint. The two claimed to be deserters, but they had been carrying weapons and were well fed, leading their captors to believe that they had been manning an observation post.

McDade halted the column and strode forward to interrogate the prisoners himself. Neither the presence of these soldiers nor the words they spoke persuaded McDade to change his plans. He summoned his company commanders to discuss the particulars of the helicopter extraction.

The company commanders headed to the front of the column, bringing their radio operators and first sergeants with them. The soldiers they left behind, strung out over a distance of six hundred yards, were exhausted after four nights with minimal sleep. When notified of the pause, they took naps, smoked cigarettes, or ate canned food known as C-rations. They had made the march in a single-file line without columns of flank security on either side of the main body as American units typically marched in a combat zone, and the companies put out little or no flank security during the pause. This carelessness would prove to be one of the most dire consequence of the battalion's leadership problems, so dire in fact that it would be taught to future generations of U.S. infantry officers as an example of how not to lead.

McDade told Alpha company's commander to have his company secure the edges of the clearing. Then he continued conferring with the company commanders about the extraction. A few minutes later, as Alpha company was entering Landing Zone Albany, it began receiving heavy fire from its front and right flank. Bullets spewed from North Vietnamese riflemen and machine gunners hidden behind trees or anthills, while other North Vietnamese soldiers ran at and around the American soldiers.

These North Vietnamese troops belonged to the 8th Battalion of the 66th Regiment, which had missed out on the battle at X-Ray. An hour earlier, they had been eating rice when they received word that an American force was approaching in the thick jungle. The North Vietnamese scouts who had delivered the report had seen only the foremost element of the American column and had concluded that the enemy consisted of a single American rifle company. As a consequence, the commander of the 8th battalion chose to attack quickly, hoping to overwhelm the Americans before they could solidify defensive positions, rather than having his men dig the foxholes and set up the protected machine gun positions that would have been most suitable for fighting a larger American foe. This haste helped them catch the Americans off guard at first but left them as ill-prepared as the Americans for what happened next.

Within a few minutes, the weight of the entire North Vietnamese battalion was bearing down on Alpha company. Having just moved into the clearing, Alpha company had not had any time to prepare defenses and hence had no protection from the bullets save for a scattering of trees and bushes. McDade undermined the protection of Alpha company further through another serious command error. Mistaking the North Vietnamese bullets for friendly rounds, he ordered his soldiers to cease fire, and repeated the order several times when the staccato of gunfire persisted and grew louder. Some of the other American officers believed that McDade had lost his nerve, although it is possible that his lack of recent combat experience had merely prevented him from distinguishing the tinny report of the North Vietnamese AK-47 from the boom of the American M-16. A new 5.56mm assault rifle manufactured by Colt, the M-16 had only recently been issued to the 1st Cavalry Division and other American units. After it became clear that the firing in question was not friendly, McDade sat down quietly against a tree and stopped providing direction to the battalion, leaving other officers to take charge.

Exploiting superiority in numbers, North Vietnamese soldiers broke through two platoons of Alpha company and fought them in a very personal and nasty fracas lasting ninety minutes. "It was like a gang fight," recounted Sergeant John Eader, one of the American survivors, "small groups of us versus small groups of them. It got down to knives. It got down to choking people."[9]

Nearly all the Americans in the two platoons had been wounded or killed by the end of the ninety minutes.

The remainder of Alpha company established a strong redoubt in a copse at the center of the would-be landing zone, from which they beat back several North Vietnamese onslaughts. After seeing his men dropping in big clusters, the North Vietnamese commander decided to encircle this strongpoint, apparently still believing that he faced only one American company. Hundreds of North Vietnamese troops swung around to the left in expectation of surrounding the clearing. They were therefore no less surprised than the Americans from Charlie and Delta companies when they ran smack into the middle of the American column.

Following the outbreak of small arms fire at the clearing, Charlie and Delta companies had hastily organized themselves into a thin defensive line. They were unable to arrange defenses in depth because of the neglect of flank security as well as the visibility problems posed by the elephant grass in which they had taken their break. Their ability to coordinate their activities with the battalion headquarters and with each other was, moreover, hampered by the absence of the company commanders, first sergeants, and radio operators, who were stuck at the front of the column.

On account of the elephant grass, the North Vietnamese and Americans did not see each other until they were almost close enough to shake hands. Spurts of bullets erupted suddenly from assault rifles on both sides, ripping through the foliage up and down the American column. For several minutes, the North Vietnamese and Americans squared off at ranges more familiar to soldiers of earlier centuries. They killed each other with bayonets, knives, and shovels as well as bullets and grenades. The North Vietnamese and Americans then recoiled into clusters, which intermittently reengaged in fits of primeval fighting.

For the first several hours, the American brigade did not direct air or artillery strikes into the area where Charlie and Delta companies were located because of the absence of radio operators and commanders. Observers surveying the battle from aircraft could not discern which trees and blades of elephant grass were concealing Americans and which were shielding North Vietnamese troops. The lack of radios in the column also prevented the brigade commander, Colonel Brown, from understanding the severity of the situation, and hence he did not rush relief forces to the area by helicopter.

The North Vietnamese, on the other hand, were feeding reinforcements into the battle as fast as they could. At the start of the fighting, the remnants of several North Vietnamese units that had been battered at X-Ray—the 33rd Regiment, the 320th Regiment, and the 7th battalion of the 66th Regiment—had been close to LZ Albany. At the command of their officers, they marched toward the sounds of battle. Exactly how many additional troops they introduced into the clash is unknown, but subsequent events suggest that they brought many hundreds. Upon reaching the scene, they reinforced North Vietnamese soldiers along all sections of the American column, including the tail, where by this time Alpha company of 1/5 was warding off attacks.

In the middle of the column, the intensity of combat subsided gradually as the numbers of North Vietnamese and American combatants declined and the survivors gravitated toward advantageous terrain. Much nastiness, however, was still in evidence. North Vietnamese soldiers methodically searched the elephant grass for wounded Americans and shot them in the head. Enraged by the dying screams of their fellow soldiers, able-bodied Americans sought to hunt down the executioners. Decades afterward, North Vietnamese leaders admitted that their men had killed wounded Americans but defended the practice with the assertion that the victims had still been capable of killing North Vietnamese soldiers.

Later in the afternoon, communications from Charlie and Delta companies improved, giving the battalion and brigade headquarters enough clarity on the location of friendly and enemy forces to apply American air power. Jet fighter-bombers raced across the battlefield to deliver aerial rockets, napalm, and 250-pound bombs. Flying at speeds in excess of five hundred miles per hour, the jets were nearly impossible for North Vietnamese machine guns to hit. Although the spotters and pilots took care to avoid harming friendly forces, the close proximity of American and North Vietnamese troops guaranteed that some of the ordnance would harm American troops.

Lieutenant Larry Gwin, a company executive officer, watched the first napalm cans tumble from the sky. "I saw them hit the tops of the trees," Gwin recounted, "and jellied napalm was coming down through the tree limbs and the NVA were jumping up trying to get away and being engulfed in the flames." Gwin witnessed the same sight again and again during the afternoon.[10] Napalm obliterated an entire North Vietnamese company as it prepared for an attack one hundred meters from the Americans.

Word of the battle reached the American forces at LZ Columbus in midafternoon. The commander of the 2nd Battalion, 5th Cavalry promptly ordered one of his companies to march to Albany. Led by Captain Walter B. Tully, the company reached the scene of battle at 5:00 p.m. and linked up with Alpha 1/5 at the tail of the American column. After learning the plight of Charlie and Delta companies, Tully took his men toward them, but on the way ran into a large contingent of North Vietnamese troops ensconced in a row of dense thickets. The Americans assaulted the row and, after a period of fierce combat, drove the enemy out. The North Vietnamese had, however, held them off long enough to exhaust the remaining minutes of daylight. Tully decided to set up defenses for the night and then send out search parties to assist the isolated soldiers of Charlie and Delta companies.

Foraying into the dark, Tully's troops and other Americans from the head and tail of the column reached several groups of wounded men that night, including twenty-one wounded from Charlie company who had established a small perimeter. The enemy applied only light pressure on organized American defenses during the night but succeeded in executing more of the wounded. In the morning, the Americans moved out from their perimeters girded for battle, only to find that the North Vietnamese had departed the area before sunrise.

The North Vietnamese left a great deal behind, for the survivors had been too few in number to haul away bodies and weapons with the thoroughness customary to North Vietnamese units. The Americans recovered 403 enemy corpses at the site of the fighting as well as 222 assault rifles and carbines, 39 light machine guns, three heavy machine guns, and 6 82mm mortars. North Vietnamese histories would recount that the battle shattered the 8th Battalion of the 66th Regiment, killing or wounding nearly all its officers, including its commander. On the American side, the casualties were not as high, but they were among the highest that an American unit would ever suffer in a single day of the Vietnam War: 151 killed, 121 wounded, and 4 missing out of the approximately 500 men whom Colonel McDade had taken to LZ Albany. Charlie company paid the highest price, with 45 of its 112 men killed and another 50 wounded.[11]

Hanoi's propagandists were to proclaim the Ia Drang campaign a heroic victory of North Vietnamese arms. Not until several decades later would Communist accounts begin to acknowledge that the Ia Drang battles had devastated North Vietnam's forces in both the military and the psychological senses. Every North Vietnamese battalion for miles around had been crippled by casualties. Having overtaxed their supply system, the North Vietnamese Army now lacked enough food to sustain its remaining troops. These problems led the commander of Communist Military Region 5 to recommend dissolving the Central Highlands Front and transferring its regiments to coastal provinces, where they could be fed from rice harvested in Communist-controlled areas. Higher authorities turned down the recommendation, evidently because they had not been given the full truth about the highland clashes and still believed that the Americans could not fight effectively in the region's mountains and jungles.[12]

The morale of the surviving North Vietnamese troops plummeted, and discipline broke down in a manner that North Vietnamese officers had never seen before. In light of the excellent leadership and training of the North Vietnamese Army, this breakdown must have been caused by the devastating effects of American firepower and the inability of the North Vietnamese to respond in kind. It is also possible that malaria, which was running rampant in these units, contributed to the despair.

Dang Vu Hiep, a senior North Vietnamese political officer, described a shocking state of affairs among the survivors of Ia Drang. "The soldiers' ties to their units weakened and they ignored orders from cadres," he remembered. "The more the commanders shouted at them, the less willing they were to listen, driving the soldiers into a spirit of negativism and resistance." Numerous soldiers wrote letters home stating that they were certain to die sooner or later in battle or from hunger or malaria. They sang melancholy and pessimistic songs. "In some units," Dang Vu Hiep noted, "as many as two thirds of the unit's personnel spent all day lolling in their hammocks, discussing all kinds of negative stories and subjects."[13]

On the American side, morale was high among most of the men who had fought in the Ia Drang Valley. It was not so high in the three companies that had lost large numbers of men at Albany, but discipline did not break down in those companies, and the same units would fight well in subsequent battles. Rick Rescorla, a vigorous officer who would survive the Vietnam War only to die while orchestrating the evacuation of the World Trade Center on September 11, 2001, recollected with pride the resilience of the American soldiers who had fought in the Ia Drang. When called back into action a short time later, Rescorla and his fellow infantrymen eagerly left the comforts of Camp Holloway to return to battle. As cooks, bottle washers, projectionists, and other rear-echelon soldiers lined up along the runway to watch helicopters pick up men and take them to the fighting, Rescorla recalled, the combat infantrymen viewed them with contempt rather than envy. "Not a man among us would swap places with these lard asses," he averred.[14]

Psychological costs were, however, beginning to accrue on the American home front, which had become unaccustomed to large numbers of casualties in the twelve years since the end of the Korean War. Betty Jivens Mapson, whose father was killed during the second day of fighting at X-Ray, recounted that when her father's body returned home, "You could have heard me screaming three states away." Several decades afterward, looking back on the suffering that many other relatives of the fallen had felt but few could articulate as well, she said, "I am so very proud of my father and wished that somehow he could know that and know that he is still very much alive with us. For a long time it seemed to me that he was just away like he usually was on Army duty, and one day he would come home. For a lot of years I waited and watched our driveway because I wanted so much for him to come home for my Momma and my brothers and me."[15]

Extensive foreign press reporting on the Ia Drang Valley battles made them the focal point of international attention during the last months of 1965, but American and North Vietnamese forces fought several other large battles of comparable military significance during this period. On November 8, as part of as search-and-destroy operation codenamed Hump, a battalion of the U.S. 173rd Airborne Brigade ran into a regiment of the 9th North Vietnamese Army Division in Bien Hoa Province. Seeking to turn the hunter into the hunted, the North Vietnamese tried three times to envelop the heavily outnumbered American battalion. To prevent the American paratroopers from summoning air and artillery strikes, North Vietnamese officers kept their men very close to the American perimeter. Nevertheless, the Americans thwarted each attack through rapid repositioning of soldiers to the hardest-pressed sections of their makeshift defenses. The North Vietnamese relented in the middle of the afternoon and withdrew under a hail of American air and artillery. The Americans reported 403 confirmed enemy killed, with some American estimates putting the number as high as 700. American losses amounted to 49 killed and 83 wounded.[16]

A few days later, at the hamlet of Bau Bang in Binh Duong Province, the 2nd Battalion of the 2nd U.S. Army Infantry Regiment fought an even larger foe, larger, in fact, than the enemy forces that Hal Moore's battalion vanquished at Landing Zone X-Ray during the same week. The battalion's commander, Lt. Col. George M. Shuffer Jr. of Palestine, Texas, had decided to encamp in a peanut field south of Bau Bang on the evening of November 11. Reinforcing his infantrymen on the perimeter that night were M-113 armored personnel carriers and tanks that had been attached to the battalion.

Reconnaissance teams from the 9th North Vietnamese Army Division located the Americans during the evening. The sighting was quickly relayed to the Central Office for South Vietnam (COSVN), the Communist Party headquarters for the southern half of South Vietnam. The headquarters decided to order all but two battalions of the 9th Division to march by night to Bau Bang and annihilate the American battalion at dawn.

Several thousand North Vietnamese soldiers coalesced at Bau Bang in the black of early morning. Weapon crews emplaced mortars within the hamlet and dug machine gun and recoilless rifle pits just to its south. Companies of infantry assembled behind high grass and rubber trees near the American perimeter, in some places within forty meters of American foxholes. Fielding ten soldiers for every American, the 9th Division would strike the American battalion at the height of its vulnerability, just after sunup, when the Americans would be leaving their foxholes and pulling their vehicles back from the perimeter in preparation for departure.

At 0605, a mammoth formation of North Vietnamese soldiers emerged from waist-high grass southwest of the American perimeter. Charging straight at the American battalion, the North Vietnamese could see friendly mortar rounds crashing into the American encampment.

The American M-113s had already prepared to move out. At the sight of the massed enemy, they drove toward the attackers and let loose with Browning .50 caliber machine guns. Blasting holes the size of golf balls in the bunched North Vietnamese soldiers, the Brownings broke the initial assault. American air and artillery strikes on North Vietnamese assembly areas wreaked havoc on support units and infantry units that were preparing to enter the fight.

Two more North Vietnamese assaults followed in quick succession, from the south and southeast. Lieutenant Colonel Shuffer staved them off by rapidly redirecting armor and infantry to the

main points of attack. He then ordered armored personnel carriers to counterattack in these sectors, which they did to good
effect, shooting down discombobulated North Vietnamese soldiers and crushing enemy equipment beneath their treads. The
heavy weapons that the North Vietnamese had entrenched in
the hamlet continued to shoot at the Americans, but Shuffer did
not direct fire at those weapons because he had been told that
civilians were in the hamlet.

At 0700, the North Vietnamese launched their fourth and
largest attack, out of the rubber trees to the north of the American
battalion. North Vietnamese crew-served weapons on the southern side of the hamlet emitted a cacophony of fire in support of
the new onslaught. Shuffer asked higher authorities if he could
unleash American artillery, air power, tanks, and heavy machine
guns into this area despite the reported presence of civilians.
Permission was promptly granted. The American firepower ended
most North Vietnamese activity in the hamlet, ruined most of the
civilian structures in the hamlet's southern section, and stopped
the fourth attack at the edge of the wire.

A fifth and final attack occurred from the north at 0900. It
was thwarted with the assistance of napalm. The remnants of
the North Vietnamese forces hobbled away from the field of
battle with whatever casualties and weapons they could carry.
Air strikes and artillery barrages imposed additional fatalities on
them during their retreat.

Afterward, the Americans collected 198 enemy bodies. Considering that most of a division had made five large and unsuccessful attacks in the open, had been pummeled continuously
with air and artillery, and had been seen dragging away some of
their dead, the total death toll was likely much higher. The 9th
Division's losses compelled it to cancel plans to assault the Dau
Tieng district capital in Binh Long Province, giving support to

Westmoreland's argument that search-and-destroy operations were an effective means of forestalling North Vietnamese attacks on urban centers. American losses at Bau Bang totaled twenty killed and seventy-six wounded.[17]

In the official report submitted by the 9th Division to Hanoi, the division's commander sought to conceal the one-sided nature of the outcome by grossly exaggerating the unit's achievements. The division had wiped out two entire American battalions, he claimed. When the division commander and a delegation of officers visited General Nguyen Chi Thanh at a secret headquarters, North Vietnam's top commander told them, "I received radio reports of your victory over the Americans at Bau Bang. I was so happy that I could not sleep!" Nguyen Chi Thanh hugged each of them, then exclaimed, "This means that we were able to fight and beat the Americans from the very first round of the match!"[18]

Misleading reports on this and other battles would color Hanoi's strategic thinking for a long time to come. General Nguyen Chi Thanh and Le Duan, North Vietnam's top civilian strategist and decision-maker, were to champion more large clashes with the Americans on the premise that North Vietnamese forces were racking up one victory after another. Their bold and confident assertions prevailed over the cautious warnings of General Vo Nguyen Giap and other North Vietnamese officers who contended that guerrilla tactics would meet the objectives of attrition warfare at a much lower cost.[19]

Two weeks after the battle of Bau Bang, the 9th Division's reconnaissance elements spotted a regiment of the South Vietnamese Army's 5th Division in the Michelin plantation, a vast expanse of rubber trees in Binh Duong Province. As at Bau Bang, North Vietnamese infantry approached in undergrowth during the night with orders to strike in the early morning light, when the unsuspecting foe was preparing to move out. Although the South Vietnamese regiment was several times larger than the American force at Bau Bang and was accompanied by U.S. advisers with access to American firepower, its lackluster leadership and lighter armaments rendered it notably less capable of self-defense. On the morning of November 27, the North Vietnamese division overran two of the South Vietnamese regiment's three battalions and the regimental command post. In the space of a few hours, the North Vietnamese inflicted 602 casualties, a toll in South Vietnamese losses second only to those suffered at the battle of Dong Xoai in June 1965.

The 1st Infantry Division of the U.S. Army rushed three of its battalions to the Michelin Plantation with instructions to smash the North Vietnamese. The North Vietnamese division commander, however, evacuated his soldiers before the Americans could lay their hands on them. The battalions of the 1st Infantry Division searched the surrounding terrain in vain for over a week.

Then, suddenly, one of the American battalions ran into a base camp that housed much of the 9th NVA Division. Whether by fate or coincidence, the American battalion was the same one that had battled the North Vietnamese at Bau Bang. It had been marching on a jungle road just north of Nha Mat hamlet when it began taking fire from North Vietnamese sentries. At the sound of the guns, American and North Vietnamese officers ordered their soldiers to form up for the attack.

Each side tried rapidly and unsuccessfully to outflank the other. Lieutenant Colonel Shuffer then consolidated his forces at sufficient distance to permit the lavish use of air and artillery. Following the inundation of the enemy camp with ordnance, the Americans assaulted frontally. Fighting their way through enemy bunkers, the Americans penetrated into the heart of the enemy camp at 1430. The North Vietnamese scattered, abandoning huge stockpiles of equipment as well as most of their dead. North Vietnamese casualties were reported to be 301 by body count with another estimated 100 killed and 204 wounded, while American losses were listed as 42 killed and 102 wounded.[20]

A similar tale of South Vietnamese failure followed by American success occurred during early December in Operation Harvest Moon, a large search-and-destroy operation involving both American and South Vietnamese units in Quang Nam Province. The intended victim of Operation Harvest Moon was the 1st NVA Regiment, which had been replenished with fresh troops after its ravaging during Operation Starlite. On December 8, a North Vietnamese battalion ambushed one of the three South Vietnamese battalions participating in Harvest Moon and overran it. The next morning, two North Vietnamese battalions decimated another South Vietnamese battalion and a South Vietnamese regimental command group.

One of the three U.S. Marine battalions assigned to Harvest Moon flew to a nearby landing zone and linked up with the South Vietnamese survivors. They then located an enemy force of several hundred men, which they thrashed with air and artillery until it was no longer capable of fighting. In an ensuing contest, a North Vietnamese ambush of a Marine battalion was thwarted when one of the battalion's companies maneuvered around the ambush position and struck the North Vietnamese from behind. More than one hundred members of the ambush force perished, and the remainder hightailed. According to American estimates, the North Vietnamese suffered a total of 407 dead during Harvest Moon.[21]

The South Vietnamese Army fared somewhat better in IV Corps, the Mekong Delta. Owing to the absence of large North Vietnamese units in IV Corps, Westmoreland had sent no American troops there and had instead beefed up the defenses by relocating South Vietnamese troops from other regions that were now filling up with Americans. Lieutenant General Dang Van Quang, the IV Corps commander, intensified military operations in the second half of 1965, resulting in increased levels of Communist casualties. Intensive combat in pro-Communist villages drove peasants to load their most prized possessions onto oxcarts and leave their homes for the safety of district or provincial capitals. The villagers, both those who fled and those who stayed, remained intent on alignment with the stronger side, and hence much of the delta's population stopped abetting the Viet Cong and started helping the government.

The changing times in the delta were captured in the official Communist history of Military Region 9, the southern half of the delta. "The enemy's ferocious military operations and bombing and poisonous chemical [defoliant] attacks unsettled the lives of the people, frightening them and causing their spirits to waver," the history stated. During the last months of 1965, "our village and hamlet guerrillas all fled with their families to evacuate to safer areas." The South Vietnamese government gave the refugees money, rice, clothing, medical supplies, and tin for building houses in order to "carry out the American neo-colonialist policy of creating false prosperity."

According to the Communist Party's own estimates, only 5 percent of its members in areas of the Mekong Delta previously "liberated" by the Viet Cong continued to perform their duties effectively. Local Viet Cong cadres became disillusioned with superiors at the regional level who refused to acknowledge the changed situation. "When we go up to Region for political training," they groused, "we are told that the enemy is spread as thin as a leaf from a blade of young rice, but when we return to our unit we see that enemy forces are thicker than the skin of an old buffalo."[22]

At a gathering in December to review village-level reports from the delta province of Dinh Tuong, Communist leaders acknowledged that South Vietnamese military activity had sharply reduced popular support for the revolution. "The increasing intensity of the war, the intensive and frequent shellings and strafings were considered the real causes of the deterioration of the people's enthusiasm," they concluded. "That is why all the policies of the Front have run into difficulties: the amount of tax collected and the number of the conscripted youths diminished noticeably."[23]

By the end of 1965, American and South Vietnamese search-and-destroy operations had robbed the North Vietnamese Army of the initiative in most of South Vietnam. Between August and December, American operations had compelled the North Vietnamese to abort attacks on Chu Lai, Saigon, Pleiku, Plei Me, and Dau Tieng. Westmoreland's command estimated Communist losses for the year to be 35,000 killed and 6,000 captured. On the other side of the ledger, U.S. losses for the year totaled 1,378 killed, 6,148 wounded, and 143 captured or missing, while the South Vietnamese lost approximately 14,000 killed, the bulk of them prior to August.[24]

Estimates of North Vietnamese casualties were at times inflated by South Vietnamese or American officers intent on demonstrating success. The overestimations, however, were offset to a large degree by casualties that American and South Vietnamese forces missed. Oftentimes those forces did not search the battlefield for casualties, or did not search it until after the Communists had hauled their casualties away, or were unable to locate enemy remains because heavy ordnance had mangled them beyond recognition. Close examination of the year's major battles showed that conventional warfare took an enormous toll on Communist forces, whatever the precise number was.

The magnitude of enemy casualties and the high ratio of enemy to friendly casualties would have given much comfort to American and South Vietnamese leaders had it not been for North Vietnam's ability to generate new combatants at high rates and its apparent indifference to losses. For most of 1965, Westmoreland's intelligence analysts had underestimated the growth of enemy forces in South Vietnam. In November, they were shocked to discover the presence of a host of new units that had recently infiltrated from the North via Laos. The discoveries led them to conclude that enemy strength in South Vietnam was rising at twice the rate previously thought.[25] According to North Vietnamese statistics, a total of 46,796 North Vietnamese infiltrated in 1965, a huge increase from the previous year's total of 17,000.[26]

The Americans now believed that North Vietnam's main force strength in South Vietnam had reached 110 battalions, with more than ninety thousand men, by the end of 1965, an increase of 35 battalions and forty thousand men since the middle of the year. Those 110 battalions served as the building blocks for five new infantry divisions formed by the North Vietnamese high command in the last months of 1965. These infantry divisions, as well as the division-sized 69th Artillery Group, purportedly comprised "volunteers" from the South, but in reality almost all the soldiers and all the division commanders were natives of North Vietnam.[27]

Westmoreland could have mandated rapid expansion of the South Vietnamese Army to offset the unanticipated increase in enemy strength, but he chose not to take that route because he knew of its deep pitfalls. Producing additional battalions and divisions would overstretch the already overstretched South Vietnamese officer corps, requiring the promotion of individuals without sufficient training and experience and hence resulting in more battlefield debacles. Westmoreland and South Vietnamese military leaders pursued a less aggressive growth plan, whereby the South Vietnamese Army would recruit additional junior officers and let them gain experience before proceeding with a major expansion of the army.[28]

As one remedy for the problem of rising enemy strength, Westmoreland pushed his field commanders to inflict casualties at a higher rate. Through improved intelligence collection and innovative tactics, he asserted, they could prevent North Vietnamese forces from slipping away when confronted by American forces, as they had often done in recent months. But Westmoreland lacked confidence that such improvements would be enough. In late November, during a visit by McNamara, he recommended increasing American troop strength to 400,000 by the end of 1966, nearly 50 percent higher than the recommendation of 270,000 he had submitted in July. This increase, he said, would allow allied forces to retain the initiative, inflict greater losses on the enemy, and ensure progress in pacification. Westmoreland cautioned that even with this increase, the enemy's strength was still likely to grow from the present 110 battalions to more than 150 battalions by the end of 1966, and consequently additional deployments of up to 200,000 American troops might be required in 1967.[29]

The unexpectedly rapid climb in North Vietnamese troop numbers and Westmoreland's resultant call for more American troops ran a lance through Robert McNamara's hopes of restraining the enemy by restraining the United States. "Limited war" theory suffered a devastating blow, one from which it would never recover. During his plane ride back to the United States, the secretary of defense ruminated and agonized. By now, he had abandoned his earlier notion that the United States could afford to cut its losses and withdraw from Vietnam after making its initial troop commitments, probably because he had come to realize the amount of damage it would have caused America's global prestige and credibility. It was no longer a question of whether to keep American troops in Vietnam, but whether to meet Westmoreland's request for four hundred thousand men or to accept a more modest increase.

By the time of his return to Washington, McNamara had the answer. He would approve the four hundred thousand. Westmoreland's arguments about the military advantages of the increase had prevailed over whatever worries McNamara might have harbored about the domestic and international consequences of deepening America's commitment. The game of mutual restraint having failed, it was time for a game of mutual escalation.

When the Joint Chiefs heard that McNamara wanted to boost the troop level to four hundred thousand by the end of 1966, they warned President Johnson against approving the increase unless he called up the reserve units of the U.S. armed forces. Composed of Americans who held civilian jobs during the week and trained on weekends, the reserve units were designed to provide additional manpower for rapid overseas deployment in times of war—the very type of deployment now contemplated. Within the reserves, noted the chiefs, resided precious leadership capabilities and technical skills that took years to develop. The admonition bounced impotently off President Johnson, who remained as opposed to a reserve call up now as he had been in July out of fear of political turmoil.

McNamara, being less interested in the Joint Chiefs' personnel concerns than Johnson's political concerns, devised a plan to obtain the four hundred thousand troops without tapping the reserves. Under this plan, the U.S. armed forces would draft more young Americans and deploy large numbers of officers and technical specialists with little to no experience. Johnson hastily approved this plan, leaving the generals to smolder.

As the Joint Chiefs had warned, the substitution of draftees and young volunteers for reservists would do serious harm to the quality of the American forces in Vietnam, as well as that of the American forces elsewhere in the world. Combat leadership was to suffer the most. The prohibition against sending the reserves also kept the U.S. military from deploying most of its civil affairs specialists, the personnel best qualified to organize nonmilitary activities. Only 1 percent of the U.S. Army's civil affairs troops would ever serve in Vietnam.[30] The percentage of Americans killed in action who were draftees would increase from 16 percent in 1965 to 21 percent in 1966 to 34 percent in 1967 and 1968.[31]

While the Joint Chiefs lost the battle over the reserves because of domestic politics, they were to lose their next major battle with the civilian leadership because of disagreements over foreign policy and military strategy. Their dispute with McNamara and Johnson on actions against North Vietnam came to a head near the end of the year in one of the few meetings between the Joint Chiefs and the president. This remarkable encounter would be described in detail three decades later by an aide to one of the Chiefs, Major Charles G. Cooper, who happened to be holding a large plywood map for the group because Johnson's staff had not provided an easel.

Standing before the map, the generals laid out their case for stronger military actions against North Vietnam. If taken promptly, the Chiefs told the president, these measures would compel North Vietnam to halt or drastically curtail its military activities in South Vietnam, and they would not provoke a major Chinese military response. If the United States did not take these measures, it would become mired in a protracted war without the possibility of decisive victory.

After listening to the Chiefs, Johnson turned away for a minute, then pivoted back on them in a fit of rage. As retold by Major

Cooper, President Johnson "screamed obscenities, he cursed them personally, he ridiculed them for coming to his office with their 'military advice.'" The president "called them filthy names—sh___heads, dumbsh___s, pompous assh___s—and used 'the F-word' as an adjective more freely than a Marine at boot camp." Johnson said that he was the one who had to carry the weight of the free world on his shoulders, and he accused them of "trying to pass the buck for World War III to him." In further clarification, Johnson yelled, "How can you f___ing assh___s ignore what China might do?"[32]

The Chiefs had not, in actuality, ignored what the Chinese might do. They had concluded that China would not fight the United States unless the Americans launched attacks on Chinese territory. The Chinese had said as much in January, May, July, and October 1965, and the U.S. intelligence community had stated the same in September 1965.[33] From what is known of the meeting, the Chiefs did not mention these facts to Johnson after the browbeating.

Postwar disclosures from the Communist camp would lend further weight to the notion that the Chinese would not have fought with the Americans unless the Americans had attacked China. On one occasion in the fall of 1965, Chinese Defense Minister Lin Piao informed fellow Communists of Southeast Asia that China did not need to provide them much military help because they were fighting "paper tigers" that could be defeated through guerrilla warfare and "self-reliance."[34] On another, Mao told Ho Chi Minh that a large increase in Chinese support to North Vietnam was unnecessary because of the inevitability of North Vietnamese victory.[35]

To his fellow Vietnamese Communist Party leaders, Ho confided dismay at China for letting North Vietnam down. To the outer world, though, he had only praise for the Chinese. When questioned by a Western newsman in December 1965 about his country's relationship with China, Ho replied that capitalists had fabricated the idea of tension between North Vietnam and China to "fool the people." He lamented that "there are still many people in the West who do not understand that the close relations among the socialist countries are based on the principles of Marxism-Leninism and proletarian internationalism." Relations between North Vietnam and China were, he said, "fraternal relations as close as the relations between lips and teeth."[36]

Discontent with the Chinese was more pronounced among North Vietnamese leaders who were a decade or two younger than Ho, a group that included the most influential members of the Politburo. They were not innately hostile to the Chinese, but they had not spent as much time as Ho in close partnership with the Chinese, and were not as close personally to China's leaders. Some members of this group resented the Chinese leadership for exhorting North Vietnam to fight relentlessly when China itself was unwilling to clash directly with the United States or increase its assistance to North Vietnam. According to a secret East German report, these North Vietnamese leaders had become convinced that "the Chinese are ready to fight to the last Vietnamese, but otherwise are content to be left alone by the Americans."[37]

Postwar Communist histories would also divulge that North Vietnamese military activity was constrained at this time by supply shortages, the sorts of shortages that could have been alleviated by additional Chinese aid, and exacerbated by additional American military action. In anticipation of decisive conventional warfare, the North Vietnamese sent far more trucks down the Ho Chi Minh Trail during 1965 than in previous years and moved 4,379 tons of supplies down the trail in 1965, exceeding the combined total for the years 1959–1964, yet they fell far short of their targets. American bombing slowed traffic on the road network, as did wet weather, which turned roads into mud of such depth that truck tires could gain no traction. The B2 region, comprising the southern half of South Vietnam, was supposed to receive 2,840 tons of weapons in 1965 but received only 880 tons. Across the country, supply shortfalls frequently prevented large North Vietnamese units from carrying out offensive operations.[38]

Once Johnson had eviscerated the Joint Chiefs' recommendations for heightened military action against North Vietnam, the generals shifted focus to Cambodia and Laos. The enemy's reliance on Cambodian territory for logistics, troop staging, and sanctuary during the Ia Drang fighting had convinced the Joint Chiefs as well as Westmoreland of the need for ground operations in Cambodia. In missives to civilian policymakers, the generals sought permission for temporary incursions into Cambodian territory to interdict North Vietnamese supply lines and blow up North Vietnamese facilities. Major General Kinnard went even further, calling for the stationing of U.S. ground forces in Cambodia.[39]

McNamara and other top civilian officials convinced President Johnson to rule out ground operations in Cambodia.[40] Speaking for many of the civilians, William Bundy cited a "lack of convincing evidence that Cambodian territory is being used as a major base or major infiltration route."[41] CIA analysts contended that North Vietnamese infiltration of supplies through Cambodia was considerably smaller than U.S. military intelligence analysts believed.[42]

The civilian leadership also thought that operations into Cambodia would foil their efforts to preserve what Bundy called "a façade of Cambodian neutrality," which they hoped would discourage greater North Vietnamese activity in Cambodia. To maintain this façade, the policymakers in Washington had prohibited the military from telling the press that North Vietnamese forces were operating in Cambodia. Critics suspected that this gag order was also intended to prevent the stirring up of hawkish sentiment in the United States. Whatever the case, Americans who had fought North Vietnamese troops based in Cambodia viewed the policy of silence as "dishonest and hypocritical," in the words of Lieutenant Colonel Hal Moore.[43]

McNamara was somewhat less dismissive of proposals for American ground operations in Laos. Prior to the Ia Drang campaign, Major General Kinnard had recommended inserting his division across the Laotian panhandle to block the infiltration routes. His recommendation had gained the backing of U.S. Army Chief of Staff General Harold K. Johnson, Army Vice Chief of Staff General Creighton Abrams, and General Cao Van Vien, the chairman of the South Vietnamese Joint General Staff.[44] Enhancing the proposal's credibility was the conclusion of a special national intelligence estimate that positioning large U.S. forces in Laos along Route 9 was unlikely to trigger Chinese intervention or a sharp increase in North Vietnamese military action.[45]

The generals and intelligence analysts made a strong impression on McNamara. On November 3, he informed Johnson that large-scale ground operations might soon be undertaken in Laos.[46] But then McNamara met objections from the most important general, Westmoreland. At the end of November, Westmoreland's staff notified McNamara that blocking the Ho Chi Minh Trail with ground forces was feasible but would require one to two years and at least four and a half divisions and support troops, a total of 100,000 to 150,000 men. Given those requirements, Westmoreland stated, such an undertaking would not "represent the most profitable use of available resources."[47] As in July 1965, Westmoreland had been swayed by General DePuy's contention that search-and-destroy operations within South Vietnam could cause greater harm to the enemy than ground operations in Laos.

Among the Americans, the last internal debate of the year concerned temporary suspension of Rolling Thunder. Proponents touted a bombing pause as a means of bringing the North Vietnamese to the negotiating table. Soviet interlocutors promised that a new pause would work out better than the seven-day pause that President Johnson had ordered in May, which had elicited nothing from the North Vietnamese other than bile. Anatoly Dobrynin, Soviet ambassador to the United States, told the Americans that the May pause had failed because its short duration had caused the North Vietnamese to dismiss it as a cynical ploy. The new pause, therefore, should last between twelve and twenty days.

Although Hanoi had not actually expressed interest in negotiations, to Moscow or to anyone else, the Soviets hoped to bring the two sides to the table by convincing both that the other really wanted peace. The Soviet leadership wanted to reduce, if not eliminate, hostilities in Vietnam to prevent the Soviet Union from getting sucked further into a war that was getting bigger by the day. The Soviets also favored a pause because, as Soviet Foreign Minister Andrei Gromyko told his Hungarian counterpart, it "would give time to the Russian specialists working in North Vietnam to strengthen the air defense system."[48]

McNamara considered it unlikely that a bombing pause would cause the North Vietnamese to negotiate, but he favored one nonetheless because he believed that North Vietnamese intransigence in the face of such a pause would make future gradual escalation of the bombing more palatable to American and international opinion.[49] The Joint Chiefs, Westmoreland, and General Ulysses S. G. Sharp, the U.S. Pacific Commander, united in opposition to a pause. In their view, it would not draw Hanoi to the conference table, and it would allow the North Vietnamese to strengthen their antiaircraft defenses and transportation systems. Similar protestations emanated from Henry Cabot Lodge, whom Johnson had returned to the post of ambassador to South Vietnam in the late summer because of Lodge's high standing in the Republican Party, and in spite of the president's abhorrence of Lodge's prior ambassadorial service.[50]

In this instance, Johnson acknowledged that the military's objections about undue restraint had some validity. While deliberating with McNamara on December 17, Johnson observed soberly that "the Chiefs go through the roof when we mention this pause."

"I can take on the Chiefs," McNamara replied. In a startling display of his disdain for the generals, McNamara added, "We decide what we want and impose it on them."

Shifting to the public, Johnson remarked, "I don't think you can sell the American people on the merits of stopping the bombing." He then opined, however, that suspending Rolling Thunder was in the best interests of the American people because the air campaign stood in the way of peace negotiations.[51] Several days later, after further handwringing, Johnson decided to initiate a bombing pause, with a start date of December 24.

News of the pause floated to the North Vietnamese on a stream of Soviet messages advising them to negotiate with the Americans. In seeking the cooperation of the North Vietnamese, the Soviets said that if the United States was not interested in meaningful negotiations, a North Vietnamese offer to negotiate would merely enhance North Vietnam's image in the eyes of the Third World. At present, the Soviets mentioned, many Third World countries were put off by North Vietnam's unwillingness to negotiate.[52]

Socialist and Communist envoys from various other countries assured North Vietnamese leaders that negotiations would end favorably for Hanoi. Rising antiwar sentiment in the United

States, they said, would ensure success. A pair of Italian leftists who visited Ho Chi Minh late in the year explained that "the movement opposed to the Vietnam War in the United States includes many important political figures, such as [Senator J. William] Fulbright and [Senator Wayne] Morse, and many professors and students."

The North Vietnamese would have none of it. Ho told the Italians, "We are prepared to roll out the red carpet and strew flowers in their path to let the Americans withdraw. But if the U.S. does not withdraw, then we have to drive them out." In case he had not conveyed the point emphatically enough, he added, "For Johnson and McNamara, it is either the red carpet or we kick their asses out the door."[53]

The bombing pause went over better with the American public. The majority of Americans were willing to give the enemy one more chance to back off before ratcheting up Rolling Thunder. A poll of Americans in late December showed that 73 percent favored a temporary ceasefire and that 59 percent favored a bombing pause. It also found that 61 percent of respondents believed that if suspension of military pressure did not yield negotiations, it was time for "all-out U.S. bombings of every part of Vietnam."[54]

At the end of 1965, fewer than 10 percent of the American citizenry wanted the United States to withdraw from Vietnam. The majority favored the Johnson administration's strategy, and 28 percent wanted to "carry war to North at risk of war with Red China."[55] Although a few antiwar protests took place in the latter part of the year, they generated more hostility than sympathy, even among most of the liberal Democrats who would later turn against the war. One such liberal Democrat, Senator William B. Proxmire of Wisconsin, asserted that the protesters were conveying the mistaken impression that the American people opposed the war and thus were encouraging the enemy. "If these peace marchers want peace," Proxmire pronounced, "the best contribution they can make is to address their plea to the Communists."[56]

To the casual onlooker, the American body politic appeared to be in the honeymoon phase of the war at the end of 1965. Some members of the Johnson administration, however, were already noticing signs of creeping disenchantment with the president's handling of the war, and they implored Johnson to change his behavior to avert a falling out. Johnson's reticence, they warned, was enhancing doubts about his honesty and preventing public and congressional support for the war from solidifying to the point that it would remain firm after the initial surge of enthusiasm subsided.

"The substantial people of the country are solidly behind the actions of our government," Maxwell Taylor told the president on December 27, but "there is wide-spread criticism that the government does not adequately explain what is going on." Taylor, the former chairman of the Joint Chiefs of Staff and ambassador to South Vietnam, had just completed a trip across the United States in his current capacity as special consultant to the president. "There is even some suspicion," he added, "that this government is holding back and perhaps concealing some of the facts."[57] Taylor and Jack Valenti, the president's special assistant, urged Johnson to speak repeatedly on television to let the American people know why the United States needed to fight in Vietnam.

Johnson paid them no heed. No stirring speeches or fireside chats, no televised addresses or White House press conferences would be forthcoming. Valenti later said he believed that Johnson kept quiet because he feared that rousing the country for war would drain energy from his domestic programs.[58]

In North Vietnam, where dissent resulted in imprisonment or worse, the nation's leaders did not have to worry about public opinion at the end of 1965, but they did have to worry about a military situation that had gone from highly promising to extremely discouraging in the span of a few months. The North Vietnamese Army's efforts to overcome American advantages in firepower and mobility by means of stealth and tactical excellence had failed uniformly and at great cost. Although the Saigon government had done little to reestablish its authority in villages outside the Mekong Delta, Communist control of the rural population had begun to ebb across the board as American and South Vietnamese military successes quashed the peasantry's belief in an inevitable North Vietnamese victory and precipitated migration from villages to urban centers.

Hanoi's allies, moreover, had proven highly disappointing. China was telling the North Vietnamese that they did not need much help, and the Soviet Union kept urging them to engage in peace negotiations that they deemed premature. Soviet entreaties to the Americans had cleared North Vietnamese skies of American aircraft for the moment, but the bombers would return unless Hanoi made concessions.

Like General Westmoreland, North Vietnam's military leaders had been forced to settle on a strategy that prioritized attrition. Neither side had any idea how much time would be required to vanquish the other side. The Americans hoped that the passage of time would allow the South Vietnamese to regain their strength, while the North Vietnamese hoped that it would erode America's will.

In the nearer term, the Americans foresaw little change in the war aside from rising troop levels on both sides. The North Vietnamese, on the other hand, anticipated drastic change during the year to come, change not of their making or to their liking.

The resolution of the 12th Plenum of the Communist Party, issued at the end of 1965, noted six times the need to prepare expeditiously for an American invasion of North Vietnam. It was equally insistent on ordering preparations for looming American ground operations against the Ho Chi Minh Trail.[59] Surely the world's most powerful nation would soon make strategic moves of such obvious benefit.

CHAPTER 4

. . .

ONE FOOT BACK IN

January–February 1966

During the first days of January 1966, the Johnson administration pressed what it termed its "peace offensive." For the role of intermediary, it chose the Polish government, which wanted to end the war as much as the Soviet government did. Averell Harriman, now serving President Johnson as ambassador at large, informed Polish diplomats that the United States was willing to accommodate two key North Vietnamese preconditions for negotiations: seating the National Liberation Front at the negotiating table and including Hanoi's main principles for a settlement in the negotiating framework.

The Poles conveyed the offer to the North Vietnamese and advised them to give at least some indication of willingness to negotiate. If the United States really sought a negotiated compromise, Polish officials explained, the North Vietnamese could engage in negotiations that would ultimately result in an American withdrawal. If the United States were simply using the pause as a ruse in escalating the war, the North Vietnamese openness to negotiations would expose the American duplicity.

"We are afraid that if you reject these suggestions out of hand,

this will lead to a defeat on your political front," Jerzy Michalowski of the Polish Foreign Ministry told Pham Van Dong, the
titular premier of North Vietnam. "International opinion, the
progressives and communists in the West will not understand
you. There also will be a lack of understanding of your position
among non-Communist Americans who are currently demanding peace." Michalowski added that American receptivity to a
negotiated withdrawal of U.S. forces would decline over time as
U.S. investment of resources and prestige rose.

"We demand independence, the liberation of South Vietnam,
and unification," Pham Van Dong shot back. "I do not think that
at this time the United States is prepared to go down the road
toward peace in accordance with our rational demands." The
Americans, he contended, were intent on intensifying the war.
Negotiations would come later, once the Communists had fully
exploited America's military weaknesses in South Vietnam and
its political weaknesses at home. American ground units "are now
being battered by our forces," Pham Van Dong explained, based
evidently on the erroneous reports Hanoi had been receiving of
North Vietnamese military successes against American forces.

At another meeting, Ho Chi Minh told Michalowski, "No one
believes that we are the aggressors. No one has ever thought that,
even those who are not communists." The Americans "started the
war, so they are the ones who must pack their bags and leave."

"The Americans are powerful aggressors," Michalowski
responded. "They want to rule your country. Because they are
strong, they do not want to pack their bags and go home. They will
continue to send more troops and more planes. We have a clear
understanding of America's military capabilities. For example,
they are capable of manufacturing 500 aircraft a day! They have
an enormous war machine. A terrible war will rage on for five
more years, ten more years. Why shouldn't we use political tactics

to achieve similar results? It is very possible that now the U.S. wants to withdraw in some form or other."

"The U.S. is more powerful than France," Ho remarked, "but today we are stronger than we were back then. Our history demonstrated that we have already defeated aggressors whose technology is superior to ours. Even if they send ten times as many troops to fight us, in the end they will surely be defeated."

Michalowski was not one to be overawed by a venerable revolutionary's airy prognostications. He had fought in the Polish Army in World War II and seen his country ravaged by massive battles between the German and Russian armies. "If the war is protracted," he told Ho, "there will be no one left to liberate."[1]

As days and weeks passed without a positive North Vietnamese response to the American overtures, derision of the bombing pause reverberated through the halls of the Pentagon. The Joint Chiefs scrawled memo after memo explaining the need to resume Rolling Thunder. McNamara and other senior civilians wanted to give the diplomatic feelers more time, so they countered with memos belittling Rolling Thunder. Six months earlier, McNamara had credited American air power with putting a ceiling on the North Vietnamese infiltration of troops, but now he was depicting the bombing as ineffectual. The North Vietnamese Army had, after all, blown through that ceiling.[2] In a meeting with President Johnson, McNamara remarked, "I told the Chiefs I would advise to resume the bombing if the Chiefs could show me how we were being hurt in the South. No answer from them, which is very encouraging."[3]

That statement was misleading at best. The Joint Chiefs had not produced quantitative data, but neither had they been mute. The generals contended that the decision to restart Rolling Thunder ought to be based on enemy infiltration capabilities, not irrefutable proof of infiltration. Past experience, they pointed out, had shown that such proof might not be available until the newly infiltrated North Vietnamese units were firing their weapons at American infantrymen.[4]

McNamara's discounting of Rolling Thunder's effects also came under criticism from men whose counsel Johnson held in higher esteem than that of the Joint Chiefs. Dean Rusk and Maxwell Taylor told the president that the bombing served as an important hindrance to infiltration.[5] From Saigon, Westmoreland and Lodge reported that the enemy was exploiting the pause by stockpiling supplies and amassing forces just north of the DMZ.[6] Thieu made the same points to Lodge and grumbled that the North Vietnamese were touting the bombing pause as an indication of American and South Vietnamese weakness.[7]

At a January 25 meeting between Johnson and U.S. congressional leaders from both parties, every senator and representative except J. William Fulbright and Mike Mansfield urged the president to resume and intensify the bombing. The congressmen of isolationist Midwestern states, liberal Northeastern states, and conservative southern states united in a remarkable demonstration of the national will. Richard Russell of Georgia said the pause had gone on for too long and that the United States was "going to lose a lot of boys as a result." To President Johnson, his longtime friend, he said, "For God's sake, don't start the bombing halfway. Let them know they are in a war. We killed civilians in World War II and nobody opposed it. I'd rather kill them than have American boys die. Please, Mr. President, don't get one foot back in it. Go all the way." If the administration fought with one hand behind its back, "the American people won't stand for it. This is an unpopular war but the people want us to win."

Everett Dirksen of Illinois, who as Senate minority leader had been instrumental in securing Republican support for Johnson's civil rights legislation, told the president to "go in to win. If we are not winning now, let's do what is necessary to win. I don't believe you have any other choice. I believe the country will support you."

Senator Bourke B. Hickenlooper of Iowa, a Republican who had been elected his state's lieutenant governor in 1939 as an isolationist and was now called a "neo-isolationist" by his peers, declared, "If only Vietnam were concerned, I'd get out. But we are confronting the Communist world. Either get out or lick them. I've been restless with our light bombing. If we win, we must take out their ability to make war."

"We get into some trouble by letting the Communists believe we are weak," intoned Russell B. Long, Democratic senator from Louisiana. The only way to prevent Chinese intervention, he said, was to convince China that "we'll lick her, too. Unless we let them know we aim to be strong, and to win, we are in for trouble."

Senator Leverett Saltonstall, a liberal Republican from Massachusetts who had been that state's governor from 1939 to 1945 and its senator ever since, urged Johnson to escalate without concern for the reaction of China. "All four Chiefs believe the Chinese will not come in," he said. "That's a risk that must be taken. You must give our boys full support."

"The American people will not follow indecision," said L. Mendel Rivers of South Carolina, the Democratic chairman of the House Armed Services Committee. "Win or get out. Let the military select the targets. My committee will follow you."[8]

Yet not even this bipartisan consensus could convince Johnson to abandon the course McNamara had prescribed. The president continued to hold out for a North Vietnamese response. It finally came on January 28, in a Radio Hanoi broadcast. Reading from a text prepared by Ho Chi Minh, a party official pronounced that the United States had undertaken the bombing pause as a "sham peace trick" that was intended simply to "conceal its scheme for intensifying the war of aggression." No negotiations could begin until the United States showed its good faith by "permanently and unconditionally ending the bombing and all other acts of war directed against the Democratic Republic of Vietnam."[9]

President Johnson convened the National Security Council the next day for a postmortem. According to one set of notes taken at the meeting, Rusk remarked, "The enormous effort made in the last 34 days has produced nothing—no runs, no hits, no errors." Another notetaker recorded that Rusk said, "I struck out completely."

The Joint Chiefs were quick to wheel out their arguments in favor of intensified bombing. General John Paul McConnell, the Air Force chief of staff, told the council, "Our bombing is ineffective because of the restrictions placed upon the Air Force. We should lift these restrictions and we would then get results." CIA Director William F. Raborn gave that argument a boost with a prediction that bombing could cut in half the number of North Vietnamese trucks moving through Mu Gia Pass, the most heavily transited pass between North Vietnam and the Ho Chi Minh Trail.[10]

President Johnson ordered the resumption of Rolling Thunder, but not at the high levels recommended by the Joint Chiefs and the congressional leaders. McNamara and his Whiz Kids had convinced him that more intensive bombing would not make much difference. The enemy, they argued, was capable of infiltrating far larger amounts of supplies than it was currently infiltrating, and hence could withstand extensive damage to its logistical capabilities. According to their statistics, the North Vietnamese had the capacity to infiltrate between 50 and 300 tons of supplies per day depending on the season, with an annual average of 200 tons per day, a whopping 73,000 tons per year, or more than seven times the U.S. intelligence community's estimate of actual infiltration for 1965. They contended that Communist forces in South Vietnam could limit their external supply requirements to 140 tons per day by refusing to go beyond "light" combat.[11]

Westmoreland's analysts anticipated much higher external supply requirements for the North Vietnamese. By their calculations, the enlargement of the North Vietnamese troop presence in South Vietnam and the heightened military activity brought on by U.S. intervention would boost North Vietnamese requirements to 260 tons per day in 1966. Were the North Vietnamese to use their combat capabilities to the maximum possible extent, they would need as much as 317 tons per day.[12] If the enemy's logistical ceiling was 200 tons per day or even 250 tons per day, any lowering of that ceiling would diminish the amount of time that enemy units could engage in combat.

As it turned out, all the Americans grossly overestimated the capacity of the North Vietnamese supply system. During 1966, Hanoi would infiltrate just 13,449 tons over the Ho Chi Minh Trail, or 37 tons per day, and a few thousand more tons by sea via the Cambodian port of Sihanoukville. The North Vietnamese had wanted to infiltrate nearly twice this amount during the year but proved unable to transport that much. There was, in other words, no unused logistical capacity.[13]

Statistics published by the North Vietnamese after the war revealed that American bombing did materially reduce the supply ceiling. Air strikes damaged or destroyed a substantial number of trucks and their cargo and slowed the rate of truck deliveries by blocking bridges, passes, and roads. During the 1965–1966 dry season, 42 percent of North Vietnamese trucks on the Ho Chi Minh Trail were incapacitated, and air attacks were a major cause along with weather and mechanical failures.[14]

For Communist commanders in much of South Vietnam, supply problems reached dire proportions in the first months of

1966. Neither the importation of supplies from the North nor the collection of rice in the South could keep pace with the needs of the growing North Vietnamese forces. Plans to create a new 6th Division in early 1966 were scrapped because of insufficient supplies of food and ammunition.[15] During preparations for a large offensive campaign in the A Shau Valley, a North Vietnamese division ran out of rice and had to scrape together manioc roots and other barely edible jungle roots to maintain a shred of combat effectiveness.[16]

While President Johnson disregarded the counsel of his military advisers to expand the bombing, he was receptive to their recommendations for further large troop increases. At a conference in Honolulu during early February, Johnson resolved to increase U.S. troop strength in Vietnam to 429,000 by the end of 1966. When the Joint Chiefs received word of the president's pledge, they notified McNamara that troops with adequate technical skills could not be provided so rapidly without mobilizing the reserves. Johnson refused to budge on the reserves, so McNamara moved the date for the 429,000 from the end of 1966 to July 1967.[17]

Later that month, McNamara confessed to Johnson that he was beginning to have grave doubts about the war. He had reached the conclusion that the chances for military victory were only one in three, and therefore he was eager for a negotiated peace. He was even willing to accept a coalition government in South Vietnam that included some Communists, similar to the one in Laos.

McNamara's words took the president by complete surprise. Afterward, Johnson told Rusk that McNamara's one-in-three reckoning had stunned him and that he considered inclusion of Communists in a coalition government to be "a very dangerous position."[18] Both McNamara and Johnson knew that in other countries where Communists had joined non-Communists in coalition governments, the Communists had almost invariably overpowered the non-Communists and taken complete control. Johnson evidently shot down the suggestion of a coalition government, for McNamara did not raise it again.

Westmoreland, who appears to have been unaware of McNamara's new ideas, remained focused on military success in South Vietnam. His campaign plan for 1966 called for penetrating enemy base areas, destroying large enemy forces, and securing the country's heavily populated areas and heavily trafficked roads. With large numbers of U.S. troops now in every region except the Mekong Delta, Westmoreland had Americans searching for the enemy around the coastal villages of the east, along the border regions of the west, and near the demilitarized zone at the northern extreme.[19] American and South Vietnamese numerical goals for the year included increasing the population in secure areas from 50 to 60 percent, increasing the critical roads open for use from 30 to 50 percent, and raising enemy casualties to the "crossover point," the point at which enemy losses surpassed enemy troop additions.[20]

In early 1966, the U.S. Army staff published a study entitled "A Program for the Pacification and Long Term Development of Vietnam," or PROVN for short, which would later be cited as an indictment of Westmoreland's neglect of population security and the political, social, and economic dimensions of counterinsurgency.[21] In actuality, PROVN's recommended strategy differed little from Westmoreland's strategy. Both emphasized the need to combine conventional warfare with counterinsurgency.[22]

Westmoreland's commitment to counterinsurgency, in all its aspects, continued to be borne out by his actions. In January, Westmoreland secured the cooperation of the South Vietnamese governments in elevating the Rural Development Cadre program and making it the centerpiece of counterinsurgency. Formed at the end of 1965 by merging two successful CIA pilot programs, the Rural Development Cadre program trained men between the ages of twenty-one and twenty-nine for twelve weeks at a CIA-supported facility at Vung Tau and then deployed them to their native provinces. Teams of fifty-nine men went into the hamlets to perform the military, political, social, and economic tasks that the strategic hamlet militias had performed, from training self-defense forces to organizing political rallies to issuing identification cards. Initial plans called for training 19,000 Cadres per year, of whom the first 4,500 would graduate on May 21.[23] In its incipient stages, the Rural Development Cadre program received praise bordering on euphoria from some U.S. officials, particularly those who believed that the enlightened use of nonmilitary tools was the key to turning the war around. Some of these enthusiasts pushed for an increase in the annual output to 39,000 cadres.[24]

The main point of disagreement between the PROVN study and Westmoreland was the extent of U.S. intrusion into the South Vietnamese government. PROVN favored greater American involvement in the government's day-to-day operations and greater influence over its leadership appointments. Westmoreland believed that such measures would impede the development of South Vietnamese capabilities and leave the United States responsible for everything.[25] He urged the South Vietnamese to undertake reforms and make better decisions, but did not resort to strong-arm tactics when they ignored his advice.[26]

North Vietnam's military strategy for 1966 put as much emphasis as Westmoreland's on destroying the opposing side's conventional forces through offensive operations. "If we want to take the defensive position, we should withdraw to India," remarked Le Duc Tho, one of the most influential members of the North Vietnamese Politburo. "In this dry season, if we do not attack the enemy, he will attack us. We must therefore try by all means to take the offensive position."²⁷ Communist commanders were directed to launch attacks "everywhere," which was expected to increase the vulnerability of the Americans and South Vietnamese by compelling them to disperse their forces and fight beyond the protection of established defensive positions.²⁸

For the year of 1966, Hanoi set a goal of inflicting fifty thousand casualties on the Americans. Achieving that target would require a tripling of the actual American casualty rate during the last five months of 1965, though it did not require such a multiplication if one relied on the inflated North Vietnamese reports of American casualties from that period. Even higher targets were set for South Vietnamese forces, with the objective of making them too weak to protect the Saigon government when the Americans tired of the war and went home.²⁹

The Central Military Party Committee designated the mountain jungles of the central highlands and the provinces north of Saigon as the primary battlefields for 1966. Offensive operations would surge during three "waves," each two months in duration, with start dates in February, July, and October. Operations would continue on a less intensive basis during the other months. To provide forces for these offensives, the committee sent twelve infantry regiments, three field artillery regiments, and a variety of smaller units from the North to the South. The North Vietnamese kept several divisions in North Vietnam for use in countering an American invasion of North Vietnam or Laos.³⁰

With the American and North Vietnamese armed forces both intent on large attacks, the year 1966 appeared destined for a flurry of uppercuts and roundhouses. Yet the year's opening months saw neither side throw many punches. Because of shortages of food and other supplies, most North Vietnamese Army regiments spent the early months of 1966 sitting passively inside Laos, Cambodia, southern North Vietnam, or at secret bases in remote corners of South Vietnam.[31] When the Americans went into the mountains and jungles looking for a fight, the North Vietnamese rarely obliged them. The few major battles, and the much more numerous North Vietnamese harassing actions, were concentrated in populous regions of the country where North Vietnamese forces had gone in search of food.

During the first months of 1966, the U.S. military stepped up its efforts to locate North Vietnamese forces inside South Vietnam by advanced technological means. The results left the Americans badly disappointed. Airborne radar and infrared devices that were supposed to find enemy troops concealed by dense foliage turned out to be "virtually useless," according to Westmoreland's chief of intelligence. One new airborne contraption, called the "people sniffer," did show initial promise. Flown by helicopter over jungles and forests, it could detect human urine through the thickest jungle canopy. The North Vietnamese, however, soon learned of this innovation and foiled it by hanging buckets of urine wherever they went.[32]

In III Corps, U.S. forces began the year with spoiling attacks around Saigon and gradually increased the radius of their operational circle. The estimated 4,600 enemy forces in the immediate vicinity of the capital and the 39,000 others believed to be within eighty kilometers receded, unwilling to give battle.[33] North Vietnamese units fled base areas even when it meant abandoning large amounts of supplies.[34]

The one place in III Corps where the Communists chose to stand and fight was their north-south infiltration corridor in Binh Duong Province. To the leadership in Hanoi, the corridor possessed too much strategic value to yield it willingly. The first major clash occurred during Operation Rolling Stone, which began on February 11. The 1st Brigade of the 1st U.S. Infantry Division carried out the search-and-destroy component of Rolling Stone while the division's 1st Engineering Battalion repaired roads near Route 13. Almost immediately, reconnaissance elements from the 9th North Vietnamese Army Division caught sight of Operation Rolling Stone, but the division's commander, Hoang Cam, avoided contact for two weeks. He decided to wait until the Americans made a careless mistake, such as lingering near jungle terrain where his troops could mass, before hitting them with his whole division.

Identifying a prime opportunity to attack proved more difficult than Hoang Cam had foreseen. He was interested in striking during the night or at dawn, but North Vietnamese scouts discerned that the Americans shifted the shapes, sizes, and locations of their perimeters in the middle of every night, so an assault during those hours might strike the wrong places or subject the attackers to fire from unseen strongpoints. "They were not using magic to hide their positions," Hoang Cam recounted, "but the enemy was indeed very crafty."

As the days went by, the Americans put themselves in no especially vulnerable positions. Exasperation mounted for Hoang Cam, who could not wait indefinitely given the division's limited food supplies. He eventually had to choose between leaving empty-handed or attacking under conditions that were less than ideal. He chose the latter.

Something of an opportunity presented itself on February 23, when North Vietnamese scouts saw a large American force setting down for the night in a flat field. That evening, Hoang Cam ordered his division to ready themselves for a night attack. The North Vietnamese would face both the inherent difficulties of night operations and the inherent disadvantages of open terrain, but they would possess superior numbers, and the Americans would have only a few hours to establish their field defenses before hostile forces showed up on their doorstep.

At 0145 on the morning of February 24, the full panoply of the North Vietnamese division's armaments commenced an extended barrage. Deluged by flashes and explosions, Americans who were located at listening posts outside the wire attempted to withdraw inside the perimeter. Advancing North Vietnamese soldiers raced to cut them off and killed those whom they caught.

The American force that had bivouacked in the field consisted of a reinforced infantry battalion, an armored cavalry troop, and three batteries of artillery. In the opening phase of the battle, the Americans in these units estimated that they were under attack by five North Vietnamese battalions, with between 1,500 and 1,800 men. The actual number participating in the initial assault may have been close to that estimate, but the attack force included the entire 9th Division, which was roughly three times that size.

At a distance of approximately seventy-five meters from the main U.S. defenses, North Vietnamese soldiers assembled in groups of thirty to forty men, then dashed forward together. American infantrymen engaged them with automatic and semiautomatic fire while American tanks and armored personnel carriers let fly more potent projectiles. American artillerymen inside the perimeter fired some of their guns at high angles to hit North Vietnamese staging areas and brought others down parallel to the ground to fire directly into the assault troops.

With American bullets and shrapnel mincing the air across the field, one North Vietnamese assault group was shredded after another. The North Vietnamese overran a few of the outermost American foxholes, but they never penetrated the main lines of defense. At 0645, after five hours of fruitless attacks, Hoang Cam ordered his division to withdraw. American infantry and armored cavalry moved out from the perimeter fifteen minutes later in a counterattack. The 9th Division, however, was by that time moving away on concealed routes, and few of its men were caught by the pursuers.

Afterward, the Americans found 142 enemy bodies on the field, and they estimated that another 250 had been killed. The casualty count was complicated by the presence of civilian porters within the enemy ranks. "The poor civilians," remarked one observer. "The VC forced them to carry their ammo and stores and go in with them as porters. So a large number of women and youths were also mown down." American losses were 11 killed and 74 wounded.[35]

The failure of this attack did not stop Hoang Cam from ordering another a few days later. This time, the 9th Division's intended prey was the 2/28 battalion of the 1st U.S. Infantry Division, which was in Binh Duong for Operation Cocoa Beach. The Americans had encamped in an open field whose soil was so hard that it could not be dislodged with entrenching tools. Hoang Cam did not write about this battle in his memoirs, so one can only speculate that he chose to strike because he expected that the Americans would have to spend the night without the protection of foxholes and weapons pits.

As it turned out, the American battalion commander had sent a request for picks and shovels that afternoon, and these tools were flown in quickly enough for the men to dig into the ground during the night. When the 272nd Regiment of the North Vietnamese Army attacked the next morning, the excavations gave the Americans the protection they needed to repulse the assault with only light losses. The Americans then counterattacked by flying another battalion, the 1/16 Infantry, into the rear of the North Vietnamese regiment. Catching the North Vietnamese forces off guard, the soldiers of 1/16 Infantry turned the North Vietnamese retreat into a rout. The American ground pounders found 199 enemy bodies, and airborne observers estimated that at least another 300 had been killed. U.S. losses totaled 15 killed and 15 wounded.[36]

In the central highlands, the North Vietnamese only occasionally attacked South Vietnamese forces during the first part of 1966, and they studiously avoided combat with American units. Large attacks would await the onset of the monsoon season in May, when the clouds and rain would impair American mobility and close air support. The American forces in II Corps were able to bring large enemy forces to battle only twice in the year's opening months, which they achieved by targeting North Vietnamese rice-gathering operations in villages near the coast.

In Operation Van Buren, which began on January 19, elements of the U.S. 101st Airborne Division, the 2nd South Korean Marine Brigade, and the 47th South Vietnamese Army regiment entered the Tuy Hoa valley of Phu Yen Province to find and destroy the 95th North Vietnamese Army regiment. Unwilling to abandon the valley's rice, the 95th Regiment clawed at the intruders repeatedly. In the open terrain, the regiment saw its claws badly mangled by American air power. Allied forces killed an estimated 679 North Vietnamese, captured 49, and induced 177 to defect. With few men still capable of fighting, the 95th regiment broke into small groups and headed to the mountains. The Americans suffered 55 dead and 221 wounded.[37]

The other major confrontation took place in the fertile plains of northern Binh Dinh Province. In late January, American and South Vietnamese battalions joined forces in this area for a search-and-destroy operation that was initially dubbed Operation Masher but was subsequently renamed Operation White Wing because of concerns that the original title sounded excessively brutal. The 2nd, 12th, and 22nd regiments of the North Vietnamese Army's 3rd "Yellow Star" Division had recently occupied positions near the north-south artery of Route 1 and were preparing attacks on the district capitals of Bong Son and Phu My.[38] The Yellow Star Division was not yet ready to execute its offensive when it was blindsided by Operation White Wing.

The 1st U.S. Cavalry Division, the 22nd South Vietnamese Army division, and six South Vietnamese Airborne battalions began the first phase of Operation White Wing on 28 January. The 3rd Brigade of the 1st Cavalry Division quickly found the 12th North Vietnamese Army Regiment on the coastal Bong Son plain, to the north of the town of Bong Son. For a week, the two units grappled for control of the plain and its villages. The Americans had heard that the people of the Bong Son Plain had been under Communist domination for most of the war and would be implacably hostile. Upon entering the hamlets, however, the GIs found the residents to be opportunists who would provide information to Americans in direct proportion to the strength of the American forces in their area.

The U.S. Army also learned, as the South Vietnamese Army had learned at the battle of Ap Bac in 1963, that an opposing force entrenched in hamlets surrounded by rice paddies could inflict crippling losses on assaulting infantrymen. Like the South Vietnamese before them, the Americans decided to pound the hamlets with ordnance before moving in, rather than see their soldiers shot to pieces trudging through the flat paddies. The Americans urged the population to evacuate prior to major strikes, and they limited the use of air and artillery strikes where civilians were believed to be located, but civilian casualties could not be avoided altogether.

Communist cadres accused the Americans of deliberately slaughtering the population. The Americans blamed the carnage on the North Vietnamese practice of using civilian dwellings for cover and concealment. Many Americans, nevertheless, found the sight of the suffering disturbing. Hal Moore, now the commander of the 3rd Brigade of the 1st Cavalry Division, recounted, "The same awesome firepower—artillery, air strikes, and ARA [aerial rocket artillery]—that had saved our lives in the unpopulated Ia Drang Valley now, despite our best efforts, began taking a toll of innocent civilians killed and maimed, villages destroyed, and farm animals slain."[39]

At the conclusion of the fighting on the Bong Son Plain, Moore's brigade reported killing over 600 enemy by body count and capturing 357. The 12th Regiment had been virtually annihilated, and nearly all its crew-served weapons were in American hands. American losses totaled 75 killed and 240 wounded.

In the middle of February, exploiting information gleaned from a captured North Vietnamese battalion commander, the 2nd Brigade of the 1st Cavalry Division attacked the Yellow Star Division's 2nd Regiment to the southwest of the Bong Son Plain, near the Kim Son Valley. Three U.S. battalions jousted with the North Vietnamese for several days and then executed a rapid withdrawal so that B-52s could carpet the area with bombs. Developed by Boeing in the 1950s to drop atomic bombs on the Soviet Union from high altitudes, the B-52 Stratofortress measured 160 feet in length and had a wingspan of 185 feet. Its massive bomb bays allowed the B-52 to carry much larger payloads than any other U.S. aircraft. A B-52 bombing run was unique in its ability to confound the protections that foxholes and bunkers offered from conventional American bombardment.

Two large waves of B-52s hit the North Vietnamese regiment late in the day, too late for American troops to inspect the results before nightfall. The North Vietnamese hauled away some of their dead that night, but when American troops moved in the next morning, they still found 339 bodies. The Americans surmised that hundreds more had been carried away, based upon the blood stains, body parts, and lingering odors.

For Operation White Wing as a whole, the 1st Cavalry Division claimed 1,342 enemy killed by body count and estimated additional enemy losses at 1,746 killed and 1,348 wounded. The division also captured 633 prisoners, an unusually high number for a North Vietnamese Army that trained its men to fight to the death. The South Vietnamese Army and South Korean forces reported killing 1,150 during their operations. Intelligence indicated that five of the nine battalions of the Yellow Star division had been rendered combat ineffective. The division's survivors fragmented into small groups and fled to the north and west, which allowed the South Vietnamese government to regain authority over 140,000 residents of coastal Binh Dinh and to control more than 80 percent of Binh Dinh's rice harvest.[40]

In I Corps, the opening months of 1966 saw North Vietnamese soldiers streaming from the mountains eastward toward the coast. The flow was thickest in the northernmost provinces of Quang Tri and Thua Thien, where North Vietnamese forces massed for several attacks on South Vietnamese Army and militia units.[41] The U.S. Marines, concentrated as they were in coastal enclaves, were too far away to rescue the beleaguered South Vietnamese forces. Once reports of devastating South Vietnamese defeats started arriving, however, the Marines became more amenable to Westmoreland's exhortations to move inland.

In late January, General Walt sent four U.S. Marine battalions and the 2nd ARVN Division on a search-and-destroy mission in the hinterlands of Quang Ngai Province. Dubbed Double Eagle, the operation targeted two enemy regiments believed to be operating in the area. The Marines encountered little resistance on landing, and as they patrolled on foot they encountered only small groups of enemy soldiers. After three weeks of light contact with the enemy, Marine forces shifted to Quang Tin Province for Operation Double Eagle II, based on intelligence indicating the presence of an enemy regiment. Double Eagle II, which lasted until the end of February, likewise produced only small altercations.

Interrogation of prisoners revealed that the North Vietnamese had received advance warning of the Double Eagle operations and had fled before the Marines arrived. How they had obtained the information was not determined; the most likely source was either a spy in the South Vietnamese Army or a North Vietnamese radio intercept team. Double Eagle I and II did, however, disrupt the operations of several enemy regiments and kill 437 confirmed North Vietnamese soldiers, against 27 U.S. Marines killed and 292 wounded.[42]

Although the battle had yet to be fully joined in I Corps, the Americans and North Vietnamese were now on a collision course, which would soon put the U.S. Marines into the big battles of the sort that the U.S. Army was already fighting in II Corps and III Corps. To General Walt, the first months of 1966 marked a critical turning point in I Corps. "Early in 1966," he wrote later, "we began increasingly to encounter regular soldiers of the North Vietnamese Army, coming out of the western mountains with warm sweaters in their packs for use on the mountain trails that led from their own country to Laos and South Vietnam. They were sturdy, well-fed men with good weapons and equipment, uniformed, disciplined, and organized into companies, battalions, and regiments—a contrast in these respects to the guerrillas." In Walt's view, the arrival of these forces transformed the war from a low-intensity conflict, which could be handled with light infantrymen employing counterinsurgency tactics, into a conventional war, which required "the application of total resources: light and heavy artillery, tanks, motor transport, vast supply trains, and all the other equipage that spells the difference between light infantry battle and sustained heavy combat."[43]

CHAPTER 5

. . .

RETURN OF THE BUDDHISTS
March–April 1966

General Walt faced a new threat from North Vietnamese conventional forces in early March. By snaking through the jungles of the Annamite mountain spur that had so worried Westmoreland, the 21st North Vietnamese Army Regiment had crept up to the South Vietnamese coast near the Chu Lai plain. It was about to initiate an offensive campaign that would include attacks on South Vietnamese and American forces, destruction of supply convoys on Route 1, and a large assault on either Quang Ngai City or Chu Lai City. On March 3, American radio intercepts and prisoner interrogations located the 21st Regiment at a position just seven miles from Quang Ngai City. U.S. aircraft bombed the regiment's suspected location that night, while U.S. Marine infantrymen and South Vietnamese paratroopers rushed toward helicopter assembly points for a heliborne assault, codenamed Operation Utah, that was to begin early the next morning.

The 2nd Battalion, 7th U.S. Marines and the 1st ARVN Airborne battalion landed near the mountain spur in the morning without incident. The Marines took their preliminary objectives, two hills, unopposed. Matters were different for the South

Vietnamese paratroopers, who met heavy resistance when they tried to secure a donut-shaped hill. Just as the first paratroopers reached the peak, two battalions of khaki-clad soldiers from the 21st NVA Regiment came up the slopes toward them. American advisers brought a shower of air and artillery onto the North Vietnamese, compelling them to crouch behind boulders and thick vegetation. Bullets and grenades soared back and forth, but neither side was able to drive the other off the hill.

At 1330, the South Vietnamese battalion commander asked the Marines for help. The Marines obliged, advancing on the flank of the South Vietnamese unit until they met a large clump of North Vietnamese soldiers. Rather than pulling back and summoning air and artillery, the audacious Marine battalion commander, Lieutenant Colonel Leon Utter, ordered his battalion into the attack.

As the Marines were scurrying forward, North Vietnamese soldiers found a seam between the American and South Vietnamese forces. The North Vietnamese commander swiftly filled it with troops and 12.7mm machine guns. Firing on the exposed American and South Vietnamese flanks, the machine guns felled a considerable number of Marines from Utter's F company. The remainder of F company found cover, but neither they nor the rest of the Marine battalion were in a position to counterattack the North Vietnamese machine guns. By radio, the Marines asked the South Vietnamese battalion commander to assault the North Vietnamese machine guns. The commander refused, based on an earlier agreement that he would not move until his wounded had been evacuated.

For the next several hours, the Americans exchanged heavy volumes of fire with the two North Vietnamese battalions. A third North Vietnamese battalion, from the 1st Regiment, joined the battle at approximately 1620. By late afternoon, all three of the U.S. Marine companies were running low on ammunition, causing some of the Marines to scavenge the AK-47s or 12.7mm machine guns of dead North Vietnamese.

As darkness approached, Utter ordered his Marines to pull back to the hamlet of Chau Nhai 4. They did not leave any wounded on the battlefield, but they did have to leave most of their dead where they lay, a bitter pill for a service that prided itself on leaving no man behind, dead or alive. The North Vietnamese soldiers who attempted to pursue the Marines into the hamlet were obliterated by American bombs, rockets, and napalm.

Both sides brought reinforcements into the battle on the next day. Several additional South Vietnamese and U.S. Marine battalions arrived, boosting South Vietnamese strength to two thousand and American strength to three thousand. The North Vietnamese committed the remaining elements of the 1st and 21st Regiments, giving them close to three thousand soldiers. In the map rooms of American and South Vietnamese headquarters, officers plotted the locations of units and directed the movement of friendly forces into encircling positions. Fighting raged all day on hilltops and in hamlets, draining the life force from numerous young men.

As night came, American and South Vietnamese commanders laid plans to tighten the noose on the North Vietnamese forces the next morning. The North Vietnamese, however, decided to make a night withdrawal, and through considerable cleverness they managed to sneak most of the survivors of six battalions past five thousand American and South Vietnamese noses. Enemy dead in Operation Utah numbered 636 by body count, with another 325 listed by the Americans as "possible." The North Vietnamese threat to the coastal cities had been thwarted for the moment. The Marines suffered 83 dead and 205 wounded, while the South Vietnamese sustained 30 dead and 120 wounded.[1]

Just as Operation Utah ended, General Walt received word of an imminent attack farther north, in Thua Thien Province. The reported target was the U.S. Army Special Forces camp in the A Shau Valley. Forbidding and remote, the A Shau Valley began at a point just two miles from the Laotian border and ran twenty-five miles from northwest to southeast between two five-thousand-foot ridgelines. The valley floor was a primitive wilderness of double-canopy jungle, bamboo, and ten-foot elephant grass. The North Vietnamese considered the Special Forces camp a serious menace because it overlooked three trails that were ideally suited to infiltration of North Vietnamese soldiers from Laos to the coast of Thua Thien Province.[2]

Four days before the attack, two North Vietnamese soldiers had walked out of the elephant grass near the camp with their hands in the air and turned themselves in to a startled South Vietnamese jeep mechanic. Claiming to belong to the 325th North Vietnamese Army Division, the two men explained that hardship, fear of death, and the government's amnesty program had convinced them to defect. Four North Vietnamese battalions, they said, were preparing to pounce on the camp.

On a normal day, the camp had a garrison of 210 paramilitary troops, most of them from tribal minorities known as Uplanders or Montagnards, under the command of ethnic Vietnamese officers and advised by ten U.S. Army Special Forces soldiers. In response to the claims of the defectors, the camp's Special Forces detachment implored General Nguyen Chanh Thi's I Corps headquarters to reinforce the garrison with two infantry companies. General Thi, however, was embroiled in political matters, and he did not send any reinforcements to A Shau. The parent unit of the Special Forces detachment, the U.S. Army's 5th Special Forces Group, then ordered to the camp another unit under its authority, consisting of 149 troops of the ethnic Nung minority and 7 Green Berets. Arriving late on the afternoon of March 7, the new troops took up defensive positions inside the camp's central fort.

Shaped in an equilateral triangle, the walled fort measured two hundred yards on each side. Machine guns scowled outward at each corner of the triangle and at the midpoint of each side. Amid the strands of barbed wire surrounding the fort, the defenders had positioned claymore mines with electronic detonators. Developed by Norman McLeod of the Explosives Research Corporation in the late 1950s, the claymore mine was one of the most potent antipersonnel weapons in the American arsenal. Packed with C-4 explosive, it threw seven hundred ball bearings in a sixty-degree arc, with a kill range of a hundred meters.

The attack came on March 9 in the dead of night. Hearing the sound of wire cutting at 0130, garrison troops set off a claymore mine in the sector whence the noise was coming. Quiet returned until 0350, when the air filled with the din of North Vietnamese mortars and recoilless rifles. During a three-hour barrage, the heavy weapons of the 95th North Vietnamese Army Regiment inflicted sixty casualties on the defenders and destroyed the camp's main supply area.

At daylight, the 95th Regiment initiated probing attacks on the camp's perimeter but with less urgency than was customary for North Vietnamese units. They may have taken their time because they believed that the camp stood beyond the range of friendly artillery, which was true, and that the weather was so awful as to prevent American aircraft from coming, which was not entirely true. Or they may have wished to keep the garrison alive for the moment to lure in relief forces.

At 1120, a single Douglas AC-47 Spooky gunship appeared over the A Shau Valley. The camp's defenders greeted its arrival with boisterous cheers, believing that the North Vietnamese would now be repaid with the wrath of the Spooky's three Gatling guns, each one capable of firing six thousand rounds per minute. The crew of this Spooky, like many of the other American air crews in South Vietnam, was willing to take extraordinary risks to help fellow Americans who stood on the verge of death. The AC-47 gunship normally conducted combat missions at an altitude of three thousand feet, but with the cloud ceiling over the A Shau at just four hundred feet, it would have to fly below that altitude to see what it was shooting, and at so low an altitude, the slow-moving, twin-propeller airplane would be highly vulnerable to North Vietnamese antiaircraft fire.

The Spooky made only one pass at the enemy before North Vietnamese munitions struck its engines. Unable to keep the gunship in the air, the pilot crash-landed on a mountain slope five miles away, with enough skill and good fortune to spare the lives of the crew. Climbing out of the wreckage, the six crewmen prepared to meet the enemy, who did not take long to arrive. The American airmen held off three North Vietnamese attacks. At one point, Lieutenant Delbert R. Peterson, the copilot, charged an enemy 12.7mm machine gun position with an M-16 assault rifle and succeeded in capturing the weapon. A rescue helicopter arrived and picked up three of the crewmen, but not Peterson, who could not be found at the time of the helicopter's arrival. He was never seen again.

Other air operations achieved better results. A CH-3C Sea King helicopter touched down inside the camp's perimeter, onloaded the most seriously wounded men, and hauled them to the nearest medical facility. Two C-123 transport aircraft dropped ammunition and medical supplies to the garrison at low altitude. With guidance from a propeller-driven A-1E Skyraider, two B-57 jet bombers fired their 20mm cannons and dumped their bombs on major enemy troop concentrations.

On the ground, many of the Uplanders, Nungs, and Americans acquitted themselves well in mortal combat with the North Vietnamese. The same could not be said of the camp commander, an officer of Vietnamese ethnicity who disappeared into a bunker and provided no leadership to anyone. Because of his cowardice, an entire company of the garrison refused to fight.

In the early afternoon, the Special Forces detachment requested reinforcements. Without them, said the Green Berets, the camp was unlikely to survive the coming night. The weather showed signs of improving, which led General Walt's headquarters to order the movement of an infantry company to the camp by air. But before the reinforcements could reach the valley, dense clouds returned, forcing the cancellation of the reinforcement order.

The defenders held out into the night. Several hours before dawn, three North Vietnamese battalions launched human wave attacks on the southern side of the camp while North Vietnamese mortars and recoilless rifle fire turned many of the fort's remaining defenses into rubble. North Vietnamese infantry pierced the southern wall, but the defenders contained the penetration and consolidated defenses on the northern side of the fort, assisted by U.S. Marine jets, which dropped bombs through the darkness and clouds under the guidance of radar.

Radio contact with the defenders was lost at 0730, then reestablished at 0807 when the defenders reported that air strikes were preventing the enemy from overrunning the rest of the camp. Captain David Blair led three counterattacks against the southern wall of the fort. With only a handful of Americans and Nungs, however, it proved impossible to drive back the much more numerous North Vietnamese.

At 1100, the defenders reported that they could not hold out for more than an hour. They radioed soon thereafter that no ammunition should be air dropped because they would be unable to reach it. Very few crew-served weapons remained in their possession, and those that did were perilously low on ammunition. Nevertheless, their arms kept the North Vietnamese in check for several more hours, during which time General Walt's headquarters worked up plans for their evacuation.

In the middle of the afternoon, the camp garrison received word that American aircraft were preparing to extricate them. Captain Blair objected, arguing that the better option would be to send reinforcements to the camp.

"I didn't want to quit," Blair said later. "If you're a combat soldier, you just don't want to get whipped. Plus, we were killing a bunch of them." Slaying as many of the enemy as possible had become "an obsession for many of us," Blair recalled, "because I don't think any of us thought we were going to live through it, and you get over being scared and you're just fighting."[3]

Blair's objections failed to dissuade higher headquarters from proceeding with the evacuation. After destroying their communications gear, classified documents, and heavy weapons, the camp's survivors clambered over the parapets on the north side of the fort and scrambled toward a clearing three hundred meters to the north. The able-bodied were supposed to carry the wounded, but some of the Vietnamese abandoned their wounded and made a run for the landing zone, with the pusillanimous camp commander in the lead. When the helicopters arrived, a number of these same individuals refused to wait their turn to embark, and when they were not allowed on board, they grabbed onto the helicopter cables, nearly bringing the aircraft down. Americans clubbed the offenders, knocking some of them off. Those who continued to hang on were shot.

The first flight of helicopters carried away 69 of the defenders, including four Americans. Two helicopters were shot down, and some of their crewmen were left stranded. Other men were killed in the landing zone as North Vietnamese weapons zeroed in on them. Night fell before additional helicopters could reach the landing zone, so the remaining survivors broke into groups and headed into the jungle. The next day, sixty of them were located and evacuated by helicopter, and the day after that, another thirty-four were rescued.

When it was all over, a total of 248 of the defenders were reported dead or missing. Five Americans appeared on the roster of the dead, and the other twelve left the battlefield with wounds. Enemy dead were later estimated at one thousand.[4]

In the days after the battle, the South Vietnamese corps commander pleaded with General Walt to send U.S. Marines into the A Shau Valley to reestablish a permanent camp. After conducting an aerial reconnaissance, Walt decided that the mission would require more battalions than he could spare, and therefore no forces were sent to the valley. When the North Vietnamese realized that they had the A Shau Valley to themselves, they built it into a major base area and infiltration corridor.[5]

Westmoreland sought other ways to disrupt the enemy's cross-border activities in light of General Walt's refusal to retake the valley. Reversing his stance of November 1965, he now wanted to insert U.S. ground forces into Laos.[6] Joining him in this position was the U.S. Army Pacific, which recommended deploying two American divisions into Laos along the seventeenth parallel.[7] Westmoreland also requested permission to conduct ground operations in Cambodia.[8]

U.S. Ambassador to Laos William Sullivan objected strongly to the proposals for ground operations in Laos. In his estimation, they would cause Laotian Prime Minister Souvanna Phouma to resign, provoke the Soviets into assisting the Laotian Communists, and induce the North Vietnamese to enter Laos in greater strength. As an alternative, he suggested an amphibious landing at the city of Vinh in southern North Vietnam.[9] Sullivan's opposition to large-scale ground operations in Laos would win the day with McNamara and Rusk. His argument for invading North Vietnam would not.

Americans who bemoaned Hanoi's largely unfettered use of the Ho Chi Minh Trail had for years called it the "Averell Harriman Memorial Highway," after the architect of the 1962 agreement for the neutralization of Laos. The United States had honored that agreement, removing its military personnel, while North Vietnam had incessantly violated it by infiltrating troops and supplies destined for South Vietnam. Westmoreland now decided to give it a new namesake: "Sullivan's Freeway."[10]

McNamara and Rusk also shot down Westmoreland's request to operate in Cambodia. Such operations, they explained, would cause Cambodia to collaborate openly with Hanoi, and the Vietnamese Communist forces "would find it far easier than at present" to exploit Cambodian territory for basing, infiltration, and sanctuary. They said, in addition, that "questions of law and of international and domestic opinion also weigh heavily with us."[11]

Since the accession of Ky and Thieu in June 1965, the stability of the government in Saigon had receded as an issue demanding intensive American attention. Their leadership and the mighty buttresses of American military power had brought a relative political tranquility in the second half of 1965 that had continued into the first months of 1966. In Saigon and Washington, a sense of relief had settled in. No one in either place anticipated the shattering of the calm in early March by what would be the last and bloodiest of the Buddhist crises.

This crisis arose not from a clash between the Buddhists and the South Vietnamese government, as in previous instances, but from a falling out between the government's leaders in Saigon and its senior representative in I Corps, General Nguyen Chanh

Thi. Prime Minister Ky had allowed General Thi and the other corps commanders great latitude in running their provinces to such an extent that some reputable observers were referring to the corps commanders as "warlords." During January and February of 1966, General Thi had betrayed Ky's trust.[12] Ky's frustration with Thi boiled over at the beginning of March as the result of a personal slight suffered during a visit to Hue. While conversing with an aide in a voice loud enough to be heard by Ky's entourage, Thi had uttered the insult, which was said to consist of a single question: "What is this little man doing here anyway?"[13]

Convening a meeting with the country's top generals on March 9, Ky called for the removal of Thi. The generals replied that Ky should seek Lodge's opinion on the matter. Ky proceeded to tell Lodge that he was thinking of sacking Thi because "his judgment is poor, he has delusions of grandeur, he does none of the things that are expected of him." In elaboration, Ky said that when Thi received written orders from the government, he scribbled "this crazy government" on the orders and sent them back.

Lodge replied that the generals should act only if they had concrete evidence of insubordination or malfeasance and were certain that Thi could be removed without trouble. Ky told Lodge that these conditions could be met.[14]

At a meeting with Lodge later in the day, Thieu, whose steadier personality made him a more reliable source of information for the Americans, also predicted that the removal of Thi would be a cinch. "We can easily relieve him," Thieu assured Lodge. "There will be no reaction."[15]

On the following day, Ky presided over a meeting of the military directorate, a ten-member body composed of South Vietnam's most important generals. He asked the other members for a vote of confidence, which he would use to remove Thi. If he did not receive their vote, Ky said, he would resign as prime minister and Thi would remain in office. All nine of them, including General Thi himself, cast ballots in Ky's favor. Ky thereupon pronounced that General Thi would be relieved, and his place would be taken by General Nguyen Van Chuan, commander of the 1st Infantry Division.

General Thi did not voice objection to his removal, but he protested when Ky said that he would need to leave the country for several months. It could turn into a permanent exile, Thi groused. After receiving assurances that he would be permitted back into the country, Thi agreed to write a letter requesting that he be relieved of command because of a chronic sinus condition. He would proceed to the United States imminently for the ostensible treatment of the ailment.[16]

American officials in Vietnam applauded the change, though a number of military officers who respected Thi's military talents worried that the country was losing a capable commander. Among senior U.S. leaders in Washington, the mood was uniformly celebratory. McNamara told Johnson that the ousting of Thi had been a splendid idea. Taylor commented, "He's a bad character and good riddance."[17] Providing further evidence of the advisability of Thi's removal was the issuance of new CIA reports indicating that Thi had been plotting with General Tran Van Don and others against the Ky government.[18]

The sacking of Thi would indeed have been a windfall had Thi not confounded the predictions of a trouble-free exit. On March 11, at the instigation of Thi loyalists within the government, two thousand people gathered in the streets of Da Nang to demand Thi's reinstatement. "Down with the Generals' Command in Saigon!" they chanted. Additional demonstrations followed in Da Nang and Hue during the next several days. Such was Thi's influence over local army and police units that none of them interfered with the protests.[19]

Ky and Thieu, who were monitoring events from Saigon, underestimated the peril of the situation. Thus, they allowed General Thi to return to Da Nang on March 16 for the purpose of retrieving his personal belongings. When Thi arrived in Da Nang, he was greeted by large cheering crowds, whose leaders proclaimed their desire for Thi to remain in office. Thi decided that instead of packing up his things, he would stay in Da Nang and connive against the central authorities. Reinstalling himself in his prior official residence, he had the staff fly his general's flag on the building's flagpole.[20]

New street demonstrations ensued in Da Nang and Hue. Few residents in either city displayed enthusiasm for the agitators; when protest organizers attempted to undermine the national government by stopping commercial activity for half a day, they had to use intimidation to get shop owners to shutter their doors.[21] But momentary snapshots, of the sort sometimes provided in press reporting or diplomatic correspondence, suggested that the protesters enjoyed substantial backing. Political artistry and propaganda proved to be strong suits of Thi's political appointees, and of the Buddhists and Communists who became the principal exploiters of the breach that Thi's loyalists had opened.

The initial brouhaha had taken the militant Buddhists and the Communists by surprise.[22] Members of both groups had participated in some of the protests on the first day, but as junior partners to Thi's personal supporters. Before long, however, the Buddhists and Communists were capitalizing on the disorder in Da Nang and Hue to organize protests of their own, the objectives of which went well beyond the restoration of Thi.[23]

Tri Quang, the central figure in the Buddhist protests of 1963 to 1965, reemerged from months of quiescence to assume the role of chief operator and orator. Borrowing heavily from the scripts of his prior campaigns, Tri Quang and his acolytes accused the government of religious persecution and demanded the ousting of Ky. Under the banner of the Struggle Movement, his militant Buddhists organized a plethora of "struggle groups," which could, at a moment's notice, mobilize thousands of demonstrators in a manner that seemed a spontaneous manifestation of popular discontent.[24]

Just as vigorously, but far less conspicuously, Communist leaders sought to organize acts of protest in the same northern cities where Thi's supporters and the Buddhists were agitating. A National Liberation Front directive instructed urban Communist organizers to "keep ready banners, slogans, leaflets, explosives, grenades, etc. so we can work in every state of confusion." At each demonstration organized by another movement, "we must strive to rally the people to take part in the parade" and "to make every effort to infiltrate into its leading organ or to win the sympathy of certain leaders so we can place our slogans." More broadly, they were to build a popular movement that would demand eradication of the most dangerous groups, particularly veterans of Diem's Can Lao Party and other "leftovers of Diem-Nhu rule who are still hidden in the rebel government."[25]

Several North Vietnamese histories would recount that Communist cadres, masquerading as students or Buddhists, brought unwitting urbanites into the anti-government and anti-American protests at this time. Typically, the cadres recruited disaffected or impressionable laborers, civil servants, and students into ostensibly non-Communist opposition organizations, including some that the Communists had only just swallowed up. In the retelling of one Communist history, Viet Cong agents in Da Nang "inserted themselves into the management of the radio station, the leadership council of the provincial Buddhist association, and the 'people fighting for revolution' forces organized by the Nguyen Chanh Thi faction." In Hue, Communists infiltrated the leadership of a prominent Buddhist youth organization and several associations of university and high school students.[26]

As in prior years, foreign opinions varied widely on the degree of Communist involvement in the disturbances. Some CIA analysts contended that Communist participation was minimal. While acknowledging that the Communists were working hard to recruit urban youths, they maintained that only "unconfirmed evidence" showed that the Communists had penetrated the Struggle Movement. These analysts noted that Communist ideology held little appeal for educated urban youths, which in general was true, but then drew the mistaken inference that the Communists could not have manipulated youths into supporting their activities.[27]

Concerning Tri Quang, a CIA assessment concluded that he wanted the United States out of South Vietnam, but he "probably desires an independent South Vietnam" that would be "under Buddhist control and not under Communist political dictation." Such a government, the authors wrote, might actually improve the situation by rallying more nationalists and Buddhists to the government's cause.[28] These analysts appear to have been unaware that the Buddhists had dominated the South Vietnamese government in the spring of 1965 and that they had alienated most nationalists during that period. That alienation had accelerated the decline in South Vietnam's armed forces and would have ended with Communist control of South Vietnam had it not been for American intervention.

Most other informed observers believed the Communist role in the protests to be much larger and the activities of Tri Quang and his militant Buddhists to be much more dangerous. A CIA staff officer in Saigon reported that the Communists were "unquestionably involved in many of the Struggle groups" and had penetrated the leadership of the Struggle Movement in Da

Nang.[29] The American consul in Hue asserted that Tri Quang was engaged in a "power play" in which he "covered his effort with a highly bogus propaganda operation designed to project a fictitious image of a public opinion opposed to the Saigon government and resentful of the American presence."[30] As in the case of the 1963 crisis, no one found incontrovertible evidence that Tri Quang was colluding with the Communists, but an ever greater number of people now concluded that he was. Ky, who at one time had praised Tri Quang as a "visionary," declared that Tri Quang "is a Communist and undoubtedly we face a great Communist conspiracy to take over the government, ask the Americans to leave, and turn the country over to Hanoi."[31]

Ambassador Lodge, whose sympathy for Tri Quang and the rest of the militant Buddhists in 1963 had resulted in the catastrophic overthrow of the Diem government, was now the monk's foremost American detractor. In a cable to Washington on the subject of Tri Quang, Lodge wrote, "I am sure that everything he is doing is totally consistent with Communist aims, that the Communists are utilizing the opportunity which he creates, and that he either cannot or will not in any way seek to dissuade them."[32] In another report, he commented that "it makes very little difference whether Tri Quang is or is not an official card-carrying Communist, for what he is doing is actively helping them."[33] To convince Washington that the Communists were in league with the ostensibly non-Communist Buddhist and student oppositionists in Da Nang and Hue, Lodge forwarded intelligence reports detailing covert meetings between them.[34]

In public, Lodge and other senior American officials announced that the United States would stay out of the conflict between the government and the Struggle Movement. In secret, they passed South Vietnamese officials information on Struggle leaders in order to have them arrested.[35] When Tri Quang offered Lodge a plan to remove Ky, Thieu, and the other generals from the civil government by means of a national convention, Lodge rejected it as nonsensical and said the government was on the right track.[36] Lodge's rebuffs of Tri Quang enjoyed the blessing of President Johnson, whose memory of the State Department's circumvention of President Kennedy in 1963 had caused him to insist that the State Department keep him apprised of all South Vietnamese political developments.[37]

Neither Ky nor Thieu sought to appease Buddhist leaders with a string of lavish concessions as some of their unfortunate predecessors had done. Ky and the majority of the government's top military and civilian leaders were Buddhists, which lessened their vulnerability to militant Buddhist accusations of religious persecution.[38] The South Vietnamese leaders did, however, offer to accelerate the transition to civilian government, in order to deflate Buddhist charges of military despotism. Elections would be held by the end of the year, Ky announced on March 25. The protesters responded to the announcement by amplifying their denunciations of the government.[39]

When it became clear that the government's personal diplomacy and hastening of transition to civilian rule would not quell the protests, Ky and the rest of the directorate laid plans for suppressing the demonstrators with military force. On March 29, Ky gave notice of the planning to Lodge, who responded that the United States would welcome this type of action while cautioning Ky to be careful about the timing.[40] Explaining his approval in a subsequent cable to the State Department, Lodge asserted that Tri Quang had his mind set on bringing down the government and could not be induced to change his position. "He will have to be taken care of by Vietnamese, in a Vietnamese way," Lodge stated. "This may involve either a compromise, or a gesture with a measure of force, or just plain force."[41]

News of an impending showdown stimulated both excitement and apprehension in the White House. President Johnson told McNamara and Rusk that the United States had to back Ky and his plans for transition to civilian rule but at the same had to be prepared for a drastic change of strategy in case the situation fell apart. Possible strategic alternatives to consider, the president said, were the installation of a new South Vietnamese leader, the abandonment of I Corps, and the withdrawal of American forces from all of South Vietnam.[42]

Johnson directed a small group to look at the last of these options, under the assumption that the United States would fall back to Thailand and make a stand there. Chairing the group was George Ball, the senior administration official who had been the most skeptical of American involvement in Vietnam. The group's findings, issued several weeks later, stated that a rapid American departure from Vietnam would demonstrate to all of Southeast Asia that the United States did not have the stomach for war and was not committed to the region. For most Thais, the group concluded, an American withdrawal from Vietnam would constitute "a US failure and a proof that Communism from the north was the decisive force in the area. Faced with this reaction, we must still conclude that Thailand simply could not be held in these circumstances, and that the rest of Southeast Asia would probably follow in due course."[43]

Generals loyal to the Saigon government were still drawing up their plans for forcible suppression when, on April 3, a throng of three thousand South Vietnamese soldiers marched against the government in Hue and ten thousand civilian protesters of especially venomous demeanor congealed in Da Nang.[44] Ky responded by holding a press conference to announce military preparations for retaking Da Nang, a city that was now "held by the Communists." He denounced Da Nang's mayor Nguyen Van

Man, a dentist who had been appointed to public office by General Thi, for underwriting the demonstrations with government funds. "Either the government will have to fall or the mayor of Da Nang will be shot," Ky declared. "But perhaps we will not have to shoot him. Perhaps when he hears my voice saying this over the radio he will run off to the Viet Cong."[45]

At a meeting the next day, Ky informed Lodge that the generals had decided to move several battalions of elite troops to Da Nang and impose martial law. Ky believed that the restoration of order in Da Nang would make a strong impression on people elsewhere in Vietnam, particularly in Hue. "I will have no trouble with Hue once Da Nang is disposed of," Ky promised. The South Vietnamese armed forces did not have enough aircraft to move the battalions to Da Nang, so he asked Lodge to contribute American airlift to the mission. Lodge agreed, sending General Westmoreland an order to provide the necessary transport planes immediately.[46]

That night, Ky and several other generals flew to the Da Nang airbase with two South Vietnamese Marine battalions. A third South Vietnamese Marine battalion and two Ranger battalions came soon thereafter. But General Chuan, the new I Corps commander, opposed the use of these battalions in Da Nang and blocked the routes from the airbase to the city center.[47]

Ky warned the Struggle Movement's leaders that they had until midnight on April 6 to surrender. Should they refuse, he would send tanks and infantry into the city to crush them. Lodge gave encouragement to Ky. "The government has to establish its authority in the city of Da Nang," Lodge told him. The Struggle Movement had been given many opportunities to negotiate, and if they persisted in their unwillingness to work out their differences with the government, "then ultimately the time of testing could not be avoided."[48] Lodge subsequently informed

Washington, "As the government sought to compromise and tranquilize, the Buddhists have steadily but surely persisted in laying down conditions which the government can only accept if it is willing to give up power."[49] Lodge's words sounded eerily similar to the language Ngo Dinh Diem's American advocates had used in the fall of 1963, when Lodge was endeavoring to oust the South Vietnamese president for resisting the demands of these same Buddhists.

Before the midnight deadline arrived, several South Vietnamese leaders convinced Ky to keep the elite battalions in their pens and seek a political solution. They had apparently been unnerved by General Chuan's obstructionism and his devious treatment of the minister of defense, whom Chuan had incarcerated when he had shown up at Chuan's headquarters. On the following day, Ky reversed course again, telling Lodge that if the Saigon government did not use force now, the entire northern section of the country would be lost.[50]

Ky's vacillation unsettled President Johnson. The White House had Lodge warn the generals against resorting to force on the grounds that it would result in bloodshed and "drive major elements in Struggle movement into arms of Viet Cong."[51] This admonition convinced Ky to withdraw the troops from Da Nang and pursue a more patient strategy. He would cut off supplies into the Struggle strongholds and publicize plans for a National Political Congress that would form a new government.[52]

The Buddhists responded to the government's restraint and promises of democratic transition with new protests and demands for prompt elections to replace the current government. When asked if a new elected government might seek peace with the Communists and demand the withdrawal of U.S. forces, Tri Quang's lieutenant Thien Minh remarked, "If that is what the people want, then that is what they will get."[53] Other Buddhist leaders announced that they were forming "kamikaze" squads of Buddhist youth to send against government forces.[54]

Westmoreland, meanwhile, worked behind the scenes to undercut support for the Struggle Movement within the South Vietnamese officer corps. As a demonstration of American displeasure, he withdrew U.S. advisers to all South Vietnamese military units that appeared to be collaborating with the rebels. He directed General Walt to talk sense into South Vietnamese officers and sent one of his most artful officers, Brigadier General John F. Freund, to I Corps with instructions to "do all possible to put the Struggle forces in a bad light by blaming the entire situation in I Corps on the group of hot headed students."[55] Those actions soon paid dividends. The leaders of the 1st ARVN Division recanted their anti-American rhetoric and promised to protect U.S. installations.[56]

The convening of the National Political Congress in Saigon from April 12–14 momentarily eased tensions in Da Nang and Hue. The Congress and the government's leadership agreed to elections for a constitutional convention within three to five months, to be followed immediately by the creation of a new government. The government also consented to amnesty for individuals who had participated in anti-government demonstrations.[57]

During the week following the National Political Congress, Da Nang and Hue remained relatively quiet, but Buddhist chicanery returned. Members of the Da Nang Struggle Committee raided the offices of the Vietnam Nationalist Party and kidnapped more than a dozen anti-Communist leaders, of whom at least two were murdered. The committee notified the police chief of Da Nang that he would be killed unless he followed the committee's orders.[58] Tri Quang told a young American diplomat named John Negroponte that the Buddhists would not tolerate the replacement of the I Corps commander or the 1st Division commander, their most powerful allies in the government.[59] Within South Vietnamese Army units, Buddhist chaplains incited soldiers to turn their backs on the government and participate in anti-government demonstrations.[60]

Because the political entanglements in Da Nang and Hue were preoccupying the greater part of the 1st ARVN Division, the U.S. Marines had to abort a series of operations they had planned to conduct with that division.[61] From Westmoreland's perspective, the timing of this diversion of South Vietnamese forces could not have been worse. He badly needed forces to impede the North Vietnamese soldiers that had begun streaming east through the A Shau Valley following the fall of the Special Forces camp.

Westmoreland suspected that the North Vietnamese were preparing to attack Hue, owing to the city's symbolic importance and its potential use as the launching pad for an offensive to seize the entirety of the two northernmost provinces, Quang Tri and Thua Thien. From a logistical perspective, those two provinces were the easiest in all of South Vietnam for the Communists to support, and the most difficult for the Americans and the South Vietnamese. The North Vietnamese had their shortest lines of supply into Quang Tri and Thua Thien, through the DMZ and Laos. The Americans and the South Vietnamese could not supply Quang Tri and Thua Thien primarily by sea as they supplied other South Vietnamese provinces because they lacked deep water ports. Separated from the rest of South Vietnam by a mountain spur, they could be reached by truck only through the Hai Van pass, whose narrow and winding road presented tantalizing opportunities for ambushes.

Recent intelligence supported the theory that the North Vietnamese intended to capture the two northernmost provinces. According to some of Westmoreland's intelligence analysts, two entire North Vietnamese divisions had already entered Quang Tri and Thua Thien, and the North Vietnamese had established a large new headquarters twenty miles west of Hue. *Nhan Dan,* an official mouthpiece of the Vietnamese Communist Party, published an article claiming that a North Vietnamese division was practicing how to infiltrate stealthily for fifty kilometers and then assemble for a concerted attack.

General Walt and other senior U.S. Marine officers were somewhat less concerned than Westmoreland about the enemy threat to Quang Tri and Thua Thien. They believed that they had clear-cut evidence of only one regiment in northern I Corps and did not think the North Vietnamese were on the verge of major lunge at Hue. Although North Vietnamese forces made repeated strikes at South Vietnamese forces in Quang Tri and Thua Thien during March and April, they disappeared when the Marines went looking for them, which seemed to indicate a lack of strength and ambition.[62]

The largest battles the Marines fought during this period took place in the southernmost province of I Corps, Quang Ngai. Near the end of March, in Operation Texas, several U.S. Marine and South Vietnamese Army battalions clashed with three battalions from the 1st and 21st North Vietnamese Army regiments. After locating the North Vietnamese forces in a constellation of fortified hamlets, the Marines opened with a long symphony of air and artillery strikes, causing men's eardrums to burst and the earth to tremble. American and South Vietnamese armor and infantry then charged the hamlets.

The preparatory strikes had done less injury to enemy battalions than the Marines had hoped. Inching their heads out of bunkers and tunnels, the North Vietnamese opened fire on the advancing allied forces with bazookas, 82mm mortars, B-40 rocket launchers, heavy machine guns, and pack howitzers. With both sides brandishing heavy weapons at short ranges, the casualties piled up rapidly. The North Vietnamese clung to their defensive positions until the end, killing as many of their opponents as they could before being pulverized.

The Marines sustained 99 dead and 212 wounded. One American report put the enemy dead at 283, while another showed 623. The North Vietnamese themselves later acknowledged that they were never able to locate 250 of their soldiers who had taken part in the battle.[63]

The ability of North Vietnamese entrenchments to withstand American bombardments would prove an enduring feature of the South Vietnamese battlefield. U.S. military researchers determined that the North Vietnamese employed fortifications in 63 percent of their engagements with U.S. forces over the course of 1966. They also discovered that even rudimentary fortifications offered the North Vietnamese formidable protection from American heavy weapons. A 750-pound bomb stood less than a fifty-fifty chance of inflicting a single casualty on an entrenched North Vietnamese unit, and a 105mm artillery round stood less than a 1 percent chance. In addition, research showed North Vietnamese fortifications to be very effective at impeding infantry assaults, as measured by the high levels of casualties incurred by American infantrymen who attempted to close on them.[64]

One solution that American commanders tested was the employment of extraordinary volumes of air and artillery strikes against fortified North Vietnamese positions. Lieutenant Colonel Boyd T. Bashore, an American infantry battalion commander, wrote in the periodical *Army* that the infantry should simply step aside while bombs and shells gradually wore down the enemy's fortifications. "The 'traditional assault' is delayed until the position has been so devastated and the enemy so cut up that the trip becomes a cake walk," Bashore stated.[65]

That approach did, in fact, gain in popularity. But it seldom resulted in cake walks. After even the fiercest of bombardments, American assault forces often encountered stubborn resistance from North Vietnamese survivors. In many instances, the American infantry could not wait very long to attack unless they wished to allow the enemy an opportunity to slip away through tunnels or other avenues of escape. Some American infantry officers, moreover, were by instinct and training inclined to attack quickly and aggressively in situations that might seem, in the cold rational analysis of a distant observer, to be best suited to prolonged bombardment. Eventually, most American commanders dealt with enemy fortifications by alternating between probing infantry attacks and air and artillery strikes, capped by a final ground assault once the enemy resistance had ebbed to a whimper.

American commanders also sought to circumvent the enemy's use of fortifications by engaging enemy troops that were on the move. This feat could be accomplished by intercepting enemy forces, enticing enemy forces into an attack, or pursuing enemy forces in retreat. The North Vietnamese were, in fact, often willing to fight without the protection of field fortifications when they believed it would prevent the Americans from fighting from fortifications because American fortifications were even more effective than those of the North Vietnamese, being supplemented by weaponry that the North Vietnamese lacked, such as claymore mines and preregistered artillery support.

On April 21, intelligence from a North Vietnamese defector led U.S. and South Vietnamese forces to the 1st Regiment of the North Vietnamese Army. The turncoat showed them the precise locations of the regiment's four battalions in the rolling hills of Quang Ngai Province, first on a map and then from a helicopter. Following a lengthy bombardment, two U.S. Marine battalions and three South Vietnamese battalions flew by helicopter to positions near the regiment in what was dubbed Operation Hot Springs. The North Vietnamese regimental commander did not like what he saw, so he ordered most of his men to withdraw while a rearguard of several companies stayed behind to prevent a pursuit.

The 2nd Battalion of the 7th U.S. Marine regiment skirmished with some of the rearguard units. The most significant action, though, involved Mike company of the 3rd Battalion, 7th Marine Regiment, which was sent to the hamlet that the defector had identified as the site of the 1st Regiment's headquarters. As Mike company neared the hamlet, North Vietnamese machine guns and mortars opened fire. Making effective use of cover and concealment, some of the Marines moved forward to probe the enemy position. They reported back that the North Vietnamese were large in number and deep in entrenchment. The company commander, Captain Thomas Draude, called for fire support. For several hours, artillery, mortars, fixed-wing aircraft, and helicopter gunships took turns bashing the unfortunate piece of land.

In the late afternoon, the American company headed into the hamlet to clean out any remaining North Vietnamese soldiers. Large numbers of North Vietnamese automatic weapons opened up on the Marines. For thirty minutes, machine guns barked at each other from close range. Noticing that the sun was starting to go down, Draude decided that his only option for defeating the enemy before nightfall was a bayonet charge. Word was passed down the line to fix bayonets.

Two of the Marine platoons stormed the enemy positions while the third provided flanking fire. The bayonets dispatched a sprinkling of North Vietnamese who served as the final rearguard while the rest of the North Vietnamese fled. Within thirty minutes, the Marines were in full control of the hamlet.

A number of the North Vietnamese soldiers who had recently left the hamlet now began firing at its new occupants. The Marines were not sure whether these rounds were the harbinger of a counterattack or merely a ploy to delay a pursuit. Draude decided to move his company back to a more defensible position four hundred meters away. After reaching that position, Draude received word that the body of one dead Marine, Corporal Frederick Miller of Berlin, Ohio, had been left behind. North Vietnamese shots continued to zip across the hamlet, and darkness was descending.

Draude decided to go back into the hamlet himself to retrieve Miller's body, taking with him two Marines who had a rough idea of its location. Three Marines might well have disappeared into the dark and never reemerged had the North Vietnamese returned in force, but the North Vietnamese were not in the hamlet. Some huts that had caught fire during the fighting were still burning, providing enough light to search the hamlet and locate Miller. Draude picked up the body and carried it on his shoulders back to the defensive position.

The next day, Draude received a visit from his battalion commander, Lieutenant Colonel Charles H. Bodley. When Bodley heard that Draude had ventured into the hamlet with two Marines to get Miller's body, he lit into Draude, saying that he should not have gone himself and should have sent a larger force or else waited until morning. Draude, said Bodley, had been "stupid, foolish, and had endangered himself and his Marines needlessly." After five minutes of verbal flaying, Bodley swore that he would relieve Draude if he ever did anything like that again.

Draude replied, "I understand what you are saying, sir, however, given the same situation with a dead or wounded Marine left behind, I'm afraid I would have to do the same thing."

Shedding his last remaining layer of calm, Bodley accused Draude of becoming emotional. He said that Draude had left him no choice but to fire him, effective immediately.

Their conversation was interrupted by the approach of a helicopter, whose long blades blew a gale of dust in their faces. The assistant division commander, Brigadier General William A. Styles, jumped out of the helicopter.

"Where is the company commander of Mike company?" Styles demanded. Draude surmised that the general had come to take him into custody in preparation for a court martial.

Guided to Draude, General Styles pumped the captain's hand like an oil derrick, slapped him on the back, and told him over and over how proud he was to have him in the division. After several minutes of congratulations, the general turned to Lieutenant Colonel Bodley and remarked, "How can you go wrong with such a fine young man as this?"

Styles got back in his helicopter and flew away. Draude kept his job and subsequently received a Silver Star for his actions that day.

After the battle, the Marines recovered a total of 257 enemy bodies, 96 individual weapons, and 14 crew served weapons. Total enemy dead were estimated to be 327. The Americans also took 16 enemy soldiers prisoner. American casualties totaled 4 dead and 27 wounded.[66]

Outside of I Corps, the Buddhist crisis had much less impact on the military situation. Most South Vietnamese officers had no sympathy for the militant Buddhists, and they went about their duties no differently than they had before. Only a few South Vietnamese Marine and Airborne battalions were diverted from military operations outside I Corps to deal with Da Nang and Hue.

In III Corps, the major military development of the spring was the partnering of the 1st and 25th American divisions with the 5th and 25th ARVN divisions. The latter were two of the worst units in the South Vietnamese Army on account of their ineffectual commanders. These divisions had made a practice of operating in areas known to contain no hostile forces and ending all contacts with the enemy by the early afternoon so that they could find safe accommodations for the evening. When the Americans had beseeched the South Vietnamese high command to relieve the 25th Division's commander, nothing came of it because he was a personal friend of Ky.[67]

In March, soldiers of the 25th U.S. Army Division began combined operations with the 25th ARVN division in Hau Nghia Province. Under the direction of American officers, South Vietnamese and American soldiers toiled side by side. They conducted search-and-destroy operations together and participated in population-security operations in concert with South Vietnamese policemen and civil administrators.

In the villages, South Vietnamese troops helped the Americans communicate with the population, and the Americans helped the South Vietnamese keep their hands off the population's chickens. The government recruited 1,100 of Hau Nghia's men into militias, and the RD Cadre program spread into the hamlets. The Americans organized "county fairs" patterned after American events of the same name, in which bands played concerts of American music and cooks served American food, though they were discontinued after it was determined that the Vietnamese peasantry did not have a taste for John Philip Sousa or mashed potatoes. By American estimates, governmental control of the province's population and food supplies increased from 20 to 53 percent in a few months.[68]

In the highlands, Westmoreland sent the 1st Cavalry Division on search-and-destroy operations against enemy forces and supply areas prior to the arrival of the monsoon season. On March 30, during Operation Lincoln, the reported presence of a few NVA soldiers near the Chu Pong massif led to the helicopter insertion of an Air Cavalry platoon into the midst of what turned out to be the entire 18th NVA Regiment. American reinforcements arrived rapidly, landing half a kilometer away and then advancing on foot while American air strikes arrived on top of the 18th Regiment. Several hundred North Vietnamese soldiers perished in the battle.[69] Most other search-and-destroy operations in the highlands failed to bring the enemy to battle, and the same was true in the lowlands of II Corps.

For infantrymen on both sides, the main adversaries on most days were booby traps, malarial mosquitoes, leeches, oppressive heat, rain, dysentery, bad officers, sleep deprivation, and boredom. Much of the chatter among these men, as among soldiers since the beginning of time, consisted of complaints about these various problems. For the most part, they had joined the military to fight for their country, but now they fought above all for each other. Good leadership, which was common although not universal on both sides, as well as camaraderie sustained men's spirits through hardship and trauma. Deputy Secretary of Defense Cyrus Vance, who would later serve as secretary of state during the Carter administration, reported to President Johnson on an April visit to Vietnam: "The morale of our forces is magnificent. Even the men in the hospitals are in good spirits. They have a sense of dedication and display a professional competence which makes one proud to be an American."[70]

In Washington, where the decisions to deploy American forces had been made by civilians who were only dimly aware of the infantryman's travails, civilian officials were giving greater attention than before to military matters outside of South Vietnam. As the Joint Chiefs and congressional hawks kept up their lobbying for intensifying Rolling Thunder and mining North Vietnamese ports, they were joined by Walt Rostow. A hawkish professor of economics, Rostow had replaced McGeorge Bundy as national security adviser at the beginning of April. Like other bombing proponents, Rostow singled out for special attention the North Vietnamese facilities for receiving, storing, and distributing petroleum, oil, and lubricants (POL). These facilities were becoming less vulnerable by the day as the North Vietnamese feverishly dispersed their POL facilities in anticipation of American air attacks.[71]

Public sentiment for expanding the bombing against POL and other targets in the Hanoi-Haiphong area was on the rise.[72] A new CIA report predicted better outcomes for bombing in the North than previous CIA estimates, noting that the "self-imposed restrictions" on the bombing campaign had spared from destruction nearly 80 percent of North Vietnam's modern industry and all its critical military supply installations and routes. Of the major target systems in North Vietnam, the CIA analysts stated, "not one has been attacked either intensively or extensively enough to provide a critical reduction in national capacity."[73]

Neither public opinion nor the CIA estimate altered the thinking in the State Department, where most officials still opposed expansion of the bombing. Leonard Unger, deputy assistant secretary of state for far eastern affairs, contended that in convincing Hanoi to give up in the South, "we can influence their calculation by one strike practically as much as by ten."[74] Senior State officials continued to warn that bombing in the Hanoi-Haiphong sanctuaries risked war with China or the Soviet Union or reprisals by North Vietnam.[75]

This fear of foreign intervention took into account neither China's many indications of unwillingness to intervene, nor rising discord in the Communist camp that was rendering intervention even more unlikely than before. The boost in Soviet aid to North

Vietnam that had begun in 1965 was improving relations between Hanoi and Moscow, to the detriment of relations between Hanoi and Beijing.[76] In March, Le Duan attended the 23rd Congress of the Communist Party of the Soviet Union, an event that the Chinese Communists had boycotted and wished for other Communist parties to skip as well. In Chinese eyes, his mere attendance was appalling, but even more abhorrent was Le Duan's comment at the event that the Soviet Union was his "second motherland."[77]

Chinese Deputy Premier Deng Xiaoping was so disturbed by North Vietnamese behavior that he raised the possibility of withdrawing China's forces from North Vietnam. If the North Vietnamese did not trust China, he notified Le Duan, the Chinese would pick up their marbles and go home. "We have a lot of things to do in China," he remarked acidly.

The North Vietnamese did not want the Chinese troops to leave. Their departure would compel North Vietnam to redirect its own manpower to the road construction, engineering, and air defense tasks that more than one hundred thousand Chinese troops were performing. Le Duan assured Deng that Hanoi had no suspicions of Chinese motives, saying that "Chinese comrades came to help us out of proletarian internationalism." Le Duan added that North Vietnam might eventually need more than five hundred thousand Chinese troops, presumably in the event of an American invasion of North Vietnamese territory.[78]

The Chinese troops would stay in the North for the time being. But China did cut back its aid to North Vietnam as punishment for dallying with the Soviets.[79]

CHAPTER 6

. . .

SHUTTING THE LID

May–June 1966

With the start of the heavy rains in early May, North Vietnamese commanders in the highlands unleashed a series of battalion-sized attacks on South Vietnamese Army and militia posts. Each attack was crafted with an eye toward preventing American forces from engaging North Vietnamese forces except on terms most favorable to the North Vietnamese.[1] American search-and-destroy operations in the highlands during May and June were unable to bring the North Vietnamese to battle, with a few exceptions, of which the most significant was Operation Paul Revere.

Initiated on May 10 by the 3rd Brigade of the U.S. Army's 25th Infantry Division, Operation Paul Revere ensnared three North Vietnamese regiments near the Chu Pong massif. Using small patrols to locate enemy forces, the Americans made frequent contact with North Vietnamese units and in several cases turned small skirmishes into major fracases. When North Vietnamese forces ran into dire trouble during these exchanges, they scampered toward the Cambodian border for sanctuary and usually made it across. Nevertheless, Paul Revere killed a reported 546 North Vietnamese and captured 69.[2]

In the extreme north of the country, the lead elements of the 324th North Vietnamese Army Division began entering Quang Tri Province in May, starting a military buildup that would soon erase any Marine doubts about the presence of a conventional enemy threat in Quang Tri. Unlike previous North Vietnamese units, which had made the southward journey in Laos, the 324th Division came straight across the DMZ. This route permitted the infiltration of men and materiel in a much shorter time. Whereas the trip down the Ho Chi Minh Trail took a minimum of forty days, the troops of the 324th Division marched from the northern edge of the DMZ into the mountainous interior of Quang Tri in just twelve.[3]

The newly arrived North Vietnamese units intended to lure the U.S. Marines into combat by attacking South Vietnamese forces in the rugged interiors of Quang Tri and Thua Thien. The targets chosen were far from the coast so that the U.S. Navy could neither land Marine reinforcements amphibiously nor fire their massive guns into the fray. According to a Communist history, the North Vietnamese believed they could defeat the Marines in the jungle-covered mountains of Quang Tri and Thua Thien because this terrain "reduced to the maximum the strengths of the U.S. troops but utilized to the maximum our troops' familiarity with fighting in mountain jungle terrain."[4]

On May 19, North Vietnamese attacks of multi-battalion size smashed South Vietnamese Army outposts at Gio Linh and Con Thien, near the demilitarized zone. In response, General Walt launched Operation Reno to find the culprits and any other North Vietnamese units that might be lurking in the area. The Marines were meticulous in limiting their vulnerability to surprise attacks, so meticulous that the North Vietnamese chose to stay well away from them. As a result, the Marines could bring no sizable North Vietnamese formations to battle during the operation.[5]

Ky, meanwhile, was contending with the growth of Struggle Movement influence over the South Vietnamese Army in the northern provinces. If the movement obtained the allegiance of key Army leaders there, Ky believed, those leaders would attempt to detach those provinces from the rest of the country. Some of the younger military officers who had been sent to Da Nang in early April for the abortive seizure of the city were calling for the government to retake Da Nang by force. All the key South Vietnamese military commanders in II, III, and IV corps as well as the leaders of the 2nd Division in I Corps were loyal to the Saigon government, as were most militia commanders, and many of them were similarly fed up with the Buddhists and the Struggle Movement. As these officers knew from experience, continued toleration of the Struggle Movement's insolence would cause the government to lose face and hence would erode support for the government among its own personnel as well as the general population.[6]

Whether or not Ky intended to stick to the plan for electing a constitutional convention, as laid out by the National Political Congress, was never clear. Buddhist machinations in Da Nang and Hue and the headquarters of adjacent South Vietnamese Army units in early May ensured that he would not. On May 7, Ky reneged on his deal with the National Political Congress during a speech in Can Tho. His government would stay on for at least one year, he informed a group of foreign journalists who were huddled beneath umbrellas in the monsoon rains. Clad in a canary-yellow flight suit with a lavender scarf, Ky displayed good humor to match, which may have originated with the Jim Beam that he was sipping from a paper cup between utterances. "If the sky and the airplane and particularly my wife don't force me to resign," he quipped, "then I'll be in power at least one more year—why not?"[7]

Ky made his next move on May 15. Although Da Nang appeared on the surface to have regained an air of normalcy, Ky had become convinced that the government needed to assert its authority decisively to suppress the Struggle Movement and dispel the widespread perception that the government was weak in confronting its antagonist. "Any chief of government would feel badly if, under his administration, the second largest city in the country was lost," Ky commented in private. "Any averagely manly chief of government would try to get it back."[8]

Ky took care to prevent the Americans from learning of his scheme in advance. He planned to execute the operation during overseas trips by Westmoreland and Lodge, the two Americans who could do the most to interfere. In his memoirs, Ky would write that he had kept the Americans in the dark because "the United States government did not always understand the Buddhist problem in Vietnam" and because "Lodge had already told me, before leaving for the United States, that in general terms the White House was convinced that if I could establish a policy of firmness it would help the war effort."[9]

At Ky's command, South Vietnamese aircraft carried South Vietnamese Marine and Airborne battalions to Da Nang. On May 15, these battalions headed from the Da Nang airbase into the city with instructions to seize the I Corps headquarters, the Da Nang military and police garrisons, the mayor's office, the radio station, and a pagoda that served as the Struggle Movement's command center. They were authorized to fire on anti-Ky forces only if fired upon first. Cheering crowds lined the streets as the columns of loyalist troops filed past, while the troops guarding the targeted installations melted away and the Struggle group ringleaders withdrew into pagodas, where they erected barricades. The Marine and Airborne units took all of their objectives in just one hour and fifteen minutes.[10]

In Washington, the president's foreign policy counselors were less concerned with the rapid success of the mission than with the absence of advance notification from the Saigon government. Upon learning of the events in Da Nang, Secretary of State Rusk wrote to William Porter, the acting American ambassador in Saigon, "It is intolerable that Ky should take such far reaching move as that against Da Nang without consultation with us." Porter duly informed Thieu and Ky that "my government is extremely annoyed that you would carry out an operation of this importance without in any way consulting or informing us." Considering that great numbers of Americans were now fighting in South Vietnam, Porter said, the absence of consultation on this matter "was not only highly unsatisfactory, it was unacceptable."[11]

Thieu and Ky tried to defuse the tension by offering Washington a number of tenuous excuses, including claims that they did not have enough time to notify American officials and that they believed the operation would not bring harm to any Americans. They were less diplomatic in dealing with General Walt, if Ky's memoirs are to be believed. In Ky's retelling, Walt complained that as the senior American military commander in the region, he should have been notified in advance, to which Ky responded, "This is an internal problem—the people versus the government. If I may speak frankly, it's none of your business and you don't have to know about it."[12]

As in previous crises of this sort, dating back as far as 1954, senior officials in Washington opted against public expressions of support for the Saigon government, and instead tried to serve as mediator. They instructed the embassy to seek a compromise between the government and its adversaries in order to forestall further bloodshed.[13] As before, this behavior served only to alienate the leaders of the government in Saigon, who were convinced that compromise was a recipe for damaging the government's prestige and encouraging rebellion.

Ky continued forward with forceful suppression. On May 18, he ordered South Vietnamese Marine and Airborne battalions to encircle the Struggle forces who had barricaded themselves in the pagodas. Then he put Struggle Movement and Buddhist leaders on notice that he would use force to retake the pagodas if necessary because the presence of rebel forces inside them meant that they could no longer be treated as places of worship.[14]

In response, militant Buddhists set up funeral pyres outside the Tinh Hoi pagoda and threatened to conduct self-immolations if the government forces tried to enter. Tri Quang levied false accusations of violence against Buddhists, while his deputy announced that unless the government provided ammunition and food to the Struggle forces, they would accept ammunition and food from the Communists.[15] Hanoi sought to exacerbate the crisis by lauding the oppositionists on Communist Liberation Radio and proclaiming that the National Liberation Front would be pleased to assist them.[16]

In another reprise of past crises, seasoned American journalists like Charles Mohr of the *New York Times* and Ward Just of the *Washington Post* provided reasonably fair reporting of the political turmoil. They did not accept Buddhist allegations at face value, and they pointed out similarities between Struggle Movement propaganda and actions and those of the Communists. Younger reporters played up the aspects of the crisis that reflected most negatively on the South Vietnamese government, parroted wild Buddhist claims about the government's killing of monks and desecration of pagodas, and disregarded contrary evidence. They jockeyed to become the next David Halberstam, the next correspondent to attain celebrity by discrediting the South Vietnamese government and its American supporters.[17]

Lodge, who had collaborated with Halberstam and like-minded journalists in destroying the Diem government during the fall of 1963, rued the monster he had set loose. "The success which the Buddhists have in winning the American press over to them is marvelous to behold," Lodge remarked in a cable to Washington. "Our journalists seem to accept without question the Buddhist Institute pretense that they speak for Buddhism as a whole—which I think is palpably untrue. They regard the U.S. Government and the Government of Vietnam with undisguised cynicism and disbelief, but if a Buddhist says it or does it, it is carried without a change and without a doubt."[18]

Most prominent among the sensationalist reporters in the spring of 1966 was Neil Sheehan, a veteran of the 1963 Buddhist crisis who had returned to Vietnam with a different employer, the *New York Times.* "Although the government physically controlled most of Da Nang, it did not appear able to solidify its position politically," Sheehan reported on May 16. "It was unclear what Marshal Ky had accomplished by seizing Da Nang other than to exacerbate an already grim situation." Sheehan suggested that the blame for this sorry state of affairs belonged to the Americans by invoking these words from a senior Buddhist monk in Da Nang: "In the end the responsibility for this is with the Americans because the Government used all the American aid and American weapons to attack the people."[19]

R. W. Apple Jr., another *New York Times* correspondent, strummed notes of comparable gloom. In one dispatch, he wrote, "As the situation continued to deteriorate in the northern provinces of South Vietnam, with anti-Government and pro-Government troops fighting two gun battles in the streets of Da Nang, some American officials privately said the country was headed for chaos."[20] A *New York Times* editorial published on the same day as Apple's piece berated Ky for breaking his agreement with the Buddhists and called on the U.S. government to withdraw American troops to their bases in order to "bring Saigon to its senses." The editorial complained that "with Saigon concentrating on internecine feuding, American troops are being forced to carry the brunt of the anti-Communist struggle; their casualties now are beginning to exceed those of the South Vietnamese Army."[21]

The despairing texts of the reporters and editors leeched the morale of both the American leadership and the American people. On May 20, Wheeler wrote to Westmoreland, "We have had adverse reactions here in the past arising from the numerous political imbroglios in that country," but "the effect of the present situation on the public and in the press and in the Congress (both of the latter in this instance reflecting early and muted public opinion) is far more adverse than heretofore."[22] On the following day, President Johnson notified Lodge by telegram that "we regard situation as extremely serious, both in substance and because of press reports tending to exaggerate matters." The "situation now appears to American public to be getting out of hand with US in helpless position." In this context, Johnson mentioned a new Gallup poll indicating that 54 percent of Americans favored withdrawal from Vietnam if South Vietnamese infighting intensified.[23]

Rising dissatisfaction among the American press and government gave Ky additional incentives to complete the suppression campaign expeditiously. He acted accordingly. On Ky's command, South Vietnamese Marine and Airborne battalions besieged the remaining Struggle Movement strongholds in Da Nang, including the pagodas, on May 20. Two days later, rebel leaders offered to negotiate, but Ky rejected the offer and announced that anyone who did not surrender by 6:00 p.m. that day would be considered a deserter. Rebel soldiers and noncommissioned officers abandoned their cause in droves prior to the deadline. By the next day, most of the others had surrendered, and all the rebel strongholds had been occupied by loyalist forces.[24]

The Americans who entered the city afterward determined that Buddhist reports of mass civilian casualties and horrendous damage to pagodas had been fictitious. American estimates of fatalities on both sides during the nine days of fighting in Da Nang ranged from 60 to 150, and the available accounts indicate that all or nearly all the dead had been armed combatants.[25] In this instance, as in previous political crises, the government's use of force did not drive the people into the arms of the Communists, but rather increased the government's prestige and its ability to obtain the people's cooperation.[26]

The retaking of Da Nang did not, however, end the troubles in Hue as Ky had prognosticated. General Thi, elements of the First Division, and armed civilians remained in defiant control of the city. Lobbying with the Americans for Ky's removal, Thi told one American officer, "People have no confidence in him, and will not support him. The way Ky dresses and conducts himself is a joke."[27] Thi threatened to use the 1st Division to defend Hue against Ky's forces. In a radio broadcast, he exhorted South Vietnamese soldiers to turn their weapons against the government.[28]

Westmoreland, working frantically to avert a military clash, negotiated with Ky and Thi and eventually convinced the two of them to get together on May 27 for a tête-à-tête. At the meeting, Ky promised to give Thi a new job in the army, and Thi in turn said he would help end the demonstrations. The Americans most probably exerted additional influence on Thi behind the scenes, for he would soon leave the country without receiving the promised job, purportedly to undergo a medical checkup in Washington. Thi and his family took up residence in the United States and did not return to Vietnam.[29]

Thi's withdrawal from the scene did not alleviate the crisis conditions in Hue to the extent the Americans had hoped. On May 29, a Buddhist nun burned herself to death in the city center before a throng of civilians and foreign journalists. Buddhist monks showed the press a letter, ostensibly written by the dead nun, that accused the American government of "approving the massacre of our monks, nuns, and Buddhist followers." At the conclusion of the suicide, Tri Quang pronounced to the correspondents of the international media that President Johnson had "taken advantage of the anti-Communist aid extended by the United States people to support Thieu and Ky in their attempt to wipe out Vietnamese Buddhism."[30]

Additional burnings followed in Hue and several other cities. In each instance, the Buddhists called foreign reporters to notify them where the immolations were taking place.[31] Once, when the journalists did not arrive until after the fire had gone out, the Buddhists poured more gasoline on the smoldering corpse and lit it for the benefit of the cameras.[32] On another occasion, the Buddhists asked a French doctor for morphine to inject into the self-immolator before she set herself alight, which corroborated prior allegations that the Buddhists were drugging individuals before the burnings.[33]

On June 1, eight hundred demonstrators marched on the U.S. consulate in Hue. Some were bearing firearms. The Americans had convinced General Pham Xuan Nhuan, commander of the 1st ARVN Division, to send troops to protect the building, but these troops fled when the wall of armed protesters moved toward them. The mob tore the consulate's steel gates from their hinges and broke through the front door. After engaging in various acts of vandalism, which included smashing a photo of Lyndon Johnson, the ruffians set the building on fire. That evening, according to a dispatch written by R. W. Apple, "all semblance of governmental authority had vanished from the streets of Hue, and the city had drifted into a state of anarchy." Students toting carbines, pistols, and grenades lorded over the city, unchallenged by soldiers or policemen.[34]

The burning of the consulate convinced Ky and General Hoang Xuan Lam, the new I Corps Commander, to accelerate plans to move loyalist forces into Hue. They intended to send an armored regiment from the 1st Division to the city center. General Nhuan, however, caught wind of the plan and moved other armor and infantry into Hue first. Announcing that he would take action against the Buddhists as a newly loyal commander, Nhuan asserted that action by other forces was unnecessary.

Upon entering the city, Nhuan's infantry did not carry out the house-to-house searches for weapons that he had promised, nor did they interfere with the students who were menacing the population with their weapons and ransacking the houses of government officials. Instead, they drove to a park on the north bank of the Perfume River, dismounted from their vehicles, and lounged at the riverside. Officers and enlisted men sunbathed in aluminum chairs and swam in the river.[35]

In a further effort to discourage the introduction of loyalist forces, Buddhist organizers filled Hue's streets with makeshift "altars," which in many cases were nothing more than tables draped with saffron cloths and topped with incense sticks or Buddha figurines. The militant Buddhists decried as sacrilege any attempt by South Vietnamese forces to move the altars. The theatrics, however, aroused condemnation by many of the city's other Buddhists, who, in the reporting of Charles Mohr, "seem to feel that the orders to place altars on busy streets to block traffic are cynical and sacrilegious."[36] Buddhist leaders in Thailand, Burma, and Ceylon formally denounced the use of altars in this manner, and called upon Vietnamese Buddhists to purge

Communists from their ranks and to avoid further involvement in politics.[37]

Ky and General Lam did not tolerate the shenanigans for long. On June 7, two Airborne battalions and one Marine battalion flew to Phu Bai airport, ten miles south of Hue, and the next day they swept into the city to seize the principal military installations. Thanks to back-room negotiations and the imposing figures cut by the South Vietnamese Airborne and Marine units, the 1st Division did not put up a fight. Although Struggle Movement spokesmen had vowed to "fight to the death," the movement's armed civilians receded in sheep-like fashion before the advancing loyalist battalions, eventually surrendering or fleeing the city.

In the wake of the elite troops came combat policemen, who disarmed the local police and replaced their commanders. Combing the city for the ensuing two weeks, the loyalist forces arrested all the Struggle Movement leaders they could find and put government employees back to work. All told, government forces arrested several hundred Buddhist monks and students, including Tri Quang, as well as a small number of military officers. Only a handful of lives were lost during the restoration of governmental control in Hue.[38]

Once the Saigon government had retaken Da Nang and Hue, American public support for the war rebounded, as did confidence in the war's outcome.[39] In the U.S. Congress, leaders expressed uncertainty as to whether the political situation had stabilized, but they generally supported intensification of the war in order to prevent a Communist victory.[40] At the White House, the Pentagon, and Foggy Bottom, fretting over the possibility of losing some or all of South Vietnam melted away, replaced by cautious hopes that the Saigon government had shut the lid on the Buddhist problem for the last time.

During the dénouement in Hue, the prolonged futility of American search-and-destroy operations in the highlands came to an end. In Operation Hawthorne, the 1st Brigade of the 101st Airborne Division made contact with the newly infiltrated 24th NVA Regiment in Kontum Province. Following initial exchanges of fire between small elements of the two units, the North Vietnamese commander ordered his entire regiment to engage the Americans, in expectation that monsoon rains would severely constrain the use of American air power.

That expectation would prove to be misplaced. In one of the most impressive airlifts of the war, a total of fifteen thousand U.S. troops were flown to blocking positions on all sides of the 24th Regiment. The North Vietnamese regiment did not attempt to sneak away in the face of large American forces, as had become the norm, but instead stayed in Kontum and used the cover of jungle and low clouds to seek positions from which to attack with surprise and numerical superiority.

For some of the days of Operation Hawthorne, the monsoon weather did prevent the Americans from employing close air support and repositioning artillery. The American paratroopers were thus compelled to fight a series of skirmishes against the 24th Regiment in which they lacked any advantage in firepower. They gave better than they took, and marked enemy positions for possible destruction when the weather improved. "The amazing thing about our troops is that they fought with all they had, never complaining," said 1st Sergeant Walter I. Sabralowski, a paratrooper who was interviewed immediately after Operation Hawthorne. "The men out there were outstanding, and if I have to go into battle again I hope the same type of men are with me."

Lieutenant Colonel A. P. Abood, a battalion commander in the 101st Airborne Division during the operation, saw many wounded men who had been evacuated to the rear line up to board resupply helicopters so that they could return to their units. When Abood told them they were in no condition to fight, they replied that he was mistaken. Arguments were resolved by a capability test. "Those who had severe limps," said Abood, were "asked to walk ten paces, and when they couldn't walk ten paces they broke down and cried."[41]

During patches of clear skies, B-52 bombers were summoned to sow devastation on ground held by large North Vietnamese units. American forces had to be withdrawn at least three thousand yards from the planned targets to ensure their safety. Unless the enemy moved out quickly during the American withdrawal, they were in for great trouble. An American officer gave this description of an area that had been hit by B-52s during Operation Hawthorne: "The damage, in places, resembled that which could be expected from a low yield nuclear weapon. The blowdown and cratering effect were enhanced by the use of 1,000 pound bombs, which seemed to have significantly greater effect than the 750 pound bombs." This B-52 strike, he said, "contributed significantly to the annihilation of the better part of an NVA battalion."[42]

The 24th North Vietnamese Regiment hung on for a week. Then, in belated recognition that its position was untenable, the division's tattered remnants made a break for Laos. The Americans never determined how many North Vietnamese survivors reached Laos, but post-battle searches led them to estimate North Vietnamese killed in action at approximately 1,200, which was not far from the total strength of the average North Vietnamese regiment. American losses in Operation Hawthorne came to 48 killed and 239 wounded. For the next year, the 24th Regiment was nowhere to be found in South Vietnam.[43]

Early June also witnessed an upsurge in military activity north of Saigon, owing to the arrival of Major General William DePuy as commander of the U.S. 1st Infantry Division. DePuy took the place of Major General Jonathan O. Seaman, whom Westmoreland had relieved for failing to instill the aggressive spirit and tactical dexterity that could be seen in other American divisions. To avoid a dustup with Seaman's supporters in the Army, Westmoreland gave him a promotion to the command of II Field Force, the corps-level headquarters responsible for all U.S. units in III Corps. That promotion actually made him the direct boss of the 1st Division's new commander, but DePuy's personality and his higher standing with Westmoreland ensured that Seaman would have no say in how DePuy ran the division.

At 5′8″ and 140 pounds, DePuy was several sizes smaller than most of the U.S. Army's division commanders. He compensated for his slightness of body through exceptional intensity and acumen. Later in his career, after he had pinned on his fourth star, he would mastermind a rewrite of U.S. Army doctrine that transformed the post-Vietnam army. At this moment, however, he was not thinking ahead in time but back. During the Normandy invasion, as a twenty-five-year-old officer in the 90th Division, DePuy had seen poor American commanders squander American lives in appalling numbers. Determined to prevent the same from happening to the 1st Division on his watch, DePuy immediately scrutinized all his battalion and brigade commanders. Within a few days of taking command, DePuy fired a large number of them and replaced them with officers reputed for aggressiveness, some of whom he had pried away from other units.

Although General Seaman had never relieved any of his commanders, he did not object to any of DePuy's personnel changes. Army Chief of Staff Harold K. Johnson, on the other hand, sent DePuy a private letter informing him that the Army did not have enough officers to permit wholesale relief of commanding officers. DePuy defended his decisions in a detailed reply: "Col. A was a fat, disheveled officer without any soldierly characteris-

162 • **TRIUMPH REGAINED**

tics whatsoever who made a bad impression on all those people whom he briefed as a representative of 1st Division. Lt. Col. B was completely without talent of any kind whatsoever. He had no initiative, no imagination and repeatedly performed his duties in a sluggish, unintelligent manner.... [Lt. Col. C] lost complete control over his battalion and suffered a number of unnecessary casualties while inflicting none on the VC.... [Artillery Battalion Commander A] refused to admit responsibility personally or for any of his people for gross errors in artillery firing which led to civilian and friendly military casualties."[44]

When DePuy relieved some of his handpicked officers, General Johnson scolded him again. "I can't have you be the filter for all the best officers we have in the Army to see if they meet your approval," Johnson told DePuy during a face-to-face meeting later in the year. "You get the army's best officers assigned, and then you relieve them. I need division commanders who make the best of the human material they are assigned."

"I'm not here to run a training ground," DePuy countered. "They get people killed!"[45]

While some of DePuy's personnel changes may have been open to question, the improvement in the 1st Division's performance could not be doubted. Its first major operation under the new commander was El Paso II, which kicked off at the beginning of June. Based on intelligence reports that the 9th North Vietnamese Division was making ready for major offensive activity, DePuy sent two of his brigades into Binh Long Province for a preemptive strike.

General Hoang Cam, the irrepressible commander of the 9th Division, did not need long to identify the presence of intruders in his staging area. He ordered his 272nd Regiment to prepare an ambush along Route 13, undaunted by the fact that the Americans had already smashed 9th Division forces near this same road twice since the beginning of the year, during Operations Rolling Stone and Cocoa Beach. For the ambush site, the 272nd Regiment selected a three-kilometer section of Route 13 near the village of Tau O. It was bounded at each end by a small bridge, beneath which flowed streams of sufficient size to obstruct vehicular traffic should the bridges be disabled. Along this stretch, both sides of the road were saturated with heavy vegetation, ideal for concealing ambush forces, and they were specked with revetments made of sandbags and dirt-filled barrels that Communist forces had used for roadside ambushes in prior years.

The 272nd Regiment planned to destroy the two bridges once an American convoy was strung out between them, thereby preventing the column from escaping forward or backward or receiving reinforcements. Then the North Vietnamese infantry would assail the column from the flanks and rip it apart. One infantry battalion of the 272nd Regiment would block the head of the American column and attack the vehicles near the front, a second would assault the middle of the column, and a third would seal the rear and attack the last vehicles. Three heavy weapons companies were positioned to provide supporting fire, and one company of civilian laborers was on hand to move supplies and retrieve casualties.

On June 8, after the North Vietnamese had been sitting in their ambush positions for several days, an American armored convoy of the desired size approached the ambush site. The number of American soldiers in the convoy totaled 135, roughly one-tenth the number of North Vietnamese soldiers who were laying in waiting. Most of these 135 men were riding atop the convoy's seventeen tanks and armored personnel carriers because of the threat of mines.

Once the convoy had passed completely into the three-kilometer ambush zone, the North Vietnamese sprang the trap.

Sappers blew the bridges, the heavy weapons of the 272nd Regiment cried out, and infantrymen emerged from their foxholes to charge the vehicles. Initial North Vietnamese salvos knocked out several American armored personnel carriers and compelled the American infantrymen to jump inside the remaining vehicles or seek cover behind them. The surviving armored personnel carriers responded quickly with their machine guns, and the tanks fired beehive rounds, save for one that was equipped with a flamethrower, which disgorged a fifty-meter jet of burning liquid from a 250-gallon tank.

The ambush site lay beyond the range of American artillery, a problem that would lead post-battle investigators to recommend avoidance of future operations outside artillery range. American aircraft, however, soon arrived to shower the North Vietnamese with napalm and bombs. American drivers brought their vehicles together into clusters and backed them up to one another so that they could protect each other's backs. North Vietnamese 82mm mortar rounds closed in on the clusters and North Vietnamese recoilless rifle crews concentrated their weapons on them.

The North Vietnamese attack soon fell into disarray, which North Vietnamese histories would blame on both heavy American fire and poor North Vietnamese leadership. At the front of the column, North Vietnamese companies failed to coordinate their actions with one another, and one of them became so spread out that its officers were unable to direct their soldiers. In the North Vietnamese battalion at the center of the American column, a platoon leader "lost control of his men," as one North Vietnamese account described it. "When he reached the road he found that he had only one man with him."[46] During the attack on the rear of the column, a North Vietnamese company got lost, and some of the other platoons advanced too slowly and did not fire simultaneously as had been planned.

Only a few North Vietnamese soldiers managed to reach the American vehicles and climb on top of them. They were shot off by the weapons of other vehicles before they could harm the occupants. The North Vietnamese did, however, continue to land punishing blows with their crew-served weapons. Recoilless rifle rounds struck several more armored personnel carriers and a tank, killing their crewmen or leaving them severely burned. A North Vietnamese mortar scored a direct hit on another American tank, setting it ablaze and killing all its crew except the driver, who drove the tank into a stream to douse the fire.

After four hours, the North Vietnamese abandoned the ambush. As they were withdrawing, American armored reinforcements ran into and over a North Vietnamese company. Large numbers of North Vietnamese infantrymen were suddenly standing within grenade distance of American vehicles, but they had run out of grenades, and they had no more ammunition for their heavy weapons, so they were reduced to throwing empty recoilless rifle shell casings at the vehicles. A North Vietnamese history explained that this tactic was intended "to trick and frighten the enemy."[47]

After the battle, the Americans counted a total of 170 enemy bodies. On one corpse, they found documents identifying the man as an adviser from the Chinese Communist People's Liberation Army. They also captured four enemy soldiers and forty-two weapons. The American forward air controller estimated that between 200 and 250 more dead men had been dragged away. The American cavalry troop had sustained 14 killed and 37 wounded.[48]

In the northernmost provinces of I Corps, the Marines were beginning to enjoy some success in engaging large North Vietnamese units. On June 22, General Walt sent a force of Marines to Cam Lo, in central Quang Tri, in his latest effort to find the North Vietnamese units prowling the province. This time, the enemy was everywhere to be found. The first Marine reconnaissance patrol and each one thereafter ran into North Vietnamese regulars. "No patrol was able to stay in the field for more than a few hours, many for only a few minutes," one witness recalled. General Walt readied large forces for combat in central Quang Tri.[49]

In Thua Thien Province, the action began near the populous coast rather than in the inland wilderness. On June 25, the opening day of Operation Jay, two U.S. Marine battalions ran into three North Vietnamese Army battalions that had entrenched themselves in fortified hamlets. Extensive pounding from U.S. naval gunfire, artillery, and bombers did little to soften up the North Vietnamese, and multiple Marine assaults on the hamlets came to naught. After dark, the North Vietnamese counterattacked the Marines but were repulsed. The counterattack may have been intended merely to preoccupy the Marines while most of the North Vietnamese sneaked away, for all three of the North Vietnamese battalions were gone by dawn. The Marines counted twenty-three of their own dead and fifty-eight wounded, while they retrieved eight-two enemy bodies and estimated that another two hundred had perished.[50]

As the middle of the year approached, the debate in Washington over Rolling Thunder took a new turn on account of heightened interest from McNamara in bombing POL sites. McNamara was particularly impressed by the fact that increased North Vietnamese infiltration of supplies by gas-guzzling trucks had made North Vietnam much more reliant on POL. McNamara's conversion on this topic led promptly to the president's.

"The effect of not disrupting POL shipments to the North Vietnamese forces in the field is to pay a higher price in U.S. casualties," President Johnson pronounced at a meeting of the National Security Council on June 17.[51] Within a week, the White

House ordered strikes on seven POL storage sites in the Hanoi-Haiphong area. The first bombs were supposed to drop on June 24, but the sorties were delayed because someone in Washington leaked the plans to the press, whose publication of the information gave advance warning to the North Vietnamese. The first POL strikes took place on June 30.[52]

Although the POL strikes represented a significant concession to the hawks, Johnson persisted in his unwillingness to wield the most powerful of the military tools that the generals were exhorting him to use. Rolling Thunder continued to operate under most of the longstanding restrictions in the Hanoi-Haiphong area, and it was not striking other key targets with the intensity and repetition required for complete and enduring destruction. Johnson also kept rejecting the advice of Westmoreland to take the war into enemy sanctuaries in Laos and Cambodia, which were becoming ever more valuable as the North Vietnamese increasingly fought their big battles near South Vietnam's borders.

In June, the North Vietnamese leadership engaged in their own contentious debate on strategy and tactics. On one side was Nguyen Chi Thanh, who wanted to keep fighting large battles. His position received support from anonymous articles in official party publications, most of which seem to have been written by other senior strategists, though one article praised Nguyen Chi Thanh so profusely as to arouse speculation that the general had written it himself. In defense of the current strategy and tactics, the pro-Thanh faction argued that North Vietnamese forces in the South were destroying entire American battalions at little cost to themselves. Shifting to guerrilla tactics, they contended, would play into the enemy's hands because the American objective was to force North Vietnam's main forces into dispersing and fighting a guerrilla war.[53]

Vo Nguyen Giap articulated a contrary position in private meetings with the rest of the party leadership, and received reinforcement from other anonymous articles. In his view, the time had come for a strategy of protracted guerrilla warfare. The large-scale conventional warfare of the recent past, he stated, had led only to massive North Vietnamese casualties at relatively low cost to the Americans.[54] North Vietnamese sources have not explained why Giap thought the war was going poorly, but he undoubtedly had spoken with North Vietnamese officers who had witnessed battles in the South firsthand, and he also had access to the articles of Western journalists who reported seeing hundreds of dead North Vietnamese soldiers after battles that claimed only a few dozen American lives. Evidently he trusted these sources more than the rosy official reports produced by North Vietnamese combat commanders for Hanoi's consumption.

Although Giap still held the titles of supreme commander of the armed forces, minister of defense, and secretary of the Central Military Party Committee, his authority was smaller than those titles suggested, having been constricted in 1964 during the party's campaign against "revisionism." Key strategic decisions were now made by a five-man Politburo subcommittee that consisted of Le Duan, Le Duc Tho, Van Tien Dung, Pham Hung, and Giap, and other committee members had repeatedly voted to take Nguyen Chi Thanh's military advice over Giap's.[55] At least some of them had been taken in by Nguyen Chi Thanh's blithe depiction of the military situation, and had no doubt been behind some of the anonymous articles extolling his strategic acumen.

At a meeting in the middle of June, the majority of the five-man committee voted to stick with the strategy of attrition and the tactics of large conventional attacks. They would "keep the enemy continuously under attack" through conventional operations, though there would be two surge periods. The first would be a "winter wave" that ran from mid-October to the end of November 1966, and the second a "spring wave" that ran from the end of January to the end of March 1967. The persistence of offensive operations, said the committee, would "force the U.S. and the puppets to disperse their strategic reserve mobile forces to deal with North Vietnam's main force army" and "force the enemy to passively react to our actions," which together would "create favorable conditions for other battlefields."[56]

The top geographic priority for the offensive waves was to be the region north of Saigon, followed in second by the Quang Tri–Thua Thien region, with the central highlands third. The North Vietnamese leaders considered the terrain and weather in these areas to be well suited to attacks on American and South Vietnamese forces, and all three were close to the sanctuaries of Cambodia, Laos, or North Vietnam. Resource limitations necessitated that the North Vietnamese forswear major campaigns in most other areas of South Vietnam and thus to concede the bulk of the country's rice to the enemy.

According to Nguyen Chi Thanh, the fighting would continue into the summer of 1967 but would lead to a "decisive victory" by the end of 1967.[57] By "decisive victory," General Thanh appears to have meant the collapse of the South Vietnamese armed forces and the withdrawal of the American military. Official statements on the subject were, however, deliberately left vague. Having already promised a "decisive victory" in 1965, some North Vietnamese leaders were wary of new predictions, particularly those involving the defeat of the world's strongest power in one year. Hopes could be raised and dashed only so many times before debilitating disillusionment set in.

Yet Hanoi's leaders also knew that numerous Communist leaders at lower levels, particularly those native to the southern half of the country, were growing impatient. A North Vietnamese officer who defected to the South Vietnamese government in July 1966 said that while officers from the North had steeled themselves for a long and bloody struggle, the Southern cadres "are resolved to end the war in South Vietnam as quickly as possible" so that they can "return to civilian life."[58] Somehow the Northerners would need to reassure the Southerners that Hanoi had realistic plans for victory without overpromising.

The North Vietnamese decided to issue new guidance that reiterated the current strategy while explaining away the forecast of victory in 1965 and avoiding a raising of expectations. The deputy commander of the General Staff, General Nguyen Van Vinh, decreed that when selling the coming offensive to those below, Communist leaders were to explain that the party's 1965 promise of a "decisive victory within a relatively short period of time" might have been taken too literally. "In speaking of winning victory over the enemy in the special war," the general lectured, "we did not mean a total victory but a decisive victory." No explanation of the difference between total victory and decisive victory was provided.

General Nguyen Van Vinh continued, "When we speak of achieving success within a relatively short period of time, it means that we assert our determination." It was unduly pessimistic, he noted, to rule out a defeat of the Americans in a short period of time, and total victory would surely be won within a few years. Nevertheless, "In indoctrinating the cadres and party members ideologically, we must speak of protracted fighting and the determination to fight and win, and must not disseminate to the lower echelons the idea of achieving decisive success within a few years."[59]

CHAPTER 7

· · ·

THE REAL GRAND MARSHAL

July–September 1966

A t the beginning of July, the lightning bolts of Rolling Thunder crashed down on North Vietnam's POL storage sites and transportation assets. While Douglas EB-66 Destroyers and Lockheed EC-121 Warning Stars flew long-range jamming missions above the Gulf of Tonkin and eastern Laos, strike aircraft swooped into North Vietnamese air space to drop their payloads. In conformance with the theory of gradual escalation, the overall rate of bombing was incrementally higher than in preceding weeks.

When the crews of North Vietnam's antiaircraft radar realized that American jamming signals were blinding their equipment, they employed all the anti-jamming measures known to the Communist bloc. They could, however, find no antidote to the newest American techniques. According to an official history, the North Vietnamese Air Defense Service was forced to conclude that "the most effective tactic for dealing with enemy jamming is to destroy the source of the jamming." Neither North Vietnam's fleet of jet aircraft nor its ground-based missiles were able to shoot down any of the Destroyers or Warning Stars that were emitting the jamming signals.[1] Although North Vietnamese antiaircraft artillery still fired flak at any American strike aircraft they could see or hear, the likelihood of hitting a high-flying jet aircraft was much lower in the absence of radar guidance.

Within a matter of days, the bombs were landing on all the major POL targets near the Hanoi-Haiphong area. They detonated oil held in storage containers, triggering massive secondary explosions that served as confirmation that the bombers had found their marks. Thick black smoke, penetrated occasionally by orange flames, puffed up from the ruins of bulk storage containers. It was visible in every direction for dozens of miles.

The destruction of oil storage facilities evoked rage and despair among North Vietnamese officials and citizens, with the exception of individuals who secretly despised the Communist regime. It was simultaneously cause for rejoicing among the group in North Vietnam that most uniformly detested the regime, the American prisoners of war. By the middle of 1966, the North Vietnamese had captured and incarcerated several hundred American servicemen, most of them airmen whose planes had been shot down over North Vietnamese territory. Aside from a small minority who readily collaborated with their captors, the American prisoners had tried at first to abide by the official U.S. Code of Conduct, which prohibited them from divulging any information beyond their name, rank, serial number, and date of birth. Staunchly patriotic, they abhorred the thought of disclosing information that the North Vietnamese could use to harm the Americans who were continuing to fight the war.

When prisoners refused initial demands for their cooperation, the North Vietnamese subjected them to a systematic program of torture, degradation, and deprivation, in violation of commitments it had made under the Geneva Convention Relative to the Treatment of Prisoners of War. Interrogators sought to extract information on American military tactics and technology, as well as "confessions" to participation in the "crimes" of the United States. The North Vietnamese were especially intent on obtaining testimonials affirming Hanoi's propaganda line that Rolling Thunder deliberately targeted North Vietnam's civilian population.

Making statements in support of North Vietnamese propaganda on Rolling Thunder was especially revolting to the American airmen because they knew, from firsthand experience, that it was fraudulent. During their missions over North Vietnam, they had been prohibited from striking residential areas and had incurred considerable risks to avoid harming civilians during their attacks on military targets. The political and military leaders of the Johnson administration had refused to target population centers as their predecessors had done in World War II, because they viewed the deliberate bombing of civilians as morally objectionable and believed it would undermine domestic and international support for the American cause. Rolling Thunder did take the lives of large numbers of North Vietnamese civilians, but mainly because they had been located at or near military targets or had been hit by stray bombs. The total number of North Vietnamese civilians who would be killed from the start of Rolling Thunder in March 1965 to its end in November 1968, estimated at fifty-two thousand, was smaller than the death tolls of single bombing raids on Tokyo, Hiroshima, and Nagasaki in 1945.[2]

The favorite method of North Vietnamese torturers was strappado, a cruelty that was medieval in both its historical origins and its inhumanity. The torture staff began by binding the victim's arms behind his back. Then, using a rope tied to his wrists, they suspended him from a meat hook. By tightening ropes or putting weight on various parts of the body, the interrogator could squeeze off circulation and produce the most excruciating of bodily pain.

If the victim refused to give in promptly, the procedure could go on for days, long after his shoulders had been dislocated and his soft tissue had been torn to shreds.

One American who lived to tell of his experience in "the ropes," as the Americans called the technique, was Gerald Coffee. A Navy pilot from Modesto, California, Coffee had been shot down on February 3, 1966, while flying a reconnaissance mission in an RA-5C Vigilante. The torture was administered by a fiendish North Vietnamese interrogator whom the Americans nicknamed Pigeye because of his pig-like face and a dysfunctional eye. When Pigeye began to tighten the ropes, Coffee recounted, "I could feel the rending of tendons and cartilage in my hip sockets and my lower back." One of Pigeye's assistants stood on an iron bar that kept Coffee's feet from moving, with the result that the tightening of ropes pulled Coffee's shoulders toward his ankles and compressed his lungs. "I could hardly breathe," Coffee remembered, "so constricted were my lungs from being bent over in a tightening little ball." Once Pigeye began jumping on Coffee's shoulders, "The pain was all there was. The pain in every joint, bone, muscle in my body filled my entire consciousness."[3]

Other common torture techniques included leg irons, whips, and water torture. For the most recalcitrant prisoners, interrogators resorted to the removal of fingernails, the burning of flesh with cigarettes, and the administration of electric shocks. The North Vietnamese methods eventually caused most of the prisoners to cooperate to one degree or another, even men of extraordinary toughness and patriotic conviction like James Stockdale, the senior naval officer among the prisoners, who ultimately earned the Congressional Medal of Honor for his leadership of the prisoner community and later ran for vice president of the United States.

Stockdale and other imprisoned officers concluded that because of the Hanoi government's gruesome practices, prisoners could not be expected to adhere strictly to the U.S. Code of Conduct. Instead, the senior officers told the rest of the servicemen to avoid cooperation until they were subjected to severe physical coercion. "We set a line of resistance we thought was within the capability of each POW to hold, and we ruled that no man would cross that line without significant torture," Stockdale explained afterward.[4]

Another very tough man who was broken by torture was Jeremiah Denton. When the ropes failed to elicit his cooperation, the torturers jumped up and down on an iron roller placed across his shins. Denton held out for several days before the pain became so horrific that he capitulated. He agreed to confess to America's crimes on videotape—after devising an ingenious scheme to use the video against his antagonists. As Japanese cameramen recorded Denton on May 2, 1966, he blinked a one-word message in Morse code: TORTURE. It was the first confirmation received by the United States of Hanoi's treatment of the prisoners.[5]

During the first week of July, as the prisoners milled around prison camp radios, they heard commentary on the new bombing campaign from an English-speaking North Vietnamese newscaster they called "Hanoi Hannah." As described by historian John G. Hubbell, who interviewed a large number of the survivors after their return to the United States, Hanoi Hannah railed against the air strikes so venomously that the prisoners became convinced that "at last, Washington had taken off the gloves and was hitting the enemy where it hurt."[6] The sullenness of prison existence dissipated, and in its place came hopefulness that the bombing would compel Hanoi to end the war and relinquish the prisoners to the U.S. government.

On July 6, guards blindfolded and handcuffed fifty-two of the captives, then loaded them aboard trucks. To the prisoners, this unusual development appeared to confirm that the bombing had convinced the North Vietnamese government to send them home. Abounding in glee, the Americans surmised that they were being moved to Hanoi in preparation for their plane ride to the United States.

The trucks did, in fact, take the Americans to Hanoi. When the prisoners disembarked from the trucks and had their blindfolds removed, they were facing down a wide city street. Bleachers had been erected on both sides of the thoroughfare, as one would see at a parade, and they were packed with North Vietnamese civilians. At the end of the street was a stadium. The prisoners were not sure what to make of this scene. Some guessed that they were being given an official sendoff prior to returning to their homeland.

A man with a battery-powered megaphone promptly disabused the American of that notion. "Now you are going to see the hatred of the Vietnamese people," he said in English to the captives. "We are going to try to protect you, but we are not going to kill any Vietnamese in doing so. So if the people want to kill you they are going to kill you. Now I give you advice: do not look to the right or to the left, do not look behind you. Do not speak. Walk straight ahead. Show a proper attitude to the Vietnamese people. Bow your heads in shame for your crimes."[7]

Prodded by the guards, the prisoners moved forward in rows of two, each row separated by ten feet. From the bleachers, the throng erupted in angry shrieks and shaking of fists. Cruising alongside the column to document the proceedings was a truck loaded with Cuban, French, and other foreign journalists and cameramen sympathetic to Hanoi.

Although the prisoners were by now having considerable doubts about the imminence of their return to the United States, they also doubted that the North Vietnamese were serious about letting the spectators hurt prisoners of war, let alone kill them. Probably, the Americans told themselves, the North Vietnamese just wanted to take some photos of bedraggled Americans in humiliating poses for use in their propaganda. A few of the prisoners broke into open defiance. Jeremiah Denton shouted to the other Americans, "You are Americans! Keep your heads up!"[8] He waved a V for Victory sign at the cameras and gave the middle finger to the hecklers in the grandstands.

Suddenly, a dozen men burst past the guards and set upon the POWs, punching and kicking. The guards watched impassively. Spectators took it as a cue to pour from the bleachers and sidewalks into the street. Their faces full of anger and malice, the civilians spit on the Americans and screamed at them to bow and kowtow. Men and women alike beat the prisoners and pelted them with stones, bricks, and bottles. A number of the guards joined the mob in punching and kicking the prisoners, reserving special viciousness for those who refused to bow their heads.

Soon, the Americans were convinced that the North Vietnamese had not been kidding about the possibility of death. Some of them fought back against their assailants and pushed their way forward through the crowd toward the stadium, which appeared to be a safer place than the street. Denton saw prisoners ahead of him shoving and jostling, and although he did not know who they were, he was proud to call them his countrymen.

At some point, higher authorities made clear that the prisoners were not to be killed, for the guards started pushing the frenzied civilians away and shepherding the prisoners through toward the stadium. All of the prisoners were able to make it inside the stadium alive. The guards, seeming nearly as relieved as the prisoners to escape the mob, locked the entrance shut.

A number of the Americans wondered whether they would now be thrown to the lions, as in early Christian times. No such danger awaited. They had time to regroup and look each other over. From the bruises and bloody gashes, they could tell that no man had escaped a severe thrashing.

Over the public address system, a voice informed the POWs, "You have seen the just wrath of the Vietnamese people. Those of you who have seen the light and want to apologize for your crimes and join the Vietnamese people will receive lenient and humane treatment. If you are true Americans, you will follow the way of Fulbright, the way of Morse, the way of Mansfield." Otherwise, the voice said, the prisoners would be handed back to the justly wrathful Vietnamese people.[9] The prisoners were returned to their camps and advised to produce confessions in order to avoid further trouble.

Radio Hanoi promptly issued official spin on the event. "Angry people," a spokesman proclaimed, had berated American airmen on Hanoi's streets because they "had committed unpardonable crimes by bombing and strafing populated areas, economic and other public utility establishments." Omitting mention of the violence, the announcer asserted that "the Hanoians, though seething with anger at the crimes committed by the U.S. air pirates, showed themselves to be highly disciplined. Otherwise, the sheer thought of these crimes might have prompted them to tear [Lyndon] Johnson's 'skywarriors' to pieces."[10]

For neither the first nor the last time, the Hanoi government had miscalculated how the American people would react. The North Vietnamese had anticipated that the violent and demeaning parade would demoralize American supporters of the war and compel the Johnson administration to ease off the bombing. Instead, the news of the event demoralized only American opponents of the war, some of whom went so far as to censure the North Vietnamese regime. Senator Robert Kennedy announced, "I have dissented at many points from this war and its conduct, but I am at one with all Americans in regarding any reprisal against these young men as an intolerable act—contrary to the laws of war, contrary to all past practices in this war, a plunge into barbarism."

Nineteen additional Senate doves, including Senators Church, Fulbright, McCarthy, McGovern, and Morse, issued a "plea for sanity" to Hanoi. In their plea, they urged the North Vietnamese to "refrain from any act of abuse against the American airmen," who "are prisoners of war, fully entitled to the protection extended to men in uniform when captured in the performance of their duty." The Senators warned that if the North Vietnamese government executed the prisoners as war criminals, as it was reportedly considering, it "would drastically reduce the influence of all those in the United States who have tried to curtail the fighting" and "would incite a public demand for retaliation, swift and sure."[11]

Chastened, the North Vietnamese would not stage another prisoner parade. Nor would they drop any more hints that they would try the prisoners as criminals. In the hidden world of the "Hanoi Hilton" and other prison camps, though, the torture continued. For years to come, prisoners would be strong-armed into regurgitating North Vietnamese propaganda on camera or to pro-Hanoi visitors from the West. One of the most senior of the POWs, Navy Captain James A. Mulligan Jr., told the press after his release in 1973 that 95 percent of the prisoners had been tortured and that 80 percent had provided statements denouncing the purported crimes of the United States.[12]

Lyndon Johnson was no more intimidated than any other American by the Hanoi parade. Rolling Thunder continued apace.

By the end of July, it had obliterated all the large POL facilities in North Vietnam and disabled all the rail lines that carried POL tank cars. According to U.S. intelligence estimates, July's campaign destroyed 78 percent of targeted POL capacity.

Despite the spectacular pyrotechnics and the large quantities of enemy assets destroyed, however, the air campaign did not have the crippling impact that its American proponents had originally projected. During the many months when the Americans had been debating among themselves whether to hit the POL targets, the North Vietnamese had dispersed oil storage to small containers across the country. Much of the oil was now in barrels that lined city streets, which the North Vietnamese knew the Americans would not bomb for humanitarian reasons. Dispersion introduced new inefficiencies into the North Vietnamese logistical system and added many thousands of people to the several hundred thousand North Vietnamese who were fully occupied with counteracting the effects of Rolling Thunder. The North Vietnamese, nevertheless, could still store enough of the Soviet oil received at Haiphong Harbor to fuel the trains and trucks that transported armaments to South Vietnam.[13]

From the perspective of the White House, the bombing achieved better results in the United States than in North Vietnam. Large numbers of Americans who had previously opposed expansion of the bombing zones rallied behind the president once the bombs started falling on the POL targets, which by their obvious relevance to Hanoi's war machine were more palatable to some Americans than other targets. Heretofore the American public had been split 50-50 on expanding the bombing into the Hanoi-Haiphong area, but after the POL strikes began, public support swung to 85 percent in favor.[14] The POL campaign was also accompanied by an increase in support for Johnson's handling of the war, from 42 percent to 54 percent.[15]

As evidence mounted that the POL campaign would not wreck Hanoi's supply system, Cambodia gained in prominence as a means of disrupting North Vietnamese logistics. MACV intelligence was reporting heavy Communist infiltration of rice and military supplies from Cambodian territory into South Vietnam. According to their figures, Chinese Communist supplies were now coming through the port of Sihanoukville at a rate of over one thousand tons per year. On the basis of these reports, Westmoreland and the Joint Chiefs advocated ground operations on Cambodian soil and covert operations in Cambodia to outbid the enemy for rice and ammunition.

The CIA, however, contended that Westmoreland's intelligence staff overestimated the importance of Cambodia to the North Vietnamese war effort in South Vietnam. Communist forces, its analysts asserted, still depended "primarily on the South Vietnamese countryside" for food supplies. Westmoreland considered the attitude of the CIA to be "disturbing" and suspected that the agency was "reflecting what Washington wanted to hear." The State Department stoked that suspicion by invoking the CIA's interpretation in denying Westmoreland's requests for action in Cambodia. The proposed actions, asserted the State Department, would not have enough impact on North Vietnamese activities to justify the risks of provoking Sihanouk into overt collaboration with Hanoi.[16]

In hindsight, it appears doubtful that overt collaboration could have been worse for the United States than the status quo. North Vietnamese historians have revealed that North Vietnamese logistical activities in Cambodia were by this time more significant than even Westmoreland's command recognized. The severing of the maritime infiltration routes to the South Vietnamese coast in early 1965 had led Hanoi to seek new maritime routes for infiltration of weapons and ammunition, and by early 1966 the North

Vietnamese were scheduling shipments from North Vietnam, China, and the Soviet Union into Sihanoukville. In July 1966, the North Vietnamese set up an ostensibly capitalist company in Cambodia that paid the Cambodian armed forces in gold to transport weapons and ammunition from Sihanoukville to the South Vietnamese border.[17]

The new maritime infiltration program made use of ships that dwarfed their predecessors. One Chinese freighter that berthed in Sihanoukville in the fall of 1966 delivered three thousand tons of weapons and ammunition for transshipment to North Vietnamese forces.[18] By comparison, the eighty-nine maritime infiltration voyages from North Vietnam to the South Vietnamese coast between February 1962 and February 1965 had altogether delivered approximately five thousand tons.[19] In this one shipment to Sihanoukville, the North Vietnamese delivered more weapons and ammunition than the Ho Chi Minh Trail had delivered to South Vietnam in all of 1965.[20]

The infiltration of weapons by land and sea during 1966 permitted the arming of North Vietnamese forces with unprecedented quantities of assault rifles, machine guns, rocket launchers, recoilless rifles, mortars, and flamethrowers. In the hands of North Vietnamese soldiers, there began to appear state-of-the-art Soviet and Chinese heavy weapons, such as the 82mm recoilless rifle and the 120mm mortar. The latter was capable of hitting American and South Vietnamese bases from twice the distance of other mortars, thereby quadrupling the amount of territory that base security units had to patrol.[21]

The organic weapons of North Vietnamese conventional forces now rivaled those of American forces, and were much superior to those of the South Vietnamese Army. American factories were manufacturing enough machine guns and M-16 assault rifles to outfit all U.S. Army and Marine Corps units, but few were left over for South Vietnamese forces. It would be another year before the United States would produce sufficient numbers of M-16s to allocate as many of the rifles to South Vietnamese as American units.[22] Because the North Vietnamese Army possessed far more automatic weapons than the South Vietnamese Army, South Vietnamese commanders were loath to close with enemy forces and instead relied on air and artillery strikes as much as possible, which often allowed the enemy to escape unwanted engagements at minimal cost.[23]

The North Vietnamese were also procuring food in Cambodia on a scale larger than any of the Americans knew. During 1966, in response to a growing gap between the needs of North Vietnamese forces and the food available to them from South Vietnamese sources and the Ho Chi Minh Trail, North Vietnamese logistical personnel established front organizations in Cambodia to acquire foodstuffs and transport them to South Vietnam. To prevent the Americans from catching on to their scheme, they operated under the cover of plantation owners or businessmen, living in large villas, driving large automobiles, and dressing in fancy clothes.[24] Communist histories do not provide figures for the amount of food purchased each year, but they do reveal that the amount surged in 1966 and that between 1965 and 1974, the North Vietnamese bought a startling 268,000 tons of rice in Cambodia, enough to keep 150,000 soldiers fed continuously throughout those ten years.[25]

Despite the upsurge in the acquisition of food in Cambodia, the North Vietnamese were unable to keep their forces in South Vietnam adequately fed during 1966. At the time, CIA and State Department analysts doubted that enemy units were experiencing debilitating food shortfalls.[26] Westmoreland and others in the military, however, concluded that by August shortages of food were seriously constraining enemy activity, particularly in the highlands.[27] North Vietnamese sources published after the war confirmed the accuracy of Westmoreland's assessment.

Nguyen Huu An, who was now a division commander in the highlands, recalled that rice shortages necessitated that every soldier, from the senior commanders on down, spend a considerable part of his time cultivating manioc. This crop, known in other lands as cassava or yuca, was easy to cultivate in any type of soil, and it could withstand both droughts and monsoon rains. Manioc yielded tubers resembling sweet potatoes, rich in carbohydrates, which could sustain men for extended periods with little or no rice. But manioc alone was incapable of maintaining combat-ready troops, for unlike rice it lacked the protein required for strenuous activities like protracted marching and fighting. Hence rice, whether cultivated in South Vietnam or imported from elsewhere, was to remain an obsession of the North Vietnamese Army for the remainder of the war.

"We often joked to one another that, 'Rice is the real grand marshal of our army,'" Nguyen Huu An recalled. "This was true. If we wanted to launch a combat campaign of even the shortest duration, one of the major questions was, 'Do we have enough rice?'"[28]

Shortages of rice and medical supplies kept the entire 7th Division out of action from the middle of 1966, when it was nominally assigned to the strategic infiltration corridor near Route 13, until the spring of 1967.[29] The incapacitated troops would have been very useful in the first major battle of July, in which the U.S. 1st Division fought the North Vietnamese Army's 9th Division in Binh Long Province once more. This time, the site of combat would be the Minh Thanh road, which linked Route 13 to the Saigon River. The principal North Vietnamese combat element would be the 272nd Regiment of the 9th Division, replenished with eight hundred soldiers who had just completed the march down the Ho Chi Minh Trail.

U.S. intelligence had detected the presence of the 272nd Regiment well before the engagement, although American reports on the battle did not divulge the means by which it had been detected. North Vietnamese officers may well have concluded that radio intercepts had led the Americans to the 272nd Regiment, for North Vietnam's senior leaders were at this moment deeply worried that American interception of their communications were making possible numerous American attacks on their forces. The Central Party Secretariat had just issued a directive declaring that "the protection of secrecy in communication-liaison by radio is the number one problem of importance in the protracted war between ourselves and the enemy."[30]

Based upon the intelligence concerning the 272nd Regiment, the U.S. 1st Infantry Division formulated a plan to lure the North Vietnamese into battle on terms favorable to the Americans. The 1st Infantry Division would dangle before them a convoy that appeared weaker, more isolated, and more heavily laden with valuable supplies than it actually was. American officers produced a fake operational plan for the convoy stating that bulldozers and richly stocked trucks were traversing the Minh Thanh road with only a small escort of armored cavalry, then passed it to a South Vietnamese office suspected of harboring spies. The Americans actually assigned the convoy three full cavalry troops and an infantry company, and positioned four infantry battalions nearby to serve as rapid reaction forces. In advance of the convoy's departure, artillery tubes were pointed at the road, and aircraft were sent into the skies nearby.

The division commander, General DePuy, spoke to the troops before they headed out. "In this war, we have to kill more of the enemy than they kill of us in order to win," DePuy said, looking into the eyes of men whose faces conveyed a seriousness beyond their years. "We are going to use our advantages, and we are going to kill a lot of the enemy. And we are going to win." At the conclusion of his remarks, DePuy told them, "Now it's up to you. Be tough. Be aggressive. Do your job. This is the 1st Infantry Division. We have a reputation to live up to."

Colonel Sidney B. Berry Jr., commander of the brigade that was directing the operation, spoke next. The 272nd Regiment was their principal adversary in this section of Vietnam, Berry said. "Because of our operations, 272nd Regiment forces do not stay inside South Vietnam for very long now," he explained. "They move across the border, attack a target, and move back to their base sanctuaries in Cambodia. It is an ideal situation for them—we cannot follow them into Cambodia. Do not ask me how they arranged this with our Congress."

Colonel Berry was followed by Brigadier General James F. Hollingsworth, the assistant division commander. One of the most decorated soldiers of what became known as the Greatest Generation, Hollingsworth had come out of World War II with three Distinguished Service Crosses, three Distinguished Flying Crosses, four Silver Stars, four Bronze Stars, and six Purple Hearts. As an officer in the 2nd Armored Division, he had been steeled for battle by the speeches of General George S. Patton. Echoes of Patton could be heard in the remarks Berry delivered now.

"These sons of bitches are going to be surprised all to hell," Hollingsworth barked. "We don't get 'em like that often." Because they were so close to the Cambodian border, Hollingsworth said, they had to strike quickly and pursue relentlessly. "Get your men ready, get 'em mean. There are times to go slowly, and there are times to lock and load—kick ass. This is that time, won't be a long period. Gotta get in there fast and move fast. Kill fast. The ambush could take place less than ten miles from a line we cannot cross. That doesn't give us much time to muck around. Don't stop because one of your men gets hurt. Press on. Leave a medic behind or a guard and push on."

The three infantry battalions of the 272nd Regiment had established themselves in covered ambush positions along a two-kilometer stretch of the Minh Thanh road. The distance between their foxholes and the road's laterite surface ranged from one hundred to four hundred meters. The convoy moved in their direction at just a few miles per hour, with a platoon of American infantrymen walking on either side of the road in wedge formation. When the American vehicles reached the first section of red laterite soil on the Minh Thanh road, their wheels and treads kicked up clouds of the dirt. The red powder stung the eyes and lungs of the passengers and made their column visible to the North Vietnamese long before the column could see the North Vietnamese.

Periodically, the Americans fired small arms and artillery into the roadside foliage, seeking to draw the enemy into battle before the column had walked all the way into the ambush zone. The North Vietnamese forces, however, maintained strict discipline and refrained from prematurely discharging their weapons.

Just when the convoy reached the stretch of road that the Americans had considered the most likely trigger point, the heavy weapons of the 272nd Regiment loosed their first fusillade. North Vietnamese soldiers popped out of foxholes and dashed toward the vehicles. Charging the road at a multitude of points, the North Vietnamese intended to isolate the American vehicles and prevent them from forming defensive clusters, as the American armor had done so effectively at Tau O one month earlier.

Armor-piercing rounds slammed into the tank at the head of the American convoy and several other vehicles, bloodying their crewmen and igniting fires. The other vehicles in the convoy and the accompanying infantry returned fire with an arsenal of powerful weapons. The beehive rounds discharged by the tank main guns proved especially deadly to the onrushing infantry. North Vietnamese efforts to break the convoy into small pieces failed, for the American drivers had kept their vehicles close together during the approach and were able to compress quickly into two clusters.

American artillery immediately raked one side of the Minh Thanh road, and American jets flogged the other. Stacked by altitude at six levels, the jets took turns strafing the North Vietnamese and scalding them with napalm. In the few hundred meters on either side of the road, the earth was scorched a smoky black, pocked with dead and dying North Vietnamese soldiers. Few of the North Vietnamese ever made it across the kill zone between their foxholes and the American vehicles.

Helicopters landed three battalions of American soldiers in the surrounding area to cut off exit routes and initiate counterattacks, while a fourth American battalion advanced through the jungle on foot. Lieutenant James E. Parker Jr., an infantryman riding aboard one of the helicopters, recalled, "I caught myself whistling, looking ahead, tense. My stomach was queasy." Parker could hear explosions, faintly at first. Ahead, jets hurtled downward, parallel to the road, and then pulled back up, followed each time by the blossoming of a giant fireball. As Parker's helicopter made a diving run to the landing zone, he could see trees that had been denuded by napalm. Between them were black holes that had been gouged in the jungle surrounded by rings of fire.

The American infantry counterattacked the dwindling 272nd Regiment at several locations. Unexpectedly thick jungle slowed the movements of some American units, permitting a number of North Vietnamese soldiers to slip away before the encirclement had been completed. As the North Vietnamese retreated,

American spotters in the air fed their coordinates to helicopters and jets waiting to swoop in, resulting in further loss of life.

Once again, the 9th Division had been dealt a lopsided and devastating defeat. During searches of the battlefield, the Americans found 238 enemy bodies, and they estimated that an additional 305 North Vietnamese had been killed. American losses totaled 25 killed and 113 wounded.[31] After the battle of Minh Thanh road, the remainder of the 9th Division left Binh Long Province for Cambodia to recuperate.

During the remainder of the summer, the 1st Infantry Division conducted futile searches for the 9th Division in Binh Long. As a whole, III Corps was relatively uneventful for several months after the Minh Thanh engagement. The remaining North Vietnamese forces largely confined their attacks to small strikes on outmanned and outgunned South Vietnamese units.

The one major exception was a clash in August between the Australians and the North Vietnamese in Phuoc Tuy Province. As part of Operation Sheffield, an Australian battalion entered the Long Tan rubber plantation on August 18 and ran straight into the 5th North Vietnamese Army Regiment and the 445th local force battalion just as they were getting ready to attack an Australian headquarters. Monsoon rains prevented the Australians from employing air strikes or reinforcing by helicopter, but they made superb use of artillery and brought in a company of reinforcements by armed personnel carrier for a devastating counterattack. According to captured documents, North Vietnamese casualties from the battle totaled eight hundred dead and one thousand wounded, versus Australian losses of seventeen killed and twenty-one wounded.[32]

In the highlands, the only large battle of the summer took place during Operation Paul Revere II, a search-and-destroy operation launched by the U.S. 1st Cavalry Division and South

Korean forces. The search began in Pleiku Province, near the Cambodian border. Enticed by the proximity of hostile forces to its base area, the 88th NVA Regiment Army crossed over from Cambodia to attack the Americans and South Koreans. Having prepared themselves well for battle, the allied forces inflicted crippling damage on the North Vietnamese regiment, killing more than seven hundred of its men and capturing nearly a hundred. In the ensuing Paul Revere III, which began on August 25, the North Vietnamese avoided repetition of the mauling by staying inside Cambodia.[33]

To the east, in the coastal provinces of II Corps, a rise in the number of American combat battalions was followed in swift succession by a surge in search-and-destroy operations. Aimed primarily at the 3rd and 5th North Vietnamese Army divisions, these operations were intended to destroy enemy forces and deny them access to the rice harvest. The operations achieved these objectives and also disrupted Communist guerrilla operations and political activities in the villages. Because of the resultant food shortages, North Vietnamese soldiers had to steal rice, livestock, and other belongings from the population, which, in the words of one North Vietnamese account, "affected the fine traditions of the army and damaged the people's confidence in us."[34]

Southern and central I Corps witnessed one large battle in the summer, in the Que Son Valley. Straddling the border between Quang Nam and Quang Tin provinces, the valley was prized by the North Vietnamese for its high rice yield and its accessibility to both the Laotian infiltration routes and the coast. In August, during Operation Colorado, the U.S. 1st Marine Division and six South Vietnamese battalions located the North Vietnamese Army's 21st Regiment on the valley floor, and a series of firefights ensued. Lt. Colonel Ton That Soan, commander of the South Vietnamese Marine units that participated in the operation, recounted that "the volume of air support provided by U.S. aircraft from the Chu Lai Airbase and from the U.S. 7th Fleet off the coast was terrifying, precise, continuous, and incredibly powerful."[35]

The 21st Regiment, badly bloodied, was forced to slink away before it could seize appreciable amounts of rice or inflict much damage on opposing forces. The history of the 2nd North Vietnamese Army division, the parent unit of the 21st Regiment, attested, "while our forces were able to annihilate a number of enemy troops, our level of combat efficiency was low and our own casualties were high.... During the course of the ferocious, continuous, and tense fighting, a fear of combat and fear of death and sacrifice appeared among the troops of some of the units."[36]

A principal reason for the scarcity of combat in the southern and central provinces of I Corps was the allocation of most U.S. Marine mobile forces to the northernmost province of Quang Tri. After the upsurge in sightings of North Vietnamese units in Quang Tri during late June, intensified American reconnaissance operations located the 324B Division in the mountains of north-central Quang Tri, where layers of brush and hundred-foot jungle canopies concealed its nine thousand men from view. American intelligence agencies learned that the 324B Division intended to attack toward the coast, as the spearhead of an offensive to seize complete control of Quang Tri and Thua Thien provinces. Soon thereafter, additional reports confirmed that two more North Vietnamese regiments had infiltrated into western Quang Tri and another fifteen thousand North Vietnamese troops had taken up residence in Laos between Tchepone and the South Vietnamese border. These units could rapidly reinforce the 324B division in either Quang Tri or Thua Thien.[37]

General Walt decided to attack the 324B Division in its staging ground before it could venture forth. Employing the same military logic as Westmoreland, he considered an American spoiling attack to be preferable to an unexpected North Vietnamese attack at the time and place of North Vietnamese choosing. In the middle of July, a task force of four U.S. Marine infantry battalions and an artillery battalion headed toward the central section of the DMZ to hunt for the 324B division. The South Vietnamese committed part of the 1st ARVN Division and five battalions of their strategic reserve to the operation, which was dubbed Operation Hastings.

In conjunction with Operation Hastings, Westmoreland requested authorization for B-52 strikes in the DMZ, where he knew enemy logistical forces were hauling supplies to the 324B Division, and where enemy reinforcements might be gathering. The State Department authorized the employment of tactical bombers but rejected the request for the B-52s. It offered the following explanation: "At this time, such action would be regarded in many circles and the press as escalation and possibly even a misinterpretation as a softening up for more direct military action on the ground."[38] The reaction of Westmoreland and the Marine commanders to this statement was not recorded, but it is difficult to imagine their concurrence in the view that bombing division-sized violators of the demilitarized zone with large aircraft would invite much more severe and injurious reproach than bombing them with smaller aircraft.

The initial focal point of Operation Hastings was the Ngan Valley, where the 324B Division's command post and the 1,500 men of its 90th Regiment were believed to be located. On July 15, two U.S. Marine battalions entered the Ngan Valley by helicopter while South Vietnamese units scoured adjacent areas. One of the American battalions occupied blocking positions, toward which the other battalion would sweep the enemy.

The original plan was frustrated by unexpected problems of terrain and weather. Seven-foot-high elephant grass and oppressive heat and humidity slowed the advance of the sweeping battalion such that from midmorning to midafternoon, it advanced only two miles. During that period, it came across a two-hundred-bed hospital made of bamboo and several large supply caches, guarded by a few North Vietnamese soldiers, whom the Marines shot. The Americans also exchanged fire sporadically with North Vietnamese snipers, with each side losing several men.

At nightfall, the battalion was one mile short of its planned objectives. Surmising that large enemy forces were not far off, the battalion commander set up a perimeter for the night rather than continue on in the dark. The decision likely saved a large number of American lives, for soon after the Marines had dug their foxholes and eaten their C rations, they were attacked by a reinforced North Vietnamese company whose scouts had spotted them in the afternoon.

"It was so dark we couldn't see our hands in front of our faces, so we threw out trip flares and called for a flare plane overhead," recalled Captain Robert J. Modrzejewski, a company commander. "We could hear and smell and occasionally see the NVA after that."[39] The North Vietnamese assaulted in vain for three hours before running out of steam and taking leave of the Americans.

Brigadier General Lowell E. English, commander of the Marine task force, scrapped the original plan the next day and ordered the two battalions to come together. After linking up, the battalions probed through the elephant grass during the remaining hours of sunlight, making only light contact with the enemy. That night, they faced another North Vietnamese assault. Just one Marine died and five were wounded during the battle, whereas the Marines found seventy-nine enemy bodies around their perimeter the next morning.

On July 17 and 18, English inserted his third and fourth Marine battalions near the Ngan Valley. Neither was able to find any enemy forces. Late on the afternoon of July 18, just as the Marines were starting to believe that the enemy had skipped town, a thousand North Vietnamese attacked two platoons from the 3rd Battalion, 4th Marines.

The two platoons, with a strength of sixty-five men between them, were serving as rearguards for engineers who were detonating captured ammunition while the rest of the battalion headed to its next destination. With the enemy close upon them, the platoon commanders worried that a withdrawal in the direction of the rest of the battalion would trigger an enemy charge that would catch them in terrain less favorable than the high ground they currently occupied. They decided to stay put, hoping to hold out long enough for the rest of the battalion to arrive.

The thousand North Vietnamese, who in the accounts of American witnesses were wearing tennis shoes, surged toward the two isolated platoons. From their advantageous positions on the high ground, the Marine platoons kept the thronging North Vietnamese at bay with automatic weapons and air and artillery strikes. Bombs and napalm turned Communist forces from well-organized masses of men, charging aggressively in rows with their shoulders almost touching, into heaps of charred flesh. An American medic found that the bullets were flying so profusely in both directions that he gave up trying to tend to the wounded and instead fired at the enemy with the rifle of an incapacitated American. He killed five North Vietnamese soldiers before being shot dead himself.

The remainder of the American battalion was able to reach the stranded platoons before the North Vietnamese did. Widening and deepening the defensive position, they ensured that no Marines would be overrun. Although the North Vietnamese were steadily dwindling in number and élan, they kept fighting for the better part of four hours. When they withdrew, they left 138 of their dead on the ground. American estimates put the total enemy dead as high as 500. American losses came to 14 dead and 49 wounded.

Subsequent Marine efforts to trap enemy forces in the Ngan Valley resulted in little contact save for a hilltop clash on July 24 between a Marine battalion and a battalion of the 324B Division. Allied forces ended Operation Hastings on August 3, having concluded that all the remaining enemy soldiers had crept back across the DMZ to North Vietnam or into the dense jungles of western Quang Tri and Laos. Total North Vietnamese killed were reported at 736 confirmed and 600 probable. Eleven others had been taken prisoner. The U.S. Marines sustained a total of 116 killed and 448 wounded, while the South Vietnamese incurred 21 dead and 26 wounded.[40]

Soon after the completion of Operation Hastings, seven U.S. Marine infantry battalions took part in Operation Prairie in central and western Quang Tri. The targets of Operation Prairie were the newly detected 31st and 32nd regiments of the 341st Division and the remnants of the 324B Division. During a series of small and medium-sized battles spanning August and September, the Marine battalions killed a reported 943 North Vietnamese, of whom a considerable number had belonged to the 324B Division. That division, greatly reduced in size, hobbled back across the DMZ into North Vietnam to avoid further damage.[41] General Walt's preemptive strikes had foiled the North Vietnamese drive toward the coast before it had left the starting gate.

For the U.S. military, this victory marked a fitting conclusion to a summer of unalloyed success. Search-and-destroy operations had repeatedly brought the North Vietnamese to battle and crushed them before they could attack on their terms or reach the populous regions where they could obtain desperately needed food. Among the North Vietnamese, the successive defeats provided reason for independent thinkers to doubt the strategy and tactics in whose service so many young men were being sacrificed.

In South Vietnam's cities, South Vietnamese and American officials spent the summer of 1966 preparing for the Constituent Assembly elections of September 11. The centerpiece of the government's plans for political transition, the Constituent Assembly would be responsible for drafting a new constitution. The constitution, in turn, would provide the foundation for a new government, whose leadership would be elected in 1967.

Ky announced that anyone could run for a seat in the Constituent Assembly, with a few major exceptions. Those exceptions included the militant Buddhists, other veterans of the Struggle Movement, and avowed neutralists and Communists. Washington officials voiced displeasure at the absence of Struggle Movement veterans on the candidate lists, but Lodge snuffed out their objections with the assertion that they were "similar to our being disappointed in the U.S. because there is not a large number of active, card carrying Communists running for the House and Senate."[42] On instructions from Ambassador Lodge, the CIA transferred 10 million piasters, the equivalent of $85,000, to the chief of the National Police for use in supporting Ky allies who were running for assembly seats.[43]

The South Vietnamese government surprised skeptics with its efficiency in organizing and publicizing the assembly elections. The Communist presence in the countryside prevented the government from registering approximately one-third of the country's adults, but where government officials could operate, they registered nearly every adult to vote. They were equally thorough in getting voters to the polls. On election day, more than 80 percent of the registered voters, a total of 4.3 million South Vietnamese citizens, cast ballots.[44]

American diplomats were delighted by the high turnout and the ability of the South Vietnamese government to protect the elections from fraud and Communist interference. Election observers determined that the South Vietnamese government did not pressure the citizenry to vote for candidates favored by the government. In fact, only four of the nearly one hundred candidates favored by Ky were elected to the assembly. The election winners included representatives of all the major political, regional, and religious groups, aside from those that had been banned.[45]

American and South Vietnamese proponents of democratization applauded the elections as the start of a democratic revolution.[46] Ambassador Lodge was more restrained in his assessment. "Cynics claim that most people went to the polls simply to avoid future difficulties with the authorities and that the Vietnamese people fear they will be required to show canceled voting cards whenever they come into contact with officialdom," the ambassador wrote. "No doubt this is part of the explanation. But if 80.8 percent of the registered voters went to the polls simply because the GVN pushed them into it, it at least shows that the GVN has some authority and standing with the great majority of the population. And adherence by the population to the government is what this political-military war is about."[47]

Following the elections for the Constituent Assembly, Ky and Thieu moved ahead with plans to complete the new constitution and hold elections for the new national government. They appeared to be interested in retaining some sort of governmental role for the military in the long term but also evidenced a desire to shift primary responsibility for governance to civilians. The interest in governing that South Vietnamese military officers had gained in 1964 and 1965 as a result of civilian incompetence had been eroded by the thankless tedium of civil administration and the corruption arising from payments to generals for supporting or opposing a government.[48]

While the South Vietnamese government's prestige among the population was slowly improving, the image of the United States was moving in the opposite direction. As more American troops arrived in Saigon and other cities during 1966, they more often gave offense to the civilian society. American vehicles congested city streets and at times ran smaller vehicles off the road or struck pedestrians. With the influx of cash-carrying Americans, inflation spiked, reducing the buying power of Vietnamese consumers. The South Vietnamese population witnessed sharp rises in prostitution and dating between American soldiers and Vietnamese women, which offended the sensibilities of most Vietnamese, especially young Vietnamese men, who griped that the Americans won the prettiest Vietnamese girls because they had the thickest wallets.[49]

Every night, thousands of American servicemen consumed alcohol at South Vietnamese establishments, sometimes to excess. Their carousing inevitably resulted in behaviors admired by no society, particularly not a reserved society like Vietnam's. In August, Lodge told his staff that the Saigon police had become vehemently anti-American because of "the rowdy behavior of certain Americans up and down the streets and through the nightclubs and bars—not once, but night after night."[50] President Johnson responded later that month by ordering Operation MOOSE—Move Out Of Saigon Expeditiously—which would eventually reduce the U.S. troop presence in Saigon from seventy-one thousand to thirty-six thousand.[51]

Within the South Vietnamese government and armed forces, the massive influx of American troops and dollars led to graft on an unprecedented scale. The American troops afforded the

South Vietnamese more time for siphoning resources through illicit activities, and the American dollars multiplied the amount of resources available for siphoning. Practices like bribery, extortion, contracting fraud, and misappropriation of funds that had been occasional during the Diem era and more frequent during the upheaval following Diem's assassination were now chronic. A debilitating diversion for the leadership, corruption was also a source of discontent among the South Vietnamese who did not profit from it.[52]

Still, many Vietnamese were pleased by the presence of hordes of young Americans with thick wallets. American GIs shelled out money not only to prostitutes and barkeepers but also to small businessmen and vendors who swarmed around American bases. The U.S. government hired huge numbers of Vietnamese to cook their food, clean their laundry, and maintain their installations, and American contractors hired thousands more for construction projects. "It seemed the Americans wanted to build everything at once—warehouses, barracks, roads, bridges, helipads, ports, airports," one South Vietnamese official commented.[53]

The lodgment of the American behemoth on South Vietnamese soil was also buying time for South Vietnamese entrepreneurs, financiers, lawyers, and regulators to learn the arts and sciences of economic development. The South Vietnamese did not have a long tradition of industrial enterprise, but then neither had the South Koreans, who under American tutelage had figured out how to build large and complex businesses. Now, sixteen years after the Americans had come to fight in their country, the South Koreans were starting to develop advanced industries. The Samsung Corporation and Goldstar, the forerunner of LG, were making radios, televisions, and kitchen appliances. Kia Industries was manufacturing automobiles under license from Mazda, and a startup auto manufacturer called Hyundai Motor Company was about to open its doors. If the Americans could stick around in South Vietnam as they had in South Korea, there seemed no reason why the South Vietnamese could not build a comparable economic powerhouse.

CHAPTER 8

. . .

INTERNAL CONTRADICTIONS

October–December 1966

Secretary of Defense McNamara traveled to South Vietnam at the beginning of October to take another look at the situation. Although the South Vietnamese government appeared to be stable and the North Vietnamese Army was losing one battle after another, McNamara was distressed by the enemy's ability to field new soldiers and its ability to limit its casualties by avoiding battle under unfavorable circumstances. The number of men who infiltrated from the North and the number of men recruited by Hanoi's agents in the South were hotly debated, but there was general agreement among the Americans that the total number of Communist troops in South Vietnam was still increasing. Intelligence analysts expected the number to be forty thousand higher at the end of 1966 than at the beginning.

"The prognosis is bad that the war can be brought to a satisfactory conclusion within the next two years," McNamara notified President Johnson upon his return. "The large-unit operations probably will not do it; negotiations probably will not do it." He presented Johnson with a new strategy for bringing the war to an acceptable conclusion, founded upon "girding, openly, for a longer war and in taking actions immediately which will in 12 to 18 months give clear evidence that the continuing costs and risks to the American people are acceptably limited, that the formula for success has been found, and that the end of the war is merely a matter of time."

In the interest of stimulating negotiations, McNamara advocated another bombing pause, and he recommended a ceiling on Rolling Thunder strikes if the bombing had to be resumed. McNamara asserted that the bombing, including the recent POL strikes, had failed to halt or severely impede North Vietnamese infiltration, and he prophesied that higher strike rates were unlikely to cause more disruption than the current rates. In making his recommendations, McNamara acknowledged that restraints on the bombing would "cause serious psychological problems among the men who are risking their lives to help achieve our political objectives; among their commanders up to and including the JCS; and among those of our people who cannot understand why we should withhold punishment from the enemy."[1]

What no one but the president knew was that McNamara wanted to go even further after the midterm elections of November 1966, by ending Rolling Thunder once and for all. "I myself am more and more convinced," he confided to the president in a phone call, "that we ought definitely to plan on termination of the bombing in the north but not until after the election, and I hate to even talk about it before then for fear of a leak." McNamara did not explain why he wanted to wait until after the election, but the president did not need to be told that eliminating Rolling Thunder now would hand the Republicans the votes of the millions of Americans who were unable to see the logic in withholding punishment from the enemy.

Another central element of McNamara's new long-term plan that would be kept secret until after the midterm elections was a ceiling on U.S. troops of between five hundred thousand and six hundred thousand. Without such a ceiling, McNamara told Johnson, troop levels could rise indefinitely, which would ruin South Vietnam's economy, turn the majority of Americans against the war, and convince the North Vietnamese that the Americans could not afford to continue much longer. Recent experiences in Vietnam had shown that large U.S. troop increases resulted in only modest increases in Communist losses, McNamara claimed, and the North Vietnamese could continue to limit their casualties by retreating into Laos and Cambodia as necessary. By keeping the U.S. troop ceiling at a reasonable level, the Johnson administration could retain the domestic support required to maintain forces at that level indefinitely while the South Vietnamese put their house in order.[2]

To bolster the American position in ways that air power and troop increases purportedly could not, McNamara chose to push two initiatives: an anti-infiltration barrier and intensified U.S. support for pacification. Earlier in the year, the inability of bombing to stop the infiltration through Laos had led McNamara to begin exploratory planning for a ground barrier that was to run along the northern border of South Vietnam and then due west across Laos to Thailand. By the time of his October trip, he was championing the barrier with the zeal of a Carmelite monk. "I keep looking back for five years, and as far as I am concerned it is a failure," he told Westmoreland in reference to anti-infiltration efforts. "I keep asking where did we make a mistake? The first mistake was not putting in a barrier five years ago instead of talking about it today." McNamara vowed to push it forward with the utmost vigor, promising, "I will absolutely guarantee you that a year from today there is going to be a barrier up there. I guarantee that. It may not be all that we talked about today, but it will be 95 percent of what we talked about."[3]

Whereas the generals wanted a ground barrier across Laos that was manned by ground forces, McNamara's ground barrier relied primarily on air forces. The preliminary plans for the barrier, drawn up by prominent scientists from Harvard and MIT at McNamara's behest, called for a five-kilometer-deep barrier that would be seeded with acoustic sensors and tiny mines that looked like gravel. When the mines exploded beneath the weight of a human foot or vehicle tire, they would cause some damage but, more importantly, they would produce a sound loud enough to be picked up by the sensors, which would then transmit a signal to a U.S. communications facility. The location data would be fed to the pilots of U.S. aircraft, who would strike the coordinates with Sadeye cluster bombs. Newly developed under the official name of CBU-75, the Sadeye consisted of 1,800 bomblets, each one weighing one pound. The beastly munition could spray an area the size of 157 football fields with razor-sharp shrapnel.[4]

Designating pacification "the main talisman of ultimate U.S. success or failure in Vietnam," McNamara recommended allocating massive quantities of additional U.S. resources and half of the South Vietnamese Army to pacification. He noted that the solution required not only more money and men, but also better behavior by the South Vietnamese. "The first essential reform is in the attitude of GVN officials," McNamara posited. "They are generally apathetic, and there is corruption high and low. Often appointments, promotions, and draft deferments must be bought; and kickbacks on salaries are common." The second critical reform, he stated, was "in the attitude and conduct of the ARVN." McNamara conceded that because of these human factors, the odds for success in pacification were "less than even."[5]

McNamara also championed a major reorganization of American support to pacification. This reorganization had been conceived by Robert Komer, whom President Johnson had put in charge of coordinating pacification support activities in Washington earlier in the year.[6] Komer advocated a single chain of command for the 2,540 U.S. military personnel in the field who worked on pacification, mostly in the security sector, and the 470 civilians who worked in the sectors of civil administration, development, and law enforcement. The senior individual in each province or district, whether civilian or military, would serve as the team chief and report through a chain of command that fed up to a pacification support manager in Saigon who was a deputy to General Westmoreland. Komer argued in favor of putting pacification under the U.S. military's umbrella because security came first in pacification and because the military possessed far more human and material resources than any civilian agency.[7]

Komer's reorganization would allow the United States to speak with a single voice to the South Vietnamese provincial and district chiefs, the local leaders who exerted authority over all South Vietnamese pacification operations except those of the South Vietnamese Army. It would also compel all American personnel to work together in pursuit of a unified, coherent strategy. Experience had shown that, when left to their own devices, some of the agencies would go in different directions and do nothing to support one another. For instance, the U.S. Agency for International Development had funded projects in villages without convincing American military advisers that those villages deserved priority in the counterinsurgency effort, and therefore the military advisers did not entreat the South Vietnamese to allocate troops to protect those villages.[8]

Although McNamara and President Johnson liked Komer's concept, most of the other civilian authorities in Washington and Saigon threw fits when they learned of it. One reason for their ire was Komer himself, who, in addition to being energetic and smart, was also brash, abrasive, supercilious, and devious, except when dealing with President Johnson, before whom he fawned and flattered like a sixteenth-century Florentine courtier.[9] The main source of discontent, though, was the placement of civilian agency personnel inside a military chain of command. In the view of embassy civilians and agency heads in Washington, Komer's reorganization would give undue influence to American and South Vietnamese military officers who were less familiar than the civilians with the nonmilitary components of pacification, and would demoralize the civilians because they would recoil at the very thought of taking orders from the military.[10]

Opposition from Secretary of State Rusk, Ambassador Lodge, and other senior civilian officials convinced President Johnson to give the civilians a trial period of 120 days to show that they could lead a unified pacification structure. In November, Deputy Ambassador William J. Porter was made the head of a new organization called the Office of Civilian Operations, and under his jurisdiction each province and district had a single official with authority over all U.S. civilian personnel as well as military personnel "to the extent that civilian functions have been assigned to them." When the trial period was up, the president would decide whether to make the arrangement permanent or put pacification under Westmoreland's military command.[11]

The military found some aspects of McNamara's new strategy appetizing, others distasteful. Both the Joint Chiefs and Westmoreland approved of the heightened emphasis on pacification and the reorganization of pacification support. Westmoreland also endorsed McNamara's troop ceiling, albeit for reasons different from McNamara's. If McNamara and Johnson remained unwilling to call up the reserves, Westmoreland reasoned, then increasing the number of American troops above five hundred thousand would degrade the quality of U.S. forces.[12]

The generals welcomed McNamara's new interest in impeding North Vietnamese infiltration, a matter about which they had been agitating for years. They had serious reservations, however, about the practicalities of his anti-infiltration barrier. In their view, McNamara's plans assigned too many U.S. combat forces to the construction and maintenance of the South Vietnamese section of the barrier and relied too heavily on air power for the Laotian section. The number of troops tied to barrier activities would be the subject of contentious debate until the end of the year.

What the generals found most unsettling about the barrier was McNamara's invocation of the project as a substitute for heavier bombing. To frustrate McNamara's efforts to replace the bombing, senior military officers belittled the barrier concept behind his back. They called it the McNamara Line, in an unkind comparison to the Maginot Line that had failed to prevent the German conquest of France in 1940.[13]

Westmoreland and the Chiefs assailed McNamara's proposed ceiling on Rolling Thunder with the argument that Rolling Thunder could achieve much more if it were intensified and freed from the restrictions of the White House and Office of the Secretary of Defense. The generals wanted to bomb new fixed targets in the North and hit the old ones again to reduce Hanoi's will and ability to support the war. Although Rolling Thunder was dumping bombs on North Vietnam at a rate three times that of the previous year, few new fixed sites had been struck since late 1965. Of the 242 targets on the Joint Chiefs' list of fixed targets in North Vietnam, 158 had been struck in 1965, and only 27 more had been hit in 1966. Whereas 30 percent of Rolling Thunder sorties in 1965 had been directed at fixed targets, just 3 percent of the 1966 sorties were similarly aimed, the remainder having been directed at trucks, trains, air defenses, supply stations, and other moving targets.[14]

Of the fixed targets, the Joint Chiefs were particularly concerned about ports and airfields. By the fall, none of North Vietnam's six major ports had suffered significant damage from aerial attack, and only four of eleven airfields had been hit.[15] North Vietnamese aircraft were using the airfields to attack and disrupt American aircraft during Rolling Thunder missions. During the last three months of 1966, North Vietnamese MiGs were in the air almost every day.

MiG-21s, which were capable of speeds exceeding a thousand miles per hour, were seeking battle with American aircraft at high altitudes, while subsonic MiG-17s were prowling closer to the ground. The tactical cunning of American pilots, the shortage of skills and experience among their North Vietnamese adversaries, and the technical superiority of American aircraft over the MiG-17 resulted in many more North Vietnamese losses than American losses, but the MiG presence interfered with American operations and required additional precautions that reduced operational effectiveness. During one stretch of major bombing in December, MiG operations compelled 20 percent of U.S. strike flights to jettison their bombs.[16]

The North Vietnamese were, in the meantime, busy finding ways to improve the performance of their aircraft. High quality pilots could not be produced overnight, so Hanoi looked to fraternal socialist countries for help. During the fall, the North Korean government agreed to send enough pilots to man three of North Vietnam's MiG companies.[17] According to a North Korean air force officer who defected to South Korea in 1998, more than eight hundred North Korean pilots eventually flew Soviet MiGs over Vietnam.[18]

Of even greater concern to American pilots and generals than the MIGs were the 122 surface-to-air missile sites in North Vietnam, many of which were positioned in areas off limits to

American bombers. At first glance, the missiles did not appear to pose a serious threat to Rolling Thunder. They were hitting few American aircraft and were killing more friendly civilians than American pilots as missiles frequently fell into populous residential areas after missing their targets.[19] American radar jamming and the destruction of North Vietnamese radar sites by American Shrike air-to-surface missiles contributed to the low success rate. But so did the U.S. policy of flying aircraft at less than half the preferred bombing altitude, which the Americans instituted because it greatly reduced vulnerability to the missiles. Flying at lower altitudes, however, made American aircraft much more vulnerable to conventional antiaircraft guns. Those guns accounted for nearly all the 318 Rolling Thunder aircraft that were lost to hostile action in 1966.[20]

In early November, the Joint Chiefs pushed for approval of Rolling Thunder 52, a package of bombing strikes more ambitious than any that had come before. The package reduced the sanctuaries around Hanoi and Haiphong from a radius of thirty nautical miles to ten nautical miles for the former and from ten nautical miles to four nautical miles for the latter. Those reductions would make fair game of many fixed military and logistical targets that hitherto had been off limits. The proposal for Rolling Thunder 52 also included new industrial, infrastructure, and air defense sites that lay outside the existing sanctuaries.[21]

McNamara and Rusk objected to the proposed shrinkages of the sanctuaries and assented to only one third of the new fixed targets advocated by the Joint Chiefs.[22] President Johnson sustained most of their objections, and Rolling Thunder 52 was modified accordingly. The bombing of North Vietnam, Johnson decreed, "should be steady and as undramatic as we can make it." In his opinion, too much bombing could undermine efforts to negotiate with the North Vietnamese by "rubbing their nose in it in front of a television camera." Johnson believed that "if we're causing 'em damage and they're hurtin' but we haven't got their children's hospitals afire and so forth, I think Moscow can say to Hanoi, 'Goddammit, this thing is gettin' awfully costly on you and on us and on everybody else. Let's try to find an answer here.'"[23]

The first bombs of Rolling Thunder 52 fell on November 22. As the American aircraft made their daily bombing runs, the Joint Chiefs renewed their pressure for expanding the target lists, and found to their surprise that they were beginning to make headway with the president. Exhortations from Asian leaders to intensify the bombing were raising some of Johnson's first doubts about Robert McNamara's approach to the bombing. On November 26, McNamara vented his frustrations to Harriman, who recorded them in a memo under the heading "Personal: Absolutely No One to See." Harriman's assessment, with which McNamara agreed, was that Johnson was acting upon "a feeling that the world was with him," having been influenced by recent discussions "with the Thais and Koreans who were war-like and wanted to finish up China, while we were at it."[24]

The first major U.S. ground operation of the fall was Operation Irving, which unfolded in Binh Dinh Province. It was the successor to Operation Thayer of the previous month, in which two brigades of the 1st Cavalry Division had combed the same general area for the 3rd NVA Division but had encountered only a smattering of North Vietnamese soldiers. The eminent military historian S. L. A. Marshall, who was visiting the American division at the time, observed that Operation Thayer had been "incredibly boring, wasteful, and exhausting. Rarely in warfare has so much heavy artillery been brought up to shoot at clay pipes." According to Marshall, senior American officers later talked of "Operation Thayer-Irving" as if they were a single operation in an effort "to redeem the whole by implying that all along the hounds had been on the trace."[25]

The participants in Operation Irving included five battalions and a squadron of the 1st Cavalry Division as well as several South Vietnamese and South Korean units. On the opening day of Operation Irving, October 2, small detachments of troops fanned out to the rice paddies, villages, and forests to look for North Vietnamese troop concentrations.

Alpha company of the 1-9 Cavalry Squadron was assigned to Hoa Hoi, a village near the coast. Hoa Hoi seemed a most unlikely place for the North Vietnamese to put troops, which may have been why they had put troops there. Only twelve hundred meters from the South China Sea and just a short walk east of Highway 1, the village could be reached rapidly by helicopter, truck, or amphibious landing craft. Hostile forces could easily block the sea to the east and the highway to the west, and the sand flats to the north and south of the village offered no cover or concealment.

At 0800, an H-13 Sioux light helicopter headed toward the village carrying a scout party from the cavalry squadron tailed by two UH-1 Huey gunships. They flew "nap of the earth," their skids only twenty feet above the treetops. Leading the mission was Major Joseph A. Koehnke, a blond thirty-two-year-old from Alliance, Nebraska. Marshall wrote of the major, "Though he talks in a very gentle voice, faster than a horse can trot, he seems to measure every word. His manner radiates self-assurance, which with his personal warmth makes him that happy combination—a man worth following and a topnotch technician."

Scanning the terrain from the helicopter, the scout party glimpsed a few men in khaki uniforms. Major Koehnke called the gunships forward to strafe them. The amount of return fire directed at the helicopters led the Americans to conclude that the North Vietnamese had a platoon in the area, so an American platoon was flown to a nearby beach and ordered to advance on the enemy. This platoon, dubbed the Blue Team, encountered no one until it reached the edge of the village, whereupon North Vietnamese weapons spat an even greater volume of ammunition than they had expended on the helicopters. Three of the Blue Team's soldiers fell dead, and three more sustained wounds.

Now the Americans decided that the enemy had at least a company in the village. Major Koehnke ordered the Blue Team to pull back to the beach and await the dispatch of a larger U.S. force. The American platoon, however, was pinned down by the unexpectedly intense enemy fire and could not return to the beach. American helicopter gunships flew in at low altitude to pelt the North Vietnamese positions that were tormenting the platoon. Raking the North Vietnamese with machine guns, the helicopters knocked out some enemy strongpoints, but in the process hostile fire crippled three of the aircraft, causing them to limp away toward the sea. All three had to crash-land before reaching the beach.

The helicopters carrying the 1st Battalion, 12th Cavalry were on their way to another objective when the battalion was ordered to shift course to Hoa Hoi. Captain Harold T. Fields Jr. of Orlando, Florida, a twenty-eight-year-old graduate of the Citadel who commanded one of the battalion's companies, told his soldiers, "We've got a target now, a real one, and no mistake." These men, having been thoroughly frustrated by the fruitless and monotonous days of Operation Thayer, stood up and cheered.

Bravo company of 1/12 landed first, touching down three hundred meters to the east of Hoa Hoi. Barreling toward the enemy's fortified positions, the company overran a North Vietnamese trench line on the village periphery. By drawing the attention of the North Vietnamese, Bravo company reduced the fire aimed at the Blue Team, permitting it to break free. The two American units linked up, and the Blue Team transferred operational authority to Bravo company. The two groups barely spoke to each other and shared no information, as a result of erroneous assumptions that each had made about the other. According to Marshall, "The newcomers rather took it for granted that the Blue Team had been too hard-charging, had gotten itself quickly compromised in consequence, and had then given up on a bad job." The Blue Team, on the other hand, "reckoned that they had all but shattered the NVA resistance and were leaving the larger force only the credit for what would prove to be a tiresome mop-up."

The next company from the 1st Battalion, 12th Cavalry to arrive, Alpha company, landed to the southwest of Hoa Hoi. Its advance toward the village compelled a forward line of North Vietnamese defenders to scamper back into the village. Because of uncertainty about the presence of civilians, the Americans did not fire at enemy positions in the village but instead asked higher headquarters for guidance.

Over the course of 1966, the international media had been reporting extensively on civilian casualties caused by U.S. air and artillery strikes. Westmoreland, concerned that these reports could erode support for the war in South Vietnam and the United States, had responded by imposing more stringent rules of engagement. Foremost among the changes was the requirement that South Vietnamese officials approve any use of heavy firepower in populous areas.[26] Westmoreland's constraints would ultimately ensure that civilian casualties were not appreciably more prevalent than in most other twentieth-century conflicts. Civilian fatalities over the course of the Vietnam War were to total 45 percent of military fatalities, which was only slightly higher than the 40 percent inflicted in World War II and much lower than the 70 percent of the Korean War.[27] The revised rules of engagement also became a source of visceral frustration for American infantrymen, who knew that the rules could give the enemy precious time to make combat preparations or run away.

While American officials awaited South Vietnamese permission to fire into Hoa Hoi, a Huey circled overhead to blare warnings in Vietnamese from its loudspeaker. The voice called on the citizenry to depart the village and advised the armed men to surrender. For an hour, the Americans held their weapons in abeyance and watched frightened civilians emerge from the village. A total of 171 civilians walked out, to be hauled away to refugee camps. Only a few North Vietnamese soldiers came out to surrender.

By the time the hour had passed, the Americans had received authorization from the South Vietnamese authorities to shoot into the village, on the assumption that anyone remaining in Hoa Hoi was hostile. Helicopter gunships unleashed machine guns and rockets on enemy strongpoints while Alpha and Bravo companies and the latest arrival, Charlie company, pushed toward the village. As the American infantry advanced, they ran into concealed North Vietnamese machine guns, which hit several Americans with their first rounds. The Americans then stepped back and radioed the locations of the enemy weapons to American gunships and recoilless rifles teams, which doused them with liberal amounts of ammunition.

Renewing the assault, the American infantry attempted to overrun all of the North Vietnamese positions before day's end. The North Vietnamese, however, fought on with sufficient strength and tenacity to retain control of the village center when darkness arrived. By this juncture, it had become evident to the Americans that the North Vietnamese had an entire battalion in the village.

During the evening, the American division commander dispatched two more companies to Hoa Hoi by air to thicken the cordon around the village. American artillery, warships, and aircraft took turns firing illumination rounds throughout the night to deny the enemy the protection of darkness. In an unbroken cadence, American howitzer shells crashed on the village center.

The North Vietnamese could see and hear the Americans flying in reinforcements and beefing up their lines on all sides of the village. Lacking any escape tunnels or trenches, the North Vietnamese battalion could not leave Hoa Hoi except by slipping through gaps in the American cordon, a very difficult proposition given the presence of the illumination rounds and the density of the American lines. The North Vietnamese commanding officer decided, nevertheless, that fleeing was a better option than trying to hold the village for another day against the multiplying American forces and their inexhaustible supply of artillery shells. Setting out in groups of four to five men, North Vietnamese soldiers endeavored to find holes in the American encirclement.

The North Vietnamese had built an impressive record of sneaking past encircling Americans. This time, however, the Americans were too numerous, the terrain too unfavorable, and the sky too bright. The Americans espied and gunned down each group that tried to escape, including one that tried to conceal itself by driving water buffalo in front of them. After a while, the North Vietnamese commander recognized the futility of the escape plan and ordered his remaining troops to stay in their defensive positions.

In the morning, the Americans entered the village center in overwhelming numbers. The remaining North Vietnamese were swiftly killed or taken prisoner.

Estimated North Vietnamese losses during the twenty-four hours of fighting at Hoa Hoi included 233 killed and 50 captured. An entire battalion had been wiped out. Six Americans had been killed and 35 wounded.

In the ensuing days, U.S. ground forces flew into the valleys neighboring Hoa Hoi and swept through them on foot. Heavy-lift helicopters carried bulldozers and backhoes from one place to the next to help clear and improve landing zones. B-52s, tactical aircraft, artillery, and naval gunfire blasted the ground before, during, and after the infantry operations. On October 4, 11, and 16, American and North Vietnamese infantry clashed in substantial numbers, although the carnage was not as extensive as at Hoa Hoi. By the time Operation Irving ended on October 24, the 1st Cavalry Division added another 450 enemy killed and 700 prisoners to their scorecard against an additional 16 of their own killed.[28]

Other American, South Vietnamese, and South Korean operations in Binh Dinh against the 3rd NVA Division tallied several thousand additional casualties during October. At the end of the month, numerous North Vietnamese bases and supply stores lay in ruin, and most of the rice land in Binh Dinh was in the hands of the Americans and the South Vietnamese government.[29] The fighting made refugees of close to one third of Binh Dinh's total population of 875,547.[30]

The "winter wave" offensive that the North Vietnamese Politburo had conceived in June as a step toward "decisive victory" began in the highlands in mid-October. In Pleiku and Kontum provinces, several regiments of the 1st and 325B North Vietnamese Army divisions attacked Uplander units near the Cambodian border. The U.S. Army's 4th Infantry Division moved to the border region, precipitating a series of clashes that ran into December. The mountains and valleys where they fought were coated so thoroughly with jungle vegetation that most North Vietnamese troop movements could not be seen from the air, and American helicopters seldom could land unless American engineers first cleared a hole in the jungle with chainsaws and demolitions. The proximity of the fighting to the border also permitted North Vietnamese forces to make maximum use of their Cambodian sanctuary. An after-action report produced by the 4th Infantry Division observed, "The availability of the sanctuary enabled the enemy to stockpile large quantities of supplies well forward with no risk of destruction, to withdraw into sanctuary when his forces became threatened, and to maintain significant forces in complete safety which could be employed at will to reinforce units in contact or to conduct attacks against U.S. forces."[31]

The North Vietnamese could not, however, turn these formidable advantages into battlefield success against the 4th Infantry Division. By carefully analyzing the terrain, the Americans stayed clear of areas where they would be most vulnerable to a large attack. North Vietnamese commanders, under pressure by higher authorities to kill Americans, had no choice but to attack American units in their encampments. Each time, American weapons halted the North Vietnamese before they could claw their way to American foxholes. During this campaign, more 4th Infantry Division soldiers would be laid low by malaria than by hostile fire. The Uplanders, who had less firepower at their disposal, suffered much heavier casualties in combat with the North Vietnamese.[32]

The winter battles in Pleiku and Kontum shattered North Vietnam's 95B, 101B, and 101C regiments. When the fighting ended in December, the 101C Regiment was downgraded to a battalion and merged with the depleted 101B Regiment to form the 33rd Regiment, which itself was too thinly manned to engage in combat operations for the next year. General Nguyen Chi Thanh considered the damage to his highland regiments so serious that he ordered his forces in the region to shift from conventional combat to guerrilla warfare and political mobilization, the very activities he had strenuously opposed during the strategic debates of the summer.[33]

In the region north of Saigon, which was Hanoi's top priority for the winter wave, the North Vietnamese Army began offensive operations at the beginning of November. Primary responsibility for the winter wave attacks in this region was given to the 9th Division, which had been rejuvenated once more by large infusions of infiltrators from the North.[34] The 9th Division moved to a well-stocked base area near the Michelin Plantation, in Binh Duong Province, from which it intended to attack several South Vietnamese outposts and the newly arrived and inexperienced 196th Light Infantry Brigade.

Westmoreland had put the U.S. Army's 196th Light Infantry Brigade in a corner of Tay Ninh Province that he expected to be devoid of major fighting. Shortly after the brigade's arrival, Westmoreland replaced the colonel who had commanded it with Brig. Gen. Edward H. de Saussure, because he believed that independent brigades like the 196th ought to be commanded by a general officer. Although an excellent staff officer and an expert on artillery and missiles, de Saussure had never commanded infantry before.

In the middle of September, the 196th Brigade had initiated Operation Attleboro, a search-and-destroy operation that took its name from Attleboro, Massachusetts, where the brigade had been reactivated one year earlier for service in Vietnam. Because of the brigade's inexperience, Operation Attleboro was intended to provide on-the-job training, not to cause serious harm to the enemy. The brigade made little contact with enemy forces during the first six weeks of the operation.

When the 196th sent its units on patrol the morning of November 3, its officers expected just one more punch into thin air. Instead, one of the companies ran into reconnaissance units from the 9th NVA Division in high elephant grass. North Vietnamese reinforcement arrived swiftly, blocking the American company's possible avenues of retreat. In the vicious, fragmented melees that followed, dozens of men on both sides were killed or wounded. American relief companies were flown into the area, and during the afternoon they drove the North Vietnamese off.

The next day, the entire 9th NVA Division went on the offensive against the 196th Light Infantry Brigade. Each of the 9th Division's three regiments struck a different piece of the American brigade, attaining great numerical superiority by virtue of the fact that the American brigade was dispersed in company-sized units. The North Vietnamese did not overrun any of the American companies, but they did pin some of them down and inflict sizable casualties.

Major General William DePuy, the commander of the 1st Division, and MACV deputy commander Lieutenant General John A. Heintges arrived during the day to assess the situation. Both became convinced that de Saussure did not understand what was going on and was making poor decisions. If he continued to bungle, they believed, some of his companies could be annihilated. At the recommendation of General Heintges, General DePuy took command of all American forces in the area, turning de Saussure into his subordinate. One of DePuy's assistant division commanders joined the 196th Light Infantry Brigade with instructions from DePuy to relieve de Saussure and take command of the brigade should de Saussure not carry out the orders from DePuy's headquarters.

In the evening, the sky was jammed with helicopters bringing the headquarters of DePuy's division and one of his battalions to the scene. Additional American and South Vietnamese battalions began preparations for rapid deployment to the site of battle. DePuy ordered de Saussure to break contact with the enemy the next day and bring all his units together so they could disentangle themselves.

De Saussure complied. During the consolidation of his units, several American companies fought inconclusive clashes with large North Vietnamese forces. It took most of the day for all the American companies to reach other friendly units.

The first phase of Attleboro had come to an end. Sixty Americans lay dead and 159 had been wounded. The Americans estimated North Vietnamese losses at 200 dead, a figure that seemed reasonable in light of a North Vietnamese after-action report stating that a battalion of the 101st Regiment had been rendered combat ineffective. DePuy urged Westmoreland to fire de Saussure and send him back to the United States in order to demonstrate the command's commitment to accountability and provide a warning to other commanders. Westmoreland demurred, choosing instead to transfer de Saussure to another position.

For the second phase of Attleboro, DePuy intended to marshal the strength of nearly twenty thousand American and South Vietnamese troops that Westmoreland was airlifting into Tay Ninh. He would use some to search critical areas for the enemy, others to block enemy routes of escape, and still others to serve as rapid reaction forces. DePuy did not, however, wait until all the forces were in place before launching into the next phase, for he worried that the North Vietnamese would soon sneak back into Cambodia. On November 6, he rushed small detachments of the 1st Infantry Division to suspected locations of the enemy's 9th Division. Making repeated contacts on the first day, the Americans called in large volumes of air and artillery support. They reported killing 170 enemy that day while suffering one killed and twenty-three wounded.

In the succeeding days, the North Vietnamese mounted several large attacks on DePuy's forces and were repulsed with heavy losses in every instance. North Vietnamese histories attributed some of these setbacks to a lack of antitank weapons, which allowed American M-41 and M-48 tanks to run roughshod over North Vietnamese defensive positions. They also heaped blame upon officers who "failed to place the proper emphasis on small-unit tactics using appropriate-sized forces and were not sufficiently flexible when confronted with unexpected situations."[35]

Fighting raged until November 15, when the last North Vietnamese troops departed the area. On the battlefields of Operation Attleboro, the Americans counted a reported 1,106 North Vietnamese corpses, including those of four battalion commanders and five company commanders. They also held 44 North Vietnamese prisoners. The material take included 2,400 tons of rice, 19,000 grenades, and 400 Bangalore torpedoes. American losses totaled 155 killed and 494 wounded. Hanoi's hopes of striking a mighty blow to American and South Vietnamese forces in Tay Ninh had been dashed.[36]

In the far north, along the DMZ, Westmoreland and his intelligence analysts expected a major NVA offensive to materialize during the last months of the year on the heels of the large engagements of July, August, and September. Westmoreland and the Joint Chiefs urged McNamara and the State Department to authorize land-based and naval artillery to fire in the northern half of the DMZ, where the North Vietnamese were building field fortifications and antiaircraft positions from which substantial numbers of U.S. aircraft had already been shot down. The State Department did not respond to the request before the year ended.[37]

To the immediate south of the demilitarized zone, the U.S. Marines who awaited the North Vietnamese deluge saw only trickles. During the last three months of 1966, the big Communist units sat idle in hideouts within the DMZ or the strip of North Vietnamese territory to its north.[38] Some Marine officers took the inactivity as evidence that the enemy threat in Quang Tri had receded, and hence they advocated withdrawing Marines from the DMZ to the coastal areas for pacification duty. Westmoreland, however, remained convinced that the enemy would soon resume major combat operations in northern Quang Tri. He directed the Marines to build a network of strongpoints near the DMZ, to be labeled the "strong point obstacle system," which would facilitate the location and destruction of enemy infiltrators. The largest forward points would be at Gio Linh, which lay astride Route 1, and at Con Thien, several miles to the west. A second line of firebases was to be built along Route 9, from Lang Vei and Khe Sanh in western Quang Tri, to Cam Lo in the center, and to the town of Dong Ha in the east.[39]

Westmoreland had to make a series of trips to I Corps to prod the Marines and check whether they were making progress on the strongpoints. "During frequent visits to Lew Walt's headquarters," Westmoreland recollected, "I gained the impression that the Marines in their supreme self-confidence, however admirable that might be, were underestimating the enemy's capabilities." Of greatest concern to Westmoreland was Khe Sanh, six miles from the Laotian border. The enemy was likely to seek a second Dien Bien Phu in the coming months, Westmoreland told Walt, and Khe Sanh seemed the most likely target. Westmoreland favored reinforcing Khe Sanh, not only because it would impede infiltration but also because Khe Sanh's proximity to Laos made it an excellent launching pad for operations to cut the Ho Chi Minh Trail should Washington authorize them. When Westmoreland suggested that the Marines position a full battalion at Khe Sanh, Walt initially balked, believing that Khe Sanh was less imperiled than his boss thought, but changed his mind after receiving reports of a major North Vietnamese troop concentration only fourteen kilometers north of Khe Sanh.[40]

Because food and other supply shortages constrained North Vietnamese military activity throughout 1966, American forces did not kill as many North Vietnamese troops for the year as Westmoreland had wanted. But the scarcity of activity also meant lower American and South Vietnamese casualties, and it provided breathing space for the rebuilding of the South Vietnamese government and the resuscitation of pacification. During the last months of 1966, top American and South Vietnamese generals agreed to commit the bulk of South Vietnamese Army units to population security. South Vietnamese commanders at the corps level and below were, however, slow to act on Saigon's implementing orders, owing to a marked preference for the glamor of offensive operations over the quiet grind of counterinsurgency.[41]

The reluctance of the South Vietnamese Army to alter its mission, though, was not its biggest problem. No matter what mission the armed forces took on, their accomplishments were still hindered by deficiencies in leadership. Heavy casualties ensured ongoing shortfalls of experienced officers, leaving many South Vietnamese units under the command of junior officers who lacked basic skills. "The fundamental weakness within RVNAF continues to be inadequacy of leadership at all levels," Westmoreland remarked in December.[42] Near the end of the year, American advisers rated the leadership of close to one third of South Vietnamese Army battalions as "unsatisfactory" or "marginal."[43]

Insufficiencies of leadership were similarly detrimental on the civil side. Although American and other allied military operations were driving North Vietnamese troops out of hundreds of villages, the Saigon government still struggled to fill those villages with capable administrators, Revolutionary Development Cadres, and militiamen. Only with good leaders could the rank-and-file be motivated and empowered to keep the enemy out. As in the case of the regular army, many of the individuals most suitable for leading these organizations had been killed in previous years or had been forced out of the government for supporting Ngo Dinh Diem or other political figures.[44]

Despite the ineffectiveness of South Vietnamese pacification programs, governmental control over the population increased during the second half of the year. According to a captured North Vietnamese document, the number of South Vietnamese civilians living under governmental control at the end of 1966 was one million higher than it had been in the middle of 1965. Allied military operations were reducing the presence of North Vietnamese forces and cadres in the villages and eroding the willingness of Southerners to resist the Saigon government. Masses of civilians were continuing to flow from Communist-held rural areas to government-held towns and cities because of both voluntary relocations and forced evacuations. Although the refugees did not necessarily feel an affection for the Saigon government, and some resented it for herding them into overcrowded refugee facilities, they generally cooperated with the government and let their sons serve in its armed forces.[45]

Interviews with Communist defectors and prisoners during this period told a story of reduced Communist activity and morale, a story that differed little from the jagged mountains of I Corps to the flatlands of IV Corps. A Communist defector from Darlac Province informed an interviewer that South Vietnamese military operations in his district had "demoralized the cadres. All they did was run into hiding. They couldn't carry out the instructions, policies and plans which had been proposed by the [National Liberation] Front."[46] A political cadre from Tay Ninh recounted that popular support had shifted away from the Communists because "although they had good speeches," they "still kept running away at the sight of the GVN soldiers."[47] In Binh Dinh Province, a captured district-level cadre explained that because of intensive American and South Vietnamese military operations in the second half of 1966, many cadres requested dismissal from their positions. Those who remained in office "became less rigid in carrying out the Front polices, allowed the peddlers more freedom in their movements, and avoided as much as possible frictions with the villagers in the hope that they wouldn't later be denounced to GVN or American troops during some possible operation."[48]

Hanoi's supply deficiencies, military defeats, and diminishing control over the population in the South were compounded by ominous problems on the international front. In China, Mao was unleashing the Great Proletarian Cultural Revolution. His objective was to cleanse the Chinese Communist Party of petty ambitions, attachment to private property, ideological laxity, pro-Soviet sentiments, and bourgeois culture, among other things. As Chinese Premier Zhou Enlai put it, the Cultural Revolution was necessary because too many party leaders had "found it easy to revolutionize others' lives, but hard to avoid privatization of their own privileges."[49] Accusations of corruption and bourgeois thinking were employed to destroy individuals whose real offenses had been the holding of opinions at variance with those of Mao. One of the topics most subjected to thought policing was China's role in exporting revolution, and much of the recrimination stemmed from the foiling of Chinese efforts to promote revolution in neighboring Southeast Asia in 1965, most notably the counter-coup in Indonesia and the American intervention in Vietnam.[50]

Mao recruited high school and college students into bands of radical agitators and terrorists, known as the Red Guards, who were to impose the philosophy of the Cultural Revolution by obliterating "old ideas, culture, customs, and habits of the exploiting classes." In August and September, the Red Guards launched a terror campaign in the cities against teachers, intellectuals, and former businessmen who had "bourgeois" family backgrounds. More than three thousand people perished and nearly four hundred thousand were forced to leave the cities on the grounds that they were spouses or children of "monsters and freaks." Others were compelled to spend all their waking hours cleaning toilets. Torture was commonplace. The subsequent campaigns of the Cultural Revolution would kill far larger numbers of people, probably in the vicinity of two to three million, though the actual total may never be known.[51]

North Vietnamese leaders, like many of their brethren in other Communist countries, were appalled by the excesses of the Red Guards. They did not voice their displeasure directly to the Chinese leadership, but instead showed it with the practiced aloofness of a jilted friend. Officers of the 2nd Chinese Division who rotated out of North Vietnam in October reported that the warm welcome shown by the North Vietnamese leadership upon the division's arrival in June 1965 had given way to a frosty reserve.[52] In Laos, North Vietnamese advisers to the Laotian Communists halted the routine sharing of intelligence with their Chinese advisers. When the Chinese government sent a song-and-dance troupe to Laos to entertain Communist soldiers, the North Vietnamese advisory mission prohibited the Chinese actors and actresses from singing songs that praised Mao and distributing badges bearing his likeness.[53]

North Vietnam's behavior fueled Chinese suspicions that the North Vietnamese were becoming too cozy with the Soviets, at a time when rising levels of Soviet aid to North Vietnam signaled a desire in Moscow for greater influence in Hanoi. From the Chinese perspective, the North Vietnamese appeared to be following Soviet recommendations to seek a negotiated peace with the Americans. To derail this perceived Soviet chicanery,

Chinese leaders told their North Vietnamese counterparts that they could not prevail at the conference table until they had won on the battlefield, which they said would require fighting at least through 1968.[54]

China's fears of deep Soviet influence in Hanoi were, in actuality, unwarranted. The North Vietnamese were paying little attention to Soviet advice and were leaving the Soviets in the dark about their negotiating positions and plans. Conscious that Soviet aid was motivated by a desire for influence not only in North Vietnam but across the Communist world, the North Vietnamese were banking on the continuation of Soviet aid regardless of Hanoi's stance on negotiations, which was how events were indeed playing out.[55]

The North Vietnamese were becoming more interested in negotiations during the last months of 1966, but not for the purpose of achieving the peace for which the Soviets longed. Instead, they hoped to use promises of peace talks to trick the Americans into suspending Rolling Thunder. At a meeting of the North Vietnamese Politburo on October 18, Ho Chi Minh declared that "our immediate goal is to make the enemy end the bombing of North Vietnam so that we can transport supplies to help South Vietnam and make preparations to launch more powerful attacks."[56]

The North Vietnamese chose to rely on Polish intermediaries for a new diplomatic initiative, which became known as Marigold. In conversations with American officials during November and early December, Polish diplomats said that Hanoi had expressed serious interest in negotiations, based on conditions that were largely consistent with the U.S. diplomatic position. But Hanoi's list of conditions included one key item that the Johnson administration had repeatedly rejected: termination of Rolling Thunder prior to the start of negotiations.

In spite of that demand, leading figures in the Johnson administration were hopeful that a diplomatic breakthrough was at hand. The State Department informed the Poles that the United States was ready to negotiate, but added that some of Hanoi's conditions, particularly the bombing cessation, would have to be clarified. After hearing this response through the Polish channel, the North Vietnamese accused the United States of equivocation and demanded that the Americans accept the conditions without alteration.[57] After a December 4 Rolling Thunder strike hit areas of Hanoi that had been spared until now, Pham Van Dong notified the Poles that the bombing had shown the "highest cynicism and effrontery" of the Americans, and that as a consequence North Vietnam was no longer interested in talks with the United States.[58]

The North Vietnamese nonetheless continued to pursue sham negotiations for the purpose of stopping Rolling Thunder. Shifting from the Poles to the Soviets, Le Duc Tho told General Secretary Leonid Brezhnev on December 15 that the North Vietnamese wanted the Soviets to facilitate peace negotiations as a "tactical move" that would be accompanied by continued military action. Le Duc Tho explained that the time for real negotiations had not yet arrived, because the Americans "still have not admitted... that they are losing the war."[59]

The Soviets did not enter the negotiating fray directly, but they were likely behind ensuing Polish efforts to move the negotiations forward. Those efforts included exhortations to the Americans to stop bombing near Hanoi as a means of bringing the North Vietnamese to the negotiating table. Although President Johnson remained wary of Hanoi's motives, he eventually made a partial concession. On December 24, the U.S. ambassador in Warsaw told Polish officials that the United States had indefinitely suspended all bombing within ten miles of Hanoi as a gesture of good faith.

The Americans added that the North Vietnamese could show their good faith by stopping attacks within ten miles of Saigon.[60]

North Vietnam's only response was an increase in southbound military traffic. American opponents of unilateral restraint seized on Hanoi's intransigence as more proof that goodwill gestures were politically ineffective and militarily harmful. "We were just starting to put some real pressure on Hanoi," Admiral Sharp wrote to General Wheeler. "Our air strikes on the rail yard and the vehicle depot were hitting the enemy where it was beginning to hurt." Sharp urged full resumption of Rolling Thunder as the only way to end the war quickly, before the American public turned against it. "This war is a dirty business, like all wars," stated the U.S. Pacific commander. "We need to get hard-headed about it. That is the only kind of action that these tough Communists will respect. That is the way to get this war over soonest."[61]

The year 1966, like the years 1964 and 1965, ended with the senior leadership of the U.S. military distraught at the civilian leadership's restraints and half measures. McNamara remained intent on curtailing Rolling Thunder and supplanting it with aerial interdiction across Laos and the DMZ. He continued to rebuff the military's recommendations for ground operations to disrupt the enemy's burgeoning logistical operations in Cambodia and Laos. The Joint Chiefs were convinced that new measures beyond South Vietnam's borders would exacerbate North Vietnamese supply problems that had become much more serious than before, and much more serious than McNamara recognized. The leaders in Hanoi, who knew their nation's logistical shortfalls and vulnerabilities to be even greater than the American generals thought, were trying, through deceitful diplomacy, to dupe the Americans into ending the ravages of Rolling Thunder.

Within South Vietnam, the war was going well for the Americans at year's end. Hanoi's winter wave offensive had failed to achieve its objectives of seizing the initiative and inflicting large losses. Wherever and whenever Nguyen Chi Thanh had concentrated North Vietnamese forces for offensive operations, the Americans had smashed them with heavy firepower and sent their remnants to flight. Supply shortages were compelling the North Vietnamese Army to curtail its military operations and keep more of its forces in the sanctuaries of Cambodia, Laos, and North Vietnam. The expanding distances between Communist forces and the South Vietnamese citizens were reducing Hanoi's ability to exploit the population's resources and disrupt South Vietnamese counterinsurgency activities. The lone consolation for Nguyen Chi Thanh, which was likely not very consoling to an ambitious general like him, was Lyndon Johnson's unwillingness to take sterner actions in Cambodia, Laos, or North Vietnam.

CHAPTER 9

. . .

ESCALATION

January–April 1967

Having halted the American bombing near Hanoi through negotiating overtures at the end of 1966, the North Vietnamese government was inspired to extend the ruse at the beginning of 1967. During a speech on January 5, Mai Van Bo dangled the prospect of negotiations in exchange for a halt across all of North Vietnam. "If the U.S. permanently and unconditionally ends the bombing of North Vietnam," he announced at the Latin American Conference Hall in Paris, "that action will be taken into account by the Government of the Democratic Republic of Vietnam."[1]

To step up the pressure on President Johnson to stop the bombing, the North Vietnamese cultivated American journalists and intellectuals who opposed their own country's involvement in the war. One of them was Harrison Salisbury, assistant managing editor of the *New York Times*. The North Vietnamese government admitted Salisbury into the country and escorted him to various sites to see damage caused by American bombs. In a series of *Times* articles, Salisbury published what he saw and what he was told by his hosts. The latter included allegations that the United

States was wantonly bombing civilian targets, in contravention of official U.S. government statements. Critics of the war in the United States and other Western countries seized on Salisbury's reporting as proof that a morally bankrupt American government was deliberately targeting North Vietnamese civilians under the guise of striking military targets.[2]

In responding to Salisbury's reporting, spokesmen for the Johnson administration were forced to concede that American bombs had inadvertently hit some civilian structures in North Vietnam. They added, truthfully, that the United States had taken extraordinary precautions and put pilots at additional risk to avoid harming the civilian population. The only damage to civilians and their property, said the spokesmen, had been caused by bombs that had missed their intended targets. They did not mention that at least a few civilian targets had been hit inadvertently because they had been mistaken for other structures.[3]

Salisbury's credibility came under fire within a few days as it was learned that information in his stories had been lifted straight from North Vietnamese propaganda tracts. North Vietnamese facilities identified in Salisbury's reporting as "civilian" turned out to have been essential military targets. In response to Salisbury's publication of a photograph that he had denoted as the bombed-out ruins of the Phat Diem cathedral, the Johnson administration issued fresh reconnaissance photographs showing the cathedral to be intact.[4]

During interviews with Salisbury, top North Vietnamese officials expounded on the righteousness of their cause. Pham Van Dong gave the most consequential interview, a partial transcript of which was published in the *Times* on January 8. Seated on a Louis XVI sofa in the formal drawing room of Hanoi's presidential palace, the North Vietnamese premier held forth to Salisbury on the weightiest matters of war and peace. "De Gaulle said that the Americans started this war and that this is an unjust and despicable war," Pham Van Dong opened. "From this, he drew the following conclusion: the U.S. must withdraw from South Vietnam. What is your opinion on this subject?"

According to a North Vietnamese transcript, which included dialogue omitted from the accounts of the meeting that Salisbury was to publish, Salisbury answered this question by saying, "In my personal opinion, that view is correct. Unfortunately, that is not the opinion of my government."

After a lengthy commentary on American failures in South Vietnam, Pham Van Dong voiced confidence that the United States would eventually have to recognize that it must withdraw from Vietnam. "I think that people such as you must contribute to clarifying the truth," he told Salisbury. "For the Americans, this is an unjust, senseless war fought in a region in which Americans cannot gain any advantages. For us, however, this is a holy war. It is a war for our independence, for our freedom, for our lives. For us, this war is everything, both for the current generation and for future generations. For that reason we are determined to fight and determined to win." In the struggle for South Vietnam, "we have the just cause, and that is why we will defeat the Americans. Because of this, we have already defeated the Americans. We are now winning. If we have to fight into next year, we will win. If we have to fight for thirty more years, we will still win, for the same reason."

"I do not doubt your ability to fight for another ten or twenty years," returned Salisbury. "I do not doubt that you have support from your friends. I also have no doubt that the White House can still mobilize more troops and manufacture more aircraft and more bombs. I do not think that doing so will enable the U.S. to win the war, but it will make the war drag on for many more years. In the end, occupiers cannot win. The issue is, however, what can be done to end the war and lessen the suffering of the people."

In another segment of the meeting that was omitted from Salisbury's accounts, Salisbury assumed the role of peace broker. He proposed "exploratory feelers" between North Vietnam and the United States, so that "a basis could be found to trust one another more, and a practical solution could be found to end the war." Salisbury suggested that "if the U.S. stops the bombing and stops sending additional troops, then you should stop sending troops into South Vietnam also in order to maintain the present balance of forces. Or perhaps you could take some other, equivalent action."

Pham Van Dong objected to reciprocity. He made clear, in addition, that North Vietnam would not be rushed into negotiations. "We cannot press history forward," he lectured. "If this does not come today, it will come tomorrow. It is no use to make haste. If we show haste, it will be wrong and we will have to wait again. We must let the situation ripen."

Pham Van Dong presented Salisbury with the four points that had long served as Hanoi's official negotiating stance. Salisbury, who was unfamiliar with the history of the diplomatic discourse, misinterpreted them as a new, softened stance on negotiations. He reported them as such in his *New York Times* story on the conversation, as well as in a private report to Secretary of State Rusk.[5]

When Salisbury's analysis appeared in the newspaper, readers who favored negotiations seized upon it as proof of Hanoi's desire for a peace agreement and hence of the need to end Rolling Thunder, the ostensible main obstacle to diplomacy. Four hundred and sixty-two members of the Yale faculty signed a letter calling for "an unconditional halt to the bombing of North Vietnam," citing "Pham Van Dong's interview with Harrison Salisbury in which a new flexibility seems to have been indicated." Lest anyone doubt the righteousness of their indignation, the signatories asserted that "we believe we speak for men of goodwill everywhere in the world."[6]

Officials of the Johnson administration and other supporters of the war denounced Salisbury as a dupe of the Communists. Arthur Sylvester, the assistant secretary of defense for public affairs, publicly ridiculed him as "Harrison Appallsbury" of the "New Hanoi Times."[7] Senator Barry Goldwater declared, "It's rather sad commentary on the state of the press in the United States when the most influential of it . . . becomes the mouthpiece for Communist propaganda."[8] Hanson Baldwin, the *New York Times's* own military editor, sent a complaint to the newspaper's managing editor about Salisbury's reporting, asserting, "I do not think it is fair or accurate to make judgments based on statistics from Communist sources and print them as gospel without some qualification."[9]

Following Salisbury's departure from Hanoi, the North Vietnamese Politburo rejoiced at their success in convincing him that they had softened their diplomatic position without actually softening it. "Our reception of the American journalist Salisbury and the press conference held by our representative in Paris [Mai Van Bo] have had a great impact on public opinion and have created a new opportunity to take another step forward in the struggle to demand that the U.S. stop the bombing of North Vietnam," the Politburo noted in a secret cable to its headquarters in the South. "The U.S. is experiencing internal confusion and disputes about whether to continue or to end the bombing."[10]

Throughout January, Westmoreland, Lodge, and the Joint Chiefs urged Johnson to resume the bombing in the Hanoi area and strike new targets. The halt was, in their opinion, achieving nothing except allowing Hanoi to increase its support for North

Vietnamese forces in the South.[11] McNamara, however, wanted to continue the suspension of bombing within ten miles of Hanoi as a means of enticing Hanoi into negotiations. He claimed that the suspension could not be producing any adverse military effects because his analysts had determined that Rolling Thunder had never been able to reduce the infiltration of North Vietnamese men and materiel.[12] Unbeknownst to the Americans, North Vietnamese Foreign Minister Nguyen Duy Trinh was telling the 13th Plenum of the Party Central Committee at this very time that stopping the bombing of North Vietnam would be a military windfall for North Vietnam.[13]

Although President Johnson doubted that renewed diplomatic initiatives would bear any fruit, he decided to make one more overture to the North Vietnamese before resuming Rolling Thunder strikes near Hanoi. Having achieved little by communicating through intermediaries, he sent a personal letter to Ho Chi Minh. "I am writing to you in the hope that the conflict in Vietnam can be brought to an end," the letter began. "That conflict has already taken a heavy toll—in lives lost, in wounds inflicted, in property destroyed, and in simple human misery. If we fail to find a just and peaceful solution, history will judge us harshly." Johnson proposed direct and secret talks between trusted representatives of the two sides. The United States would not accept permanent cessation of bombing as a precondition for talks but would agree to stop the bombing and refrain from increasing the number of U.S. troops in South Vietnam if the North Vietnamese discontinued their infiltration into South Vietnam.[14]

One week later, a North Vietnamese diplomat delivered Ho Chi Minh's reply to the U.S. embassy in Moscow. Ho accused the U.S. government of "war crimes and crimes against peace and against humanity" in South Vietnam and alleged that in North Vietnam, "thousands of American planes have rained down hundreds of thousands of tons of bombs destroying towns, villages, factories, roads, bridges, dikes, dams and even churches, pagodas, hospitals and schools." If the United States wanted direct talks with North Vietnam, the letter stated, it first had to discontinue the bombing and "all other acts of war" against North Vietnam.[15]

Johnson held Ho's rebuff aloft to show Americans that North Vietnam would not negotiate unless the United States surrendered its most valuable bargaining chip in advance. He informed members of Congress that the United States could not obtain peace "crawling on our stomachs. We can't have it with a cup in our hands. We can't have it begging." American troops would remain in South Vietnam, he told the congressmen, "until we have an honorable and just peace."[16]

New polls showed that the American public believed, by a margin of three to one, that more vigorous U.S. military actions were required to bring the war to a successful conclusion. Citing these poll numbers, Johnson told his top advisers on February 17 that now was the time to take stronger action.[17] He resolved to lift the restrictions he had placed on Rolling Thunder in December. Wheeler urged him to go further, hitting targets that had hitherto been off limits, to include power plants, steel plants, and a cement plant.

McNamara, who had hoped to talk Johnson into ending Rolling Thunder after the midterm election, now sought the more modest objective of blocking the military's attempts to expand the bombing beyond December's parameters. Hitting the targets proposed by the Chiefs, he contended, would not affect the movement of supplies to the South, because North Vietnam's logistical capacity greatly exceeded current usage. Furthermore, warned McNamara, such strikes could provoke America's enemies into fighting a larger war. After hearing the arguments, Johnson came down between the positions of McNamara and the Joint Chiefs. He authorized the bombing of a select fraction of Wheeler's targets, as well as an increase in the monthly rate of Rolling Thunder sorties from 13,200 to 14,500.[18]

While this enlargement of Rolling Thunder satisfied the majority of Americans, it evoked protests from liberal Democrats in Congress, who increasingly believed that the bombing was a senseless impediment to the diplomacy needed to end the war. At the head of the liberal charge was Robert F. Kennedy. Having been an ardent supporter of South Vietnam as the attorney general of his late brother, the younger Kennedy had shifted his position after his brother's death in November 1963, mainly because of the souring of his relationship with Lyndon Johnson. Elected to the Senate at the end of 1964, he had aligned himself with the liberal wing of the Democratic Party and adopted the liberal position that the Johnson administration was not trying hard enough to solve the conflict through diplomacy. The younger Kennedy was now considered the man most likely to run against Johnson in 1968 should the liberals decide to abandon the president. On March 2, Kennedy declared publicly that the United States should halt all bombing of North Vietnam unconditionally for the purpose of facilitating a negotiated settlement. "We are not in Vietnam to play the part of an avenging angel pouring death and destruction on the roads and factories and homes of a guilty land," Kennedy pronounced.[19]

On the following day, Johnson vented his frustration with Kennedy and like-minded liberals in a phone call with Henry "Scoop" Jackson, a hawkish Democratic senator from the state of Washington. In a thinly veiled dig at Secretary McNamara, the president said that he did not buy the argument made at a recent cabinet meeting that Rolling Thunder had no military benefits. Jackson assured Johnson that he was in the right. If the bombing were not hurting the North Vietnamese, he told the president, they would not be trying so strenuously to stop it. "You know, I'm just a country boy," Jackson said, "but we understand that at home."[20]

The president promptly directed Westmoreland to hold a press conference describing the positive results of the bombing campaign. Appearing before the Saigon press corps one day later, Westmoreland announced that Rolling Thunder "saves American and Vietnamese lives on the battlefield" by constraining the enemy's infiltration of military resources into the South. Therefore, suspension of bombing would "cost many additional lives and probably prolong the conflict."[21]

Johnson continued to weigh further actions against North Vietnam. At his behest, the CIA Office of National Estimates assessed several options, the most aggressive of which combined heightened bombing of North Vietnam's industrial and transportation targets with mining of North Vietnamese ports. The estimate, issued on April 12, concluded that this maximal option would "threaten Hanoi's ability to support the war and maintain its own internal situation." It would not provoke Soviet or Chinese intervention, in the estimation of the analysts, and "there would be a good chance that the Soviets would at this juncture begin to exert greater efforts to bring about peace."[22]

Like earlier prognostications of Soviet and Chinese restraint, this one would be vindicated by postwar revelations. Soviet Ambassador to the United States Anatoly Dobrynin wrote in his 1995 memoirs that the Soviets were intent on avoiding a direct confrontation with the United States at this time for fear that a confrontation would bolster China and undermine the development of the socialist system within the Soviet Union.[23] In the late 1990s, the Chinese released the memorandum of a conversation on April 10, 1967, in which Zhou Enlai informed the North Vietnamese of China's contingency plan for an American blockade of the ports—the most provocative of the proposed actions. This plan, Zhou said, involved no Chinese intervention in Vietnam but instead redirected Soviet supply shipments into Chinese ports for transshipment to North Vietnam by road or railroad.[24]

Johnson, however, once more refused to trust predictions that the Soviets and Chinese would keep their weapons holstered. He would not mine the ports. He did authorize incremental increases to Rolling Thunder on April 22 for the purpose of imposing additional strains on the North Vietnamese logistical system. The newest iteration, Rolling Thunder 55, included ten new targets in the Hanoi-Haiphong complex, among them the lines of communication in northeastern North Vietnam, the Haiphong cement plant, the Hanoi transformer station, and the Hoa Lac and Kep airfields.[25] This intensification produced enough consternation in Hanoi that the North Vietnamese regime withdrew most of its air defense forces from infiltration and supply routes to defend the capital region.[26]

In the South, the war was intensifying in conjunction with rising American combat troop strength. The guidance that Westmoreland issued to his commanders at the beginning of 1967 emphasized attacks on enemy bases and logistics, which Westmoreland termed "the Achilles heel of the VC/NVA."[27] In recognition of the value of controlling the rural population, Westmoreland enjoined his commanders to accord highest priority to the enemy forces and base areas that posed the greatest threats to pacification.[28]

The first enemy base in Westmoreland's crosshairs for 1967 was the Iron Triangle, a three-hundred-square-mile plot of jungle, rubber plantations, and open rice paddies thirty kilometers to the northwest of Saigon. It was the closest North Vietnamese redoubt to the South Vietnamese capital, yet friendly forces had not set foot in it since an October 1965 foray by the 173rd Airborne Brigade. Close to two-thirds of American combat units in III Corps would take part in the operation to disinfect the triangle, which was christened Operation Cedar Falls.

Lieutenant General Jonathan Seaman, the commander of II Field Force, planned to begin the operation by surrounding the Iron Triangle with American forces and evacuating all civilians from its interior. From that time on, anyone found in the triangle could be engaged as an enemy combatant. American units would search for and destroy a regional North Vietnamese headquarters that intelligence had located in the triangle, as well as enemy military forces. Fearful of North Vietnamese spies within the South Vietnamese government, the Americans would not notify their South Vietnamese counterparts of the operation until the U.S. forces had cordoned off the triangle, at which time the South Vietnamese would be asked for help in removing the civilian population.

Operation Cedar Falls began on January 8 with an air assault by six U.S. brigades. Some helicopters ferried infantry to the outer edges of the Iron Triangle, while others headed for the village of Ben Suc, considered the most likely place for enemy resistance to develop. Adjoining a loop of the Saigon River at the northwest corner of the triangle, Ben Suc had an estimated population of six thousand, many of whom were believed to serve in Viet Cong logistical companies that moved rice and other supplies by sampan on the rivers, loaded and unloaded the goods, and stored them in the jungle nearby.

The 1st Battalion of the 26th Infantry headed for Ben Suc aboard UH-1 Huey helicopters. Commanding the battalion was Lt. Col. Alexander M. Haig, the future secretary of state. The aircraft first took a diversionary route at a cruising altitude, then dropped to treetop level and flew twelve kilometers to Ben Suc.

Upon reaching the village at 0800, the Hueys split up and set down at three landing zones on the village outskirts.

Within the span of ninety seconds, all 420 of the battalion's men disembarked from the helicopters. As they marched toward the center of the village, helicopter loudspeakers announced in Vietnamese, "Attention people of Ben Suc. You are surrounded by Republic of South Vietnam and allied forces. Do not run away or you will be shot as VC. Stay in your homes and wait for further instructions."[29]

A bombardment of the adjacent jungle ensued, primarily as a means of discouraging anyone from leaving the village. The helicopters then informed the villagers to gather their possessions and assemble at the village school. By the early afternoon, 3,500 people had gathered on the school grounds.

Three platoons of the South Vietnamese field police and a South Vietnamese infantry battalion arrived via air at Ben Suc. The field police searched the mass of people at the school for military-aged males, and the infantrymen combed the village for men who had disregarded the summons to the school. All the men found in the village were flown to the provincial capital for questioning, while the women and children were evacuated by boat.

After emptying Ben Suc of its inhabitants, the Americans evacuated all remaining civilians from the Iron Triangle. American bulldozers and "tankdozers," M-48 medium tanks with bulldozer blades, flattened nine square kilometers of jungle terrain. Search parties found vast underground networks of tunnels and chambers, which had been used for storage, medical treatment, and the manufacture of mines and booby traps.

To explore and map these subterranean networks, the Americans sent in volunteers who bore the affectionate nickname of "tunnel rat." The men who volunteered for this task were, in the words of an official U.S. Army history, "either extremely brave or extremely foolish."[30] The tunnel rat went into the tunnels with a flashlight, field telephone, silencer-equipped pistol, and compass. At each turn, he reported his azimuth and estimated distance traveled by telephone. To ensure that the tunnel rats could breathe, air was pumped into the tunnels using air compressors or auxiliary helicopter engines.

The tunnel rats of Operation Cedar Falls discovered massive document caches, containing 491,553 pages of documents, of which 52,797 pages were deemed important enough to translate. The underground scouts also found a signal and cryptological center replete with code books, an intelligence facility from which the enemy had neglected to remove a notebook containing the names of spies within the South Vietnamese armed forces, and a one-hundred-bed hospital. From the reports of the tunnel rats, engineers were able to map out miles of tunnels and underground chambers. The engineers proceeded to collapse the subterranean complexes with explosives, unless they were encased in concrete, in which instance the engineers filled them with acetylene gas and ignited it. All the major facilities of the enemy's regional headquarters were demolished, including 400 tunnels, 1,100 bunkers, and 500 other structures.

The Americans also seized 3,700 thousand tons of rice in the Iron Triangle. They hauled some away and destroyed the rest with flamethrowers, diesel fuel, explosives, and bulldozers. At a time when food shortages severely constrained the operations of North Vietnamese Army, the loss of this stockpile was an excruciating blow.

In terms of inflicting casualties, Operation Cedar Falls was less successful. Preparatory American air strikes had caused large numbers of North Vietnamese soldiers to flee the Iron Triangle before the American ground forces arrived. Out of 5,987 persons evacuated from Ben Suc, only 28 were determined to be insurgents, and most of them were low-level locals. As the American and South Vietnamese forces scoured the Iron Triangle, most of the remaining enemy fighters attempted to sneak through the American cordon. The Americans skirmished intermittently with enemy squads and platoons, but most of the Communists whom the Americans encountered belonged to small work parties of two to three men harvesting rice from the paddies.

Combat engagements were still numerous, more numerous than might have been expected considering the early exodus of North Vietnamese troops. The Americans reported killing 738 of the enemy, capturing 283, and detaining 512. Another 543 defected. American losses came to 72 killed and 337 wounded, and the South Vietnamese Army sustained 11 killed and 8 wounded.[31] For the North Vietnamese, the loss of men was less significant than the loss of food and the denial of a major sanctuary near Saigon. The operation's ultimate impact would depend upon how long the North Vietnamese could be kept out of that sanctuary.

In early February, Westmoreland shifted focus to another base area to the north of Saigon, War Zone C. Measuring four thousand square kilometers in area, War Zone C was much larger than the Iron Triangle and much farther from the capital, its northern and western boundaries touching the Cambodian border. The North Vietnamese had been very careful in moving personnel in and out of War Zone C and communicating about their activities, so the United States had only the most fragmentary of information on the units and installations inside. During Operation Attleboro in November 1966, the Americans had obtained a piece of information that pointed toward War Zone C as the home of COSVN, the central Communist Party headquarters in the South. Other bits of information suggested that the headquarters of the 9th

Division and its 271st Regiment were also located in the zone, and that three other regiments were nearby.

The offensive into War Zone C, Operation Junction City, would be the largest operation of the war to date. It began on February 22 with the movement of twenty-two U.S. battalions by air and land into the zone's marshes, forests, rubber plantations, and rolling hills. American airborne and airmobile assault elements formed a horseshoe around the northern end of War Zone C, while infantry and armored cavalry pressed into the open end of the horseshoe from the south.

The Americans who advanced into the middle of the horseshoe found the area to be largely deserted. During six days of small firefights, American troops killed fifty-four of the enemy at a cost of twenty-eight of their own. Unlike the North Vietnamese forces in the Iron Triangle, the enemy units in War Zone C had received no forewarning of an American onslaught but had escaped after the Americans had entered the horseshoe through tunnels they had dug for such an eventuality. Some North Vietnamese had departed so hurriedly that they had left partially cooked food in their field kitchens. American search parties discovered large enemy base camps with cavernous mess halls and lecture theaters, which appeared to have been used quite recently and were extensively booby trapped.[32]

On the sixth day of Junction City, North Vietnamese forces initiated a series of attacks along the American supply routes into War Zone C. This creatively devised campaign marked the start of the "spring wave" offensive Hanoi had conceived during June 1966. First came the ambush of a company of the U.S. 1st Division by a battalion of the 101st North Vietnamese Army Regiment. Under heavy fire, the American company established a stout perimeter and called in air strikes. In four hours of battle, the North Vietnamese battalion inflicted losses of 25 killed and

28 wounded on the American company, although at great cost to itself, leaving 167 bodies and 40 weapons on the battlefield.[33]

On the night of March 10, two North Vietnamese battalions attacked a firebase belonging to the U.S. 1st Division's 3rd Brigade. American air and artillery strikes fell on the attackers with such alacrity that most of the assault force never got near the perimeter wire. Only 3 Americans were killed and 38 wounded that night, while a search of the surrounding area the next morning turned up 197 North Vietnamese corpses.[34]

General Seaman, as the commander of Operation Junction City, transferred forces to the east on March 18 to look for more North Vietnamese units. He established new firebases in locations that made them irresistible targets for the enemy. Tempted, in particular, was the nearest North Vietnamese Army division to these firebases, the 9th.

The audacity that had previously characterized the 9th Division had recently given way to passivity, which in turn had generated pressure from higher headquarters for activity and results. During an internal review, the 9th Division's Party Committee and command group had confessed that for too long the unit "had missed many opportunities to destroy the enemy because of fear of enemy tanks, artillery, and air strikes," its forces preferring "to disperse and fight only small-scale battles." The new American firebases appeared to offer the best available opportunities for the division to bleed the Americans.[35]

On March 20, the 9th Division's 273rd Regiment attacked the American firebase at Bau Bang, the hamlet where, in November 1965, American tanks and armored personnel carriers had mowed down five waves of North Vietnamese attackers in a peanut field. Bau Bang was now held by a U.S. armored cavalry troop, which had just arrived with six tanks, twenty armored personnel carriers, and 129 men. To cover all approaches to the firebase with heavy weapons, troop commander Captain Raoul H. Alcala had positioned the vehicles in a circular formation called the "wagon train" by American troops in homage to their pioneer ancestors.

At the sound of North Vietnamese weaponry, Captain Alcala summoned flareships to light up the night sky and then ordered a succession of air and artillery strikes. The tanks and armored personnel carriers fired their assortments of weaponry into the North Vietnamese ranks. Some of the North Vietnamese shock troops reached the armored personnel carriers on the firebase's perimeter and climbed on top of them, but were knocked off when American tanks fired beehive rounds at the carriers. Once the Americans ran out of beehive rounds, they launched high-explosive shells with delayed fuses into the ground in front of the North Vietnamese, producing showers of deadly fragments. North Vietnamese rocket-propelled grenades destroyed several of the American vehicles, but Captain Alcala sealed the holes in the defensive circle by pulling the remaining armor back into a tighter formation. American armored cavalry troops from nearby bases eventually arrived to reinforce the perimeter.

As in the first Battle of Bau Bang, the North Vietnamese chose to call it quits after their fifth futile charge. The defeat that they conceded was at least as lopsided as the preceding one. The Americans reported 227 enemy dead by body count and 3 enemy captured against U.S. losses of 3 killed and 63 wounded.[36]

The next morning, another regiment of the 9th Division attacked Fire Base Gold, which had been established in an egg-shaped clearing two days earlier by the 3rd Battalion of the U.S. 22nd Infantry and the 77th Artillery Battalion. Although the jungle around the clearing had been thinned by defoliants and napalm, it retained enough foliage for large North Vietnamese formations to approach undetected during the night. At 0630, a small group of Americans was returning from a night patrol when it ran into enemy soldiers moving from the woods toward the firebase. An enormous North Vietnamese force overran the American patrol in five minutes, killing or wounding all its members. The North Vietnamese regiment then sent waves of troops to assault Firebase Gold, oriented by the blares of bugles.

From high perches on the branches of trees, North Vietnamese snipers fired into the American base, to deadly effect. By the American commander's estimate, the sniper rounds were coming from a distance of three hundred yards and an elevation of forty feet. The M-16 assault rifle, which had recently been distributed to the units holding Fire Base Gold, lacked accuracy at that range, so the defenders gathered the few M-1 rifles the unit still possessed and fired them at the trees. Nearby U.S. firebases discharged their artillery at the North Vietnamese attackers, and U.S. armor and infantry departed those bases to assist Gold. Air support, however, was delayed by the downing of the O-1 Cessna Bird Dog that had been carrying the forward air controller, and was further impeded by a one thousand-foot cloud ceiling.

At 0756, North Vietnamese soldiers broke through the southeastern side of the American perimeter. Ahead of them they saw American artillery pieces, which they resolved to seize. Before they could close in, however, American artillerymen fired beehive rounds into their ranks. The bursting of thousands of spikes put an abrupt halt to the intrusion. Subsequent breaches on the eastern and northeastern sides met the same fate.

The 2nd Battalion of the 12th U.S. Army Infantry Regiment had set out on foot toward Firebase Gold after receiving word of the attack. It had to cut its way through 1,500 meters of bamboo to reach the firebase, which it achieved in the space of only two hours through energetic chopping. Upon reaching Firebase Gold at 0840, its soldiers solidified the base's perimeter, then initiated counter attacks.

At 0912, an American armored column arrived from the west. Smashing into the side of the main North Vietnamese assault force, it fired beehives into exposed infantry. With the attack now in total shambles, the North Vietnamese regimental commander requested and received permission to break contact and withdraw.

By 1000 the North Vietnamese were gone from the scene, and American helicopters were arriving to evacuate the wounded. Sweeps conducted afterward found 647 enemy bodies, and an additional 200 enemy were estimated to have been killed and dragged away. The Americans lost 31 killed and 109 wounded.[37]

The 9th Division's last major counterthrust to Junction City occurred on April 1, when its 271st Regiment and 70th Guard Regiment attacked Landing Zone George. Two days earlier, Lieutenant Colonel Alexander Haig had arrived at Landing Zone George with his battalion, the 1st Battalion of the 26th Infantry. Haig had directed his soldiers to dig what had become known as "DePuy fighting positions," after Major General William DePuy. Each man dug a hole deep enough that he could stand in it with his helmet on, then covered the hole with logs or steel rods topped by camouflage. The fighting position had two firing ports, each at a forty-five-degree angle from the front so that enemy soldiers charging the position could not fire straight into it and could be cut down by others firing at them from angles.

Thanks at least in part to the virtues of the DePuy fighting position, American casualties during the initial North Vietnamese mortar, rocket, and recoilless rifle barrages were only twelve wounded. Haig responded with cluster bombs and artillery, which caused far greater damage to the North Vietnamese infantry since they were massed and in the open. A few of the attackers penetrated the American perimeter, but the Americans promptly threw them back. Post-battle sweeps turned up 609 bodies. American casualties amounted to 17 killed and 102 wounded.[38]

Brigadier General Bernard William Rogers, a former Rhodes Scholar who served as assistant commander of the 1st Infantry Division during Junction City, reflected upon the operation in a speech at the Yorktown Day Celebration in Virginia a few months later. "Who is this American soldier in Vietnam?" Rogers asked. "He is a boy, about 19 years of age, armed and in uniform, who did not choose to be there. He would have preferred to remain at home, comfortable, enjoying the many attractions and conveniences available to Americans, secure in the company of his family, his friends, his sweetheart. Thoughts of those persons at home creep into his mind, even at times when he is trying to force himself to concentrate on the battle at hand.

"In the jungles and rice paddies of Vietnam, this smooth-cheeked, bright-eyed, enthusiastic boy becomes a man. He lives with fear, he lives with carnage, he lives with death. Burned forever into his memory are ugly sights and awesome sorrows which at times are almost too much for a boy, just turned man, to bear. He kills the enemy but questions the waste and folly of war. He sees his buddy killed beside him and asks why? Why was it his turn to go today and not mine?

"He exults in the victories won by his outfit, but he weeps with grief while attending the memorial services for his buddies who fell in the fight. He understands the cause for which he is fighting; his enthusiasm, dedication and motivation are contagious. He looks with disgust at reports of those back home who question his being and fighting in the far-off place. He dismisses such reports with a shrug, remarking 'Those guys back home just don't know what it's all about.'"[39]

The battles initiated by the North Vietnamese during the latter part of Operation Junction City raised the American tally of North Vietnamese dead for the operation to 2,728. Nevertheless, Major General John H. Hay, commander of the 1st Infantry

Division, acknowledged afterward that the operation had not inflicted as many casualties on the enemy as he had hoped. Too often, he lamented, the enemy had been able to avoid casualties when he so desired by slinking into the jungle or moving across the border into Cambodia.

Hay would have found some solace had he known that the North Vietnamese were themselves highly displeased with the outcome of Junction City. The mauling of the 9th Division's units in large attacks caused the North Vietnamese high command to suspend regimental-sized assaults throughout South Vietnam. As a consequence, American forces were able to operate in smaller units at less risk in the months to come. U.S. ground operations of battalion size or larger decreased by 40 percent in 1967 over the previous year, and hence U.S. units could cover more territory in their hunts for hostile forces.[40]

In reviewing Operation Junction City, American military intelligence analysts concluded that the North Vietnamese units encountered during the operation had been equipped with weapons shipped through the Cambodian port of Sihanoukville, as opposed to weapons hauled from North Vietnam via the Ho Chi Minh Trail. The CIA and the State Department disputed that contention, arguing that North Vietnamese forces in the South were getting what they needed from the Laotian infiltration routes.[41] Postwar Communist histories would reveal that large numbers of the weapons had indeed come from Sihanoukville. In February 1967, a Chinese ship had arrived in the Cambodian port to deliver three thousand tons of armaments. Transported to the COSVN base area in War Zone C later that month, they were then distributed to North Vietnamese units, including some of those assigned to countering Junction City.[42]

In the sparsely populated border region of II Corps, American forces continued to hound the North Vietnamese in early

1967, Westmoreland's guidance about safeguarding pacification notwithstanding. At Westmoreland's direction, the 4th Infantry Division went after two North Vietnamese divisions that had been spotted on the high plateau near the Cambodian border. The primary objective, on top of the standard one of inflicting casualties, was to prevent the enemy from penetrating the interior of Pleiku Province. "If we let the enemy get a foothold in here," Westmoreland warned, "he could cut the roads to Pleiku and we could be in very difficult shape."[43]

In January, the 4th Infantry Division initiated Operation Sam Houston to find and destroy the enemy on the high plateau. After the beating that North Vietnamese units had suffered in the highlands at the end of 1966, the North Vietnamese commanders near Pleiku now had little interest in battle. Making lavish use of their Cambodian safe haven, they only occasionally crossed back into South Vietnam to fight on the high plateau, when the terms of battle heavily favored them. During the four months of Operation Sam Houston, nine of the eleven encounters between American and North Vietnamese forces transpired within five kilometers of the Cambodian border, and most began with North Vietnamese ambushes of American companies that were moving through terrain well-suited for ambushing. Total American casualties during Sam Houston were 172 killed and 767 wounded. The Americans estimated North Vietnamese fatalities at 733. Although the dearth of battle frustrated American commanders, the operation did achieve the objective of keeping Pleiku safe.[44]

To the east, in Operation Pershing, the 1st Cavalry Division sought to clean the 3rd North Vietnamese Army Division out of northern Binh Dinh Province and Quang Ngai Province. North Vietnamese forces ambushed the Americans from time to time, but for the most part tried to steer clear of them. By April, most of the 3rd Division had taken refuge in the jungles of Quang Ngai Province, where, with only tree roots and leaves to eat, they did not have the sustenance required to fight. The inability of the 3rd Division to engage the Americans caused the North Vietnamese commander for the region to sack the division's commander and order his replacement to get the division back into combat.[45]

In the far north of the country, the relative calm of late 1966 continued into January 1967. It ended abruptly in February when patrols of the 3rd Marine Division received heavy and accurate fire from North Vietnamese mortars in the DMZ. Westmoreland sought and received permission from Washington to fire artillery into the DMZ and southern North Vietnam.[46]

As projectiles flew back and forth over the DMZ, officials in Washington and Saigon quarreled over plans for McNamara's anti-infiltration barrier. Advocates of the barrier touted a growing array of sensors that would be deployed into the barrier zone, including balanced pressure systems, which were buried in the ground and could sense the change in pressure caused by a human footstep; seismic sensors, which detected ground vibrations like those from the movement of men or vehicles; and infrared systems, which were triggered when an object passed between an infrared beam and a sensor. Technology enthusiasts also trumpeted pulse doppler radars that could detect personnel and vehicles up to ten thousand meters away, and night observation telescopes that used the reflected light of the moon and stars to provide night vision capability with a range of one thousand meters.[47]

McNamara gained a degree of support from Westmoreland by incorporating Westmoreland's strong point obstacle system into the barrier plans. Barrier proponents asserted that the strongpoints would prevent enemy forces from traversing the flat terrain of eastern Quang Tri and advancing on Hue. To cross the DMZ, therefore, the North Vietnamese would have to move through the mountains of western Quang Tri, which were not conducive to the large-scale transportation of supplies.[48]

Opposition to the barrier and its strong point obstacle system percolated among General Walt and the Joint Chiefs. The strongpoints, they said, would divert 11,500 American and South Vietnamese troops for little gain. Few infiltrators and even fewer supplies were moving through the thirty kilometers of eastern Quang Tri where the strongpoints would be concentrated. The enemy was not trying to move supplies across any section of the demilitarized zone adjacent to Quang Tri, they asserted, but instead was using the safer routes in Laos. In lieu of McNamara's barrier, General Walt advocated mobile operations by Marine battalions based along Route 9, the main east-west route near the DMZ.[49]

The objections of the generals made no impression on McNamara. Ground clearing for the barrier was to commence in April, McNamara decreed. The 3rd Marine Division was assigned the mission of guarding and constructing the strongpoint system.

As if intending to validate the objections of the American generals to the barrier, two North Vietnamese Army divisions now began trekking across the DMZ into the mountains of western Quang Tri. Their supplies came down the Ho Chi Minh Trail, traveling south through Laos past the seventeenth parallel before scooting east into Quang Tri to meet their users. Additional North Vietnamese units were taking the Ho Chi Minh Trail to reach Thua Thien Province.

These new threats compelled Westmoreland to reposition Marine forces and reinforce I Corps with the division-sized Task Force Oregon, an amalgam of three Army brigades. It marked the first time in the war that large U.S. Army units operated in I Corps, hitherto the exclusive preserve of the U.S. Marine Corps.[50] Westmoreland also requested the transfer of the 9th Marine

Amphibious Brigade, a theater reserve unit, from Okinawa to the coast off Quang Tri. Based aboard ships, the brigade's special landing forces could fly by helicopter to the battlefields of Quang Tri in a matter of minutes. "The forthcoming summer campaign in I Corps could be a decisive period of the war," Westmoreland notified the Joint Chiefs in making the request. "It is essential that we provide every reinforcement available to insure that the campaign is a success and the enemy suffers a decisive defeat."[51] Secretary of Defense McNamara agreed to the deployment of the amphibious brigade.

At this same time, Westmoreland approved a recommendation from Major General DePuy to increase direct U.S. military participation in village security. DePuy had recently returned to Washington to become the special assistant for counterinsurgency and special activities for the Joint Chiefs of Staff. In the early spring, he had told Westmoreland that the South Vietnamese armed forces continued to fare poorly in their primary mission of pacifying South Vietnam's rural population because of leadership deficiencies. Pacification had improved when U.S. forces were in or near the villages, but when American forces departed to fight big enemy units in remote locations, there was "a marked adverse impact."[52] Westmoreland's order to increase U.S. participation in the village war would cause the percentage of American forces involved in direct support of counterinsurgency to increase from 22 to 40 percent over the course of 1967.[53]

By allocating more American forces to securing villages where South Vietnamese forces had failed, Westmoreland would curtail the enemy's access to recruits, food, and information. But he would also relieve pressure on South Vietnamese leaders to prosecute the war more vigorously and effectively. General Nguyen Duc Thang, one of the most dynamic of the South Vietnamese generals, later complained that the willingness of the U.S. military to take over tasks from the South Vietnamese "was accepted by many ARVN leaders as an excuse to spend more of their time on personal, selfish affairs," such as diverting government funds for personal use and maintaining mistresses at cafes and nightclubs.[54] Whereas the 9,378 Americans who would be killed in action in 1967 amounted to an 87 percent increase over the previous year's total, the annual total for the South Vietnamese would barely change.[55]

The need for American forces in both supporting pacification and battling North Vietnamese units in jungles and mountains, at a time of persistently high North Vietnamese infiltration, convinced Westmoreland in March that he needed to raise the troop ceiling again. On March 18, he asked Washington to increase the number of U.S. troops in Vietnam from 470,000 to 550,000. The optimal troop strength, he stated, would be still higher, at 678,000.[56]

Westmoreland's floating of the 678,000 figure provoked a brusque rebuttal from General John P. McConnell, the chief of staff of the Air Force, who believed that the proposal did not give due weight to his service's capabilities. McConnell maintained that "effective application of our superior air and sea power against North Vietnam's vulnerabilities" would obviate the need for a troop increase of that magnitude. Air and sea power could "cripple his capabilities to continue to support the war" and "destroy his resolution to continue." McConnell convinced the other Joint Chiefs that they should ask McNamara for a smaller troop augmentation, which would bring the total to 568,000, in tandem with recommendations for increasing the use of air and sea power and calling up the reserves.[57]

At the end of April, Westmoreland made the case for troop increases to President Johnson during a visit to Washington. "Without these forces, we will not be in danger of being defeated," the general informed the president, but "progress will be slowed down." The previous month, Westmoreland noted, friendly forces had reached the "crossover point." That was the point where enemy losses exceeded enemy gains from infiltration and recruitment. More American troops, Westmoreland argued, would ensure sustained momentum even if North Vietnamese troop infiltration increased.

"When we add divisions, can't the enemy add divisions?" asked the president. "If so, where does it all end?"

"The enemy has eight divisions in South Vietnam," Westmoreland responded. "He has the capability of deploying twelve divisions, although he would have difficulty supporting all of these." If the United States did not increase its troop level, "the war could go on for five years," whereas "with a force level of 565,000 men, the war could well go on for three years. With the second increment of 2-1/3 divisions, leading to a total of 665,000 men, it could go on for two years."

Westmoreland also took the opportunity to recommend large ground operations in Laos, which he now believed essential to success.[58] He urged the president to authorize Operation High Port, in which a South Vietnamese division would move into Laos with the support of U.S. firepower and logistics. "Laos would become more and more the battlefield and this would take the pressure off the South," Westmoreland explained. He also advocated ground operations in Cambodia and an amphibious landing in North Vietnam.[59]

Neither Westmoreland's arguments on the troop numbers nor those of the Joint Chiefs swayed Johnson. The president was likewise unreceptive to proposals for air, naval, or ground operations outside South Vietnam, despite intelligence community estimates that these courses of action promised high reward at low risk. On most subjects, he still put greater faith in McNamara than in the intelligence experts. Only on the issue of Rolling Thunder was he willing to break with McNamara and heed some of the recommendations of the hawks.

For all its import, this meeting had not been the primary purpose of Westmoreland's April trip to Washington. President Johnson had summoned the commanding general to the United States to speak to the press, and after refusing two presidential requests to speak in the United States the previous year, Westmoreland had been unable to turn this one down. Confident assertions of military progress from the charismatic Westmoreland, the White House hoped, would quell rising public dissatisfaction with the war.

Early in April, Gallup had reported that approval of Johnson's handling of the war had fallen to 42 percent. The disapproval rating had risen to 45 percent, and among Democrats it had reached 38 percent—twice what it had been one year earlier. A majority of Democrats and nearly two-thirds of all those surveyed said that the administration was not telling Americans everything they needed to know about the war.[60]

On April 4, the Rev. Dr. Martin Luther King Jr. had called upon blacks and "all white people of goodwill" to boycott the Vietnam War. Young men, he said, should avoid military service by declaring themselves conscientious objectors. "Negroes and poor people generally are bearing the heaviest burden of this war," King thundered. The U.S. government was the "greatest purveyor of violence in the world today," and its use of new American weapons in Vietnam was comparable to Nazi Germany's testing of "new medicine and new tortures in the concentration camps of Europe." King demanded an end to all bombing in North and South Vietnam, a unilateral ceasefire in Vietnam, the setting of a date for all U.S. troops to leave, and reduction of American support to other Southeast Asian countries in order to avert wars there.[61] Lastly, he proposed merging the civil rights movement with the antiwar movement.

King's speech drew harsh reproach from other civil rights leaders, many of whom did not oppose the war. In their view, the recklessness of King's accusations about Vietnam undermined his credibility and that of the civil rights cause and demonstrated the risks to the civil rights movement of tying it to an antiwar movement whose rhetoric could alienate American moderates. An editorial in the *Washington Post* blasted King for spouting "sheer inventions of unsupported fantasy." King had "done a grave injury to those who are his natural allies" and "an even graver injury to himself." *Life,* which three years earlier had anointed King its man of the year, denounced the speech as a "demagogic slander that sounded like a script for Radio Hanoi."[62] On April 11, the sixty-member board of the NAACP voted unanimously against the proposed merger of the civil rights and antiwar movements. In a public statement, the board asserted, "Civil rights battles will have to be fought and won on their own merits, irrespective of the state of war or peace in the world."[63]

Into this fray of partisan squabbling and malaise stepped Westmoreland to say things that the president should have been saying for the past two years. Appearing at the annual meeting of the Associated Press in New York's Waldorf Astoria Hotel, the general declared that the United States and its South Vietnamese allies were engaged in "a single, all-pervading confrontation in which the fate of the people of Vietnam, the independence of the free nations of Asia, and the future of emerging nations, as well as the reputation and the very honor of our country, are at stake." South Vietnam was faced not with a civil war but with "a massive campaign of external aggression from Communist North Vietnam." During the last nine years, Westmoreland said, the Vietnamese Communists had killed or kidnapped fifty-three thousand South Vietnamese civilians, "a large share of them teachers, policemen, and elected or natural leaders," which in a country with America's population "would be more than 600,000 people."

The American military intervention had rescued South Vietnam from defeat and inflicted immense losses on the enemy, Westmoreland stated, but the enemy was not yet prepared to give up. "I foresee, in the months ahead, some of the bitterest fighting of the war," he intoned. "I have confidence in our battlefield capability. And I am confident of the support we and our allies will continue to receive from our President and from the Congress. The magnificent men and women I command in Vietnam have earned the unified support of the American people."

In the course of his remarks, Westmoreland warned that antiwar protests in the United States were leading the enemy to believe that American morale was crumbling, for the North Vietnamese did not understand the role of debate in American politics. This perception was giving Hanoi hope and bolstering its will to persist. In reference to the burning of an American flag at a recent antiwar demonstration in New York City's Central Park, Westmoreland stated that he and his troops were "dismayed" by "recent unpatriotic acts here at home."[64]

Opponents of the war, who had heretofore received few public rebukes from administration officials, erupted in protest over Westmoreland's speech. Senator Fulbright asserted that the Johnson administration was portraying dissent as tantamount to treason. According to Senator George McGovern, the general's statements represented an attempt by the administration to blame its failed policy on its critics. In the *New York Post*, a pundit labeled Westmoreland's speech "a forum of domestic psychological warfare."[65]

Westmoreland's statements drew plaudits from other voices, including the *Denver Post,* which asserted that Westmoreland's commentary on the antiwar demonstrations "ought to stimulate reappraisal by many of those who protest against the U.S. presence in Vietnam."[66] Although many influential cultural figures had joined the antiwar movement by this time, others expressed agreement with Westmoreland's concerns about wartime dissent. This group included some of the foremost writers of the day, among them John Steinbeck, John Dos Passos, Ralph Ellison, John Updike, and Jack Kerouac.[67]

Steinbeck was at this moment wrapping up a four-month trip to Vietnam and other Southeast Asian countries. In one of his dispatches, he reported, "The most hysterical objector to this war is the man or woman farthest from it." No opposition to the war was to be found among the South Vietnamese, Australians, South Koreans, Thais, Laotians, or Malayans. Steinbeck wished that antiwar Americans "would go out where the fighting is—sit behind the sandbags with the kids they call murderers, fly with the airmen, or if they are particularly adventurous, go in with a First Cav strike, hit the ground and take cover, or if they wish really to know something about fear and gallantry, I could wish that they might go on a night patrol in the Delta, where every tuft of grass may hiccup a burst of fire and any small stab of pain is probably a needle-pointed punji stick smeared with human excrement and poisonous as a snake bite."[68]

Within the U.S. government, Westmoreland's forecast of more violent fighting in the months ahead met with some skepticism. Shortly before his trip to the United States, the Office of National Estimates had concluded that the North Vietnamese would persevere in their current strategy of wearing down American will through an attrition-based strategy, rather than ramp up combat in the South in pursuit of a swift victory. The analysts speculated that Hanoi was content to stick with its strategy because of overconfidence resulting from the massive exaggeration of allied casualties in reports sent to Hanoi.[69]

North Vietnamese commanders were indeed grossly inflating American and South Vietnamese losses, but North Vietnam's leaders were becoming more aware of that problem and hence more skeptical of their existing strategy. In April, the leadership of the North Vietnamese General Staff convened to assess that strategy and contemplate alternatives. The deliberations opened with an analysis of the current situation from the Combat Operations Department, which put forth a number of sobering facts and observations. It highlighted, in particular, the incongruity between reports of high enemy losses and persistent enemy strength. "Each year we have annihilated or caused the disintegration of 200,000 to 250,000 enemy personnel," the department reported, citing Hanoi's official figures, and yet "the puppet army still basically has as many personnel as ever."

Following the department's presentation, the commander of the General Staff, Van Tien Dung, described the war in still gloomier terms. The Combat Operations Department, he remarked, had understated the severity of Communist military difficulties in the South. Most notably, he said, the department's analysis had not adequately considered the inability of the North Vietnamese Army to win large battles.

After much discussion and debate, the senior leadership decided to jettison its strategic focus, in effect since August 1965, of wearing down America's will through protracted attrition. North Vietnam would now adopt a strategy aimed at breaking America's will more rapidly, through military escalation that culminated in urban revolts. The North Vietnamese Army was to initiate a campaign of intensified military operations, stretching from the middle of 1967 to the middle of 1968, to inflict devastating losses on American and South Vietnamese forces. In the middle of this campaign, North Vietnamese units would assail the major cities and provincial capitals, which would spark mass urban revolts against the South Vietnamese government, comparable in impact to the uprising in Hanoi during 1945.

The men in Hanoi predicted that North Vietnam's military victories and its mobilization of the urban masses would convince the United States to withdraw its forces from South Vietnam. Shorn of American protection, the remnants of the Saigon government and its armed forces would swiftly collapse. The unification of Vietnam by the Communist Party would inevitably follow.[70]

CHAPTER 10

. . .

RECORD LOSSES

May–August 1967

I n the plains of eastern Quang Tri, two 158-meter hillocks protrude from the flat red earth at a location fourteen miles from the South China Sea and two miles from the demilitarized zone. Long ago, French missionaries gave this place the name Con Thien, which in Vietnamese means "Hill of Angels." Mike McKenna, an eighteen-year-old Marine radio operator, was highly impressed when he learned in the spring of 1967 that he would be sent to the Hill of Angels. Upon arriving at Con Thien, however, he discovered that the barren hills "more resembled Golgotha, the Place of Skulls, the location of the crucifixion."[1]

In February 1967, the Marines had turned Con Thien into a combat outpost, making it one of the strongpoints in the McNamara barrier. It was now the closest American base to North Vietnam. To American officials and military officers, Con Thien was an observation post, a firebase, a tripwire, or a salient. To critics of American military strategy, Con Thien was an act of folly, a bullet magnet, a piece of bait, or a death trap. To those who defended it, Con Thien was protracted boredom punctuated by spurts of terror.

The twin peaks of Con Thien afforded ideal observation of the demilitarized zone and its north-south infiltration corridors. On a clear day, Marines looking northward could see a North Vietnamese flag fluttering atop a distant pole on the other side of the DMZ, and to the southeast they had a fine view of the Marine headquarters on the high ground at Dong Ha, ten miles away. "Visitors to Con Thien could look back at the vast logistics complex at Dong Ha and know instantly why the Marines had to hold the hill," remarked Colonel Richard B. Smith, commander of the 9th Marine Regiment. "If the enemy occupied it, he would be looking down our throats."[2]

The Marines had bulldozed the top of each mound into a small plateau, roughly the size of a basketball court. Into the soil, they had burrowed artillery revetments, bunkers, and trenches. To impede ground assaults, they had strewn rolls of barbed wire around the plateaus and the grassy saddle between them. Two U.S. Marine infantry companies, a South Vietnamese CIDG unit, and three M-48A3 tanks were guarding Con Thien on May 8, the day the North Vietnamese attacked.

May 8 marked the thirteenth anniversary of the fall of Dien Bien Phu. The selection of the date of attack, however, may have had more to do with weather than historical commemoration, for the attack was to occur during a heavy monsoon storm that would dilute the potency of American air power. The North Vietnamese intended to overrun the base, occupy its fortifications, and defend it against an American counterattack. Other North Vietnamese forces in the vicinity of the DMZ would spring from their hiding places and clamp their jaws on unsuspecting Marine columns heading to the relief of Con Thien.

At 0250, a North Vietnamese soldier fired a green flare. Five minutes later, North Vietnamese mortars and artillery pounded Con Thien, and North Vietnamese sappers surged toward the base's perimeter, with infantry following close behind. Using Bangalore torpedoes, the sappers blew holes in the barbed wire, then crawled through the openings and tossed satchel charges into outer trenches and bunkers, collapsing them into piles of fractured wooden beams and sand.

Two battalions of the North Vietnamese Army's 812th Regiment charged the Hill of Angels at 0400. Because of low rain-clouds, the American flare ship sent to provide illumination for the garrison was delayed in its arrival, which gave the North Vietnamese precious extra minutes of darkness. North Vietnamese flamethrowers flashed on and off, burning several Marines to death. Rocket-propelled grenades disabled two American tanks.

The North Vietnamese infantry broke through the defensive perimeter in two places. Their efforts to exploit the breaches, however, were thwarted by the Marines, who quickly shifted troops to contain them. The Marines held the North Vietnamese at bay for the next two hours. With the approach of sunrise, which would be sure to bring American aircraft with it, the North Vietnamese decided to withdraw.

Unbeknownst to the North Vietnamese, the Marines had, in the intervening hours, sent nearby units to cut off potential escape routes. Armored vehicles interposed themselves between Con Thien and the DMZ, trapping large numbers of North Vietnamese soldiers. Unwilling to surrender, the North Vietnamese fought where they stood and were slaughtered in the early morning light.

For the day, Marine losses totaled 44 killed and 110 wounded. Of the CIDGs, 14 were killed and 16 wounded, and 4 of their U.S. Special Forces advisers were wounded. North Vietnamese casualties were reported as 212 dead and 8 captured.[3]

The Americans did not need long to determine conclusively that the North Vietnamese participants in the Con Thien attack had used the demilitarized zone as their staging ground. When presented with that fact, the White House authorized the Marines to conduct ground operations into the southern DMZ and fire their weapons into the northern half. Eight U.S. Marine battalions and five South Vietnamese battalions mounted up for Operation Hickory, an offensive into the southern half of the DMZ, scheduled to begin on May 18.

In preparation for departure, the Marines were issued supplies in a profusion that few had ever witnessed. Every battalion received new field utilities, crates of rifle ammunition, cases of hand grenades, and belts of machine gun rounds. The total load for each Marine—including food, water, weapons, tools, and ammunition—came to approximately one hundred pounds. For most of the Marines, this bounty was the first indication that the operation would differ from previous ones.[4]

Some of the American and South Vietnamese battalions crossed into the DMZ on trucks and armored vehicles. Others arrived by boat or air. On the first day of the operation, the temperature hit 106 degrees Fahrenheit, with high humidity. The wet heat sucked energy from the Americans, except those who hailed from southeastern states, who did not seem to mind. Logisticians had to send forward additional water to compensate for the gallons of sweat pouring off the troops.

Operation Hickory met stern resistance in certain places, usually where the North Vietnamese could fight from deftly camouflaged bunkers. More often the allied forces found only abandoned fortifications and tunnels. During the eleven days of Operation Hickory, the North Vietnamese incurred 789 killed and 37 captured, according to American figures. U.S. Marine casualties were 142 killed and 896 wounded, and the South Vietnamese Army recorded losses of 22 killed and 122 wounded. The incursion put a halt to North Vietnamese depredations against Con Thien and other strongpoints near the DMZ.[5]

The assault on Con Thien constituted the opening act of the midyear offensive approved by the North Vietnamese Politburo in April. I Corps would see the most violence during the first phase of the offensive because of both heightened North Vietnamese activity and the arrival of U.S. Army forces. In Quang Ngai Province, elements of the 101st Airborne Division and 1st Cavalry Division spent May clobbering three North Vietnamese regiments, each of which sustained severe losses that forced them to depart for more remote locations.[6]

To the north, in Quang Tin and Quang Nam provinces, the 1st Marine Division battled two regiments from the 2nd NVA Division that were trying to control the Que Son basin. For the Marines, engaging a large enemy force that was willing to stand and fight was a welcome reprieve from prolonged periods of fruitless searching. Captain Jim McElroy, a company commander in the 3rd Battalion of the 5th Marine Regiment, recounted the prevailing mood on the brink of combat. "I have never seen troops so excited in my life," he remembered. "We had been walking around there for two and a half weeks, and they finally got into something. I was just amazed. I had guys that I thought were dunderheads who were mapping our coordinates and setting in for the night."[7] During the fighting in and around the Que Son basin, the Marines killed a reported 1,566 enemy troops against Marine casualties of 220 killed and 714 wounded.[8]

In the extreme northwest of the country, the Marines were heavily engaged around the Khe Sanh plateau during the month of May. Marines swept out of Khe Sanh's central combat base in early May to battle soldiers of the 18th NVA Regiment who had begun to lurk in the nearby hills. Backed by artillery and air power, the Marines ejected the North Vietnamese from the high ground around Khe Sanh within two weeks. Confirmed enemy dead were 940, and the Marines estimated that hundreds more had perished. American casualties came to 155 killed and 425 wounded.[9]

Some of the most intense fighting of May took place in the highland province of Pleiku, where North Vietnamese forces launched a series of battalion-sized attacks along the Cambodian border. To lure American companies into ambushes, a small group of North Vietnamese soldiers would expose itself and then run toward a site where a battalion was laying in waiting. The North Vietnamese battalion held its fire until the Americans were very close, to prevent them from bringing their air and artillery power to bear.

The North Vietnamese battalions often succeeded in ambushing company-sized American units at close range, but they were unable to overrun any of them. When air and artillery could not be employed, as was often the case, the American companies fought the North Vietnamese off by keeping together and coordinating the use of rifles, machine guns, grenades, and claymore mines. "These engagements were won within a fifty-yard area of heavily jungled terrain where the fighting was man to man, our guys against the bad guys," observed Colonel Charles A. Jackson, commander of the 1st Brigade of the 4th Infantry Division.[10]

In nine days of combat in Pleiku, the 4th Infantry Division reported killing 369 of the enemy, primarily by small arms. Total North Vietnamese losses for the nine-day period may well have been much higher, given the profuse bombing of enemy bases and staging areas that were not subsequently searched. American losses during the nine days totaled 69 killed and 259 wounded.[11]

The North Vietnamese employed similar tactics in neighboring Kontum Province. Although the results usually mirrored those in Pleiku, the North Vietnamese did succeed in one instance in inflicting heavy losses on an American company, Alpha of the 2nd Battalion, 503rd Infantry. Grappling with a North Vietnamese battalion five kilometers outside the town of Dak To on June 22, the American company radioed its battalion headquarters for reinforcements. American infantry battalions normally positioned their companies close enough to one another that any one company could be reinforced quickly by a sister company. In this instance, however, the nearest sister company, Charlie, was exceedingly slow in responding to the reports of the initial contact, a problem for which the Charlie company commander and his battalion commander would later blame each other. To guard against an enemy ambush, Charlie advanced with the most cautious and time-consuming of tactics.

For several hours, Alpha company stood its ground alone against the North Vietnamese battalion. The North Vietnamese attacked every side of the American company and succeeded in killing all the American platoon commanders. The able-bodied Americans eventually withdrew to the company command post, leaving behind a large number of seriously injured men. The company command post hung on until Charlie company arrived in the early afternoon, more than five hours after it had begun its movement. Confronted by well-positioned North Vietnamese machine guns, the commander of Charlie company did not attempt to retrieve the stranded survivors of Alpha company during the afternoon or the night.

The patrols sent by Charlie company the next morning discovered an appalling scene of butchery. Of the seventy-six Americans found dead, forty-three had received ghastly head wounds at close range, a telltale sign that they had been executed by the North Vietnamese. Ears and fingers were missing from some of the American corpses. The patrols also located a few paratroopers who had survived the night outside the American perimeter by feigning death. One of these men had remained inert while a North Vietnamese soldier severed his finger with a trench knife.

The official American report on the battle stated that 106 enemy bodies had been found and that another 407 had been killed by artillery fire as the enemy departed the area. Americans who had been on the battlefield suspected that the actual numbers were considerably lower. Witnesses reported finding only 18 enemy bodies on the battlefield and none in the areas into which the artillery had been fired. The North Vietnamese, though, had possessed ample time to evacuate their casualties, and the sheer intensity of the battle suggested that the North Vietnamese losses were likely very high, if not as high as what the Americans reported.[12]

American estimates of enemy forces killed in action during May and June were nearly double the numbers for the same months in 1966. The May tally of 9,808 set a new record for the most enemy killed in a single month. The highest North Vietnamese losses were reported in I Corps, where a whopping 6,119 were killed in the month of May alone. Accompanying the surge in enemy losses was a similarly large rise in American casualties. In May, the monthly total of American fatalities exceeded 1,000 for the first time.[13]

The intensification of combat did little to diminish the resolve of the American troops. That was the conclusion of Philippa Schuyler, a famous pianist who was reporting on the war for the *Manchester Union Leader* during this period. Traveling from one end of the country to the other, Schuyler sounded out Americans of every rank, race, and religion. Most of the servicemen she met voiced dissatisfaction with the self-imposed restrictions on American military power, but they were unanimous in the belief that the United States ought to stay in Vietnam until the war was won. "At no time did I meet any American who felt we should withdraw without having achieved victory," Schuyler reported. Support for the war, she added, was equally strong among black and white troops and among the able-bodied in the field and the wounded in the military hospitals.[14]

On the pacification front, the month of May saw President Johnson reach a decision on the reorganization of American support. Having been persuaded by Robert Komer that the experimental Office of Civilian Operations had been a failure, Johnson scrapped that office and created a new Department of Defense entity to manage the American side of pacification, entitled Civil Operations and Revolutionary Development Support (CORDS). It was placed within General Westmoreland's military command structure, giving it access to the command's abundant resources. Johnson appointed Komer as its head.[15]

At each organizational echelon, down to the district, CORDS assigned a single American authority over all the U.S. personnel involved in pacification. If that individual was a civilian, the deputy was a military officer, and vice versa. Civilians who thought they could continue working independently soon learned that they now took direction from Komer's officials. The instruments of American power were all following the same conductor at last.[16]

Komer convinced Westmoreland to form a new intelligence program under CORDS, separate from existing military intelligence organizations, to focus on the "Viet Cong Infrastructure." That term referred to the political cadres and other hidden subversives who wielded political control over villages and facilitated the movement, sheltering and feeding Communist guerrillas and soldiers. In Komer's view, the U.S. military's intelligence programs were inordinately focused on armed combatants and were incapable of identifying and locating the members of this shadow government.

The first title assigned to this intelligence program was the anodyne Intelligence Coordination and Exploitation. Soon, though, it would receive the name under which it was to acquire fame and notoriety, the Phoenix Program. Komer, who had served in the CIA for thirteen years, gave the CIA a leading role in the program because of the agency's familiarity with the subject matter and its sponsorship of several key intelligence organizations. The head of the new program, CIA officer Evan J. Parker Jr., established intelligence coordination centers at district and provincial headquarters, to which the relevant agencies sent representatives. Komer enjoined Parker to pursue a "rifle shot" approach, eliminating individual enemy leaders with surgical military strikes, instead of the "shotgun" approach employed by regular forces, whereby troops surrounded a hamlet and searched it for suspicious individuals.[17]

Komer's programs reorganized only the American side of pacification, not the South Vietnamese side, which was by far the greater problem. Komer recognized, as did most other American officials, that the effectiveness of pacification depended primarily on the quality of South Vietnamese leaders, not on the quality of their American advisers. He also believed, more controversially, that the Americans ought to exert greater influence to improve South Vietnamese quality. Komer urged Westmoreland to merge all the South Vietnamese armed forces into the American military command so that Americans could appoint South Vietnamese officers based on merit, not political or personal considerations as was often the case now. Westmoreland rejected this proposal, as he had done when the PROVN study had proposed the same arrangement in 1966.[18]

Following the creation of CORDS and Phoenix, leadership deficiencies continued to plague all the South Vietnamese organizations involved in pacification except the Provincial Reconnaissance Units, an elite, CIA-supported force of a few thousand men.[19] One American official noted in the fall that the leaders of Revolutionary Development Cadre teams "often give the impression of the blind leading the blind."[20] Attrition of the cadres climbed to 36 percent in mid-1967, and the average size of hamlet teams fell to thirty cadres, barely half of the fifty-nine on the books.[21] Other South Vietnamese security forces, beset by their own leadership woes, often failed to protect the cadre teams from the predations of Communist guerrillas and soldiers.[22]

While Westmoreland and Komer were pressing their programs forward in the South, Admiral Sharp was bombing targets near Hanoi and Haiphong that had hitherto been spared. In reaction to the unprecedented destructiveness of Rolling Thunder 55, the North Vietnamese air defense command sent its MiGs to defend the skies in numbers never before seen. When the Americans came for the Hoa Lac and Kep air bases, MiGs shot down three American aircraft, but were unable to prevent American bombs from obliterating the runways and facilities. Fearing that the same fate would befall their remaining airfields, the North Vietnamese relocated most of their remaining MiGs to Chinese bases. Thereafter, North Vietnamese aircraft flew missions from China into their own country, and at heavy cost.

During the first month of Rolling Thunder 55, American aircraft destroyed thirty MiGs in air-to-air combat, just twelve fewer than in the preceding twenty-two months combined. Only eleven American aircraft were lost in 1,600 sorties, a marked improvement over preceding iterations of Rolling Thunder.[23] Contributing to the low loss rate was the fielding of two new devices mounted aboard American aircraft: the QRC 160-1, which jammed North Vietnamese radar, and the QRC 248, which enabled American aircraft to decipher the communications of MiG transponders.[24]

The intensified air campaign devastated North Vietnam's power plants and other electric infrastructure. It wiped out an estimated 165,000 kilowatts of power-generating capacity, amounting to 87 percent of total national capacity. This loss of power halted what little industrial activity remained in North Vietnam and slowed the unloading and movement of cargo at the port of Haiphong. According to CIA estimates, the North Vietnamese would need between three months and one year to repair the damaged facilities and return them to operation.[25]

Encouraged by these achievements, the Joint Chiefs called for further loosening of Rolling Thunder's shackles.[26] McNamara, however, downplayed the impact of the latest strikes and advocated contraction rather than expansion of the bombing. Rolling Thunder, he advised President Johnson, should be discontinued altogether in the northern sectors of North Vietnam because aircraft loss rates were six times higher there than in southern North Vietnam and intelligence reports indicated that the bombing in these sectors had not diminished Hanoi's ability to prosecute the war in the South. "We cannot by bombing reach the critical level of pain in North Vietnam," stated a memorandum cowritten by McNamara, Vance, and McNaughton. "Below that level, pain only increases the will to fight."[27]

Those last words particularly nettled the Joint Chiefs, to whom it appeared but the latest act of hubris by civilian eggheads who thought they knew more than battle-tested military officers.[28] In a written retort, the Chiefs asserted, "Anyone who says that 'pain only increases the will to fight' can only speak from ignorance of the battlefield."[29] Aircraft loss rates were higher in the northern bombing zones, argued the generals, because the North Vietnamese had concentrated antiaircraft weaponry there, which must have reflected a view that North Vietnam had more valuable assets to protect in those areas than in the southern sectors. If the United States chose to curtail the bombing, it would persuade the North Vietnamese that American will was wavering and hence would harden their negotiating stance.[30]

The CIA weighed in on the side of the Joint Chiefs. After speaking with the agency's top Vietnam specialists, CIA Director Helms reported to President Johnson that in the view of these experts, halting the bombing or concentrating it in the southern sections of North Vietnam "would be regarded by Hanoi as a victory and would intensify Hanoi's determination to persist in the struggle. It would harden Hanoi's position and would not make Hanoi more amenable to negotiation or settlement."[31]

The arguments of the military and the CIA did not alter McNamara's views. On May 22, he convinced Johnson to withdraw all authorizations to strike targets within ten nautical miles of Hanoi.[32] Johnson, however, paid some heed to the conclusions of the generals and intelligence professionals, for he rejected McNamara's recommendation to stop the bombing of other targets in northern North Vietnam.

The Pentagon's civilian and military leaders were, at the same time, locking horns over the question of the troop ceiling. On May 19, McNamara sent President Johnson a lengthy memorandum recommending that he cap the U.S. troop level at five hundred thousand and avoid calling up the reserves. The secretary of defense stated that the military's plan for a much larger troop increase and reserve call-up would increase opposition to the war and "stimulate irresistible pressures in the United States for further escalation against North Vietnam, and for ground actions against 'sanctuaries' in Cambodia and Laos." Such escalation, he warned, would be "likely to get us in even deeper in Southeast Asia and into a serious confrontation, if not war, with China and Russia." McNamara acknowledged that Hanoi was unlikely to consider changes to its negotiating posture until it saw the outcome of the U.S. presidential election in 1968, but he maintained that his strategy would "lay the groundwork by periodic peace probes."[33]

When this memorandum found its way onto the desks of the Joint Chiefs, it brought relations between the generals and the secretary of defense to new lows. Rumors swirled that the Joint Chiefs were planning to resign in unison.[34] The generals did not resign, but they did issue a scathing rejoinder to McNamara's claim that maintaining public support required rejecting the troop increase and reserve call up. "The Joint Chiefs of Staff firmly believe that the American people, when well informed about the issues at stake, expect their Government to uphold its commitments," the Chiefs wrote. "History illustrates that they will, in turn, support their Government in its necessary actions." McNamara's option might arouse less criticism from the American citizenry in the short term, they noted, but in the long term it would create greater problems because the people would become disenchanted with the slow rate of progress.[35]

National Security Adviser Walt Rostow endorsed the recommendations of the Joint Chiefs for additional troops and the call up of reserves, telling the president that "nothing you could do would more seriously impress Hanoi that the jig was up." If the president gave Westmoreland another two hundred thousand men, stated Rostow, "We may never have to use the 200,000 men—just as we never had to conduct the great offensive of 1919 or actually invade Japan at the end of 1945."[36]

Johnson considered the competing views in silence. He would wait until summer before making up his mind on the troop ceiling and the reserves.

Across the Potomac River from the Pentagon, at Foggy Bottom, State Department leaders were at this time preoccupied with a different part of the Vietnam problem, the revitalization of the South Vietnamese government. "If we can get a reasonably solid GVN political structure and GVN performance at all levels," William Bundy wrote at the end of May, "favorable trends could become really marked over the next 18 months, the war will be won for practical purposes at some point, and the resulting peace will be secured." Without these results, "no amount of U.S. effort will achieve our basic objective in South Vietnam." In the view of Bundy and other State Department leaders, the rejuvenation of the South Vietnamese hinged upon their upcoming presidential election, scheduled for early September.[37]

Protecting American equities in the South Vietnamese elections would be the job of the man who had just replaced Henry Cabot Lodge as U.S. ambassador, Ellsworth Bunker. Like Lodge, Bunker was a tall, gray-haired patrician from the northeastern Protestant elite. He could trace his ancestry back through generations of Nantucket seafarers to George Bunker, who had landed in Boston in 1634. A member of the Yale class of 1916, he had rowed on the crew team with two other future titans of American diplomacy, Dean Acheson and Averell Harriman. After graduating from Yale, Bunker worked for his father's business, the National Sugar Refining Company, where he spent the spring and summer of his career.

At the beginning of 1951, Bunker's thoughts had been turning to a genteel retirement when Acheson, by then the secretary of state, asked him to serve as Harry Truman's ambassador to Argentina. Bunker agreed to leave his company and take the ambassadorship, and he served the Truman administration so well that the Eisenhower administration decided to keep him around. Under Eisenhower and then under Kennedy and Johnson, Bunker held a succession of ambassadorships, during which he evidenced an uncanny ability to influence foreigners and resolve disputes. Bunker facilitated an end to the longstanding feud between the Netherlands and Indonesia over West New Guinea and helped competing factions in the Dominican Republic form a new government after the assassination of

Rafael Trujillo. His displays of exceptional diplomatic talent had made him the most compelling candidate to fill the most important ambassadorship in the world.

Although Bunker was seventy-three years of age when Lyndon Johnson appointed him ambassador to South Vietnam, he possessed the energy and physical presence of a man several decades younger. Standing six foot two, he glided about with an athletic and regal bearing. One journalist observed that at the time of his departure for Vietnam, Bunker had "the air of having bathed every day of his life in cold spring water."[38]

Serious and reserved in personality, Bunker preferred work over the entertainment of foreign dignitaries and visiting American officials. In Saigon, he worked seven days a week, breaking only now and then to read books—his favorite author was Robert Conrad—or watch films of the Yale football team. Despite his affinity for solitude, however, Bunker exuded personal warmth and charm. His temperament immediately drew plaudits from embassy staff and foreign diplomats, who found him a refreshing contrast to his haughty predecessor.

"There was an air of impenetrability about him, a shield of dignity that marked him instantly as an aristocrat," remarked one South Vietnamese official, recalling his first impression of Bunker. "Before long, the cool demeanor had earned him the nickname Old Man Refrigerator among the Vietnamese." Over time, however, the South Vietnamese realized that they "had in Bunker a dedicated friend whose aloof manner belied his warm heart."[39]

Shortly before Lodge's departure, the outgoing ambassador had adjudged Thieu the best available candidate for the presidency. In his current capacity as chief of state, Lodge had stated, Thieu "has been prominent, yet dignified, to which the Vietnamese attach importance, while avoiding public connection with controversial issues."[40] This assessment reflected an understanding of Vietnamese politics and culture that had been tragically lacking four years earlier when Lodge had instigated the cataclysmic coup against Ngo Dinh Diem.

Bunker possessed a more insightful and open mind than Lodge, but he too arrived in the country without fully appreciating Vietnam's peculiar cultural characteristics, such as the extraordinary importance attached to dignity and prestige. At Bunker's first glance, Thieu appeared less promising than Ky as a presidential candidate because Thieu did not display the mien or behaviors of a Western politician. One of Bunker's earliest cables from Saigon stated that Thieu was likely to stay out of the presidential race because he "is not the kind of man who enjoys the rough public give-and-take of a campaign. Throughout his tenure as chief of state, he has remained in the background, leaving the limelight to Ky."[41]

Bunker's opinion of Ky soon began to sour, however, as a result of allegations that Ky's henchmen were undermining Thieu through bribery, slander, intimidation, and censorship. The lead organizer of the dirty tricks was reported to be General Nguyen Ngoc Loan, the head of the National Police and Military Security Service. On May 30, Bunker admonished Ky to avoid "acts of repression and indiscriminate use of press censorship" because it was "essential that the elections be carried out fairly and honestly." Bunker also emphasized the need to maintain unity within the armed forces in the event that both he and Thieu ran for the presidency. Ky replied, "Don't worry. I know how to handle the situation. It is like a western movie, it will come out all right in the end." In Bunker's reporting of the conversation, he commented that "I hope he is right and that the happy ending of the western movie which he envisages will not be preceded by the gun play which is a normal part of every western."[42]

Bunker's warning did not bring a halt to the skullduggery. Ky's minions reportedly tried to coerce Thieu into withdrawing from the race by making threats against his life. In a message to Rusk sent via CIA channels, Bunker lamented "the rather blatant election-rigging tactics of General Loan," which were "so widely known that, as long as he remains in his present position, the results of the September election will remain in doubt regardless of how well in the end it may be conducted."[43]

Bunker's solution at this point was to reform Ky, which he rationalized by arguing that Ky was "virtually certain to win, whether by proper or improper means," and was "on balance the best available candidate, though not exactly a prize package." The United States, Bunker proposed to the White House, should tell Ky quietly that it would back him in the presidential race and give funding to his campaign provided that he got rid of General Loan. Bunker asked the State Department to explore the possibility of displacing Loan by sending him to military training in the United States. In addition, Bunker recommended consideration of "measures which we can take to exert behind-the-scenes pressure on Thieu to withdraw from the Presidential race."

This proposal ran aground as soon as it reached Washington. White House officials objected that if the United States sided with Ky, word would be certain to get out, which would undermine the legitimacy of the election and alienate Thieu, who was unlikely to withdraw even under pressure. An attempt to oust Loan could incite him to stage a coup d'état, and if it did not so incite him, Ky had other thugs besides Loan who could continue to manipulate the electoral process. On June 20, the State Department notified Bunker that the United States would urge Ky to bring Loan under control but would not side with Ky or any other candidate.[44]

Ten days later, without any apparent prodding from the United States, a group of South Vietnam's top generals tried to convince Thieu to drop out of the presidential race. In a smoke-filled room, with Thieu and Ky in attendance, the generals promised Thieu the jobs of both defense minister and chairman of the Joint General Staff in return for his cooperation. Thieu refused to bow out, saying that if necessary he would resign from the military and run for president as a civilian. Several generals responded that having two generals in the presidential race would wreck the unity of the armed forces. The majority then demanded that Thieu and Ky run on the same ticket and vowed that a refusal to accept this solution would cause all the generals to resign. That threat extracted promises from Thieu and Ky to run together.

Then came the knotty question of who would run on the top of the ticket. Neither Thieu nor Ky volunteered to take the number two position. The generals therefore decided to follow military protocol and rely upon rank. Thieu held three stars to Ky's two, and therefore Thieu would run as president and Ky as vice president. To placate Ky, the generals promised that he would get to select cabinet members and control the armed forces.[45]

After the meeting, Ky and some of his supporters contended that the arrangement put all the real power in Ky's hands, leaving Thieu a mere figurehead. But others who had been present in the smoke-filled room did not share that impression. In their version of events, the meeting had not resulted in a clear delineation of the authorities of the president and vice president. Many within Ky's own camp were dissatisfied with the outcome because it appeared to give Thieu the position with the most prestige and power.[46] Whether Ky or Thieu would ultimately end up as the nation's actual leader remained unsettled.

As the election approached and Bunker learned more about South Vietnam, he warmed to Thieu. In a cable to Washington, dated August 23, the new ambassador reported, "I think Thieu has made a good impression in this campaign. He has handled himself with dignity, restraint and modesty and has not reacted to criticisms by other candidates. During tours of the countryside and in contacts with the press he has quite consistently made constructive remarks reflecting a sober and mature approach toward the evolution of the constitutional process."[47]

With Bunker keeping track of politics in Saigon, Westmoreland was focusing on I Corps, where he expected the North Vietnamese to mount their largest offensive of the summer. American intelligence indicated that the bulk of the North Vietnamese Army was in or near I Corps, with three divisions in the DMZ, two in the northernmost provinces of South Vietnam, and two in southern I Corps. Seeking to maintain the initiative, Westmoreland began a major offensive of his own before the North Vietnamese could begin theirs.[48]

The North Vietnamese forces in I Corps kept their distance from the initial American operations, indicating a lower appetite for battle than Westmoreland had expected. Their first major riposte came not from the infantry but from artillery in the DMZ. In late June, North Vietnamese guns renewed the bombardment of Con Thien, ending the respite that the Marines had bought by crossing the DMZ in Operation Hickory. To prevent the Americans from zeroing in on the location of their artillery, the North Vietnamese periodically moved their weaponry around the DMZ.

This time, Westmoreland was unable to obtain White House permission to send troops into the DMZ to end the North Vietnamese troublemaking. Marine officers and NCOs at Con Thien went around each morning to talk cheer into eighteen- and nineteen-year-old grunts who were distraught at their inability to hit the enemy back. Westmoreland himself flew into the base by helicopter to give pep talks. While he was touring the base, one Marine told him, "General, I lost my best buddy to incoming yesterday—why can't we go into the DMZ after those bastards?" Westmoreland replied, "Son, I wish we could, but the politics of the situation are such that we can't violate the DMZ."[49]

As Marine casualties mounted, some Marine officers suggested withdrawing Con Thien's garrison to positions more distant from the DMZ, beyond the range of North Vietnamese howitzers. Westmoreland ruled out that option. The North Vietnamese, he believed, would respond to abandonment of the outpost by moving artillery to Con Thien and points farther south, allowing them to bombard bases that were closer to the heavily populated areas.[50]

By early July, neither Westmoreland nor the Marines could bear the status quo any longer. If they could not enter the DMZ, they could at least probe areas near the DMZ for enemy forces. By operating in the field and keeping on the move, the Marines would be more difficult for the North Vietnamese artillery to target. On July 2, in what was termed Operation Buffalo, Marines marched out of Con Thien's gate and headed north.

On the first day of the operation, an American Marine company walked into a large ambush. Two full North Vietnamese battalions had set it up on an eight-foot-wide cart path flanked on both sides by hedgerows. To trick the American company into thinking it enjoyed numerical superiority, only a few North Vietnamese soldiers opened fire at the outset. When the Marines attempted to outflank the North Vietnamese, they ran into large concentrations of enemy soldiers, who held them in place while other North Vietnamese infantry assailed the Marine flanks. North Vietnamese flamethrowers torched the hedgerows, driving Marines to run for open spaces, where they became easy targets for rifles and machine guns. The North Vietnamese fired medium artillery and 122mm rockets in support of their infantry, the first time they had done so in the war.

North Vietnamese fire killed the American company commander, Captain Sterling K. Coates, putting the company in the hands of the forward air controller, Captain Warren Keneipp. A fighter pilot by trade, Keneipp had joined the Marine company only two weeks before and was scheduled to stay with the unit for just a few more days before reassignment to NASA's astronaut program. Keneipp was unable to establish radio contact with two of the platoons. In the last broadcast he made to the command post at Con Thien before his death, Keneipp said, "I don't think I'll be talking to you again. We are being overrun."[51]

Small, scattered Marine fire teams continued to hold out. Sister companies from the 1st Battalion, 9th Marines and several tanks came to the assistance of the battered company, sparing it from complete annihilation. When the relief forces began evacuating the casualties, North Vietnamese artillery and mortars followed their paths, striking corpsmen, litter bearers, and the previously wounded. The 3rd Battalion 9th Marines arrived late in the afternoon and attacked the North Vietnamese flank at twilight, which prompted the North Vietnamese to withdraw.

The total losses sustained by the 1st Battalion, 9th Marines for the day were 84 killed, 190 wounded, and 9 missing. American casualty recovery teams discovered that a substantial number of the Marines had been killed at very close range. Some had been unable to defend themselves because they had been wounded, while others had been cut down because their M-16 rifles—a weapon that the Marine Corps only recently had begun fielding—had jammed. The first M-16s suffered from several design flaws, which would be corrected a few months later by adding a chrome-plated chamber and reducing the rate of fire.[52] The Americans also saw that the North Vietnamese had cut the genitals off the bodies of several American corpses and stuffed them in the men's mouths.

One of the Marines to witness the mutilated bodies was Corporal David J. Gomez. "I have never seen so many people ready to kick somebody's ass," he remembered. "We wanted to fight. We wanted to even the score. We wanted to prove to the NVA that you just can't do this and fucking walk away. I cannot believe that human beings would do that to other human beings, and I can't believe—though I did it—how much of an animal you can become once you've seen something like that, once you've seen what they've done to your brothers. That anger becomes the determination to become the best combat Marine there was, and when you get the chance you do the same fucking thing to them that they did to you."[53]

Operation Buffalo continued despite its inauspicious start and despite the discontent the initial calamity had generated among Marines who suspected that it could have been avoided had Washington permitted them to return fire into the DMZ. During the ensuing days, seven American battalions jousted sporadically with North Vietnamese forces near the DMZ, both sides making extensive use of artillery. American aircraft spotted several large North Vietnamese troop concentrations in the open, which were subjected to the cudgels of American artillery and air power. On two occasions, a Marine reconnaissance team called artillery onto unsuspecting North Vietnamese units, resulting in 152 deaths. Total reported North Vietnamese losses in Operation Buffalo were 1,290 killed, while Marine losses came to 159 killed and 345 wounded. Half the Marine casualties were attributed to North Vietnamese artillery.[54]

During July, American bulldozers began clearing a six-hundred-meter-wide strip near the DMZ for the eastern portion of McNamara's barrier. By the end of the month, the strip extended from the coast thirteen kilometers inland. The official plan called for completing the first phase, consisting of four strongpoints and three battalion base areas, no later than November 1. The second phase, which would establish strongpoints west of Con Thien to block infiltration through the mountains of western Quang Tri, would be completed after the monsoon season, by July 1968.[55]

In III Corps, Westmoreland had expected that the onset of the southwest monsoon would cause combat to subside during the summer. The North Vietnamese, however, chose to concentrate much of their summertime combat activity in III Corps, with the 7th and 9th divisions once more attempting to inflict heavy casualties on the U.S. 1st Infantry Division north of Saigon. Although the monsoon weather complicated North Vietnamese logistics, the interminable downpours and low cloud ceiling also interfered with American air operations. The North Vietnamese employed the usual tactic of attacking small American detachments at close range to obtain numerical superiority and prevent the use of American artillery and air strikes. In nearly every case, their efforts ended with North Vietnamese losses that far outstripped American losses.[56]

The North Vietnamese also executed several large attacks on South Vietnamese outposts north of Saigon. On July 11, the 141st Regiment of the 7th Division assaulted Tan Hung, ten kilometers outside the provincial capital of An Loc. Measuring 200 by 175 meters, the camp was described by one American as "an oversized football field cut out of the middle of a large rubber plantation." Crammed inside the perimeter of Tan Hung was a battalion of the 9th South Vietnamese Army Regiment.

That night, the soldiers of the 141st NVA Regiment headed to assembly positions near Tan Hung. A blanket of clouds dumped rain on them and blotted out the moon, complicating the navigation of unfamiliar jungle trails. Moreover, because the regiment was rife with malaria, all but the most severely infected troops had to take part in the operation, and thus malaria impaired the night vision of many of those present. Several battalions lost contact with the regimental headquarters and failed to reach their attack positions on time. The regimental commander had to push the start time back thrice as he waited for his forces to arrive.

While the North Vietnamese assault units were accumulating at the assembly positions, a South Vietnamese patrol sighted one of them. The patrol notified the camp commander, who put out an alert to all his subordinates. Every man in the South Vietnamese battalion would be awake by the time the shooting started.

At 0215, the North Vietnamese attack order came at last. Mortar rounds sailed into the camp, and North Vietnamese infantry rushed its northern and eastern sides. The North Vietnamese penetrated the perimeter at several points, but the South Vietnamese sent reinforcements to drive them out, and they succeeded in killing every North Vietnamese soldier who made it inside. According to a report filed by an American adviser, the South Vietnamese company commanders "were outstanding and displayed great initiative. Each of the leaders reacted rapidly to each penetration, executing counterattacks when needed without waiting for guidance."

The North Vietnamese retreated before dawn. In the morning, the South Vietnamese victors found seventy-two North Vietnamese bodies inside their perimeter and seventy-two more outside. They also took ten North Vietnamese soldiers alive. Of the defenders, nineteen were dead, forty-seven wounded, and five missing.[57]

The next month, another North Vietnamese regiment attacked the Tong Le Chon CIDG camp in War Zone C, an outpost that the U.S. Army Special Forces had established after Operation Junction City to prevent the enemy's return. Malaria-induced vision problems again slowed the attacking regiment's advance.

"The march formations frequently became separated and split, and the soldiers had to take each other's hands to stay in contact," a North Vietnamese history recounted. The regiment needed nearly the entire night to reach its attack positions.

Following a preparatory artillery barrage, North Vietnamese engineers used DH-10 directional mines and Bangalore torpedoes to blow through the camp's perimeter wire and fences. Hundreds of North Vietnamese soldiers scampered through the gaps. American gunships arrived in time to cut down the first wave of attackers, but the second wave broke into a section of the camp. Twenty of the CIDG defenders threw up their hands in surrender, only to be shot dead. As the rest of the garrison attempted to stave off the North Vietnamese, the camp's ammunition bunker blew up, felling many men on both sides. Gunfire slackened as the stunned survivors attempted to locate and treat the wounded. The North Vietnamese attacked twice more that night but were frustrated each time by machine gun fire and well-placed air strikes. At daybreak, the camp's garrison counterattacked the North Vietnamese, who had already begun to withdraw. The North Vietnamese left behind 152 bodies and 60 weapons. The garrison suffered 26 killed and 87 wounded.[58]

In the gloomy light of the spring and early summer defeats, the top North Vietnamese military leaders held another conclave in Hanoi to review their strategy. The Combat Operations Department of the General Staff offered an analysis of the military situation that was even more pessimistic than the one it had delivered in April. "With the exception of the U.S. battalion our troops annihilated in the Ia Drang Valley in November 1965," the department reported, "our troops have not been able to completely annihilate another such American unit, because the American air and artillery firepower has been too strong, because they have been so mobile, and because American campaign-level commanders usually have not accompanied their units on the ground in battle."[59]

Some of the North Vietnamese leaders recommended that the army eschew all large assaults and concentrate exclusively on guerrilla warfare. General Nguyen Chi Thanh countered that sole reliance on guerrilla warfare would play into the hands of the Americans, who were intent on scattering the Communist main force units and limiting them to guerrilla operations. It would, he said, permit the United States to "end the war by launching major attacks, so as to enter a period of pacification, stamp out the guerrilla war, and consolidate the rear base."[60]

Le Duan concurred with Nguyen Chi Thanh. He threw his weight behind the sustained offensive in the South and the decisive urban offensive in January 1968 that the party leadership had approved in April. Communist forces would prevail, he asserted, by attacking "the enemy in his lair, in the cities and province capitals," which were "the nerve centers of the enemy's forces."

Within South Vietnam's cities, Le Duan said, the party now had a prime opportunity to mobilize labor unions, intellectuals, high school and college students, and religious groups. The seizure of power in Hanoi in August 1945 had demonstrated how a decisive victory could be obtained rapidly through a popular uprising. "When discussing the possibility of revolution breaking out," Le Duan explained, "Lenin said that revolution can break out wherever the network of imperialism is weak, and that when it does break out the revolution on its own will surge forward with tremendous force, a force sufficient to combat and to defeat the violence of the enemy's army."[61]

Giap objected that the time for urban uprisings had not yet come. Not until the American and South Vietnamese armed forces had been crippled, he argued, would the urban masses join with the revolution in toppling the government. He failed to persuade the other senior leaders.

At the conclusion, the Central Military Party Committee reaffirmed the current strategic plans. Field commanders were informed that intensive military operations, in battalion strength, would continue for the remainder of 1967. To map out the details of the coming urban offensive, the committee organized a series of meetings. Giap was excluded from the meetings, presumably because of his pessimism.[62]

General Thanh was in Hanoi in early July preparing for upcoming operations when he died suddenly from a heart attack. According to one North Vietnamese version of the story, he consumed too much alcohol and was stricken by the heart convulsion in his bathtub, where he perished.[63] Another version had it that he was rushed to a hospital for emergency treatment and expired on the operating table.[64] Whatever the case, North Vietnam had lost an able combat commander, although not a very able strategist. Responsibility for carrying out the decisive offensive would thence be entrusted to Pham Hung, the deputy prime minister of North Vietnam, who went to the South to assume the two positions held previously by Nguyen Chi Thanh: Communist Party secretary and political commissar of the South Vietnamese People's Liberation Army.

Hanoi's review of its strategy coincided with a visit by Secretary of Defense McNamara to South Vietnam for the purpose of discussing America's strategy with Westmoreland. The principal items on McNamara's agenda were Westmoreland's request for more troops and the future of Rolling Thunder. According to General Douglas Kinnard, whom Westmoreland charged with selling McNamara on the troop augmentation, Westmoreland believed that the visit constituted his last chance to obtain additional forces. As a consequence, Kinnard recounted, "enormous energy was used in making the briefings for McNamara as persuasive as possible."[65]

Westmoreland and his staff explained to McNamara in exacting detail why more troops were needed, emphasizing heightened North Vietnamese infiltration and the weak performance of South Vietnamese forces in pacification. Admiral Sharp and his staff made the cases for unfettering Rolling Thunder and mining Haiphong. Despite the high quality of the presentations, McNamara gave every appearance of having already made up his mind against the military's recommendations.[66]

"McNamara went out of his way to show his arrogant disinterest in the presentations," recollected one military officer who witnessed the meetings. "During most of the briefings he read or worked on papers spread out before him, and he asked almost no questions of the briefers."[67] After Admiral Sharp delivered one briefing, McNamara demonstrated his disdain by ignoring Sharp completely and talking only to Westmoreland.[68]

When it came time for McNamara to share his own thinking, he informed Westmoreland that no more than forty-five thousand additional troops were needed. That number had been provided by one of his premier number crunchers, Alain Enthoven. A thirty-six-year-old economist with a PhD from the Massachusetts Institute of Technology, Enthoven was a Whiz Kid par excellence, convinced that quantitative analysis was central to all strategic thinking and hence that his ability to marshal statistics demonstrated the superiority of his strategic insights to those of the commanders in the field.

According to Enthoven's calculations, forty-five thousand was the most troops that could be provided without calling up the reserves.[69] In addition, he argued, a larger increase was unnecessary because a comparison of friendly troop strengths and enemy casualties at various junctures revealed that "the size of the force we deploy has little effect on the rate of attrition of enemy forces." The North Vietnamese had shown the ability to evade U.S. forces when they so desired, and therefore it was up to Hanoi to decide how many casualties North Vietnam would incur.[70] Enthoven also maintained that sending more U.S. forces would not improve pacification, citing as evidence a decline in South Vietnamese civilians living in secure areas of I Corps during 1966 despite a simultaneous increase in the U.S. Marine presence. Because adding U.S. forces would help with neither attrition nor pacification, it would merely reduce the American public's patience with the war and discourage the South Vietnamese from taking responsibility for their own problems.[71]

For all his emphasis on quantitative reasoning, Enthoven's own use of statistics was misleading at best. There was, in fact, a strong correlation between the size of American forces and the attrition of enemy forces. Between the first half of 1966 and the first half of 1967, the longest period of comparison available, American forces had increased in number by 83 percent, and enemy casualties had increased by 85 percent.[72]

Enthoven's analysis also suffered from unfamiliarity with local context and complexity. The enemy could and did limit casualties by hiding in Laos and Cambodia or remote areas of South Vietnam, but if the enemy wished to influence events in South Vietnam, it had to be near the country's populous regions. The more allied troops it faced in these regions, the more likely it was to bump into a hostile patrol and thus to fight on terms not of its choosing. This point was verified by a subsequent CIA analysis of the period 1965 to 1967, which concluded that the larger the number of allied battalions, the higher the effectiveness of each battalion in inflicting casualties on the enemy.[73]

Similar defects were to be found when it came to the impact of U.S. troop strength on pacification. As General DePuy had highlighted in his April assessment, the increase in the American presence near the villages since the middle of 1965 had greatly diminished enemy control over the villages, while the withdrawal of American forces from populous areas had led to pacification setbacks. To link U.S. troop levels to pacification woes in 1966 in I Corps was to ignore the fact that many of those troops had been diverted from the villages to the hinterlands because of Hanoi's flooding of I Corps with conventional units.

During the meetings with McNamara, Westmoreland also advocated raids by South Vietnamese units, in battalion or brigade strength, against enemy base areas in Laos. This recommendation enjoyed the endorsement of Ambassador Bunker. Already Bunker had discerned that ground operations in Laos were the only practicable means of preventing the North Vietnamese from endlessly funneling replacements into the South to offset heavy casualties.[74]

For McNamara and his Whiz Kids, Bunker was in many ways a more formidable foil than Westmoreland. Whereas the Pentagon's defense intellectuals, with their lofty academic pedigrees and social scientific methods, were known to deride Westmoreland and Sharp as uncouth yokels of mediocre intellect, Bunker was a prototypical product of the East Coast Ivy League establishment. His age, wealth, and Northeastern Protestant lineage put him on a social plane at which a fifty-one-year-old Irish Catholic of middle-class origins like McNamara was obliged to peer upward. Whether out of deference to Bunker or some other motive, McNamara said that he would consent to battalion-size South Vietnamese Army operations inside Laos.[75]

The sincerity of that promise soon came under suspicion, because it was soon to be broken. McNamara never revealed whether he had intended to break the promise all along, or had changed his mind in response to subsequent opposition from

Ambassador Sullivan or others. As had become customary, Sullivan piped up in opposition at the first whiff of an intention to send South Vietnamese forces into Laos. His newest list of objections to this measure included a prediction that the South Vietnamese forces would be decimated in Laos, and a prediction that the North Vietnamese would take control of the whole Mekong Valley.[76]

Sullivan was proposing that infiltration through Laos be stopped with two secret programs that had shown promise in their experimental stages: Popeye and Commando Lava. Under the Popeye program, American aircraft sprayed chemicals into clouds to induce heavy rainfall. The aircraft assigned to Commando Lava dropped chemicals onto enemy lines of transit, which chelated under rain to such a degree that the soil turned to a thin mud, so soupy that it could not support a vehicle. According to Sullivan, these programs, in conjunction with McNamara's barrier and bombing, could "make enemy movement among the cordillera of the Annamite chain almost prohibitive." Indulging in one of his most memorable rhetorical flourishes, Sullivan quipped, "In short, chelation may prove better than escalation. Make mud, not war!"[77]

Suggestive of Sullivan's influence in convincing McNamara to shelve the plans for South Vietnamese operations into Laos was his role, a few weeks after McNamara's trip, in killing a proposal from Admiral Sharp's headquarters to put American ground troops into Laos. Inserting U.S. forces into Laos, Sullivan protested in a cable to the State Department, would alienate the Soviets, which would be ruinous because Soviet diplomatic pressure on Hanoi was the only means of bringing the war to an acceptable end.[78] In another message, Sullivan wrote that the officer who issued the proposal "had better bring out the 200,000 U.S. troops with him to 'pacify' the area he wants to occupy in

Laos and to defend it against North Vietnamese forces operating against it on short DMZ-type logistics lines." Sullivan added, "I am disappointed that messages of this type are permitted to move in official channels and receive wide dissemination. It is the sort of thing which is giving marijuana a good name."[79]

McNamara returned from Saigon to Washington on July 12, having accomplished little except demonstrating, rather unconvincingly, that he wanted to consider the views of the leaders in the field before settling on his recommendations to the president. No changes were made to the bombing program. American troops strength would be increased by the amount McNamara had conceived prior to the trip, 45,000, bringing the total number to 525,000.

With the federal budget deficit already soaring, President Johnson decided to seek additional tax revenue to pay for the additional troops. On August 3, he called upon Congress to impose a 10 percent tax surcharge. Conservatives opposed the tax hike on the grounds that additional taxation would remove pressure on Johnson to rein in domestic spending. Liberals were opposed because they thought it would insulate Johnson from pressure to reduce American commitments in Vietnam.[80]

The tax debate also fueled general dissatisfaction with Johnson's approach to the war. Senators and representatives from both parties took the opportunity to question publicly the validity of the Tonkin Gulf Resolution and the administration's honesty in presenting the resolution to Congress. House Minority Leader Gerald Ford of Michigan declared that the United States did not require more taxes or more troops, but instead needed to remove the restrictions on Rolling Thunder and undertake a naval blockade of Haiphong.[81]

During the summer, Democratic Senator J. William Fulbright became the first prominent member of Congress to turn completely against the war. The defection was particularly humiliating for Johnson because Fulbright had been instrumental in shepherding the Tonkin Gulf Resolution through Congress.[82] At a meeting on July 25, Fulbright caused further embarrassment by thumbing his nose at the president in front of most of the congressional leadership.

"Mr. President, what you really need to do is to stop the war," Fulbright inveighed. "The Vietnam war is a hopeless venture. Nobody likes it."

Johnson erupted in fury. "Bill, everybody doesn't have a blind spot like you do," he fired back. "You say don't bomb North Vietnam on just about everything. I don't have the simple solution you have. We haven't delivered Ho yet. Everything which has been proposed to Ho has been rejected. As far as stopping the bombing in North Vietnam, I am not going to tell our men in the field to put their right hands behind their backs and fight only with their left. General Westmoreland told me when he was here that the bombing is our offensive weapon. And it will be just like tying his right hand behind him if we were to stop it." Referring to the Tonkin Gulf Resolution, Johnson said, "If you want me to get out of Vietnam, then you have the prerogative of taking the resolution under which we are out there now. You can repeal it tomorrow. You can tell the troops to come home. You can tell General Westmoreland that he doesn't know what he is doing."[83]

The fact that the most strident opposition to the American presence in Vietnam was coming from Johnson's own party stuck in the president's craw. On August 16, Lady Bird Johnson penned in her diary, "Lyndon and I watched Senator John Tower for the Republicans and Senator Joe Clark for the Democrats on television—the *Today* show—talking about Vietnam. What a twist of fate it is to see the Administration—indeed us—being explained, backed—yes, even defended—by John Tower, while that red-hot Democrat Joe Clark slashes at the administration's policy with rancor and emotion."[84]

The split between liberal elites and the working-class Americans of whom they were the ostensible champions was also becoming more pronounced. The factory workers, truck drivers, farm hands, stevedores, and carpenters who had flooded the American armed forces in World War II were enormously proud of their military service and of the large number of their sons who were now serving in Vietnam. These families, like many other American families with sons in Vietnam, tended to view liberal elite opposition to the war as unpatriotic and harmful to the Americans fighting the war. Particularly offensive to them were the burning of draft cards and fluttering of Viet Cong flags by well-to-do young men who had found ways to avoid military service.

Working-class Americans composed a large fraction of the participants in a massive parade that took place in New York City on May 13. The "We Support Our Boys in Vietnam" parade, as it was called, received endorsements and large contingents of marchers from veterans' groups, religious organizations, and labor unions populated predominantly by the working class. Among these were the American Legion, the Veterans of Foreign Wars, the Teamsters, the International Longshoremen's Association, the National Maritime Union, the Knights of Columbus, and the Police and Fire departments of New York City.[85]

Although the parade's organizing committee had stated that the event was not an endorsement of any particular policy in Vietnam, some of the organizers acknowledged that it was intended to influence events in America's favor. "We are interested in showing our boys in Vietnam that all Americans aren't kooks," explained Thomas W. Gleason, president of the International

Longshoreman's Association. "More than this, we want to show the Vietcong, the Red Chinese and anybody else who thinks we're soft and gutless that we aren't."[86]

For nine hours, marchers numbering somewhere between 70,000 and 140,000 paraded down thirty-four blocks of New York's Fifth Avenue. The signs they carried evidenced a desire for robust use of American military power against the Vietnamese Communists, or "Reds" as they were termed by many of the inscribers. In a news report on the event, Murray Schumach of the *New York Times* wrote that the "enthusiastic spectators, frequently standing in crowds three deep, applauded and cheered in the sunshine for hours while the legion with their flags and pennants swept by, singing, chanting, shouting."[87]

Another journalist who was on hand, Leroy F. Aarons of the *Washington Post,* noted that many of the marchers had "the rough hands and unfashionable checkered suits of the working man." Whereas protesters at peace rallies had given Aarons a multiplicity of answers when asked what needed to be done with respect to Vietnam, the demonstrators on this day all gave him essentially the same answer. "I would support our boys over there," said a typical respondent. "I wouldn't go around burning flags and setting fire to my draft card. I would bomb Haiphong and get the whole damn thing over with."[88]

A group of eighteen men and women calling themselves the "Flower Brigade" showed up to protest against the war. Led by the radical activist Abbie Hoffman, they belonged to the Flower Power movement, a leading element of the budding counterculture, whose utopian visions promised liberation from the foibles of American political and cultural traditions. Hoffman and his fellow Flower Children informed parade attendees that they supported the troops, just not the war in Vietnam. At least some of those on the receiving end of this information, however, were not of the opinion that opposing the war was compatible with supporting the troops. Marchers grabbed placards from the hands of the Flower Children and ripped them up. Others sprayed paint at them. Eventually, the police decided that it was best to escort Hoffman and his brigade away from the march.[89]

The martial spirits on display during the parade gave encouragement to the hawks of the Johnson administration, but this encouragement was alloyed with worries that the spirits could be dissipated by mounting opposition to the war among liberal journalists, professors, and congressmen. Four days after the "We Support Our Boys in Vietnam" parade, White House political adviser James Rowe made this point to President Johnson. "The common people, in the form of the American Legion, the labor unions, the boiler makers and the bartenders, may parade down Fifth Avenue to 'support the boys' in Vietnam," Rowe observed, but "the 'opinion makers' in the press, on the magazines and in the universities are more and more attacking the Vietnam policy." Rowe warned the president that "eventually these 'opinion makers' may convert the people, particularly if unopposed."[90] This admonition proved no more effective than previous ones in rousing administration officials to rebut the doves.

Nor was the administration dealing effectively with criticisms from the hawks. Those criticisms were about to reach a fever pitch thanks to Senator John Stennis. A conservative Democrat from Mississippi, Stennis exemplified the impatience of conservatives in both parties with the strategy of gradual escalation. To pressure the administration into removing the shackles from Rolling Thunder, the senator scheduled hearings on the bombing campaign, to begin on August 9.

The effects began to be felt before the hearings even began. On August 8, McNamara briefed President Johnson on the latest bombing recommendations received from the Joint Chiefs. The generals wanted to restrike the Hanoi thermal power plant, which had been hit in May but was back to operating at 75 percent of capacity. The Joint Chiefs also advocated hitting the Paul Doumer Bridge in Hanoi, several additional targets in the Hanoi-Haiphong area, and ten targets near the Chinese border. McNamara opposed all these targets except the power plant. Additional bombing near Hanoi and Haiphong, he said, unduly risked causing civilian casualties, poisoning the negotiating environment, and arousing domestic opposition to administration policy. The strikes near China could result in an inadvertent crossing of U.S. aircraft into Chinese air space.

Johnson shared McNamara's aversion to strikes near Hanoi, Haiphong, and the Chinese border, and for the same reasons. But he wanted to bomb more targets, both to achieve military effects and to mute criticism from the hawks. "We have got to do something to win," the president said. "We aren't doing much now." Johnson approved the strike on the power plant.[91] The next morning, just as the Stennis hearings were beginning, the president authorized the bombing of the Doumer Bridge and railroad bridges, railroad yards, and rolling stock close to China.[92]

Johnson's sudden authorization of targets he had refused to strike for the past three years led hawks in Congress and the military to denounce it as a cheap ploy to undercut the points they would make during the hearings. Admiral Sharp, the first witness to be called on August 9, said later, "It was obvious to me that the Secretary of Defense had hoped to spike my guns by granting these new targets right before I was to testify."[93]

For the next three weeks, Stennis and his committee listened to the testimony of ten general officers, including all the Joint Chiefs of Staff.[94] The generals all had the same basic story to tell. Since the inception of Rolling Thunder, they had opposed the gradualism of the bombing campaign, issuing recommendations for intensive strikes that had been swatted down time and again. The low intensity of the bombing in the early stages, the generals explained, had given the enemy time to disperse supplies and build up air defenses. In the past eighteen months, the number of surface-to-air missiles in North Vietnam had more than doubled, and antiaircraft guns had increased by 250 percent.

For all its self-imposed problems, the generals said, Rolling Thunder had constrained the enemy's ability to supply the war in the South, particularly as the bombing had grown in size and scope during the past few months, and thus had saved American lives. The Joint Chiefs explained that they had studied McNamara's idea of restricting the bombing to the southern region of North Vietnam and had found fault with its principal premise, that suitable bombing targets in northern North Vietnam had been exhausted. One hundred important fixed targets remained in Hanoi, Haiphong, and the area near the Chinese border, all of which the generals wanted to strike in order to reduce infiltration of war materials into the South and shorten the time required to make Hanoi relent. The military men saw an ongoing need to strike these fixed targets because of the North Vietnamese government's capacity for regenerating and relocating them.

The generals informed the committee that Rolling Thunder had forced North Vietnam to divert between five hundred thousand and six hundred thousand people to repair bomb damage and reroute supplies. This diversion had reduced the availability of manpower for farm labor, in turn necessitating greater imports of food into North Vietnam. Rolling Thunder was also compelling the North Vietnamese to import vast amounts of ammunition for air defense, estimated by the U.S. military at 300,000 tons of antiaircraft rounds per year. That figure called into serious question the estimate of some American intelligence analysts that the

North Vietnamese were importing only 125,000 tons of weapons and ammunition annually.[95]

The generals recommended mining Haiphong Harbor as a means of slashing Hanoi's importation of weapons, ammunition, oil, and other essential supplies. Several of them told the committee that they had opposed McNamara's barrier, which they thought would be especially futile if the United States remained unwilling to block the Ho Chi Minh Trail or mine the ports. "It is like closing the window and leaving the door open," commented General Johnson, the Army chief of staff.[96] McNamara's rejection of Westmoreland's recommended troop level also elicited criticisms. General Greene, the Marine Corps commandant, noted that defeating the enemy quickly would require additional Marines to fully meet the dual imperatives of foiling large enemy incursions into I Corps and supporting pacification.

President Johnson watched the avalanche of reproach with mounting dismay. He would later say to Wheeler that the generals "almost destroyed us with their testimony before the Stennis committee. We were murdered on the hearings."[97] In mid-August, Johnson authorized additional Rolling Thunder strikes in an attempt to mitigate the criticism. "I would like to be able to say that we have hit six out of every seven targets requested," he told his top advisors. To achieve that objective, he said, "Let us find the least dangerous and the most productive targets." That instruction, unfortunately, ignored the basic logic of the North Vietnamese air defense system. The North Vietnamese had placed their most dangerous defenses around the most productive targets.[98]

On August 24, just one day before McNamara was to appear before the committee, Johnson undercut his own escalatory efforts by imposing a moratorium on bombing near Hanoi. This action grew out of a peace initiative that had begun the previous month.

Herbert Marcovich and Raymond Aubrac, left-wing French professors who were sympathetic to North Vietnam, had traveled to Hanoi in July to present a diplomatic proposal received from an American academic colleague, Professor Henry Kissinger. The proposal, Kissinger had informed them, had been approved by the White House.[99]

Marcovich and Aubrac had laid out the proposal in a meeting with Pham Van Dong on July 24. The United States would end the bombing of North Vietnam, the Frenchmen explained, and all sides would keep external military support to South Vietnam at existing levels. Negotiations would then commence. Pham Van Dong replied that Hanoi would participate in negotiations if the United States stopped the bombing, but he objected to the stipulation about levels of military support. "We will not agree to any reciprocal action," he insisted. "We are in our own country. They, not us, are the ones who escalated the war.... They are the ones who came here. They must get out!" Pham Van Dong added, however, that American troops could leave gradually under a peace settlement.[100]

This position was not substantively different from previous North Vietnamese positions, but the slightly less hostile North Vietnamese tone convinced the peace-hungry Johnson to follow up with another goodwill gesture. His reply to Hanoi, supplied by Kissinger on August 18 at Marcovich's house in Paris, stated that the United States was willing to halt the bombing of North Vietnam if it would "lead promptly to productive discussions" and if the North Vietnamese would "not take advantage" of the halt by increasing the movement of men and supplies into the South.[101] As a demonstration that the U.S. government was serious about this negotiating track, the Johnson administration would refrain from bombing within ten nautical miles of Hanoi area for ten days, from August 24 to September 4.[102]

McNamara thus had one more reason to be on the defensive when he appeared before the Stennis committee on August 25. His testimony began at 10:10 a.m. in room 224 of the Old Senate Office Building. After reading a prepared statement in which he defended the administration's handling of the air war, he faced a barrage of questions from the committee members, stretching the hearing into the afternoon.

Senator Howard Cannon, Democrat of Nevada, asked McNamara why he and the president had so often rejected the recommendations of the Joint Chiefs on Rolling Thunder. McNamara was evasive, saying merely that "there are many, many reasons, political and other reasons."[103] Senator Margaret Chase Smith, Republican of Maine and chair of the Republican Conference, asked McNamara if he agreed with previous witnesses that greater bombing of the North in the past two years would have reduced American casualties in the South. McNamara answered that he had seen no information to support that view and considerable information supporting the opposite view.

Senator Stuart Symington, Democrat of Missouri, brought up a statement by General Walt that a prior bombing pause had enabled the enemy to bring forward heavy equipment in I Corps, resulting in greater Marine casualties. McNamara ignored that particular case and fell back on the general argument he had long made in private. "All of the evidence is so far we have not been able to destroy a sufficient quantity to limit the activity in the south below the present level, and I do not know that we can in the future," McNamara responded. For the average North Vietnamese battalion in the South, he said, the present level meant fighting one day out of thirty. The North Vietnamese had the excess logistical capacity to withstand additional bombing, as they only needed to move seventy-five tons per day to the South, whereas their infiltration system had a capacity of more than two hundred tons per day.[104]

As America's generals had pointed out earlier in the hearings, the North Vietnamese Army would have preferred to fight much more often than one day per month, given that its main objective was to inflict casualties on its opponents.[105] The North Vietnamese also would have preferred to make greater use of heavy weapons on that one day when they were fighting, since heavy weaponry increased the lethality of most of their operations. North Vietnamese forces were not fighting multiple days per month or making liberal use of heavy weapons because they lacked the requisite food and ammunition, which was proof that their infiltration system did not possess unused capacity. Consequently, every truck, rice bag, and ammunition crate destroyed by Rolling Thunder spelled a further reduction in the amounts of manpower and firepower that the North Vietnamese Army could commit to the battlefield.

At one point in his testimony, under heavy pressure to explain his refusals to heed the military's advice, McNamara blurted out, "I don't believe that there is this gulf between the military leaders and the civilian leaders in the executive branch." During a break, McNamara told the press that "My policies don't differ with those of the Joint Chiefs and I think they would be the first to say it."[106]

When the hearing came to a close, McNamara climbed into his private car and headed for the Pentagon. En route, he received a phone call from the president, who directed him to come to the White House. For three hours, Johnson tore into McNamara for his performance before the Stennis committee.[107]

According to journalist Mark Perry, McNamara's testimony provoked an emergency meeting of the Joint Chiefs of Staff, at which the generals decided to resign together in protest of the administration's contemptuous and duplicitous disregard for their advice. They reportedly changed their minds the next day after concluding that a group resignation would result only in their

replacement with yes-men.[108] Several senior officers and relatives
of the Joint Chiefs were said to have confirmed this account, but
two of the Joint Chiefs themselves later denied it.[109]

On August 31, the Stennis committee issued its report. In an
indication of enduring consensus among moderates and conservatives of both parties, the document received the endorsement
of all Democrats and Republicans on the committee. The report
faulted America's civilian authorities for vitiating Rolling Thunder
through gradualism and for consistently opposing recommendations from the military to escalate the air campaign. Disputing
McNamara's claim that mining Haiphong Harbor would achieve
little, the committee asserted that the military witnesses had all
testified that mining the port in concert with aggressive bombing
"was the single most important thing which could have been done"
and that it could still "have a substantial impact on the course of
the war and the American and allied casualties in the South."[110]

The fallout from the Stennis hearings drove Johnson to do
something he had almost never done: hold a press conference on
Vietnam. "While the Joint Chiefs and the Secretary of Defense,
the Secretary of State and the President, are not in complete
agreement on everything, there is no deep division," President
Johnson told the media on the day after the committee issued
its blistering report. "There is a very surprising and very agreeable amount of unanimity, with the men of the same general
opinion. There are no quarrels, no antagonisms." In fact, the
president remarked, during his thirty-six years in Washington,
"I have never known a period during that time when I thought
there was more harmony, more general agreement, and a more
cooperative attitude." As evidence of the harmoniousness, Johnson
stated that he had authorized the bombing of 300 of 350 targets
recommended by the Joint Chief of Staff, the six of seven he had
previously mentioned to his inner circle.[111]

The misleading statements of McNamara and Johnson about unanimity compounded the anger of moderates and conservatives in Congress and the general public at what they had heard during the Stennis hearings. At the same time, the administration's intensification of Rolling Thunder at the start of the hearings alienated liberals. A Harris poll showed that the public approval rating for Johnson's handling of the war fell from 47 percent in mid-July to 33 percent in late August.[112] Another poll showed that the percentage of Americans satisfied with the conduct of the war was just 13 percent, down from 39 percent a year earlier, while the percentage of those dissatisfied increased from 54 percent to 75 percent during the same period.[113]

Had polls been taken in North Vietnam, they likewise would have shown dissatisfaction with the national leadership's handling of the war. After sustaining costly military defeats early in the year, Hanoi had reduced the size of its attacks and relied more heavily on combat near South Vietnam's borders, but it had been unable to regain control of villages, cause greater harm to the enemy, or reduce its own casualties. As in the United States, ongoing difficulties spurred sentiments both for and against escalation. But whereas the American advocates of escalation were achieving modest changes to American strategy by influencing a hesitant decision maker, the North Vietnamese advocates of escalation included the decision makers themselves. The North Vietnamese did not, however, have supplies to escalate as much as they wanted, so they would have to keep escalating on the cheap until the time came for the cities to rise up.

Marines from company E, 2nd Battalion, 4th Marines move out from Landing Zone White during Operation Starlite.

Indonesian President Sukarno, left, and General Suharto.

A CH-47 Chinook helicopter delivers artillery equipment and supplies to the 1st Cavalry Division in the Ia Drang Valley.

Tuesday lunch in the White House dining room. From left: George Christian, Walt Rostow, Robert McNamara, Tom Johnson, Richard Helms, Dean Rusk, Lyndon B. Johnson.

Captured photograph of Vietnamese Communist soldiers.

F-105 Thunderchiefs assigned to Operation Rolling Thunder bomb North Vietnam.

South Vietnamese armored units enter Da Nang to suppress the Struggle Movement, May 1966.

North Vietnam's leaders attend an Independence Day celebration in Hanoi. From left:
Vo Nguyen Giap, Truong Chinh, Le Duan, Ho Chi Minh.

American and South Vietnamese leaders meet at Cam Ranh Bay. From left:
Lyndon B. Johnson, William Westmoreland, Nguyen Van Thieu, Nguyen Cao Ky.

U.S. Marine Corps tanks and infantry near Con Thien.

Secretary of Defense Robert McNamara speaks at the Stennis hearings, August 25, 1967.

U.S. Army soldiers prepare to assault a North Vietnamese position during Operation Hawthorne.

From left, William Westmoreland, Earle Wheeler, Ellsworth Bunker.

South Vietnamese Rangers search for Communist fighters in Cholon during the Tet Offensive.

U.S. Marines disembark from a CH-46 Sea Knight helicopter near Khe Sanh.

South Vietnamese citizens and officials observe funerals for victims of the Hue Massacre.

In Operation Pursuit, a column of American troops traverses rice paddies near Da Nang.

General Creighton Abrams addresses President Lyndon Johnson and the "Wise Men," March 26, 1968.

North Vietnamese rockets strike Saigon during the second wave offensive of May 1968.

Protesters clash with police at Chicago's Grant Park during the Democratic National Convention, August 28, 1968.

CHAPTER 11

SAMSON'S FLIGHT

September–December 1967

S outh Vietnam's citizens gathered at polling stations on September 3 to cast their ballots for the presidency. The nation's security forces, arrayed in great numbers around the facilities, ensured that few acts of violence disrupted the voting. According to the reports of foreign observers, the election was generally conducted in a free and fair manner, with little evidence of irregularities.

Once the votes were tallied, the ticket of Nguyen Van Thieu and Nguyen Cao Ky was pronounced the winner. It came as little surprise that the most powerful men in the country won a Vietnamese election, but their fraction of the total was a far cry from the usual 99.9 percent, coming in at just 34.8 percent. The preponderance of votes for the Thieu-Ky ticket had been cast in rural areas. Phan Khac Suu, the chief of state during the tumult of late 1964 and early 1965, received the most votes in Hue and Da Nang, collecting 10.8 percent overall, while former prime minister Tran Van Huong earned the most from Saigon's voters and finished with 10 percent. Truong Dinh Dzu, a demagogue who had campaigned on a farfetched promise to negotiate an immediate withdrawal of all North Vietnamese forces, received 17.2 percent of the vote.[1]

Some American and South Vietnamese observers hailed the low percentage of votes for Thieu and Ky as proof that South Vietnam had made the transition from rigged elections to legitimate democracy. Others construed it as evidence of either a lack of popular enthusiasm for the pair, a lack of familiarity with all the candidates, or a lack of national solidarity. Still others believed that the election made little difference to the South Vietnamese people or nation, given the country's lack of democratic traditions. From the perspective of the ruling elites in Saigon and Washington, the election's most significant consequence was the solidification of Thieu's position as national leader.[2]

North Vietnamese military activity heated up in I Corps in early September, beginning as in May and June with the launching of large projectiles at Con Thien. More than three hundred mortar, artillery, and rocket rounds flew each day from the demilitarized zone into Con Thien. Concealed in caves north of the Ben Hai River, the North Vietnamese weapons were difficult for the Americans to locate and even more difficult to damage with air strikes. As in July, the U.S. Marines were not authorized to enter the demilitarized zone. They patrolled the ground near Con Thien and crossed swords with North Vietnamese infantry, though the North Vietnamese did not appear in multi-battalion formations as they had during Operation Buffalo. The Con Thien garrison sustained nearly two hundred killed and two thousand wounded during the month of September.[3]

Frustration with the state of affairs at Con Thien welled up inside Marine Corps Commandant General Greene until, on September 24, he took it up with the other Joint Chiefs. "The casualty level currently being experienced by the Marines in the

DMZ region is too high, considering the operational benefits received," he notified his fellow generals. Greene recommended reinforcing Con Thien with two regiments and increasing air and naval gunfire into the DMZ.[4]

Greene's complaint persuaded General Westmoreland to unleash a new array of firepower on the demilitarized zone. The section to the north of Con Thien was brutalized by an unprecedented deluge of naval gunfire, B-52 strikes, tactical air strikes, and artillery fire. As described by Westmoreland to President Johnson, it was "much more than was ever poured on Berlin or Tokyo."[5] This prodigious exercise in destruction led to a slackening of the North Vietnamese bombardment of Con Thien in late September.[6]

Elsewhere in I Corps, the North Vietnamese moved about in large numbers to obtain rice and fight battles where conditions were auspicious. During September, the entire 2nd Division of the North Vietnamese Army swept into the Que Son Valley to scarf up the rice harvest. Such was the power and vigor of the North Vietnamese tempest that Westmoreland sent an entire brigade of the 1st Air Cavalry Division to smite them. In Operation Wallowa, the cavalrymen rode into the valley on a vast fleet of helicopters, saturating the skies in a manner unknown to either the Marines who had operated in the valley previously or the North Vietnamese who had fought them. For North Vietnamese soldiers accustomed to walking the valley unmolested during daylight, the sudden appearance of helicopter gunships firing machine guns and rockets was a most unwelcome surprise. The gunships killed a reported 210 North Vietnamese in the first two weeks of Operation Wallowa. Cavalrymen dismounted from their helicopters to grapple with the North Vietnamese on the valley floor, lifting the total of enemy casualties to 1,600 by the end of October.[7]

In II Corps, allied forces were similarly effective in disrupting the North Vietnamese initiatives of the early fall. The U.S. Army 4th Infantry Division launched Operation Francis Marion against North Vietnamese forces in Pleiku, which killed or captured over 1,600 enemy at a cost of 300 Americans. When the North Vietnamese moved large forces from the mountains toward the coastal farms of Phu Yen Province to take the rice harvest, South Vietnamese and South Korean forces sallied out and caught them in several hamlets to the west of the provincial capital of Tuy Hoa. Exercising restraint in the use of firepower to avoid harming civilians, the South Vietnamese and South Koreans took a week to expel the North Vietnamese from the hamlets and sustained numerous casualties in the process. When the North Vietnamese reoccupied the same hamlets a week later, the South Vietnamese and South Koreans made more extensive use of air and artillery in the hamlets to limit casualties to their infantry. They killed a reported 400 North Vietnamese troops and chased the rest back into the mountains, but also destroyed 3,700 dwellings, created 20,000 refugees, and killed or wounded an undetermined number of civilians.[8]

North of Saigon, the North Vietnamese Army's 7th and 9th Divisions and the 69th Artillery Group massed in October near Loc Ninh, a district capital close to the Cambodian border. Their offensive largely followed the patterns of past offensives in the border regions, with North Vietnamese battalions and regiments attacking American companies and suffering much greater losses than the Americans. The most damaging North Vietnamese attack took place on October 17 at Ong Thang stream, where the 271st NVA Regiment assailed two companies of the U.S. Army's 2nd Battalion, 28th Infantry. The North Vietnamese killed fifty-six Americans, including the battalion commander, Colonel Terry de la Mesa Allen Jr., who had chosen to stay with the badly wounded while the able-bodied pulled back, and Major Donald W. Holleder, a former all-American football player at West Point, who was shot by an enemy sniper while trying to rescue debilitated Americans.[9]

On the diplomatic front, the North Vietnamese remained noncommittal on negotiations through September 4, the day when Johnson's ten-day bombing pause expired. Johnson nonetheless extended the pause another three days, without result, then extended it again for an indefinite period while sending word to the North Vietnamese that his patience was running out. On September 10, the North Vietnamese replied that they were rejecting the American proposal because they would not accept any preconditions for the suspension of bombing. Johnson resumed the bombing the next day.[10]

On September 26, Under Secretary of State Katzenbach urged Johnson to authorize yet another bombing pause in order to facilitate communications and negotiations. The president's patience, however, had truly been exhausted. "I think they are playing us for suckers," Johnson snapped. "They have no more intention of talking than we have of surrendering."[11] At a subsequent meeting, Johnson said that the North Vietnamese were exploiting American interest in dialogue through the Marcovich-Aubrac channel merely to gain a respite from Rolling Thunder. "I know if they were bombing Washington, hitting my bridges and railroads and highways, I would be delighted to trade off discussions through an intermediary for a restriction on the bombing."[12]

Once more the Joint Chiefs pressed for intensification of Rolling Thunder, and once more they were subjected to a torrent of objections from McNamara.[13] The secretary of defense invoked a September CIA report that characterized North Vietnam's use of countermeasures and alternative routes as so effective that "the North Vietnamese transport system has emerged from more than 30 months of bombing with greater capacity and flexibility than it had when the Rolling Thunder program started." The system for infiltrating supplies from North to South was still operating well below capacity, the CIA contended, and thus "logistics problems have not placed a relevant ceiling on force structures or levels of combat."[14]

Rostow disputed this CIA analysis, noting that if the enemy had so much logistical capacity, one would expect the North Vietnamese to double or triple the infiltration of supplies so that Communist units in the South could double or triple the number of days per month they could fight.[15] A few months later, the CIA would itself back away from the bold assertion that Rolling Thunder was not constraining North Vietnamese combat activities in the South. In an assessment produced jointly with the Defense Intelligence Agency, it asserted that the "cumulative effects of the airstrikes have clearly degraded North Vietnam's capability for sustained large-scale conventional military operations against South Vietnam."[16]

Decades afterward, the North Vietnamese published histories confirming that logistical problems continued to put a ceiling on their military activities during this period. The North Vietnamese had wanted to attack the highland town of Dak To in October 1966 but were unable to do so until October 1967 because they needed a year to stockpile the necessary supplies, which included nine hundred tons of rice, ammunition, and weapons.[17] The history of the 9th NVA Division revealed that the unit was constrained in its operations north of Saigon by severe shortages of food brought on by low amounts of supplies from external sources as well as by enemy sweep operations.[18]

The intensification of Rolling Thunder was reaping even larger rewards in North Vietnam, though they were even less visible to the outside world. The bombing of entry points from China into North Vietnam during the summer greatly reduced the importation of critical supplies into North Vietnam, of which the most critical was food. American ordnance blew away a span of the Paul Doumer Bridge, the only bridge over the Red River between Haiphong to Hanoi, and knocked out additional transportation targets that were critical to the distribution of food and weapons.[19]

American intelligence analysts possessed very little information on the supply situation in North Vietnam. The North Vietnamese, knowing that their enemies would seek to exploit any vulnerability, strenuously avoided public acknowledgment of shortages in food and other essential supplies. To the outside world, they proclaimed that North Vietnam's agricultural system was achieving exceptionally high yields.[20] They also stayed away from the topic of food imports in internal communications, presumably for fear that American intelligence would gain access to those communications.

The few foreigners from non-Communist countries who visited North Vietnam during the summer and fall of 1967 were not permitted to move freely or speak with ordinary citizens but were herded to Potemkin villages and to meetings with regime loyalists who stuck to the party line. According to that line, nothing done by the American imperialists could stop North Vietnam's glorious march toward victory.[21] Trusted visitors from Communist countries were able to learn more, but they generally knew to keep their mouths shut in public. One Hungarian visitor to Hanoi, though, did comment on the food crisis to a Western news outlet after departing the country. Istvan Szabo, the foreign news editor of the Hungarian Communist Party's official newspaper, told a correspondent of United Press International that during a recent visit he had found that "the North Vietnamese were depending mainly on supplies from friendly Communist countries but that despite this help, distribution problems as a result of the bombings had caused serious food shortages."[22]

On October 10, a CIA intelligence cable on North Vietnam's economic situation reached the desk of Lyndon Johnson. The information in the report was dated to late August, and the source was listed as Truong Cong Dong, a member of the National Liberation Front's "permanent mission" to Hanoi. "The food situation can be referred to as chronic famine," the report stated. "The majority of the population eats only one meal a day, consisting of rice, vegetables and fruit." According to the report, "All food products are rationed, and the rations initially provided for many products such as cigarettes, tea, sugar and meat, have recently been reduced."[23]

John Colvin, the British consul-general, was one of the few Western diplomats living in Hanoi at this time and hence one of the few Westerners who could see beyond the Potemkin villages. His observations from the period, which were published in a postwar memoir, offered the most detailed analysis of the situation and its implications. By the beginning of September, Colvin observed, the loss of food supplies from China was sapping the customary resilience of North Vietnamese population. "The evidence of malnutrition was now clear, and among adults as well as children," Colvin related. "In the streets, offices and factories, the population could barely get about their duties.... The hospitals were filled with cases of hunger edema as well as wounds."

Because of the famine and the disruption of North Vietnamese logistics by the bombing, the economy of North Vietnam "was at last breaking down," Colvin concluded. "The country and its people were close to a collapse which, for the first time, no amount of excited exhortation could correct." This turn of events led him to abandon his earlier view that the North Vietnamese "would pursue the conflict even if they had, like Samson, to pull the pillars down on themselves and on all of us." If the Americans kept up the military pressure on the North much longer, Colvin believed, the North Vietnamese would have to concede defeat in the South.[24]

Although contemporaneous North Vietnamese documents were silent on the famine, the topic of North Vietnam's dependence on food imports would surface in a party document that was circulated in May 1969, after the North was no longer under air attack. In that document, Le Duan divulged that if North Vietnam "did not receive the 900,000 tons of rice they [the Chinese] give us, we would face unimaginable problems," and "we would not be able to win victory." In what may have been a hint at the misery imposed by the breaching of this vulnerability in 1967, Le Duan remarked, "If we did not receive these several hundreds of thousands of tons of rice, our people would starve!"[25]

The fragmentary reports of North Vietnamese famine to emerge at the time made little impression on American intelligence analysts and policy officials. Although the intelligence community was aware that North Vietnam was importing hundreds of thousands of tons of food from China, the intelligence estimates and strategy papers from the period noted neither the vulnerability of the imported food to interdiction nor the limited evidence indicating that Rolling Thunder had disrupted these imports.[26] McNamara and many analysts at the CIA and DIA were heavily invested in the belief that no amount of bombing could bring North Vietnam to its knees, and they had a history of clinging to this and other long-held beliefs when contradictory evidence materialized.[27]

Had the intelligence community told Johnson that North Vietnam was on the brink of starvation, he might have kept Rolling Thunder on full blast until North Vietnam cried uncle. Starving an enemy into submission was not the preferred method of military victory for most nations, least of all those like the

United States that aspired to promote fair play on the world stage, yet it often became the actual method of victory after other methods had failed. During the last year of the American Civil War, Abraham Lincoln had brought famine to the Confederacy through the destruction of crops and railroads. The Allied Powers had forced the Central Powers to surrender in 1918 with blockades that starved hundreds of thousands of civilians to death. In April 1945, the United States had launched Operation Starvation to prevent the importation of food and other supplies into Japan, though the operation was cut short by the atomic Armageddon at Hiroshima and Nagasaki.

Whether the North Vietnamese government could have remained in power and found a way to continue the war in the face of sustained American bombing would never be known, because the bombing was not to be sustained. Johnson's suspension of the bombing around Hanoi at the end of August, which was to extend into late October, allowed North Vietnamese and Chinese engineers to revive the supply network. The Doumer Bridge and other key lines of transportation were back in operation by the end of September.[28]

During the middle of October, McNamara urged Johnson to undertake another bombing pause. In support of his case, he wheeled out a new argument that was as tortuous as any he had made in his nearly seven years in office. McNamara contended that the North Vietnamese would not agree to substantive negotiations until they were persuaded that they could not defeat South Vietnam by force, and the only way to persuade them on that score was to demonstrate that the American people were steadfast in their support of an independent South Vietnam. The steadfastness of the American people, McNamara continued, would be solidified if they knew that Johnson was pausing the bombing to exhaust every possible avenue toward peace.[29]

By this time, McNamara was nearly alone among senior officials in believing that another unilateral pause would serve American interests. Most of Johnson's other advisers now opposed suspension of the bombing because they thought it would produce the opposite of the effects predicted by McNamara, depressing the morale of the American people and bolstering the will of Hanoi to persist. When the CIA was asked to predict the results of a pause, its analysts responded that the North Vietnamese would view the pause as "a sign the U.S. will was weakening" and would henceforth reject diplomatic proposals unless the United States made concessions on points where it had previously refused to yield.[30]

Clark Clifford, returning from a trip with Taylor to Southeast Asia, reported strong opposition to a bombing halt among Southeast Asian leaders. "Without the bombing, Southeast Asians feel there is no inducement for the North Vietnamese to seek peace," stated Clifford, a Democratic senior statesman who was serving as chairman of the President's Foreign Intelligence Advisory Board. "This thing could go on for twenty years. If we stop bombing, they will build up their industries, their transportation lines, their food supplies, and their communications."[31]

In a stinging setback for McNamara, the chorus of opposition to a bombing pause prevailed. On October 23, Johnson authorized Rolling Thunder 58, which not only extended the air campaign but intensified it. The target list included sites that the president had consistently refused to bomb in the past, most notably the Phuc Yen Air Base, as well as sites near Hanoi that had been off limits since late August.[32] Sixty-four American aircraft bombed Phuc Yen the very next day, and smaller contingents hit it again for two more days, wrecking three MiGs, damaging three more, and putting the runway out of service.[33] Rolling Thunder 58 would push the total tonnage of munitions dropped on North Vietnam in 1967 to 246,328, nearly twice the previous year's sum.[34]

Johnson's break with McNamara on the bombing appears to have been a leading cause of a larger rift between the two men, one that would lead to McNamara's departure from the administration. Sometime during the fall, Johnson and McNamara both came to believe that McNamara should move on to a new job, though it was never clear who reached that conclusion first. The World Bank was chosen as McNamara's next destination and February 1968 as his departure date. For McNamara's successor as secretary of defense, Johnson selected Clark Clifford.[35]

Another reason for McNamara's fall from grace may have been his reluctance to keep cheerleading for the administration's policies. "It is time that this Administration stopped sitting back and taking it from the Vietnam critics," Johnson said at an October Cabinet meeting. "We have got a psychological war as well as a military war on our hands and the Communists are winning the psychological war with our help." Congressmen from his own party, he lamented, were parroting the enemy's propaganda. As far as he could tell, the only person sticking up for the administration was Republican Senate Minority Leader Everett Dirksen.[36]

The activities of the antiwar movement were ballooning at this time, owing to an upsurge in antiwar sentiment on college campuses. Some college students found the war objectionable because they opposed war in general. Such individuals could obtain exemption from military service through conscientious objection, which required demonstrating to the local draft board a deeply held belief in pacifism. Conscientious objectors, though, were a miniscule minority. During 1967, when more than thirty-four million American men were registered with the Selective Service, just 22,733, or about 0.07 percent, held conscientious objector status.[37] Many of the conscientious objectors, it should be added, were willing to assist the nation's cause in Vietnam to such an extent that they went to Vietnam to serve in noncombatant roles.

Other students objected to the war on the grounds that it was strategically unnecessary or morally wrong. From the middle of 1965 to the middle of 1967, this type of opposition had not been appreciably more common on college campuses than elsewhere in America. Then it skyrocketed. Campuses suddenly became islands of antiwar activism in an American sea that experienced no comparable change. Some students gravitated toward the viewpoint of liberal Democratic politicians who had turned against the war, while others aligned with radical groups like Students for a Democratic Society and the Student Nonviolent Coordinating Committee that sympathized with the Vietnamese Communists.

The rise in antiwar activity among college students had multiple roots. One was generational change. The Baby Boom generation had begun arriving on campuses in 1964, and by 1967 it accounted for most of the undergraduate population. Reared by the Greatest Generation, which had overcome the tribulations of the Great Depression and carried the United States to victory in World War II, the Baby Boomers had grown up in the unprecedented affluence and comfort of the 1950s and 1960s. Rather than engendering gratitude and respect, as the Greatest Generation had hoped, prosperity and pleasure had filled large sections of the Baby Boom generation with self-absorption and self-indulgence, at the expense of the patriotic spirit that had driven their parents across the oceans to vanquish the Axis powers.[38] One member of the Greatest Generation, Harvard history professor John V. Kelleher, spoke for many when he described the Boomers as "spoiled brats with an underdeveloped sense of history and a flair for self-protection."[39]

The spread of leftist ideas at American colleges and universities also played a part in the youth rebellion, especially its more extreme elements. For several decades, the professoriate had been accumulating proponents of radical ideologies like socialism, Marxism, Freudianism, atheism, humanism, structuralism, and nihilism. European-born intellectuals such as Herbert Marcuse, Claude Lévi-Strauss, Paul de Man, Jacques Derrida, and Theodor Adorno brought much of this material across the Atlantic, and their thinking inspired a wide range of American public intellectuals and professors, from Benjamin Spock and Richard Hofstadter to Angela Davis and Abbie Hoffman. Other strains of radicalism were largely homegrown, such as the politicized Christianity of William Sloane Coffin and Martin Luther King Jr. and the Beat counterculture of Alan Ginsberg and William S. Burroughs.

The radicals had encountered few receptive listeners among the Silent Generation, the generally conservative cohort sandwiched between the Greatest Generation and the Baby Boom generation. With the restless youth of the Baby Boomers, whose self-preoccupation and infrequent exposures to life's pains and tragedies left them less respectful of tradition and authority, the radicals found a much more welcoming audience. Leftist faculty appealed to the vanity of the Boomers by promising membership in a new cultural elite and to their longing for adventure and meaning by promising liberation from the humdrum of bourgeois society.[40]

Radical professors were especially effective stimulants of antiwar ferment where they possessed sufficient numbers to reinforce one another. At the University of Wisconsin, for instance, the combined weight of faculty radicals like Harvey Goldberg, George Mosse, William Appleman Williams, and John R. W. Smail helped turn the student body into an epicenter of opposition to the war. In a retrospective account of the university's antiwar movement, journalist David Maraniss described the scene in 1967: "Goldberg and Mosse drew the largest crowds, their lecture halls buzzing with hundreds of students filling the aisles and leaning over the balconies. Radical students formed a cult around Goldberg and sat spellbound as he delivered lectures laced with revolutionary allusions, cultural anecdotes, literary references, reflections on the day's *New York Times,* and arcane sociological data from French archives."[41]

Of much greater influence than the faculty radicals, though, was the draft. The federal government curtailed student draft deferments in July 1967, which precipitated a spike in draft calls to college students. Male students who wanted to avoid the perils and discomforts of military service latched on to opposition to the war as a vehicle for hastening the end of the war and the draft, and for justifying—to themselves and to others—their pursuit of less than honorable opportunities for draft avoidance, most commonly the fraudulent use of medical deferments.

At Yale, a 1966 poll had found that more than two-thirds of students favored the Johnson administration's Vietnam policy, and only 10 percent favored withdrawal. When the draft deferments were slashed, however, support for the war plunged, and antiwar groups sprouted up. Michael Medved, who became active in the Yale antiwar movement at this time, recalled, "For college students of the late 1960s, our strident opposition to the war didn't inspire our overriding determination to shun military service; rather, our overriding determination to shun military service inspired our strident opposition to the war."[42]

A similar swing in attitudes toward the war and military service took place at Harvard. In the fall of 1966, the heckling of Robert McNamara by antiwar students during a campus speech sparked so much revulsion that an astounding 2,700 Harvard undergraduates signed an apology to McNamara. Support for the war and the Johnson administration persisted among students until the modification of the draft deferments in the middle of 1967, at which point it nosedived. "When we came back in the fall," recounted student Steven Kelman, "suddenly everyone was against the war."

Kelman, a self-identified radical socialist, reflected a few years later that "students should have realized that in many cases it was not our oft-praised idealism and sensitivity—those traits which we frequently and stupidly believe we are the first generation in world history to possess—which led us into mass action against the war. It was something close to self-interest." Instead of humble introspection, however, "a self-righteousness, of the type that engulfs either the newly converted or the guilty conscienced, a new Cotton Matherhood of burning frenzy, suddenly enveloped Harvard in the months between September and November.... To say one supported the war in Vietnam quickly became a rough equivalent of saying one supported Bull Connor's police dogs in Birmingham."[43]

Harvard student James Glassman remembered that in 1966 it had been commonplace to hear students assailing the draft as "highly discriminatory, favoring the well-off." Conscription, they believed, was taking in too few young men from affluent families, the sort of men who attended Harvard and other colleges. But when the draft began scooping up large numbers of college students in 1967, they no longer favored the drafting of the well-off but instead opposed the draft altogether and with it the war. "The altruism was forgotten," Glassman recounted. "What was most important now was saving your own skin."[44]

Another Harvard student of this period, James Fallows, wrote some years later of the disparate outcomes he had witnessed between Harvard students and poor Boston whites during the draft board screening at the Boston Navy Yard. Four out of every five

Harvard men who showed up with Fallows managed to avoid the draft by feigning suicidal thoughts, losing large amounts of weight, gaming tests for colorblindness, or throwing urine specimens in the faces of orderlies. Four out of every five working-class men who went through the screening were accepted into the military.

Fallows concluded, pityingly, that it had never occurred to the young men of the working class that they could find a way to circumvent the draft.[45] It is also possible, however, that these men knew the draft could be dodged but chose against that option because they viewed it as unpatriotic, unmanly, and unfair to other men of draft age. Or as "gutless and soft," as Thomas Gleason had put it.

Fallows went on to infer what many others were also to conclude: that most of the young Americans who went to Vietnam were uneducated, poor, and non-white men who lacked the know-how and privileges to avoid the draft.

That reasoning was flawed in several important respects. One was the assumption that draftees accounted for most of the men who fought and died in Vietnam. In actuality, two-thirds of those who served in Vietnam had not been drafted, but had instead voluntarily enlisted or joined the officer corps. Volunteers, in fact, constituted a much larger share of American manpower in the Vietnam War than they had in World War II, a war widely perceived to have inspired a higher degree of patriotic volunteerism. Americans who volunteered for service in World War II fulfilled only one-third of the military's needs, necessitating the use of the draft to obtain the other two-thirds.

For the young men of the Vietnam War, as for those of previous wars, the motives for volunteering ranged from the selfless to the self-serving, and there was no way of gauging the percentages of individuals who fell on each point along that spectrum. Numerous volunteers specified a sense of patriotic duty as a leading factor in their decision to join the military. Many also cited belief in the cause of anti-Communism as a motive. Others, who tended to be more reticent, volunteered primarily to obtain a better or less dangerous job than a draftee typically would.

While the gaming of the draft system became commonplace among certain segments of society by the end of 1967, these segments were not defined purely by age, education, class, or race. Region and ethnicity were also large factors, particularly when it came to college students. Whereas draft resistance and anti-war protest proliferated at the Ivy League schools of the Northeast and the large universities of the upper Midwest and Pacific Northwest, they did not feature prominently at the campuses of the South and West.[46]

For the country as a whole, the educated, the affluent, and the white did a large share of the fighting and dying. Americans who served in Vietnam were, on average, substantially better educated than those who had served in World War II, thanks to the more stringent induction standards the military could maintain when fighting a smaller war. Eighty percent of them had high school degrees, as opposed to only 45 percent of World War II veterans. The men sent to Vietnam were also better educated than the total population of military-age males during the Vietnam era; only 65 percent in that category possessed high school degrees. Of the American officers in Vietnam, a group accounting for 12.5 percent of the total force in Vietnam, most had college degrees, in contrast to World War II, when a large fraction of men without college degrees had been made officers to meet the demands of a global conflict.[47]

Well-educated Americans were generally more attuned than the average American to the threats that Communism posed to the United States. They were more familiar with the many dark chapters that Communism had already written into history during its first fifty years, to include Lenin's Red Terror, Stalin's purges and famines, Mao's Great Leap Forward and Cultural Revolution, the overthrow of the coalition governments in Eastern Europe, the North Korean invasion of South Korea, and the suppression of the Hungarian uprising. Although antiwar sentiment was on the rise at numerous American college campuses, it did not overwhelm countervailing viewpoints. The American professoriate of the late 1960s included large numbers of World War II and Korean War veterans who supported the war and encouraged students to serve in the military. Antiwar events and publications incited a prowar backlash, manifesting itself in activities by existing campus groups like the Intercollegiate Studies Institute and College Republican National Committee and by new groups such as Young Americans for Freedom and the Victory in Vietnam Association.[48]

Although select groups of affluent and well-educated Americans dodged the draft more frequently than the rest of the population, their behavior did not result in gross underrepresentation of the upper and middle classes in the fighting forces. After the war, MIT researchers analyzed a random sample of 1,510 Americans killed in Vietnam and found that Americans of all income levels were well represented. A disparity existed between lower and upper classes, but it was not the massive disparity often assumed; 34 percent of the fatalities came from families in the lowest 30 percent of society by income, while 25 percent came from families in the top 30 percent of the income scale.[49]

During the war's early years, black troops died in combat at higher rates than white troops, a first in American history. Blacks accounted for 20.8 percent of Americans killed in 1965 and 1966, nearly twice their representation in the general population. Black fatalities had constituted 8.4 percent of the American dead in the Korean War, the first war with racially integrated units, and much smaller fractions of the total during previous conflicts, when most blacks had served in segregated support units. To some Americans, the increased participation of black soldiers in combat was a sign of progress in racial integration. To others, it signified invidious discrimination and callousness toward black lives. Complaints from the latter perspective caused the armed forces to reduce the allocation of black servicemen to combat units, and as a result the distribution of fatalities for the war as whole would ultimately mirror the percentage of each group in the general population. Of all the Americans to die in Vietnam, 85.6 percent would be white and 12.4 percent would be black.[50]

On October 16, nearly one thousand young men in eighteen American cities turned in their draft cards to the organizers of the national Stop the Draft Week. The cards went to Washington, DC, where they were received by a group of intellectuals that included Yale chaplain William Sloan Coffin, Harvard professor George Williams, pediatrician Benjamin Spock, and novelist Norman Mailer. Leading a march to the Justice Department, the intellectuals declared that they supported the draft resisters and would be willing to be arrested for abetting those who had handed over the cards.

"In the face of what to us is insane and inhuman, we can fall neither silent nor servile," proclaimed Coffin, their chief spokesman. "Nor can we educate young men to be conscientious only to desert them in their hour of conscience." A Justice Department official agreed to meet with the group in a conference room, but he refused to take the draft cards or arrest any of the delivery men. Unprepared for such a tepid reaction, the intellectuals ended the matter by leaving the draft cards on the conference room table and walking out.[51]

Other antiwar activists organized a much larger rally in the nation's capital, scheduled for October 21. As the date approached,

U.S. Attorney General Ramsey Clark informed President Johnson that the participants would include droves of people from "extreme Left-wing groups with long lines of Communist affiliations." Clark assured the president that governmental efforts were underway to limit attendance by creating "other diversionary events on day and night of march." The Army Intelligence Command and the FBI dispatched plainclothes agents to infiltrate the protest groups and convinced a number of charter bus managers to cancel buses to Washington that would have carried protesters.[52]

Despite the administration's efforts, more than fifty thousand demonstrators attended the protest. Most were college students. Congregating at the Lincoln Memorial, they listened to speeches and music and took part in chants of the anti-draft slogan "Hell, no, we won't go!"

The words that attracted the most media attention came from Dr. Spock, the pediatrician who had risen to fame by authoring *The Common Sense Book of Baby and Child Care*, which had convinced millions of Americans to desist from corporal punishment of their children. "We don't consider the Vietnamese people—North or South—as the enemy," Spock's voice boomed over the loudspeakers. "They wish no harm to the United States. They are only defending their country from the unjust onslaught of arms and planes." In case anyone failed to infer the source of this injustice, Spock stated that "the enemy, we believe in all sincerity, is Lyndon Johnson, who we elected as a peace candidate in 1964 and who betrayed us within three months, who has stubbornly led us deeper and deeper into a bloody quagmire in which uncounted hundreds of thousands of Vietnamese men, women, and children have died, and 13,000 young Americans, too."[53]

Dr. Spock had apparently not been following recent North Vietnamese public rhetoric, much of which described the Hanoi government's objectives as offensive rather than defensive in nature and named the United States as the main target of the offensive activity. "The Vietnamese revolution is a component of world revolution and its successes have never been separated from the latter's," Le Duan had announced during one Radio Hanoi broadcast. "The tremendous strength of world revolution is none other than the integrated strength of the many political forces which from various directions attack U.S.-led imperialism."[54] During the fall, the chiefs of state of Indonesia, Malaysia, and Singapore were all expressing fear of North Vietnamese and Chinese offensive ambitions and saying that their countries would succumb to those ambitions if the United States withdrew from South Vietnam.[55]

After the speeches at the Lincoln Memorial, the demonstrators marched across the Memorial Bridge toward the Pentagon. Some were seen waving the flag of the National Liberation Front, half red and half blue with a yellow star in the middle. Others waved the flag of the United States.

At the Pentagon, protesters taunted the 2,500 soldiers who had been positioned around the building for protective purposes. Pulling up parking lot stakes, they lit bonfires, then tossed draft cards into the flames. On a few occasions, mobs tried to breach the line of soldiers, but were beaten back with rifle butts, night sticks, and fists. A small contingent from the Students for a Democratic Society that made it through a door into the Pentagon was quickly subdued and arrested by the Federal Marshals and military personnel inside. The authorities took at least 250 protesters into custody.[56]

A few days later, Johnson asked the CIA to assess the extent of foreign collusion with American antiwar groups. The CIA reported back that "contact between Hanoi and the leaders of the U.S. peace movement has developed to a point where it is now almost continuous." The CIA did not find evidence that the peace groups were under direct foreign control, but it did determine that American Communists were highly influential in the leadership of the antiwar organizations. Many of the organizers of the October 21 demonstration, the CIA concluded, had "known and associated with Communists and Communist-front groups over the years."[57]

To the North Vietnamese, the protests provided heartening evidence of declining will in the United States.[58] So did public polling that indicated the flagging of support for the war among the general U.S. population. In early November, public approval of LBJ's handling of Vietnam slumped to an all-time low of 23 percent.[59]

As Johnson himself recognized, presidential silence in the face of the protests was a central reason for the decrease in support for the commander in chief and the war. In a remarkable private meeting with Robert Manning of *The Atlantic* on October 19, Johnson admitted that he had avoided rallying the American people around the war because he "had to be careful not to get the country on an anti-communist binge." Such a binge, he said, would "tear up what we have gained with the USSR," such as the Consular Convention and the Treaty on the Non-Proliferation of Nuclear Weapons. "If history indicts us for Vietnam," Johnson confided to Manning, "it will be for fighting a war without trying to stir up patriotism."[60]

Because of his continued reluctance to speak to the American people on the war and his lack of confidence that McNamara and other cabinet officials would speak on his behalf, Johnson leaned again on Westmoreland.[61] The White House summoned Westmoreland and Bunker to the United States for ten days of public and media appearances, beginning on November 13. The two men were resolved to highlight the positive, because of both pressure from the White House and their own convictions that they needed to counteract unduly negative press coverage. "The media were inclined to accentuate the negative," Westmoreland later said of this period. "To balance the picture," he and other senior leaders "were prone and encouraged by Washington to accentuate the positive."[62]

During the scheduled appearances, Westmoreland and Bunker reported on gains in pacification and emphasized the effectiveness of Rolling Thunder in tying down North Vietnamese personnel and impeding infiltration. "I have never been more encouraged in my four years in Vietnam," Westmoreland pronounced at one gathering of reporters. On NBC's Meet the Press, he averred, "I find an attitude of confidence and growing optimism. It prevails all over the country, and to me this is the most significant evidence I can give you that constant, real progress is being made." He also ventured, albeit cautiously, into the forecasting of future U.S. commitments, stating, "It is conceivable that within two years or less the enemy will be so weakened that the Vietnamese will be able to cope with a greater share of the war burden."[63]

As Johnson had hoped, the upbeat performances of Westmoreland and Bunker were followed by an uptick in popular opinion. Between the beginning and end of November, public approval of Johnson's handling of the war rose from 23 percent to 34 percent.[64] Sentiment for escalating the war reached an unprecedented high, with 63 percent of Americans favoring heightened military action. When asked in December for their views on a ground invasion of North Vietnam, 49 percent of Americans said they favored it and only 29 percent were opposed.[65]

Johnson and the war effort also profited from a growing popular backlash against the antiwar movement. "A rising reaction against anti-Vietnam demonstrations is developing among the American people," pollster Louis Harris observed in December. The public had responded to the antiwar protests with "a firming up of support for President Johnson and the military effort in Vietnam." In a survey conducted by Harris, 76 percent of respondents said they believed that the recent antiwar demonstrations "encourage Communists to fight all the harder," and 68 percent thought that the demonstrations amounted to "acts of disloyalty against the boys in Vietnam."[66]

During Westmoreland's visit to Washington, he met privately with the Joint Chiefs to lay out his plans for the coming year. Those plans included ground operations into North Vietnam and Laos. Westmoreland's planners were drawing up Operation York, a multiphase operation that would culminate in the insertion of American troops by sea and air into southern North Vietnam.[67] They were also working on Operation El Paso, in which two American divisions and one South Vietnamese division would be airlifted into Laos. These divisions would establish bases along Route 9, from which they would attack enemy units and logistical complexes and block the road junctions at Tchepone, Muong Phine, and the Four Corners, the choke points transited by all southbound trucks on the Ho Chi Minh Trail. To keep the American and South Vietnamese divisions supplied, convoys of trucks would travel from South Vietnam into Laos on Route 9. Although the Laotian sections of Route 9 were in poor shape at the moment, American engineers believed they could make them passable by truck, with a capacity of 750 short tons per day, within three weeks.[68]

Ambassador Sullivan was at this same time making new arguments against the use of U.S. ground forces in Laos. The bombing of the Ho Chi Minh Trail was now spectacularly effective, he contended, so effective that it was preventing the delivery of virtually all cargo stockpiled by the North Vietnamese for transport during the dry season.[69] Reports from Chinese military observers, published by the Chinese government after the war, indicated that the bombing was indeed causing serious damage to supply shipments sent down the trail, destroying more than half the total cargo en route.[70] The rain-inducing Popeye and the mud-making Commando Lava, however, were not gumming up the infiltration routes. Although Popeye had succeeded in generating additional rainfall, Commando Lava had been unable to produce mud in the expected quantities.[71]

The trucks kept moving, and some of them kept making it through. By inserting more supplies at the top of the trail, the North Vietnamese were able to increase the amount that reached South Vietnam. As a North Vietnamese history would eventually reveal, the amount of supplies delivered to South Vietnam via the Ho Chi Minh Trail climbed to 25,536 tons in 1967, up from 7,903 in 1966.[72]

The subject of ground operations in North Vietnam, Laos, and Cambodia surfaced publicly at the end of November in a televised interview with two of America's most eminent national figures. One of them, Dwight Eisenhower, voiced strong support for incursions into these countries and belittled the notion that the United States had to honor national boundaries that the enemy had been dishonoring. "This respecting of boundary lines on a map, I think you can overdo it," the former president commented.[73]

The other man in the interview was General Omar Bradley, who like Eisenhower was one of only five men in American history to attain the rank of five-star general. In World War II, Bradley had commanded the Twelfth Army Group, whose fifty-four divisions constituted the largest U.S. military formation ever assembled, and after the war he had become the first chairman of the Joint Chiefs of Staff. Bradley focused his comments on the role of American willpower in ensuring victory. The North Vietnamese, he said, were counting on wearing down

America's will, as they had worn down France's. "I just don't believe the American people are that weak," asserted Bradley. "I think their fiber is stronger than that. They're not going to give up and get out."[74]

Westmoreland was still in Washington when one of the biggest battles of the year came to a climax. The origins of the clash dated back to the end of October, when U.S. signals intelligence and long-range reconnaissance patrols had revealed the departure of four North Vietnamese regiments from their bases in Cambodia and their passage across the South Vietnamese border into Kontum Province. The regiments were on a course for Dak To, a small town fifteen miles from the intersection of the Laotian, Cambodian, and South Vietnamese borders.[75]

As soon as this information reached the American 4th Infantry Division, the division commander rushed combat units to the defense of Dak To. The division's 1st Brigade moved by air to the Dak To Special Forces camp, where it set up its headquarters before dispatching infantrymen to reconnoiter the ridge lines and hills outside the town. American aircraft swept the area with infrared sensors and personnel detectors. Soon American headquarters were abuzz with reports of large enemy troop movements and the buildup of ammunition storage areas and base camps.[76] Why exactly the North Vietnamese Army was advancing on Dak To remained a puzzle to the Americans and the South Vietnamese.

The true intention of the North Vietnamese was to lure American and South Vietnamese forces into battle in the hills south of Dak To. Foreboding in appearance, those hills offered the North Vietnamese some of the best defensive terrain in all of South Vietnam. A dense canopy of teak and mahogany trees, up to two hundred feet in height, concealed the jungle floor from overhead view. Thickets of bamboos, vines, and shrubs grew beneath the trees, and between the flora flowed a multitude of streams and rivers that prevented rapid movement of troops on the ground. The red basalt soil was ideal for the digging of trenches, bunkers, and fighting positions.

The North Vietnamese high command entrusted the Dak To campaign to one of its best generals, Nguyen Huu An. Pulled from another unit, the general was put in command of the 1st NVA Division, to which the four participating regiments were attached. En route to the 1st Division's headquarters in Cambodia, Nguyen Huu An received reports of widespread illness and low morale in the unit. When he reached the division's headquarters, "the situation was even worse than had been reported," he recounted. "The soldiers lay motionless in the huts, those who were healthy as well as those who were ill, and a few of the men stood around in small groups outside the huts whispering together nonchalantly. I saw very few of the smiles that I expected on the faces of young men."

Part of the problem, Nguyen Huu An discovered, was the discrepancy between what soldiers had heard in training and indoctrination in the North and what they had seen of the war in the South. At training camps, propaganda cadres had spoken of glorious victories over American and South Vietnamese opponents and of the imminent unification of the country. When newly minted soldiers began the southward march, they told one another, "Move faster. If we're too slow all that will be left for us to do is pick up the used cartridge casings!"

As the infiltrators progressed down the Ho Chi Minh Trail, they ran into friends and acquaintances returning from the South, whose stories and missing limbs revealed a far different picture of the battlefield. The infiltrators held whisper sessions about each unpleasant story received from the veterans. "The rose-colored lenses they had been issued in the rear began to fall from their eyes," in the words of Nguyen Huu An.[77]

Through force of personality, Nguyen Huu An restored a measure of fighting spirit in the 1st Division. During the final days of October, the four infantry regiments under his command left their Cambodian bases and marched toward Dak To on mountain trails, which their officers named the Roads to the Annihilation of Americans. North Vietnamese artillerymen carried the disassembled pieces of pack howitzers and recoilless rifles, and supply personnel hauled ammunition and food on bicycles. Rainfall pelted the mountains, making dirt trails muddy and rock trails slippery. While traversing steep mountainsides, a number of the men lost their footing and fell to their deaths.

When the North Vietnamese regiments reached the jungled hills south of Dak To, they began building stout fortifications on the slopes. Nguyen Huu An expected his men to complete that task over a period of two weeks. Then, on November 15, they would fire the big guns at Dak To and the nearby base of Tan Canh to bait the Americans. When the Americans came to fight them in the hills, some of his infantry would be waiting for them in unexpectedly formidable entrenchments, and other North Vietnamese soldiers would emerge from nearby hiding places to attack the unsuspecting Americans from the flanks and rear. The North Vietnamese set a goal of crushing one to two American battalions in the first phase of the battle and another one to two of the American battalions that they anticipated would be sent as reinforcements after the initial drubbing.

Circumstances conspired to precipitate a clash of arms far sooner than Nguyen Huu An had desired. On November 2, with North Vietnamese units still arriving at the hills outside Dak To, a North Vietnamese soldier turned himself in to the Americans and spilled the entire North Vietnamese campaign plan. The soldier, Sergeant Vu Hong, testified that nine thousand North Vietnamese troops were converging on Dak To, and he supplied precise details on the locations and sizes of the intended North Vietnamese attacks.

At the headquarters of the 1st Brigade, 4th Infantry Division, Hong's story met skepticism from much of the staff. The young sergeant seemed to know too much for a man of his rank. It was just like the North Vietnamese to send a phony defector to mislead their adversaries about their plans. But when the Americans checked Sergeant Hong's information against other intelligence sources, those sources corroborated his story without exception. Once the Americans became convinced of the sergeant's veracity, they decided to move additional infantry battalions and artillery to Dak To to initiate preemptive attacks.

At the headquarters of the North Vietnamese Army's 1st Division, where Hong had worked, the sergeant's absence was quickly noticed. The possibility that someone with his comprehensive knowledge had defected or been captured alarmed the division's officers, all the way up to the commander. Nguyen Huu An recollected that when he learned of the sergeant's disappearance, "I felt as if my head were about to explode." Fearing that his units would soon come under American attack, Nguyen Huu An ordered all his soldiers to dig field fortifications and report any signs of enemy activity immediately.

By the next morning, Nguyen Huu An had received enough reports of American troop movements to leave no doubt that the Americans were sending forces to all the places where his 1st Division soldiers intended to go. For this reason, he altered his plan and accelerated its execution. The general directed his troops to remain in place and keep digging until they were well entrenched, at which time they were to use the advantages of terrain and fortification to repel any and all Americans who showed up. Those who could not build adequate fortifications before American forces arrived were to attack the Americans from the flanks and rear as soon as possible to prevent them from consolidating defensive positions.

The first contact took place on November 3. On a ridge south of Dak To, a battalion of the American 4th Infantry Division ran into a company from the 1st NVA Division that was in the process of digging trenches. Throwing down their spades and grabbing their weapons, the North Vietnamese generated enough gunfire to dissuade the Americans from charging into them. The American battalion commander ordered his soldiers to pull back so that he could soften up the North Vietnamese with artillery and tactical air strikes.

Following the barrage, the American infantry assaulted the North Vietnamese position but found that enemy resistance remained stiff. Again, the American commander drew his troops back and summoned artillery shells and bombs. After this bombardment, the American infantry were able to dislodge the North Vietnamese from the ridge. The Americans lost four killed and counted thirteen North Vietnamese bodies, though they believed that many more North Vietnamese had been dragged away or entombed in rubble. In an omen of the battles to come, the Americans discovered that the North Vietnamese fighting positions had been encased in thick mahogany logs, hewn from the surrounding forest with handsaws, which protected the occupants from most anything other than a direct hit by a bomb or artillery shell.

For the next two weeks, similar scenes played out intermittently in the hills above Dak To. After American infantry located North Vietnamese positions, they scurried away and watched American bombs and defoliants clear the vegetation concealing North Vietnamese positions. In some instances, napalm was employed to incinerate bunkers and their occupants. American infantry attacks followed, and the cycle was repeated until the North Vietnamese were too feeble to ward off a concerted assault. North Vietnamese losses greatly outnumbered those of the Americans and South Vietnamese.

On November 14, Nguyen Huu An decided that it was time to draw American forces toward Hill 875. This hill, which was farther from Dak To than the other hills his troops had occupied, had not yet felt the sting of any weapon. North Vietnamese soldiers and engineers had been fortifying it undisturbed for the full two weeks of labor Nguyen Huu An had originally wanted for all his forces. Hill 875 overlooked a valley that could serve as an escape route for North Vietnamese forces withdrawing from Dak To to Cambodia and hence would be coveted by both sides when the North Vietnamese attempted to return to their sanctuary.

The North Vietnamese had constructed an elaborate underground fortress on Hill 875, excavating layers of combat trenches and a series of deep communications trenches that enabled their occupants to mass and fight on all four sides. Along the back wall of the trenches were small holes where soldiers could take refuge during a bombardment. The North Vietnamese dug bunkers beneath the roots of wide trees to provide both concealment and cover, and they burrowed a tunnel into the bowels of the hill for storing food and water and sheltering the wounded.[78]

In preparation for what he expected to be the climactic battle, Nguyen Huu An massed several thousand troops in concealed positions on and around Hill 875. To trick the Americans into sending a relatively small force to the hill, North Vietnamese radio operators sent out messages indicating that a much smaller force held the hill, and the North Vietnamese units on the hill were instructed to direct only modest volumes of fire at the Americans when they first came. Once the American troops began climbing the slopes, the bulk of Nguyen Huu An's division would pounce on them from all sides.

On November 18, the Americans decided to take Hill 875 after receiving intelligence reports that it was occupied by the battered remnants of the 66th NVA Regiment. As Nguyen Huu An had hoped, underestimation of North Vietnamese strength caused the Americans to send only one battalion. Brigadier General Leo H. Schweiter, commander of the 173rd Airborne Brigade, dispatched the 2nd Battalion of the 503rd Infantry to take Hill 875 and destroy the retreating North Vietnamese before they could escape to Cambodia.

The 2nd of the 503rd had arrived at Dak To two weeks earlier with 450 troops, but by this time the hill fighting had whittled down its strength to 290. On the evening of November 18, the battalion's three companies encamped 750 meters north of Hill 875. Lieutenant Colonel James R. Steverson, the battalion commander, met with his company commanders to review the plan of attack. They would move out early in the morning in a standard infantry formation, with two companies assaulting up the north slope of Hill 875 and the third remaining in reserve at the encampment. "If you run into any heavy contact, pull back," Steverson said. "Then we'll bomb the shit out of them."[79]

The night passed uneventfully. Early on the morning of November 19, the battalion's forty-year-old Catholic chaplain, Major Charles J. Watters, held a mass. Attendance was unusually high, with many non-Catholics attending. After the service, quiet prevailed across the battalion, save for the sounds of the packing of gear.

Soon after sunrise, Charlie and Dog companies marched out, watched by the men of Alpha company, the battalion's reserve. As the soldiers carried their heavy packs toward Hill 875, they heard the jet engines of F-100 Super Sabres screaming past, then saw the aircraft drop cluster bombs on the face of the hill. Next came artillery strikes.

The two American companies began clambering up the hill at 0943. No one spoke. Ahead, they saw piles of leaflets strewn across the hillside. "You are here under the orders of your Imperialist Government," the leaflets read in English. "Sit down and hold your weapon over your head. You will not be shot."

The words did not scare Specialist 4 Raymond Zaccone, but the presence of the leaflets did. If the leaflets were here, he thought, then the North Vietnamese who had put them on the ground must be nearby. In an effort to calm his nerves, Zaccone recited a refrain that had become popular among the American infantry: "Yea, though I walk through the Valley of the Shadow of Death, I will fear no evil for I am the meanest motherfucker in the valley."[80]

At 1030, the point teams reached a clearing in the vegetation, newly created by the detonation of American bombs. When a few men ventured into the open space, the wall of jungle in front of them erupted in gunfire. The North Vietnamese aimed three shots at the foremost American, Specialist Kenneth Jacobson, and at least one bullet hit him in the head. A medic, seeing blood and brains spray from Jacobson's head, crawled toward him. The medic was promptly shot dead.

The other Americans scrambled for cover. Unable to see any of their foes, they loosed bullets in what sounded like the direction of the hostile fire. The North Vietnamese weaponry was roaring more loudly than most of the Americans had ever heard, despite Nguyen Huu An's injunction to his troops to begin the battle with only modest doses of bullets. The American return fire was not nearly as boisterous at first, but gradually it crescendoed as more paratroopers moved up the slope to the front line.

Lieutenant Colonel Steverson, who was flying overhead in a command-and-control helicopter, ordered the two companies to press forward. One of the men on the ground radioed Steverson a reminder that he had directed them to pull back if they made heavy contact with the enemy. Unconvinced that the current situation amounted to heavy contact, Steverson replied that the companies should advance.

At a lull in enemy fire, the paratroopers began another ascent. The first platoon to move ahead was stopped after five meters by bursts of bullets. One of the company commanders urged Steverson to withdraw the troops to a lower elevation and inundate the enemy with artillery and bombs, and this time the battalion commander consented. After the American platoons moved down the slope, they popped smoke and told friendly aircraft to drop their bombs above the smoke clouds.

Following the bombardment, the paratroopers endeavored to advance up the hill again. After thirty meters, hostile fire compelled them to halt, at which time Steverson ordered another round of air strikes. At 1258, four F-100s commenced bombing and strafing runs that lasted nearly an hour. The Americans drove forward again.

With the two American companies now well up the hillside, Nguyen Huu An unleashed the units that he had hidden nearby to attack the American flanks and rear. Making use of tunnels, North Vietnamese soldiers emerged from bunkers that the Americans had cleared on their way up. When Charlie and Dog companies realize they were under attack from all sides, they ceased all efforts to climb the hill and braced to defend themselves. Steverson ordered Alpha company to head from the encampment site to Hill 875 to assist Charlie and Dog.

Alpha company had to cross 750 meters to the reach the hill. After only a few hundred meters, a huge cluster of North Vietnamese infantry emerged from trees on the western side of the hill and burst into its flank. North Vietnamese soldiers overwhelmed Alpha company's command group, killing the company commander and everyone else. The company, however, remained intact, and it was able to reach the hill with the help of Private First Class Carlos J. Lozada, who kept large numbers of North Vietnamese occupied for several minutes with his M-60 machine gun while the rest of Alpha company moved toward Charlie and Dog companies. Refusing to fall back, Lozada was eventually shot dead by the North Vietnamese. He received the Medal of Honor posthumously.

The survivors of Alpha company battled their way up the hill until they reached the rest of their battalion. The new arrivals thickened the defensive perimeter while air strikes punished the rest of the hill. In the late afternoon, the American officers decided to hunker down for the night and resume the attack up the hill in the morning with the help of reinforcements that were reported to be on their way. The battalion had sustained between thirty and forty killed and one hundred wounded during the day's fighting.

Just before 7:00 p.m., a propeller-driven American aircraft flew over Hill 875 on a bombing run, locating its target by its proximity to a burning fire that a previous aircraft had set as a reference point. Unbeknownst to the pilot, the fire identified previously had burned out and a new one had started in a different location. As a consequence, the pilot bombed the wrong patch of ground. That patch happened to be the American battalion's aid station.

The blast killed twenty men and wounded somewhere between twenty and thirty. The fatalities included Captain Harold J. Kaufman, who as the commander of Charlie company had been the senior infantry officer on the ground, and Major Watters, the chaplain. Watters had left the American perimeter six times that day to retrieve wounded paratroopers, for which he would receive a posthumous Medal of Honor.

The friendly fire disaster ensured that the Americans could not collect all their dead and wounded before nightfall. It also destroyed ammunition reserves and decimated the battalion's medical staff. Only two of thirteen medics remained alive, and both of them were wounded.

The Americans expected the North Vietnamese to attack after dark. They consolidated their perimeter and prepared to fight a pauper's battle, firing their small remaining supply of ammunition only when absolutely necessary. "If the NVA had known how little ammunition we had," Sergeant Ed Placencia said later, "they surely would have overrun us."[81]

Nguyen Huu An had decided to wait until the morning to renew the fight. During the night, he concerned himself with setting favorable conditions for the next round. He ordered his troops to fire at American soldiers who attempted to leave their perimeter in the dark to retrieve their wounded. By keeping wounded Americans stranded in no-man's land, Nguyen Huu An would compel the Americans to attack into that space in the morning, exposing them to further damage.

The next morning, however, the American battalion's ammunition shortage prevented it from launching any attacks. Helicopters arrived to deliver supplies and troops, but a fierce North Vietnamese response forced them to turn back. The beleaguered paratroop battalion remained in a defensive crouch throughout the morning and early afternoon, awaiting the arrival of reinforcements on the ground.

The 4th Battalion, 503rd Infantry had departed its encampment for Hill 875 that morning. After a grueling march through thick jungle, the battalion reached the hill at 4:00 p.m. Nguyen Huu An, having already lost many of his troops and having expended large quantities of his ammunition, did not attack the newcomers as they ascended the hill to link up with the beleaguered American battalion. He would wait for the Americans to attack his entrenched units farther up the hill. The two American battalions spent the evening enlarging landing zones for aircraft to bring in supplies and evacuate the wounded.

The next morning, American aircraft collected in the skies above Hill 875 and took turns plastering it with their most destructive armaments. Over a six-hour period, they deposited fifteen tons of bombs and seven tons of napalm on suspected enemy positions, including some that were very near the American infantry. "The strikes were so close that the impact of the rounds lifted you off the ground," remembered Lieutenant Mercer Vandenberg. "I prayed we'd only find pulverized dirt on top of the hill."[82]

At three in the afternoon, the aerial symphony came to an end, which was the cue for the 4th Battalion of the 503rd to charge up the hill. One company headed straight for the summit at a brisk pace while another advanced on its left flank. They soon ran into enemy entrenchments that remained camouflaged, fortified, and occupied by living men. American paratroopers fell in substantial numbers to small arms and to the North Vietnamese mortar rounds that began landing in the middle of their formations. Grenades flew profusely in both directions. The throwing of grenades into narrow North Vietnamese firing slits often provided the sole means by which the Americans could advance.

For the next two hours, the Americans clawed slowly up the hill in bitter fighting. Just as they appeared to be on the verge of taking the hilltop, they were ordered to pull back so that air and artillery could pound the remaining defenders one more time. Some of the paratroopers believed that they could take the hill quickly by pressing on, but they were overruled by officers at higher headquarters who preferred the less costly and risky approach of blasting the summit and waiting until morning to make the final charge.

Late in the day, Nguyen Huu An climbed an observation post near Hill 875 to survey the battlefield through his binoculars.

He barely recognized the terrain. "When we had conducted our reconnaissance of the area, the entire wide Hill 875 area had been covered in groves of bamboo and thick clusters of jungle trees," he related. "Now the green had been stripped from the ground, exposing the raw, red dirt, almost the color of blood. Our troops in the fortified position on the top of the hill had to camouflage their positions with charred tree trunks. Many sections of their trenches had been plowed flat by the bombing."[83]

On the morning of November 22, two fresh companies from the 4th Infantry Division arrived by helicopter to take part in the coup de grâce. By midmorning, these companies were making their way up the south slope of Hill 875. Encountering concerted North Vietnamese opposition near the top of the hill, they methodically drove the North Vietnamese from their last strongpoints, in some cases battling the North Vietnamese hand-to-hand inside their trenches. Once more, the American infantrymen were nearly to the finish line when, in the interest of limiting friendly casualties, they were withdrawn so that one more dose of destruction could be administered from above. Silver canisters of napalm tumbled onto the hilltop, scorching the last remaining teak trees.

At 1300, Nguyen Huu An convened his officers. The time had come, he said, to withdraw from Dak To. "The objectives of the campaign have been achieved," he explained. The division had "completely annihilated two U.S. battalions" and "inflicted heavy casualties on a number of other U.S. battalions." It is not known whether he mentioned the most compelling reason for the withdrawal, one he disclosed after the war. The division had to depart at this juncture, Nguyen Huu An wrote in his autobiography, because "we had expended all our supplies."[84]

By design or not, Nguyen Huu An had grossly exaggerated the damage his division had inflicted on the Americans. The 2nd

Battalion of the 503rd Infantry, which had borne the brunt of the North Vietnamese wrath after stepping into Nguyen Huu An's elaborate trap, had sustained 95 killed, of whom 20 had been the victims of the friendly fire incident. The 4th Battalion of the 503rd Infantry had lost 18 killed in action. These two battalions had killed a reported 322 North Vietnamese soldiers.

For the three-week Dak To campaign as a whole, the official American toll listed 2,188 North Vietnamese killed against 283 Americans and 61 South Vietnamese. As was often the case, the American figures on North Vietnamese dead included estimates of the numbers who had been blown apart beyond recognition, hauled away by their comrades, or killed in areas never searched by American troops. According to an American intelligence report, the 1st Division of the North Vietnamese Army had entered South Vietnam with 6,600 troops and retreated with 5,000. If that report was indeed accurate and those were the only troops fighting at Dak To, then the American tally of 2,188 total enemy killed was 37 percent higher than the actual total of 1,600, a significant rate of inflation, though not as egregious as what skeptics often presumed to be standard U.S. practice. It is possible, though, that considerable numbers of additional North Vietnamese troops had taken part in the battle, as was suggested by the statement of the well-informed Vu Hong that a force of nine thousand was attacking Dak To, and thus the communications intercepts did not tell the full extent of North Vietnamese losses.[85]

At Dak To, the North Vietnamese had once again determined the place of battle and compelled the Americans to fight in terrain advantageous to the North Vietnamese. That fact attracted more attention than the tactical benefits the Americans had gained by striking the NVA division before it had been able to entrench itself. The American and South Vietnamese casualties incurred during the battle provoked a resurgence in grumbling about Westmoreland's tactic of fighting enemy forces any time they showed up near a border. The disparagement of this tactic received so much attention that Westmoreland decided to pen a forceful riposte, which he forwarded to General Wheeler.

The document was one of the most persuasive defenses of American tactics in Vietnam that Westmoreland ever produced. If allied forces allowed the North Vietnamese to run free near South Vietnam's borders, he penned, they would overrun government bases and towns, reaping propaganda victories and demoralizing the South Vietnamese. Left unchecked, the North Vietnamese could creep from the border regions to populous areas in the country's interior, where the allies could not employ their air and artillery as freely and where the enemy could take food from the population. North Vietnamese divisions that had reached the country's interior were inflicting casualties on U.S. forces in proportions similar to those at Dak To and were tying down American divisions for many months, whereas the U.S. forces sent to Dak To were able to go back to other missions after just three weeks.[86]

Once Nguyen Huu An's 1st Division left Dak To, American intelligence tracked it back to its Cambodian sanctuary. Through shallow incursions across the Cambodian border, American reconnaissance teams from the Studies and Observation Group located the division's base camps. In early December, Westmoreland requested permission to bomb the division inside Cambodia with B-52 bombers for at least seventy-two hours.[87]

"The enemy's dangerous activities fulfill all the criteria for substantiating the hot pursuit concept," Westmoreland apprised the Joint Chiefs of Staff. "Reports state that enemy units are not disposed in an alert or defensive posture; rather, they are utilizing their Cambodian sanctuary to rest, regroup and reconstitute openly and unmolested. There is no evidence of heavy bunker construction." Because the area was remote, Westmoreland pointed out, it was free of civilian bystanders, and free of impartial observers who would report the arrival of American bombers. Admiral Sharp and Ambassador Bunker endorsed Westmoreland's recommendation.[88]

Within hours of receipt of Westmoreland's recommendation, President Johnson sat down with his senior advisers in the White House to discuss it. "These are the troops who were defeated at Dak To," General Wheeler explained to the president. "They are licking their wounds and getting re-equipped and having their manpower replenished." Once the North Vietnamese division recuperated, it "will come out of Cambodia and attack our men." In response to a question from the president about the expected results of the air strikes, Wheeler said that Westmoreland hoped that they would kill five hundred troops and raze enemy supply depots and transportation infrastructure.

"How long can we let Sihanouk get away with giving the enemy this type of protection?" Johnson demanded of his civilian advisers.

Secretary of State Rusk spoke up against a tougher Cambodian policy. "The action which General Westmoreland is proposing would be a significant act of war against Cambodia," he posited. "This would change the entire character of the war. If Cambodia is attacked, they may ask the Chinese to side with them. Then we will really have a new war on our hands."

"Aware as I am of the mistakes generals have made in the past, I place great confidence in General Westmoreland," the president told the group. "Both he and Ambassador Bunker have recommended this action. We must tell Cambodia that we will not continue to permit them to house and protect these killers."

McNamara came down on the side of Rusk. "I believe, Mr. President, that it is most unwise to expand the war beyond the

South Vietnamese borders," the secretary of defense remarked. "This action would further divide this nation. This action would further increase our problems in the United Nations."

"The Joint Chiefs do not want to widen the war either," Wheeler countered. "We only wish Cambodia would be neutral—honest to God neutral, too. Anyone else would not permit enemy troops to use their territory for sanctuaries."

Johnson weighed the arguments for and against. "I do not look forward to the day when somebody will say that General Westmoreland asked for this action and we refused it and then a lot of American boys were killed as a result," he said. And yet, "this act could result in Cambodia declaring war against us and in their inviting the Chinese in."

Clark Clifford came up with something of a compromise. Rather than dropping bombs on the North Vietnamese division, the United States should take pictures of the North Vietnamese forces from aircraft and then use the photos to pressure the Cambodian government into evicting the North Vietnamese.

Johnson found Clifford's idea appealing. At the conclusion of the discussion, the president ordered the collection of photographic evidence of the North Vietnamese presence in Cambodia for presentation to Sihanouk. "I think we have been derelict in our duty in bringing this thing to a head," he asserted as they adjourned. "Let's give it top priority."[89]

The Americans subsequently sent photographs of the North Vietnamese division's presence to Sihanouk. The Cambodian leader talked with an American diplomat and offered promises to address the problem, then did nothing to fulfill those promises. Johnson complained about Sihanouk's inaction in private but took no action himself.[90]

Johnson's reluctance to act in Cambodia and the fear of Chinese intervention that drove it might have been considerably less had the White House been better informed on the deterioration of relations between China and North Vietnam at this time. The continuation of China's Cultural Revolution had repeatedly injected poison into those relations over the course of 1967. Through official party media organs, Chinese and Vietnamese officials were exchanging rhetorical grenades. One North Vietnamese Communist Party mouthpiece contrasted the virtues of Ho Chi Minh with a leader who went unnamed but sounded suspiciously like Mao. "If a certain leader, at a certain time, regardless of the objective rules and the objective situation, acts in accordance with his subjective wishes, he will not be able to avoid falling into a situation in which every move will be in vain, like Don Quixote's struggle against the windmill," the author wrote. "The Marxist-Leninist parties set forth the principle of collective leadership," the article stated, in order to prevent "one-sided and erroneous decisions."[91]

By turning the Chinese Communist Party inward to deal with alleged cancers in the body politic, the Cultural Revolution had diminished the interest of China's leaders in ideological crusades abroad. China's capabilities for supporting such crusades, moreover, had been reduced by purges in the security apparatus and by the economic regression resulting from the upheaval.[92] When the North Vietnamese Politburo sent a delegation to China in the summer of 1967 to request weapons, ammunition, and other aid, the North Vietnamese diplomats found the Chinese bereft of any desire to fight the Americans or their allies in Cambodia, Laos, or Vietnam. The Chinese recommended that the North Vietnamese concentrate their military activities in southern South Vietnam and avoid large attacks in northern South Vietnam, which convinced the North Vietnamese diplomats, in the words of one of their number, that the Chinese "are afraid that if we make powerful attacks in the north, the enemy will invade North Vietnam and there will be a danger that China might become involved."[93]

Ongoing American disputes over intelligence on the Communist powers were supplemented by several new intelligence controversies concerning South Vietnam in the last months of 1967. Westmoreland's MACV and the CIA became embroiled in a row over which categories of enemy personnel should be included in the order of battle, the military's term for the roster of enemy combatants. Several CIA analysts sparked the quarrel by proposing the inclusion of approximately two hundred thousand personnel from the categories of political cadres, self-defense forces, and secret self-defense forces.

Westmoreland, Bunker, and a large number of intelligence experts objected to the CIA's proposal on the grounds that information on these categories was sketchy and individuals in these categories did not pose a direct threat to U.S. forces because they were typically unarmed civilians who provided intermittent support to the Communists. Westmoreland and Bunker also worried that suddenly adding two hundred thousand people to the order of battle would be misconstrued by the press as evidence that the enemy was getting stronger, when in fact enemy strength had begun to diminish in March.[94]

During September, the CIA leadership and Westmoreland's intelligence officers came to an agreement to exclude the civilian categories from the order of battle.[95] By the end of the year, the controversy had receded. It would have remained a very small part of the Vietnam story had it not been for the zeal of one of the CIA analysts, Samuel Adams, who for years afterward accused Westmoreland and other officials of conspiring to conceal the enemy's true strength from the White House and the American people. Adams's efforts would reach their apex in a postwar CBS News program in which journalist Mike Wallace alleged that "a conspiracy at the highest levels of American military intelligence" had sought to "suppress and alter critical intelligence on the enemy."

The CBS documentary would insinuate that Westmoreland had suppressed intelligence reports indicating that the North Vietnamese possessed two hundred thousand more troops than previously recognized and were infiltrating twenty-five thousand men per month in late 1967. To keep President Johnson and the American people in the dark, it was alleged, Westmoreland had compelled his staff to keep estimates of enemy troop strength below three hundred thousand by reducing estimates of guerrillas and excluding the self-defense personnel from the order of battle. Lieutenant Colonel Everette Parkins and Lieutenant Richard McArthur were reportedly fired for refusing to bow to pressure to reduce the estimates.[96]

Westmoreland, by then in retirement, believed that the documentary's producers had twisted the facts so egregiously that he sued CBS for libel. The case went to trial, resulting in the declassification of vast numbers of documents and the recording of statements from a multitude of first-hand witnesses. Westmoreland ultimately was unable to collect damages because it required demonstrating that CBS had acted out of malicious intent, which his lawyers were unable to demonstrate. But the case did reveal a host of inaccuracies in the CBS production and in the narrative of Sam Adams that undergirded it.[97]

The CBS defense lawyers produced documents and witnesses showing that Westmoreland had tried on occasion to limit the estimated size of enemy forces, including political cadres, to three hundred thousand in the summer of 1967. Several members of his intelligence staff testified that estimates of support troop and irregular categories were kept lower than some analysts would have liked.[98] The evidence also showed, however, that

Westmoreland had assented to an intelligence estimate that exceeded the three hundred thousand ceiling.[99]

Affidavits from key witnesses undermined the accusations that Westmoreland had compelled subordinates to falsify or suppress information. Everette Parkins attested that he had neither been pressured into reporting false numbers nor fired for refusing to participate in a conspiracy.[100] Another witness recounted that Lieutenant Richard McArthur had been relieved not because he objected to Westmoreland's numbers but because he had developed a drinking problem and had disappeared for three days without telling anyone.[101] Walt Rostow and several other witnesses stated that Westmoreland had hidden none of the details of the debate from President Johnson.[102]

The lawsuit also revealed that in the summer of 1967, American intelligence analysts had investigated the question of whether the two hundred thousand political cadres, self-defense forces, and secret self-defense forces posed a sufficient threat to American and South Vietnamese units to qualify as combatants. The analysts had concluded that these groups did not post such a threat, except in a few places in the Mekong Delta where they had fired potshots at South Vietnamese Army patrols.[103] John L. Hart, who had been the CIA station chief in Saigon in 1967, excoriated Sam Adams and CBS for exaggerating the importance of these groups in a *Washington Post* op-ed published during the trial. "In redefining and narrowing his count of the enemy," Hart wrote, "Westmoreland was not simply exercising a prerogative, but, more important, fulfilling a duty, when he specified which enemy forces were crucial to North Vietnam's conquest of the South, and which were not." Hart, like Westmoreland, had concluded that the enemy's conventional warfare had long since supplanted guerrilla warfare as the principal threat to South Vietnam, and "it was not therefore Westmoreland's revised order of battle, but rather those persons who overvalued the people's revolution in the South as against the invasion from the North who, if you will pardon the expression, 'misled the president.'"[104]

The evidence accumulated for the trial revealed that the estimates of twenty-five thousand infiltrators per month in late 1967 had come from a few analysts who had extrapolated from prisoner interrogations, captured documents, and agent reports. Those analysts had not taken into account other relevant information, particularly classified signals intelligence, because they had not possessed access to that information.[105] During 1967, the North Vietnamese infiltration command had increased its use of unenciphered voice communications in order to transmit information more rapidly, enabling the U.S. National Security Agency to intercept and analyze a multitude of messages on the North-South infiltration. This intelligence gold mine, nicknamed the "Vinh Window," was rich enough to permit a precise count of the human traffic on the Ho Chi Minh Trail by the fall of 1967.[106] During the last four months of 1967, according to the Vinh Window data, the monthly average of North Vietnamese infiltration was 7,387. This information had led Westmoreland and others with access to it to discount the estimate of 25,000 per week.[107]

The dispute over the size of the order of battle obscured the fact that Adams and others at the CIA did not differ much from Westmoreland's intelligence staff in their estimates of what were universally recognized as the enemy's principal fighting forces: the regulars, guerrillas, and support troops. According to American estimates, the strength of those forces fell from 278,000 to 220,000 between the beginning and end of 1967. Total enemy strength, which also included the political cadres and self-defense forces, declined by roughly 55,000 during the year.[108] Revised estimates, produced several years later on the basis of additional information, found that the number of enemy combatants had not fallen as sharply during the year, declining from 290,000 to 262,000.[109]

The CIA also concurred in the U.S. military's estimates of enemy manpower losses for 1967, which totaled 169,000. That amount consisted of approximately 88,000 killed, 32,000 permanently lost from wounds, 18,000 defected, 7,000 taken prisoner, and 24,000 non-battle casualties. The tendency of some South Vietnamese and Americans to inflate enemy casualty numbers would eventually generate considerable skepticism about the accuracy of the aggregate figures, but these figures were not based solely on the reports of enemy casualties in combat engagements. They reflected, in addition, information contained in captured Communist documents, which in general showed that American estimates of Communist losses were fairly close to the Communists' own numbers.[110]

No one on the American side possessed solid information on the other key manpower figure, Communist recruitment in the South. In November, the intelligence community consensus placed enemy recruitment for the main, local, and guerrilla forces for 1967 at somewhere between thirty-six thousand and sixty thousand, a sharp drop from the estimate for 1966.[111] Revelations that came, much later, from North Vietnamese sources would suggest that Communist recruitment in the South fell much further during 1967 than U.S. intelligence officials realized. According to the official history of the North Vietnamese Army, the Communists recruited just 7,600 new troops in South Vietnam in 1967.[112] Another account noted that in the B2 theater, covering the southern half of South Vietnam, local recruitment plummeted from 6,351 in 1966 to just 1,000 in 1967.[113] These figures probably did not include individuals recruited as guerrillas, support troops, or political cadres, but they did offer compelling evidence of a precipitous fall in overall recruitment.

The plunging of Communist recruitment in the South constituted one of the most important developments of the year, as it multiplied Hanoi's manpower difficulties at a time of severe combat losses and simultaneously facilitated the inflow of more young men into the South Vietnamese armed forces. It reflected the reduced access of Communist recruiters to the population as well as the diminishing attractiveness of service in a cause that had suffered one military setback after another. The root cause of these developments was the heightened involvement of American ground forces in ejecting Communist forces from South Vietnam's villages.[114]

According to U.S. estimates, the number of South Vietnamese citizens living in areas under governmental control increased by 1.2 million over the course of 1967. The proportion of those experiencing this change without the trauma of relocation was higher than in prior years; 61 percent of the total remained in their villages as the South Vietnamese government took charge of security and governance, while only 39 percent migrated from Communist-held villages to towns or cities.[115] North Vietnamese figures suggest that the shift in control of the rural population may have been even greater than the American estimators realized. In the B2 theater, the only region for which statistics were published, the North Vietnamese recorded a decline in the population living in "liberated" or "contested" zones from 5.6 million to 3.4 million during the year.[116]

The other big intelligence controversy of late 1967 concerned Hanoi's military intentions in the coming year. In November, U.S. intelligence agencies obtained numerous Communist documents that pointed toward a large-scale offensive in early 1968. An unusually high volume of probing attacks on district and provincial capitals gave cause for speculation that the Communists were sharpening their knives in preparation for powerful slashes at the urban centers.[117]

On November 19, the U.S. 101st Airborne Division captured a North Vietnamese cadre's notebook that described orders for "a general offensive and general uprising in order to achieve a decisive victory for the Revolution within the 1967 Winter and 1968 Spring and Summer." According to the notebook, the North Vietnamese central command had directed its forces to "use very strong military attacks in coordination with the uprisings of the local population to take over towns and cities. Troops should flood the lowlands. They should move toward liberating the capital city [Saigon], take power and try to rally enemy brigades and regiments to our side one by one."[118]

This discovery, along with other recent finds, led CIA analyst Joseph Hovey to predict that the North Vietnamese intended to strike South Vietnam's towns and cities in January 1968. Hovey's report went to Westmoreland in late November and, on December 15, to President Johnson. Other CIA analysts, however, found fault with Hovey's analysis. Signals intelligence unavailable to Hovey, they said, contradicted his predictions. With these criticisms attached, the report lost credibility in Saigon and Washington. Most U.S. military and intelligence officials concluded that the North Vietnamese were gearing up for intensified military action in the areas where they had been most active in 1967, the northern provinces and the border regions.[119]

North Vietnam had its own intelligence controversies with respect to the upcoming offensive. Communist cadres who traveled from South Vietnam to Hanoi late in the year to brief the Politburo presented conflicting estimates of the offensive's prospects. Some expressed confidence that the offensive would result in urban uprisings and the annihilation of the South Vietnamese government. Others said that they were not sure whether the masses would rise up or whether the attacking troops could hold their ground in the towns and cities.[120]

In some of Hanoi's elite circles, worries about the fate of the offensive exacerbated a sense of angst that had been built up over time by the destructiveness of Rolling Thunder in the North and the American scything of North Vietnamese forces in the South. To avert further devastation, some North Vietnamese officials had begun recommending peace negotiations with the United States. Regime hardliners were alarmed by the prevalence of this sentiment and by reports that those who favored negotiations were colluding with the Soviets. According to some of the Hanoi government's secret sources, a cabal of pro-Soviet North Vietnamese leaders was plotting to overthrow the leadership of the Vietnamese Communist Party.

The hardline elements become so fearful near year's end that they decided to unleash the internal security services. The secret police arrested three hundred military officers, civil officials, professors, writers, and journalists on suspicion of conspiring with the Soviets. Roughly thirty were senior party figures and several had close ties to General Giap. Later it was learned that the interrogators had grilled the detainees about Giap's involvement in the pro-Soviet plot. Apparently the interrogators did not obtain much incriminating information, for Giap was not arrested.[121] The regime also cracked down on suspected oppositionists in the general population. Near the end of 1967, it sent 230,000 people to "reformatories" for their alleged opposition to the government.[122]

Although the rounding up of the Soviet Union's friends in Hanoi surely displeased Soviet leaders, it did not cause them to shut off the flow of aid to North Vietnam. In the last months of 1967, Soviet ships were docking at Haiphong to unload unprecedented quantities of military hardware, most of which Hanoi intended to use in the upcoming offensive. The cargo manifests included aircraft, antiaircraft weapons, artillery, ammunition, oil products, ferrous and nonferrous metals, medical supplies, and food. Soviet aid to North Vietnam, which had accounted for 37 percent of aid received by North Vietnam at the beginning of 1967, amounted to half the total by the end of the year.[123]

On December 30, North Vietnamese Foreign Minister Nguyen Duy Trinh issued a public statement on negotiations. It was intended to distract the United States and counteract the impression in other countries that the Americans were more interested than the North Vietnamese in peace. "After the United States ceases, without conditions, the bombings and any other acts of war against the DRV, the DRV will talk to the United States on appropriate questions," the foreign minister said. The rhetoric made little impression on the Johnson administration, which had been receiving the same one-sided offer since the middle of 1965, though the mere fact of its enunciation aroused interest in the West among the minority that trusted the leaders in Hanoi more than those in Washington.

After the speech, a Vietnamese Communist leader in Hanoi confided to a Soviet diplomat that the foreign minister's statement was a "propaganda ball" tossed up in response to the "balls" floated by President Johnson. "The talks will begin," Dong said, "when the Americans have inflicted a defeat on us or when we have inflicted a defeat on them. Everything will be resolved on the battlefield."[124]

CHAPTER 12

. . .

TET

January 1968

Major James F. MacGill of Fayetteville, North Carolina, awoke on January 31 at his usual hour of 6:00 a.m., shaved, and donned his uniform. He then walked to the tactical operations center of his battalion, the 3/7 Infantry Battalion of the 199th Light Infantry Brigade. The battalion was nicknamed the Cottonbaler Battalion, because in 1815 it had fended off the British at New Orleans from breastworks made of cotton bales. With the Tet holiday truce in effect, MacGill expected to find the operations center quiet and uneventful. Instead, he discovered a hive of activity, the staff bustling with nervous energy, fielding an inundation of reports concerning hostile forces and combat.

"Every unit that we could talk to or heard about was in contact with the enemy," MacGill remembered. "We were wondering why we were the only ones who were not in contact."[1]

At 0808, the Cottonbaler Battalion received an urgent call for help from Saigon. A platoon of U.S. military policemen was surrounded and under attack near the Phu Tho racetrack. The battalion commander, Lt. Col. John K. Gibler, decided to launch a relief operation, which he entrusted to his best company, led by

Captain Antonio V. Smaldone. In the eyes of Gibler and MacGill, Smaldone personified the great combat leader who thrived in war and who would have gone nowhere in the peacetime military.

Smaldone loaded his company aboard a convoy of trucks and armored personnel carriers. MacGill, in the meantime, boarded an OH-23 light observation helicopter to oversee the operation. As the battalion's operations officer, MacGill was to scout the battlefield and direct the movements of the battalion's other two companies, which were preparing to be airlifted into the city. By the time the vehicles were ready to depart the base, the sun had floated well above the horizon, and MacGill could see plumes of smoke jetting upward from Saigon.

Setting off at 0905, the ground vehicles drove in a single file at thirty miles per hour. The trip to the Phu Tho racetrack, a straight shot up Highway 4, was expected to take about one hour. As the column motored ahead, Vietnamese corpses came into view along the highway. The Americans could not tell whether the bodies were those of innocent civilians, Communist operatives in civilian garb, or South Vietnamese soldiers on leave. Soon they began to see dead American soldiers as well, slumped over in their jeeps or strewn across the road. Stopping to collect the Americans, Smaldone's company accumulated a truckload of bodies en route to the racetrack.

At an intersection on the outskirts of the city, the houses and rooftops erupted with gunfire. Captain Smaldone ordered the infantry to dismount. First Lieutenant Richard W. Harper, riding aboard an armored personnel carrier at the front of the column, knocked out the main enemy position with a 106mm recoilless rifle. The enemy's resistance having been broken, the soldiers scampered back onto the trucks, and the drive resumed.

Harper's lead carrier turned north onto a side street, and the rest of the convoy followed. Drivers and passengers shot glances in all directions for signs of the enemy. Several hundred feet above, MacGill in his helicopter radioed directions to Smaldone. Although South Vietnam was not their native country, MacGill and Smaldone knew the city better than most of their opponents as both of them had spent time there during previous tours. In finding their way and synchronizing their movements, they used bars and brothels as points of reference.

One kilometer from the racetrack, the column was ambushed by a well-concealed enemy company. A rocket-propelled grenade crashed into the lead vehicle, killing Lieutenant Harper. Machine gun fire sprayed the length of the convoy. Several Americans were wounded, but they refused to be evacuated. To avoid getting bogged down in a place of the enemy's choosing, Smaldone ordered his vehicles to back up and take a different route to the objective.

A few blocks from the racetrack, the Cottonbalers encountered machine gun fire again. Leaping from the trucks and armored personnel carriers, infantrymen probed for opportunities to bypass or overrun the enemy. Higher authorities had prohibited the relief force from employing mortars, artillery, and tactical air strikes in the city, but had authorized use of plastic explosives as well as recoilless rifles, either of which could destroy the masonry structures that shielded the enemy. By blasting their way through the neighborhood's tightly packed buildings and backyard walls, the Americans advanced slowly toward the enemy machine gun nests.

In the middle of the afternoon, the Americans reached the last major thoroughfare that stood between them and the racetrack. Barring their way was an enemy machine gun, whose position in the upper floor of a building gave its crew the ability to shower any section of the street with rivulets of bullets. The machine gun drove back every American probe toward the street.

Smaldone stepped off his armored personnel carrier to reconnoiter the enemy redoubt. Proceeding on foot with his driver and gunner, he spotted the machine gun's exact position in a corner window of the building. Returning to his carrier, Smaldone gave orders for infantrymen to provide covering fire while his vehicle maneuvered to a position with an unobstructed view of the target.

The moment that Smaldone's driver reached the intended spot, the gunner launched a 106mm recoilless rifle round at the machine gun nest. Traveling at 1,100 miles per hour, the round promptly struck its mark and exploded. The blast obliterated the machine gun and ignited a cache of mortar rounds, producing a chain reaction of larger explosions. Spears of red flame and chunks of black debris were hurled up a hundred feet.

The men of the 199th Light Infantry Brigade surged across the street. Before they reached the racetrack, they encountered another enemy strongpoint, this one protected by snipers. The sniper fire forced the American infantry to stay behind walls and await heavier weaponry. One of the Americans to witness the skill of the enemy sharpshooters was Specialist Four Doug McCabe, who had left California Polytechnical University to enlist in the Army because, as he put it, he "got so angry with the draft dodger professors that I just couldn't take it anymore." At the line of contact, McCabe observed, the Communists "were well trained and damn good shots because after three steps they fired at us and one round grazed the top of my helmet and another hit the machine-gun ammo I was carrying on my back."[2]

Sufficiently stubborn did Communist resistance remain that Gibler requested and obtained permission to send helicopter gunships to support the infantry. The mighty automatic weapons of the gunships caused the enemy forces to break contact with Smaldone's company and scurry back into the racetrack. After barricading the track's entrances, they fell in with other Communist soldiers, who were positioned behind concrete benches or in the concrete towers atop the grandstands.

Smaldone's first effort to penetrate the walls of the bowl-shaped structure stalled in the face of fierce enemy opposition. He pulled his troops and vehicles back and sent them to a different section, on the southeastern corner. An armored personnel carrier rammed the racetrack's cinder-block wall repeatedly until a hole opened up. American recoilless rifles and gunships pelted the defenders near the breach while American soldiers swarmed in.

Communist fighters withdrew to the highest and most defensible sections of the grandstands. Once the full magnitude of the American force became evident, however, they decided to evacuate the entire racetrack. The American infantry sought to obstruct the evacuation while simultaneously contending with snipers perched in surrounding buildings.

At 1555, Captain Smaldone reported that he had secured the racetrack at the cost of just three Cottonbalers killed and fifteen wounded. Major MacGill directed the battalion's other two companies to insert by helicopter onto the racetrack, which at a half-mile long and a quarter-mile wide constituted the largest landing zone in the city. To pass the twenty minutes it would take the other companies to arrive, Smaldone sat down in a folding chair on the racetrack's infield and opened a copy of the *Wall Street Journal*. Lieutenant Bill Trotter remembered, "It had a calming effect on the men to see the old man reading his *Wall Street Journal* while chaos was running wild."[3]

Huey and Chinook helicopters landed on the racetrack with fresh, unblemished soldiers. Among the arriving passengers was Lieutenant Colonel Gibler, who set up a command post in the office of the racetrack director. A group of enterprising young Americans found a dozen small Vietnamese horses in the racetrack's stables and took them for a gallop around the track, defying the whizzing of bullets overhead. Officers chased after the equestrians, barking at them to get down before the snipers hit them.[4]

Smaldone's Cottonbalers exalted at the punishment they had meted out to their adversaries and at the low number of casualties they had sustained in so doing. "It got frustrating beating around in the jungle and the rice paddies all the time and having sporadic contact, when the enemy wanted it, on their terms," said William A. Johnson of Dixon, Tennessee, a nineteen-year-old radio operator. "They came to us this time, and they paid dearly for it."

• • •

The Tet Offensive was the surprise ending to a month of American and South Vietnamese speculation about Hanoi's next move. January witnessed an upsurge in captured North Vietnamese documents that mentioned or hinted at a looming offensive. In a report to Washington on January 15, General Westmoreland gauged that there was a 60 percent chance that the Communists would undertake a major offensive before Tet and a 40 percent chance that it would come after Tet. Both Westmoreland's intelligence staff and the CIA shared his view on the likely timing of the North Vietnamese offensive.[5]

An offensive during Tet, the week-long celebration of the Lunar New Year, appeared to defy reason. The North Vietnamese had honored a ceasefire at Tet in recent years, and violating the holiday truce would carry a high risk of alienating the populace because Tet far surpassed all other Vietnamese holidays in revelry and reverence. Despite the hardships of the war, Vietnamese households still sold off prized belongings to host a respectable Tet celebration for their families. Brothers from opposing sides left their units for a few days to come together at the homes of their parents. No one on the American side seemed to have been aware that the war had begun with an attack on the ARVN 32nd Regimental headquarters during Tet of 1960, or that Vietnamese forces had attacked Chinese occupation troops during Tet of 1789.

As for the location of the offensive, the Americans continued to dismiss the possibility that the North Vietnamese would target South Vietnam's major population centers. Communist defectors and informants had spoken of preparations to attack various military and governmental installations in South Vietnam's towns and cities, but this evidence was explained away as diversionary chaff. It did not make military sense to strike large numbers of urban areas simultaneously.[6] Teeming with government policemen and soldiers, the towns and cities could be taken only with large assaults that would expose the attackers to devastating counterattacks. Most of the important towns and cities, moreover, lay far from the North Vietnamese logistical lines in Laos and Cambodia. Lt. Gen. Phillip B. Davidson, Westmoreland's top intelligence officer at the time, later remarked, "Even had I known exactly what was to take place, it was so preposterous that I probably would have been unable to sell it to anybody."[7]

Westmoreland, Davidson, and most of the American intelligence analysts preferred to base their forecasts on the capabilities of the opposing forces, rather than their intentions. Reliable information on the location and number of enemy troops was much easier to obtain than reliable information on the enemy's strategic intentions, and an adversary could attain a major victory only if it could bring superior capabilities to bear. Speculation about enemy intentions without due regard for capabilities could easily lead to disaster if that speculation were mistaken, as had been the case in late 1964 and early 1965, when the Americans had incorrectly predicted that Hanoi would not commit its available forces to battle in South Vietnam. Capabilities analysis led Westmoreland and his senior military intelligence officers toward the conclusion that the principal objectives of the Communists' offensive plans in early 1968 lay in the two northernmost provinces, Quang Tri and Thua Thien.

During January, Quang Tri and Thua Thien witnessed the arrival of an alarming number of North Vietnamese troops, including most of an infiltration surge that brought twenty-three thousand men into South Vietnam for the month.[8] At Khe Sanh, a North Vietnamese assemblage of forty thousand soldiers surrounded the Marine combat base in the middle of January. Bristling with artillery on a scale they had never fielded before, the North Vietnamese ringed Khe Sanh with five artillery regiments, four separate artillery batteries, and two antiaircraft artillery regiments, which were equipped with howitzers up to 152mm in caliber, 140mm rockets, and 120mm and 82mm mortars.[9] If the northernmost provinces fell into North Vietnamese hands, their geographic isolation and lack of deep water ports would make their recapture a most difficult proposition for the Americans.

After the war, a handful of North Vietnamese leaders were to claim that they had not planned to overrun the Marine base at Khe Sanh but merely had sent troops there to lure allied forces away from the targets of the Tet Offensive. Several of Hanoi's leading generals and multiple North Vietnamese histories, however, decisively debunked that claim. These sources revealed that Hanoi's objectives in assailing Khe Sanh included both drawing American forces away from the Tet targets and overrunning Khe Sanh.

No one knew better what North Vietnam was trying to achieve than General Tran Quy Hai. At the beginning of 1968, General

Hai was North Vietnam's commanding general for the Route 9 Front, the North Vietnamese military region encompassing Khe Sanh. In a book written after the war, he stated that "the primary objectives of the campaign conducted by the People's Liberation Armed Forces along Route 9 in early 1968 were to annihilate enemy manpower strength, to liberate Khe Sanh, and to support our other battlefields throughout South Vietnam."[10] Another account, an official Communist history of the war in the northern provinces, asserted that the North Vietnamese forces in northern Quang Tri Province intended to "liberate Khe Sanh, shatter a section of the enemy's defensive line, and annihilate and lure in many additional enemy forces to support our other theaters of operations."[11]

With a force of forty thousand men plus a large fraction of the ammunition and artillery that had been laboriously hauled down the Ho Chi Minh Trail in recent months, the North Vietnamese Army tied down a mere six thousand American troops. If the North Vietnamese had not intended to overrun Khe Sanh but were merely menacing it to draw American forces away from towns and cities, military logic would have dictated commitment of more forces to the urban attacks and fewer to Khe Sanh. It also would have dictated the discontinuation of North Vietnamese offensive activities at Khe Sanh after the urban offensive had run its course, yet those activities did not abate until weeks afterward.[12]

To the North Vietnamese leadership, Khe Sanh presented an opportunity to replicate the victory at Dien Bien Phu in 1954. In that climactic battle, the Viet Minh had overrun an isolated French base by marshaling superior numbers of troops, disrupting French logistics with artillery, and refusing to flinch after sustaining casualties on a horrific scale. Hanoi's leaders thought they could prevail in the same way this time.

Initial preparations for the battle fed Hanoi's confidence that it could achieve a second Dien Bien Phu. By exploiting Khe Sanh's proximity to the sanctuary and supply lines of Laos, the North Vietnamese Army was able to mass forces near Khe Sanh that greatly outnumbered the garrison of six thousand. North Vietnamese artillery units were able to bring large numbers of howitzers within range of the base's airstrip. In the middle of January, the North Vietnamese cut the roads into Khe Sanh, making the base and its satellite outposts reliant for supplies on air assets, which could by shot down by North Vietnamese artillery or grounded by the poor weather that plagued Khe Sanh at this time of year.

The parallels between Khe Sanh and Dien Bien Phu were as plain to the Americans as to the North Vietnamese. Some American military experts believed that Hanoi was justified in believing the conditions favorable for a replay of 1954. The most distinguished of them, Maxwell Taylor, recommended that the president abandon the base.[13]

Westmoreland concurred that the enemy was seeking to replicate Dien Bien Phu, but he was convinced that Khe Sanh could and should be held. If the North Vietnamese took possession of Khe Sanh, Westmoreland argued, they would have easier access to eastern Quang Tri Province. In his opinion, losing Khe Sanh "would be a major propaganda victory for the enemy" and "would seriously affect Vietnamese and U.S. morale."[14] The fall of Khe Sanh would also confound Westmoreland's plans for moving American and South Vietnamese forces into Laos later in the year under Operation El Paso, as it would deprive him of the best available base near the Laotian border. Westmoreland believed, furthermore, that Khe Sanh presented an opportunity to destroy a large chunk of the North Vietnamese Army. Distant from civilians and the restrictions that their presence imposed on American military power, Khe Sanh could function as the chopping block on which several North Vietnamese divisions could be hacked apart.

The Americans would frustrate enemy designs on Khe Sanh in 1968, Westmoreland contended, because they had created better conditions for battle than had the French at Dien Bien Phu in 1954. The French garrison at Dien Bien Phu had sat in a deep valley surrounded by mountains under enemy control, whereas the Khe Sanh combat base was located on a plateau surrounded by hills that the hill fights of 1967 had left in the hands of three thousand U.S. Marines. The French defenders at Dien Bien Phu had received relatively little air or artillery support and had run short on ammunition and food because of logistical difficulties. At Khe Sanh, the Americans could employ B-52s, tactical aircraft, and a formidable array of light, medium, and heavy artillery, and they possessed a broad and deep set of capabilities for resupply by air. Westmoreland's arguments were reassuring enough to President Johnson that he waved off the recommendations to abandon Khe Sanh.

Westmoreland laid plans for massive air strikes in the area environs of Khe Sanh under the code name Niagara, foreshadowing a cascade of bombs. With prompting from Wheeler and Sharp, Westmoreland asked his staff to study the use of tactical nuclear weapons in the event that the situation at Khe Sanh or elsewhere in northern I Corps deteriorated. A small team began a top-secret analysis, examining how the wind, terrain, blast patterns, and locations of Marine positions would affect the use of nuclear devices near the isolated plateau. Referring to the administration's many futile attempts to communicate resolve via military force, Westmoreland later reflected, "If Washington officials were so intent on 'sending a message' to Hanoi, surely small tactical nuclear weapons would be a way to tell Hanoi something, just as two atomic bombs had spoken convincingly to Japanese officials during World War II and the threat of atomic bombs induced the North Koreans to accept meaningful negotiations during the Korean War."[15]

The American press soon heard and disseminated rumors that the administration was contemplating the use of nuclear weaponry in Vietnam. Johnson worried that news of the military's secret analysis would scare the American people and possibly even provoke a nuclear confrontation with Hanoi's allies, so he terminated the study. In a public announcement, he denied that the Department of Defense had been considering the use of nuclear weapons in Vietnam.[16]

In mid-January, at the 14th Plenum of the Vietnamese Communist Party's Central Committee, Le Duan outlined his expectations for the coming struggle. The offensive, he declared, was intended to achieve a "decisive victory" through the combination of main force warfare and a general uprising. The South Vietnamese government's troops were "extremely weak," so weak that "some of our people say that when we attack them, they just break down and burst into tears." By striking both Khe Sanh and the population centers, Hanoi would prevent the allies from concentrating their forces at any one place. North Vietnam's overall plan, Le Duan disclosed, was "to stretch the enemy throughout the Southern battlefield, drive his main force to battlefields advantageous to us and deal it crushing blows."

Le Duan sought to put to rest any doubts about prospects for the urban uprisings. "Almost all of the cities are boiling and ready to rise," he insisted. "The masses are now ripe, and they want to seize control of the government. Millions of people are ready to take to the streets, and the masses have just been waiting for our military forces to support them."

Once North Vietnam's forces took control of Saigon and other major cities and key rural areas, Le Duan divined, the South Vietnamese regime would slide into oblivion. The United States, already wracked by internal conflicts, would then have to pull out of South Vietnam. "Back in the United States, the morale of the warmongers will collapse," Le Duan asserted. "Millions of people, the popular masses, will march out into the streets to oppose the warmongers. The warmongers will have lost their base."[17]

The directives issued to troops in the South on the eve of battle brimmed with confidence that the Tet Offensive would incite mass uprisings. "We were told the cities were like pregnant fish, filled with eggs," recalled Nguyen Ngoc, a North Vietnamese soldier who later became a writer. "We just needed to tickle the fish a little, and all the eggs would pour out." The assault units readily accepted the prediction, he noted, because "we believed the cities were oppressed by the Americans and South Vietnamese."[18]

Ahead of the attacks, thousands of Communist cadres infiltrated the major cities and the provincial and district capitals. Carrying false identification papers and wearing the clothing of merchants or farmers, they could seldom be distinguished from the countless other South Vietnamese who were traveling to family celebrations. Some smuggled weapons aboard trucks or sampans laden with lumber or flowers for delivery to hiding places in cemeteries, drainage ditches, the homes of sympathizers, or Buddhist pagodas. The armed combatants filed out of tunnel complexes and jungle hideouts in the dark of night and marched toward South Vietnam's population centers. Taking all possible precautions to evade detection, they restricted their movements to nighttime and bypassed hamlets and government outposts. Communications technicians avoided sending any messages about the attacks except at the highest levels of encryption.[19]

According to an official American postmortem, eighty-four thousand Communist troops took part in the urban offensive.

That figure, however, did not include substantial numbers of headquarters personnel, cadres, guerrillas, and civilian laborers. The total number of Communist personnel converging on the cities at the end of January likely exceeded a hundred thousand.[20] Hanoi arrayed additional forces near key towns and cities, poised to join the fray once victory came into view.

In most of the country, the attackers escaped the notice of the South Vietnamese government and the Americans prior to reaching their targets, in no small part because most South Vietnamese soldiers, militiamen, and policemen had gone on leave for the holiday and patrolling had been suspended. Communist forces and plans did not, however, remain entirely invisible. One week before the urban offensive began, the South Vietnamese Army captured a Communist colonel named Nam Dong who divulged the actual plans for the attack, including the start date. The South Vietnamese officers who received this information did not share it with the Americans because rumors of American contacts with the Vietnamese Communists had led them to believe that the United States was colluding with the Communists and already knew about this offensive.

During a raid at Qui Nhon on January 28, government forces apprehended Communist cadres carrying audio tapes with messages imploring the people to support the revolution, which was said to have seized control of Saigon, Hue, and Da Nang. Upon interrogation, the captives confessed that the Communists planned to attack Qui Nhon and other cities during the holiday truce. The discovery prompted the South Vietnamese Army leadership in II Corps to put its troops on alert.[21]

In the last days before the Tet ceasefire, numerous allied patrols and informants brought word of Communist units gravitating toward the population centers, setting in motion a variety of last-minute allied preparations. Radio intercepts and other information pointing toward attacks near the urban areas of III Corps during Tet caused Lt. Gen. Frederick Weyand to beef up the defenses of Saigon and other cities.[22] Westmoreland became so concerned by the signs of an impending ceasefire breach that he went to Thieu with a plea to cancel the holiday truce. Thieu agreed to cancel it in I Corps but refused to do so elsewhere, arguing that it would weaken South Vietnamese morale and reduce support for the government among the populace.[23]

According to the official North Vietnamese campaign plan, the urban offensive was to commence on the first night of the Lunar New Year. That seemingly straightforward detail proved to be Hanoi's first major problem. In early January, North Vietnam's Maritime Meteorological Department had chosen to adjust its lunar calendar, moving the date of the new year one day forward, but word of the adjustment reached only the coastal areas of central Vietnam before the end of the month. As a result, the North Vietnamese attacked six towns near the central coast on the night of January 29–30, twenty-four hours ahead of North Vietnamese forces in the rest of the country.[24]

At each of the six locations, the allies drove off the assault force within a few hours. Word of these attacks prompted the Saigon government to order all personnel to return to their units from holiday leave at once, but most of them could not be reached before the main event began. American commanders were more successful in summoning their troops to duty stations. Westmoreland, however, did not redeploy any additional forces to the population centers, and he and his subordinate commanders still did not expect the attacks to occur in as many places or with as much force as they soon would. Just a few hours before the Communists started shooting in Saigon, two hundred U.S. military intelligence officers were sipping cocktails at a pool party in the South Vietnamese capital.[25]

Most of the remaining urban attacks began on the night of January 30–31. Masked by the blackness of night and the popping of holiday firecrackers, Communist troops struck five of South Vietnam's six cities, thirty-six of forty-four provincial capitals, sixty-four of 242 district capitals, and fifty hamlets. Their primary targets were South Vietnamese bases, headquarters, radio stations, and leaders. With a few notable exceptions, they stayed away from American installations.

For reasons of operational secrecy, the Communist assault units had neither studied the cities they were attacking nor received training in urban warfare. Nearby Communist Party headquarters were supposed to provide guides for the combat forces, but many of the guides never linked up with the units they were supposed to steer. The absence of guides caused numerous formations to arrive late at their intended targets or to miss them entirely.[26] Other units were delayed by tardiness in the issuance of the attack order. In one battalion that failed to receive the attack order, the commander took leave to get married during the holiday, and his deputy commander drank himself into a stupor on the night before the offensive, as was discovered by Communist officers who encountered the battalion during their march to Saigon.[27]

When the surge of the Communist storm met the breakwaters of the South Vietnamese government installations, some of the structures gave way immediately. Others had enough armed men on hand to withstand the preliminary Communist onslaught, and their chances of survival increased as other personnel returned to duty. Communist political cadres rushed from house to house exhorting the people to stand alongside them, unless those people were identified as government leaders, in which case they were killed on the spot.

At 3:00 a.m., nineteen commandos drove up to the American embassy in Saigon aboard a Renault Dauphin sedan and a

Peugeot 304 light truck. From the vehicle windows, they opened fire on the two American military policemen stationed outside the wall. The policemen, Specialist Charles L. Daniel and Private First Class William M. Sebast, scrambled inside the compound and locked the outer gate. Over their radio, they transmitted the code "Signal 300," meaning that the embassy was under attack.

The commandoes, attired in civilian clothes with red armbands, climbed out of the two vehicles. Using plastic explosives, they blew a hole in the protective wall encircling the embassy compound. Then they rushed through the breach, firing into the smoke.

"They're coming in," one of the military policemen radioed. "They're coming in! VC in the compound!"[28] Daniel and Sebast gunned down the first two commandos to enter but were then killed by other commandos pouring through the hole.

Now in control of the compound's courtyard, the commandos fired B-40 antitank rockets at the fortified door of the chancery, the embassy's main building. The rockets failed to pierce the door's six-inch-thick teak slabs. Although the commandos were carrying more than enough plastic explosive to demolish the door, none of them attempted to use it. Their first priority was not entering the embassy but rather linking up with Communist soldiers and two hundred pro-Communist students who were scheduled to arrive at the embassy as reinforcements. The disinterest of the attackers in the immediate seizure of the chancery was a godsend for the Americans inside, whom the attackers outnumbered by a wide margin. Just two twenty-year-old Americans—Sergeant Ronald W. Harper of Cambridge, Minnesota, and Corporal George B. Zahuranic of Uniontown, Pennsylvania—were guarding the first floor of the chancery, and Zahuranic had been seriously wounded at the outset.

From the windows and rooftops of nearby buildings, American military policemen, Marines, and embassy officials traded fire with the commandos, who had taken cover behind large concrete shrubbery pots in the courtyard. As minutes turned into hours, no other Communist soldiers or students materialized. At dawn, U.S. Marines and military policemen charged the compound and made quick work of the remaining commandos, shooting them down on the embassy's manicured lawn. A search of the premises turned up sixteen dead and three wounded commandos, as well as the bodies of five American servicemen and four of the embassy's Vietnamese employees.[29]

The din of gunshots had drawn a throng of American reporters to the embassy compound, which lay near the quarters of the international press corps. An American news crew captured part of the action, and their handiwork was broadcast that evening to America's living rooms. Initial press reports stated, on the basis of erroneous remarks from military policemen, that the Communists had entered the chancery.[30] Although the security situation at the embassy had no bearing on the military situation elsewhere or on the American command and control apparatus—Westmoreland's military command was headquartered at Tan Son Nhut air base—the spectacle gave the impression that the Communists were threatening to overwhelm the American expeditionary forces in Vietnam.

Across South Vietnam's towns and cities, the reaction of the residents to the offensive was astonishingly consistent. Refusing the entreaties of Communist cadres and soldiers to stand beside them, the citizenry chose instead to hide, run away, or report the location of the attackers to allied troops. Even youth organizations that had routinely protested against the Saigon government chose to side with that government.[31] Ninety percent of Communists who were taken prisoner during the offensive would tell interrogators that they had received no assistance from the population, and only 2 percent said they had received unsolicited help.[32]

Truong Van Man, deputy commander of a North Vietnamese company, had expected that at least 60 percent of the population would rise up in support of the offensive. In actuality, Man recounted, "None of them were enthusiastic about our offensive, let alone taking part in a general uprising." Rather than abetting the revolutionaries, "The people either ran away or barred their doors to the VC troops."[33]

One reason for the people's behavior was their disgust with the violation of the holiday ceasefire.[34] But, as Quang Trung's successful attack on Chinese troops during Tet of 1789 had demonstrated, a ceasefire violation alone did not suffice to alienate the entire population. The primary reason for the population's behavior was its preference for the Saigon government over the Hanoi government. Most residents of the towns and cities had relatives serving in the government and did not want to see them killed by Communist commissars. Most had been imbued with hatred for Communism and its adherents through experience, education, or both.

Their behavior was also influenced by the alacrity of South Vietnamese soldiers and policemen in returning to duty and resisting the offensive, which itself was driven by the desire to protect family members who lived in the towns and cities. Despite profuse Communist appeals to government personnel to defect, no South Vietnamese units and very few individuals joined forces with the attackers. American analysts determined that 141 of 149 South Vietnamese battalions performed satisfactorily during the offensive and that 30 of them fought exceptionally well.[35]

South Vietnamese and American forces employed tanks, armored personnel carriers, and recoilless rifles against Communist forces, who, in the interest of speed and stealth, had brought along few weapons heavier than a machine gun. "The spearhead battalions were not able to advance rapidly," recounted

General Huynh Cong Than, commander of seven Communist battalions that took part in the attack on Saigon, "because they carried only small, light weapons and had little ammunition, while enemy forces were numerous and used the thick building walls and the tangle of streets and alleys in the cities to put up a ferocious resistance."[36]

In the jungles and the mountains, Communist forces could fight from prepared defensive fortifications and could break away from their adversaries and escape by trail or tunnel when it suited them. In the cities, they did not have the time or materials to build fortifications yet were nonetheless supposed to hold ground, and if they did decide to flee, the potential escape routes were either unknown or obstructed by enemy forces. Hostile civilians were reporting their locations and movements to the enemy. Under these circumstances, the hammers of South Vietnamese and American firepower could come down on their heads until the forces of life had been drained from the last man.

For Communist soldiers who were not trying to hang on to a particular patch of ground, the odds of survival were only marginally better. Hanoi had not provided its forces with backup plans in the event that the offensive proceeded differently than anticipated. To do so, presumably, would have undermined the zealous confidence of the offensive. As a result, Communist forces did not know where they could rally when they failed to reach their intended destinations, or how they could get supplies after expending their initial issues of bullets and grenades. Battered units disintegrated into small groups or individuals and fled blindly, to be crushed piecemeal.

Only in a few cases did the Communists gain control of large sections of the urban landscape. One was Ben Tre, the capital of Kien Hoa Province in the Mekong Delta. An assault force of 2,500 Viet Cong overran most of Ben Tre and surrounded the

American advisory compound and South Vietnamese government headquarters. The invaders captured a set of 105mm howitzers, which they fired into the American advisory compound. Lacking expertise in the aiming of these weapons, the Communists fired many errant rounds, some of which flattened civilian dwellings near the compound.

Two companies of American combat troops rushed to the relief of Ben Tre. Out of concern for civilian life and property, the South Vietnamese corps commander refused to allow these companies to direct air or artillery strikes into the town. Enmeshed in brutal street battles against Viet Cong who were fighting from fortified homes and public buildings, the American soldiers were unable to reach the American compound.

With American and South Vietnamese troops outnumbered and facing renewed attacks, the South Vietnamese corps commander eventually agreed to lift the prohibition on air power and artillery. Their firepower thus multiplied, the American infantry dislodged the Viet Cong from strongpoints that stood in their way and broke through to the advisory compound. They then wiped the town clean of enemy fighters.

Journalist Peter Arnett was among the newsmen who arrived at Ben Tre to cover the battle. In narrating the destruction visited upon the city, he mentioned only the American and South Vietnamese employment of heavy weapons, omitting the Communist use of artillery. Arnett reported that an American major told him, "We had to destroy Ben Tre in order to save it."

Whether anyone actually spoke these words would become a matter of dispute, one that has never been satisfactorily resolved. Doubters noted that Arnett had previously acquired the reputation of a sensationalist who was prone to exaggeration, if not fabrication. That reputation would be amplified by several incidents after the war, most notably the 1998 Tailwind documentary, in which

Arnett falsely accused the United States of killing American military defectors with poison gas during a 1970 raid in Laos. Arnett further aroused suspicion about the Ben Tre quote by providing conflicting accounts of the source's identity, including an about-face in 2003 in which he attributed the remark to a soldier who was answering a question from the major.[37]

Whatever the truth about its origins, the quote was circulated widely as fact, and it turned Ben Tre into a microcosm of the war in the eyes of the war's opponents. To Americans unfamiliar with urban warfare and skeptical of the nation's cause, it showed that the United States had resolved to annihilate South Vietnam and its people in order to achieve victory.[38] To Americans who had witnessed the destruction of cities in World War II and the Korean War, by contrast, Ben Tre reconfirmed that combatants who used residential housing as fortresses and did not evacuate the residents bore responsibility for the ensuing damage to property and persons.

"The way we selected these targets was determined by the VC," remarked a U.S. forward air controller who directed strikes during the battle. "They chose the battleground and we really had no choice where we put the target. There were American soldiers lying dead on the road and there were going to be a lot more if we didn't put ordnance into the town."[39]

The place where the Communists seized the most ground was the one where they had sent the most troops, the city of Hue. Although American ground forces had been tearing up and plowing under Communist base areas for more than two years, they had neglected a key base area to the west of Hue, the A Shau Valley. It was an extraordinarily damaging oversight. The valley had remained in North Vietnamese hands since the fall of the A Shau Special Forces camp in March 1966, permitting North Vietnamese engineers and logisticians to build it into a supply depot and transit channel for North Vietnamese forces heading from the Ho Chi Minh Trail into South Vietnam.

Throughout January 1968, the North Vietnamese had funneled men and materiel through the A Shau Valley toward Hue. On the first night of the Tet Offensive, a total of ten thousand soldiers arrived in Hue, nearly all of them North Vietnamese Army regulars, in contrast to the other sites of attack, where soldiers and cadres of Southern origin participated in large numbers. The soldiers also came equipped with more heavy weapons and ammunition than any of the other assault forces.[40]

Former gem of the Annamese emperors, Hue was at the beginning of 1968 perhaps the most beautiful and beloved city in South Vietnam. Its architecture reflected an illustrious history of religion and bygone power, from dark pagodas and forbidding royal tombs to towering French churches and grand colonial villas roofed with red tile. At the center of Hue stood the citadel, a sprawling fortress that had been constructed by Emperor Gia Long and his European allies at the beginning of the nineteenth century. The citadel contained the Palace of Perfect Peace, from which the emperors had exercised their authority. Around this three-square-kilometer area, the French military had erected stone ramparts, twenty feet thick and thirty feet high, which were still fully intact in January 1968. Close to half the city's population resided in densely packed houses within the citadel's walls.

Among the Vietnamese, Hue was said to be a lotus flower that had risen up through the dirt and muck and weathered the whims of war. North Vietnam's armed forces had largely steered clear of Hue until this time, even during the Buddhist turbulence of 1966, and hence the South Vietnamese had seen no need to keep large numbers of soldiers in the city. The Americans had not stationed forces in Hue, partly because of the tranquility, partly because of the residents' xenophobia and the past misbehavior of

American servicemen at Hue's royal tombs. For that reason, the city had been spared from the neon lights and honkytonk bars that had overrun Saigon and other large South Vietnamese cities.

At 2:30 a.m. on January 31, a North Vietnamese soldier sent up a bright flare to inaugurate the attack on Hue. Four North Vietnamese sappers, clad in South Vietnamese Army uniforms, killed the guards at the western gate of the citadel. Signaling with flashlights, they directed North Vietnamese units to the gate and inside. Other North Vietnamese soldiers rode nylon rafts across the river to reach the fortress.[41]

Possessing both numerical superiority and the element of surprise, the attackers quickly vanquished most of the citadel's garrison. North Vietnamese officers dispersed their soldiers along the stout walls and interior buildings to prepare defenses. Inside the palace's colossal throne room, they established a military command center.

The North Vietnamese Army flooded the rest of Hue with equal dispatch. By dawn, North Vietnamese troops held most of the city, including nearly all the governmental and military headquarters. At eight o'clock that morning, they hoisted the gold-starred flag of the National Liberation Front on the towering pole at the Zenith Gate, where the Viet Minh had flown a gold-starred flag upon Emperor Bao Dai's abdication in August 1945. All that remained in allied hands were the U.S. advisory compound, located on the south bank of the Perfume River, and Mang Ca, a fortified stronghold in the northern corner of the citadel.

Mang Ca was serving as the headquarters of the 1st ARVN Division. The night before the offensive, the division's reconnaissance company had spotted two enemy battalions advancing on Hue, prompting the division commander, Brigadier General Ngo Quang Truong, to put his soldiers on alert and position platoons at key points in the city. He had kept only a single platoon, with fifty soldiers, at the division's headquarters. That platoon, supplemented by the division's doctors and clerks, spent the first hours of the battle in a desperate close-quarters struggle to keep the North Vietnamese out of Mang Ca.

One of General Truong's best officers, 1st Lt. Tran Ngoc Hue, had been asleep in a residential area of the city that night, together with his parents, his wife, and their four-week-old daughter. Born and raised in the city on the Perfume, Tran Ngoc Hue had been given the city's name as his own. Bolting awake at the booms of exploding rockets, Lieutenant Hue herded his family members into an underground bunker, then jumped on a bicycle and headed for his unit's headquarters.

The elite unit that Tran Ngoc Hue commanded, the Black Panther Company, was headquartered at a small airfield inside the citadel. As the lieutenant was making his way through the citadel's streets, he crossed into a current of North Vietnamese soldiers, hundreds of them, streaming through the dark. In his civilian clothes, he did not attract the attention of the North Vietnamese, who were mainly concerned with large concentrations of men in uniform. The only way to reach his unit was to proceed in the same direction as the assault troops, so he ditched his bike and let the current of North Vietnamese troops take him.

Splitting off from the North Vietnamese column unobserved, Lieutenant Hue dashed to the citadel's airfield, which some of his soldiers were defending against onrushing North Vietnamese. He retrieved an antitank weapon and fired it into a dozen enemy soldiers on the opposite side of the field, sending three of them into the air. All the other North Vietnamese who attempted to cross the runway during the remaining hours of darkness were gunned down by the Black Panthers.

At dawn, General Truong ordered the Black Panthers to join him at the beleaguered division headquarters. Using back alleys where Lieutenant Hue had played as a child, the Black Panther Company made its way to Mang Ca. As they neared the fortress, they saw three enemy machine guns lined up in preparation for an attack. The Black Panthers blew them away, then used a smokescreen to cover their advance into the compound.

General Truong put Lieutenant Hue in charge of the defense of Mang Ca. During the morning, North Vietnamese soldiers climbed over the fortress's eight-foot walls in several places and penetrated the hospital and parade ground. Lieutenant Hue organized what a North Vietnamese account termed "ferocious" counterattacks, recapturing the hospital and parade field and pushing the remaining North Vietnamese soldiers out. U.S. Marine Captain James J. Coolican, an adviser to the Black Panther Company, later described Lieutenant Hue as "bigger than life in the field." Other advisers deemed him "absolutely fearless."[42]

So shocked were the North Vietnamese by the repulse at Mang Ca that they discontinued all efforts to take the stronghold. This decision not only ensured the safety of the 1st Division's headquarters but also set the stage for a counteroffensive into the rest of the citadel.[43] The retention of Mang Ca would permit the South Vietnamese, and later the Americans, to inject fresh troops into the fortress without having to fight through or over the immense ramparts and gates.

Once the North Vietnamese had snuffed out organized governmental resistance in the rest of the city, they set up a new administration called the "People's Alliance for Democracy and Freedom." For propaganda purposes, they named as its head a cultural anthropology professor from Hue University. The administration's primary objective was the extermination of government leaders and other "enemies of the revolution." Brandishing typewritten lists of names compiled by their agents in the city, Communist cadres rounded up South Vietnamese officials, soldiers, teachers, intellectuals, clergymen, and Catholics. All foreigners were marked for execution, with the partial exception of French citizens, whose lives were to be spared if they were not priests.[44] A large number of the victims were shot at once. Others were beaten to death during attempts to glean information.

Hanoi's other major target in I Corps, the Khe Sanh plateau, was curiously quiet at the start of the Lunar New Year. The North Vietnamese had originally intended to mount a massive assault on Khe Sanh ten days before Tet but had changed their minds in mid-January, just after completing the encirclement of the Marine combat base. American strength, North Vietnamese logistical shortfalls, and delays in the arrival of North Vietnamese combat units had convinced them that the original plan was likely to fail. "Instead of launching a powerful assault to swiftly liberate Khe Sanh," a North Vietnamese history explained, "we switched to the use of siege attack tactics, to gradually squeeze and liberate Khe Sanh."[45]

During the second half of January, the North Vietnamese had engaged the U.S. Marines in a series of small clashes outside the Khe Sanh combat base. The Marines had kept hold of the hills, denying the enemy platforms for observation and artillery fire. The North Vietnamese almost certainly intended to intensify their attacks at the time of Tet, but the U.S. Air Force derailed their plans right before the start of the urban offensive.

On January 30, a flotilla of B-52s was summoned to a location in eastern Laos that was emitting radio messages and receiving large numbers of North Vietnamese trucks. Forty-five of the Stratofortresses, the most ever assembled for a single strike, drenched the site with explosive ordnance. The crumpling of broad sections of the valley floor revealed the existence of vast underground complexes, and eighty-five secondary explosions confirmed the presence of multitudinous munitions stockpiles. North Vietnamese officers captured near Khe Sanh in the coming days would tell interrogators that the bombing had devastated the command and control apparatus in South Vietnam's northern provinces.[46]

By the end of the first full day of the Tet Offensive, the hopes of the North Vietnamese leadership had been shattered. The South Vietnamese people had uniformly refused to rise up in support of Communism. South Vietnamese soldiers were returning from leave and fighting for their families and their government. With Communist forces spread across more than one hundred towns and cities, they lacked overwhelming numbers in any one place except for Hue. Holding unfamiliar ground against hostile forces with larger weapons and the support of the population, their outlook appeared bleak. At Khe Sanh, American air power had thrown the North Vietnamese campaign into such disorder that a force of forty thousand had been unable to muster an attack of any significance.

The futility of the first day was evident to most of the Communist troops. Even the most gifted party orators found it difficult to reconcile the day's events with the euphoric prophesies that had preceded them. "On the march to the delta, all the soldiers firmly believed in the great victory," recounted one young Communist soldier. But enemy air and artillery tore up his unit en route to its objective, killing many of its soldiers and stopping the rest from reaching their destination. "This never happened when we fought in the jungle," he recollected. "The troops' morale decreased a great deal."[47]

American and South Vietnamese leaders were still not sure what to make of the opening round of the offensive. Some interpreted the urban offensive as a feint, aimed at diverting attention from the big-unit war in the northern provinces. That interpretation helped dissuade Westmoreland from shifting large numbers of American forces to the urban centers. So did the fact that the South Vietnamese appeared to be stamping out most of the attacks with their own boots.

CHAPTER 13

...

REACTION

February 1968

A n estimated four thousand Communist fighters were holed up in Saigon on the morning of February 1. It was the most in any city that morning aside from Hue. As South Vietnamese military and police units congealed, seven American battalions joined them in the effort to retake the capital city. Employing heavy weapons and plastic explosives, the counterattackers began expunging the invaders from one building after another.

South Vietnamese policemen screened young men to catch Communists who tried to sneak away in civilian guise. Their work would not have garnered much attention had it not been for the photograph that would become the most infamous image of the Tet Offensive. Two days into the offensive, Associated Press photographer Eddie Adams and a handful of other journalists went searching for newsworthy material in a Saigon neighborhood where the South Vietnamese were reported to be rousting out the Viet Cong. While walking the streets, they happened upon a group of South Vietnamese policemen escorting a prisoner in civilian clothing.

As the journalists followed the procession, General Nguyen Ngoc Loan, head of the South Vietnamese National Police, approached the captive. Adams focused his camera on the two men and started snapping photos. The camera's film captured Loan loading his pistol, shooting the prisoner in the head, and watching the lifeless body tumble to the ground.

Loan, seeing the photographer five feet away from him, remarked, "He killed many of my men and many of your people."[1] The deceased man had, in fact, executed the family of a government official a short time earlier.

One of the photos taken by Adams, in which the prisoner grimaced while his head was blown sidewise by a pistol shot, was soon splashed above the fold in the newspapers of the world's largest cities and smallest towns. It ultimately earned Adams a plethora of prestigious awards, including the Pulitzer Prize. Although execution had been the standard punishment for combatants cloaked in civilian garb throughout the history of warfare, some Americans knew nothing of that fact and hence were susceptible to concluding that America's ally had sunken into moral turpitude. Among the first to voice this interpretation in public was Senator Robert F. Kennedy, who told CBS News, "The photograph of the execution was on front pages all around the world—leading our best and oldest friends to ask, more in sorrow than in anger, what has happened to America?"[2]

Eddie Adams himself did not sympathize with those who viewed the photograph as proof of South Vietnamese or American depravity. "I thought absolutely nothing of it," Adams recalled later. "He shot him, so what? Because people die in fuckin' war. And I just happened to be there this time. This is not an unusual occurrence." Adams would also deplore the way in which his photo came to be perceived in the United States. "It was very one-sided," he said ruefully. "I didn't have a picture of that Viet

Cong blowing away the family. It was very detrimental—perfect propaganda for North Vietnam."[3]

As American and South Vietnamese troops spread through the suburbs of Saigon, they engaged lingering Communist forces and blocked those who endeavored to flee the city.[4] Those forces included the battalions commanded by General Huynh Cong Than, who, after several days of unsuccessful attempts to penetrate the center of Saigon, had been ordered to keep his units near the capital in preparation for subsequent operations. While awaiting further instructions, the general's command group became the target of an American operation. An American artillery barrage, fired to protect helicopters as they inserted an American infantry unit, killed the general's own son.

"I sat beside the body of my 17 year-old son with my heart breaking and spoke to him as if he were still alive," Than remembered. He told the lifeless boy, "You joined the army at an early age and you were killed in a big battle against an American sweep operation. Rest in peace, my son. You have done your duty for the revolution."[5]

By February 5, the Communists had been driven from most neighborhoods in the greater Saigon area. Hundreds of their dead lay in the streets and fields, picked at by dogs and rats. Sporadic fighting continued around Saigon, extending into March in outlying areas.

In every other town and city besides Hue, the offensive played out in similar fashion. The government's security forces, with help from the Americans in some cases, vanquished the Communist soldiers, guerrillas, and political cadres within a few days. The detritus of war was swept away, construction crews went to work on buildings scarred by the fighting, and citizens returned to their daily routines. From the point of view of the allied armed forces, the war had taken a monumental swing toward the better.

From the point of view of the American press, however, the war had turned sharply for the worse. Among journalists who had previously doubted the sincerity of American officials when they had spoken of military progress, the scale of the urban offensive demonstrated enduring Communist strength and hence disproved the official optimism once and for all. In a February 4 dispatch, for instance, Peter Lisagor of the *Philadelphia Inquirer* asserted that the "cozy assumption that the South Vietnamese government has been winning the confidence of the people has been virtually exploded by the daring Vietcong attacks."[6]

Some reporters contended that the attacks had bolstered the Viet Cong's standing among the South Vietnamese populace and erased what little sympathy had remained for the Saigon government. With no public opinion polls available, they invoked unnamed South Vietnamese sources, drawn heavily from the tiny class of urban intellectual malcontents. "Many South Vietnamese feel that the Communists have scored political and psychological gains that may have significant consequences in the months to come," wrote Stanley Karnow in the *Washington Post.* "At the same time, judging from local opinion, President Nguyen Van Thieu's Administration has suffered a severe loss of prestige that could lead to the kind of internal political instability that has plagued South Vietnam in recent years."[7]

While some of the negativity was longstanding and predictable, Tet also saw a number of hitherto dispassionate newsmen turn into open doubters on the war. Walter Cronkite, the venerable anchorman of the *CBS Evening News*, reported mournfully from South Vietnam in late February that America's nation-building project in South Vietnam had degenerated into a chaos of bloodletting, comparable in its destructiveness to World War II. Cronkite concluded that no form of American escalation, not even the invasion of North Vietnam or the use of nuclear weapons, could secure victory.

"We have been too often disappointed by the optimism of American leaders, both in Vietnam and Washington, to have faith any longer in the silver linings they find in the darkest clouds," Cronkite announced on national television. "To say that we are mired in stalemate seems the only realistic, yet unsatisfactory conclusion." Shifting from journalism to punditry, Cronkite contended that the United States should negotiate its way out of the war, "not as victors, but as an honorable people who lived up to their pledge to defend democracy, and did the best they could."[8] Like most other Americans who were calling for negotiations, Cronkite did not mention that the North Vietnamese habitually refused to negotiate except on terms that would precipitate South Vietnam's destruction, and thus he obscured the damage to America's international credibility and alliances likely to result from a rush to peace.

Several American journalists were appalled by what they believed to be the biased and ill-informed reporting of their colleagues. The liberal columnist and ABC-TV commentator Howard K. Smith denounced his fellow correspondents for their one-sided coverage of the war and lamented the passing of what had been "a great age in journalism."[9] Peter Braestrup, who worked for both the *New York Times* and *Washington Post* in South Vietnam during 1968, was so distressed by the inaccuracies of the media in covering the Tet Offensive that he wrote a 1,400-page study on the subject. "Rarely has contemporary crisis-journalism turned out, in retrospect, to have veered so widely from reality," Braestrup wrote in the book's conclusion.[10]

For Robert Elegant of the *Los Angeles Times*, the media's most contemptible error at Tet was its willful disregard of the massacre perpetrated by the North Vietnamese at Hue.[11] During February, few American correspondents reported the mounting evidence of Communist atrocities in that city. The violence was enveloping governmental personnel of progressively lesser prominence and civilians whose only transgression had been the witnessing of acts of cruelty.

One of the few American journalists to cover the bloodbath was Don Oberdorfer of Knight Newspapers. Among the stories he related was that of Pham Van Tuong, a man who earned his living as a janitor at a government information office in Hue. When the Tet Offensive began, he and his wife, eight children, and three nephews hid in a bunker next to his house. Several days later, a handful of men wearing black pajamas came looking for him and discovered the bunker.

"Mr. Pham, Mr. Pham the information office cadre, come here!" they shouted.

Pham pulled himself out of the bunker along with two of his children and two nephews. The remaining family members heard shooting above. When they emerged from the bunker, they found all five dead.[12]

On the fifth day of the occupation, North Vietnamese troops came to the cathedral in Phu Cam, a predominantly Catholic district of Hue that had once been the Diem regime's nerve center in Annam. The soldiers had received orders to "encircle the reactionaries who exploit Catholics and isolate them" and to "destroy the power and influence of reactionary ring leaders" in Phu Cam.[13] Inside the cathedral, the North Vietnamese found close to one thousand men, women, and children, fearful and in prayer. The soldiers separated out four hundred men and boys, some because they had been identified in advance, others because they appeared to be wealthy or of military age. A Communist cadre assured the crowd that the detainees were simply going to the Tu Dam pagoda for three days of political reeducation.

Two days after the males had been led away, the Communists ordered the women in the cathedral to provide food and clothing for their husbands and sons. The women complied. Residents subsequently reported seeing the four hundred men and boys marching southward from the city. It was the last time Hue's citizens ever saw them.

In July 1969, three Communist defectors guided U.S. paratroopers to a hidden site in double-canopy jungle outside Hue. Carving a path through the brush in the dim jungle light, they eventually reached a creek bed, whose sight made the stomach churn. For a hundred yards, the bed gleamed white from the bones of four hundred skeletons, washed clean of flesh by the current. An inspection of the skulls revealed that the males of Phu Cam had been either shot or brained with blunt objects.[14]

Colonel Le Minh, commander of one of the North Vietnamese Army units in Hue, acknowledged later that "there were those unjustly sentenced in the situation at hand." Unlike many of the other North Vietnamese officers who survived the battle, he acknowledged his role in the atrocities and expressed remorse. "The responsibility for such injustice must belong to the leadership, in which I had a part," he admitted.[15]

While the top Communist leadership in Hanoi was never directly implicated in the Hue massacre, culpability undoubtedly went higher than the commanders on the scene. The North Vietnamese military commanders in the South served in an army renowned for order and discipline, making it all but impossible that they would have even considered killing thousands of people in cold blood without sanction from above. Further evidence of direction from higher authorities came from Communist efforts to execute government officials and supporters systematically in other locales. The Communists executed small numbers of government leaders in many of the other cities they attacked during

Tet and would have done so in larger numbers had they gained control of those cities as they had in Hue. A North Vietnamese postmortem on the failed attack on Da Nang, for instance, noted that only the "prompt countermeasures of the army of the puppet government and of the U.S. forces" prevented the Communists from achieving all their objectives in the city, which included "the massacre of the cruel elements."[16]

South Vietnamese investigators ultimately discovered the remains of three thousand victims of the Hue massacre in jungles and schoolyards, in tree-lined parks and salt flats. An additional two thousand residents of Hue who disappeared were never found. When the Hue City Communist Party Committee convened at a distant mountain stronghold after the event, party officials reported that the death toll of government personnel alone exceeded 2,700. "We eliminated 1,892 administrative personnel, 38 policemen, 790 tyrants, 6 captains, 2 first lieutenants, 20 second lieutenants, and many NCOs," they stated in self-congratulation. "Hue was the place where reactionary spirit had existed for over ten years. However, it took us only a short time to drain it to its root."[17]

While the apparatchiks were liquidating their enemies, the North Vietnamese soldiers in Hue were contending with efforts by the 1st ARVN Division and other South Vietnamese Army units to retake the citadel. They also faced a counterattack from the U.S. Marine Corps, which had been assigned the task of removing the North Vietnamese from the city's southern side. Owing to a lack of information about the North Vietnamese presence in Hue, the Marine command initially underestimated its size and hence dispatched only three battalions to Hue.

The commander of one of these battalions, 2nd Battalion, 5th Marine Regiment, was Lieutenant Colonel Ernest C. Cheatham. Known to his peers as "Big Ernie," Cheatham had played professional football during the 1950s as a defensive tackle for the Pittsburgh Steelers and Baltimore Colts. Cheatham received his marching orders from Colonel Stanley S. Hughes, commander of the 1st Marine Regiment. "I want you to move up to the Hue University building, and your flank is the Perfume River, and you're going to have an exposed left flank," Hughes said at an impromptu conference of commanders. "Attack through the city and clean the NVA out." Cheatham looked at Hughes expectantly for further clarification, but Hughes did not know any more about the situation in the city than did Cheatham.

"If you're looking for any more, you aren't going to get it," Hughes barked. "Move out!" Then, in a less harsh tone, Hughes added, "You do it any way you want to, and if you get any heat from above, I'll take care of that."[18]

Sketching out their initial thrusts into Hue, the Marine commanders planned to bring armor and infantry forward in unison, the armor blasting enemy positions and providing cover for the Marine infantrymen, who would flush out North Vietnamese troops and finish them off with grenades and small arms. American forces had not fought an urban battle this large since the battle for Seoul in September 1950, when most of the Marines at Hue had been infants. Institutional memory of urban fighting had faded in recent times, the attention of the Marine Corps having been riveted on the jungles and mountains and rice paddies of Vietnam. Marine headquarters therefore rushed Korean War–era manuals on urban combat tactics to the combat units. Some of the Marines did not have time to read the texts until they reached Hue.

When the first Marine tanks entered the city, they were rudely greeted by North Vietnamese recoilless rifles and antitank rockets. From well-prepared defenses along a wide frontage of buildings, the North Vietnamese could bring antitank fire on any vehicle that approached them. "The moment a tank stuck its nose around the corner of a building," said Lieutenant Colonel Cheatham, "it looked like the Fourth of July."[19]

Chastened by heavy damage to armored vehicles and their crews, the Marines shifted to a slower and more deliberate approach. Concentrating on one North Vietnamese defensive line at a time, they identified enemy firing positions and strongpoints and then devised plans for destroying them. They sought to keep Marine casualties to a minimum, but the strength of the enemy's defenses ensured that the Marines could not attain their objectives at a low cost. From concealed locations inside buildings and on rooftops, North Vietnamese soldiers shot at Marines as they crossed streets or sought cover behind walls. On numerous occasions, the Marines suffered so many casualties that they had to halt their assault, bring forward fresh troops, and find a new point of attack.

The casualties suffered during assaults across well-defended streets led the Marines to create their own streets, as their forbearers had done in the Korean War and World War II. They rammed tanks into the sides of buildings. They fired recoilless rifles and bazookas into walls, or demolished them with C4 plastic explosives. South Vietnamese government officials began complaining that the Marines were causing excessive damage to the city's buildings, but the Americans paid them no heed.

"I have no sympathy—not after I've seen what happened to the Marines," remarked Army Lieutenant Colonel Howard L. Moon, the senior American adviser to the South Vietnamese province chief. "There have been times when the wounded and the dying have been coming in here every two or three minutes. The Marines don't know how to quit. If you can save a Marine by destroying a house to get at Charlie, then I say destroy the house."[20]

The Marines did honor a South Vietnamese request to refrain from the use of air and artillery support inside the city. In terms of firepower, therefore, the Marines lacked their usual superiority. Arrayed against Marine recoilless rifles, antitank rockets, mortars, and machine guns were North Vietnamese weapons of comparable quality. The only Marine weapon for which the enemy lacked a match was the tank, and tanks were of limited value in this battle because of the narrowness of the streets and the abundance of antitank weapons.

Unlike the Communist forces who had attacked the other towns and cities, the North Vietnamese units at Hue were at the end of a steady stream of fresh men, supplies, and equipment. Anticipating American efforts to stop the inflow, the North Vietnamese had positioned large units along the length of their supply lines from the A Shau Valley into the city. American advances toward those lines were thwarted by stiff resistance from forces of superior size.

The Americans supplied their forces in the city through a well-protected artery that fed into the city from the east. Logistical units brought men and supplies at a brisk rate, rushed casualties out, and ensured that troops had access to amenities that could relieve the strain of battle. "This is a funny kind of war," remarked Lieutenant Colonel Cheatham. "A block in front of us, Marines are getting shot. Six blocks behind us, they are buying cigars and cigarettes at the PX in the Army compound."[21]

On February 6, the Marines made ready to assault a complex that had been the South Vietnamese government's provincial headquarters one week earlier. Ringed by a stone wall, it contained a large school and a two-story stone building that was shaped in an L, both of which now had a North Vietnamese machine gun nest in every window. Hotel company of the 2/5 Marines, which had taken up positions near the compound, was awaiting the final attack order when a 6x6 truck loaded with replacement troops approached. Instead of stopping at Hotel company's forward line as it should have, the truck sped past and headed straight at the stone wall.

The driver did not realize his error until the North Vietnamese opened fire. Throwing the truck in reverse, he pressed the gas pedal as far as it would go. The truck escaped to safety, but in the process it tossed two of its passengers into the street. Both of them were promptly shot by the North Vietnamese. The two Marines lay prostrate in the dirt, neither man able to get to his feet.

One of the men kicked his way to Hotel company while remaining prone. A corpsman rushed over to him and found that he was gasping for air. He had a sucking chest wound, from which blood was bubbling. The corpsman wrapped the Marine's chest with cellophane and loaded him on a vehicle destined for the nearest military hospital.

The other wounded man had crawled away from the middle of the street to the bottom of a driveway, but could go no further. Private First Class Walter R. Kaczmarek of Port Reading, New Jersey, volunteered to rescue the stranded Marine. Nineteen years of age, Kaczmarek had been in Vietnam less than two months. After graduating from high school in 1966, he had gone to work as a sheet metal apprentice but one year later had decided to enlist in the Marine Corps.

"I wanted to get into the war," Kaczmarek later said. "I grew up in a town where everyone was a veteran of World War Two. My grandfather was a World War One veteran, and my uncles were veterans of Korea. I grew up on patriotism." When enlisting, Kaczmarek had told the Marine Corps recruiter that he wanted to fight in Vietnam. "Okay, son," the recruiter had replied, "I'll have you in a combat squad before the year is out."[22]

With North Vietnamese bullets flying across the street, Kaczmarek began crawling on his belly. After he had advanced only a few yards, a bullet hit a nearby wall and sent a chip of brick into his face, just below his left eye. Blood seeped over the chip, which was sticking out like an arrowhead. Kaczmarek returned to his platoon momentarily so that a buddy could remove the piece of brick, and then he resumed the rescue mission.

This time, Kaczmarek decided to approach the street by sneaking through a hedge. Taking off his web belt and other gear, he slithered into the shrubs, then darted into the street. A hail of North Vietnamese fire flowed in Kaczmarek's direction but did him no harm. Kaczmarek removed himself from the enemy's view by diving to the ground next to the injured Marine. The man flopped around intermittently, screaming that he had been hit in the chest and felt intense pain every time he breathed. It was later determined that his collarbone had been shattered by two gunshots.

In a calming tone, Kaczmarek reassured the Marine that all would be well. Then, when the moment seemed right, Kaczmarek grabbed the man's arm, sprang to his feet, and ran for the hedge. The wounded man yelled that his arm was being torn off. Kaczmarek let go of the arm and slid into the hedge, and from there he was able to drag the injured Marine to safety.

Hotel company began its assault at 9:50 a.m. Immediately the Marines ran into heavy enemy fire and had to halt in place. Forward came two M-48 tanks and a tripod-mounted 106mm recoilless rifle, while 81mm mortars dropped one hundred rounds on the North Vietnamese positions. The North Vietnamese fired back with a 75mm recoilless rifle and antitank rocket launchers.

On the order of the Marine battalion's executive officer, the Americans donned gas masks and fired tear gas pellets, which had only recently been authorized for use in Vietnam. They launched a frontal attack into the clouds of tear gas, but a sudden breeze swept the tear gas away, causing the Marines to abort the assault on the two main buildings. They redirected their attention to an outlying building, which they took at a cost of five wounded. Inside they found twelve dead North Vietnamese.

The Marines paused for the rest of the morning and the early afternoon, intermittently exchanging fire with the North Vietnamese. In the middle of the afternoon, the Marines subjected the main headquarters building to a new pelting of 81mm mortar and 106mm recoilless rifle rounds. The company commander, Captain George R. Christmas, informed 2nd Lieutenant Leo Myers that his platoon would lead the way into the building. Myers in turn assigned the duty to the squad led by Private First Class Alan V. McDonald. The men in the squad drew straws to see who would kick in the door. The short straw was pulled by Private Kaczmarek.

Lieutenant Myers's men fired smoke into the street to conceal their movements. Kaczmarek prayed to God for survival, then he and the rest of McDonald's squad dashed forward while other Marines provided covering fire. To nullify the concertina wire that the NVA had strewn around the headquarters building, the squad threw a long board on top of it. Kaczmarek went across first.

The Marines had been told to avoid tossing grenades into this building because the walls inside were believed to be made solely of plaster and lathe, too weak to contain grenade fragments. Crawling up a short staircase to the front porch, Kaczmarek fired a full M-16 magazine into the doorway. While still on his hands and knees, he pushed open the door and wriggled into the lobby.

Kaczmarek saw stacks of books that the North Vietnamese had used to fortify the walls. He did not see any people or hear any noises. The rest of his squad came in behind him while he continued to scan for signs of individuals with hostile intent.

The North Vietnamese, it turned out, had retreated into the deeper recesses of the building. Marine riflemen poured into the long hallways on the first and second floors. Their advance slowed when they began receiving ripostes of gunfire from the North Vietnamese rearguard, to which the Marines responded in kind.

As Kaczmarek was peering out the window of a second-floor bathroom, he saw a bevy of North Vietnamese troops exiting the building. They were heading down an ally toward a narrow exit. An American with an M-60 machine gun also caught sight of the group, and he sprayed 7.62mm bullets into their backs, knocking down six of them.

After the main headquarters building had been cleared, a burly and fearless gunnery sergeant named Frank A. Thomas espied a series of square spider holes along the outer wall. The stubborn occupants of these holes were continuing to fire their rifles and lob grenades at the Marines. Shotgun in hand, Thomas went over to the nearest hole and dragged out a North Vietnamese soldier by his shirt collar.

"This one's still alive," Thomas pronounced.[23]

Most of the other holes turned out to contain North Vietnamese soldiers, some of them already dead. Those who evidenced any residual fighting spirit were shot, while the remainder were taken prisoner.

The Marines found considerable evidence that the main building had been serving as the headquarters of the North Vietnamese Army's 4th Regiment. In the haste of their retreat, the North Vietnamese had left behind bundles of important paperwork and a large collection of maps. The recapture of this building appeared to exert a harmful effect on all the North Vietnamese forces south of the Perfume River. From here on, the Marines south of the river encountered less resistance in their relentless advance.

To the north of the river, in the citadel, progress was considerably slower. The 1st ARVN Division and other South Vietnamese units were embarking on one brutal assault after another into the jaws of heavily armed North Vietnamese infantry. Having commandeered most of the citadel's private houses, the North Vietnamese used the thick masonry and stone walls as shields. The South Vietnamese retook ground only in small bites and at large costs in lives. Some of the Americans suspected that insufficient South Vietnamese resolve accounted for the slow rate of advance, but in reality these units were led by some of the most resolute and courageous officers on either side of the conflict. What kept them from advancing as speedily as the Americans on the south bank was a dearth of weapons heavy enough to blow holes through walls and enemy strongpoints.

Eleven days into the contest, the South Vietnamese reluctantly asked the U.S. Marines for help in evicting the remaining North Vietnamese from the citadel. The First Battalion, Fifth Marine Regiment entered the citadel on February 12 through the back gate that led into Mang Ca. The next morning, the Marines departed the 1st ARVN Division's headquarters on a southeasterly course, toward the dividing line between the North Vietnamese and South Vietnamese forces inside the citadel.

The Americans planned to assault frontally, with South Vietnamese soldiers on their right flank. Several tanks accompanied the American infantrymen, but the tank commanders were prohibited from firing their main guns in order to limit the damage to the citadel's structures. Owing to a miscommunication between South Vietnamese and the American personnel, the Marines stumbled into the North Vietnamese at a street that they had expected to be held by South Vietnamese forces. When the first

Marine company reached the street, North Vietnamese soldiers opened fire from windows, doorways, rooftops, alleys, and the high Dong Ba tower on the northeastern citadel wall. The Marine company sustained thirty casualties, including all its officers.

The Marines pulled back. Battalion headquarters insisted that the Marines press onward, but repeated attempts met with further casualties and minimal progress. The North Vietnamese had every street and intersection covered by interlocking fields of fire, with shooters on the fortress walls and the Dong Ba tower providing further support.

The next morning, the Marines again attacked the North Vietnamese head-on, and with similarly disappointing results. In the afternoon, the Marine battalion commander received permission to wield the complete suite of American weaponry against the enemy. Jet fighter-bombers pummeled targets along the citadel walls with bombs and rockets. American artillery and naval gunfire crashed down on the fortress into the night.

On the following day, the Marines focused their fury on the Dong Ba tower. From this structure, the North Vietnamese had been able to bring machine gun fire on almost any location in the citadel. The Americans unleashed every available 3.5-inch rocket launcher and tank gun on the tower, not stopping until it had been reduced to a large mound of rubble. Marine riflemen then scrambled forward to secure the site.

To the surprise of the approaching Marines, North Vietnamese soldiers suddenly cropped up at the top of the rubble heap to fire automatic weapons. They were, however, too few in number to keep the Marines off the pile and soon had to flee. North Vietnamese counterattacks would steal the position back on several occasions during the ensuing period, but the North Vietnamese would not again hold it long enough to operate it as a machine gun platform.

Following the toppling of the Dong Ba tower, the American advance through the streets of the citadel gained momentum. The North Vietnamese nonetheless remained tenacious in defense of their positions in the masonry and stone houses. Once the Americans established a foothold in a house on one block, the North Vietnamese pulled back to the next block, where they had already prepared a dense line of defensive positions. In this way, the North Vietnamese avoided prolonged exposure of their flanks and forced the Americans to attack frontally throughout the battle.

The weight of American firepower and the unending flow of American and South Vietnamese infantrymen in its wake eventually ground the North Vietnamese down. To defend a city block was to put oneself in the path of the steamroller, and many North Vietnamese men were crushed underneath, including the senior North Vietnamese commander. At times the destruction was so thorough that the North Vietnamese had to leave their dead behind. The Americans bulldozed the corpses into piles, or incinerated them with flamethrowers to eliminate the stench of decaying flesh.

On the night of February 16, the new North Vietnamese commanding officer in the citadel radioed higher headquarters to request permission to leave the city. The dead and wounded, he relayed, had reached horrific proportions. His superiors told him to stay in the citadel and fight.

Continued North Vietnamese resistance to the southward churn of American and South Vietnamese forces in the citadel prolonged the short-range combat for another week. Finally, on February 23, after North Vietnamese forces had yielded nearly all of the citadel, the North Vietnamese high command ordered a retreat from Hue. The surviving soldiers made a rapid but orderly exit, leaving the dead where they lay.

Whatever relief the North Vietnamese might have felt from their successful evacuation did not last long. After departing the city, they came under attack from American forces that had penetrated the North Vietnamese logistical lines between Hue and the A Shau Valley. One North Vietnamese officer remembered that during the westward retreat, the Americans "expanded their attacks outwards in all directions." They were "pursuing our troops out to the foothills, driving our forces up into the mountains, blocking our supply lines, and destroying our lines of communications and supply caches." American forces "launched attacks deep into our rear areas, causing us a great many difficulties."[24]

The battle for Hue ended with 142 American and 421 South Vietnamese troops dead. The wounded numbered close to 1,100 Americans and over 2,100 South Vietnamese. An additional 80 Americans gave their lives in combat on the city's periphery. Although low in absolute terms for such a battle, these totals represented a large proportion of the strength of the units involved. American estimates of North Vietnamese killed in the city ranged from 2,500 to 5,000, and another 3,000 in the outskirts. The fighting claimed the lives of more than 1,000 civilian bystanders and damaged or destroyed 80 percent of Hue's houses, turning 115,000 residents into refugees. Much of the citadel was damaged beyond repair, though the imperial palace and some other imperial buildings escaped with only minor scratches.[25]

On the far side of I Corps, at Khe Sanh, the North Vietnamese spent the first part of February regrouping. They formed a new headquarters to replace the one that American B-52s had obliterated in Laos, and concocted fresh plans for assaulting the American combat base. Digging trenches and tunnels similar to those at Dien Bien Phu, the North Vietnamese legions crept toward the base, pausing only when the bombs of Operation

Niagara fell close by. They hoped to burrow so close to the Marines that when they stepped from trench and tunnel mouths, the Americans would not bomb them for fear of hitting their own men. Eventually, some trenches reached within fifteen yards of the base's barbed wire.[26]

Media coverage of Khe Sanh was colored by the broader press reaction to the Tet Offensive. American news articles and the accompanying photographs depicted the Marine garrison as beleaguered and ineffective. Of the twenty-five photographs of Khe Sanh to appear in the *New York Times*, ten showed Marines dead, wounded, crouching under fire, or examining destruction wrought by the Communists; four featured Marines in non-combat situations; and eight showed either U.S. supply aircraft under fire or air strikes falling close to the American perimeter. Only one showed Marines firing at the North Vietnamese.[27]

Some American journalists, particularly those inclined to view the Tet Offensive as a Communist success, asserted that the North Vietnamese were on the verge of achieving a second Dien Bien Phu at Khe Sanh. On the February 14 broadcast of the *CBS Evening News*, Murray Fromson announced: "Here, the North Vietnamese decide who lives and who dies, everyday, which planes land and which ones don't, and sooner or later they will make the move that will seal the fate of Khe Sanh."[28]

For a time, the situation at Khe Sanh appeared so ominous that it transfixed President Johnson, who heretofore had shown little interest in the war's battles. To him, the parallels to Dien Bien Phu were unmistakable. On Johnson's orders, aides constructed a miniature model of the battlefield in the White House basement. Wearing a bathrobe and slippers, the president spent sleepless nights next to the model, poring over the most detailed reports out of Khe Sanh and imagining the action described therein on the model.[29]

The North Vietnamese heavy weapons fired frequently upon the American positions at the combat base and the hill outposts, most of which had not been dug in very deeply or fortified with timber, steel matting, or the like. At the sound of incoming rockets or shells, Marines took shelter in bunkers strewn with trash and infested with rats. North Vietnamese bombardments did not, however, inflict heavy casualties as they had at Dien Bien Phu, because the Americans excelled at locating and striking enemy weapons once they had opened fire.

Nor did the North Vietnamese sever Khe Sanh's aerial lifeline as it had severed Dien Bien Phu's. Each day, flotillas of American helicopters and cargo planes carried several hundred tons of supplies to the base's airstrip and the surrounding hills. Radar-guided parachutes and low-altitude drag parachutes allowed some aircraft to deliver their payloads without touching the ground.

The Americans also proved remarkably effective at detecting the location of North Vietnamese troops around Khe Sanh. In January, Westmoreland had commandeered ground sensors that had been scheduled for insertion on the Laotian section of McNamara's barrier and diverted them to Khe Sanh. The Americans seeded these devices across the approaches to the combat base. When North Vietnamese troops marched through, constellations of sensors transmitted radio signals that enabled American intelligence personnel to estimate the size, speed, and bearing of the enemy forces. The Americans could then calculate where the enemy would be by the time American munitions landed on the ground.[30]

A never-ending procession of American aircraft dropped bombs near Khe Sanh, based on identified or suspected locations of North Vietnamese artillery and infantry. On an average day, approximately 350 fighter aircraft, 60 B-52s, and 40 reconnaissance aircraft were flying missions in the area. Over the course of the battle, more than one hundred thousand tons of American bombs fell on a five-square-mile area around the combat base, making it the heaviest battlefield bombing in the history of warfare. The fields of Khe Sanh, on which French planters had been growing lush green coffee plants when the battle began, were turned into a wasteland of cratered, lava-colored rock.

On several occasions, battalion-sized North Vietnamese assaults nearly overran Marine positions on the hills. They came nearest on the night of February 5, at Hill 861-A. Named for its elevation, this hill had been populated with Marines for the purpose of obstructing the approach to Khe Sanh through the Rao Quan Valley. On top of its peak was Echo company of the 2/26 Marines, commanded by Captain Earle Breeding.

The Marine company was crowded inside an area a hundred yards long by twenty-five yards wide. Breeding had organized the defenses on the presumption that the enemy would attack from the north, because heavily armed Marine units on other hills and the combat base looked directly into the eastern, western, and southern faces of hill 861-A. The leathernecks dubbed the perimeter's northern section "the point."

The mission of defending the point belonged to Echo company's 1st platoon, commanded by Second Lieutenant Donald E. Shanley. Blond-haired and blue-eyed, Shanley had been the best backstroker on the nation's top high school swimming team in Winnetka, Illinois, then joined Stanford University's swimming team in 1962. Upon completion of his undergraduate studies, Shanley had enrolled at the University of California, Berkeley business school, but at the end of the first year he had dropped out to enter the Marine Corps Officer Candidate School because he wanted to take part in what he called "this great defining social struggle" in Vietnam.[31]

The North Vietnamese chose to assault Hill 861-A on a night when the hilltop was smothered in a gravy of thick fog. A mortar barrage commenced at 4:00 a.m., followed by salvos of rocket-propelled grenades. The bombardment knocked out an American M-60 machine gun and 60mm mortar at the point. North Vietnamese sappers blew apart the wire in front of the point with Bangalore torpedoes, clearing the way for a battalion from the 325C Division to charge what remained of Shanley's defenses.

As the North Vietnamese assault force rushed the foremost American trench line, they traded rifle fire and grenades with the outnumbered Marines. Where the North Vietnamese met no resistance, they jumped into the trench and ran along it to hit Marines from their sides. Although American flares filled the sky, the enshrouding fog scattered most of their light waves, allowing only a dim glow to reach the eyes of the combatants. The opposing sides were, however, often so close that they could see each other clearly. Private First Class Newton Lyle recalled, "You could actually see the Gooks running around on the lines, laughing and throwing Chicoms [grenades] in bunkers, and you could hear the screams of your buddies, your friends."[32]

At nearby American firebases, reports of the attack brought howitzers to life. Showering the slopes of 861-A with burning metal, the American artillery swept the hill from its base to a line two hundred meters below Breeding's perimeter. Breeding's own mortarmen dropped rounds on the northern side of the hill at ranges as close as thirty-five yards. The American heavy weapons may have felled considerable numbers of North Vietnamese soldiers, but they were not able to stop the large group that was already inside the American perimeter.

One of Shanley's Marines, Corporal Thomas Eichler, sprinted to the machine gun on the point. He found three severely wounded Marines, one of whom he slung over his back before heading toward safety. As he was walking, a North Vietnamese soldier appeared out of the fog in front of him. Having dropped his rifle to carry the wounded Marine, Eichler chose flight over fight. Spinning around, he ran as fast as his legs would take him and his burden.

The North Vietnamese soldier opened fire. Eichler felt the thud of bullets as they struck the wounded Marine on his back. As Eichler would later learn, the bullets did no harm, having been stopped by the man's flak jacket.

By taking advantage of the fog, Eichler eluded this North Vietnamese soldier, but then he ran into another, who was firing rockets at other Americans. Eichler seized the strap from this man's rocket pouch, wrapped it around his neck, and strangled him to death. Eichler brought the injured Marine to safety, then rescued two other machine gunners.

Most of the Marines were trying to keep low in the trenches and bunkers that remained in American hands, but after Eichler returned with the last member of the machine gun crew, he stood erect above the trench line. He pitched grenades at the North Vietnamese and screamed at them. "There must have been an angel of the lord protecting him," one witness stated. "It was a miracle he was not killed."[33]

By this time, the North Vietnamese had taken complete control of the front trench line. The intensity of the fighting slackened as the North Vietnamese paused to regroup in the trench line and collect American equipment, along with magazines, books, and other souvenirs. The pause bought time for Captain Breeding to send Marines from other sections of the perimeter to reinforce Shanley's battered platoon. Shanley consolidated a new defensive line along a secondary trench, which was the last line of defense for the company's command post and ammunition dump.

Scurrying around in the fog, Shanley and other officers and NCOs tried to find men and give them orders in preparation for a counterattack. The crash of artillery rounds was so loud at times that the issuer of instructions had to cup his hands over the listener's ear and yell directly into it. After several minutes, Shanley gave the signal to commence the counterattack.

The Marines began by hurling fragmentation grenades at the enemy-held trench line. They had to guess at the proper distance, for the fog obscured everything beyond a range of ten yards. Then, climbing up from their trenches, the Americans charged straight at the North Vietnamese. Shanley led the assault, striding without crouching, his indifference to danger inspiring others to follow him.

According to one American account, the counterattack took the enemy by such surprise that the Americans caught North Vietnamese soldiers perusing newly acquired issues of *Playboy*. Most of the North Vietnamese, though, were ready for battle by the time the Americans set upon them. The combatants struggled for control of the trench line with bayonets, knives, entrenching tools, and fists. Both sides tossed grenades, at considerable risk to themselves since the fifteen-yard blast radius of the grenades exceeded the visibility radius. The Marines' flak jackets gave them a decided advantage in the grenade contest, as they could coil up and absorb the fragments in their jackets while the North Vietnamese were riddled with shrapnel.

"The M-16 didn't come into play too much because of the hill we were on," Captain Breeding recollected. "There were really no fields of fire to speak of, and it turned out to be a hand grenade war." The struggle for the trenches "was just like a World War II movie," with "knife fighting, bayonet fighting, hitting people on the nose with your fist and all the rest of that."[34]

420 • TRIUMPH REGAINED

The North Vietnamese were on the receiving end of most of the damage inflicted in the close-quarters fracas. Some Marines attributed the one-sided outcome to superior Marine training and adaptiveness. Others contended that the North Vietnamese did not fight well because they had been given drugs before the battle to remove their fear, a conclusion based on their giddiness in the midst of combat.

Half an hour after the first North Vietnamese had pierced the Marine perimeter, the much-reduced assault force departed whence it had come. As the North Vietnamese retreated down the hillside, American artillery shells chased after them. A North Vietnamese battalion had been held in reserve below the summit, but it had lost so many men to American bombardments that it made no effort to attack and instead trickled away with the remnants of the assault battalion.

The Marines on the hill, oblivious to developments more than ten yards away, were still worried that the North Vietnamese would strike again before dawn. "We sat there just praying for daylight to come," Private First Class Lyle recounted, "'cause we knew by daylight they would either have to pull back or they'd really get their ass kicked because we could call in air strikes and artillery. So we sat there and prayed for the sun to come up. It seemed like that last hour and a half was like a year. And the next morning, when the sun finally did come up, we thanked God that the ones of us that had lived God let us live."[35]

Eight U.S. Marines perished on Hill 861-A that night, most of them killed at the point during the opening moments of the battle. The Marines counted 109 North Vietnamese bodies inside the perimeter. Larry Jackson and another Marine assigned to burial detail used C-4 plastic explosive and a shovel to excavate a grave for nineteen North Vietnamese corpses. "I never thought that I could ever throw nineteen human beings in a hole and just cover them up," Jackson recounted. But the death of his squad leader, Private First Class Jack C. Bogard, had erased any sympathy he might have felt for the enemy. "That was the first time I'd ever seen a dead Marine," Jackson stated. "I remember helping take him to the LZ to be transported out. And I remember just falling down on my knees, crying just like my three-year-old baby." So intensely did Jackson burn with hatred of the North Vietnamese that he urinated on the nineteen bodies before filling in the hole.[36]

Fearing enemy ambushes and mines, the Marines did not police the battlefield beyond their perimeter. Lance Corporal Lance E. Tibbett could see approximately one hundred dead and wounded North Vietnamese in a gully down the slope and heard some of them crying out in pain.[37] Captain Breeding could have ordered his men to shoot these wounded North Vietnamese, or the North Vietnamese soldiers who later came to rescue the wounded and retrieve the dead, but he did not.[38]

The North Vietnamese would win only one military victory in the vicinity of Khe Sanh. It occurred on February 6 at the village Lang Vei, eight kilometers to the southwest of the Marine combat base and just two kilometers from the Laotian border. The U.S. Army Special Forces had operated a camp at Lang Vei since 1966 and, owing to the presence of large North Vietnamese forces in nearby Laos, had developed the camp into one of their most formidable redoubts. The United States had spent one million dollars on its fortifications and equipped the garrison of twenty-four Americans and five hundred indigenous troops with a large arsenal of mortars, machine guns, and recoilless rifles. In late January, the Special Forces had delivered M-72 light antitank weapons to the camp after an American pilot beheld five North Vietnamese tanks near Lang Vei, the first time North Vietnamese tanks had been seen in the war.

Major General Rathvon Tompkins, commander of the 3rd Marine Division, had assured Westmoreland's headquarters in the middle of January that he could protect the Lang Vei camp from a concerted North Vietnamese onslaught. Within range of Lang Vei, the Marines possessed sixteen 175mm howitzers, sixteen 155mm howitzers, and eighteen 105mm howitzers. If the North Vietnamese attacked the camp in dangerously large numbers, Tompkins planned to send Marine armor and infantry to the rescue.

Spearheading the North Vietnamese attack on February 6 were sixteen Soviet-made PT-76 amphibious tanks. An estimated four hundred North Vietnamese infantrymen and sappers accompanied the armor during the approach to Lang Vei, the infantry using the steel hulls of tanks for cover. In another unusual display of heavy equipment, the North Vietnamese positioned four 152mm howitzers to fire at Lang Vei.

In the dark of night, the North Vietnamese hit the camp from the north, south, and west simultaneously. The North Vietnamese tanks rolled through the camp's barbed wire, scanned for targets with their searchlights, and eviscerated bunkers with their 76mm main guns. To the dismay of the American Green Berets and their indigenous counterparts, the tanks suffered no ill effects from exploding claymore mines and most of the other ordnance that the garrison threw at them.

The American commander at the Lang Vei camp phoned the Khe Sanh combat base for artillery support. The artillery officers at the other end of the call were at that moment organizing responses to North Vietnamese weapons that were shelling the Khe Sanh base. They said they needed more information before they would redirect their howitzers toward Lang Vei. It was unclear to them, and to the rest of the Americans, whether one or both of the enemy's two targets was merely a feint, intended to draw attention away from the real target.

Fifteen precious minutes ticked away before the officers at the main camp decided that the attack on Lang Vei might not be a feint. By the time the first American shells whistled into Lang Vei, North Vietnamese tanks and infantry had already broken into the eastern side of the camp's perimeter. Those forces were now so close to friendly personnel that Marine artillery could not risk firing at them.

The Green Berets asked the Marines to send a relief force, in accordance with the previously approved contingency plans. Col. David Lownds, the Marine commander at the Khe Sanh combat base, refused. As he saw it, the presence of large North Vietnamese forces between Khe Sanh and Lang Vei made overland routes too dangerous, and the North Vietnamese tanks posed too grave a danger to helicopters. Continued North Vietnamese shelling of the Khe Sanh base, moreover, led Lownds to believe that the North Vietnamese might attack it on the ground at any moment. Major General Tompkins and the senior Marine commander in the country, Lieutenant General Robert E. Cushman Jr. concurred in the decision.

For the next few hours, the 106mm recoilless rifles and M-72 rocket launchers of the Lang Vei camp dueled with the North Vietnamese tanks. The garrison's indigenous troops fought bravely, more than half of them perishing while attempting to hold their ground. But the North Vietnamese attack force was not to be denied. The North Vietnamese overran the base before sunrise.

Eight Americans held out in the tactical operations center, which had been built underground and encased in concrete. After unsuccessfully trying to collapse the tactical operations center by placing a tank on top of it, the North Vietnamese chipped away at its concrete shell with explosives and threw grenades into its vent shaft. The Americans hung on until the next afternoon, when a series of bombing and strafing runs by American aircraft permitted everyone except one seriously wounded man to escape to safety.[39]

The fall of Lang Vei occurred in the wake of multiple rebukes from General Westmoreland to General Cushman, the officer who had succeeded General Walt as the senior Marine commander in Vietnam. Westmoreland and his staff had previously faulted General Cushman for a lack of preparedness among the Marine units near the DMZ, a problem most evident in the extensive casualties suffered by Marines who had not entrenched themselves adequately. Late in January, Westmoreland had become so dissatisfied with Cushman that he had ordered the creation of a new headquarters in the northern provinces to supersede Cushman's authority.[40] Westmoreland's deputy, General Creighton Abrams, was slated to take command of this headquarters on its opening date in mid-February.

Upon learning of the defeat at Lang Vei, Westmoreland flew to Cushman's headquarters, whereupon he received two hours of briefings. As the two hours unfolded, Westmoreland became, by his own account, "more and more shocked at things that virtually begged to be done yet remained undone." Especially galling to Westmoreland was the unwillingness of the Marine leadership to meet the request of the Special Forces commander at Lang Vei for relief forces. Convinced that the circumvention of Cushman's authority could come none too soon, Westmoreland decreed that he would henceforth give orders directly to Marine units.[41]

The largest Communist attack at Khe Sanh took place on February 29. That night, a regiment of North Vietnamese infantry marched toward the Marine combat base in tunnels and trenches for an assault on what they believed to be the weakest section of the base's perimeter, which was defended by a contingent of South Vietnamese Rangers. American sensors detected the motions of the North Vietnamese soldiers long before they were visible to the garrison. The information gleaned from the sensors caused Colonel Lownds to request the use of the heaviest of weapons against the two main axes of approach. "I need a B-52 strike NOW!" he hollered over the phone. "Any later than two hours from now, forget it because he's going to have closed with me."[42]

At the front of the assault force was a team of sappers. They glided through the dark toward the perimeter wire, which they intended to destroy with satchel charges. Next came an infantry battalion that would burst in behind the sappers. The other two battalions trailed behind, ready to rush reinforcements to the points where the first battalion penetrated the South Vietnamese defenses.

Nguyen Van Tuan, an infantryman in the lead North Vietnamese battalion, was close enough to the sappers to see them in the blackness of night. When the sappers approached the wire, hostile artillery shells flew straight into them. "The sappers died at the edge of the trench, still gripping their charges," Tuan remembered. The accuracy of the American artillery fire left no doubt that the North Vietnamese had lost the element of surprise.

Tuan's battalion rushed ahead toward the wire, seeking to close with the defenders before the artillery could flatten them. Flares filled the sky, exposing the battalion's position to American pilots and forward air controllers. "Illumination lighted the killing ground as we attacked into certain death," Tuan remembered. "Within moments, aircraft were upon us spitting orange streams of fire into our trenches. The assault stalled."

The lead battalion's radio teams pleaded for reinforcements from the trailing battalions. The voices on the other end sounded panicked. American artillery shells and bombs were exploding in the middle of those battalions as well. Soon the radio operators from the other battalions went off the air, replaced by the empty cackle of static on the receivers. With no support from the rear, the commander of the lead battalion decided to drive his men forward in another assault.

"The second assault was much worse," Tuan remembered. "The enemy had bracketed the killing field with all ordnance available. Only when the aircraft attacked did the artillery cease, and then, as if working in unison, when one stopped the other commenced."[43]

In response to the request from Lownds, a group of fully loaded B-52s had been diverted from its original target to Khe Sanh. Flying six miles above the earth, the bombers could be neither seen nor heard from the ground. When the B-52s reached Khe Sanh, the American artillery paused and the bays of the aircraft opened to release twenty-seven-ton payloads of 250-, 500-, and 750-pound bombs. After tumbling for forty-five seconds, the bombs produced explosions that engulfed most of the terrain occupied by the attacking regiment. "This was the only time the kids on the line told me that they actually saw bodies being thrown in the air," Lownds later said.[44]

A small number of North Vietnamese troops reached the combat base's outermost barbed wire in a third and final assault. The South Vietnamese Rangers, supported by American heavy weapons, stopped them before they could get near the defensive positions. Resigned at last to defeat, what was left of the North Vietnamese regiment withdrew.

According to one North Vietnamese history, the regiment lost half its men that evening.[45] The actual toll may well have been higher. Tuan's company suffered so many casualties that it did not have enough men left to constitute a single platoon. The garrison's total casualty count during the engagement was one wounded Ranger.

The North Vietnamese began pulling forces out of Khe Sanh after this debacle. Among the troops who remained, demoralization set in. The official history of one of the principal siege units, the 304th NVA Division, told of a division whose resolve and discipline had been shattered by the combination of massive casualties and minimal achievements. One battalion disobeyed orders from its regimental headquarters to relieve a fortified defensive position. Another battalion withdrew from its assigned location without notifying its headquarters. After one company was denied permission to abandon what it considered an inordinately dangerous position, its political officer convened a Communist Party chapter meeting and passed a resolution sanctioning the unit's withdrawal. The 304th Division imposed disciplinary punishments on 399 men, of whom 186 were party members. The divisional history noted, in addition, that "the lack of a high and uniform spirit and resolve and combat discipline throughout the division was also demonstrated in the number of incidents of desertion and of self-inflicted wounds."[46]

The leading hawks of the Johnson administration—the Joint Chiefs, Westmoreland, Bunker, Sharp, and Rostow—spent much of February urging the president to initiate a strategic counteroffensive. They recommended the usual items on the escalation menu: intensified bombing of the North, the mining of Haiphong Harbor, and large ground operations into Laos, Cambodia, and southern North Vietnam. Enough of the American public wanted military success in Vietnam, they argued, to support these initiatives.[47] In early February, 61 percent of Americans told pollsters that they favored military escalation, slightly more than before Tet, while 23 percent preferred de-escalation. General support for the war stood at 74 percent, up from 61 percent in December.[48]

Johnson was not prepared to implement most of these measures, but he did agree to intensify the bombing of the North. On February 6, he reduced restrictions on Rolling Thunder near Hanoi and Haiphong and authorized strikes on fourteen targets that had been off limits until now. He also sent aircraft to bomb the MIGs at the Phuc Yen airfield.[49]

General Wheeler encouraged Westmoreland to request reinforcements, in order to facilitate the extension of the ground war beyond South Vietnam and to force Johnson to call up the reserves.[50] In his initial reply, Westmoreland said that he did not need reinforcements. Wheeler, however, had become so fed up with Johnson that he was willing to mislead the president on the point and solicit Westmoreland's participation in the misleading. Wheeler's persistent prodding eventually induced Westmoreland to send an official message on February 12 stating that "I desperately need" reinforcements to fend off the enemy.[51]

This distress call, coinciding as it did with the American media's dire reports of the situation in Vietnam, rattled the president. With an election coming up in November, Johnson was acutely conscious that his political career would be over if he denied a request for reinforcements and then catastrophic defeat followed. He spoke repeatedly of General George McClellan and President Abraham Lincoln, worried that Westmoreland might follow McClellan in charging that his president had failed to provide what was needed.[52]

In late February, Johnson dispatched Wheeler to South Vietnam to confer with Westmoreland on the reinforcement question. Wheeler spent his visit with Westmoreland developing a three-stage troop request. The first increment, totaling 108,000 reinforcements, would arrive in South Vietnam by May 1. The other two increments, totaling 97,000, would be prepared for deployment later in the year and, depending upon conditions, would either be sent to Vietnam or assigned to the nation's depleted strategic reserve. The two generals envisioned a variety of contingencies that would require the 97,000, including the expansion of U.S.

ground operations into Laos and Cambodia, which Westmoreland continued to advocate.[53]

In his trip report, Wheeler attempted to sell Johnson on the troop request by depicting the situation in Vietnam as much worse than what both he and Westmoreland actually believed it to be. The Tet Offensive had "nearly succeeded in a dozen places," Wheeler asserted. "In short, it was a very near thing." Wheeler warned that the United States could face renewed Communist attacks and that in the absence of American troop reinforcements, the nation must be "prepared to accept some reverses."[54] The report avoided discussion of operations in Laos and Cambodia as well as the strategic reserve, for, as Westmoreland explained later, Wheeler "saw no possibility at the moment of selling reinforcements in terms of future operations." Wheeler preferred to exploit the civilian leadership's "belief in crisis to get the troops, then argue new strategy later."[55]

Upon his return to Washington, Wheeler went to the White House to brief President Johnson on these and additional ominous findings. If the president did not authorize an additional 205,000 men, Wheeler said, it would precipitate "the collapse of the ARVN." The United States would be compelled to "give up the two northern provinces of South Vietnam."[56]

By the end of the briefing, Johnson was, in the words of Clark Clifford, "as worried as I have ever seen him."[57]

CHAPTER 14

. . .

HAWKS AND DOVES

March 1968

L yndon Johnson once more was forced to choose between several unappetizing options, each likely to create as many problems as it solved. If he accepted General Wheeler's recommendation to add another 205,000 troops, he would have to raise taxes or cut spending or both, to the detriment of his domestic agenda. He would also have to call up the reserves, which he found as abhorrent as ever, or else he would leave the U.S. military without enough troops in its active strategic reserve units, which would raise the hackles of the military and Congress and put the nation at heightened risk.

If Johnson did not heed Wheeler's advice on the 205,000 troops, he would come under renewed criticism for ignoring the military leadership. The large number of Americans who wanted to punish the enemy for the deceitful surprise attack would feel the president had let them down. And, according to the generals, the U.S. military could suffer reverses that would then be blamed on the commander in chief.

In years past, Lyndon Johnson had turned to Robert McNamara when Vietnam had entangled him in such a predicament.

McNamara would have eagerly devised a plan to limit the risks to the president and prevent the discontents of hawks and doves from boiling over. Now McNamara was gone, and into his shoes had just stepped Clark Clifford, who did not possess his predecessor's intimate familiarity with Vietnam. To compensate for this lack of knowledge, Johnson asked Clifford to organize an expert review of American policy, which would then serve as the basis for responding to Wheeler's proposal.

A long-time friend of Johnson, Clifford had consistently expressed support for the president's Vietnam policies in years past, and he was seen as something of a hawk. During February, however, Clifford had grown doubtful about the war, a fact that appears to have escaped Johnson's notice. Clifford had accepted the view of the media and some elements of the intelligence community that Tet had shown the enemy to be stronger than previously believed and hence had discredited American claims of military progress.[1] At a time when President Johnson's conviction in staying the course was hardening, his new secretary of defense was going soft.

In assembling a task force to evaluate policy options, Clifford gave the appearance of possessing an open mind, an impression that he reinforced in a 1969 *Foreign Affairs* article.[2] In a memoir published in 1991, however, Clifford told a different story, in which he had already made up his mind on at least one of the key issues: reinforcements. By this juncture, he wrote, he "was already unalterably opposed to the request for more troops."[3] Casting further doubt on his professions of open-mindedness was his decision to side immediately with the dovish faction of the Johnson administration and empower them to produce a draft report within a mere two days and a final report two days after that.

The dove who exerted the most influence on Clifford was Paul C. Warnke, the assistant secretary of defense for international security affairs. According to another leading dove, Townsend Hoopes, the Tet Offensive had convinced Warnke that Westmoreland's military strategy was "foolish to the point of insanity."[4] Warnke and the other doves opposed increasing American troop strength, intensifying Rolling Thunder, and widening the war geographically. These measures, they believed, would not enable the United States to win the war and would not be supported by the American public.[5]

In the preliminary draft of their report, the task force expressed opposition to escalation in any form. As a strategic alternative, they proposed shifting the focus of American troops from destroying enemy forces to securing populous areas.[6] But by venturing into the particulars of military strategy, they provoked a swift counterstroke from the generals. In a biting reply to the task force's proposal, General Wheeler argued that pulling American forces back to the populous regions would invite large North Vietnamese attacks on the towns and cities, the government's main sources of power.[7]

Westmoreland had been making this argument persuasively since 1965, and it had been further validated by the events of Tet. At Hue, the North Vietnamese had proven that they could bring ruin all the way to the coast if they possessed unfettered access to the hinterlands between the nation's borders and its strongholds. In the space between Laos and Hue, North Vietnamese forces had staged enough large units, heavy weapons, and supplies to attack and overrun one of South Vietnam's most important cities. If the North Vietnamese were allowed to make more such assaults, American forces would have to launch counterattacks that devastated the targeted cities, as Hue had been devastated. Communist initiatives in the rest of the country during Tet had quickly fizzled because, among other reasons, the North Vietnamese did not have major staging areas close to any city besides Hue thanks to American operations that had driven large North

Vietnamese forces from base areas like Van Tuong, the Ia Drang Valley, the Bong Son Plain, the Ngan Valley, the Iron Triangle, and the Pleiku plateau.

Wheeler's objection forced Clifford into a major revision of the document. Clifford may have been swayed to some degree by Wheeler's arguments, though in his memoir he stated merely that he acquiesced because "after only four days at the Pentagon, I was not ready to take on the collective weight of Rusk, the Joint Chiefs, Westmoreland, and Rostow."[8] In the revised memorandum, the task force largely avoided the topic of overall military strategy, which was said to deserve further study.[9]

At this same time, Johnson was receiving information suggesting that the war was turning in America's favor. The North Vietnamese legions had been driven from Hue and were pulling back from Khe Sanh. Positive data from the U.S. military on conditions in town and country were beginning to outmuscle the negative reporting from the press and the CIA.

On March 7, the *New York Times* quoted a "senior military spokesman" in Saigon as saying that the Communists had incurred terrible damage during the offensive and squandered their capabilities for large-scale offensive activity.[10] That spokesman was Westmoreland himself. He had made the comment to inspire the South Vietnamese, but it had the side effect of deflating the sense of impending doom that Wheeler had wanted to use to rouse Johnson.[11] Westmoreland's single statement may have done greater harm to the proposal for more troops than all the months of lugubrious clamoring by the doves. Two days after the article was printed, a dispirited Wheeler notified Westmoreland that he was unable to muster sufficient support in Washington for the reinforcements.[12] Johnson would end up adding just 13,500 more troops to the total in Vietnam.

If the brightening of the situation in South Vietnam and the obviation of the troop increase assuaged Johnson's angst, the relief did not last long. The New Hampshire presidential primary, held on March 12, gave his adversaries within the Democratic Party a chance to bruise him in front of a global grandstand. Entered on the Democratic ballot was the name of a little-known and eccentric senator from Minnesota, Eugene McCarthy. The name Lyndon Johnson was not inscribed on the ballot because the president had not yet officially declared his candidacy, but his supporters had orchestrated a write-in effort.

That evening, electoral officials announced that Johnson had defeated McCarthy by just three hundred votes. Among the intelligentsia, the outcome was interpreted as proof of mounting opposition to the war in Vietnam. Later analysis, though, would reveal that the majority of McCarthy voters had described themselves as hawks and were unaware of the antiwar position of McCarthy, who had campaigned in New Hampshire on his opposition to Johnson rather than the war. Theirs had been a protest vote against Johnson for his refusal to wield more of America's military might in Vietnam.[13] But whether voters thought Johnson was going too far in Vietnam or not far enough, the overriding fact for Johnson was that they were against him.

An even sharper political dagger was about to pierce Johnson, in the form of an ultimatum from Robert F. Kennedy. The American press was rife with speculation that Senator Kennedy would enter the Democratic primary to challenge Johnson for the presidential nomination, using his critique of Johnson's Vietnam policy to draw liberals away from the incumbent. On March 14, Kennedy delivered his ultimatum in person to Secretary of Defense Clifford. He told Clifford that Johnson had to acknowledge publicly the waywardness of his efforts in Vietnam and organize a commission to devise a new strategy. For the commission's members, Kennedy proposed himself and a list of national security dignitaries, most of whom were known doves. If Johnson refused these demands, Kennedy would have no choice but to declare himself a presidential candidate in order to rescue the United States from disaster.[14]

Johnson, and probably also Kennedy, knew that no president could afford to flagellate himself in this manner or turn his foreign policy over to a committee. The president rejected the ultimatum outright.

Two days later, Kennedy announced his candidacy for the presidency. As the charismatic brother of a martyred president, he presented a much more formidable challenge to Johnson than McCarthy. While McCarthy had been able to gain the support of liberals in the media and Congress, those liberals could be expected to support Kennedy if given the choice between Kennedy and Lyndon Johnson.

On March 22, the White House's attention was diverted to Khe Sanh for one last time. An uncharacteristically large number of Communist howitzers opened fire simultaneously at Khe Sanh, and American sensors detected the movement of North Vietnamese infantry formations toward the combat base. American artillery and B-52 bombers struck swiftly and decisively. Whatever North Vietnamese forces survived this bludgeoning were unable or unwilling to charge the base. The event signified the end of serious offensive action at Khe Sanh, and the end of Hanoi's dream for a second Dien Bien Phu.

The battle for Khe Sanh had played out much as Westmoreland had intended. American forces had crippled multiple North Vietnamese divisions at low cost to themselves. American estimates put the number of North Vietnamese killed at between ten and fifteen thousand, an assessment supported by captured documents and the testimony of North Vietnamese witnesses. Fewer than five hundred U.S. Marines died during the contest.[15] Although few people knew it yet, the world had just seen the first battle of the sensor era and the first indication that the new technology would transform warfare in the decades to come.

Intense fighting was to persist in other areas of South Vietnam long after the Communist tide had receded from the cities and Khe Sanh. In anticipation of a need to reinforce the successes of Tet, Hanoi had continued to send infiltrators at a rapid clip, with 13,752 entering the South in February and 23,477 in March.[16] As American and South Vietnamese units pushed out from the population centers, they found the enemy unusually willing to stand and fight, resulting in unusually heavy casualties on both sides.[17]

The surprisingly good performance of South Vietnam's armed forces during Tet was followed by additional improvement in March. Communist atrocities in Hue and elsewhere had brought home to the South Vietnamese what the Communists had in mind should they prevail. The realization had invigorated some hitherto lackluster leaders and given Thieu license to sack those who were not sufficiently invigorated.[18] During March, South Vietnamese combat deaths exceeded 2,500, well above the American tally of 1,543 and far below the estimated Communist total of 17,371.[19]

One significant exception to the trend of ongoing Communist pugnacity was the 48th Local Force Battalion, which according to American intelligence was operating in Quang Ngai Province during March. American patrols that went in search of the battalion rarely found signs of the enemy except for mines and booby traps, which inflicted considerable losses on the Americans. Adding to the frustration of the Americans was the unwillingness of local villagers to disclose the locations of the deadly devices.

Countless American units had experienced the same agony at other times and other places in South Vietnam and had felt the same indignation at the seeming complicity of the civilian population. On occasion, the Americans had lashed out against civilians in acts of violence ranging from punches to gunshots. But military discipline, enforced by officers, had usually prevented the loosing of violent rage upon civilians and had ensured

438 • TRIUMPH REGAINED

that it had never occurred on a large scale. Such fundamental
leadership was, however, absent when the 1st Battalion, 20th
Infantry went in search of the 48th Local Force Battalion on
March 16.[20]

That morning, according to American intelligence reports,
the enemy battalion was located in the hamlets of My Lai 4 and
My Khe 4. Lieutenant Colonel Frank Barker, commander of the
operation, had informed his officers the previous evening that
the civilian population would depart these hamlets for a weekly
market by 0700, before the Americans were scheduled to arrive.
Anyone found in the village, therefore, could be considered an
enemy. The American soldiers, said Barker, were to destroy homes,
crops, and livestock, because the hamlets gave sustenance to the
enemy and constituted an enemy stronghold. He did not explicitly say that his troops should kill anyone found in the village,
and his death in a June 1968 helicopter crash would prevent later
investigators from asking him whether he had intended to order
the mass slaughter of civilians. Some of the officers who were
present said later that they had interpreted his remarks to mean
that they had license to kill whomever they found, but others
asserted that Barker had implied nothing of the kind.

The 1st platoon of Charlie company, under the command of Lt.
William H. Calley Jr., landed by helicopter at 0730 on the morning
of March 16. Helicopter pilots spotted a small number of armed
Vietnamese men running away and opened fire on them. The
chattering of guns led other Americans to believe that the 48th
Local Force Battalion was present and hence that large numbers
of enemy combatants were likely to appear at any moment.

The killing of civilians began with the shooting of a few adults
who came into the view of Lieutenant Calley's platoon and were
presumed to be members or supporters of the 48th Local Force
Battalion. It likely would have ended there had the officers on the

scene notified the troops that they had found unarmed women and children and reminded them to avoid harm to civilians, as American officers had done routinely in the past. Instead, Calley ordered his platoon to kill the large groups of women, children, and elderly men whom they found in the two hamlets. Two other platoon commanders, Lieutenant Stephen Brooks and Lieutenant Thomas Willingham, followed Calley's example. Some of the soldiers indulged eagerly; others hesitated and participated only when ordered; still others refused to take part in the murders. The Americans killed somewhere between 347 and 504 civilians and raped approximately twenty women and girls.

Warrant Officer Hugh Thompson Jr., flying overhead in an OH-23 Raven observation helicopter, caught sight of the butchery at approximately 9:15 a.m. Aghast at the behavior of his fellow Americans, he set his helicopter down to rescue some civilians who had been shot but were still alive. Upon returning to his company headquarters at 11:00 a.m., Thompson reported the mass shootings of unarmed civilians to his commanding officer, who in turn passed the report up the chain of command. When the pilot's report reached Lieutenant Colonel Barker, the commander ordered his officers to cease fire. As soon as the platoon commanders relayed the order to their soldiers, the atrocities came to an end.

Word of the massacre spread quickly through the Americal Division, the parent division of Barker's battalion. The commander of the Americal Division, Major General Samuel W. Koster, directed his subordinates to investigate the episode. While most of the officers privy to the investigation disapproved of the killings, some of them worried that acknowledgment of what had happened could undermine the broader American war effort or could destroy their careers or those of officers at higher levels of authority. In the final report, the investigating officers stated that no civilians had been deliberately killed, though twenty or so might have been inadvertently caught in the crossfire between American and hostile forces. Other Americans who knew about the massacre kept quiet out of fear of retribution by higher authorities or fear of enemy exploitation of the event. The crime would remain a secret for the next year.[21]

Between January 29 and March 31, 1968, Communist forces killed roughly 3,700 American and 7,600 South Vietnamese troops.[22] In so doing, they suffered losses, as estimated by the Americans, of over 54,000 dead.[23] Many thousands more defected to the South Vietnamese side after their hopes for a rapid and glorious victory had been dashed.[24] Losses had been especially heavy among underground urban cadres, whose identities had been exposed when they had tried to organize popular uprisings, and village guerrillas and political cadres, who had flocked to the towns and cities to take part in the offensive.[25]

As South Vietnamese forces began returning to the countryside in March to reassert governmental authority, they often found that the Communists had no one left to oppose them. The people who had organized political meetings, beheaded government officials, and controlled the rural population had been killed or captured during the failed uprisings. Hanoi's ability to recruit rural South Vietnamese youth, already in steep decline in 1967, suffered an irreparable blow.[26]

Neither the magnitude nor the implications of Hanoi's losses were fully appreciated in Washington at the end of March. Although the fear of a colossal American defeat had petered out, few in the White House discerned the dawning of a strategic upturn in Vietnam. Instead, they foresaw the persistence of bloody stalemate, as described by Walter Cronkite. If the war continued to grind on as before, Lyndon Johnson knew, it would play into the hands of Eugene McCarthy, Robert F. Kennedy, the Republican presidential nominee, and whoever else promised the American people a new and improved approach to Vietnam.

As he had done so many times with McNamara, Johnson phoned Clifford near the end of March to talk over the best solution to the current morass. "I think what we've got to do," the president told his new secretary of defense, "is to get out of the posture of just being the war candidate that McCarthy has put us in and Bobby is putting us in, the kids are putting us in and the papers are putting us in." Spelling out his general strategic principles, Johnson said, "Our right hand is going after their jaw with an offense on the war front, but we ought to have a peace front too simultaneously and use both fists—not just one, not fight with one hand behind us, so that we can say we are the peace candidate—but we are the true peace candidate. We're not the Chamberlain peace—we're the Churchill peace."

For the fist of peace, Johnson tossed around the idea of suspending bombing in Hanoi and Haiphong during an upcoming stretch of bad weather. It needed to be "something that will not hurt our men materially," Johnson explained. "We're not going to get these doves, but we can neutralize the country to where it won't follow them if we can come up with something."

"Yes, that's right," Clifford responded. "I think you put your finger right on it. We have a posture now in which Kennedy and McCarthy are the peace candidates and President Johnson is the war candidate. Now we must veer away from that and we can do it."[27]

To provide backing for the peace fist, Clifford assembled a group of "Wise Men," akin to that which had met in the fall of 1967, on March 25 and 26. Displaying a penchant for plotting much like McNamara's, Clifford altered the group's membership to guarantee majority support for his preferred outcome. He supplemented the 1967 group with three individuals who opposed hawkish escalation—Arthur Goldberg, Cyrus Vance, and General Matthew Ridgway.

On the first day, the Wise Men received briefings from Philip Habib of the State Department, Major General William DePuy of the Defense Department, and George Carver of the CIA. The most forceful briefer was Habib, who depicted the South Vietnamese government and military in grim terms. The South Vietnamese were now so weak, he said, that it might take five to ten years of American effort to make them viable. In response to a question about American policy, Habib advised that the United States should "stop the bombing and negotiate."[28]

The views of Ambassador Bunker did not appear to have been conveyed to the Wise Men. Bunker had recently expressed opposition to a bombing halt, warning that it would jeopardize the newfound aggressiveness of the South Vietnamese forces and "reverse the favorable trend of opinion in the urban areas." In the event of a pause, Bunker believed, the North Vietnamese "might well conclude that the situation in South Vietnam has been shaken more than they probably now think and that in the U.S. our resolve with respect to Viet-Nam has been weakened."[29]

The Wise Men did hear from General Creighton Abrams, Westmoreland's deputy, on the following day. Johnson had just selected Abrams to replace Westmoreland as commander of U.S. forces in Vietnam. Johnson had made the decision not because of dissatisfaction with Westmoreland or his strategy, as was conjectured in the media, but because he had been planning since November to rotate Westmoreland home after an unusually long tour.[30]

Having just flown in from Saigon, Abrams met with President Johnson and General Wheeler on the morning of March 26 to prepare for the meeting. During the session, the president urged the two generals to tell the Wise Men of the positive achievements of American and South Vietnamese forces over the past two months. "I want you to tell them all the things that are true," Johnson said. "If you soldiers were as gloomy and doomy as the civilians you would have surrendered."[31]

Speaking to the Wise Men in the afternoon, Abrams and Wheeler asserted that the North Vietnamese were reeling from the blows of highly effective American and South Vietnamese forces. Questioned about the progress of South Vietnam's military in comparison with South Korea's armed forces during the Korean War, Abrams replied, "The Koreans had the same problem of building their army and fighting at the same time. I would say the Vietnamese are doing as well if not better than the Koreans." When asked whether the South Vietnamese could start taking over more of the war after a period of expansion, Abrams answered in the affirmative. "I would have to quit if I didn't believe that," he averred.[32]

At the end of the conclave, six of the Wise Men concurred in the view that "we can no longer do the job we set out to do in the time we have left and we must begin to take steps to disengage." Preferring Habib's depiction of the situation to that of Abrams, they concluded that the outlook in South Vietnam was so bad that the war could not be turned around except with inordinate American commitments of time and resources. The changes on which these Wise Men agreed, however, went only as far as the measures Johnson and Clifford already intended to implement: capping U.S. troop levels, instituting a bombing halt, and pushing for negotiations. What the United States should do if the negotiations failed to yield something better than capitulation to the North Vietnamese was left unsaid. Four Wise Men took a hawkish position, opposing a bombing halt and urging the president to heed the advice of his generals. The American people, they argued, could be rallied in support of continued military operations long enough to gain a satisfactory outcome. The other two Wise Men advocated a middle position between the doves and hawks.[33]

Having secured the blessing of a plurality of the Wise Men for the peace fist, Johnson next delivered a televised speech to the nation on the evening of the thirty-first. From the Oval Office, with a plain, cream-colored curtain behind him, the president addressed the American people in a somber tone. He began by recounting his prior efforts to achieve peace in Vietnam and the repeated rebuffs of Hanoi. The Tet Offensive had been "a savage assault on the people, the government, and the allies of South Vietnam," he intoned, and had failed to produce a popular uprising or a collapse of the South Vietnamese government. Further North Vietnamese attacks would likewise end in failure.

To encourage Hanoi to negotiate an end to the senseless bloodshed, the president continued, he had decided to halt Rolling Thunder strikes except in the southernmost sections of North Vietnam. "We ask that talks begin promptly, that they be serious talks on the substance of peace," he said in his Texas drawl. "We assume that during those talks Hanoi will not take advantage of our restraint."

Johnson made clear that he would stand by the South Vietnamese government, whose recent improvements he touted. "The United States," the president said, "will never accept a fake solution to this long and arduous struggle and call it peace." He vowed to keep up the military pressure on the North Vietnamese as necessary, asserting that "if peace does not come now through negotiations, it will come when Hanoi understands that our common resolve is unshakable, and our common strength is invincible."

At the end of the speech, Johnson read a section of teletype that had been inserted at the last minute without the knowledge of most of his staff. "I have concluded that I should not permit the Presidency to become involved in the partisan divisions that are developing in this political year," he stated. "With America's sons in the fields far away, with America's future under challenge right here at home, with our hopes and the world's hopes for peace in the balance every day, I do not believe that I should devote an hour or a day of my time to any personal partisan causes or to any duties other than the awesome duties of this office—the Presidency of your country. Accordingly, I shall not seek, and will not accept, the nomination of my party for another term as your President."[34]

In his 1972 memoir, Johnson would write that he had been considering withdrawal from the presidential race for more than one year prior to his March 31 speech. Among the reasons that he listed for his decision to withdraw were concerns over his health, doubts about his influence with Congress, and the difficulties inherent in handling civil unrest during an election year.[35] He may also have been motivated by rising popular opposition to his stewardship of the war and to his presidency more generally following the Tet Offensive. Between the end of January and the end of March, the percentage of Americans who approved of Johnson's handling of the war had fallen from 39 to 26, and that of the disapprovers had risen from 47 to 63. His overall approval rating had tumbled from 48 to 36 percent during that period.[36] When Democratic voters had been asked to choose between Johnson and Robert F. Kennedy for the Democratic presidential nomination, 52 percent had picked Johnson and 40 percent had chosen Kennedy in January 1968, but in late March only 41 percent preferred Johnson while 44 percent favored Kennedy.[37]

The precipitous drop in support for Johnson was not accompanied by a similar decline in American popular support for the war. Following the surge in hawkish sentiment in February, support for hawkish measures subsided in March as Johnson rejected escalation and pursued diplomacy, but there was no rise in sentiment for American withdrawal. On March 25, pollster Louis Harris reported that a poll just taken had found that 72 percent of Americans believed that "we are right in trying to stop the Communists without getting Chinese or Russian troops into the war," while only 13 percent disagreed with that statement. Harris concluded that "the prevailing desire of the American people is that the country's leaders find a way to bring the Communists to the negotiations table by using present troop commitments and forces in Vietnam."[38]

The American people persisted in supporting the war in February and March 1968 because of their enduring perception that international Communism threatened the United States and because of their conviction that the nation had to stand firm when subjected to a devious sneak attack. At Tet, as at other times of international crisis, most Americans rallied around the flag, believing that national security demanded national unity.[39] Contrary to what doves had hoped and hawks had feared, the gloom-ridden and unduly negative reporting of the press did not cause a loss of heart among many Americans, excepting the liberal elites.

By this time, most Americans had spoken with young men back from the war and in general had found them to be more positive about the war and their participation in it than media reports suggested. These veterans had seen war in all its ugliness, the blowing off of limbs, the dying breaths of wonderful young men, the bloodlust of soldiers after the death of friends. And yet, for all the trauma and anguish, they had also found redeeming value in the brotherhood of arms and the sacrifices of patriotic service. When Gallup surveyed returned veterans in the spring of 1968, it found that "while only 26 percent wanted to go to

Vietnam in the first place, 94 percent, having returned, say they are glad for the experience."[40]

The impact of the Tet Offensive on American policy was relatively small. By the end of March, Johnson had abjured both a major U.S. troop increase and a geographic widening of the war, but it is highly unlikely that he would have authorized such measures in the absence of the offensive, given how frequently and strenuously he had resisted them before Tet. Johnson had decided to initiate a bombing halt over northern North Vietnam, but it was a temporary measure at a time when foul weather all but precluded air operations in that region. As an internal State Department policy document explained, the pause would have a "maximum testing period" of four weeks, and "a major change in the military situation might require full scale resumption at any time."[41]

In the wake of Tet, Johnson had unequivocally rejected the demands of congressional doves for rapid disengagement from Vietnam and had authorized a modest addition of 13,500 troops. The American troop commitment would continue a gradual climb to the end of his presidency, when it peaked at 542,000. Johnson had also spurned the recommendation of Pentagon doves for an unrealistic military strategy of abandoning the hinterlands of South Vietnam. As long as Johnson remained in the White House, there would be no Chamberlain peace.

. . .

CHAPTER 15

THE SECOND WAVE

April–June 1968

For the first days of April, the world could talk about little except Lyndon Johnson's speech. Depending on where one stood politically and geographically, the president's words conjured surprise, delight, despair, recrimination, intrigue, or a combination thereof. The speech was widely misinterpreted thanks mainly to Johnson's incomplete accounting of his intentions and objectives.

In the immediate aftermath of the speech, American doves showered Johnson with praise for halting the bombing and stepping out of partisan politics to achieve peace. Senator J. William Fulbright called Johnson's announcement "an act of a very great patriot." UN Ambassador Arthur Goldberg told the president, "You looked ten feet high when you stood there not thinking of any other consideration but what would serve the country best."[1]

The euphoria lasted scarcely twenty-four hours. Congress had been notified that bombing would continue up to the 20th parallel, but few congressmen knew where the 20th parallel was, and many presumed it to be far from Hanoi, based on Johnson's promise to bomb only those areas where enemy activities threatened American forces. The location of the line became clear as the result of bombing raid on Thanh Hoa, just south of the 20th parallel, on April 1. Press reports noted that Thanh Hoa was 205 miles north of the DMZ and just 81 miles south of Hanoi.

On the Senate floor, Fulbright berated Johnson for dropping bombs so close to Hanoi. The bombing halt, he declared, "was of no consequence and certainly not an inducement for North Vietnam to come to the conference table." By squandering this chance for peace, the president had left "no alternative but to go down the road to all-out nuclear war."[2] As a consequence of Fulbright's outcry, Johnson agreed to stop bombing north of the 19th parallel, seventy miles to the south of the 20th parallel.[3]

Johnson had fewer problems obtaining support for the bombing halt from American hawks and moderates. Generally supportive of the bombing of North Vietnam, they were placated by the fact that the suspension of Rolling Thunder over northern North Vietnam was offset by intensified bombing of the southern part of the country. In April, with weather improving, the overall number of Rolling Thunder strikes actually increased by 43 percent, and the number would increase again in the months ahead, reaching an all-time high of 14,382 in July.[4]

In South Vietnam, many politicians and civilians interpreted Johnson's suspension of the bombing, his offer to negotiate, and his forswearing of another presidential term as the first steps toward abandonment of South Vietnam. Some were so fearful of postwar Communist retribution that they sought to avoid being seen talking with Americans, smoking American cigarettes, or drinking American beer.[5] Thieu warned Bunker that there was "an atmosphere of apprehension among the South Vietnamese people which resembled that before the 1954 Geneva talks when it became apparent that the French were about to give up." To his advisers, Thieu expressed a fear that Washington was negotiating with Hanoi behind South Vietnam's back and would sacrifice South Vietnam's interests for the betterment of American relations with the Soviet Union.[6]

Johnson sought to allay Thieu's concerns in a personal letter dated April 2. The speech of March 31 "does not in any way dilute our commitment to our goal of peace and self-determination," Johnson wrote. "We are ready to seek an honorable peace but at the same time a vigilant America stands ready to defend an honored cause whatever the price, whatever the burden, whatever the sacrifice that duty may require."[7]

In the ensuing days, Thieu used this letter and the tougher phrases from Johnson's speech to persuade other South Vietnamese that the Americans were not preparing to sail away.[8] Bunker wrote to his wife on April 7 that Thieu's reassurances had proven highly effective in alleviating pervasive worries about America's plans. "Had it not been for Thieu's calmness and common sense," Bunker observed, "we could have been in considerable trouble."[9]

In North Vietnam, Johnson's speech of March 31 was both highly unexpected and highly welcome.[10] As in South Vietnam, his words were taken as "clear signals that the United States was preparing to back out of Vietnam," in the retelling of Bui Tin. After the heavy losses of the Tet Offensive, Bui Tin stated, "it was a joy to hear about the new developments coming from Washington."[11]

Le Duan promptly concluded that the American offer to negotiate should be accepted. He did so not to reach an expeditious diplomatic settlement, but to establish a diplomatic forum for use once North Vietnamese forces had emerged victorious on the battlefield. He still expected the victory to come before the end of the year, despite all the defeats experienced to date. "Unless a major military victory is achieved, nothing can be

452 • TRIUMPH REGAINED

expected from diplomatic struggle," the North Vietnamese leadership informed the party faithful in a missive on the decision to negotiate. "Diplomatic debate should be regarded as a means to confirm the enemy's defeat and our victory."[12]

On April 3, Le Duan announced publicly Hanoi's willingness to enter into talks with the United States. He did it without first consulting either Ho Chi Minh, who was receiving medical treatment in China, or the leaders of the Chinese Communist Party. According to one senior North Vietnamese official, Le Duan was afraid that Ho Chi Minh and the Chinese would oppose the immediate acceptance of Johnson's diplomatic offer since they had earlier demanded greater concessions from the United States prior to the start of negotiations.[13]

When the Chinese heard the announcement, their shock was mixed with suspicion that Le Duan was conniving behind China's back.[14] Summoning North Vietnamese officials to Beijing, the Chinese made their displeasure known in extraordinarily blunt terms.

"So many people don't understand why the Vietnamese comrades were so hurried in making this statement," Zhou Enlai told Pham Van Dong. "The world's people can't help thinking that you are facing some difficulties in your struggle. That you changed your positions has increased the number of expected votes for Johnson, increased the price of stocks in New York, and decreased the gold price in free markets." Zhou asserted that Johnson's March 31 statement was "a wicked and deceitful scheme" that was not an effort to end the war, "only a means for them to overcome the difficult time." Just when Johnson was in desperate straits, "your April 3rd statement solved his difficulties."[15]

After taking this browbeating, Pham Van Dong withdrew, then returned six days later to provide his government's response. Endeavoring to dispel any notion that Hanoi had gone soft, the

North Vietnamese premier told Zhou that North Vietnam's massive deployments of troops to South Vietnam demonstrated that "this will of ours is like iron and stone, which is unshakable." Then, with a bluntness of his own, Pham Van Dong informed the Chinese that Hanoi was entitled to make its own decisions on the war. "We are the ones fighting against the U.S. and defeating them," he said icily. "We should be responsible for both military and diplomatic activities."[16]

Hanoi's public agreement to negotiate produced as much delight in Washington as it did dejection in Beijing. One of Johnson's advisers, unaware like everyone else in the United States that Le Duan had cut Ho Chi Minh out of the process, quipped, "Apparently it's easier to satisfy Ho Chi Minh than it is Fulbright."[17] The Johnson administration quickly informed Hanoi that Averell Harriman was available to meet with North Vietnamese diplomats to begin the negotiations.

For the next several weeks, Hanoi and Washington traded proposals on the location of the talks. The Americans offered up fifteen different sites in countries that were neutral or friendly to the United States. The North Vietnamese, who appeared to attribute more importance than the Americans to the site and to the appearance of making concessions on the site, countered with only two cities: Warsaw and Phnom Penh.[18]

Harriman phoned Johnson on April 11 to recommend acceptance of Warsaw. "I feel very strongly that Warsaw has a number of advantages over any other place," Harriman said.

"I have rejected it outright, flat, all the way," Johnson responded. Coloring Johnson's thinking on Warsaw were the meetings between American and Chinese diplomats that had taken place there since 1958, which had devolved into a circus of propaganda and acrimony. "As long as I am President, we are not going to Warsaw where we have been once before and negotiate in that kind of atmosphere. I feel strongly it ought to be neutral, have adequate communications. Some of the other people with experience feel the same way, such as Ellsworth Bunker."

Harriman replied, "I would also hope to be among those consulted."

"Yes, you have told me your opinion now," the president shot back. Then he needled Harriman further, warning against trying to sneak the decision past the White House. "I would also like to be consulted and decide before the State Department decides."

"I will obey orders," Harriman said.

"I hope so."

"I have to tell you this was a major step forward in kicking the Chinese out of the situation," Harriman continued. "The people in Eastern Europe want to end this conflict and have a reasonable settlement. It doesn't bother me to negotiate in an Iron Curtain country."

"It does bother me," Johnson snapped. "I don't want any part of Warsaw, Czechoslovakia, or any of these other Eastern European countries. I think it ought to be in Asia, in a neutral territory."

"I have dealt with these countries for a long time," Harriman pleaded, "and I think my judgment is better than Bunker's."

"It may be," said the president. "It may be better than mine."

"But I would like to be able to tell you how I feel."

"You did, you see."[19]

Later that day, Johnson remarked to one of his congressional confidantes that Bunker was "the wisest man we've got in our whole State Department."[20]

American military operations in the South, like American bombing in the North, were intensifying in tandem with Johnson's pursuit of a negotiated peace. At the direction of Westmoreland, who still had a few months left in office, American and South Vietnamese forces picked up the operational tempo during the first weeks of April. In III Corps, forty-two American and thirty-seven South Vietnamese battalions took part in Operation Toan Thang, meaning Complete Victory, which consisted primarily of small-unit patrols and ambushes. By the end of May, it would claim 7,600 enemy killed. To the north of Hue, large U.S. units initiated Operation Carentan II, which mauled the 90th and 803rd North Vietnamese Army regiments.[21]

In Operation Pegasus, Westmoreland sent nineteen battalions to lift the siege of Khe Sanh. Early in April, those battalions moved westward along Highway 9, while Marines at Khe Sanh fanned out into the wasteland surrounding the base. A few of the North Vietnamese units that remained near Khe Sanh attempted to stand their ground and were annihilated by overwhelming American firepower. The others fled in great haste, leaving behind humongous quantities of equipment and ammunition. Those who sought refuge in Laos were blocked by South Vietnamese paratroopers who had been dropped between Khe Sanh and the Laotian border, and the rest were chased by the 1st Cavalry Division. American estimates put North Vietnamese losses during Operation Pegasus at 1,325 against friendly losses of 82 American and 33 South Vietnamese troops.[22]

On the heels of Pegasus came Operation Delaware, the first large operation by American and South Vietnamese forces in the A Shau Valley since the abandonment of the valley's Special Forces camp in March 1966. Allied units received orders to eliminate the estimated three thousand North Vietnamese troops occupying the valley and to shut down the infiltration corridor running through it. The operation promised high potential rewards, including heavy attrition of enemy forces and the long overdue closure of the main North Vietnamese gateway to Hue, but they were matched by high risks. Operation Delaware would be the first large air assault outside the range of friendly artillery, and air support was expected to be hindered by inclement weather and exceptionally dense enemy antiaircraft fire. With the valley only two miles from Laos, the North Vietnamese could rapidly introduce reinforcements.

These perils had caused Westmoreland to question whether to move forward with the operation. His doubts had been overcome by the confident assurances of Major General John Tolson, who as commander of the 1st Cavalry Division would also serve as overall commander of Operation Delaware. Tolson emphasized that his troops had surmounted difficulties of comparable magnitude before. In this operation, he saw a prime opportunity to engage and smash an enemy that had so often been able to elude American firepower. "I would like to see the enemy come after us for a change," said Tolson, "particularly the forces from Laos."[23]

On April 19, two brigades of the 1st Cavalry Division sped toward the A Shau valley in helicopters, while a brigade of the 101st Airborne Division and three battalions of the 3rd ARVN Regiment converged on the valley over land. During the preceding days, American bombers had soared high above the A Shau to blast numerous North Vietnamese antiaircraft positions that had been spotted from the air. As the Americans were about to discover, however, large numbers of 37mm antiaircraft guns had survived the bombardment by virtue of superior protection or camouflage.

At the appearance of the first two heliborne battalions, the valley erupted in a deadly crossfire from the 37mm guns, each one flinging 1.5-pound shells in rapid succession. As the helicopters reduced speed and altitude to unload their passengers, they became easy targets. The fragments of bursting 37mm shells sliced through the hulls and windows of helicopters, several of which crashed to the ground.

Michael Ward, a crewman on one of the choppers, recounted, "From the moment the assault on the A Shau Valley began, the radio was full of talk about aircraft taking hits and getting shot down. All that day, we went into LZ after LZ knowing in our minds that it was probably our last sortie before we got killed. I had never been so afraid in all my life. But we all kept going."[24] Of the helicopters carrying the first two Cavalry battalions, ten were destroyed and twenty-three damaged.

The North Vietnamese forces in the A Shau Valley had spent the previous weeks preparing for another attack on Hue. The initiation of Operation Delaware prompted them to set aside their thoughts of Hue and focus on the threat to the A Shau Valley and the supply corridor of which it was a part. Hanoi instructed the North Vietnamese units in the valley to "annihilate a portion of the U.S. and puppet's manpower strength, liberate our transportation route, and crush the enemy's plot to cut our strategic transportation corridor and destroy our logistical installations."[25]

For reasons never divulged, the North Vietnamese officers in the valley did not end up carrying out this instruction. Rather than mass for large attacks, most of the North Vietnamese troops dispersed and headed out of the valley.[26] Some of them were caught in the dragnet of Operation Delaware, while others escaped to fight another day.

A North Vietnamese rearguard remained in the valley, presumably to fix the attention of the Americans while the rest of the North Vietnamese slipped away. On April 25, the first and third platoons of Delta company of the 5/7 Cavalry bumped into elements of the rearguard on a ridgeline overlooking the valley floor. While advancing along a road that twisted through jagged rocks and broken trees, the Americans began receiving fire from what turned out to be a reinforced North Vietnamese Army company. The quality of the enemy defenses indicated that the

North Vietnamese had spent at least a few days preparing to fight on this ground. North Vietnamese soldiers occupied fortified bunkers, spaced twenty to thirty meters apart, that were well situated to cover one another.

The American company commander took his first platoon and company command group up a cliff on the enemy's right flank. When they reached a saddle, sheets of North Vietnamese fire came at them from multiple directions. Hunkering down, the Americans exchanged blows with the North Vietnamese for the next three hours. During that period, the American company commander was wounded, the platoon commander was killed, and half of the other Americans became casualties.

Once the fighting on the saddle had erupted, third platoon of Delta company had marched toward the sound of the guns. The North Vietnamese, however, detected the maneuver and positioned automatic weapons to cover the path between the two American forces. Their bullets compelled third platoon to halt its advance.

As dusk approached, the American company commander decided that the troops in the saddle should stay put for the night. With so many casualties to carry, first platoon and the command group would have found it exceedingly difficult to fight through the enemy positions in the dark. Having lost radio contact with third platoon, moreover, the company commander would have been unable to bring his other forces into the fight.

At nightfall, the members of third platoon were unsure where the rest of their company was, and they knew even less about the location of the North Vietnamese. They guessed, however, that they could get closer to the other Americans by moving farther up the road. First Lieutenant James M. Sprayberry, the company's executive officer, decided to take a rescue party in that direction. In response to his call for volunteers, twelve men stepped forward.

The group collected as many grenades as they could carry, then walked silently into the abyss of night. After three hundred meters, a North Vietnamese machine gun opened fire. One of the Americans went down with a bullet wound in the foot. Sprayberry sent that man back along with two others, then told his remaining men to lie down against a bank next to the road and stay low.

Crawling into the center of the road by himself, with nothing to shield him from view except the dark of night, Sprayberry headed in the direction of the North Vietnamese machine gun. He kept so quiet that the North Vietnamese crew, on high mental alert though they were, did not hear his approach. When he was close enough to make out the crew's bunker, he tossed in a grenade, killing them.

On the rock wall next to the road, Sprayberry discerned a series of spider holes. He threw a grenade into one from just a few feet away. Sounds of moaning came from the hole, so he tossed in another, and the sounds ceased. Sprayberry went to the next spider hole, and again he needed two grenades to eliminate the occupant.

Lieutenant Sprayberry wriggled back to the rest of the volunteers, took some grenades from them, and headed toward the enemy once more. The resumption of his advance caused the North Vietnamese to lob several grenades in his direction, but he escaped injury. He then charged the bunker whence the grenades had come and snuffed it out with a grenade of his own. Sprayberry demonstrated a "total disregard for his personal safety," in the words of one witness.

Sprayberry told two of the volunteers, Specialist 4 Delbert R. Mack and Specialist 4 Barry P. Tranchetti, to cover either side of the road while he advanced still farther. He destroyed three more enemy positions with grenades. At this point, he was able to establish radio contact with the stranded Americans, who provided information on their location. Sprayberry assured them that he was on his way.

As the lieutenant continued ahead, he was startled by a North Vietnamese soldier who emerged from a spider hole to charge at him. Sprayberry squeezed off three shots from his .45 pistol, killing the soldier. Shortly thereafter, Sprayberry linked up with the survivors of first platoon and the company command group.

Summoning the able-bodied, Sprayberry organized them into litter parties to carry back the wounded. The North Vietnamese eventually figured out what was afoot, and they directed fire into the saddle, but to little effect. Sprayberry stayed on until the last man had been evacuated. Then, with Mack and Tranchetti covering him, he destroyed one more enemy machine gun emplacement by sneaking within two feet of it and dropping in grenades.

The whole ordeal lasted seven and a half hours. During that time, Sprayberry killed a total of twelve enemy soldiers. "This feat was so remarkable," attested one American, because "Lieutenant Sprayberry did not know exactly where the platoon was," and "he eliminated all of the enemy between him and the platoon." Sprayberry would eventually receive the Medal of Honor for his actions that night.[27]

As the Americans and South Vietnamese combed the A Shau Valley, they discovered vast storage depots and truck parks. Power lines led away from the valley in several directions to satellite bases, where additional goods were found. All told, the forces assigned to Operation Delaware seized 2,500 individual weapons, fifty-nine crew-served weapons, thirty flamethrowers, eighteen trucks, twelve 37mm antiaircraft guns, and three tons of automotive spare parts. The Americans also took possession of the packed-earth road on whose surface the North Vietnamese had moved supplies from Laos toward Hue, throwing into chaos the enemy's plans for new mischief in Hue. A reported 869 North Vietnamese troops were killed in the month-long operation. Allied units withdrew from the valley in May, but they continued to make forays into the area to hound any enemy forces that sought to return.[28]

Near the end of Operation Delaware, the *New York Times* interrupted its usual regimen of short war-related articles with a startling three-part series on black servicemen in Vietnam. It was written by Thomas A. Johnson, one of the newspaper's first black overseas correspondents, who had just spent several months traveling across the country. In the articles, Johnson told of remarkable advances in racial integration, cooperation, and equality in Vietnam. Integration proponents would hail the findings as evidence of the potential for progress in the United States, where the enactment of the landmark civil rights laws and anti-poverty programs of Lyndon Johnson's Great Society had been followed not by comparable advances in race relations but by race riots, black separatism, and persistent poverty.

"Fourteen weeks of interviews with black and white Americans serving here reveal that serving in Vietnam is like a speeded-up film of racial progress at home," Johnson wrote. "In the job of battle, fighting prowess and dependability quickly erase color barriers. Staying alive becomes more important than keeping stateside racial patterns." The young black and white men he witnessed cheered each other on in the game of war, displaying team spirit of a strength possible only when death was the cost of defeat.

Vietnam offered blacks "an environment almost free of discrimination," Johnson had found. Black soldiers were now doing everything white soldiers were doing and going everywhere white soldiers were going. Blacks and whites were fighting and dying in the same fierce battles along the country's frontiers. They were eating at the same restaurants in Saigon and in the same dining rooms.

"There are reports of racial discrimination, racial fights, and instances of self-segregation," Johnson noted, "but most Negroes interviewed said these instances were greatly outweighed by racial cooperation." During breaks from duty, black troops frequently congregated for "soul sessions" where they could "get the black view" and "get away from 'the man,'" yet even here blacks allowed whites to attend if they were considered "for real" whites. The attitudes of black soldiers toward their experiences in the military were so positive that they were reenlisting at three times the rate of whites.

In a distinctly less positive vein, Johnson pointed out that the progress in Vietnam brought into starker relief the problems that remained in the United States. The high reenlistment rate of black soldiers was fueled in part by the perception that blacks enjoyed higher incomes, more promising career paths, and better relations with whites in the armed forces than in the rest of American society. Blacks in Vietnam were also wary of returning to the United States "at a time when the loudest black voices—if not the most representative—clamor for racial separation." Most of the black troops rejected the political radicalism of separatist leaders like Stokely Carmichael and H. Rap Brown but believed that the black grievances fueling the separatist movement were real and in need of redress. Black servicemen foresaw intensified violence between whites and blacks in the United States in the time to come, though they differed as to whether black rioters were justified in their actions or were "just hoodlums" who had to be "stopped before they all give us a bad name." No one could be sure how many black veterans would side with the militants, how many would join the police forces standing in the way of the militants, or how many would sit on the sidelines.[29]

The next phase of the war began in early May. Until Operation Delaware, Hue had been one of the targets for what the North Vietnamese termed the second wave of the general offensive and uprising, which was scheduled to start on May 4. The second wave would be similar to the first wave offensive at Tet, with North Vietnamese forces attacking the cities and inciting popular uprisings. Although Operation Delaware had foiled the planned strike on Hue, the North Vietnamese proceeded with plans to seize other cities, Saigon being the foremost target. In preparation for the offensive, eight North Vietnamese Army regiments and fifteen field artillery battalions traveled from the North to the South.[30] North Vietnamese infiltration into South Vietnam during the month of April exceeded twenty thousand.[31]

To maintain this high rate of infiltration, the North Vietnamese Army was sending young men with less training and experience than ever before. Half the enemy prisoners questioned in May 1968 said that they had been in the military for less than three months, including the transit time from North to South, which meant that their training had been whittled down from the three months of previous years to one month. Officer training at the Infantry Officers' School near Son Tay had been shortened from two years to eight months. This abbreviation of training manifested itself in markedly decreased North Vietnamese performance on the battlefield.[32]

Within the North Vietnamese officer corps, the plans for the second wave encountered much more skepticism than had the Tet plans. Methods that had failed the first time were now to be employed under even less favorable conditions. "We were concerned that the orders revealed no changes in our organization, equipment, and tactics for this new round of attacks," remembered Huynh Cong Than. "Anyone with even a basic understanding of military matters and anyone who had commanded troops during the first wave of attacks on Saigon could immediately see the difficult nature of our mission."

This time, unlike during the Tet Offensive, Communist forces would lack the element of surprise, and no South Vietnamese forces would be away on holiday leave. Around Saigon and other cities, the Americans and South Vietnamese had thickened their defenses. Huynh Cong Than noted that in the urban combat to come, "the attacker would need extremely powerful weapons to be able to expel defenders from areas with large, well-constructed buildings," yet Communist forces would possess "only light infantry weapons."

Huynh Cong Than and many others shared their concerns with senior military and party leaders. Although numerous debates took place, the man with the most important vote, Le Duan, remained convinced that a second urban offensive would win Hanoi its decisive victory, or at least bring it much closer to that outcome. The North Vietnamese leadership made no changes to the plans in response to the complaints from below.[33]

Because of the confusion and mishaps resulting from the limited circulation of plans before the Tet Offensive, the North Vietnamese disseminated documents more broadly this time. They thereby reduced the confusion and mishaps but also multiplied the leakage of planning information to their enemies. The most damaging compromise came from Colonel Tran Van Dac, a North Vietnamese colonel who had been slated to lead four North Vietnamese infantry regiments in the attack on Saigon. After his superiors ignored his objections to the battle plan, he defected and gave the South Vietnamese all the details for the Saigon assault. Communist agents in Saigon learned of the betrayal before battle was joined, but the North Vietnamese high command decided it was too late to change the timing of the onslaught or make more than minor adjustments to the positioning of forces.[34]

On May 3, the eve of the offensive, the North Vietnamese notified the Americans that they would be willing to meet for negotiations in Paris, one of the fifteen locations the Americans had proposed. From Hanoi's point of view, the designation of a site would provide a venue where the Americans could sign the documents of their capitulation as soon as North Vietnamese arms prevailed upon the battlefield. For the Americans, Hanoi's concurrence spelled welcome progress in the diplomatic process.

The only people displeased by the selection of Paris as the negotiating site were the Chinese. As had occurred one month earlier, North Vietnamese leaders did not consult with the Chinese before taking this action, and as before the Chinese were incensed when they learned that they had been kept in the dark.[35] This time, Xuan Thuy was the North Vietnamese diplomat to receive a blistering harangue from the Chinese. "It is our opinion that you have agreed to negotiate too fast and too hurriedly, which might have left the Americans with an impression that you are eager to negotiate," Zhou Enlai fumed. "The Americans, the subordinate countries, and the puppets have a military force of over 1,000,000, and, before their backbone has been broken, or before five or six of their fingers have been broken, they will not accept defeat, and they will not leave."[36]

North Vietnamese forces marched toward the cities on the night of May 3. By navigating through jungles and swamps, many units evaded detection en route to the cities. Few, however, escaped notice once they reached the edges of the urban population, where soldiers, policemen, and citizens were too numerous to miss them.[37]

In the case of Saigon, most North Vietnamese forces became entangled in the webs of American and South Vietnamese forces on the city outskirts. Only a small fraction of the attackers would make it to the city center, and none would reach the city's major military and administrative installations. Units that attempted to hold their ground were smashed by larger and more heavily equipped allied forces, and those that attempted to escape fared only marginally better. Many units were shorn of half their strength in the opening hours of the onslaught. By the third day of battle, few North Vietnamese companies were capable any longer of functioning as coherent combat units.[38]

Nguyen Thanh, who commanded two North Vietnamese infantry regiments and an artillery battalion during the assault on Saigon, recounted that his troops "suffered heavier losses than we had suffered during the first wave, and we suffered the greatest defeat I have ever experienced during my entire career as a combat commander." The South Vietnamese and American forces "were prepared and waiting for us. They blocked us, hit us from the front, and made counterattacks that surrounded us and hit us from the rear. They rained savage air and artillery attacks down on us, and inflicted extremely heavy losses on the forces under my command." By the time he received permission to withdraw from Saigon, his forces had lost most of their officers and half of their weapons. "My command was crippled, unable to fight, and the morale of our troops deteriorated as the men wavered in fear and lost confidence in victory."[39]

The North Vietnamese met with similar failure in the other cities they attacked. Bogged down in the urban periphery, they attempted to hang on much longer than they should have, and paid dearly for it.[40] What was left of the underground Communist apparatus attempted to assist the assault forces and, as had occurred during Tet, their participation exposed their identities and enabled the South Vietnamese government to round them up. In the description of one North Vietnamese history, "our secret forces concealed inside the cities and most of our agents and secret facilities—the places where we hid our weapons and equipment, the places where our troops were based, the places from which we had launched our attacks—were exposed and were virtually eliminated and destroyed."[41]

At Dong Ha, the northernmost town in the country, the battle evolved into a broader contest for control of northeastern Quang Tri Province. In the midst of fighting between the 3rd U.S. Marine Division and the 320th NVA Division, the Marines received a new division commander, Major General Raymond Davis. General Davis brought with him new energy and new ideas. In recognition that the enemy was bypassing the bases of McNamara's barrier by infiltrating troops to their west, Davis shifted from a micromanaged defense of the bases to a decentralized offense against the 320th NVA Division. He pulled troops from the McNamara barrier and sent them out in company-sized patrols. Once the patrols located North Vietnamese forces, the Marines encircled them using helicopters and armor, then pummeled them with heavy weapons.

Aggressive Marine implementation of these tactics inflicted crippling losses on the 320th NVA Division. By the American count, the North Vietnamese lost more than 3,600 to death or capture during fighting near Dong Ha in May. American casualties totaled 327 killed and roughly 1,200 wounded. At the end of May, the North Vietnamese survivors withdrew north of the DMZ, and quiet returned to Quang Tri.[42]

The one noteworthy departure from the pattern of overwhelming Communist military defeat during May played out far from any of the cities targeted by the second wave offensive. The site of battle was Kham Duc, a Special Forces camp ten miles from Laos. Seated in an oval-shaped valley, the camp was surrounded by steeply climbing mountains whose blankets of triple canopy jungle prevented anyone in an aircraft from seeing military preparations underneath.

The North Vietnamese began probing attacks at Kham Duc on May 10. In response, an American battalion task force from the 196th Infantry Brigade flew to the camp to reinforce the Vietnamese CIDG garrison and its U.S. Army Special Forces advisers. As the battalion task force was landing, two North Vietnamese regiments attacked a forward operating base at Ngok Tavak, three miles southwest of Kham Duc, which was held by 173 CIDG soldiers and 41 Americans. Outnumbering the defenders by more than ten to one, the North Vietnamese broke into the camp and slew large numbers of defenders in close-quarters battle. After ten hours, the base's survivors retreated under cover of air strikes into the jungle and cleared a landing zone, from which four CH-46 helicopters retrieved them. Sixty-two CIDG troops and seventeen Americans did not make it out.

The next day, the whole of the 2nd North Vietnamese Army Division assembled in the mountain slopes around Kham Duc. Emerging from the jungle en masse, they lunged at the camp from every direction. American air strikes prevented the North Vietnamese from penetrating the camp's perimeter, but the size of the North Vietnamese force and the superiority of the terrain it held convinced the American leadership that a sustained defense of the camp would be too costly. Shortly before midnight, Westmoreland gave the order to evacuate Kham Duc.

U.S. Air Force transport aircraft arrived on May 12 to extract the defenders and the dependents of the South Vietnamese troops. To hold back the North Vietnamese infantry and suppress North Vietnamese antiaircraft weapons, an armada of American and South Vietnamese aircraft soaked the surrounding area with munitions, from the upper reaches of the mountain slopes to the camp's perimeter fence. Whenever North Vietnamese troops attempted to rush the perimeter, American aircraft swooped down and inundated them with bombs and napalm canisters, some of them landing as close as one hundred meters from friendly troops. Every North Vietnamese unit that attempted to breach the American perimeter had to turn back after suffering cataclysmic losses. Astonishingly, the air crews and air controllers executed the voluminous strikes with such skill that not a single friendly fire casualty was recorded.

North Vietnamese weapons downed just seven aircraft during the evacuation. The loss of American and South Vietnamese life was very low, with the exception of a C-130 crash in which more than 150 South Vietnamese dependents were killed. When the battle was over, a total of 46 American and 130 South Vietnamese troops were dead or missing.

American forces would not return to Kham Duc for more than one year, precluding any valid estimation of North Vietnamese losses. Although the exact number of North Vietnamese troops killed at or near Kham Duc in May 1968 may never be known, the evidence suggests that the number was very large. Numerous eyewitnesses attested to repeated obliteration of North Vietnamese formations by bombs and napalm on May 11 and May 12. During the three days following the evacuation, B-52 strikes on suspected North Vietnamese assembly areas and evacuation routes triggered 130 secondary explosions, causing additional damage to personnel and materiel.[43]

Although Hanoi's May offensive was sometimes described as "mini Tet," the fighting was, in many places, more violent than that in January and February. American battle fatalities reached 2,169 in May, topping the spike of 2,124 in February. It was to be the most Americans killed in any month of the war.[44] The Americans estimated that 26,000 Communist troops perished during the month.[45]

Hanoi's launch of the second wave offensive and the high butcher's bills resulting therefrom did nothing to derail the

Johnson administration's pursuit of peace talks. After accepting Hanoi's proposal of Paris as the negotiating site, Johnson sent Averell Harriman to Paris to head the U.S. delegation. He also sent Lieutenant General Andrew Goodpaster, whom the president could trust to keep Harriman from deviating from the administration's policies.

Goodpaster would have to perform this function even before he arrived in Paris. During their transatlantic flight, Harriman told Goodpaster, "Now it's our job to end this war, to get the best terms we can, but to end the war."

"That's not my understanding," countered Goodpaster, shaking his head. "We have not been instructed to end the war on 'the best terms we can.'" President Johnson's instructions, said Goodpaster, stipulated that the negotiators would "not in any way compromise the maximum pressure being put on North Vietnam by American troops."[46]

The meetings between North Vietnamese and American diplomats in Paris began on May 13 at the Hotel Majestic, a palatial Beaux-Arts hotel that had served as Nazi Germany's headquarters for occupied France from 1940 to 1944. Lacking military successes upon which they could stake diplomatic claims, the North Vietnamese representatives avoided substantive matters and instead engaged in polemics about American perfidy and aggression. One American official reported, "The Hanoi representatives are prepared to stay in Paris and even read the telephone directory if necessary to keep nonproductive talks going for a long time."[47]

The lack of seriousness in Paris soon precipitated recommendations from American hawks to lift the restrictions on Rolling Thunder. The Joint Chiefs pointed to American intelligence reports showing that the suspension of bombing near Hanoi and Haiphong had led to a surge in imports by sea. Haiphong was receiving so many shipments that supplies were piling up on the quays and streets. North Vietnamese and Chinese construction crews were rapidly repairing bridges and roads that had been damaged by Rolling Thunder, facilitating a sharp rise in the number of trucks carrying supplies toward the south.[48]

At a meeting on May 21, Wheeler urged President Johnson to resume bombing at least up to the 20th parallel. Clark Clifford objected that even this limited step could jeopardize the Paris negotiations. "We have made progress in Paris," Clifford claimed, disregarding the extensive reporting on the fruitlessness of the talks. "We are waiting for them to de-escalate. The heat is on them. If we go back in, we remove some of this heat."

President Johnson found Clifford's argument unconvincing. "How long can we go on with the 19th [Parallel] without getting trapped into never being able to do anything above the 19th?" he demanded. "I think our force brought them to table, not our eloquence of March 31. All we are doing now is to let them build it back up."

Clifford countered that extending the bombing to the 20th parallel would reduce the infiltration flow by no more than 25 percent, which in his view was not worth the risk of undermining the negotiations. Going to the 20th parallel "will make it more difficult for him to take a step down," Clifford insisted. "I do not want to appear stubborn."

Johnson refused to buy the idea that the use of force would torpedo the negotiations. He pointed out that the newest North Vietnamese military offensive "hasn't blown up the peace conference."[49]

The discussion carried through to a meeting of the National Security Council on the following day. "The North Vietnamese made a pretty good trade," Johnson commented. "They get partial suspension of the bombing for merely sitting and talking in Paris."

Clifford shot back that the very presence of North Vietnamese diplomats at Paris was a success. "It is important that we have forced the North Vietnamese to talk even though we are still bombing a part of North Vietnam," he said.

"There is no evidence that the North Vietnamese will negotiate seriously," Johnson responded. "They will do no more than remain in Paris to talk rather than negotiate until the next Administration takes over."[50] That interpretation was supported by recent analysis from the intelligence community, which had concluded that Hanoi had no intention of reaching a diplomatic settlement that would leave the South Vietnamese government in power.[51] Yet instinctive suspicion of the North Vietnamese could not entirely suppress Johnson's hunger for diplomatic progress. At the end of the meeting, Johnson decided to retain the restrictions on Rolling Thunder for the time being.

In the waning days of the second wave offensive, President Thieu formed a new South Vietnamese cabinet, with Tran Van Huong as prime minister. The U.S. embassy reported that the new cabinet included many of the best ministers from the previous cabinet as well as some able new civilians.[52] Huong's appointment received praise from student and youth groups, including some that had long been critical of the Saigon government, owing to Huong's reputation for integrity and his history of supporting youth organizations.[53]

More outspoken than Thieu and more dignified than Ky, Huong gave the Saigon government its most compelling spokesman since the last time Huong had been prime minister, at the beginning of 1965. In an address to the nation at the end of May, Huong issued bold appeals for national unity and the combating of corruption. "South Vietnamese are determined to fight to the end," he proclaimed, "if the enemy mistakenly believes mortar attacks, destruction of homes, and other such aggressive acts will lead them to victory."[54]

Thieu and Huong accelerated the replacement of ineffectual and corrupt officials at the provincial and district levels, in some cases at the recommendation of the Americans, who fed them lists of individuals deserving of removal. Of the thirteen province chiefs sacked by Thieu in the spring, twelve were replaced by individuals who, in the view of the American embassy, were notably better than their predecessors. American field advisers reported that these leadership changes led to improved South Vietnamese performance in pacification.[55]

Huong persuaded Thieu that some relaxation of wartime security measures would be useful in bolstering national morale. Thieu directed each provincial government to release detainees for whom the government lacked evidence of complicity with the Communists. He lifted press censorship and allowed the reopening of seven newspapers that had been shuttered in recent years for criticizing the government.[56]

Ky was less than pleased with the formation of the Huong cabinet. At the end of May, he complained to Bunker that Thieu had not kept him informed of his plans for changing the cabinet's personnel. The Americans, said Ky, were mistaken to view the new cabinet as an improvement over its predecessor.

"Some have approached me to make a coup, but I have told them that a coup is out of the question," Ky told Bunker. "I tell them they must be patient. They must wait." In an unprecedented display of animosity toward Thieu, Ky snarled, "There are a thousand ways to destroy a leader without a coup."

Bunker, mortified by the idea of top South Vietnamese leaders destroying each other, warned Ky that unity at the top of the South Vietnamese government was imperative if the country were to thwart the Communists.

"Americans are innocent and don't understand the Orient," Ky scoffed.

"There are some of us who do," Bunker parried. "In Japan, which has one of the most effective governments in the world, there are always the most serious divisions among the leaders, differences of temperament, personality, outlook and policy, and competition for the top job. But once a leader is elected, the top leaders know they have to work as a team; they close ranks and they support and reinforce each other. This is what gives the Japanese leadership its great strength."[57]

On June 2, during a battle with Communist holdouts in Saigon, an American helicopter fired one of its rockets into a South Vietnamese Army command post where several of Ky's most powerful supporters were standing. The blast killed six of them, including the commander of the capital military district and the police chief of Saigon. The Americans described it as an accident, and there was no evidence indicating that it was otherwise.[58] Among the conspiratorially minded South Vietnamese, however, rumors abounded that it was a deliberate American effort to bolster Thieu and diminish Ky.[59]

Accidental though the deaths may have been, they did lead to a sharp and lasting reduction of power for Ky. Thieu replaced the deceased with men who were not loyal to Ky and who exceeded their forerunners in competence and integrity. As a result of the substitutions, a variety of political groups gravitated toward closer alliance with Thieu.[60]

Later in the month, Thieu formed the Lien Minh, an umbrella organization that was intended to bring the nation's largest political factions into a strong pro-government party for the first time since Diem's Can Lao. At the first meeting of the Lien Minh, Thieu emphasized that a robust nationalist political organization would be required when the struggle with the

Communists shifted from the battlefield to the political realm.[61] Washington was sufficiently impressed with the concept that it authorized $1,150,000 in covert financial support for the Lien Minh, enough for Thieu to establish local party committees and train cadres.[62]

Thieu capitalized on his growing power and the surge in anti-Communist sentiment sparked by the Tet Offensive to expand national conscription. During June, he secured the South Vietnamese legislature's cooperation in lowering the draft age to eighteen and authorizing conscription of men between eighteen and thirty-eight for service until the end of the war. The legislature further mandated that males of ages sixteen to seventeen and thirty-nine to fifty serve in the People's Self Defense Forces, unpaid hamlet militia units that could offer a modicum of resistance until reinforcements arrived. By the middle of August, the number of men in South Vietnam's armed forces and paramilitary units would surpass the December 1967 sum by 120,000, bringing their total strength near one million.[63]

The coalescing of political support for the Thieu government also suggested that South Vietnamese elites were rallying around commonly held principles and beliefs, including nationalism, anti-Communism, representative government, and protection of civil liberties. Such was the perception and worry of at least some of the leaders in Hanoi. At a conference on May 5 commemorating the hundred and fiftieth birthday of Karl Marx, the Communist Party theoretician Truong Chinh stated that the party needed to find ways of "opposing the Western reactionary theories which are in vogue in the southern part of our country." Those theories, he warned, "are serving the aggressive policy and neocolonialism of the imperialist clique headed by the U.S. imperialists."[64]

General William C. Westmoreland turned over command of U.S. forces in Vietnam to General Creighton W. Abrams on

June 10. Departing Saigon the next day, Westmoreland headed to Washington to replace General Harold K. Johnson as U.S. Army chief of staff. Having commanded the American war in Vietnam for four years, Westmoreland had held up well under the stress. At the time of his exit, the military situation in South Vietnam had never looked better, and he enjoyed a strong reputation among most of America's military and political leaders.

His successor was also an impressive man, albeit of a different type. Creighton Abrams had grown up in Feeding Hills, Massachusetts, a small farming community along the Connecticut River. The pride of the town during his high school years, he had attained most of his school's top positions: class president, captain of the undefeated football team, editor of the school newspaper, class orator, and president of the scholastic honor society. When West Point offered him admission at the nadir of the Great Depression, he accepted the offer without hesitation.

Like most of his peers, Abrams found it far more difficult to move ahead of the pack at West Point. At five foot, nine inches and 165 pounds, he was too small for the football team. An unexceptional student, he graduated 185 out of 276 cadets in the class of 1936. The penny-pinching peacetime military of the late 1930s made Lieutenant Abrams an officer in the horse cavalry, an anachronism that should have been removed from the army decades earlier.

Had peace continued, Abrams might well have lived his entire career in obscurity, like so many other talented military men who missed out on war. The onset of World War II, with its mass conscription and its unquenchable thirst for officers, gave Abrams his chance. Promoted to command of the 37th Tank Battalion at an early age, Abrams proved the most aggressive and effective American armor officer during the breakout from Normandy in the summer of 1944. He kept his own tank at the front of the battalion with its hatch open so that he could maintain an unobstructed view of the battlefield, a practice that led fellow tankers to forecast his early demise. Abrams demanded that all of his tanks fight with open hatches, and when he saw that one tank had closed its hatch, he persuaded the crew to get with the program by threatening to weld the hatch shut.

Owing to its successes during the Normandy breakout, the 37th Tank Battalion became the vanguard for the subsequent advance toward Germany. Abrams led the battalion on daring raids into the enemy's rear, where they destroyed unsuspecting German vehicles and installations. During the Battle of the Bulge, his tanks spearheaded the relief of the American garrison at Bastogne, an event that catapulted him into the national consciousness. Among his greatest admirers was General George S. Patton, who remarked, "I'm supposed to be the best tank commander in the Army, but I have one peer—Abe Abrams. He's the world's champion."

Abrams was less polished in appearance than Westmoreland, his uniform gathering wrinkles in a manner that had never seemed to afflict his predecessor. As an inspirational leader, however, he was no less gifted. One journalist observed that Abrams could "inspire aggressiveness in a begonia." Abrams publicly cultivated the air of a beer-swilling, cigar-chomping warrior, yet he also had a powerful intellect, which he kept in shape by reading books on history and philosophy.[65]

The most immediate problem confronting General Abrams was the persistence of North Vietnamese military pressure on Saigon. Despite the terrible defeats the North Vietnamese had suffered in the Saigon area during the second wave offensive, Hanoi continued assigning the city highest priority for the North Vietnamese Army. North Vietnamese forces were prowling the outskirts, launching forays closer in, and shooting weapons into the city center. By the second week of June, Communist rocket and mortar fire into Saigon had killed 189 civilians and wounded 614. The number of residents displaced from their homes since the beginning of May surpassed 100,000.

Bunker warned Washington that the continuation of such attacks would undermine South Vietnamese morale. Juxtaposed with the suspension of Rolling Thunder over Hanoi, they conveyed the impression that the United States and South Vietnam were weak. The South Vietnamese information minister, expressing a displeasure that was becoming endemic among South Vietnamese officials, proposed that whenever the North Vietnamese fired a mortar or rocket at Saigon, the United States should drop a bomb on Hanoi.[66]

To remedy the situation, Abrams moved additional troops near Saigon. At the end of June, seventy-seven of ninety-six allied battalions in III Corps were operating in Saigon or the provinces immediately surrounding it. By saturating the area with ground and air patrols, these battalions brought the rocket and mortar attacks on Saigon to a standstill.[67]

Saigon was at this moment very much on the mind of Le Duan as he plotted his next move. In late June, he flew to Phnom Penh under an assumed name to meet the men who would have to carry out his newest plans. From the airport, Le Duan was taken by car toward the east, and then he disembarked to cover the last stretch on foot. A group of senior North Vietnamese military leaders and a dozen Chinese advisers were waiting at a secret Cambodian base to greet him.

The opening minutes were spent discussing the first and second wave offensives. Some attendees complained that North Vietnamese strategy "had not been in keeping with the reality of the situation." The recent offensives, they said, had sacrificed too much for too little gain. Whether Le Duan was paying attention or daydreaming was uncertain, but in either case their opinions had no effect on his thinking.

After the military men had presented their views, Le Duan said that in August they would undertake a third wave of the general offensive and general uprising. It would resemble the first two, concentrating on urban targets. The North Vietnamese officers agreed to comply, although they had little reason to think that the third wave had better prospects than its antecedents. The Chinese advisors, however, registered strong objections to Le Duan's plans. When Le Duan refused to budge, the Chinese stormed out of the meeting in protest.[68]

The third wave would proceed in the manner that had been in Le Duan's mind upon his arrival in Cambodia.

CHAPTER 16

. . .

THE THIRD WAVE

July–September 1968

During the first months of his tenure as commander of American forces in South Vietnam, General Creighton Abrams showed little inclination toward new strategy or tactics. After listening to his commanders explain how they were conducting operations at a conference in July, Abrams remarked that he "saw no reason to issue new instructions. We appear to be doing what we ought to be doing."[1]

Like Westmoreland, Abrams told his commanders to seek out and engage the enemy in remote areas rather than waiting for them to come to the villages, cities, and military installations. "I intend to accommodate the enemy in seeking battle and in fact to anticipate him wherever possible," Abrams vowed. "We must anticipate him, fix his major forces as far away as possible from our vital areas, and defeat him quickly."[2] Abrams directed subordinates to avoid using the term "search and destroy," but only for semantic reasons. In its place, they would use terms that Westmoreland had instituted shortly before his departure because of concerns that the original term had been misunderstood: "spoiling operations" and "reconnaissance in force."[3] Abrams emphasized the value of attrition in such operations, noting that "the payoff is getting a hold of this fellow and killing as many of them as you can."[4]

In only one case, that of the U.S. Marines in the far north, did Abrams depart immediately from Westmoreland's way of war. During his final months as commander, Westmoreland had kept the Marines at Khe Sanh so that the base could serve as the launchpad for a ground invasion of Laos, which he hoped would take place in the fall of 1968. He had approved distribution of plans for Operation El Paso, the occupation of the Ho Chi Minh Trail, just four days before leaving the country. The feasibility study accompanying the planning documents was particularly promising; it deemed force requirements for the operation to be only two divisions, the 1st Cavalry Division and the ARVN Airborne Division, not the three divisions cited in prior planning, let alone the two hundred thousand troops that Ambassador Sullivan had previously claimed to be necessary.[5]

Abrams did not foresee an imminent need for Khe Sanh as a staging area because he was less optimistic than Westmoreland that the White House would approve ground operations into Laos in the near future. Abrams had previously advocated such operations to higher authorities, and he would continue to advocate them, but he did not see a need to maintain an American outpost at Khe Sanh in the interim. Like the Marine Corps leadership, he believed that Marines near the DMZ were generally more effective and less vulnerable when conducting search-and-destroy operations than when sitting in fixed bases. If and when an incursion into Laos were authorized, American forces could reoccupy the Khe Sanh plateau and turn it back into a military base. Soon after taking office, therefore, Abrams ordered the Marines to leave Khe Sanh. The Marines demolished the base's bunkers and burned down its buildings before withdrawing the last troops on July 11.[6]

For the remaining months of 1968, the United States would have to depend on bombing and the innovations of Ambassador Sullivan to disrupt the North Vietnamese traffic in Laos. Sullivan's concept of stopping the North Vietnamese by muddying up the Laotian roads suffered further discredit in the spring, when American intelligence determined that the North Vietnamese had built new all-weather roads along the Laotian infiltration routes. With these roads, the CIA estimated, the North Vietnamese could truck a hundred short tons per day into South Vietnam throughout the year.[7]

Sullivan came up with another panacea, the insertion of international observers on the roads leading from North Vietnam to the Ho Chi Minh Trail. "We would assure observation and control of all the means which sustain and support the North Vietnamese in Laos," Sullivan explained in a cable to Washington. "This would mean that the North Vietnamese supply system would disappear and they would have to bring their troops home."[8] This idea would bear no more fruit than the mud war.

During the summer, the North Vietnamese logistical system in Laos transported enough equipment and supplies to maintain large North Vietnamese Army units and conduct combat operations, although it was still not enough for them to fight as often as Hanoi wanted. Infiltrators from the North were pouring in at a rate of fourteen thousand per month. Most of them joined combat units that had been thinned by recent battles and were scheduled to participate in the third wave offensive.[9]

This influx coincided with persistently high North Vietnamese Army battlefield casualties and a drop in Communist recruitment of South Vietnamese men. It therefore accelerated the predominance of North Vietnamese personnel in the People's Liberation

Armed Forces and National Liberation Front, organizations that most Westerners still called the "Viet Cong" and that some Westerners still believed to be independent of Hanoi. By the late summer, forty-six of fifty-eight Communist regiments in South Vietnam, including the "Viet Cong" regiments, were composed entirely of men from North Vietnam, and Northerners accounted for the majority of troops in nine of the other twelve regiments.[10]

At the end of July, American hawks seized on intelligence reports of profuse North Vietnamese infiltration as proof of the need for stronger military actions beyond South Vietnam's borders. Harriman and Vance countered that the reports proved the need to extend the bombing halt to all of North Vietnam. According to the hopeful forecasts of Harriman and Vance, an extension would dissuade the North Vietnamese from attacking again and thus would save the lives of American troops.[11]

President Johnson notified Harriman and Vance that he would not alter the bombing so long as the North Vietnamese failed to respond positively on the diplomatic front.[12] The president was incensed at what he viewed as a coordinated effort by Harriman, Vance, Clifford, and others within his own administration to stop Rolling Thunder on the basis of spurious logic.[13] He told Governor Richard Hughes of New Jersey, "What they're asking me to do is be the biggest boob of our time. Just as the Communists get ready to hit us, they want me to do what I did at Tet—take a vacation, let our men accept a Tet holiday, and as I do it, and call off our bombing, let them hit me full length, and I just—I just—I just don't see it."[14]

Johnson was receiving reports from Abrams that depicted Rolling Thunder as much more effective than Harriman, Vance, and Clifford were claiming. According to these reports, the bombing was destroying or damaging ninety North Vietnamese trucks per week, amounting to 15 percent of the trucks headed to South Vietnam. The bombing of choke points in southern North Vietnam, Abrams reported, had caused the enemy to slash the number of trucks going south and to restrict truck movements to nighttime. Rolling Thunder was tying down 80,000 North Vietnamese soldiers and between 110,000 and 200,000 laborers in air defense activities. A cessation of the bombing, Abrams predicted, would result in a several-fold increase in enemy logistical capability and combat activity in I Corps and hence in a proportionate rise in friendly casualties in that area.[15]

The intensified bombing effort in southern North Vietnam was hurting the enemy more than Abrams or any other American appreciated. As would be revealed in postwar histories, the restriction of American bombing below the 19th parallel concentrated the bombing in areas where North Vietnamese truck traffic was especially vulnerable. Every North Vietnamese truck hauling cargo to the Ho Chi Minh Trail had to pass through the panhandle of North Vietnam below the 19th parallel before moving westward into Laos. Only a small number of roads in the panhandle could accommodate trucks, and therefore all trucks had to traverse at least one of a few key intersections. With far more bombs to drop south of the 19th parallel than before, the Americans were now subjecting these choke points to sustained and devastating attack.[16]

The North Vietnamese at first rushed antiaircraft weapons to protect the choke points, but potent attacks by American aircraft put most of these weapons out of commission.[17] Mindful that the Americans could end the geographic restrictions on Rolling Thunder at any time, the North Vietnamese kept nearly all their surface-to-air missiles in Hanoi and Haiphong, which guaranteed that American aircraft losses in the campaign below the 19th parallel would be far lower than in the Hanoi-Haiphong area. The U.S. Air Force was now losing fewer than two aircraft per one thousand sorties, as compared with the more than twenty per thousand it had been losing in northern North Vietnam.[18] Within this relatively safe environment, American pilots could fly at lower altitudes and stay near their targets for longer periods.

According to North Vietnamese sources, the new bombing campaign caused monthly supply shipments through the critical junction at Ha Tinh to fall from 6,500 tons to 1,430 tons.[19] During the late summer, the North Vietnamese were able to deliver only 20 percent of the supply tonnage planned for delivery to the Ho Chi Minh Trail.[20] The revised air campaign in the North eventually became a leading cause of severe shortages of ammunition and food among North Vietnamese units in the South.[21]

In July, the North Vietnamese high command disseminated detailed plans for the third wave of the general offensive and general uprising. To commence on August 17 and continue through September 28, the third wave would consist of conventional assaults on Saigon and other major population centers. Upon receipt of these plans, some of the North Vietnamese leaders in the South refrained from expressing their doubts, for fear that they would be accused of cowardice or lack of ideological conviction.[22] Others objected that the prospects for further urban attacks were poor and recommended focusing the third wave instead on the countryside and mountain jungles.[23] Once more, Le Duan ignored the warnings.[24]

The upcoming American presidential election may well have been one of the factors in Le Duan's decision to press forward against so much contrary advice. The third wave offensive coincided with the national convention of the U.S. Democratic Party, which was scheduled for August 26 to 29 in Chicago.[25] Attacking Saigon would generate press stories on fighting and American casualties thanks to the concentration of American reporters in the capital. Those stories could, in turn, fan antiwar sentiment in the United States, encourage the Democrats to nominate a candidate averse to continued prosecution of the war, and give the Democratic nominee better odds in the general election against the Republican nominee, Richard Nixon, whom the North Vietnamese believed would be more dangerous to Hanoi than any Democrat.[26]

The North Vietnamese knew Nixon to be one of America's staunchest anti-Communists, the man who had led the accusations of espionage against Alger Hiss and jousted with Nikita Khrushchev about the merits of capitalism in a model American kitchen. Their fear of Nixon was shared by the Soviets; Moscow was so desirous of his defeat that it had secretly offered to provide money and other support to Hubert Humphrey, who had become the Democratic Party's front-runner after the assassination of Robert F. Kennedy on June 5. Soviet Ambassador Anatoly Dobrynin, the bearer of the offer, recounted that Humphrey politely declined with the comment that "it was more than enough for him to have Moscow's good wishes, which he highly appreciated."[27]

Nixon had been a strong advocate of American intervention in Vietnam in 1964 and 1965, and had subsequently credited the rescue of South Vietnam with saving all Asia from Communism. Following a trip to the Far East in 1967, he had written that the American stand in Vietnam had been "a vital factor in the turnaround in Indonesia," a country that "constitutes by far the greatest prize in the Southeast Asian area." The war had "diverted Peking from such other potential targets as India, Thailand, and Malaysia" and had "bought vitally needed time for governments that were weak or unstable or leaning toward Peking as a hedge against the future—time which has allowed them to attempt to cope with their own insurrections while pressing ahead with their political, economic and military development."[28]

From 1965 to 1967, Nixon had joined other hawks in demanding that the Johnson administration hit North Vietnam and the
Ho Chi Minh Trail harder with air power. During the Republican
primary, however, he struck a more moderate tone. When the
subject of Vietnam policy arose, he spouted generalities about
achieving a peace that preserved a non-Communist South Vietnam through a diplomatic settlement. Such statements appealed
to Republicans who believed that diplomacy, undergirded by the
threat and use of force, could resolve the conflict quickly as it had
when Eisenhower had ended the Korean War in 1953.

At the same time, Nixon's record of diehard anti-Communism
provided assurance to Republicans who foresaw further bitter
fighting ahead. Nixon reinforced that perception with comments
on the campaign trail about the need for perseverance. "This is
a war we cannot lose," he declared at a stop in New Hampshire.
"For we are fighting in Vietnam not for Vietnam alone, but
for peace in the Pacific." The American commitment to South
Vietnam was "the cork in the bottle of Chinese expansionism
in Asia."[29] In an interview on the subject of the war, he averred
that "We have to stop [the war] with victory, or it will start all
over again in a few years." Pulling out of Vietnam "may save the
lives of boys in their twenties, but not of their younger brothers
who will have to fight all over again."[30]

Nixon resisted media efforts to draw out his specific plans for
Vietnam, having no desire to tip his hand to the enemy or make
commitments that could hamstring him once in office. When a
reporter asked whether he possessed a "secret plan" to end the
war, he responded that he would end the war as president, but
he did not profess to have formulated a secret plan. Nevertheless,
one news report asserted that Nixon had claimed to have a secret
plan to end the war, and other media outlets continued this story
line with such persistence that it soon became accepted as fact.[31]

Over the course of the campaign, though, Nixon did express elements of what would later become his plan, and sometimes he expressed them in public. If elected, he intended to strengthen South Vietnam's armed forces, keep the U.S. military machine rolling, prod Moscow and Beijing to apply diplomatic pressure on Hanoi, and warn the North Vietnamese to negotiate an end to the war promptly or face devastation. By building up South Vietnamese forces, he would get them to do more of the fighting and reduce the costs in American lives and money without compromising the war effort.[32]

Privately, Nixon voiced optimism that his combination of military and diplomatic measures would compel North Vietnam to call it quits during his first months in office, just as Eisenhower's measures had forced North Korea to relent in 1953.[33] His reputation as an implacable anti-Communist would intimidate the North Vietnamese into a peace agreement. "They'll believe any threat of force that Nixon makes because it's Nixon," he told H. R. Haldeman, his chief of staff. "I call it the Madman Theory. I want the North Vietnamese to believe I've reached the point where I might do *anything* to stop the war. We'll just slip the word to them that, 'for God's sake, you know Nixon is obsessed about Communism. We can't restrain him when he's angry—and he has his hand on the nuclear button'—and Ho Chi Minh himself will be in Paris in two days begging for peace."[34]

Nixon's public reticence about policy plans and his pandering to the views of disparate voting blocs on the campaign trail served him well in courting the full ideological spectrum of the Republican electorate. Nixon's principal challengers, California Governor Ronald Reagan and New York Governor Nelson Rockefeller, staked out clearer positions on Vietnam and failed to gain broad appeal. Neither came close to matching Nixon's tallies in most of the primary votes.[35]

By the time of the Republican National Convention, held at the Miami Beach Convention Center from August 5 to 8, the nomination of Richard Nixon was a foregone conclusion. In accepting his party's nomination, Nixon was only slightly more specific than he had been during the primary. As was customary on such an occasion, he spent more time denouncing the opposing party and its sitting president than presenting alternative solutions.

"Let's never forget that despite her faults, America is a great nation," Nixon proclaimed in his acceptance speech. "America is great because her people are great. With Winston Churchill we say we have not journeyed all this way, across the centuries, across the oceans, across the mountains, across the prairies because we are made of sugar candy. America is in trouble today not because her people have failed, but because her leaders have failed. And what America needs are leaders to match the greatness of her people."

On Vietnam, Nixon intoned, "Never has so much military and economic and diplomatic power been used so ineffectively. If after all of this time, and all of this sacrifice, and all of this support, there is still no end in sight, then I say the time has come for the American people to turn to new leadership, not tied to the mistakes and policies of the past. That is what we offer to America. And I pledge to you tonight that the first priority foreign policy objective of our next Administration will be to bring an honorable end to the war in Vietnam."

Elsewhere in the speech, Nixon called upon other nations to bear a greater share of the war's burdens. "In Korea, and now again in Vietnam, the United States furnished most of the money, most of the arms, most of the men to help the people of those countries defend themselves against aggression," the nominee said. "Now, we're a rich country, we're a strong nation, we're a populous nation, but there are 200 million Americans and there are two billion people that live in the free world, and I say the time has come for other nations in the free world to bear their fair share of the burden of defending peace and freedom around this world."[36]

On August 17, nine days after the Republican convention and nine days before the Democratic convention, the third wave offensive commenced. In contrast to the simultaneous attacks of the January and May offensives, the North Vietnamese attacks were staggered geographically, which meant that some of them would kick off during the Democratic convention. The largest of the preliminary strikes took place at Tay Ninh City, initiated by the 5th and 9th North Vietnamese Army Divisions.[37]

Having detected the presence of the 7th and 9th divisions in Tay Ninh Province the previous month, American and South Vietnamese forces had been keeping vigilant watch around the city. By day they patrolled the environs, and by night they set ambushes on the roads, trails, and waterways. At 2230 on the night of August 17, an American platoon spotted a North Vietnamese battalion marching on Tay Ninh City. The Americans radioed the enemy's location, and soon American artillery, mortars, and gunships pounded the North Vietnamese unit. Stuck in the open, the battalion suffered horrific losses, estimated by the Americans at two hundred.

This initial encounter caused the other U.S. and South Vietnamese forces near the city to go on full alert. Among these were the 250 Americans at Fire Support Base Buell II, seven kilometers north of the city, who would face the first major North Vietnamese assault. At 0130, three North Vietnamese infantry battalions and an antiaircraft battalion, with 1,400 North Vietnamese soldiers all told, attempted to overrun Buell II.

Having already brought their barrels down parallel to the ground, the base's artillerymen immediately fired Beehive rounds into the North Vietnamese attackers. Artillery units at other

American firebases ringed Buell II with high-explosive shells, while Air Force fighter-bombers dropped napalm and 500- and 750-pound bombs. The North Vietnamese battalions never made it through the firebase's perimeter wire.

At 0500, the North Vietnamese withdrew from Buell II in haste, leaving many of their dead behind. The Americans retrieved 187 enemy bodies outside the wire and later identified the graves of substantially more. American losses were three killed and twenty-five wounded.

American aircraft took to the skies over Tay Ninh City at dawn to search for North Vietnamese units. Quickly reinforcing the South Vietnamese Regional Forces defending Tay Ninh City was a brigade of the U.S. 25th Infantry Division, which had been based nearby. The American brigade blunted North Vietnamese thrusts toward the city with a methodical orchestration of ground and air assets that made an impression on at least one North Vietnamese witness. Chronicling the American reaction to an attempted North Vietnamese ambush, that individual related: "enemy L-19 observation aircraft and armed helicopters arrived on the scene in approximately five to eight minutes. After forty minutes to one hour, artillery began firing. About one to two hours after the ambush started, enemy mechanized infantry and tanks arrived. Between two-and-one-half hours and three hours after the ambush, helicopters began landing enemy troops outside our battle position to join on-site forces in launching a counter-attack."[38]

Colonel Duquesne Wolfe, the senior American commander at Tay Ninh City, asked for additional American forces. Abrams refused because he had concluded, mistakenly, that the attack on Tay Ninh was a feint to draw forces away from Saigon. The shortage of American units at Tay Ninh City allowed two North Vietnamese battalions to pierce the outer defenses and enter several neighborhoods. Nevertheless, the American brigade and the South Vietnamese Regional Forces needed only two days to drive the North Vietnamese battalions out. Fighting continued in the city outskirts for another week before the 7th and 9th divisions retreated, with much fewer men than when they had arrived. American estimates of North Vietnamese casualties at Tay Ninh City exceeded 1,500 killed and 2,000 wounded.[39]

In the case of Saigon, where Le Duan hoped for the largest victory, most of the combat occurred on the urban periphery, for Abrams had amassed more than enough forces to block North Vietnamese movements toward the city center. As in January and May, the North Vietnamese sustained heavy losses in lopsided clashes. What damage the city suffered was inflicted by North Vietnamese artillery and a small number of North Vietnamese commandos who sneaked into the city.[40]

In the Mekong Delta, American and South Vietnamese forces detected the North Vietnamese units on the fringes of provincial and district capitals, pinned them down in open rice fields, and smashed them apart with the recurring one-two punches of ground assaults and air and artillery strikes.[41] In the northern provinces, allied units quickly and easily repelled sequential North Vietnamese attacks on Da Nang, Ban Me Thuot, and Quang Ngai City. For the period from August 18 to August 29, the Americans estimated total North Vietnamese fatalities at 8,500.[42]

While U.S. forces contributed their characteristic power and vigor, the Americans were impressed by the performance of their South Vietnamese counterparts during the August battles. American observers remarked that the South Vietnamese forces fought substantially better than they had earlier in the year, when, it may be recalled, they had fought better than in 1967.[43]

On August 20, the world's attention shifted from Hanoi's third wave to an even larger military offensive half a world away. Twenty divisions from the armies of the Soviet Union and other Warsaw Pact countries invaded Czechoslovakia that day to unseat the leadership of the Czech Communist Party, which stood condemned for the heresies of the so-called Prague Spring. The party's deviations from Marxism-Leninism had included removal of censorship, decentralization of authority, economic liberalization, and disregard for the dictates of Moscow. The Czech government had not prepared for war, and it did not attempt to fight the invaders off. Within twenty-four hours, Soviet forces had occupied all of Prague and replaced the leading offenders of the Czech Communist Party with individuals who could be expected to obey Moscow's orders.

Communist nations around the world faced Soviet pressure to applaud the invasion as the rescue of Czechoslovakia from sinister counterrevolutionaries. They came under equal pressure from the Chinese to condemn the event as an act of Soviet imperialism. The Soviet overthrow of the Czech government fueled Chinese fears that the Soviets might invade other Communist countries, including Chinese allies like Albania or Romania and perhaps even China itself. The Chinese leadership concluded, for the first time, that the Soviet Union posed a greater threat to China than did the United States. In the weeks that followed, the Chinese government and its media organs hurled more insults at the Soviets than at the Americans.[44]

The North Vietnamese sided unequivocally with the Soviets. A Vietnamese Communist Party mouthpiece labeled the Soviet intervention "a legitimate and essential action which symbolized such noble principles as to protect by all means the Socialist Bloc and the Socialist Revolution." It derided the deposed Czech leaders as "reactionary socialists" and "backward intellectuals who refused to reform their thoughts."[45] To the Soviets, the North Vietnamese reaction was a godsend. To the Chinese, it was an unforgivable betrayal.

Hanoi's support for Soviet intervention in another Communist country placed them, once again, in diametric opposition to Marshal Tito on the question of Communist nationalism. In accordance with his longstanding view that Communist nations could put national concerns and national independence ahead of the cause of international Communism, Tito denounced the Soviet invasion as a violation of Czechoslovakia's sovereign rights. His Yugoslav League of Communists expressed the "deep indignation and bitterness of all the people of Yugoslavia and the members of the League of Communists over the trampling of the sovereignty of an independent socialist country."[46]

In the United States, news of the Soviet invasion of Czechoslovakia overshadowed press reports on North Vietnam's third wave offensive and the accompanying American casualties. Journalists and pundits observed that the Soviet action did considerable harm to the leading dove in the presidential race, Eugene McCarthy. The onslaught undermined his core foreign policy tenet that the United States should reconcile with a Soviet Union that had become more reasonable and less violent. Humphrey fared better than McCarthy because he had made fewer compliments about the Soviets, but he too had spoken lately of "a shift from policies of confrontation and containment to policies of reconciliation and peaceful engagement." The one candidate who clearly profited from the Czech crisis was Richard Nixon since, in the words of *New York Times* editor James Reston, he "has been more anti-Communist than the Democratic party leaders."[47]

The initial reporting of the Czech calamity interrupted a private gathering of Democratic Party elites in Chicago, where party leaders were debating the platform for their impending national convention. Antiwar Democrats, who comprised a large minority on the platform committee, had been grilling Secretary of State Rusk on the subject of Vietnam when he was handed a piece of paper. Reading aloud from the paper, Rusk announced that Soviet forces had invaded Czechoslovakia. As retold by John W. Finney of the *New York Times,* the news left the committee's doves "bewildered, speechless, and with their wings clipped." The invasion, Finney observed, appeared to strengthen the hand of those on the platform committee who viewed Vietnam as part of a larger pattern of Communist aggression.[48]

The platform committee's antiwar faction spent the next few days producing a Vietnam plank that reflected the views of the Democratic Party's most liberal wing. Invoking what had become the standard narrative of the antiwar movement, the plank's authors contended that the National Liberation Front was an independent entity and that hence the conflict was a South Vietnamese civil war, not a North Vietnamese invasion of South Vietnam. The South Vietnamese government, they stated, should negotiate with the National Liberation Front to form a coalition government in Saigon that would be "broadly representative of these and all elements in South Vietnamese society." The plank called for an unconditional end to all bombing of North Vietnam and the withdrawal of all American and North Vietnamese troops from South Vietnam "over a relatively short period of time."[49]

Rufus Phillips, a Democrat who had served in Vietnam as a member of Edward Lansdale's team during the 1950s and as the chief U.S. adviser to the strategic hamlet program in the early 1960s, protested to the antiwar committee members that their plank would abandon the South Vietnamese to the doom of Communist tyranny. A coalition government in Saigon would be certain to succumb to Communist domination, whether through a coup as had befallen Czechoslovakia in 1948 or through armed intervention by a "fraternal socialist" power as had just occurred in Czechoslovakia. The non-Communist countries of Asia, Phillips stressed, still supported America's cause in Vietnam. His impassioned pleas had no effect on the antiwar committee members.[50]

Moderate and conservative members of the platform committee drafted an alternative plank, with input from President Johnson, who injected himself into the process to ensure that his administration's Vietnam policy received favorable treatment. This plank stated that the bombing ought to be halted only if it were accompanied by reciprocal actions by the North Vietnamese and would not endanger the lives of American troops. The dueling planks set the stage for a showdown on the convention floor.[51]

Whereas Nixon's nomination at the Republican convention had been determined months in advance, the outcome of the Democratic convention remained up in the air when the delegates arrived in Chicago on August 26. Humphrey, the frontrunner, faced a party that was even more divided on Vietnam than the Republicans. Liberal Democrats implored Humphrey to run on an antiwar platform, but moderates beseeched him to support a Vietnam policy similar to Johnson's, and conservatives from Southern states wanted military escalation. Eugene McCarthy, the favorite of the party's liberals, posed the most serious threat to Humphrey's candidacy.

Humphrey could secure the nomination by winning the support of moderate and conservative delegates, but to do so he would need the president's endorsement, and Johnson had made clear that he would give that endorsement only if Humphrey vowed to run on a platform consistent with Johnson's policies, especially his Vietnam policy. Throughout his vice presidency, Humphrey had publicly supported the administration's policies, as a vice president was obligated to do. Pledging to keep those policies under a Humphrey administration, however, was an entirely different proposition. A president was supposed to be his own man, with his own ideas.

Humphrey was a liberal at heart, on matters both foreign and domestic. He subscribed to the liberal view that the United States could achieve peace by adopting a softer negotiating position on Vietnam than Johnson's. He also believed that a softer diplomatic stance would enable him to win over liberal Democrats who had lost confidence in Johnson's foreign policy. For these reasons, Humphrey had, in the weeks leading up to the convention, shown a reluctance to reaffirm Johnson's Vietnam policy. His wavering had so irritated Johnson that the president had resorted to the extraordinary tactic of threatening to enter the presidential race himself.[52]

In the end, Humphrey's desire for the presidential nomination prevailed over his ideological principles. On the third day of the convention, Humphrey told Johnson that he would stick with him on Vietnam and endorse the pro-administration plank. Later in the day, with the endorsement of Johnson and Humphrey, that plank won approval on the convention floor by a count of 1,576 votes in favor and 1,041 against. Johnson passed the word to moderate and conservative delegates that he was backing Humphrey, and with that signal the nomination of Humphrey was secure.[53]

On this same day, antiwar demonstrators gathered at Chicago's Grant Park for what was expected to be the largest protest of the convention. The event was the product of months of work by David Dellinger, the head of the National Mobilization Committee to End the War in Vietnam, and his two deputies, Tom Hayden and Rennie Davis. Earlier in the summer, their committee had issued bold exhortations for half a million peace demonstrators to descend on Chicago during the convention. To their chagrin, only ten thousand showed up at Grant Park on August 28.

A large fraction of the ten thousand were Eugene McCarthy supporters, and most of them had no particular desire to follow the dictates of Dellinger's committee. Others belonged to prolabor youth groups backed by the United Auto Workers. Dellinger, the McCarthy supporters, and the labor activists wanted to keep the protests peaceful, which put them at odds with the militant elements who were on hand, including the Yippies, the shorthand name for members of the far-left Youth International Party.[54]

At Grant Park, Dellinger presided on stage as the master of ceremonies while speakers held forth on the evils of the war, the U.S. government, and American society. It was peaceful at first, but a violent confrontation erupted when policemen tried to remove a red revolutionary flag that some of the militants had run up a flagpole. Responding to recalcitrant protesters with the swinging of batons, the police got the better of the disorganized and lightly equipped militants. Among those injured in the melee was Rennie Davis, whose head had been so bloodied that he had to be rushed to a hospital.

After the scheduled speakers had made their points, Dellinger announced that they would march peacefully to the International Amphitheater, site of the Democratic Convention. Tom Hayden jumped on the stage, pushed Dellinger out of the way, and grabbed the microphone. "Rennie has been taken to the hospital, and we have to avenge him!" Hayden exclaimed. "We must move out of this park in groups throughout the city and turn this overheated military machine against itself. Let us make sure that if blood flows, it flows all over the city!"[55]

The preponderance of the protesters ended up marching not to the International Amphitheater but to the Hilton Hotel on Michigan Avenue, where Humphrey and most of the other Democratic dignitaries were overnighting. Some of the marchers brandished Viet Cong flags, black anarchist flags, or red revolutionary flags.

Choruses of "F— you LBJ!" reverberated across the city streets, followed by catcalls of "Pig" as police gathered to protect the luxurious hotels and shops along Michigan Avenue. Democratic Party leaders watched helplessly from their hotel windows as the mob seeped onto Michigan Avenue and chucked rocks, eggs, and bags of urine at policemen.

David Horowitz and Peter Collier, who at the time were editors of the radical *Ramparts* magazine, later described the thinking that drove the protest movement into such a frenzy. "Vietnam was a universal solvent—the explanation for every evil we saw and the justification for every excess we committed," they recounted. "Trashing the windows of merchants on the main streets of America seemed warranted by the notion that these petty bourgeois shopkeepers were cogs in the system of capitalist exploitation that was obliterating Vietnam. Fantasizing the death of local cops seemed warranted by the role they played as an occupying army in America's black ghettos, those mini-Vietnams we yearned to see explode in domestic wars of liberation."[56]

The police initially showed restraint in the face of this unruliness, even when protesters shouted "Pig" or more personalized insults. But the nerves of the police were wearing thin. Many policemen had brothers or cousins or sons in Vietnam and were appalled to see the country and the war derided by privileged young men who had refused to serve in the armed forces. The term "pig," in addition to serving as an anti-police slur, was also a derogatory term for Americans of Polish descent, a group that happened to account for a large portion of the Chicago police force and also for members of the white working class, who accounted for nearly the entire force. "The Chicago policemen who were in the streets of Chicago were from blue-collar families," the city's deputy mayor, David Stahl, recounted later. "They didn't have any opportunities to go to college. And I think those Chicago police officers didn't understand why these kids, the sons of daughters of the affluent, were out in the streets trying to wreck the system."⁵⁷

On Michigan Avenue, police restraint ebbed as the afternoon turned late. In the early evening, buses arrived with additional policemen, these ones topped with sturdy helmets. With reinforcements on the scene, the forbearance of the police ended. Plunging into the protesters, the cops broke up the throng with clubs and tear gas.

A select group of protesters fought back, punching and kicking and throwing rocks. They were soon corralled into patrol wagons. The rest of the crowd fled, to Grant Park or down side streets or into hotel lobbies. By 8:30 the violence had subsided. No one had been killed, but two hundred people had been injured, including fifty policemen.⁵⁸

Footage of the melee aired on the national television networks later that evening. Antiwar activists expected that the graphic imagery of policemen clubbing and dragging protesters would elicit sympathy for their cause. "The whole world is watching," the demonstrators had chanted with delight. The whole world did watch, but it did not draw the desired conclusions. The radicalism, mob tactics, disrespect for authority, and disheveled appearance of the demonstrators offended the sensibilities of most Americans, regardless of their political persuasion. Todd Gitlin, an antiwar activist and sociologist, recalled, "To our innocent eyes, it defied common sense that people could watch even the sliver of the onslaught that got onto television and side with the cops—which in fact was precisely what the polls showed. As unpopular as the war had become, the antiwar movement was detested still more—the most hated political group in America, disliked even by most of the people who supported immediate withdrawal from Vietnam."⁵⁹

In the capitals of the Communist world, nominee Humphrey's acceptance of the administration plank appears to have made a greater impression than the antiwar protests. Although no records of internal deliberations in Moscow or Hanoi have emerged on this topic, the ensuing Soviet and North Vietnamese actions implied a recognition that the third wave offensive had failed to advance the antiwar cause within the Democratic Party and hence that the next U.S. president would keep supporting South Vietnam for years to come. In early September, Soviet diplomats informed their American counterparts that Hanoi had realized the impossibility of military victory and was interested in a political settlement.[60] As coming events were to show, that interest was stronger than ever before.

Hanoi's heightened enthusiasm for diplomacy did not, however, cause it to cut short the third wave offensive. On September 10, the last spurts of North Vietnamese urban warfare began. American and South Vietnamese forces once again walloped North Vietnamese forces until desperation drove them to return to the jungles and mountains. By the end of September, when the third wave officially came to a close, estimated North Vietnamese losses for the month had reached 12,543.[61]

The extent of North Vietnamese losses in the three offensives of 1968 was, at the time, unclear to anyone except a small number of North Vietnamese officials. The American intelligence community concluded that in spite of repeated setbacks, North Vietnamese forces were "still capable of a formidable effort" and "of enduring the next six months or more without seriously impairing their position in South Vietnam."[62] Only several decades later would it become manifest that this appraisal had grossly underestimated the damage that the offensives had done to North Vietnam's capabilities and position.

"We had thrown all our forces into the general offensive," Luu Van Loi recounted in a 1996 book. By the end of the third wave, casualties had reached staggering proportions, such that "we had no forces left" to conduct major military operations.[63] Histories published by the Hanoi regime in 2005 and 2010 attested that much of what remained of the North Vietnamese Army had retreated to remote areas or neighboring countries, where no military or political influence could be exerted over South Vietnam. Most of the Southern-born Communist local forces, guerrillas, and cadres had either departed with the North Vietnamese regulars, been killed, or quit.[64] Having rushed so many North Vietnamese troops to the South earlier in the year, Hanoi had nearly drained its manpower reservoir, such that it now had to cut the monthly average of infiltration from sixteen thousand to three thousand.[65]

Tran Bach Dang, one of the top Communist officials in the South at the time, later admitted that "we had lost virtually the entire liberated area. The cost of this error was extremely high, and we paid dearly for it, not just within South Vietnam, but throughout Vietnam and throughout Indochina."[66] The period following the third wave offensive "was one of the most difficult time periods for the South Vietnamese revolution," stated the official history of the North Vietnamese Army's General Staff. "In the face of the tremendous problems and challenges on the battlefields, our posture and our strength had seriously deteriorated."[67]

Had the United States known the magnitude of North Vietnam's problems at this juncture, the widespread perception of the war as an ongoing stalemate might have subsided. Hubert Humphrey might then have felt less pressure to steer a new course on Vietnam, and the presidential race might have taken a different course. As it was, liberals in Humphrey's entourage and the media bombarded him with recommendations to change his position on the war, which they said would cut him loose from a Vietnam policy that was weighing his candidacy down. By adopting a softer stance on negotiations, but one not so soft as to provoke moderate and conservative Democrats, he could win back the mass of liberals who had been disillusioned since Chicago by his embrace of Johnson's foreign policy.

In late September, Humphrey trailed far behind Nixon in the polls, by a margin of 43 to 28 percent, with George Wallace of the segregationist American Independent Party in third at 21 percent.[68] Humphrey and his staff had tried various stratagems to lift his poll numbers, but none had worked, and disorder and despair were setting in. Mary McGrory of the *Boston Globe* likened Humphrey's campaign to "an overnight camping trip for which someone has forgotten the tents."[69]

Whether changing his position on Vietnam would actually gain Humphrey vast numbers of new supporters, and whether it would alienate droves of moderates and conservatives, Humphrey could only guess. Certainly President Johnson would not take kindly to it. But there seemed no other option to rescue Humphrey from peril. At the end of the month, Humphrey decided to take his chances on recasting his Vietnam policy.

Humphrey laid plans to announce a new diplomatic approach in a speech in Salt Lake City on September 30. To draft the speech, Humphrey enlisted the help of George Ball, who had just quit his position as U.S. ambassador to the United Nations to join Humphrey's campaign, and Averell Harriman, who saw nothing untoward in abetting Humphrey's campaign while serving as the U.S. government's chief negotiator in Paris.[70] The final text, as approved by the candidate, stated that if Humphrey were elected, he would cease the bombing of North Vietnam, provided that Hanoi respected the DMZ. It omitted the Johnson administration's two other stated preconditions for a bombing halt: an end to North Vietnamese attacks on South Vietnamese cities and the inclusion of the South Vietnamese government in the negotiations.

Humphrey waited until the day of the speech to inform President Johnson of its contents. Johnson was appalled to learn that Humphrey was leaving out the two preconditions, and he let his vice president know it. Refusing to back down, Humphrey made the very tenuous claim that those two preconditions were implicit in a passage about resuming the bombing if Hanoi did not negotiate in good faith.[71]

On that same day, Ball and others on Humphrey's staff were spinning a very different yarn to the press. Humphrey, they asserted, had committed himself to a bombing halt without any preconditions whatsoever. While Humphrey's speech might make reference to respect for the demilitarized zone, it would be merely "window dressing" required by political exigencies. They expressed hope, in addition, that the speech would convince antiwar Democrats that Humphrey had broken with the president on Vietnam and convince Eugene McCarthy to endorse Humphrey's candidacy.[72]

On the evening of the thirtieth, with the nation watching live on the NBC television network, Humphrey delivered the speech from Salt Lake City. "My first priority as President shall be to end the war and obtain an honorable peace," the vice president pledged. He would be willing to stop the bombing "as an acceptable risk for peace" if the North Vietnamese agreed to respect the DMZ. Then he would seek a ceasefire supervised by the United Nations or another international body, to be followed by mutual withdrawals of all U.S. and North Vietnamese troops.

Humphrey vowed to press the South Vietnamese to take on more of the burden of the war because the South Vietnamese armed forces were improving, "just as the South Korean army did during the latter stages of the Korean war." To reassure moderates and conservatives, he ruled out a unilateral U.S. withdrawal. "To withdraw would not only jeopardize the independence of

South Vietnam and the safety of other Southeast Asian nations," Humphrey said. "It would be an open invitation to more violence, more aggression, more instability."[73] However desirable it might be to attract liberal voters, Humphrey's victory would depend first and foremost on his appeal among a larger group of voters that still supported the war, consisting of moderate Democrats, conservative Democrats, maverick Republicans, and independents.

CHAPTER 17

. . .

MORE ROPE

October–December 1968

On the morning of October 1, Richard Nixon held a news conference to discuss the speech Humphrey had given in Salt Lake City the previous evening. When asked by a reporter whether he thought Humphrey's speech had undercut President Johnson's diplomatic position, Nixon replied that it was "very possible" that Hanoi "could so interpret" the speech. Candidate Humphrey, said Nixon, needed to clarify whether he meant to depart from administration policy on the bombing halt, so that he would "not allow the nation to think, and particularly Hanoi to think, that he is playing both sides." Bombing was America's "trump card" in negotiations with the North Vietnamese, Nixon stated solemnly. "If that trump card is played by either of the Presidential candidates by indicating that we in January might do something that the negotiators have refused to do in Paris, it means that all chance for those negotiations to succeed will evaporate."[1]

It was a deft jab from a politician who had mastered the art of negative campaigning. The Humphrey camp, however, had virtuosos of its own. The counterpunch came the next day, but not from Humphrey or a member of his campaign staff as would have been customary. Rather, it was thrown by a senior government official, Averell Harriman. Draped in the authority of the chief negotiator, Harriman publicly denigrated Nixon's characterization of the Salt Lake City speech by adjudging that Humphrey's stance would not harm the United States in the negotiations.[2]

Whether Harriman really believed this pronouncement was uncertain. Through his daily interactions with the North Vietnamese in Paris, he may well have discerned that Humphrey's speech had weakened the American negotiating posture, as other observers discerned at this time. It was possible that Harriman spoke untruthfully in Humphrey's favor because he cared more about Humphrey's election than about the Vietnam negotiations. Two months later, Harriman would disclose his belief that Vietnam policy was less important for the United States than "not permitting it to elect Nixon as President."[3]

Humphrey's advocates, including Ball and perhaps also Harriman, fed information on the brouhaha to reporters who could be expected to use it against Nixon. In an analysis of the Salt Lake City speech that ran in the *Washington Post* on October 3, Joseph Kraft wrote that "a trap was prepared for Richard Nixon" by Humphrey's campaign and Harriman. "It was expected that the Republican candidate would reply to the Vice President by raising a question as to whether Mr. Humphrey's advance towards a total cessation of the bombing would not adversely affect the Paris negotiations," Kraft stated. "Mr. Nixon did as expected. And arrangements were immediately made for Ambassador Harriman to deny the Nixon insinuation."[4]

The Salt Lake City speech and the behind-the-scenes contrivances earned Humphrey profuse acclaim in liberal circles. The *New York Times* praised Humphrey for his intention to "move away from the errors of the past" on Vietnam. "It is significant," the editors noted, "that the former members of the Johnson administration who are rallying to Mr. Humphrey's support include its best-known doves." So impressed was the paper's leadership that it issued an official endorsement of Humphrey on October 6.[5]

The impact on the general public, however, was much more modest. A Gallup poll taken between October 3 and 12 showed only slight movements in voter preferences, with Nixon holding steady at 43 percent, Humphrey inching up to 31 percent, and the hawkish Wallace retaining 20 percent.[6] Whether Humphrey's speech had done too little to mollify doves or too much to provoke hawks was not clear; his three-percentage-point gain might have resulted solely from the attraction of disaffected doves to his candidacy, but it was also possible that the leftward shift had attracted a larger group of doves while driving away some moderates and conservatives.

The Humphrey campaign's spinning of the speech was particularly upsetting to the nation's foremost moderate. After reading Kraft's article and several others of a similar bent on the morning of October 3, President Johnson phoned Rusk in a despairing rage. "So Averell started commenting on the speech," Johnson steamed, "and saying it didn't hurt the negotiations, and now Nixon has been trapped."

"Did Averell comment publicly on the speech?" Rusk asked.

"Yes, yes," said the president. "He's a damned fool. He's been playing politics."

"The combinations of these stories will hurt our negotiations," Rusk stated.

"Of course, it hurts," Johnson replied. "It'll be hell." The North Vietnamese "are not going to do anything until the election. That's period. If Humphrey's elected, they're in clover. If he's not elected, then they can look and see what they want to do between me and Nixon. So we can just forget everything until then, in my judgment."[7]

In a subsequent phone call, Johnson told Rusk, "I think we're in serious trouble. I don't know what we're going to do about it." In reference to Harriman, the president said, "I don't think we can have people working for us that are writing campaign speeches and getting themselves involved with private citizens and breaking out to the nation speeches that neither the Secretary of State nor the President know anything about." Johnson then drew a parallel with General Douglas MacArthur's challenge of President Truman's authority in 1951, one of the most contentious episodes in the history of the American republic. "I think it's just another MacArthur deal," he fulminated.

Rusk suggested they consider recalling Harriman to Washington.

"I rather think so," said Johnson. "If at the end of that period we have any more static here, I think we just might ask Averell to come back."[8]

In advance of the next meeting with the North Vietnamese representatives in Paris, Johnson directed Harriman and Vance to stick with the administration's three main preconditions for negotiations: the DMZ, the cities, and South Vietnamese participation. At the meeting, held on October 11 in the quiet Paris suburb of Sceaux, Harriman and Vance did as instructed. In delivering the three points to the North Vietnamese, Harriman and Vance stressed that South Vietnamese participation in negotiations after a bombing halt was "utterly indispensable." Le Duc Tho, the senior North Vietnamese negotiator, asked whether this participation was a precondition, touching off a semantic joust in which the Americans sought to couch the preconditions as something other than preconditions, in light of the longstanding North Vietnamese aversion to acceptance of preconditions.

"It is not a condition or demand for reciprocity—merely a definition of serious talks," Vance informed Le Duc Tho. "As we have said, we do not think there could be serious negotiations without inclusion of representatives of the GVN on our side."

Harriman and Vance pressed Le Duc Tho to say whether the North Vietnamese would agree to South Vietnamese participation in the talks if the United States stopped the bombing. Turning the question around, Tho said that he wanted to know whether the United States would stop the bombing if Hanoi agreed to South Vietnamese participation. Harriman and Vance responded that they would have to convey Le Duc Tho's question to Washington, which they promised to do.

At the end of the conclave, Le Duc Tho told the Americans, "I am convinced that if you and we have serious intent and good-will, peaceful settlement for Vietnam's problems can be found."

Harriman replied, "We accept that in the spirit you raised it and we reciprocate your approach." According to a North Vietnamese account of the meeting but absent from the American record, Harriman then presented the North Vietnamese diplomats with caviar, which he touted as a gift from Soviet premier Alexei Kosygin.[9]

After the meeting, Vance and Harriman urged Washington to agree to a bombing halt if Hanoi consented to South Vietnamese participation in negotiations. But before the State Department could issue a reply, Soviet diplomats interceded to push matters ahead. On the twelfth, the Soviet embassy in Paris notified Vance that if the United States stopped bombing North Vietnam, Hanoi would enter into negotiations that included the South Vietnamese government. After confirming with the Soviets that the accord would include assurances on the DMZ and the cities, the White House gave its approval.[10]

News of the deal came as a welcome surprise to nearly everyone in the U.S. government. North Vietnamese consent to South Vietnamese diplomatic participation was considered so advantageous to the power and prestige of the Saigon government that few had expected Hanoi to concede it. None of the Americans knew that Rolling Thunder's recent installments had been so injurious as to drive Hanoi to desperation, though some surmised it. Nor did any of them initially surmise what many would later conclude, that the deal was both a North Vietnamese ploy to obtain relief from the bombing and a North Vietnamese and Soviet ploy to sway the American presidential election.

"We think Hanoi's decision to agree to the GVN entering the discussions is of the greatest significance," Bunker and Abrams reported from Saigon. "It suggests that Hanoi has abandoned all hope of a military victory or of a unilateral U.S. withdrawal by the next administration."[11] General Wheeler remarked, "I think this is as much a symbol of defeat as the erection of the Berlin Wall. They have been clobbered."[12] At the CIA, where most analysts had believed that Hanoi would never agree to the Saigon government's participation in negotiations, Hanoi's consent to the deal was hailed as a strategic boon that would safeguard South Vietnam's stability during the negotiating period.[13]

Just as the Johnson administration was poised to obtain from Hanoi all three of its preconditions, the politics of the Democratic Party intruded again. It began with a *Washington Post* puff piece on George Ball. In the paper's October 12 edition, columnists Drew Pearson and Jack Anderson related that before Ball had decided to leave his United Nations post for Humphrey's campaign, he had flown to Paris to learn whether this move would undermine American diplomacy. During his visit, Ball learned that by joining forces with Humphrey, he would actually help the negotiations because his views on the subject were clearly superior to those of the Johnson administration. As evidence of the administration's diplomatic hamfistedness, the columnists wrote, "On at least two occasions, Ambassador Averell Harriman had been on verge of real success in negotiating with the North Vietnamese only to have the rug pulled out from under him in Washington. Either President Johnson, or some of those close to him, obviously did not want to make any concessions toward a truce."[14] By implying that a Humphrey administration would not demand the same concessions as the Johnson administration, the article informed Hanoi that it could rescind its acceptance of Johnson's preconditions and get a better deal from Humphrey after the election.

Later that day, McGeorge Bundy further undercut the Johnson administration's diplomacy in a speech at DePauw University. Bundy told the audience that the United States should pursue negotiations, but even if diplomacy were futile, the United States should undertake a "substantial reduction in the level of our own military effort there." The former national security adviser, who in many Vietnamese minds remained an influential voice of the American ruling clique and the Democratic Party, advocated halting the bombing of North Vietnam unconditionally and reducing the number of U.S. troops over a period of several years to one hundred thousand. These measures, he said, would be "more than enough to sustain and execute the basic purpose of our forces in Vietnam—the purpose of preventing defeat."[15]

At the next diplomatic meeting, on October 15, North Vietnamese representatives informed Harriman and Vance that they were not sure whether the Politburo would move forward with the deal, and that in any case the Politburo was most unlikely to proceed as quickly as the Americans desired.[16] They did not divulge that members of the Politburo wanted to make additional demands of the Americans beyond what had been agreed on October 11.[17] Hanoi's hesitancy led Johnson to suspect that Bundy's speech had caused the North Vietnamese to drive a harder diplomatic bargain, and his suspicion was confirmed by communications intercepts received a couple of days later. At a meeting with senior Defense Department staff on October 17, Clifford observed that "LBJ is absolutely wild at Mac Bundy. He thinks Bundy's speech screwed it all up! We know from intercepts how Hanoi was elated by Bundy!"[18]

The North Vietnamese, however, would soon dispel Johnson's worries that they would back out of the deal. Le Duc Tho believed that the additional demands contemplated by the Politburo failed to give due consideration to the strength of America's military position, and that insistence on them would stymie North Vietnam's efforts to stop the bombing. Flying back to Hanoi to state his case in person, he convinced the Politburo to drop the demands. The Politburo justified its decision to the rest of the party by citing the need to advance "our stratagem to pressure the United States" into "ending the bombing of North Vietnam."[19]

After his stop in Hanoi, Le Duc Tho traveled to Beijing for consultations with the Chinese leadership. Chinese Foreign Minister Chen Yi gave him a tongue-lashing for yielding to the Americans on South Vietnamese participation in the negotiations, which the Chinese considered to be highly advantageous for the Saigon government. "Since last April, when you accepted the U.S. partial cessation of bombing and held peace talks with them, you have lost the initiative in the negotiations to them," Chen Yi growled. By allowing the South Vietnamese government to participate in the negotiations, "you lost to them once more," because "you handed the puppet government legal recognition, thus eliminating the National Liberation Front's status as the unique legal representative of the people in the South. So, the Americans have helped their puppet regime to gain legal status while you have made the Front lose its own prestige."

In case his visitor had not fully comprehended the depth of his displeasure, Chen Yi charged the Vietnamese Communist Party with betraying its own founder. "You are acting in contradiction to the teachings of President Ho, the great leader of the Vietnamese people, thus destroying President Ho's prestige among the Vietnamese people," Chen Yi seethed. He finished the dressing down by accusing North Vietnam of kowtowing to the Soviet bugbear. "In a very short time," he said, "you have accepted the compromising and capitulationist proposals put forward by the Soviet revisionists."[20]

The Chinese government would soon act upon its discontent with the North Vietnamese. In November, it began withdrawing the Chinese support troops that had been in North Vietnam since 1965. Henceforth, North Vietnamese men would have to perform the work done previously by more than a hundred thousand Chinese soldiers.[21] In a country whose manpower and engineering expertise had already been stretched to its limits by the war, this reallocation of labor would cut severely into the number of North Vietnamese men available to fight in the South.

Before the Americans had offered to halt the bombing, they had sought and obtained Thieu's consent. Thieu, however, had not thought that the North Vietnamese would actually accept the terms of the deal. Although Hanoi's consent to his government's presence at the negotiating table was a strategic bonanza, Thieu was troubled by the timing of the agreement. He feared a ruse by the North Vietnamese to promote the election of Humphrey, who Thieu and most other South Vietnamese believed would be less inclined than Nixon to stand firm against North Vietnam.[22]

Thieu attempted to delay the bombing halt by issuing his own list of preconditions for negotiations. The South Vietnamese delegation, he demanded, had to sit behind a table board emblazoned with "Government of the Republic of Vietnam," and the National Liberation Front could be permitted no such board on their side of the conference table. He insisted that whenever someone on the Communist side claimed to represent the National Liberation Front, the South Vietnamese delegation would "reiterate that they are part and parcel of the North Vietnamese delegation, speak on behalf of North Vietnam, and that we do not consider them as a separate entity from the North Vietnamese delegation."[23]

The North Vietnamese, meanwhile, began proposing starting dates for the bombing halt and the first substantive meeting. They wanted a week or more between these two dates. The Americans countered that the dates should be no more than a few days apart. Soviet diplomats repeatedly intervened with the North Vietnamese and Americans to find ways to compromise on this and other points.[24]

The diplomatic maneuvering among the governments in Hanoi, Saigon, Washington, Moscow, and Beijing was further complicated by the intrusion of the American presidential candidates at the end of October. On October 25, Nixon learned that members of the Johnson administration were suddenly participating in a flurry of meetings on a bombing halt. As he wrote later in his memoirs, he suspected that Johnson was seeking to move toward peace just before the election in an effort to secure victory for Humphrey.[25] William Safire, a member of the Nixon campaign, recollected that "Nixon felt the only way to counter this was with a pre-emptive strike."[26]

Nixon's strike took the form of a public statement that raised the issue of nefarious motives while seemingly avoiding a partisan attack on Johnson. In describing the reported meetings on a bombing cessation, Nixon apprised the press that he had been "told that this spurt of activity is a cynical, last-minute attempt by President Johnson to salvage the candidacy of Mr. Humphrey. This I do not believe." He went on to say, "President Johnson is profoundly concerned about our half-million servicemen, including his two sons-in-law, in Vietnam. In every conversation I have had with him he has made it clear that he will not play politics with this war."[27]

As intended, Nixon's remarks sparked a surge in media interest on the secret peace negotiations. With so many newsmen digging around, details on the talks and their political undercurrents came into the open. Vietnam, which had receded from the campaign after Johnson's speech of March 31, returned to the fore, where it would remain until election day.

On October 27, North Vietnamese diplomats made their best offer yet on the start of negotiations, proposing to begin the talks on November 2 if the bombing were stopped on October 30. The interval between those two dates was short enough that even Johnson's hawkish advisers recommended accepting them.

"They have made the major step," Rusk said at a meeting of senior foreign policy officials.

"If ten steps separated us," Clifford interposed, "they have taken eight and we have taken two."

"I would say it is nine to one," Rusk returned.

Rusk, Rostow, and Taylor said they believed that the North Vietnamese would respect their promise to leave the DMZ and the cities alone. "I have been a hard-nosed man, Mr. President, but I am for this," Taylor said. "They are hurting."

Only Johnson himself voiced skepticism. Thieu and Nixon were convinced that the North Vietnamese were trying to hand the election to Humphrey, he knew, and they would view him as a coconspirator if he rushed the deal forward before election day. "I still think this is a political move to affect this election," he grumbled. "November 2 is a bad, dangerous date. Nearly everybody will interpret it as being connected with the campaign."[28]

The unanimity of his advisers, however, convinced Johnson to agree to the timeline proposed by Hanoi. Bunker went to work with Thieu to formulate an announcement on the start of talks. But Thieu remained determined to delay the halt and the talks, coming up with new preconditions to demand of the North Vietnamese and new reasons for pushing the dates back.

This problem, nettlesome as it already was, took on a new dimension on the evening of October 27 when the White House received a decrypted cable from Ambassador Bui Diem to Thieu that smacked of collusion between the South Vietnamese government and the Nixon campaign. "Many Republican friends have contacted me and encouraged us to stand firm," the South Vietnamese ambassador had written to his president. "They were alarmed by press reports to the effect that you had already softened your position."

In the White House, the report fueled worries that Republican pressure was causing Thieu to keep stalling until the date of the election. Nixon, it was suspected, was promising Thieu staunch support after his electoral victory if Thieu would act now to deny Humphrey the benefits of the preelection peace surge. Johnson decided to tap the phones of the South Vietnamese embassy, record the identity of every person seen entering and departing the embassy compound, and place under surveillance a one Anna Chennault, who was suspected of passing information between the Thieu government and the Republicans.[29]

Born into a family of Chinese diplomats, Anna Chennault was the widow of Claire Chennault, who had commanded the American Flying Tigers in China during World War II. After the war, she had emigrated to the United States and become one of the nation's most prominent Asian Americans. As cochair of the Republican Women for Nixon, she had helped raise $250,000 for Nixon's presidential campaign. In another effort to gain favor with the presidential nominee, she had taken it upon herself to serve as unofficial conduit between the South Vietnamese embassy in Washington and the Nixon campaign.[30]

Bui Diem had been drawn to Chennault because of her ties to the elites of the Republican Party. With the Republicans poised for electoral victories in the executive and legislative branches, cultivating influential Republicans was especially important in the fall of 1968. If Bui Diem wanted to make South Vietnam's case to leading Republicans, he could ask Chennault for an introduction, or attend one of the numerous cocktail parties she hosted at her penthouse apartment in the Watergate building.[31]

As often befalls those seeking to ingratiate themselves with a presidential campaign, Chennault was unable to gain the access and influence she desired. When she tried to speak with Nixon's inner circle, she was rebuffed and redirected to the campaign's foreign policy advisers.[32] Melvin Laird, whose support for Nixon during the campaign would earn him the position of secretary of defense, later characterized Chennault as a freelancer on the campaign's fringes.[33]

At the end of October, Walt Rostow pressed the CIA for more information on Chennault's activities. George Carver, the CIA's special assistant for Vietnamese affairs, responded by questioning the notion that Thieu's opposition to Johnson's negotiating plan was the product of collusion with Nixon. As Carver saw it, Thieu had plenty of reasons of his own to believe that the White House's diplomatic plan would imperil South Vietnam, and Carver said he would have felt the same way had he been in Thieu's position.[34]

Of late, the CIA had received considerable evidence that Thieu viewed the diplomatic deal as a threat to his nation's survival. He was reported to be worried that South Vietnam would get nothing in return for relinquishing the huge military and political benefits of the bombing. CIA reporting highlighted Thieu's concern that acceptance of a halt under American duress would undercut South Vietnamese nationalism and his own prestige. Some of Thieu's most important subordinates, including Ky and

Huong, were warning that South Vietnam could be perceived as a puppet of the United States if it went along with the entirety of Washington's plan.[35]

Thieu himself was bristling under what he perceived to be inordinate American pressure. In private moments with Vietnamese friends and relatives, he expressed unwavering determination to resist that pressure, using language that bore a striking resemblance to the defiant intonations of Ngo Dinh Diem in 1963. In the account of one of the CIA's South Vietnamese sources, Thieu vowed that he "would never concede to the Americans and was prepared to leave the Presidency if the Americans cut off financial aid to the GVN, or to die if there was an attempt against his life." Thieu preferred "a respected name in history to living shamelessly like a dog obeying its master's every command."[36]

Thieu did not need the Nixon campaign to tell him that the bombing halt would abet Humphrey, or that a Humphrey presidency would be less favorable for South Vietnam than a Nixon presidency. These truths had long been evident to virtually every informed observer in Saigon and Washington. Thieu had been wary of Humphrey since the two had met the previous year, at which time Humphrey had warned Thieu that he should not expect American assistance to continue at the same level in future years.[37] Thieu and other South Vietnamese leaders were by now convinced that the North Vietnamese, the Soviets, and the Americans were all trying to time the bombing halt to get votes for Humphrey. In Thieu's mind, his delaying of the halt did not amount to meddling in American politics, but merely to denying a contrived boost to a candidate who, if elected, might consign South Vietnam to its annihilation.[38]

While Bunker continued his Sisyphean attempts to gain Thieu's concurrence on the timing of the halt, Johnson lined up evidence to show that the halt would not harm the war effort in order to justify it to himself and to the American people. The top brass was saying that the time was right to suspend the bombing because the monsoon rains in southern North Vietnam would preclude effective bombing for the next three months. During the monsoon season, air strikes could be shifted from North Vietnam to Laos and South Vietnam, which in the view of the generals would be a more effective use of America's bombing resources.[39]

Johnson wanted to speak in person to the general whose opinion counted the most, General Abrams. He summoned Abrams to Washington for a climactic discussion, scheduled for the early morning hours of October 29. Flying into Andrews Air Force Base in the dead of night, Abrams was driven straight to the White House and escorted into a 2:30 a.m. meeting with the president. The administration's top national security officials, crisply attired in business suits and dress uniforms, sat in attendance.

Johnson peppered Abrams with questions. "Do you think they will violate the DMZ and the cities?"

"I think they will abide by it on the DMZ," Abrams answered. "On the cities, I am not sure. I am concerned about Saigon." The threat to Saigon, however, was small. "I am talking about a half dozen rockets, or a few—twenty-five to fifty—sappers into Saigon."

"If the enemy honors our agreement," queried Johnson, "will this be an advantage militarily?"

"Yes."

Johnson asked Abrams why the current situation was different from that in August, when the generals had believed that a bombing halt would allow the enemy to multiply its military capabilities. Abrams explained that the enemy had pulled out of northern South Vietnam and that thus the enemy "cannot cause the mischief he could have caused in August." In addition, the monsoon weather in North Vietnam would make Laos a more lucrative place to bomb in the next few months.

Johnson continued: "I am going to put more weight on your judgment than anybody else. Can we do this without additional casualties?"

"Yes, we can," replied Abrams.

"Do you have any reluctance or hesitance to stop the bombing?"

"No, Sir."

"If you were President, would you do it?"

"I have no reservations about doing it," Abrams said. "I know it is stepping into a cesspool of comment. I do think it is the right thing to do. It is the proper thing to do."[40]

Before Abrams departed, Johnson handed him a letter, which the general read during his flight back to Saigon. The president's letter enjoined Abrams to apply all possible military pressure on the enemy in order to facilitate diplomatic success at Paris. With a degree of optimism that he had rarely displayed in recent years, Johnson had ended the letter with a bold prediction. "With luck and with Abe," the president wrote, "we shall conquer ourselves a peace in the next three months—without the loss of a single battle or skirmish—as General Winfield Scott did 120-some years ago."[41]

Later that morning, Johnson's positive thinking was dented by a report that Thieu had firmly refused to accept the timeline for the bombing halt proposed by Hanoi and endorsed by Washington. Thieu claimed that his government needed more time for consultations and diplomatic preparations and that he wanted clarification of comments Harriman had just made casting doubt on the North Vietnamese agreement to talk directly to the South Vietnamese.[42]

Rusk urged Johnson to secure Thieu's concurrence on timing before proceeding with the halt. "If we have to take a little more time to work on it, it's better to do that than to demonstrate to everybody that we insisted on going ahead against our allies," said the secretary of state. Moving forward without the South Vietnamese "would confirm in everybody's view that the only reason we insisted on going ahead under these circumstances was because of domestic politics."

Rostow agreed, adding that Johnson should postpone the halt by one week to "get the election out of it."

Clifford, however, opposed any postponement. He accused the South Vietnamese of stalling because "they do not want to affect Nixon adversely" by agreeing to a halt before the election. "I feel it is inappropriate for us, after bearing these burdens for so many years, to turn this over to Thieu and his people and a new Administration," Clifford said.

Johnson admitted that he understood why Saigon was dragging its feet. "Thieu and the others are voting for a man they see as one who will stick with it—Nixon," Johnson remarked. "They know the Vice President [Humphrey] would be softer."

At this moment, Johnson appeared ready to side with Rusk and Rostow and against Clifford, as he had increasingly done over the course of the year. And yet Johnson suddenly took Clifford's advice over that of Rusk and Rostow. The bombing halt, the president decreed, would commence before the election no matter what the South Vietnamese did. Johnson said that Bunker should "take Thieu up on the mountain" and let him know that "we won't stand for their vetoing this."[43]

Johnson did not explain, then or later, what had convinced him to proceed with the halt before the election despite South Vietnamese opposition. He might have been most concerned about thwarting foreign meddling in the American election and the possible Republican encouragement of that meddling. Or perhaps he was most worried by the possibility that the peace talks would evaporate and with them his legacy as peacemaker. Or perhaps, despite his dissatisfaction with Humphrey for his inconstancy on Vietnam, Johnson's foremost objective was helping his vice president defeat Nixon on election day.

That evening, the White House sent Bunker detailed instructions for the discussion on the mountain. He was to state the following: "If President Thieu makes himself responsible for preventing the very peace talks which have cost so much to obtain, the people of this country would never forget the man responsible. No American leader could rescue the position of such a person with the American people." Bunker was also to tell Thieu that if the South Vietnamese government obstructed the peace effort, the U.S. Congress "would take charge of this situation and would completely undermine and would withdraw the support of the United States from the effort in Vietnam." Thieu was to be offered an additional twenty-four hours, but no more, in order to make the necessary preparations for the halt and the negotiations.[44]

Bunker, who by now had thoroughly familiarized himself with Vietnamese culture, must have worried that the message's threatening tone would only harden Thieu's resistance, but he nonetheless delivered it to Thieu on October 30. The recitation jarred the normally even-keeled Thieu. As described by Bunker, Thieu "reacted emotionally and disjointedly." Thieu would tell friends a few weeks later that he viewed the American ultimatum as a "betrayal" that was "comparable to the U.S. abandonment of Chiang Kai-Shek."[45]

During the meeting, though, Thieu maintained enough composure to refrain from acrimonious accusations. "You are powerful," he told Bunker. "You can say to small nations what you want.

We understand America's sacrifice for Vietnam. All Vietnamese know our life depends on U.S. support. But you cannot force us to do anything against our interest. This negotiation is not a life or death matter for the United States, but it is for Vietnam."

Bunker asked Thieu whether South Vietnam could agree to a bombing halt on October 31 and an initial meeting on November 4. Thieu replied that those dates did not give him enough time to consult with his colleagues. If he did not hold these consultations, Thieu said, he would be "vilified and isolated."[46]

During the twenty-four-hour extension provided by the White House, Thieu considered a last-ditch American compromise whereby the halt would start on November 1 and the initial meeting would take place on November 6. But when Bunker came back to him the next day, Thieu said that he was not ready to accept those dates, either. He proposed that South Vietnam and the United States simply announce that negotiations would begin "at an early date after preliminary agreement on the basic ground rules of the talks." In the face of continued pressure from Bunker to accede to the American timetable, Thieu snapped, "I would ask you a frank question: To have a real peace, an honorable peace after twenty years of war, why are you in such a hurry for a day or two, while the Communists took more than a month after the partial cessation of bombing last March to come to Paris and then spent five months to read the same speech at each session?" Thieu went on, "This conference will decide the fate of my nation. We need time for that. If your government says 'no' to us and decides that it has no more time, it is up to you. But I have my responsibility to my nation and my people. I have to do that to have a tranquil conscience."[47]

Johnson refused to tolerate any further delay. Painful though it would be to proceed without the South Vietnamese, he would go ahead with his announcement of the halt and the preliminary talks. He would make a speech to the world that night, October 31.[48]

In providing Thieu advance notice of Johnson's speech, Bunker said, "The President asked me to say to you that you should not be disheartened or discouraged. He would say some very fine things about Vietnam in his speech and he wants me to assure you that we intend to continue our firm support of your country and your government. We intend to continue to work together with you to achieve what we set out to do. We are all sorry that we could not be together on this."

"If we had gone into these talks with the NLF it would have meant the disintegration of the nation," Thieu responded. "The state must have stability, not trouble, not instability; that is our gravest concern." Thieu apologized that he could not make a joint announcement with the president, adding, "Please assure President Johnson that I will continue to have the greatest gratitude to him and the U.S. Government."[49]

All three of the American television networks carried Johnson's address that night. The president began by spelling out the conditions under which he was willing to negotiate. After months of fruitless dialogue with the North Vietnamese in Paris, Johnson related, Hanoi had offered to meet his terms a few days ago.

Johnson then reassured moderates and conservatives that his peace program would not harm America's troops or allies. "I spent most of all day Tuesday reviewing every single detail of this matter with our field commander, General Abrams, whom I had ordered home, and who arrived here at the White House at 2:30 in the morning and went into immediate conference with the President," he said. "The Joint Chiefs of Staff, all military men, have assured me—and General Abrams very firmly asserted to me on Tuesday in that early, 2:30 a.m. meeting—that in their military judgment this action should be taken now, and this action would not result in any increase in American casualties."

All air, naval, and artillery bombardment of North Vietnam would cease on November 1, the president announced. Talks would begin on November 6. Skipping over Thieu's opposition to the plan, Johnson said merely that the representatives of the South Vietnamese government "are free to participate" in the negotiations.

Johnson sounded a note of optimism on the time required to reach a peace agreement. Although "there may well be very hard fighting ahead," he remarked, "we know that negotiations can move swiftly if the common intent of the negotiators is peace in the world." In an admonition intended both to pressure the North Vietnamese and to assuage the American people, Johnson recalled the protracted negotiations during the Korean War at Panmunjom. "The world should know that the American people bitterly remember the long, agonizing Korean negotiations of 1951 through 1953," the president intoned. "Our people will just not accept deliberate delay and prolonged procrastination again."[50]

In living rooms across the United States, hopes for a peace agreement soared. With those hopes came a rise in support for Humphrey. Whereas Nixon had led Humphrey 44 to 36 in a Gallup poll on October 21, the poll taken by Gallup on November 2 found that the lead had narrowed to 42 to 40. In the opinion of pollster Louis Harris, this shift was the most amazing electoral twist in recent American history, a period that itself had been filled with remarkable late-breaking flips and controversies. Harris concluded that most of those who had switched were female voters who found Humphrey more appealing because of the bombing halt and the push for peace.[51]

In Saigon, the sudden improvement in Humphrey's fortunes confirmed suspicions that Johnson had timed the halt to deliver the election to his vice president. Believing that the peace fever endangered the survival of his country, Thieu resorted unabashedly to the obstructionism that the Americans had so gravely warned him to avoid. In a communiqué to the international press on November 1, he declared that the South Vietnamese government did not have "any sufficiently strong reason for associating itself with the U.S. Government" in its decision to enter talks with the North Vietnamese. To a gathering of journalists, he asserted that "South Vietnam is not a truck to be attached to a locomotive which will pull it wherever it likes."[52]

Next, at what the New York Times described as a "wildly enthusiastic joint session of the National Assembly," Thieu announced that his government would not negotiate at Paris until Hanoi acknowledged that the National Liberation Front would not participate as a separate entity. Affording the Front a delegation distinct from the North Vietnamese delegation, asserted Thieu, "would just be another trick toward a coalition government with the Communists in South Vietnam." Applause and cheers interrupted Thieu's speech fifteen times. At the conclusion of the oration, as retold in the Times dispatch, more than one hundred legislators "poured into the street, raised the red and yellow flag of South Vietnam, and began singing the national anthem."[53]

The American embassy reported that jubilant enthusiasm for Thieu extended well beyond sympathetic politicians in the National Assembly. "Many Vietnamese have observed after his Assembly speech of November 1, Thieu 'has really become our President,'" Bunker wrote to Washington. "Some have said, 'He is greater that Diem.'" By withstanding American pressure, "Thieu shed the image of the American-appointed,

American-supported chief executive and became a leader in his own right."[54]

By November 2, Thieu's vocal opposition to the talks had done much to deflate American expectations of imminent peace. It thus diminished the political advantages that Humphrey had derived from those expectations.[55] It may, in addition, have been responsible for provoking the vitriol that erupted from Ho Chi Minh on November 3, which provided further cause to doubt that peace was at hand. In a radio announcement, Ho referred to the bombing halt not as a step toward peace but as "an initial victory" against "the U.S. imperialists' war of aggression." He called upon the North Vietnamese people to "manifest a spirit of determination to fight" in order to "liberate the South."[56]

If Madame Chennault had at some point receded from the front of President Johnson's mind, she returned there on the evening of November 2. That evening, the FBI informed the White House of a phone call from Chennault to the wiretapped South Vietnamese embassy in Washington. According to the report, Chennault had told Bui Diem that "her boss" had asked her to inform South Vietnam's ambassador that he should "hold on, we are gonna win." She added that "her boss" had just called her from New Mexico.[57]

Vice presidential candidate Spiro Agnew was in New Mexico on the day that Chennault phoned Bui Diem. Upon learning that fact, Johnson deduced that Agnew's presence in New Mexico meant that either Agnew or someone connected to him was the "boss." This individual, Johnson concluded, was encouraging the South Vietnamese to shun the negotiations until the election in order to prevent Humphrey's campaign from capitalizing on the emerging hopes for peace. Whether or not Johnson realized that Thieu needed no such encouragement was not clear, but Johnson was at a minimum incensed by the appearance of collusion between a presidential candidate and a foreign power. The president promptly phoned the Republican he trusted most, Everett Dirksen.

"This is treason," Johnson bellowed at the Republican senator. "Now, I can identify them because I know who's doing this. I don't want to identify it. I think it would shock America if a principal candidate was playing with a source like this on a matter this important. I don't want to do that. But if they're going to put this kind of stuff out, they ought to know that we know what they're doing."

Dirksen said he would speak to Nixon on the matter. "I better get in touch with him, I think, and tell him about it."

"You better tell them they better quit playing with it," Johnson admonished. "You just tell them their people are messing around in this thing, and if they don't want it on the front pages, they better quit it."[58]

Dirksen relayed Johnson's comments to Nixon. On the following day, Nixon called Johnson and assured him that "any rumblings around about somebody trying to sabotage the Saigon government's attitude certainly have no, absolutely no credibility as far as I am concerned."

"I'm very happy to hear that, Dick, because that is taking place," Johnson responded. "I didn't say that it was with your knowledge. I hope it wasn't." Before they hung up, Johnson told Nixon, "You just see that your people don't tell the South Vietnamese that they're going to get any better deal out of the United States government than a conference."[59]

Johnson ordered an investigation into Agnew's phone calls, but he would not receive the results until after the election. The investigation would find no evidence that Agnew had spoken with Chennault.[60] Years afterward, Chennault attempted to clarify matters by telling a historian that the wiretap technicians must have misheard her as she had actually said "New Hampshire," the location that day of John Mitchell, Nixon's campaign manager.[61] Mitchell had not been Chennault's boss any more than Agnew had been, though it is possible that Chennault had referred to him as her boss to exaggerate her role with the campaign, considering her lengthy record of mischaracterizing events and overstating her importance. For the same reason, it is also possible that Chennault had completely fabricated the conversation with the so-called boss. The full truth of Chennault's conversations with campaign officials will most likely never be known.

At lunchtime on November 4, the day before the election, Johnson conferred with Rusk and Clifford about the information from the wiretap. Rusk strongly opposed releasing any of it to the public. "I do not believe that any President can make any use of interceptions or telephone taps in any way that would involve politics," he asserted. "The moment we cross over that divide we are in a different kind of society."

Clifford concurred with Rusk on that point and added another. "I think that some elements of the story are so shocking in their nature that I'm wondering whether it would be good for the country to disclose the story, and then possibly to have a certain individual elected," Clifford said. "It could cast his whole administration under such doubts that I would think it would be inimical to our country's interests."[62]

Johnson decided to keep the wiretap records secret. When he explained this decision to Senator George Smathers a few weeks later, he cited the two points made by Rusk and Clifford as his principal reasons.[63] He likely was also deterred by the absence of evidence linking Nixon himself to Chennault's actions, which was the reason why Humphrey chose to keep quiet when he learned of Chennault's activities on the eve of the election.[64]

Seventy-three million American voters turned out to the polls on November 5. The margin in the popular vote was narrow, suggesting that Humphrey had retained some of the support from the peace surge of October 31. Nixon received 43.4 percent of all votes to 42.7 percent for Humphrey. In the electoral college, however, Nixon won handily, finishing with 301 electoral votes to 191 for Humphrey and 46 for George Wallace.

Vietnam had loomed large in the outcome. When voters had been asked on the eve of the election what they had considered the most pressing issue, more than 40 percent had answered Vietnam. Polling showed that voters believed Nixon would do a better job than Humphrey on Vietnam and other key issues like the economy and urban rioting. Nixon won the votes of a wide array of people who had voted for Lyndon Johnson in 1964 but had then decided that Johnson's mishandling of Vietnam called for a fresh start and a different party. In light of the thin margin of victory, Humphrey supporters contended that their man would have pulled enough of those voters away from Nixon to win had Thieu not thwarted Johnson's last-minute push for peace. The magnitude of the late peace surge lent considerable credibility to their speculation, though the tightness of the race made it impossible to know for certain what would have happened.[65]

It was no exaggeration to say that the outcome meant as much in Vietnam as it did in the United States. At Saigon's Presidential Palace, Thieu's private secretary, Hoang Duc Nha, rushed to Thieu's private sitting room to deliver the news. Upon entering, he found Thieu smoking an after-dinner cigar. Word of Nixon's victory lifted months of tension from Thieu's shoulders and filled him with a newfound hope for his government and his country.

"Now at least we have bought ourselves some time," Thieu told Nha. "When the new President comes in, he has to learn something, and we have some more rope to play with."[66]

Across South Vietnam, Nixon's election was cause for celebration. In spite of nine years of war, with its bitter loss of life and its ever-expanding demands for the service of young men, South Vietnamese nationalists displayed a buoyancy not seen since the triumphs of Diem in 1962 and 1963. "To the majority of South Vietnamese, from Thieu and Ky on down, Richard Nixon's election was a reassuring event," Bui Diem observed. "They saw the new president as a hard-line anti-Communist. After the uncertainties of the last few months, there was a surge of confidence that Vietnam's cause was now in good hands."[67]

To the North Vietnamese, the outcome of the election was just as disheartening. According to one of their official accounts, they believed that Nixon "represented the most reactionary and obstinate war-loving powers in the U.S. monopoly capital circles."[68] North Vietnamese diplomat Luu Doan Huynh recalled that "the Vietnamese top leadership thought Nixon was more bellicose than Johnson, and some of the measures that were taboo for Johnson (no intensive air escalation, no operations in Laos and Cambodia, no attacks against dikes, no nuclear attacks) might be undertaken by Nixon."[69] Truong Nhu Tang, a senior Communist official in the South, described the reaction among his comrades: "As far as we were concerned, there was no question that Nixon would prove an obdurate opponent, who would bend every muscle to achieve a military resolution to the war. From this new President we could expect increased violence and, undoubtedly, new strategies to achieve the old ends."[70]

Nixon's election coincided with drastic changes in North Vietnamese strategy and tactics. The changes reflected both Hanoi's fear of Nixon and its recognition that the three offensives of 1968 had brought the North Vietnamese Army to ruin. At a meeting of the Politburo in early November, Le Duan agreed to abandon the strategy of decisive urban warfare in favor of a strategy of protracted attrition. Unlike the strategy Hanoi had pursued from 1965 to 1967, this strategy would rely primarily on low-cost guerrilla tactics rather than the conventional tactics that had led to so many large defeats. North Vietnamese forces, including conventional army units as well as guerrilla units, would launch small surprise attacks on American and South Vietnamese forces and civil administrators. In addition to conceding that his previous choices of strategy and tactics had been misguided, Le Duan was acknowledging tacitly that he should have listened earlier to Vo Nguyen Giap, who had been advocating this very strategy and these very tactics since the beginning of 1964.

The ultimate objective, as articulated by Le Duan, was still "to get the Americans to withdraw as quickly as possible." Among North Vietnam's leaders, Le Duan remained one of the most sanguine in terms of how soon the Americans would leave, yet even he no longer foresaw a rapid departure, given the necessity of foregoing large battles. Instead, he spoke of achieving victory "within the next three years." One of the least sanguine was Giap, who observed that "the way the United States is operating now indicates that they want to withdraw gradually, one step at a time, so that they can strengthen and consolidate the puppet regime."

Taking heed of Nixon's reputation for warmongering, the Politburo warned that an American expansion of the war could be on the horizon. It ordered the development of "a contingency plan to defeat a possible U.S. imperialist effort to expand the war into Cambodia and Laos" and directed the military and other relevant agencies to prepare for a resumption of American bombing of North Vietnam.[71] North Vietnamese leaders were hopeful, however, that they could spare the North from bombing, by shifting resources from provocative military action in the South to reconstruction of the battered economy in the North. To this end, they persuaded the Soviets in late November to increase the proportion of Soviet aid going toward nonmilitary items.[72]

By this time, the Americans and the South Vietnamese had already begun shifting the weight of their own efforts toward rural pacification. Later commentators would attribute this shift to General Abrams's dissatisfaction with the attrition-based strategy and search-and-destroy tactics of General Westmoreland. His dissatisfaction, it would be said, drove Abrams to replace attrition and search-and-destroy with pacification and "clear-and-hold," the latter referring to the tactic of providing continuous security in a village after clearing it of enemy forces. The reality was somewhat different. As has been seen, Abrams had insisted that his commanders continue search-and-destroy operations during his first months in command. The attrition of large enemy forces was, in his view as in Westmoreland's, an essential prerequisite for pacification. Abrams gave priority to pacification over attrition only after attrition had produced a new military environment.

Following the third wave offensive, Abrams and Thieu reassessed their military options. The exodus of North Vietnamese forces to remote base areas and external sanctuaries, they realized, spelled both a sharp decline in enemy military activity and a sharp reduction in the dangers faced by friendly soldiers and officials in the villages. The scarcity of enemy forces had made search-and-destroy operations less productive, while the diminished enemy threat to small groups of friendly personnel had made pacification operations more productive.[73]

Abrams directed his commanders to focus on small-unit pacification operations where circumstances recommended it. If the enemy assembled in large numbers, American forces were still to launch search-and-destroy operations against them.[74] "The kind of war that we have here can be compared to an orchestra," Abrams said on one occasion. "It is sometimes appropriate to emphasize the drums or the trumpets or the bassoon, or even the flute."[75]

Not every military commander made a smooth transition from the tactics of search-and-destroy to the tactics of pacification; some clung to the former or tried to apply the latter without the vigor and sound judgment required to eliminate guerrillas while simultaneously gaining the support of the civilian population. But many did adjust swiftly to the new realities. During October, the percentage of the South Vietnamese population living in secure areas rose from 66.8 percent to 69.8 percent, marking the first time since the Tet Offensive that the percentage had surpassed the January 1968 figure of 67.2 percent.[76]

On November 1, Thieu kicked off a new pacification campaign, which he named the Le Loi Campaign after the emperor who had expelled China's Ming dynasty from Vietnam during the fifteenth century. In American parlance, it was the Accelerated Pacification Campaign. The campaign plan, a synthesis of South Vietnamese and American thinking, called for intensified military and political action to regain control of one thousand hamlets in a three-month period. By increasing the government's control over the population, the campaign would both deprive the enemy of resources and strengthen South Vietnam's position at the Paris negotiations.[77]

Under the plan, South Vietnamese and American forces were to saturate the target hamlets to eliminate or drive away enemy forces and political cadres. Next, the South Vietnamese Regional Forces and Popular Forces would build outposts and patrol the villages to prevent the enemy from returning. These territorial forces would arrive with notable advantages over their predecessors, including newly formed U.S. advisory teams, newly forged M-16 rifles, and newly appointed commanders. Once security improved, South Vietnamese government officials would restart administrative activities, hold elections for local administrative positions, establish fifty-man units of the People's Self-Defense Forces, and organize economic development projects.[78]

In the aftermath of the U.S. presidential election, Lyndon Johnson remained focused on building his peacemaking legacy, while top American officials fought with one another over the ends, ways, and means of a peace agreement. On one side were Bunker, Rusk, and Rostow, who viewed the South Vietnamese government as an essential partner whose interests had to be considered at every step. This group convinced Johnson to back out of his public promise to begin the negotiations on November 6 without South Vietnamese participation.[79] Compelling the South Vietnamese to bring Communists into a coalition government would, in their opinion, be as certain to doom South Vietnam as Thieu believed it would. Bunker, Rusk, and Rostow maintained that any peace agreement had to include safeguards on issues like Communist political activity in South Vietnam and North Vietnamese troop withdrawals. Otherwise, as Bunker phrased it, "any agreement will be a temporary truce to be upset by a pragmatic and ruthless enemy not long after our forces have departed these shores."[80]

On the other side of the debate were Clifford and Harriman. As they saw it, the United States had no obligation to support or cooperate with the current South Vietnamese government. Harriman questioned the government's very legitimacy, belittling its constitution on the grounds that it "does not permit communist members or communist sympathizers to vote." He denounced its election laws because "anyone who has ever done anything to help the communists is excluded from running for public office," a stance that he called "McCarthyism at its worst."[81]

Clifford and Harriman were open to foisting a coalition government on the South Vietnamese against their will. They were also prepared to remove American troops without requiring

North Vietnamese troops to leave the South or securing other guarantees that ensured the Saigon government's survival. By Clifford's reckoning, there was "no reason to try to make the whole country safe for Thieu."[82]

Neither Clifford nor Harriman said much about the ramifications of their proposals for South Vietnam and its people. They most probably feared that other Americans would recoil at the mention of wartime allies succumbing to Communist violence and tyranny. Harriman did try to downplay the geopolitical consequences of a Communist takeover in South Vietnam by claiming that the Soviets would prevent Communism from spreading to other Southeast Asian countries in order to hurt China.[83] That theory, however, rested on several dubious assumptions: that the Soviets would abet non-Communist governments in opposing Communist movements, that the North Vietnamese could be induced to abandon their foundational ambition of spreading Communism to neighboring countries, and that Southeast Asian nations would find the promises of a retreating United States and a distant Soviet Union more compelling than the threats of an ascendant Vietnam and a maniacal China.

Clifford's disdain for the South Vietnamese government spilled into public view at a Pentagon news conference on November 12. In remarks that he had not cleared with the White House, Clifford criticized Thieu for withdrawing his support for the bombing halt shortly before the U.S. election. President Johnson, he continued, had been justified in moving ahead with the halt in the absence of South Vietnamese concurrence. "After all that we have done in that country, after the enormous contribution that's been made," said Clifford, "I believe the President was absolutely right in not giving Saigon a veto on the plan."[84]

Thieu was flabbergasted. President Johnson, he thought, must have approved Clifford's inflammatory language. "The South

Vietnamese Minister of Defense," Thieu told a confidante, "does not comment on matters of national policy without checking with the President."[85] As recounted in Clifford's own memoir, Thieu told advisers he feared that Clifford intended to overthrow or assassinate him "like Ngo Dinh Diem."[86]

Unlike 1963, however, the State Department did not move in the direction desired by the South Vietnamese president's detractors but instead took its lead from those who respected him, specifically Rusk and Bunker. On November 13, a State Department spokesman publicly voiced America's support for the South Vietnamese government on several issues of high importance to Thieu.[87] Their trust restored, the South Vietnamese and American governments spent the next two weeks producing a pair of public declarations, one to be delivered by each side, that would bring the Saigon government into the Paris negotiations on terms agreeable to both.

The declarations were issued on November 26. The American document contained two points that the South Vietnamese had viewed as paramount. First, it stated the United States would consider the "so-called National Liberation Front" as "a creation of North Viet-Nam and an agent of Hanoi's aggression against the Republic of Viet-Nam." Second, the United States expressed opposition to a coalition government in South Vietnam because "the United States does not believe aggression should be rewarded and will not recognize any form of government that is not freely chosen through democratic and legal processes by the people of South Vietnam."

The Saigon government, in its declaration, announced that it was prepared to participate in the Paris talks "to show the good will of the Republic of Vietnam and to test the good faith of Hanoi." The South Vietnamese government's concerns "have been given satisfaction in their essential aspects," it stated, and "the sovereignty of the Republic of Vietnam has been respected."[88]

In Paris, the representatives of the two Vietnams promptly entered into negotiations over the procedures for the negotiations. Both the North Vietnamese and the South Vietnamese attached great weight to procedural issues that to Western eyes seemed matters of minor import. The Vietnamese worried that conceding too easily on matters of procedure would cause them to lose face and weaken their bargaining position. They also believed that procedures could ultimately affect substance.[89]

The North Vietnamese delegation presented a seating chart with four tables, one each for North Vietnam, the National Liberation Front, the United States, and South Vietnam. The South Vietnamese delegation objected, believing that Hanoi was trying to use the seating arrangement to promote its concept of "four-power" talks, whereby the National Liberation Front was recognized as a distinct entity. The South Vietnamese and the Americans adhered to a "two-side formula," which put South Vietnam and the United States on one side and lumped the Vietnamese Communists together on the other, to demonstrate that the National Liberation Front was part and parcel of the North Vietnamese government. In keeping with this formula, the South Vietnamese insisted upon two long tables facing one another. The North Vietnamese refused to accept that configuration.

Seeking a solution that would be palatable to both Saigon and Hanoi, the Americans devised a variety of alternative seating charts. Among their suggestions were two semicircular tables, a round table, two tables facing two tables, and a diamond broken in two places. The South Vietnamese found each one unacceptable, asserting that only two long tables would do.[90]

Bunker, Rusk, and Rostow believed that the South Vietnamese had legitimate reasons for their nitpicking and inflexibility on procedural matters. They were willing to allow time for the necessary haggling.[91] Clifford and Harriman demonstrated no such cross-cultural forbearance.

By mid-December, Clifford's impatience with Vietnamese stickling had become so acute that he chose to vent in public again. During an interview on the CBS News program *Face the Nation*, Clifford blamed the North Vietnamese and South Vietnamese governments in equal measure for delaying the negotiations through bickering over procedural details. The United States, Clifford declared, was ready to begin negotiating since it had no objections on procedural grounds. He also suggested that America's disillusionment with the squabbling could cause it to withdraw troops unilaterally. "I have no idea that we should maintain 540,000 men there fighting while we wait for Saigon and Hanoi to come to some political settlement," the secretary of defense said. "That is not our obligation." Clifford also downplayed recent North Vietnamese violations of the DMZ, claiming that they were not serious enough to affect the diplomatic dialogue.[92]

In Saigon, the Clifford interview sparked even more consternation and outrage than his November 12 press conference. By faulting the South Vietnamese as much as the North Vietnamese, he gave the impression that the United States was playing the role of neutral observer rather than the role of South Vietnamese ally. His remarks about removing U.S. troops seemed to signal to Hanoi that continued diplomatic haggling would help it achieve its primary objective of securing an American withdrawal. Ky lashed out publicly, pronouncing that Clifford had "shown a gift for saying the wrong thing at the wrong time."[93] Thieu confided to a South Vietnamese press officer that he was "unable to determine the logic of public statements made by senior U.S. officials which contribute to efforts by the North Vietnamese" to divide South Vietnam and the United States.[94]

Clifford's discounting of North Vietnamese attacks near the demilitarized zone undercut efforts by U.S. leaders to hold Hanoi accountable for repeated DMZ violations. At the end of November, Rusk had urged Soviet Ambassador Dobrynin to rein in the North Vietnamese at the DMZ, which the North Vietnamese Army had violated a total of 230 times during the first month of the bombing halt.[95] In response to these violations, General Abrams had sought permission from the White House to send American forces into the DMZ to destroy the North Vietnamese provocateurs. He had received permission only to send in squad-size patrols to locate targets for American heavy weapons.[96]

Although the North Vietnamese activity near the DMZ was smaller in scale than it had been earlier in the year, it was still killing Americans. One of those Americans was Johnny Liverman, a native of the Maryland suburbs of Washington, DC. Liverman had joined the military in emulation of his father, Troy Liverman, who had fought in World War II. During the summer of 1967, Johnny had enlisted in the Marines despite the fact that he had previously injured his knee cartilage so seriously that he could have received a draft exemption.

Arriving in Vietnam in January 1968, Johnny Liverman was wounded in March and again in April. The second wound, from a gunshot to his thigh, required his evacuation to Okinawa for treatment. He could have stayed in Okinawa for the remainder of his tour, but when he heard that a close friend from his old unit had been killed, he volunteered to return to Vietnam.

"Grandma told me for yours and Mom's sake don't go back to Nam," Johnny wrote to his father. "But like you always said, Dad, 'A job worth doing is a job worth doing right.' I'm getting straight with myself. I have to go back and finish the job."

On December 11, Johnny Liverman's company was engaged in a fight along Foxtrot Ridge near the demilitarized zone. He was wounded early in the battle. Continuing to trade fire with the North Vietnamese, he did not relent until a bullet struck him in the head, ending his life.

Troy Liverman was managing the night shift at a McDonald's in Rockville, Maryland, on December 11 when a Marine officer wearing a dress blue uniform walked in. Marine officers regularly patronized the establishment, so Troy did not at first know that anything was amiss. When the officer asked for him by name, however, the father knew instantly why he had come. "You think you've had disappointments and troubles in your life," Liverman remarked later. "But they all add up to nothing when a man is telling you your son is dead."

After Johnny had been laid to rest, Troy Liverman heard that antiwar protesters intended to read his deceased son's name at their demonstrations. He decided to show up at their events to protest against them. "They had a right to protest," Liverman believed. "But they had no right to use his name to undermine his cause. My son was not a victim. He died serving his country."[97]

From a purely military point of view, the most important fighting in the last two months of 1968 was taking place in the one thousand hamlets targeted by the Accelerated Pacification Campaign. The aggressive sweeps, patrols, and ambushes of allied forces cleared the enemy from these hamlets more swiftly than anticipated. During these months, North Vietnamese scribes recorded a long succession of debilitating military defeats at the hands of a highly active adversary. "Not a day goes by without us being forced to bury another one of our comrades," stated a North Vietnamese report from the Plain of Reeds. "The enemy is all around us. Even if we wanted to retreat, I don't know where we could go. All we can do is set out booby-trapped hand grenades and try to hang on here. And our booby traps kill more of our own soldiers than they do of the enemy."[98]

In some districts, the rapid allied military progress was attributable to unexpectedly weak enemy resistance. One North Vietnamese history noted that the heavy losses suffered in the three offensives of 1968 had "left our forces in the rural areas very thin, and in some areas we had literally no one left. For that reason, when enemy troops conducted pacification sweeps, they were virtually unopposed."[99] In I Corps, the enemy offered so little opposition in the 140 target hamlets that the South Vietnamese leadership decided to increase the number of target hamlets to 198. Similarly, in III Corps, the number was increased from 250 to 279.[100]

South Vietnamese officials and their American advisers reported that security improved in a total of 857 hamlets during the first two months of the Accelerated Pacification Campaign.[101] While some reports exaggerated the extent of progress, North Vietnamese accounts left no doubt that the government's authority was spreading at a brisk pace.[102] Progress was to be seen even in the upper Mekong Delta, the site of the most controversial pacification operation of this period.

At the time of the Accelerated Pacification Campaign, the U.S. Army 9th Division, under Major General Julian J. Ewell, launched Operation Speedy Express in the upper delta. Ewell's zealous emphasis on body count led 9th Division officers to inflate the numbers, either by reporting bodies that did not exist or by including the bodies of unarmed civilians found dead on the battlefield. These practices were by no means unique to Ewell's division, but both occurred on a much larger scale than elsewhere. Whereas American forces nationwide recovered one weapon for every three enemy killed, Ewell's soldiers recovered one weapon for every fifteen killed. The division did not gun down women and children in the manner of My Lai, but it was unusually predisposed to fire liberally at enemy soldiers who were intermingled with civilians.[103]

Whatever their faults, the 9th Division's clearing operations did drive out the Communists and enable the reimposition of local security and governance. As North Vietnamese sources would attest, the Communists lost control of all the populous areas they had held in the upper Mekong Delta by the end of 1968. "The enemy established outposts in every single one of the region's 350 villages," a North Vietnamese history of the region noted, "except for one or two villages which held neither people nor outposts, villages where 'the monkeys cough, the storks call, and the fish grow beards.'"[104]

Across South Vietnam, breakneck military progress permitted the replanting of territorial forces and civil administrators ahead of schedule. Government officials in the target hamlets recruited young men into the South Vietnamese armed forces at the expense of the North Vietnamese.[105] Specially trained Armed Propaganda Teams and the Chieu Hoi amnesty program helped push Communist defections to unprecedented highs during the first two months of the Accelerated Pacification Campaign, with 2,269 defecting in November and 3,148 in December.[106]

For the North Vietnamese, the drying of the Southern wellsprings of manpower and foodstuffs made the war effort ever more reliant on infiltration of men and supplies from the North, and the infiltration contest was also going against them in the final months of 1968. By shifting air strikes from North Vietnam to Laos in early November, American air forces increased their daily sortie rate against the Ho Chi Minh Trail from 140 to 620. American aircraft bombed chokepoints in southeastern Laos and seeded them with antipersonnel and antivehicular mines, then bombed them again when North Vietnamese troops attempted to clear the mines and rebuild the roads. American ground sensors and aerial reconnaissance kept watch for the construction of bypass roads, which aircraft assailed with the same persistence.[107]

The new air campaign gouged out critical junctions on Route 12 and Route 20, the two roads that carried most of the supplies from the North Vietnamese border to the Ho Chi Minh Trail. With no other roads capable of bearing the truck traffic, the flow of North Vietnamese trucks into Laos screeched to a halt. In one North Vietnamese retelling, the situation was so serious that "the hearts of the soldiers of the Annamite Mountains, the Ho Chi Minh Trail soldiers, seemed to stop and the entire nation was cast into worry and concern."[108]

On November 14, the Communist Party Committee responsible for the Ho Chi Minh Trail declared that the choke points on the two roads had to be unblocked "no matter what the cost." Empty North Vietnamese trucks were driven around other areas in Laos and North Vietnam to draw enemy planes away. American aircraft, however, continued to smite the choke points, ensuring that the routes remained impassable. By the end of November, food and ammunition supplies dwindled to precariously low levels among the North Vietnamese forces in South Vietnam and the border regions.[109] A North Vietnamese directive dated November 29 informed units that, "as an immediate task," they had to "clear the ground for cultivation of corn and manioc for combating starvation."[110]

The North Vietnamese attempted to compensate for the troubles in Laos by moving supplies through Cambodia. U.S. intelligence agencies reported increased movement of supplies from Cambodia to North Vietnamese forces in South Vietnam, including arms and ammunition that had entered Cambodia through the port of Sihanoukville. Late in the year, U.S. military leaders renewed their advocacy of large U.S. ground operations in Cambodia to destroy North Vietnamese forces and logistics.

"More and more supplies are now being found in Cambodia," General Wheeler told President Johnson. "We are going to have to go after the Cambodian sanctuaries. It is intolerable. We must do something about it."[111]

"The policies on Cambodia have got to be changed," General Abrams said to his staff. "I think it's criminal to let these enemy outfits park over there, fatten up, reindoctrinate, get their supplies, and so on."[112] Abrams asked for authorization to send his forces up to twenty kilometers inside Cambodia, but the White House refused. Abrams then implemented what he considered the next best option, which was the redeployment of the 1st Cavalry Division from I Corps, where enemy activity had waned, to III Corps, where North Vietnamese units on both sides of the Cambodian border now posed the greatest threat to friendly forces.[113]

Among the soldiers relocated as a result of this decision was Captain Barry McCaffrey, a rifle company commander in the 1st Cavalry Division. McCaffrey landed his company three kilometers from the Cambodian border, where their mission was to intercept North Vietnamese units crossing into South Vietnam. The North Vietnamese troops who came their way made a strong impression with their clean uniforms, shiny new weapons, and military professionalism. It was plain to the Americans that the North Vietnamese owed these assets to their unfettered ability to organize and resupply in Cambodia. The U.S. government's toleration of this Cambodian sanctuary infuriated every man in McCaffrey's company. "We were forbidden to fire across the border," remembered McCaffrey. "The notion of sanctuaries was outrageous to me and to all of us who operated on the Cambodian border."[114]

After a few months of operating near the border, McCaffrey's company gradually worked their way toward Saigon through a panoply of air assaults into suspected enemy redoubts. "It was a series of running engagements," McCaffrey narrated. "Very bitter fights, heavy jungle, some scrub brush, open plains, and lots of casualties. My people got banged up or wounded, mostly from small-arms fire or grenades at very close range."

One day, McCaffrey's radio operator asked him how he always carried himself with an air of serenity during the air assaults. "It's simple," McCaffrey replied. "There's nothing I can do about anything until we're on the ground. So when we fly, I'm saying an endless loop of Catholic prayers from grade school."[115]

The year 1968 ended with casualty tolls that dwarfed those of all preceding years. By the American count, losses on both sides were close to twice what they had been in 1967. On the allied side, America's casualties for the year totaled 14,592 killed and 92,820 wounded, South Vietnam's amounted to 27,915 killed, 70,696 wounded, and 2,460 missing, and those of other allied forces came to 979 killed and 1,997 wounded.[116]

The U.S. estimate of enemy killed in action for 1968 was a staggering 181,149.[117] While that figure might well have been higher than the actual number, it was not outlandish given the massive North Vietnamese infiltration during the year, the enlistment and dragooning of Southerners before the Tet Offensive, and the abject failure of three large offensives. During 1968, according to the Vinh Window data, infiltration from the North totaled roughly 154,000 men. The American estimate of recruitment and impressment in the South added 58,000 more to the enemy rolls. North Vietnamese strength declined during the same period, from 262,000 at the beginning of the year to 251,000 at the end. From these figures, it followed that permanent North Vietnamese losses totaled 222,000, of which roughly 13,000 defected and 14,000 were taken prisoner, leaving 195,000 who were killed or permanently lost to wounds.[118]

North Vietnamese sources attest to exceptionally high losses during 1968. In the B2 theater, covering the southern half of South Vietnam, North Vietnamese casualties for 1968 exceeded those for the years 1961 to 1967 combined.[119] In an April 1969 interview with the Italian journalist Oriana Fallaci, General Giap would confirm the accuracy of American casualty estimates. "The Americans say you've lost half a million men," Fallaci said to the general. That number was actually slightly higher than the official American count of Communist dead at the time, which was approximately 480,000.[120] Fallaci expected Giap to denounce the figure as a wild exaggeration. She was thus astounded when Giap replied casually, "That's quite exact."[121]

During the last weeks of 1968, the squabbling in Paris over negotiating procedures continued without resolution. The North Vietnamese displayed no urgency to reach a compromise on procedural matters. Having reverted to protracted warfare in November because of the shattering of their army, they had no military successes that demanded immediate conversion into diplomatic gain, and they gave no indication that they were ready to accept a peace on terms acceptable to Saigon and Washington.

In a country with mechanisms for removing disastrous leaders, Le Duan would have been ousted after the three catastrophic military offensives of 1968, if not sooner. His replacement might have been someone more inclined to consider peace after so much fruitless slaughter, although it is also possible that the replacement would have been as hellbent as Le Duan on military victory. But Le Duan, through intrigue, cunning, and ruthlessness, had prevented countervailing forces from casting him out. For the time being, he could continue to pursue total victory in the South even if his own folly had greatly reduced the military power at North Vietnam's disposal and he thus would have to rely more heavily on diplomatic maneuvering.[122] The North Vietnamese people, inured by culture and experience to authority and hardship, misled by propagandists about events in South Vietnam, seemed destined to follow their government's orders as long as the government remained in power. Neither they, nor the people of South Vietnam, nor the people of the United States, had any idea how long Le Duan could persist in suppressing his critics in the North and sustaining his mismanaged crusade in the South.

The South Vietnamese were in no more hurry than their Northern adversaries to achieve a diplomatic settlement. They believed that time was on their side, for they were becoming stronger and the North Vietnamese weaker.[123] By agreeing to the inclusion of South Vietnamese diplomats in the Paris negotiations, Hanoi had bolstered the Saigon government's prestige and diminished that of the National Liberation Front. During Lyndon Johnson's final months in office, moreover, the American president had quelled the clamors from liberals in his administration and party to remove American troops and impose a coalition government on South Vietnam. Thieu and other South Vietnamese leaders were confident that the diehard anti-Communist Richard Nixon would provide the steadfast backing required to maintain this favorable trajectory.

In late December, Thieu told Bunker that he would be open to the participation of the National Liberation Front in future elections because the strengthening of the South Vietnamese government would eventually allow it to "absorb the NLF into the body politic." This absorption, Thieu believed, could begin within the next year as part of a peace settlement. During their conversation, Thieu also expressed receptivity to the withdrawal of some U.S. troops in 1969, which he knew would help maintain the American people's support for the war.[124]

U.S. military commanders and advisers shared Thieu's confidence that improvements in South Vietnamese military performance would enable the United States to reduce troop levels without putting military gains at risk. The Americans attributed these improvements to changes in leadership, the issuance of the

M-16 assault rifle, and the confidence gained through the thwart-ing of the three North Vietnamese offensives.[125] U.S. Defense Department analysts found that South Vietnamese Army battal-ions had been 56 percent as effective as U.S. battalions in killing the enemy during 1968, versus 48 percent during the previous year, and that they killed the enemy at a rate 2.6 times higher than in the previous year. This increase in capability was equivalent to the addition of 166,000 U.S. troops.[126]

The South Vietnamese armed forces were increasing in quantity as well as quality, exceeding one million in total by the end of the year. Had the United States inducted the same proportion of its men, its armed forces would have totaled eighteen million men, 50 percent more than the United States had generated in World War II.[127] Nearly every South Vietnamese young man carrying a weapon was now serving in forces loyal to the Saigon government, a fact that swept away most remaining doubts among Southerners as to whether they faced a war of aggression from the North. Nearly every man opposing them was a poorly trained North Vietnamese youth who lacked personal and cultural connections to the population of South Vietnam. While American politicians were talking about shifting military burdens to the South Vietnamese in the future, a large shift had already taken place in 1968. Whereas 1.3 South Vietnamese troops had been killed for every American in 1967, that ratio shot up to 1.9 South Vietnamese to one American in 1968.[128]

In Bunker's final cable of the year, he saw in these positive developments cause for enormous optimism about South Viet-nam's future. "I believe that 1968 will go into history as the year in which the strength and love of freedom of the South Viet-namese people was most severely tested and not found wanting," the ambassador wrote. "I am convinced that the tide is running more strongly with us now than at any time in the past." Bunker predicted that "if we continue patient and confident in our own strength, we will get next year the kind of peace we have sought through so many grim trials."[129]

Although Bunker believed that haste would undermine American diplomacy, haste was the order of the day in Washington during the Johnson administration's waning days. Johnson's hopes for conquering peace in the manner of Winfield Scott before the end of his presidency, however, diminished with each day of feuding between the North Vietnamese and the South Vietnamese delegations in Paris. Gradually, Johnson and his lieutenants had to accept the reality that the search for peace in Vietnam would be left to the Richard M. Nixon administration.

Shortly after the election, President-elect Nixon received an intelligence estimate from the Board of National Estimates that addressed the prospects for peace in the context of the momentous changes of the past three and a half years. When Johnson had faced the decision on intervention in the middle of 1965, the estimate explained, "there was the spectacle of unbroken Viet Cong successes against South Vietnamese forces, rapid Chinese advances in the field of modern weapons, and an increasingly powerful Sukarno/PKI coalition taking charge in Indonesia and bullying the newly organized and fragile Malaysian federation." Since that time, "Southeast Asians have seen China bogged down in confusion and disorder, Sukarno ousted and the PKI suffer bloody suppression, and the Vietnamese Communists pay a fearful price during long years of war."

The agencies that contributed to this intelligence estimate differed with one another on the likely consequences of a diplomatic settlement that led swiftly to a North Vietnamese conquest of South Vietnam. The majority believed that Thailand would not abandon the United States in favor of China and Vietnam unless the United States backed away from its commitments to Thailand. For other Southeast Asian leaders, these analysts contended, American support of Thailand would be the bellwether of American intentions across the region. The setbacks suffered by China and North Vietnam since 1965 and the rising strength of anti-Communist nations in Southeast Asia lent credibility to this view.

But there also remained credibility in the argument, made by a minority of the intelligence analysts, that Southeast Asian leaders would lose confidence in American commitments to Thailand and other countries after witnessing an American abandonment of South Vietnam. The Saigon government had received far larger American commitments of men and materiel than any other nation, and therefore even the most generous pledges of new American commitments to other Asian countries would be unable to allay doubts about American staying power.[130] Furthermore, a Vietnam united under Communism would be the dominant military power of Southeast Asia, capable of bending its neighbors to its will through intimidation and force.

Owing perhaps to a scarcity of information on relations between the Communist powers, the estimate did not mention that the Sino-Soviet rift had grown into a wide chasm during the past three and a half years. It did not state that China and the Soviet Union had been pulled further apart by their competition for prestige and influence in North Vietnam or that the Cultural Revolution and China's aversion to conflict with the United States had driven a wedge between Beijing and Hanoi, which in turn had spurred the withdrawal of Chinese troops from North Vietnam. The Americans did know that the Soviets had exploited their improved relationship with Hanoi and their heightened aid in urging the North Vietnamese to sit at the negotiating table at Paris but were not sure whether the North Vietnamese would agree to the sort of peace that the Soviets desired.

The war itself had been turned upside down in the period between Johnson's plunge into the ground war and his handing of the baton to Nixon. In the summer of 1965, the North Vietnamese Army had been on the verge of destroying the South Vietnamese Army and uniting the country under the flag of Vietnamese Communism. The intervention of American ground forces, with their overwhelming mobility and firepower, thwarted Hanoi's offensive and compelled the North Vietnamese to fight a war of attrition. For three and a half years, both sides repeatedly intensified the fighting to hasten the day of victory, resulting in high casualties for the armed forces on both sides and for the civilian population that had the misfortune of getting caught in between. At the end of that period, the North Vietnamese Army lay in tatters, and its Southern proxies had all but vanished, leaving Hanoi little choice but to abandon conventional campaigns and revert to guerrilla warfare. For the North Vietnamese, the change in strategy was a giant step backward as guerrilla warfare preceded conventional warfare in the sequence of Maoist revolutionary war. A return to conventional warfare was years away, and intervening events could push that day back further or prevent it from ever coming.

Between August 1965 and December 1968, North Vietnam failed to achieve the overarching objective of both the attrition strategy it pursued until January 1968 and the urban-battle strategy it pursued for the ensuing eight months, namely the breaking of America's will. The North Vietnamese overestimated their ability to inflict damage on American forces and underestimated the American people's tolerance of casualties. During this same period, the attrition strategy of the United States failed to break Hanoi's will. Some Americans made the same miscalculations about their casualty-infliction capabilities and the enemy's willpower, but President Johnson, General Westmoreland, and many other Americans never expected attrition to bring a swift North Vietnamese capitulation. Far from displaying the arrogance of power that was often attributed to them, they had seen the limits of their nation's power from the beginning. Some, in fact, had overestimated those limits by claiming that American exertions beyond South Vietnam could not alter the course of the war.

The U.S. military's attrition of North Vietnamese forces was as gruesome and full of sorrow as most grindings of the gears of war, but it was not senseless. Relentless American hammering of the North Vietnamese Army preempted Hanoi's military initiatives, diminished its military capabilities, and reduced its access to South Vietnam's villages. The confinement of American ground operations to South Vietnamese territory did allow Hanoi to limit its casualties by hiding its forces outside the country, but those forces could not accomplish much while they were in hiding. For that reason, Hanoi felt compelled to use its forces often enough to expose them to the crushing effects of American weaponry, culminating in the three colossal defeats of 1968.

The destruction of Communist forces by conventional American military power was an essential prerequisite for the considerable progress made from 1965 to 1968 toward the main strategic objectives that Westmoreland had articulated and Johnson had approved at the outset, strengthening the Saigon government and pacifying the villages. By compelling North Vietnam to revert to guerrilla warfare at the end of 1968, the U.S. military bought the South Vietnamese government additional time and space to accumulate the muscle that would be needed to wring diplomatic concessions from Hanoi and facilitate reductions in the American military presence.

Richard M. Nixon would have the opportunity to pull from the American quiver several large arrows whose use had consistently been favored by America's generals but rejected by Lyndon

Johnson. He could send ground troops into Laos and Cambodia to cut supply lines and eliminate sanctuaries. He could resume the bombing of the North with minimal restrictions and mine North Vietnam's ports to squeeze the North Vietnamese supply system. He could invade the southern section of North Vietnam to disrupt North Vietnamese logistics or land troops farther north to seize Hanoi and Haiphong. The mere threat of such measures or of even more destructive actions like bombing North Vietnamese dikes or employing nuclear weapons might compel the North Vietnamese to sue for peace, as the North Koreans had sued for peace in 1953.

Nixon would be certain to face pressure from the American public to reduce the size of the American commitment, as he had during the electoral campaign. The loudest and shrillest calls for rapid troop withdrawals would come from intellectuals, journalists, and other elite segments of society for whom opposition to the war had become de rigueur.[131] The majority of the American people, however, evidenced little desire for a precipitous withdrawal, and they would be even less inclined in that direction if the president made the effort to rally the public that Lyndon Johnson had studiously avoided. Nixon would be able to undertake a gradual reduction in troops, as Thieu had already envisioned, thanks to improvements in South Vietnam's security forces.

The evolution of American public opinion on the war was, indeed, to become one of the most widely misconstrued aspects of the war. In the most influential book on the subject, *War, Presidents, and Public Opinion*, political scientist John Mueller contended that the American public's support for the war steadily diminished after 1965 as the result of mounting American casualties. Mueller based this conclusion on the responses Americans had given to a question asked regularly during these years: "In view of developments since we entered the fighting in Vietnam, do you think the United States made a mistake in sending troops to Vietnam?" The percentage of Americans who said that it had been a mistake rose from 24 percent in August 1965 to 54 percent in October 1968.[132]

Mueller erred in assuming that those who deemed American intervention a mistake also opposed the war. As polls throughout the period from 1965 to 1968 demonstrated, the percentage of Americans who wanted the United States to withdraw from Vietnam was much smaller than the percentage who said that sending troops had been a mistake. A large and growing number of Americans supported continuation of the war in spite of their belief that the original decision to send troops had been mistaken.

The two opinion polls taken in late 1968 captured a state of American opinion on Vietnam that differed starkly from what would be remembered later. The first, conducted by Louis Harris and Associates in September, found that just 13 percent of Americans wanted to "get out of Vietnam altogether." A total of 43 percent of respondents favored maintenance or intensification of U.S. military action, and 35 percent advocated continuing the war while increasing the South Vietnamese military's share of fighting.[133]

The second poll, which was administered by the University of Michigan's Survey Research Center, asked respondents to choose from three courses of action, corresponding to the positions of doves, moderates, and hawks. Nineteen percent picked the dovish option, which was to "pull out of Vietnam entirely." Thirty-seven percent selected the moderate option, "keep our soldiers in Vietnam but try to end the fighting." Another 34 percent chose the hawkish option, which read, "take a stronger stand even if it means invading North Vietnam."[134]

The 13 percent and 19 percent who favored withdrawal in the two polls represented a significant but relatively modest increase from the 11 percent of the population who had wanted to withdraw in the middle of 1965. At the end of Lyndon Johnson's presidency, opponents of the war remained a distinct minority, albeit one that sought and sometimes attained disproportionate influence with the media and the government. Just as notable as the slow growth of the opposition was a simultaneous rise in support. The 78 percent from the first survey and the 71 percent from the second who favored continuing the war in late 1968 surpassed the 66 percent who had approved of the ground war in June 1965.[135]

Pollsters never conducted surveys to determine why an increasing number of Americans believed that sending U.S. troops had been a mistake or why a large fraction of those Americans continued to support the war. Based upon the ideas circulating in the United States during this period, it is safe to assume that the reasons for deeming the war a mistake were numerous and diverse. Individuals who were highly concerned about the war's costs could find fault with the 1965 decision because the war had proven longer and costlier than they had hoped or anticipated. Americans who preferred decisive military action had reason to believe that the Johnson administration had blundered by entering a war that it was unwilling to fight with all necessary measures. Among Americans who paid close attention to events in Vietnam, some concluded that the United States had been mistaken to take charge of the war because Americanization had undermined the development of South Vietnam's armed forces. For those attuned to international events, the defeat of Indonesia's Communists without obvious American influence may have convinced them that American intervention in Southeast Asia had not been required to save the dominoes of Asia.

Had President Johnson made a concerted effort to explain and justify the war to the American people, to "stir up patriotism" as he had put it, he could have convinced some of these disaffected Americans that his decision to enter the war in 1965 had been sound. The silence of Johnson and his lieutenants left Americans reliant for information on a press that provided useful information but also played up the negative and played down encouraging developments such as the decimation of the North Vietnamese Army and the revival of the South Vietnamese government. The American people, to their great credit, overcame the abdication of presidential leadership and the bias of the media to make their own judgments about the war, based upon their perceptions of the costs and benefits and the likelihood of success.[136]

Perceptions can be skewed by inadequacies of information or by the preconceived ideas of the perceivers. The Americans of the 1960s were not immune from these problems. On the whole, nevertheless, the American people generally demonstrated rationality and sound judgment in assessing the war. The large majority supported the war at the beginning out of a well-founded belief that the loss of South Vietnam would undermine America's credibility as an ally and lead to Communist gains in other countries, particularly in Asia.[137] Their support wavered at several points in the subsequent years when highly publicized developments appeared to have reduced the prospects for success: the Buddhist crisis, Johnson's refusal to heed the military's calls for escalation, and lack of communication from the White House at times of heavy combat. With the consolidation of the Saigon government in the middle of 1966, heightened bombing of North Vietnam in the middle of 1967, and the stateside visit of General Westmoreland and Ambassador Bunker in November 1967, public confidence in the war effort was restored. Public support held up during the Tet Offensive as Americans generally agreed that a surprise attack on American troops during a holiday truce was not the time to turn against a war.

Americans continued to support the war to the end of Lyndon Johnson's presidency because they believed that staying in, for all its problems, would serve the United States better than pulling out. In their estimation, the United States was still engaged in a global struggle against the existential threat of international Communism, and Vietnam was a key battleground in that struggle. The United States would lose its credibility as the protector of the free world if it gave up on a war to which it had committed its prestige and half a million troops. American infantry divisions and aircraft carriers and nuclear weapons would no longer have the same deterrent power, and the anti-Communist alliances built by the United States would be crippled by mistrust and fear. Americans who doubted the seriousness of the Communist threat had been contravened by the North Vietnamese atrocities at Tet, discredited by the Soviet invasion of Czechoslovakia, and thwarted by moderate and conservative delegates at the Democratic National Convention.

The endurance of popular support for the war also had foundations in morality and culture. Millions of Americans continued to believe that their nation's unique political and cultural characteristics made it a force for good in the world, one whose great power carried with it great responsibility. The participation of young men from every class, creed, color, and county gave most Americans personal connections to the war and hence greater concern about what happened in it. Americans knew that a lack of support on the home front would dishearten America's troops and strengthen the resolve of the North Vietnamese who were trying to kill them. Numerous Americans believed, furthermore, that if the United States were to walk away from the war, it would dishonor the sacrifices of tens of thousands of Americans who had perished in Vietnam.

That the large majority of Americans still supported the Vietnam War after three and a half years of mounting American casualties, weak White House leadership, misleading media coverage, and disenchantment among liberal elites was a testament to the fortitude of the national culture. America's culture provided what General Omar Bradley had called the national fiber, the moral stamina to persist in the face of adversity and steep costs. To give up on an expedition because it was arduous and violent, to yield to a foreign tyranny that had spilled so much American blood, to end an honorable war for a dishonorable peace, would have betrayed the national spirit that had made the United States the world's most powerful and beneficent country.

In their affection for the nation, Americans vested more faith in the accumulated wisdom of the people than in the character of individuals elected to political office. They had not let their disillusionment with Lyndon Johnson extinguish their faith in the American nation or its international commitments, still believing, as Theodore Roosevelt had once put it, that patriotism meant standing by the country, not standing by the president, except to the degree that the president stood by the country. The grievous errors of other Americans, like Robert McNamara and Averell Harriman and Clark Clifford, had not ruined their solidarity with their countrymen.

In the absence of White House authorization for overwhelming force in North Vietnam or Laos, the martial will of the American people had been America's most potent asset in 1965, and it remained so through the end of 1968. The voting power of pro-war Americans had compelled Hubert Humphrey to oppose abandonment of the war and had brought into office Richard Nixon, a man reputed to be one of the most ardent and cunning

562 • TRIUMPH REGAINED

anti-Communists of his generation. So long as a majority of the
voting public backed the war, American politicians would remain
comfortable keeping America's commitment to preserving South
Vietnam. At a time when reductions in draft exemptions had led
to increased draft evasion among certain segments of society,
the endurance of popular support for the war in most American
families and neighborhoods ensured that that the U.S. military
would keep receiving enough manpower to meet its needs in
Vietnam and the rest of the world. Affluent, middle-class, and
working-class Americans were still answering the nation's call
to join the military even as some of their peers derided them as
"suckers" or "fascists."

As the recent statements of Lyndon Johnson, Hubert Humphrey, and Richard Nixon had demonstrated, the last war remained
very much on the minds of American politicians and the American
people at the end of 1968. Americans who favored persistence
in Vietnam hoped that the North Vietnamese would eventually
abandon their war of conquest, as the North Koreans had abandoned theirs in 1953. President-elect Nixon appeared capable of
harnessing the will and patriotic spirt of the American nation as
Lyndon Johnson never had, which in the near term represented
the best means of convincing Hanoi that it could not win the war
no matter how many young men it sent into the slaughterhouse
of South Vietnam.

Americans had seen South Korea overcome its early failings
to take on a growing share of responsibility for its own security during the latter stages of the Korean War and then for the
duration of the postwar peace. They were heartened to see South
Vietnam beginning to do the same. By sticking with their South
Korean ally in its time of need, the United States had foiled a
Communist invasion and created a formidable anti-Communist
bastion on the periphery of Communist China. It had likewise

thwarted the Communist invasion of South Vietnam in 1965, and the development of a strong anti-Communist nation seemed very plausible in a South Vietnam of similar cultural underpinnings, a country where the events of 1968 had given nationalism and anti-Communism new life.

ACKNOWLEDGMENTS

This book took shape over a fifteen-year period that spanned multiple jobs and four other book projects, most of them related to America's wars in Iraq, Afghanistan, and elsewhere. During that time, my understanding of war in general as well as certain particularities of the Vietnam War benefited tremendously from contact with some of the nation's finest military officers and foreign service officers. I must thank them collectively rather than individually owing to their large number and the ongoing need of some for anonymity.

This book, like the preceding volume, owes much of its value to the labors of Merle Pribbenow. His translations of Vietnamese Communist documents, memoirs, and histories enabled me to present the North Vietnamese side of the war more fully, assess the impact of American and South Vietnamese actions more accurately, and solve longstanding historical mysteries. Thank you again, Merle. Elizabeth Tran Bozzi also graciously provided translations of several Vietnamese-language books.

Vietnam veterans contributed to the book's completion in ways too numerous to count. Andy Finlayson, R. J. Del Vecchio, Paul Schmehl, Steve Sherman, Bob Turner, Bill Laurie, Mike Benge, Roger Canfield, Bob Turner, John Norton Moore, Bob Baker, Bruce Kinsey, and the late Rufus Phillips provided historical materials in personal capacities and as members of the Vietnam Veterans for Factual History, an organization that has posted a wealth of historical material on its website, www.vvfh.org. James Webb, John Del Vecchio, Lewis Sorley, B. G. Burkett, Michael

Lee Lanning, Phillip Jennings, and Rich Botkin have inspired me with their writing and their encouragement of mine.

During my visits to the National Archives, Cliff Snyder, Jeannine Swift, and Richard Boylan tracked down documents in the facility's inner recesses. Jeff Hartley located obscure articles that I could find nowhere else. At the Marine Corps University Archives, Alisa Whitley went out of her way to find documents for me. Jay Veith gave me copies of valuable documents in addition to reviewing a draft of the manuscript and serving as a sounding board. Luke Nichter shared his vast knowledge of the 1968 presidential election and the Anna Chennault affair, which led to significant revisions of my initial interpretation of that episode. Nick Turner conveyed to me crucial Indonesian commentary on the momentous upheaval in Jakarta of October 1965.

Major General Donald R. Gardner (Ret.), Brigadier General Thomas V. Draude (Ret.), Kim T. Adamson, Jerre Wilson, Nadia Schadlow, Marin Strmecki, Victor Davis Hanson, Roger Hertog, Diane Sehler, Jack David, and Chris Griffin supported this project and related efforts as the writing moved along. Andrew Walworth of RealClear Media, Brett Baier of Fox News, Jonathan Towers of Towers Productions, and James C. Roberts of Radio America have been wonderful partners in spreading my research and that of like-minded scholars through other media. At Encounter Books, Roger Kimball was quick to see the promise in this project and equally quick to bring it through the gates of publication. Amanda DeMatto was extremely helpful and prompt in managing the editorial and production processes, and Michael Totten edited the manuscript with a deft touch.

Dr. Larry Arnn, Dr. Mark Kalthoff, and Dr. Matthew Spalding, all of Hillsdale College, welcomed me into a new academic home near the conclusion of this project. They afforded me flexibility that ensured the final product received the necessary rereading and fine-tooth combing. Emily-Weston Kannon assisted with the final stages of research.

Since the publication of volume one, my family has been subjected to great stress by the combination of this project with the unconventional career path of a conservative scholar and a number of other unforeseen developments. That we have been able to make it through is a testament to the fortitude of my wife Kelli and our children Greta, Trent, and Luke as well as the support of friends and family, especially my parents, Bert and Marjorie. We also owe thanks to God, source of all strength and wisdom.

LIST OF ABBREVIATIONS

ARVN	Army of the Republic of Vietnam
CDEC	Combined Document Exploitation Center
CIA	Central Intelligence Agency
CINCPAC	Commander in Chief, Pacific Fleet
COMUSMACV	Commander, U.S. Military Assistance Command, Vietnam
CREST	CIA Records Search Tool
CWIHP	Cold War International History Project
DDRS	Declassified Documents Reference System
DIA	Defense Intelligence Agency
DMUSF	Deployment of Major U.S. Forces
DRV	Democratic Republic of (North) Vietnam
FO	Foreign Office
FRUS	Foreign Relations of the Untied States
JCS	Joint Chiefs of Staff
JCSM	Joint Chiefs of Staff Memorandum
LBJL	Lyndon B. Johnson Library, Austin, Texas
MACV	Military Assistance Command, Vietnam
MCHD	Marine Corps Historical Division, Quantico, Virginia
MHI	U.S. Army Military History Institute, Carlisle, Pennsylvania
NA II	National Archives II, College Park, Maryland
NMCC	National Military Command Center
NSC	National Security Council
NSF	National Security File

RG	Record Group
RVN	Republic of (South) Vietnam
SNIE	Special National Intelligence Estimate
TTU	Texas Tech University Vietnam Archive, Lubbock, Texas
USVNR	United States–Vietnam Relations, 1945–1967
VC	Viet Cong
VNCF	Vietnam Country File

NOTES

PREFACE

1   For discussion of the schools of thought on Vietnam, see Gary R. Hess, *Vietnam: Explaining America's Lost War*, 2nd ed. (Malden, Massachusetts: Wiley Blackwell, 2015); Michael G. Kort, *The Vietnam War Reexamined* (Cambridge: Cambridge University Press, 2018); Matthew Masur, "Historians and the Origins of the Vietnam War," in Andrew Wiest, Mary Kathryn Barbier, and Glenn Robins, eds., *America and the Vietnam War: Re-examining the Culture and History of a Generation* (New York: Routledge, 2010), 35–53; Andrew Wiest and Michael J. Doidge, eds., *Triumph Revisited: Historians Battle for the Vietnam War* (New York: Routledge, 2010).

2   A significant number of histories published in the past two decades have provided valuable Vietnamese perspectives on the war. Christopher Goscha, *Vietnam: A New History* (New York: Basic Books, 2016); Ben Kiernan, *Viet Nam: A History from Earliest Times to the Present* (New York: Oxford University Press, 2017); Lien-Hang T. Nguyen, *Hanoi's War: An International History of the War for Peace in Vietnam* (Chapel Hill: University of North Carolina Press, 2012); Nathalie Huynh Chau Nguyen, *South Vietnamese Soldiers: Memories of the Vietnam War and After* (Westport: Praeger, 2016); Heather Marie Stur, *Saigon at War: South Vietnam and the Global Sixties* (Cambridge: Cambridge University Press, 2020); K. W. Taylor, *A History of the Vietnamese* (Cambridge: Cambridge University Press, 2013); Nhu-Anh Tran, "Contested Nationalism: Ethnic Identity and State Power in the Republic of Vietnam, 1954–1963," Institute for the Study of Societal Issues, 2012; George J. Veith, *Drawn Swords in a Distant Land: South Vietnam's Shattered Dreams* (New York: Encounter, 2021); Andrew Wiest, *Vietnam's Forgotten Army: Heroism and Betrayal in the ARVN* (New York: New York University Press, 2008).

3   The relevance of Indonesia has been overlooked in nearly all histories of the Vietnam War. A few have mentioned that certain U.S. officials perceived that events in Vietnam influenced events in Indonesia but have claimed that there was no actual influence. Mark Atwood Lawrence, *The End of Ambition: The United States and the Third World in the Vietnam Era* (Princeton: Princeton University Press, 2021); David Milne, *America's Rasputin: Walt Rostow and the Vietnam War* (New York: Hill and Wang, 2008); William S. Turley, *The Second Indochina War: A Concise Political and Military History,* 2nd ed. (Lanham, Maryland: Rowman and Littlefield, 2009). The few historians to give serious

consideration to the influence of the Vietnam conflict on the political tumult in Indonesia include Kort, *The Vietnam War Reexamined;* Michael Lind, *Vietnam, The Necessary War: A Reinterpretation of America's Most Disastrous Military Conflict* (New York: Free Press, 1999); R. B. Smith, *An International History of the Vietnam War, 3: The Making of a Limited War, 1965–1966* (New York: St. Martin's, 1991).

4   This book benefited from a number of excellent histories of Chinese and Soviet relations with North Vietnam and the United States, including Ilya V. Gaiduk, *The Soviet Union and the Vietnam War* (Chicago: Ivan R. Dee, 1996); Evelyn Goh, *Constructing the U.S. Rapprochement with China, 1961–1974: From "Red Menace" to "Tacit Ally"* (Cambridge: Cambridge University Press, 2005); Chen Jian, *Mao's China and the Cold War* (Chapel Hill: University of North Carolina Press, 2001); Nicholas Khoo, *Collateral Damage: Sino-Soviet Rivalry and the Termination of the Sino-Vietnamese Alliance* (New York: Columbia University Press, 2011); Xiaobing Li, *The Dragon in the Jungle: The Chinese Army in the Vietnam War* (New York: Oxford University Press, 2020); Lorenz M. Lüthi, *The Sino-Soviet Split: Cold War in the Communist World* (Princeton: Princeton University Press, 2008); Sergey Radchenko, *Two Suns in the Heavens: The Sino-Soviet Struggle for Supremacy, 1962–1967* (Stanford: Stanford University Press, 2009); Jay Taylor, *China and Southeast Asia: Peking's Relations with Revolutionary Movements*, 2nd ed. (New York: Praeger, 1976); Qiang Zhai, *China and the Vietnam Wars, 1950–1975* (Chapel Hill: University of North Carolina Press, 2000); Vladislav M. Zubok, *A Failed Empire: The Soviet Union in the Cold War from Stalin to Gorbachev* (Chapel Hill: University of North Carolina Press, 2007).

5   Most histories disregard the ongoing relevance of the Vietnam conflict to other countries in the region. Others maintain that events in Vietnam had little impact on those countries. See Robert Dallek, *Flawed Giant: Lyndon Johnson and his Times, 1961–1973* (New York: Oxford University Press, 1998); Lloyd C. Gardner, *Pay Any Price: Lyndon Johnson and the Wars for Vietnam* (Chicago: Ivan R. Dee, 1995); Herbert Y. Schandler, *America in Vietnam: The War That Couldn't Be Won* (Lanham, Maryland: Rowman & Littlefield, 2009); Turley, *The Second Indochina War.*

6   Westmoreland has often been criticized for neglecting pacification. Loren Baritz, *Backfire: A History of How American Culture Led Us into Vietnam and Made Us Fight the Way We Did* (New York: William Morrow, 1985); Robert Buzzanco, *Masters of War: Military Dissent and Politics in the Vietnam Era* (New York: Cambridge University Press, 1996); Cecil B. Currey, *Self-Destruction: The Disintegration and Decay of the United States Army during the Vietnam Era* (New York: W. W. Norton, 1981); Gary R. Hess, *Vietnam and the United States* (New York: Twayne, 1990); John Prados, *Vietnam: The History of an Unwinnable War, 1945–1975* (Lawrence: University Press of Kansas, 2009); Lewis Sorley, *Westmoreland: The General Who Lost Vietnam* (Boston: Houghton Mifflin Harcourt, 2011); Turley, *The Second Indochina War;* Marilyn B. Young, *The Vietnam Wars, 1945–1990* (New York: HarperCollins, 1991).

7 Numerous historians have maintained that Westmoreland's reliance on
   search-and-destroy operations in remote areas was wrongheaded and
   wasteful. Robert B. Asprey, *War in the Shadows: The Guerrilla in History*,
   2 vols. (New York: Doubleday, 1975); Andrew F. Krepinevich, *The Army
   in Vietnam* (Baltimore: Johns Hopkins University Press, 1986); Guenter
   Lewy, *America in Vietnam* (New York: Oxford University Press, 1978); Lind,
   Vietnam; John A. Nagl, *Counterinsurgency Lessons from Malaya and Vietnam:
   Learning to Eat Soup with a Knife* (Westport: Praeger, 2002). A few have
   viewed Westmoreland's operations in remote regions more favorably. Andrew
   J. Birtle, *U.S. Army Counterinsurgency and Contingency Operations Doctrine,
   1942–1976* (Washington, DC: U.S. Army Center of Military History, 2006);
   Gregory A. Daddis, *Westmoreland's War: Reassessing American Strategy in
   Vietnam* (New York: Oxford University Press, 2014).

8 For allegations that the Americans overestimated the effectiveness of their
   operations, see David L. Anderson, *The Vietnam War* (New York: Palgrave
   MacMillan, 2005); Buzzanco, *Masters of War*; James William Gibson, *The
   Perfect War: Technowar In Vietnam* (Boston: Atlantic Monthly Press, 1986);
   Michael Maclear, *The Ten Thousand Day War: Vietnam, 1945–1975* (New York:
   Avon, 1981); Brian VanDeMark, *Road to Disaster: A New History of America's
   Descent into Vietnam* (New York: Custom House, 2018). In a highly publicized
   documentary and companion book, Ken Burns gave great weight to the small
   number of battles where the Americans sustained heavy casualties, conveying
   the impression that American military operations were relatively ineffective.
   Geoffrey C. Ward and Ken Burns, *The Vietnam War: An Intimate History* (New
   York: Alfred A. Knopf, 2017). Numerous histories have accepted the claim
   of CIA analyst Sam Adams that the U.S. military deliberately undercounted
   the enemy as part of an effort to misrepresent the effectiveness of U.S.
   military operations. Christian Appy, *Working Class War: American Combat
   Soldiers and Vietnam* (Chapel Hill: University of North Carolina Press, 1993);
   Harold P. Ford, *CIA and the Vietnam Policymakers: Three Episodes, 1962–1968*
   (Washington, DC: Center for the Study of Intelligence, 1998); Gibson,
   The Perfect War; Jeffrey Record, *The Wrong War: Why We Lost in Vietnam*
   (Annapolis: Naval Institute Press, 1998); Neil Sheehan, *A Bright Shining
   Lie: John Paul Vann and America in Vietnam* (New York: Random House,
   1988); Young, *The Vietnam Wars*. A few histories have been more skeptical of
   Adams's claims. T. L. Cubbage II, "Westmoreland vs. CBS: Was Intelligence
   Corrupted by Policy Demands?" in *Intelligence and National Security*, 3, No.
   3 (July 1988), 118–180; James J. Wirtz, *The Tet Offensive: Intelligence Failure in
   War* (Ithaca: Cornell University Press, 1991).

9 Several recent works have provided new information and insights on the
   perceptions of North Vietnamese leaders. Nguyen, *Hanoi's War*; Taylor, *A
   History of the Vietnamese*; Turley, *The Second Indochina War*; Veith, *Drawn
   Swords in a Distant Land*.

10 Of the historians who have assessed the advisability of sending American
   ground troops into Laos and Cambodia, the large majority have concurred
   with the Johnson administration that it would not have produced strategic

benefits. Stanley Karnow, *Vietnam: A History,* 2nd rev. ed. (New York: Penguin, 1997); Lind, *Vietnam;* Record, *The Wrong War;* Schandler, *America in Vietnam;* Turley, *The Second Indochina War.* The first books to argue that U.S. ground intervention in these countries could have been strategically fruitful were written by participants. Norman B. Hannah, *The Key to Failure: Laos and the Vietnam War* (Lanham, Maryland: Madison Books, 1987); Bruce Palmer, *The 25-Year War: America's Military Role in Vietnam* (Lexington: University Press of Kentucky, 1984); Harry G. Summers Jr., *On Strategy: A Critical Analysis of the Vietnam War* (Novato: Presidio Press, 1982). Historians who have concurred in the judgment of those participants are Anthony James Joes, *Why South Vietnam Fell* (Lanham, Maryland: Lexington Books, 2014); Kort, *The Vietnam War Reexamined;* C. Dale Walton, *The Myth of Inevitable U.S. Defeat in Vietnam* (London: Frank Cass, 2002).

11 Most American accounts have underestimated the damage that more extensive American bombing could have inflicted on North Vietnam as well as the actual damage inflicted in the years 1967 and 1968. Mark Clodfelter, *The Limits of Air Power: The American Bombing of North Vietnam* (New York: The Free Press, 1989); Ronald B. Frankum Jr., *Like Rolling Thunder: The Air War in Vietnam, 1965-1975* (Lanham, Maryland: Rowman & Littlefield, 2005); Gibson, *The Perfect War;* Max Hastings, *Vietnam: An Epic Tragedy, 1945-1975* (New York: Harper, 2018); Mark Atwood Lawrence: *The Vietnam War: A Concise International History* (New York: Oxford University Press, 2008); Milne, *America's Rasputin;* Robert A. Pape, *Air Power and Coercion in War;* Schandler, *America in Vietnam;* Sheehan, *A Bright Shining Lie;* Earl H. Tilford, *Setup: What the Air Force Did in Vietnam and Why* (Maxwell Air Force Base: Air University Press, 1991); VanDeMark, *Road to Disaster.* Among the few histories that have seen greater potential and actual achievements in Rolling Thunder are Wayne Thompson, *To Hanoi and Back: The USAF and North Vietnam, 1966-1973* (Washington, DC: Air Force History and Museums Program, 2000); Walton, *The Myth of Inevitable U.S. Defeat in Vietnam.*

12 Most historical accounts of the Buddhist crisis of 1966 have overlooked or downplayed the duplicitous tactics of the Buddhists, the collaboration between the Buddhists and the Communists, and the benefits accruing to the government for putting down the rebellion. Mark Philip Bradley, *Vietnam At War* (New York: Oxford University Press, 2009); George McTurnan Kahin, *Intervention: How America Became Involved in Vietnam* (New York: Alfred A. Knopf, 1986); Prados, *Vietnam;* Robert D. Schulzinger, *A Time for War: The United States and Vietnam, 1941-1975* (New York: Oxford University Press, 1997); Robert J. Topmiller, *The Lotus Unleashed: The Buddhist Peace Movement in South Vietnam, 1954-1966* (Lexington: University Press of Kentucky, 2002); Ward and Burns, *The Vietnam War;* Young, *The Vietnam Wars.*

13 For the depiction of the North Vietnamese as supremely patient, see Daddis, *Westmoreland's War;* Gibson, *The Perfect War;* David Halberstam, *The Best and the Brightest* (New York: Random House, 1992); Karnow, *Vietnam;* Record, *The Wrong War;* Schulzinger, *A Time for War.*

14 Most histories have underestimated the magnitude of the North Vietnamese defeats in 1968. See Gregory A. Daddis, *Withdrawal: Reassessing America's Final Years in Vietnam* (New York: Oxford University Press, 2017); Philip B. Davidson, *Vietnam At War: The History, 1946–1975* (Novato, California: Presidio Press, 1988); Gardner, *Pay Any Price;* Gabriel Kolko, *Anatomy of a War: Vietnam, The United States, and the Modern Historical Experience* (New York: Pantheon, 1985); Edwin E. Moïse, *The Myths of Tet: The Most Misunderstood Event of the Vietnam War* (Lawrence: University Press of Kansas, 2017); Prados, *Vietnam;* Ronald H. Spector, *After Tet: The Bloodiest Year in Vietnam* (New York: Free Press, 1993); Stur, *Saigon at War.* Among the few to recognize the seriousness of the North Vietnamese losses are William Duiker, *The Communist Road to Power in Vietnam,* 2nd ed. (Boulder: Westview, 1996); Ang Cheng Guan, *The Vietnam War from the Other Side: The Vietnamese Communists' Perspective* (Abingdon: RoutledgeCurzon, 2002).

15 Appy, *Working Class War;* Buzzanco, *Masters of War;* Cecil B. Currey, *Victory at Any Cost: The Genius of Viet Nam's Gen. Vo Nguyen Giap* (Washington, DC: Brassey's, 1997); Daddis, *Withdrawal;* Gardner, *Pay Any Price;* Hastings, *Vietnam;* Karnow, *Vietnam;* A. J. Langguth, *Our Vietnam: The War, 1954–1975* (New York: Simon & Schuster, 2000); Moïse, *The Myths of Tet;* Prados, *Vietnam;* Schulzinger, *A Time for War;* Sheehan, *A Bright Shining Lie;* Erik B. Villard, *Combat Operations: Staying the Course, October 1967–September 1968* (Washington, DC: U.S. Army Center of Military History, 2017); Turley, *The Second Indochina War;* Ward and Burns, *The Vietnam War;* Wirtz, *The Tet Offensive.* Two early histories contended that Khe Sanh was not a diversion. Davidson, *Vietnam at War;* Ronnie E. Ford, *Tet 1968: Understanding the Surprise* (London: Frank Cass, 1995).

16 For the interpretation that the Tet Offensive led Johnson toward disengagement from Vietnam, see Buzzanco, *Masters of War;* Halberstam, *The Best and the Brightest;* Hess, *Vietnam and the United States;* Michael H. Hunt, *Lyndon Johnson's War: America's Cold War Crusade in Vietnam, 1945–1968* (New York: Hill and Wang, 1996); Kolko, *Anatomy of a War;* Maclear, *The Ten Thousand Day War;* George Donelson Moss, *Vietnam: An American Ordeal,* 6th ed. (New York: Routledge, 2016); Schandler, *America in Vietnam;* Spector, *After Tet.*

17 The changes introduced by Abrams were to become a matter of fierce debate in later years, one that eventually influenced the U.S. military's approach to the wars in Iraq and Afghanistan. In the view of one prominent group of historians, Abrams immediately shifted away from the use of U.S. forces in search-and-destroy operations aimed at attrition of the enemy in remote areas and directed U.S. forces to concentrate on combined operations with the South Vietnamese forces, aimed at pacification of the villages. The thesis of drastic change under Abrams appears most prominently in Lewis Sorley, *A Better War: The Unexamined Victories and Final Tragedy of America's Last Years in Vietnam* (New York: Harcourt Brace, 1999) and Nagl, *Counterinsurgency Lessons from Malaya and Vietnam.* The counterargument was made in Dale

Andradé, "Westmoreland Was Right: Learning the Wrong Lessons from the Vietnam War," *Small Wars & Insurgencies*, 19, No. 2 (June 2008), 145–181; Birtle, *U.S. Army Counterinsurgency and Contingency Operations Doctrine, 1942–1976*; Daddis, *Westmoreland's War*; Villard, *Combat Operations*.

18 Most histories have made no mention of the improvement in South Vietnamese performance over the course of 1968, and some have explicitly claimed that it did not take place. Gregory A. Daddis, *No Sure Victory: Measuring U.S. Army Effectiveness and Progress in the Vietnam War* (New York: Oxford University Press, 2011); Hastings, *Vietnam*; Hunt, *Lyndon Johnson's War*; Kolko, *Anatomy of a War*; Spector, *After Tet*; Ward and Burns, *The Vietnam War*. Recognition of these improvements can be found in Graham A. Cosmas, *MACV: The Joint Command in the Years of Withdrawal, 1968–1973* (Washington, DC: Center of Military History, 2006); Lewy, *America in Vietnam*; Herbert Y. Schandler, *Unmaking of a President: Lyndon Johnson and Vietnam* (Princeton: Princeton University Press, 1977); Sorley, *A Better War*.

19 For accounts that characterize Westmoreland's emphasis on attrition as unimaginative, ill-informed, or unrealistic in its ambitions, see Daddis, *No Sure Victory*; Gibson, *Perfect War*; Gordon M. Goldstein, *Lessons in Disaster: McGeorge Bundy and the Path to War in Vietnam* (New York: Times Books, 2008); Halberstam, *The Best and the Brightest*; George C. Herring, *America's Longest War: The United States and Vietnam, 1950–1975*, 6th ed. (New York: McGraw Hill, 2019); Kolko, *Anatomy of a War*; Dave R. Palmer, *Summons of the Trumpet: U.S.–Vietnam in Perspective* (Novato: Presidio Press, 1978); Schulzinger, *A Time for War*; Sheehan, *A Bright Shining Lie*; Sorley, *Westmoreland*; VanDeMark, *Road to Disaster*; Ward and Burns, *The Vietnam War*. In a subsequent book, Daddis is less critical of Westmoreland's reliance on attrition warfare, but mainly because he concludes that Westmoreland was not as obsessed with attrition as was commonly believed, rather than because attrition was strategically valuable. Daddis, *Westmoreland's War*. Although Westmoreland's attrition strategy enjoyed extensive support from senior U.S. government leaders at the time of its implementation, only a small number of historical analyses have viewed it as a sound response to the strategic environment. Birtle, *U.S. Army Counterinsurgency and Contingency Operations Doctrine*; Graham A. Cosmas, *MACV: The Joint Command in the Years of Escalation, 1962–1967* (Washington, DC: U.S. Army Center of Military History, 2006); Davidson, *Vietnam at War*.

20 A few histories have claimed that the United States missed real opportunities for a peace settlement during this period. James G. Hershberg, *Marigold: The Lost Chance for Peace in Vietnam* (Stanford: Stanford University Press, 2012); Robert McNamara et al., *Argument Without End: In Search of Answers to the Vietnam Tragedy* (New York: Public Affairs, 1999); Prados, *Vietnam*. More common has been the conclusion that a diplomatic resolution of the war was impossible between the arrival of U.S. ground forces and the Tet Offensive because neither side was prepared at this time to compromise to the extent necessary for a peace agreement. Pierre Asselin, *Vietnam's American War: A History* (Cambridge: Cambridge University Press, 2018); Dallek, *Flawed Giant*;

Goscha, *Vietnam;* Herring, *America's Longest War;* George C. Herring et al.,
"Peace Proposals, Diplomacy, and War: Was an Opportunity Lost for an Early
Settlement in Vietnam?" *Journal of Cold War Studies*, 17, No. 1 (Winter 2015),
153–180.

21 Numerous accounts have overestimated the strength of Hanoi's military and
political position at the end of 1968. Anderson, *The Vietnam War;* George C.
Herring, *LBJ and Vietnam: A Different Kind Of War* (Austin: University of
Texas Press, 1994); Gardner, *Pay Any Price;* Spector, *After Tet.* An exception
is Arthur J. Dommen, *The Indochinese Experience of the French and the
Americans: Nationalism and Communism in Cambodia, Laos, and Vietnam*
(Bloomington: Indiana University Press, 2001).

22 Histories that identify a steep decline in American public support by the
end of 1968 include Baritz, *Backfire;* Larry Berman, *Lyndon Johnson's War*
(New York: W. W. Norton, 1989); William Bundy, *A Tangled Web: The Making
of Foreign Policy in the Nixon Presidency* (New York: Hill and Wang, 1998);
Dallek, *Flawed Giant;* Hunt, *Lyndon Johnson's War;* Robert Mann, *A Grand
Delusion: America's Descent into Vietnam* (New York: Basic Books, 2001);
Moss, *Vietnam*; John E. Mueller, *War, Presidents and Public Opinion* (New
York: John Wiley & Sons, 1973); Spector, *After Tet;* VanDeMark, *Road to
Disaster.* The few that have questioned the conventional wisdom on this
subject include William C. Gibbons, *The U.S. Government and the Vietnam
War: Executive and Legislative Roles and Relationships,* 4 (Princeton: Princeton
University Press, 1995); William L. Lunch and Peter W. Sperlich, "American
Public Opinion and the War in Vietnam," *The Western Political Quarterly*, 32,
No. 1 (March 1979), 21–44.

23 The impact of American culture on public support for the war has not
received much attention from historians. Among the few exceptions are
Colin Dueck, *Hard Line: The Republican Party and U.S. Foreign Policy Since
World War II* (Princeton: Princeton University Press, 2010); Sandra Scanlon,
*The Pro-War Movement: Domestic Support for the Vietnam War and the Making
of Modern American Conservatism* (Amherst: University of Massachusetts
Press, 2013). A small number of historians have sought to attribute American
failings in Vietnam to weaknesses of American culture. Appy, *American
Reckoning;* Baritz, *Backfire;* Record, *The Wrong War.*

24 This interpretation of the impact of the antiwar movement is consistent
with most of what has been written on the subject, although the description
of the movement is more critical than most. See, for instance, Terry H.
Anderson, *The Movement and the Sixties: Protest in America from Greensboro to
Wounded Knee* (New York: Oxford University Press, 1995); Appy, *American
Reckoning;* Charles DeBenedetti, *An American Ordeal: The Antiwar Movement
of the Vietnam Era* (Syracuse, NY: Syracuse University Press, 1990); Melvin
Small, *Johnson, Nixon, and the Doves* (New Brunswick: Rutgers University
Press, 1989); Tom Wells, *The War Within: The Battle Over Vietnam* (Berkeley:
University of California Press, 1994); Ward and Burns, *The Vietnam War.*

25 Histories that attribute Thieu's decision to the conniving of Chennault
include Larry Berman, *No Peace, No Honor: Nixon, Kissinger, and Betrayal in*

Vietnam (New York: The Free Press, 2001); Bundy, *A Tangled Web*; Dallek, *Flawed Giant;* Robert Dallek, *Nixon and Kissinger: Partners in Power* (New York: HarperCollins, 2007); John A. Farrell, *Richard Nixon: The Life* (New York: Doubleday, 2017); Andrew L. Johns, *The Price of Loyalty: Hubert Humphrey's Vietnam Conflict* (Lanham, Maryland: Rowman & Littlefield, 2020); Jeffrey Kimball, *Nixon's Vietnam War* (Lawrence: University Press of Kansas, 1998); Mann, *A Grand Delusion;* VanDeMark, *Road to Disaster;* Ward and Burns, *The Vietnam War.* Histories that properly discount Chennault's influence on Thieu are Jonathan Aitken, *Nixon: A Life* (Washington, DC: Regnery, 1993); Pierre Asselin, *A Bitter Peace: Washington, Hanoi, and the Making of the Paris Agreement* (Chapel Hill: University of North Carolina Press, 2002); Conrad Black, *Richard M. Nixon: A Life in Full* (New York: PublicAffairs, 2007); Veith, *Drawn Swords in a Distant Land.*

CHAPTER 1

1 The official name for what Americans commonly called the North Vietnamese Army was the People's Army of Vietnam. The official name of the Viet Cong was the People's Liberation Armed Forces, a term the North Vietnamese assigned to some of its units as a means of concealing the subordination of those units to Hanoi. Further complicating matters was the existence of multiple North Vietnamese Army regiments that were identified with the same regimental number. The regiment that fought at Van Tuong was distinct from a regiment farther south that has been identified in North Vietnamese accounts as both the 1st Regiment and the 271st Regiment.

2 B. K. Crumley, "Starlite: The 'Magnificent Bastards' Hit a Hot LZ," *Leatherneck*, 88, No. 9 (September 2005), 54.

3 Ibid, 55.

4 Otto Lehrack, *The First Battle: Operation Starlite and the Beginning of the Blood Debt in Vietnam* (Havertown, Pennsylvania: Casemate, 2004), 143.

5 In an early example of the problems that would creep into press coverage in the years to come, Peter Arnett wrote an article on this episode entitled "Marine Supply Column Lumbers to Death," which claimed that the column was "no more" after coming under enemy attack and made no mention of the heavy losses inflicted on the North Vietnamese. Peter Arnett, "Marine Supply Column Lumbers to Death," *Washington Post,* 20 August 1965.

6 Sources on Operation Starlite include Lehrack, *The First Battle*; Otto Lehrack, *No Shining Armor: The Marines at War in Vietnam* (Lawrence: University Press of Kansas, 1992), 33–52; "Operation Starlite, 18–24 Aug 1965," TTU, Virtual Vietnam Archive, Item 1201063060; Rod Andrew Jr., *The First Fight: U.S. Marines in Operation Starlite* (Quantico: Marine Corps University, 2015); Crumley, "Starlite"; Nguyen Quang Dat and Tran Hanh, eds., *Mot So Tran Danh Trong Khang Chien Chong Phap, Khang Chien Chong My, 1945-1975* (Hanoi: Ministry of Defense, 1991), Tap I, 22–45; Jack Shulimson and Charles M. Johnson, *U.S. Marines in Vietnam: The Landing and the Buildup, 1965* (Washington, DC: History and Museums Division, Headquarters, U.S. Marine Corps, 1978), 69–83; Military History Institute of Vietnam, *Victory*

in Vietnam: The Official History of the People's Army of Vietnam, 1954–1975, translated by Merle L. Pribbenow (Lawrence: University Press of Kansas, 2002), 157–158; William M. Hammond, *Public Affairs: The Military and the Media, 1962–1968* (Washington, DC: Center of Military History, 1988), 198–199; Lewy, *America in Vietnam,* 54–55; Tom Bartlett, "Vietnam—25 Years Ago: Operation Starlite," *Leatherneck,* 73, No. 8 (August 1990), 44–49; Andrew Comer, "Amendment to 1976 Operation Starlite Statement," 26 November 1991, Marine Corps University Archives, A/30/B/5/2.

7   Richard L. Zweigenhaft and G. William Domhoff, *Diversity in the Power Elite: How it Happened, Why it Matters* (Lanham, Maryland: Rowman & Littlefield, 2006), 121.

8   William G. Mayer, *The Changing American Mind: How and Why American Public Opinion Changed Between 1960 and 1988* (Ann Arbor: University of Michigan Press, 1992), 375–376; Gallup, "Religion—Historical Trends," https://news.gallup.com/poll/1690/religion.aspx. The afterlife question was not posed in 1965, but the percentage answering in the affirmative during the closest years, 1961 and 1968, were 74 and 73 percent, respectively.

9   For American culture and its impact on the projection of American power, see Walter Russell Mead, *Special Providence: American Foreign Policy and How It Changed the World* (New York: Knopf, 2001); Samuel P. Huntington, *Who Are We? The Challenges to America's National Identity* (New York: Simon & Schuster, 2004); Walter A. McDougall, *Promised Land, Crusader State: The American Encounter with the World Since 1776* (Boston: Houghton Mifflin, 1997); Brian McAllister Linn, *The Echo of Battle: The Army's Way of War* (Cambridge: Harvard University Press, 2009).

10 On the relationship between culture and military power, see Victor Davis Hanson, *Carnage and Culture: Landmark Battles in the Rise of Western Power* (New York: Doubleday, 2001); John Keegan, *A History of Warfare* (New York: Alfred A. Knopf, 1993); Niall Ferguson, *Civilization: The West and the Rest* (New York: Penguin, 2011); John A. Lynn, *Battle: A History of Combat and Culture* (Boulder, Colorado: Westview Press, 2003).

11 For Vietnamese cultural history, see Taylor, *A History of the Vietnamese;* Goscha, *Vietnam;* Kiernan, *Viet Nam.*

12 MACV Directive 525-4, "Tactics and Techniques for Employment of U.S. Forces in the Republic of Vietnam," 17 September 1965, TTU, Virtual Vietnam Archive, Item 0240303014.

13 William C. Westmoreland, *A Soldier Reports* (New York: Doubleday, 1976), 144–145.

14 Westmoreland, "Concept of Operations in the Republic of Vietnam," 1 September 1965, NA II, RG 407, Westmoreland vs. CBS Litigation Collection, box 3; USMACV, "1965 Command History," 20 April 1966, 241–242; Westmoreland to Wheeler, 17 September 1965, LBJL, Westmoreland Papers, box 6.

15 MACV Directive 525-4, "Tactics and Techniques for Employment of U.S. Forces in the Republic of Vietnam," 17 September 1965, TTU, Virtual Vietnam Archive, Item 0240303014; USMACV, 1965 Command History, 263.

16 Romie L. Brownlee and William J. Mullen III, *Changing an Army: An Oral History of General William E. DePuy* (Carlisle Barracks, PA: Military History Institute, 1986), 160–162; William E. DePuy, "Vietnam: What We Might Have Done and Why We Didn't Do It," *Army*, 36, No. 2 (February 1986), 22—40; John M. Carland, *Combat Operations: Stemming the Tide, May 1965 to October 1966* (Washington, DC: U.S. Government Printing Office, 2000), 365–366.

17 Mark Moyar, *Triumph Forsaken: The Vietnam War, 1954–1965* (New York: Cambridge University Press, 2006), 406–409.

18 Ibid., 407–411. On August 27, the Joint Chiefs echoed Westmoreland on the possibility that the enemy would avoid large-scale combat and on the importance of building up South Vietnamese forces. "A major effort," the Chiefs stated, "must be made not only in terms of direct combat action to expand the areas under US/GVN control but also to support the GVN in its rural reconstruction program and to assist that government in the creation of new military units and the rehabilitation of its depleted units as rapidly as possible." Joint Chiefs of Staff to McNamara, JCSM 652-65, 27 August 1965, FRUS, 1964–1968, 3, 130.

19 Westmoreland, *A Soldier Reports*, 144. In order to rehabilitate South Vietnamese counterinsurgency capabilities, Westmoreland urged the Saigon government to expand and strengthen its territorial militias, the Regional and Popular Forces, and provided resources to that end. Westmoreland, History Notes, 1 September 1965, MHI, Westmoreland Papers, box 30; Westmoreland, History Notes, 2 September 1965, MHI, Westmoreland Papers, box 30; MACV Directive 525-4, "Tactics and Techniques for Employment of U.S. Forces in the Republic of Vietnam," 17 September 1965, TTU, Virtual Vietnam Archive, Item 0240303014; Jeffrey J. Clarke, *Advice and Support: The Final Years, 1965–1973* (Washington, DC: U.S. Government Printing Office, 1988), 112.

20 Westmoreland to Wheeler, 18 August 1965, LBJL, Westmoreland Papers, box 34; Westmoreland to Wheeler, 17 September 1965, LBJL, Westmoreland Papers, box 6; Sharp and Westmoreland, *Report on the War in Vietnam*, 98–99; Westmoreland, *A Soldier Reports*, 146; Richard A. Hunt, *Pacification: The American Struggle for Vietnam's Hearts and Minds* (Boulder, Colorado: Westview Press, 1995), 34; Shulimson and Johnson, *U.S. Marines in Vietnam: The Landing and the Buildup*, 58–59.

21 Westmoreland to Wheeler, 28 August 1965, LBJL, Westmoreland Papers, box 6.

22 Saigon to State, 11 July 1965, LBJL, NSF, NSC History, DMUSF, box 43. The report used the term "rural reconstruction" to describe what more often has been described as counterinsurgency or pacification in recent times.

23 Le Buoi, *Qua Trinh Cuoc Chien Tranh Xam Luoc Cua De Quoc My Va Quy Luat Hoat Dong Cua My-Nguy Tren Chien Truong B2* (Hanoi: Ban Tong Ket Chien Tranh B2, 1984), 387.

24 Walt to Westmoreland, 19 November 1965, LBJL, Westmoreland Papers, box 34; Walt, *Strange Country, Strange War*, 29; Victor H. Krulak, *First to Fight: An*

Inside View of the U.S. Marine Corps (Annapolis: Naval Institute Press, 1984), 190–192.

25 Jack Shulimson, *U.S. Marines in Vietnam: An Expanding War, 1966* (Washington, DC: History and Museums Division, Headquarters, U.S. Marine Corps, 1982), 13–15; Jack Shulimson and Edward F. Wells, "First In, First Out: The Marine Experience in Vietnam, 1965–1971," in Charles. R. Shrader, ed. *Proceedings of the 1982 International Military History Symposium* (Washington, DC: U.S. Army Center of Military History, 1984), 272. General Victor Krulak, commander of the Fleet Marine Force in the Pacific, was the general officer most critical of Westmoreland's strategy and tactics, and yet in December 1965 even he rejected what he termed "the erroneous view that pacification and civic action will solve the problem if major enemy forces are free to roam the countryside." Shulimson and Johnson, *U.S. Marines in Vietnam: The Landing and the Buildup,* 111.

26 Shulimson and Wells, "First In, First Out," 272.

27 Lehrack, *The First Battle,* 49; Shulimson and Johnson, *U.S. Marines in Vietnam: The Landing and the Buildup,* 115–116; Shulimson, *U.S. Marines in Vietnam: An Expanding War,* 13–14.

28 Shulimson and Johnson, *U.S. Marines in Vietnam: The Landing and the Buildup,* 58–59, 133–138; Michael E. Peterson, *The Combined Action Platoons: The U.S. Marines' Other War in Vietnam* (New York: Praeger, 1989), 21–27.

29 The most forceful Marine presentation of this argument is William R. Corson, *The Betrayal* (New York: W. W. Norton, 1968). For subsequent expositions, see Robert B. Asprey, *War in the Shadows: The Guerrilla in History,* 2 vols. (New York: Doubleday, 1975); Douglas S. Blaufarb, *The Counterinsurgency Era: U.S. Doctrine and Performance, 1950 to the Present* (New York: Free Press, 1977); Andrew F. Krepinevich, *The Army in Vietnam* (Baltimore: Johns Hopkins University Press, 1986); Al Hemingway, *Our War Was Different* (Annapolis, Maryland: Naval Institute Press, 1994); Michael Lind, *Vietnam, The Necessary War: A Reinterpretation of America's Most Disastrous Military Conflict* (New York: Free Press, 1999); John A. Nagl, *Counterinsurgency Lessons from Malaya and Vietnam: Learning to Eat Soup with a Knife* (Westport: Praeger, 2002).

30 Peterson, *The Combined Action Platoons,* 38, 56–60, 68, 88; Hemingway, *Our War Was Different,* 56, 80, 158; F. J. West Jr., *The Village* (New York: Harper & Row, 1972), 114–127. At this very time, the North Vietnamese leadership was trying to induce the Americans to disperse forces in order to make them more vulnerable to large conventional attacks. In urging local guerrillas to intensify their operations, Le Duc Tho observed that guerrilla warfare "compels the enemy to disperse, limits his mobility and provides the main force with the conditions for attacking the enemy." U.S. State Department, Working Paper on the Vietnam War, part II Annex, item 65, TTU, Pike Collection, unit 1, box 11. The source document incorrectly identifies the speaker, "Anh Sau," as Nguyen Chi Thanh; "Anh Sau" was the primary alias of Le Duc Tho.

31 Birtle, *U.S. Army Counterinsurgency and Contingency Operations Doctrine, 1942–1976*, 400.

32 B. G. Burkett and Glenna Whitley, *Stolen Valor: How the Vietnam Generation Was Robbed of Its Heroes and Its History* (Dallas: Verity Press, 1998), 111–138; Lewy, *America in Vietnam* 307–373; Eric M. Bergerud, *Red Thunder, Tropic Lightning: The World of a Combat Division in Vietnam* (Boulder, Colorado: Westview Press, 1993), 219–258; Ron Milam, *Not A Gentleman's War: An Inside View of Junior Officers in the Vietnam War* (Chapel Hill: University of North Carolina Press, 2009), 113–138.

33 Hammond, *Public Affairs: The Military and the Media, 1962–1968*, 186–188; Shulimson and Johnson, *U.S. Marines in Vietnam: The Landing and the Buildup*, 62–64; *The Joint Chiefs of Staff and the War in Vietnam* (Christiansburg, VA: Dalley Book Service, 2001), Chapter 23, 12; Lewy, *America in Vietnam*, 52–53.

34 On the evolution of press attitudes toward the war, see Hammond, *Public Affairs: The Military and the Media, 1962–1968;* Daniel C. Hallin, *The "Uncensored War": The Media and Vietnam* (Berkeley: University of California Press, 1986); Clarence R. Wyatt, *Paper Soldiers: The American Press and the Vietnam War* (New York: W. W. Norton, 1993).

35 Saigon to State, 26 August 1965, *FRUS, 1964–1968*, 3, 127; Sharp and Westmoreland, *Report on the War in Vietnam*, 98–100. Because North Vietnamese soldiers in the highlands also posed a serious threat to Saigon, Westmoreland assigned the U.S. Army's 1st Infantry Division and 173rd Airborne Brigade to III Corps.

36 H. Norman Schwarzkopf, *It Doesn't Take a Hero: The Autobiography* (New York: Bantam, 1992), 114–120.

37 William G. Leftwich Jr., "Decision at Duc Co," *Marine Corps Gazette*, 51, No. 2 (February 1967), 37–38.

38 Sources on Duc Co include Theodore C. Mataxis, "Monsoon Offensive in the Highlands," TTU, Theodore Mataxis, Sr. Collection, Box 1; CIA, "The Situation in South Vietnam," 8 September 1965, CREST, document number CIA-RDP79T00472A00180003000 102-8; J. P. Harris, *Vietnam's High Ground: Armed Struggle for the Central Highlands, 1954–1965* (Lawrence: University Press of Kansas, 2016), 293–299; Leftwich, "Decision at Duc Co," 35–38.

39 After the war, a top North Vietnamese general stated, "American troops poured into South Vietnam faster than we had anticipated. We had to abandon our plan for a five-pronged attack on Saigon." Vo Cong Luan and Tran Hanh, eds., *May Van De ve Tong Ket Chien Tranh va Viet Su Quan Su* (Hanoi: Military History Institute of Vietnam and Ministry of Defense, 1987), 285.

40 Pham Thi Vinh, ed., *Van Kien Dang*, Tap 24, 1965 (Hanoi: Nha Xuat Ban Chinh Tri Quoc Gia, 2003), 637. The precipitous downscaling of North Vietnam's near-term ambitions would not become clear to the rest of the world for several months, but two developments in late August provided hints. One was a shift in North Vietnamese public statements, which went

from predictions of a rapid victory to forecasts of a struggle of up to twenty-five years. Saigon to State, 26 August 1965, NA II, RG 59, Central Files, 1964–1966, box 2967. The other was a change in North Vietnam's receptivity to negotiations with the United States. On August 18, a North Vietnamese envoy told an American diplomat in Paris that the Hanoi government would negotiate an end to the war if the United States stopped bombing North Vietnam and began a phased withdrawal of troops, a sharp break from previous demands for an immediate American withdrawal. This diplomatic position was more accommodating than any the North Vietnamese had presented since the Diem era. The olive branch, however, would be snapped at the beginning of September by hardline elements in Hanoi, who overruled those favoring a more flexible negotiating stance. The North Vietnamese reverted to demands for diplomatic preconditions that were tantamount to American capitulation. Paris to State, 18 August 1965, *FRUS*, 1964–1968, 3, 122; Paris to State, 1 September 1965, *FRUS*, 1964–1968, 3, 133; Bundy to Johnson, *FRUS*, 12 September 1965, *FRUS*, 1964–1968, 3, 139; George C. Herring, *The Secret Diplomacy of the Vietnam War: The Negotiating Volumes of the Pentagon Papers* (Austin: University of Texas Press, 1983), 85.

CHAPTER 2

1 Dang Vu Hiep, *Ky Uc Tay Nguyen* (Hanoi: Nha Xuat Ban Quan Doi Nhan Dan, 2000), 45.

2 Sources on the siege of Plei Me include Vinh Loc, *Why Pleime* (Pleiku: Headquarters, II Corps, 1966), 43–69; Harry W. O. Kinnard, "A Victory in the Ia Drang: The Triumph of a Concept," *Army*, 17, No. 9 (September 1967), 73–77; William Boyle and Robert Samabria, "The Lure and the Ambush," n.d., TTU, J. D. Coleman Collection, box 4; *Time*, November 5, 1965; Chu Huy Man, *Thoi Soi Dong* (Hanoi: Nha Xuat Ban Quan Doi Nhan Dan, 2004), 424–428; Nguyen Huu An with Nguyen Tu Duong, *Chien Truong Moi* (Hanoi: Nha Xuat Ban Quan Doi Nhan Dan, 2002), 29–30; Nguyen Huy Toan and Pham Quang Dinh, *Su Doan 304*, Tap II (Hanoi: Nha Xuat Ban Quan Doi Nhan Dan, 1990), 20–25; Tran Quoc Canh, "Tran Chien Plei Me," *Da Hieu*, June 2005; Dang Vu Hiep, *Ky Uc Tay Nguyen*, 37–49; J. Keith Saliba, *Death in the Highlands: The Siege of Special Forces Camp Plei Me* (Guilford, Connecticut: Stackpole Books, 2020); Harold G. Moore and Joseph L. Galloway, *We Were Soldiers Once...And Young* (New York: Random House, 1992), 12–15; Harris, *Vietnam's High Ground*, 303–338; Military History Institute of Vietnam, *Victory in Vietnam*, 158–159.

3 Christopher C. S. Cheng, *Air Mobility: The Development of a Doctrine* (Westport, CT: Praeger, 1994), 171–189; Moore and Galloway, *We Were Soldiers Once...And Young*, 9–11, 22–25; Carland, *Combat Operations*, 54–63.

4 Moore and Galloway, *We Were Soldiers Once...And Young*, 47.

5 Melvin F. Porter, "Silver Bayonet," Project CHECO Report, 28 February 1966, TTU, Sam Johnson Vietnam Archive Collection, box 1; Kinnard, "A Victory in the Ia Drang," 77–84; Carland, *Combat Operations*, 104–111; Vinh Loc, *Why*

Pleime, 73–80; Merle L. Pribbenow, "The Fog of War: The Vietnamese View of the Ia Drang Battle," *Military Review*, 81, No. 1, (January/February 2001), 93–94; Nguyen Van Minh et al., *Luc Luong Vu Trang Nhan Dan Tay Nguyen Trong Khang Chien Chong My Cuu Nuoc* (Hanoi: Nha Xuat Ban Quan Doi Nhan Dan, 1980), Chapter 2; Dang Vu Hiep, *Ky Uc Tay Nguyen*, 49–52; Harris, *Vietnam's High Ground*, 339–364; Coleman, *Pleiku*, 82–172; Headquarters, 1st Cavalry Division, "Combat Operations After Action Report," 4 March 1966, TTU, Virtual Vietnam Archive, Item 1070422001; Moore and Galloway, *We Were Soldiers Once... And Young*, 46–50.

6   *The Joint Chiefs of Staff and the War in Vietnam*, Chapter 23, 13; Carland, *Combat Operations*, 42–43.

7   Joint Chiefs of Staff, "Effects of Accelerated Interdiction in North Vietnam," 8 August 1965, DDRS, 1985, 113; Joint Chiefs of Staff to McNamara, JCSM 652-65, 27 August 1965, FRUS, 1964–1968, 3, 130; Wheeler to McNamara, JCSM-670-65, "Air Strikes Against North Vietnam," 2 September 1965, DDRS, document number CK3100074595.

8   CIA, "Chen Yi's Press Conference," 1 October 1965, LBJL, NSF, Country File, China, box 238.

9   Goodpaster, "Meeting with General Eisenhower," 3 August 1965, FRUS, 1964–1968, 3, 104; Goodpaster, memo for the record, 20 October 1965, LBJL, NSF, Name File, President Eisenhower, box 3. On members of Congress, see *U.S. News and World Report*, December 6, 1965.

10 McNamara to Wheeler, "Air Strikes against North Vietnam," 15 September 1965, FRUS, 1964–1968, 3, 142 (quotes); Edward J. Drea, *McNamara, Clifford, and the Burdens of Vietnam, 1965-1969* (Washington, DC: Office of the Secretary of Defense Historical Office, 2011), 62–63; William C. Gibbons, *The U.S. Government and the Vietnam War: Executive and Legislative Roles and Relationships*, 4 (Princeton: Princeton University Press, 1995), 46–47; *Pentagon Papers: The Defense Department History of United States Decisionmaking on Vietnam*, Senator Gravel ed., 1 (Boston: Beacon Press, 1972), 4, 30–32.

11 For McNamara's views in the summer, see Moyar, *Triumph Forsaken*, 408, 411. For the persistence of those views into the fall, see McNamara to Johnson, 3 November 1965, FRUS, 1964–1968, 3, 189.

12 Special National Intelligence Estimate 10-11-65, "Probable Communist Reactions to a U.S. Course of Action," 22 September 1965, FRUS, 1964–1968, 3, 148. The only intelligence agency that dissented from this estimate was the State Department's Bureau of Intelligence and Research, which had proven spectacularly wrong on past Vietnam controversies like the military situation in 1963 and the enemy's intentions in mid-1965. A SNIE published in December concluded that mining of North Vietnamese ports would not cause the Communist powers to escalate. Special National Intelligence Estimate 10-12-65, "Probable Communist Reactions to a U.S. Course of Action," 10 December 1965, DDRS, document number CK3100118919.

13 Gibbons, *The U.S. Government and the Vietnam War*, 4, 77–80; Drea, *McNamara, Clifford, and the Burdens of Vietnam*, 63–64.

14 Jakarta to State, 17 August 1965, LBJL, NSF, Country File, Indonesia, box 247; Department of State, Administrative History, 1, Chapter 7, Section L, Indonesia, n.d., DDRS, 1994, 270; Jakarta to State, "The September 30 Affair," 22 October 1965, LBJL, NSF, Country File, Indonesia, box 247; Andrew Hall Wedeman, *The East Wind Subsides: Chinese Foreign Policy and the Origins of the Cultural Revolution* (Washington, DC: Washington Institute Press, 1987), 195 (first quote), 200 (second quote).

15 Green, *Indonesia*, 34–37.

16 Helen-Louise Hunter, *Sukarno and the Indonesian Coup: The Untold Story* (Westport, Connecticut: Praeger Security International, 2007), 135–140.

17 A. C. A. Dake, *In the Spirit of the Red Banteng: Indonesian Communists Between Moscow and Peking, 1959–1965* (The Hague: Mouton, 1973), 382–408; Hunter, *Sukarno and the Indonesian Coup*, 109–163; R. E. Elson, *Suharto: A Political Biography* (Cambridge: Cambridge University Press, 2001), 110–115; John Roosa, *Pretext for Mass Murder: The September 30th Movement and Suharto's Coup D'État in Indonesia* (Madison, Wisconsin: University of Wisconsin Press, 2006), 174–175.

18 Robert Shaplen, *Time Out of Hand: Revolution and Reaction in Southeast Asia* (New York: Harper & Row, 1969), 100–102; Hunter, *Sukarno and the Indonesian Coup*, 4–7.

19 Hunter, *Sukarno and the Indonesian Coup*, 3, 176; Roosa, *Pretext for Mass Murder*, 211; Elson, *Suharto*, 113–115.

20 Hunter, *Sukarno and the Indonesian Coup*, 148; Roosa, *Pretext for Mass Murder*, 220–221; Elson, *Suharto*, 100–103.

21 For earlier statements by Indonesian leaders, see Moyar, *Triumph Forsaken*, 381–382. A State Department report on Indonesia issued in June 1966 stated, "Although the U.S. had no direct part whatever in the anti-Communist takeover that began in October, unquestionably the fact that we were standing firm in Viet-Nam reinforced the courage of the anti-Communist leaders....Without our evident determination, they would have been very much less likely to have acted." Rostow to Johnson, 8 June 1966, *FRUS, 1964–1968*, 26, 210. Ambassador Marshall Green asserted that "Our efforts in Viet-Nam had a definite and favorable impact on developments in Indonesia. General Suharto could not have reacted as he did to the Sukarno-Communist coup if a serious threat from the North had existed." Rostow to Johnson, "Talk with Ambassador Marshall Green," 21 February 1967, DDRS, document number CK3100423682. A State Department history contended that "the U.S. presence in Southeast Asia enabled Indonesia's non-Communists to attack the PKI without fear of intervention by Communist China. The fact that we stood in Viet-Nam between Indonesia and China gave Indonesia's new leadership greater flexibility in responding to the PKI bid for power." Department of State, Administrative History, 1, Chapter 7, Section L, Indonesia, n.d., DDRS, 1994, 270. Those who have argued that American intervention in Vietnam had no influence on the defeat of Sukarno and the PKI cite as their most compelling source a CIA report of May 13, 1966,

which stated, "We have searched in vain for evidence that the U.S. display of determination in Vietnam directly influenced the outcome of the Indonesian crisis in any significant way. The Indonesian Army's campaign to destroy the Indonesian Communist Party (PKI) and downgrade Sukarno following the abortive coup of 1 October 1965 appears to have evolved purely from a complex and long-standing domestic political situation." As this book and its predecessor have shown, such evidence did in fact exist. Presumably the authors of this report did not have access to the relevant documentation held by other U.S. governmental offices and agencies. Often omitted is the subsequent verbiage in this report that does indicate the American stand may have played a role: "Events in Indonesia might have developed differently if the U.S. had withdrawn from Southeast Asia, leaving the way open for the spread of Chinese Communist influence.... The anti-Peking posture of the army and the students, and to a somewhat lesser extent of civilian leaders, may conceivably have been strengthened by the firm American actions in Vietnam.... It is possible—though there is no evidence for this—that U.S. determination in Vietnam did indirectly have some influence in shaping events in Indonesia. Without the U.S. intervention, most of Vietnam would presumably have been in Communist hands by 1 October 1965, and Chinese Communist power would have been extended and growing in Southeast Asia. In these circumstances, and without the barrier of U.S. force between Jakarta and Peking, it is possible that Sukarno might by that date already have accelerated his political program to the point where army leaders, with great reluctance, would have acceded to power." CIA Directorate of Intelligence, "The Indonesian Crisis and U.S. Determination in Vietnam," 13 May 1966, LBJL, NSF, Country File, Indonesia, box 248.

22 A number of commentators have contended that Vietnam did not influence the decision to resist the coup because the Indonesian military was merely fighting for its life. See, for instance, Brackman, *The Communist Collapse in Indonesia*, 192. That argument might have been persuasive had Nasution led the counterstrike, but in reality it was Suharto, who was not fighting for his life and could have sided with the conspirators had he so desired.

23 Nick Turner, email to author, 3 November 2010.

24 William Stearman, "America Lost Vietnam but Saved Southeast Asia," *Wall Street Journal*, 28 January 2019.

25 Jakarta to State, 3 October 1965, NA II, RG 59, Central Files, 1964–1966, box 2317; Jakarta to State, "The September 30 Affair," 22 October 1965, LBJL, NSF, Country File, Indonesia, box 247; Hunter, *Sukarno and the Indonesian Coup*, 30–39.

26 Jakarta to FO, 4 October 1965, UK National Archives, FO 371/180317; Blouin to McNaughton, "Situation in Indonesia," 4 October 1965, FRUS, 1964–1968, 26, 146; CIA Office of Current Intelligence, "The Upheaval in Indonesia," 6 October 1965, TTU, Ronald Frankum Jr., Collection, box 5.

27 Jakarta to State, 28 October 1965, NA II, RG 59, Central Files, 1964–1966, box 2318; Jakarta to State, 13 November 1965, NA II, RG 59, Central Files,

1964–1966, box 2318; CIA Office of Current Intelligence, "Indonesian Communist Party," 29 April 1966, CREST, document number CIA-RDP79T00826A000600010043-2; Shaplen, *Time out of Hand*, 117–127; Elson, *Suharto*, 123–126; Geoffrey B. Robinson, *The Killing Season: A History of the Indonesian Massacres, 1965–66* (Princeton: Princeton University Press, 2018); Jess Melvin, *The Army and the Indonesian Genocide: Mechanics of Mass Murder* (New York: Routledge, 2018).

28 J. A. C. Mackie, *Konfrontasi: The Indonesia-Malaysia Dispute, 1963–1966* (Kuala Lumpur: Oxford University Press, 1974), 312–315; Jakarta to State, 19 November 1965, *FRUS, 1964–1968*, 26, 177; CIA Office of Current Intelligence, "Indonesian Army Attitudes Toward Communism," 22 November 1965, *FRUS, 1964–1968*, 26, 178; Jakarta to State, 23 November 1965, DDRS, document number CK3100363543; CIA Director of Intelligence, "Leadership Prospects in Indonesia," 2 December 1965, DDRS, document number CK100390050; Jakarta to State, 3 December 1965, LBJL, NSF, Country File, Indonesia, box 248; Jakarta to State, 19 January 1966, DDRS, document number CK3100357716.

29 Jakarta to State, 9 October 1965, LBJL, NSF, Country File, Indonesia, box 247; Jakarta to State, 14 October 1965, *FRUS, 1964–1968*, 26, 155; Cooper to Bundy, "The Rice Picture," 16 October 1965, LBJL, NSF, Name File, box 2; Jakarta to State, 1 November 1965, LBJL, NSF, Country File, Indonesia, box 247; Johnson to 303 Committee, 4 November 1965, NA II, RG 59, Lot Files, Entry 5408, box 17; Jakarta to State, 4 November 1965, LBJL, NSF, Country File, Indonesia, box 247; Jakarta to State, 1 December 1965, LBJL, NSF, Country File, Indonesia, box 248; Jakarta to State, 11 December 1965, DDRS, document number CK3100357672; Jakarta to State, 12 December 1965, LBJL, NSF, Country File, Indonesia, box 248; Jakarta to State, 17 December 1965, DDRS, 1976, 83H.

30 Jakarta to State, 24 February 1966, NA II, RG 59, Central Files, 1965–1966, box 2314.

31 Jakarta to State, 12 March 1966, RG 59, Central Files, 1964–66, box 2319; Elson, *Suharto*, 135-166; Green, *Indonesia*, 97–119.

CHAPTER 3

1 Dang Vu Hiep, *Ky Uc Tay Nguyen*, 52–57; Nguyen Nam Khanh, "Chien Thang Play—me—Ia Drang (tu 19-20 den 20-11-1965): Don Phu Dau Quan My o Tay Nguyen," *Quan Doi Nhan Dan*, 13 November 2005; Headquarters, 1st Cavalry Division, "Combat Operations After Action Report: Pleiku Campaign," 4 March 1966, NA II, RG 472, USARV Command Historian, Entry UD42196, box 259; Nguyen Van Minh et al., *Luc Luong Vu Trang Nhan Dan Tay Nguyen Trong Khang Chien Chong My Cuu Nuoc*, Chapter 2.

2 Harold G. Moore and Joseph L. Galloway, *We Are Soldiers Still: A Journey Back to the Battlefields of Vietnam* (New York: Harper, 2008), 5 (quote); Moore and Galloway, *We Were Soldiers Once...And Young*, 30–39; Carland, *Combat Operations*, 113–114; Moore, After Action Report, Ia Drang Valley Operation, 9

December 1965, TTU, Operation Masher/Operation White Wing Collection, box 1.

3 Moore and Galloway, *We Were Soldiers Once...And Young,* 63.

4 Ibid., 88.

5 Pham Cong Cuu, "Trung Doan 66 Tieu Diet Tieu Doan 2 Ky Binh Bay My o Thung Lung Ia Drang (tu 14 den 17 thang 11 nam 1965)," in Military History Institute of Vietnam, *Chien Thang Plei Me: Ba Muoi Nam Sau Nhin Lai* (Hanoi: People's Army Publishing House, 1995), 99.

6 Sources on the fighting at LZ X-Ray include McCall, Command Operations After-Action Report, 4 December 1965, TTU, Operation Masher/Operation White Wing Collection, box 1; Moore, After Action Report, Ia Drang Valley Operation, 9 December 1965, TTU, Operation Masher/Operation White Wing Collection, box 1; Melvin F. Porter, "Silver Bayonet," Project CHECO Report, 28 February 1966, TTU, Sam Johnson Vietnam Archive Collection, box 1; Robert H. Edwards, "Operations of the 1st Battalion, 7th Cavalry, 1st Cavalry Division (Airmobile), In the Airmobile Assault of Landing Zone X-Ray, Ia Drang Valley, Republic of Viet Nam, 14–16 November 1965," United States Army Infantry School, 1967; John A. Cash, "Fight at Ia Drang," in John A. Cash et al., eds., *Seven Firefights in Vietnam* (Washington, DC: Government Printing Office, 1970), 3–40; Pribbenow, "The Fog of War," 94–95; Pham Cong Cuu, "Trung Doan 66 Tieu Diet Tieu Doan 2 Ky Binh Bay My o Thung Lung Ia Drang," 98–103; Nguyen Huy Toan and Pham Quang Dinh, *Su Doan 304,* Tap II, 29–35; Moore and Galloway, *We Were Soldiers Once...And Young,* 39–201; Nguyen Huu An with Nguyen Tu Duong, *Chien Truong Moi,* 32–34; Moore and Galloway, *We Are Soldiers Still,* 36–99; Harris, *Vietnam's High Ground,* 374–399.

7 Moore, After Action Report, Ia Drang Valley Operation, 9 December 1965, TTU, Operation Masher/Operation White Wing Collection, box 1. See also Headquarters, 1st Cavalry Division, "Combat Operations After Action Report: Pleiku Campaign"; McCall, Command Operations After-Action Report, 4 December 1965, TTU, Operation Masher/Operation White Wing Collection, box 1.

8 Moore and Galloway, *We Were Soldiers Once...And Young,* 308. A Soviet account written after the war provides further evidence of the presence of Chinese advisers within the North Vietnamese military at this time. Nikolay Shershnev, "No One is Forgotten; Nothing is Forgotten," *VVA Veteran,* 26, No. 4 (July/August 2006), 23–26.

9 Moore and Galloway, *We Are Soldiers Still,* 119.

10 Moore and Galloway, *We Were Soldiers Once...And Young,* 259.

11 Sources on the fighting at LZ Albany include Johnson, "After Action Report—Operation Silver Bayonet—12–21 November 1965," 24 November 1965, TTU, Operation Masher/Operation White Wing Collection, box 1; McCall, Command Operations After-Action Report, 4 December 1965, TTU, Operation Masher/Operation White Wing Collection, box 1; Headquarters, 1st Cavalry Division, "Combat Operations After Action Report: Pleiku

Campaign"; Walter B. Tully, "Company B," *Armor,* September–October 1967, 13–19; Moore and Galloway, *We Were Soldiers Once…And Young,* 207–302; Pribbenow, "The Fog of War," 95-96; Do Trung Mich, "Trung Doan 66 Phat Huy Truyen Thong va Kinh Nghiem Chien Thang Play Me trong Qua Trinh Chien Dau va Xay Dung (Bao Cao cua Trung Doan 66)," in Military History Institute of Vietnam, *Chien Thang Plei Me,* 155; Nguyen Van Minh et al., *Luc Luong Vu Trang Nhan Dan Tay Nguyen Trong Khang Chien Chong My Cuu Nuoc,* Chapter 2; Nguyen Huy Toan and Pham Quang Dinh, *Su Doan 304,* Tap II, 35–40; Le Hai Trieu, *Lich su Trung Doan 66—Doan Plei Me 1947-2007* (Hanoi: People's Army Publishing House, 2007), 39–45; Tran Doi, "Hoi Uc ve Tran Danh My Dau Tien o Tay Nguyen," in Military History Institute of Vietnam, *Chien Thang Plei Me,* 238–240; Larry Gwin, *Baptism: A Vietnam Memoir* (New York: Ivy Books, 1999), 105–159; Coleman, *Pleiku,* 228–249; Harris, *Vietnam's High Ground,* 408–424; Moore and Galloway, *We Are Soldiers Still,* 11–13, 50, 113–125.

12 Chu Huy Man, *Thoi Soi Dong,* 439. In a November letter, Le Duan stated that in the mountains and jungles, the American "superiority in weapons and technique is impaired while their vulnerable points are easily exposed." Le Duan, *Letters to the South* (Hanoi: Foreign Languages Publishing House, 1986), 64–65. Other North Vietnamese strategists objected to abandonment of the central highlands on the grounds that it would facilitate and encourage American ground operations to cut the Ho Chi Minh Trail. Chu Huy Man, *Thoi Soi Dong,* 440.

13 Dang Vu Hiep, *Ky Uc Tay Nguyen,* 86–90. For the text of a letter from a despairing North Vietnamese soldier during this period, see Vietnam Documents and Research Notes, No. 1, "Diary of an Infiltrator," October 1967, TTU, Pike Collection, Unit 2, box 4.

14 Moore and Galloway, *We Were Soldiers Once…And Young,* 266.

15 Ibid., 326–327.

16 USMACV, 1965 Command History, 20 April 1966, 170–171; Carland, *Stemming the Tide,* 76–80.

17 Brodbeck, Combat Operation After Action Report, Operation Bushmaster I, 21 December 1965, TTU, William E. LeGro Collection, box 1; William E. LeGro, "Draft of The Big Red One," n.d., William E. LeGro Collection, box 1; Starry, *Mounted Combat in Vietnam,* 60–63; Carland, *Combat Operations,* 80–84; Nguyen Viet Ta et al., *Mien Dong Nam Bo Khang Chien (1945-1975),* Tap II (Hanoi: Nha Xuat Ban Quan Doi Nhan Dan, 1993), 211–212; Hoang Cam, *Chang Duong Muoi Nghin Ngay* (Hanoi: People's Army Publishing House, 2001), 145–150, 158; "The Battle of Bau Bang- Questionnaire Sent by LeGro for Book," 12 November 1965, TTU, William E. LeGro Collection, Box 1; Tracey L. Derks, "Storm on Thunder Road," *Vietnam,* 15, No. 2 (August 2002), 26–32.

18 Hoang Cam, *Chang Duong Muoi Nghin Ngay,* 152–153.

19 Conceivably, Nguyen Chi Thanh could have received and accepted information from other sources that more accurately described the performance of Communist forces, but the available evidence does not support that interpretation.

20 Brodbeck, Combat After Action Report, Operation Bloodhound/Bushmaster II, 30 December 1965, NA II, RG 550, Command Reporting Files, 1963–1972, box 10; USMACV, 1965 Command History, 225–226; Carland, *Combat Operations*, 88–92; George M. Shuffer Jr., "Finish Them with Firepower," *Military Review*, December 1967, 11–15; Wheeler, *The Big Red One*, 424–425; Nguyen Quoc Dung, *Su Doan 9* (Hanoi: People's Army Publishing House, Hanoi, 1990), 89–91.

21 CG Task Force Delta to COMUSMACV, "After Action Report, Operation Harvest Moon," 28 December 1965, TTU, Virtual Vietnam Archive, Item 1201062030; USMACV, "Lessons Learned No 54: The Battle of Ky Phu," 27 January 1966, TTU, Bud Harton Collection, box 1; Nicholas J. Schlosser, *In Persistent Battle U.S. Marines in Operation Harvest Moon, 8 December to 20 December 1965* (Quantico: Marine Corps University, 2017); Shulimson and Johnson, *U.S. Marines in Vietnam: The Landing and the Buildup*, 101–111.

22 Truong Minh Hoach and Nguyen Minh Phung, *Quan Khu 9: 30 Nam Khang Chien, 1945–1975* (Hanoi: People's Army Publishing House, 1996), 377–378.

23 *Rand Vietnam Interviews*, ser. DT, No. 135.

24 USMACV, 1965 Command History, 262.

25 COMUSMACV to CINCPAC, 21 November 1965, LBJL, NSF, VNCF, box 24; USMACV, 1965 Command History, 44.

26 Tran Van Quang et al., *Tong Ket Cuoc Khang Chien Chong My Cuu Nuoc: Thang Loi va Bai Hoc* (Hanoi: Nha Xuat Ban Chinh Tri Quoc Gia, 1995), 196; Military History Institute of Vietnam, *Victory in Vietnam*, 170–1. The seventeen thousand figure is in Moyar, *Triumph Forsaken*, 335.

27 Dao Dinh Luyen, ed., *Tu Dien Bach Khoa Quan Su Viet Nam* (Hanoi: People's Army Publishing House, 1996); Military History Institute of Vietnam, *Victory in Vietnam*, 156–157. American intelligence recognized the number and strength of most of these units in late 1965. Westmoreland to Sharp, 9 December 1965, NA II, RG 59, Lot Files, Entry 5408, box 2.

28 Clarke, *Advice and Support*, 111–112; USMACV, 1965 Command History, 58.

29 Birtle, *U.S. Army Counterinsurgency and Contingency Operations Doctrine, 1942–1976*, 372–374; USVNR, 5, Sec IV.C.6, 24; McNamara to Johnson, 30 November 1965, FRUS, 1964–1968, 3, 212; Drea, *McNamara, Clifford, and the Burdens of Vietnam*, 118–119. McNamara reportedly sobbed while discussing the war with the wife of *Washington Post* deputy managing editor Ben Bradlee at a private party in late 1965. Bird, *The Color of Truth*, 345. McNamara disputed the idea that he had become despondently disillusioned by this time, noting that he had not been very optimistic earlier in the year. Deborah Shapley, *Promise and Power: The Life and Times of Robert McNamara* (Boston: Little, Brown and Company, 1993), 360. His account understates the extent to which his confidence had been shaken by the unanticipated rise in North Vietnamese strength but is accurate in its assertion that he had foreseen a lengthy conflict. See Moyar, *Triumph Forsaken*, 408–412. The claim that McNamara had been traumatized by late 1965 was also undercut

by McNamara's continued pursuit of gradual escalation and his cold manipulation of the Joint Chiefs.

30 JCS to McNamara, JCSM 811-65, 10 November 1965, DDRS, Document Number CK3100292141; Lewis Sorley, *Honorable Warrior: General Harold K. Johnson and the Ethics of Command* (Lawrence: University Press of Kansas, 1998), 216–218; Birtle, *U.S. Army Counterinsurgency and Contingency Operations Doctrine, 1942–1976*, 389; *Pentagon Papers*, 4, 347; Raymond G. Davis, "Politics and War: Twelve Fatal Decisions That Rendered Defeat in Vietnam," *Marine Corps Gazette*, 73, No. 8 (August 1989), 75–76; Greene, debriefing, 9 February 1966, MCHC, Greene Papers.

31 Paul Starr, *The Discarded Army: Vietnam Veterans After Vietnam* (New York, Charterhouse, 1973), 10.

32 Charles G. Cooper, "The Day It Became the Longest War," *Proceedings*, 122, No. 5 (May 1996); Christian Appy, *Patriots: The Vietnam War Remembered from All Sides* (New York: Viking, 2003), 121–123. No other record of the meeting has been found, but the meeting and its contents were confirmed after the publication of Cooper's article by both General Greene and Admiral MacDonald. Sorley, *Honorable Warrior*, 331. Although Cooper did not specify the date of the meeting, he did specify the location, month, and time of day, which together point toward November 17, when there was an empty slot in the president's daily diary at the appointed time. President's Daily Diary, 17 November 1965, LBJL. The Chiefs made similar recommendations to others during November. JCS to McNamara, JCSM 811-65, 10 November 1965, DDRS, Document Number CK3100292141; telcon, Ball and McNamara, 23 November 1965, *FRUS*, 1964-1968, 3, 206.

33 For the Chinese statements in January, May, and July 1965, see Moyar, *Triumph Forsaken*, 360–361, 500–501. For the intelligence community's position in September 1965 and the Chinese statement in October 1965, see the previous chapter.

34 Lin Piao, "Long Live the Victory of the People's War," *New China News Agency International Service*, 2 September 1965, TTU, Pike Collection, Unit 3, box 13; Robert Garson, "Lyndon B. Johnson and the China Enigma," *Journal of Contemporary History*, 32, No. 1 (January 1997), 73; Thomas Kennedy Latimer, "Hanoi's Leaders and Their South Vietnam Policies, 1954–1968" (PhD diss., Georgetown University, 1972), 227.

35 Lüthi, *The Sino-Soviet Split*, 330.

36 *American Foreign Policy: Current Documents, 1965*, 912–913.

37 Lüthi, *The Sino-Soviet Split*, 329.

38 Nguyen Viet Phuong, *Van Tai Quan Su Chien Luoc Tren Duong Ho Chi Minh Trong Khang Chien Chong My* (General Department of Rear Services, 1988), 62–64, 382; Nguyen Viet Ta et al., *Mien Dong Nam Bo Khang Chien*, Tap II, 202. Most problematic, from the point of view of the combat forces, were acute shortages of B-40 rocket launchers and 12.8mm heavy machine guns.

39 *The Joint Chiefs of Staff and the War in Vietnam,* Chapter 24, 31; JCS to McNamara, JCSM 812-65, "U.S. Policy and Actions to Deal with Cambodian Support of the Viet Cong," 12 November 1965, *FRUS, 1964–1968,* 27, 159; Westmoreland to Sharp, "Cross Border Combat Operations—Cambodia," 9 December 1965, *FRUS, 1964–1968,* 27, 165.

40 Operations into Cambodia were permitted "to defend selves while actively engaged in contact with PAVN/VC units." State to Saigon, 20 November 1965, DDRS, document number CK3100161913; *The Joint Chiefs of Staff and the War in Vietnam,* Chapter 24, 32–33.

41 Bundy to Rusk, "US/GVN Action Against VC/PAVN Forces in Cambodia," 3 December 1965, *FRUS, 1964-1968,* 27, 164.

42 CIA, "Infiltration and Logistics- South Vietnam," 28 October 1965, CREST, document number CIA-RDP82M00097R000800180009-5; CIA Directorate of Intelligence, "Cambodia and the Viet Cong," 22 December 1965, TTU, Pike Collection, Unit 1, box 4.

43 Moore and Galloway, *We Were Soldiers Once…And Young,* 315 (quote), 342. For official guidance from Washington to Saigon on this subject, see State to Saigon, 26 April 1966, LBJL, NSF, VNCF, box 30.

44 Westmoreland, History Notes, 29 August 1965, MHI, Westmoreland Papers, box 30; Bui Diem with David Chanoff, *In the Jaws of History* (Bloomington, Indiana: Indiana University Press, 1987), 156.

45 Special National Intelligence Estimate 10-10-65, "Reactions to a Certain U.S. Course of Action in Southeast Asia," 10 September 1965, *FRUS, 1964–1968,* 28, 196.

46 McNamara to Johnson, 3 November 1965, *FRUS, 1964–1968,* 3, 189.

47 Gibbons, *The U.S. Government and the Vietnam War,* 4, 106–107. McNamara and Westmoreland did agree on the use of covert ground reconnaissance in Laos. Near the end of the year, under the code name Shining Brass, they began these missions with small teams of indigenous commandos led by U.S. Special Forces sergeants from the Studies and Observations Group. Thomas L. Ahern Jr., *Undercover Armies: CIA and Surrogate Warfare in Laos, 1961–1973* (Washington, DC: Center for the Study of Intelligence, 2006), 217; Kenneth Conboy and Dale Andradé, *Spies and Commandos: How America Lost the Secret War in North Vietnam* (Lawrence: University Press of Kansas, 2000), 142–143; Richard H. Shultz Jr., *The Secret War Against Hanoi: Kennedy's and Johnson's Use of Spies, Saboteurs, and Covert Warriors in North Vietnam* (New York: HarperCollins, 1999), 50; *The Joint Chiefs of Staff and the War in Vietnam,* Chapter 24, 27. U.S. Ambassador to Laos William Sullivan also objected to the employment of U.S. ground forces in Laos during this period, contending that it was not worth the military challenges and the political problems involved. Vientiane to State, 15 December 1965, *FRUS, 1964–1968,* 28, 211.

48 Memorandum of Conversation, Secretary's Delegation to the Twentieth Session of The United Nations General Assembly, October 7, 1965, NA II, RG 59, Central Files, 1964–1966, box 2970; Memorandum of Conversation, Secretary's Dinner for Rumanian Foreign Minister Manescu, October

14, 1965, NA II, RG 59, Central Files, 1964–1966, box 2970; Bundy, "Policy Choices and Decision-Making Procedures on Vietnam," 23 October 1965, *FRUS*, 1964–1968, 3, 181; Bundy, memcon, 24 November 1965, DDRS, document number CK3100081209; János Radv ányi, *Delusion and Reality: Gambits, Hoaxes and Diplomatic One-Upmanship in Vietnam* (South Bend, Indiana: Gateway Editions, 1978), 54 (quote).

49 Drea, *McNamara, Clifford, and the Burdens of Vietnam*, 64–67; McNamara to Johnson, "Course of Action in Vietnam," 3 November 1965, *FRUS*, 1964–1968, 3, 189; Bundy, meeting notes, 11–12 November 1965, LBJL, McGeorge Bundy Papers, box 1.

50 Bundy to Johnson, "Broodings on Vietnam," 14 December 1965, *FRUS*, 1964–1968, 3, 229; Valenti, meeting notes, 21 December 1965, 1964–1968, 3, 238; Wallace M. Greene, "The Bombing Pause: Formula for Failure," *Air Force Magazine*, 59, No. 4 (April 1976), 36–39; U.S. Grant Sharp, *Strategy for Defeat: Vietnam in Retrospect* (San Rafael, California: Presidio Press, 1978), 107–108. In public, Johnson let none of his doubts about Lodge be seen. At a press conference on July 9, he announced that Lodge "had a grasp of the situation, a knowledge of the situation, that no other American had" and "was the best equipped, the best qualified, and the most experienced to do this work." *Public Papers of the Presidents*, 1965, 728–9. See also *Department of State Bulletin*, 2 August 1965, 188.

51 Meeting notes, 17 December 1965, *FRUS*, 1964–1968, 3, 231.

52 Lüthi, *The Sino-Soviet Split*, 330.

53 Luu Van Loi and Nguyen Anh Vu, *Cac Cuoc Thuong Luong Le Duc Tho-Kissinger tai Paris* (Hanoi: People's Public Security Publishing House, 2002), 98–101. The 12th Plenum of the Central Committee of the Vietnamese Communist Party, convened at the end of December, resolved that the party would not enter into peace negotiations until "the American imperialist will to commit aggression has been crushed." Pham Thi Vinh, ed., *Van Kien Dang*, Tap 24, 649. See also Nguyen, *Hanoi's War*, 78.

54 Gibbons, *The U.S. Government and the Vietnam War*, 4, 128.

55 *Washington Post*, December 6, 1965; Mueller, *War, Presidents and Public Opinion*, 85.

56 Gibbons, *The U.S. Government and the Vietnam War*, 4, 90. After a Senate committee investigated antiwar groups that were staging political protests and conducting "teach-ins" on college campuses, the committee's vice chairman, the liberal Democratic Senator Thomas J. Dodd of Connecticut, declared that the leadership ranks of these groups were dominated by Communists. Ibid., 91.

57 Taylor to Johnson, 27 December 1965, *FRUS*, 1964–1968, 3, 250.

58 Ted Gittinger, ed., *The Johnson Years: A Vietnam Roundtable* (Austin: Lyndon Baines Johnson Library, 1993), 66. In early 1966, Johnson would mislead the Congress by asking for $10 billion for the war in FY 1967 rather than for the actual projected cost of between $16 and $18 billion. He deemed the deception necessary to protect his Great Society programs and avoid tax

hikes that would be hard to sell without a presidential pep rally for the war. Shapley, *Promise and Power*, 372–375; Gibbons, *The U.S. Government and the Vietnam War*, 4, 214–219.

59 Pham Thi Vinh, ed., *Van Kien Dang*, Tap 24, 622–651.

CHAPTER 4

1 Luu van Loi and Nguyen Anh Vu, *Tiep Xuc Bi Mat Viet Nam-Hoa Ky Truoc Hoi Nghi Pa-Ri* (Hanoi: International Relations Institute, 1990), 121–137; Luu Van Loi and Nguyen Anh Vu, *Cac Cuoc Thuong Luong Le Duc Tho-Kissinger tai Paris*, 121–131. See also Radványi, *Delusion and Reality*, 125–127.

2 Moyar, *Triumph Forsaken*, 411.

3 Valenti, meeting notes, 3 January 1966, *FRUS*, 1964–1968, 4, 3.

4 Joint Chiefs of Staff to McNamara, JCSM 16-66, 8 January 1966, *FRUS*, 1964–1968, 4, 13; Drea, *McNamara, Clifford, and the Burdens of Vietnam*, 68.

5 Valenti, meeting notes, 22 January 1966, in David M. Barrett, ed., *Lyndon B. Johnson's Vietnam Papers* (College Station: Texas A&M University Press, 1997), 310–314.

6 Saigon to State, 6 January 1966, NA II, RG 59, Central Files, box 2976; Saigon to State, 13 January 1966, NA II, RG 59, Central Files, box 2978; *The Joint Chiefs of Staff and the War in Vietnam*, Chapter 30, 7–8.

7 Habib, Memcon, 15 January 1966, *FRUS*, 1964–1968, 4, 23; USMACV, 1966 Command History, 7.

8 "Meeting in Cabinet Room," 25 January 1966, DDRS, document number CK3100189606.

9 Luu Van Loi and Nguyen Anh Vu, *Cac Cuoc Thuong Luong Le Duc Tho-Kissinger tai Paris*, 132; *FRUS*, 1964–1968, 4, 55n.

10 Greene, "Summary of Conference held at White House regarding Southeast Asia," 29 January 1966, MCHC, Greene Papers; Smith, NSC meeting notes, 29 January 1966, *FRUS*, 1964–1968, 4, 55.

11 McNaughton, "Some Observations About Bombing North Vietnam," 18 January 1966, DDRS, document number CK3100260202; McNamara to Johnson, "The Military Outlook in South Vietnam," 24 January 1966, FRUS, 1964–1968, 4, 36.

12 USMACV, 1966 Command History, 48–49.

13 For the Ho Chi Minh Trail, see Nguyen Viet Phuong, *Van Tai Quan Su Chien Luoc Tren Duong Ho Chi Minh Trong Khang Chien Chong My*, 2nd ed., 64, 382. The extent of maritime infiltration is covered in the next chapter.

14 Ibid., 64. The bombing also took a toll on the infiltration of troops, though the magnitude of the damage inflicted is considerably less clear.

15 Nguyen Huu An with Nguyen Tu Duong, *Chien Truong Moi*, 52.

16 Pham Gia Duc, *Su Doan 325*, Tap II (Hanoi: People's Army Publishing House, 1986), 72–73.

17 McNamara and McNaughton, "1966 Program to Increase the Effectiveness of Military Operations and Anticipated Results Thereof," 10 February 1966,

LBJL, Warnke Papers, McNaughton Files, box 3; Cosmas, *MACV: The Joint Command in the Years of Escalation*, 257–258; *The Joint Chiefs of Staff and the War in Vietnam*, Chapter 32, 2–5. The South Korean government covered part of the shortfall as it satisfied a request from Johnson to send another division plus another regiment to South Vietnam. Seoul to State, 3 June 1966, *FRUS*, 1964–1968, 29, part 1, 81.

18 Telcon, Johnson and Rusk, 22 February 1966, *FRUS*, 1964–1968, 4, 81.

19 USMACV, 1966 Command History, 340–341.

20 McNamara and McNaughton, "1966 Program to Increase the Effectiveness of Military Operations and Anticipated Results Thereof," LBJL, Warnke Papers, McNaughton Files, box 3; *The Joint Chiefs of Staff and the War in Vietnam*, Chapter 33, 3.

21 For a detailed exposition and refutation of these interpretations of PROVN, see Andrew J. Birtle, "PROVN, Westmoreland, and the Historians: A Reappraisal," *Journal of Military History*, 72, No. 4 (October 2008), 1213–1247.

22 The PROVN report asserted that "Rural Construction can progress significantly only in conjunction with the effective neutralization of major enemy forces." It also endorsed Westmoreland's allocation of most U.S. forces to the defeat of the enemy's main force units and of most South Vietnamese forces to counterinsurgency. Office of the U.S. Army Deputy Chief of Staff for Military Operations, "A Program for the Pacification and Long Term Development of Vietnam," March 1966, https://apps.dtic.mil/dtic/tr/fulltext/ u2/377743.pdf, 5-6. Furthermore, PROVN criticized the U.S. Marines for keeping most of their forces near the coast and recommended that Marine units move inland to engage the enemy, leaving the South Vietnamese responsible for pacifying the coastal areas. Ibid., 70, 5–18.

23 Zalin Grant, *Facing the Phoenix: The CIA and the Political Defeat of the United States in Vietnam* (New York: W. W. Norton, 1991), 284; USMACV, 1966 Command History, 502–503, 507–508, 515–517.

24 State to Saigon, 19 May 1966, *FRUS*, 1964–1968, 4, 141; Leonhart to Johnson, 30 May 1966, *FRUS*, 1964–1968, 4, 149.

25 USMACV, 1966 Command History, 511–512.

26 Cosmas, *MACV*, 350. In the spring of 1966, for example, Westmoreland took no action after the South Vietnamese Joint General Staff ignored his recommendations to institute centralized and merit-based promotions. Clarke, *Advice and Support*, 153.

27 U.S. State Department, Working Paper on the Vietnam War, part II Annex, item 65, TTU, Pike Collection, unit 1, box 11.

28 Military History Institute of Vietnam, *Victory in Vietnam*, 177.

29 Pham Thi Vinh, ed., *Van Kien Dang*, Tap 24, 638; U.S. State Department, Working Paper on the Vietnam War, part II Annex, item 65, TTU, Pike Collection, unit 1, box 11.

30 Nguyen Van Minh et al., *Lich Su Khang Chien Chong My Cuu Nuoc, 1954–1975*, Tap IV, 80–81; Combat Operations Department of the General Staff, *Lich Su Cuc Tac Chien 1945–2000* (Hanoi: People's Army Publishing House, 2005),

219–221; Nguyen Viet Ta et al., *Mien Dong Nam Bo Khang Chien,* Tap II, 215–216; Military History Institute of Vietnam, *Victory in Vietnam,* 173–175.

31 USMACV, 1966 Command History, 31–45.

32 Davidson, *Vietnam at War,* 405.

33 Sharp and Westmoreland, *Report on the War in Vietnam,* 123; USMACV, 1966 Command History, 3.

34 Carland, *Combat Operations,* 165–183; USMACV, 1966 Command History, 380–381.

35 Headquarters 1st Brigade, 1st Infantry Division, Combat After Action Report, Rolling Stone, 28 March 1966, NA II, RG 550, Command Reporting Files, 1963–1972, box 9; Hoang Cam, *Chang Duong Muoi Nghin Ngay,* 163–171; Carl Bradfield, *The Blue Spaders in Vietnam* (Lakeland, Florida: Asda Publishing, 1992), 60–65; Steven Weingartner, ed., *Blue Spaders: The 26th Infantry Regiment, 1917–1967* (Wheaton, Illinois: Cantigny First Division Foundation, 1996), 129–133; Breen, *First to Fight,* 209–214; Nguyen Quoc Dung, *Su Doan 9,* 95–96. The last of these sources, the official history of the 9th Division, claimed that the American forces suffered 1,200 casualties in this battle.

36 Ponder, "Narrative of the Battle of Lo Ke," n.d., TTU, William E. LeGro Collection, box 1; "Comments of Commanding Officer of the 2nd Battalion, 28th Infantry on the Battle of Lo Ke on 5 March 1966," n.d., TTU, William E. LeGro Collection, box 1; Brodbeck, Combat Operations After Action Report, Operation Cocoa Beach, 3 April 1966, NA II, RG 550, Command Reporting Files, 1963–1972, box 10.

37 USMACV, 1966 Command History, 38, 372–374; Carland, *Combat Operations,* 185–189.

38 Nguyen Tri Huan et al., *Su Doan Sao Vang* (Hanoi: People's Army Publishing House, 1984), 58–59.

39 Moore, *We Were Soldiers Once…And Young,* 342.

40 Headquarters 1st Cavalry Division, "Combat After Action Report, Operation Masher, Operation White Wing," 28 April 1966, NA II, RG 550, Command Reporting Files, 1963–1972, box 1; Headquarters 2nd Brigade, 1st Cavalry Division, Combat After Action Report, Operation Masher, 16 March 1966, TTU, Vietnam Helicopter Pilots Association Collection, Unit Histories—1st Cavalry Division, box 1; CIA, "The Status of the North Vietnamese Divisions in Coastal II Corps," 25 November 1967, CREST, document number CIA-RDP79T00826A002900450001-5; Carland, *Combat Operations,* 202–215, 229. Some U.S. accounts make reference to the 18th NVA Regiment, which was the original unit designation of the 12th Regiment. The regiment had received a new designation when it first arrived in South Vietnam in an effort to disguise its true identity.

41 Kieu Tam Nguyen, ed., *Chien Truong Tri-Thien-Hue Trong Cuoc Chien Tranh Chong My Cuu Nuoc Toan Thang* (Hue: Thuan An Publishing House, 1985), 109–110.

42 Platt to Westmoreland, "Combat Operations After Action Report, Operation Double Eagle I and II," 15 March 1966, TTU, Virtual Vietnam Archive, Item 1201062031; Shulimson, *U.S. Marines in Vietnam: An Expanding War,* 19–36.

43 Walt, *Strange War, Strange Strategy*, 138–140. Lodge made the same point in a message to Johnson on January 12. "The entrance of the Army of North Vietnam into South Vietnam," Lodge wrote, "has transformed the nature of the war. It is in effect a new war." Saigon to State, 12 January 1966, NA II, RG 59, Central Files, box 2978.

CHAPTER 5

1 "OP UTAH," 5 March 1966, TTU, Virtual Vietnam Archive, Item 1201063062; Shulimson, *U.S. Marines in Vietnam: An Expanding War*, 109–119; Vu Anh Tai et al., *Su Doan 2, Tap I* (Da Nang: Da Nang Publishing House, 1989), 44–51; Alex Lee, *Utter's Battalion: 2/7 Marines in Vietnam, 1965–66* (New York: Ballantine Books, 2000), 241–277.

2 With respect to the A Shau camp, the history of the 325th Division noted, "the enemy could use it as a springboard from which to send out forces to attack our strategic corridor [the Ho Chi Minh Trail] and dominate and control the entire region to prevent our forces from advancing forward to operate in the province." Pham Gia Duc, *Su Doan 325, Tap II*, 71.

3 Bennie G. Adkins and Katie Lamar Jackson, *A Tiger Among Us: A Story of Valor in Vietnam's A Shau Valley* (New York: Da Capo, 2018), 96–97.

4 Kenneth Sams, "The Fall of A Shau," 18 April 1966, TTU, Pike Collection, Unit 02, box 6; After Action Report, The Battle for A Shau, 30 April 1966, TTU, Glenn Helm Collection, box 3; Thomas R. Yarborough, *A Shau Valor: American Combat Operations in the Valley of Death, 1963–1971* (Philadelphia: Casemate, 2016), 45–61; Adkins and Jackson, *A Tiger Among Us*; 1st Marine Division, "Special Interrogation Report," 1 December 1966, NA II, RG 472, 5th Special Forces Group, Records of A Detachments, box 147; Pham Gia Duc, *Su Doan 325, Tap II*, 72–73; Richard Camp, "Rescue in Death Valley," *Vietnam*, April 2012, 24–33; Shulimson, *U.S. Marines in Vietnam: An Expanding War*, 56–64; John Laurence, *The Cat From Hué: A Vietnam War Story* (New York: PublicAffairs, 2002), 360–368.

5 Sharp and Westmoreland, *Report on the War in Vietnam*, 124; Shulimson, *U.S. Marines in Vietnam: An Expanding War*, 64.

6 Westmoreland to Waters, "Operations in Laos Corridor," 2 February 1966, LBJL, Westmoreland Papers, box 35.

7 Shulimson, *U.S. Marines in Vietnam: An Expanding War*, 145. Suspecting that such action might be afoot, the North Vietnamese alerted their newly formed headquarters for Thua Thien Province and southern Quang Tri Province in April to be on the guard for "the possibility that the American imperialists might expand the war into Central and Southern Laos." The Route 9 Front was told to be prepared "to counter any enemy plots to expand the ground war into North Vietnam, especially into Military Region 4." Kieu Tam Nguyen, ed., *Chien Truong Tri-Thien-Hue Trong Cuoc Chien Tranh Chong My Cuu Nuoc Toan Thang*, 115–116.

8 *The Joint Chiefs of Staff and the War in Vietnam*, Chapter 35, 1–2. Lodge backed Westmoreland's recommendation for operations into Cambodia. Saigon to State, 21 April 1966, DDRS, document number CK2349061672.

9   Vientiane to State, 5 January 1966, *FRUS, 1964–1968*, 28, 217; Memcon, 28 June 1966, FRUS, 1964-1968, 28, 239.

10 Westmoreland, *A Soldier Reports*, 196.

11 State to Saigon, 26 April 1966, LBJL, NSF, VNCF, box 30.

12 Nguyen Cao Ky, *Buddha's Child: My Fight to Save Vietnam* (New York: St. Martin's Press, 2002), 194–197.

13 Bui Diem, *In the Jaws of History*, 166.

14 Saigon to State, 9 March 1966, DDRS, document number CK2349125666 (quotes); Smith to Johnson, 9 March 1966, DDRS, document number CK2349529304.

15 Saigon to State, 9 March 1966, NA II, RG 59, Central Files, 1964-1966, box 2936.

16 CIA to White House Situation Room, 10 March 1966, LBJL, NSF, VNCF, box 28; CIA, "Directorate Support of Prime Minister Ky's Removal of General Thi as I Corps Commander," 10 March 1966, LBJL, NSF, VNCF, box 28; Westmoreland to Wheeler, 19 March 1966, LBJL, Westmoreland Papers, box 35; Nguyen Chanh Thi, *Viet Nam: Mot Troi Tam Su* (Los Alamitos, California: Xuan Thu, 1987), 339–344.

17 George McTurnan Kahin, *Intervention: How America Became Involved in Vietnam* (New York: Alfred A. Knopf, 1986), 417.

18 Komer to Johnson, 9 March 1966, *FRUS, 1964–1968*, 4, 92.

19 USMACV, 1966 Command History, 602; Saigon to State, 12 March 1966, LBJL, NSF, VNCF, box 28; Lodge to Johnson, 16 March 1966, LBJL, NSF, VNCF, box 46.

20 CIA, "Reason for Decision to Permit General Thi to Visit Danang," 16 March 1966, LBJL, NSF, VNCF, box 28; Saigon to State, 16 March 1966, NA II RG 59, Central Files, 1964–1966, Box 2935; Saigon to State, 16 March 1966, NSF, VNCF, box 28; *The Joint Chiefs of Staff and the War in Vietnam*, Chapter 38, 3.

21 CIA Directorate of Intelligence, "Struggle Groups in I Corps," 1 April 1966, LBJL, NSF, VNCF, box 29; Charles Mohr, "Buddhist Denounces 'Rotten' Rule by Ky," *New York Times*, 16 March 1966; Neil Sheehan, "Shops in Danang Shut in Protest," *New York Times*, 14 March 1966.

22 Lodge to Johnson, 16 March 1966, LBJL, NSF, VNCF, box 46; General Westmoreland's Historical Briefing, 20 March 1966, NA II, RG 407, Westmoreland vs. CBS Litigation Collection, box 2. Le Duan said afterward, "We did not initiate or incite this uprising by the Da Nang city masses, but we knew how to exploit opposition and conflict within the enemy's ranks to widen and deepen these contradictions so that we could gather together mass forces, take over leadership, and incite the masses to struggle, in spite of the fact that we had few Party members there and that our organizations inside the city were still weak." Cao Hung et al., *Quang Nam-Da Nang: 30 Nam Chien Dau va Chien Thang, 1945-1975*, Tap II (Hanoi: People's Army Publishing House, 1988), 128. See also Le Duan, *Thu Vao Nam* (Hanoi: Su That Publishing House, 1985), 181–182.

23 Saigon to State, 27 March 1966, DDRS, document number CK3100432955; CIA, "Viet Cong Involvement in Current Political Unrest in South Vietnam: Situation Appraisal as of 9 May 1966," 10 May 1966, LBJL, NSF, VNCF, box 31.

24 CIA Directorate of Intelligence, "Struggle Groups in I Corps," 1 April 1966, LBJL, NSF, VNCF, box 29.

25 E.40 Leading Committee to Cadres in Charge of Q. E.30, V.100 and Comrades of Our Organization, 16 March 1966, TTU, Pike Collection, Unit 05, box 19.

26 Hoi Dong Bien Soan Lich Su Nam Trung Bo Khang Chien, *Nam Trung Bo Khang Chien, 1945–1975* (Hanoi: Nha Xuat Ban Chinh Tri Quoc Gia, 1995), 363–367 (quotes); Nguyen Van Minh et al., *Lich Su Khang Chien Chong My Cuu Nuoc, 1954–1975*, Tap IV, 120–121; Cao Hung et al., *Quang Nam-Da Nang*, Tap II, 126–128. Concerning Communist direction of contemporaneous disturbances in Dalat, see Nguyen Phuc Khanh et al., ed., *Chung Mot Bong Co (ve Mat Tran Dan Toc Giai Phong Mien Nam Viet Nam)* (Ho Chi Minh City: Nha Xuat Ban Chinh Tri Quoc Gia, 1993), 532–536.

27 CIA Directorate of Intelligence, "The Vulnerability of Non-Communist Groups in South Vietnam to Viet Cong Political Subversion," 27 May 1966, TTU, Central Intelligence Agency Collection, box 10. Participation in youth groups was surging at this time, with two hundred thousand South Vietnamese in youth associations, a large fraction of which were politically vocal. Many, if not most, of the youth that belonged to associations under Communist influence were unaware of the Communist influence. Van Nguyen-Marshall, "Student Activism in Time of War: Youth in the Republic of Vietnam, 1960s–1970s," *Journal of Vietnamese Studies* 10, No. 2 (Spring 2015), 51–56, 69–70; Stur, *Saigon at War*, 81–106. For a contemporary analysis of the political inclinations of educated urban youth, see David Marr, "Political Attitudes and Activities of Young Urban Intellectuals in South Viet-Nam," *Asian Survey*, 6, No. 5 (May 1966), 249–263.

28 CIA Directorate of Intelligence, "Thich Tri Quang and Buddhist Political Objectives in South Vietnam," 20 April 1966, TTU, Central Intelligence Agency Collection, box 10.

29 CIA, "Viet Cong Involvement in Current Political Unrest in South Vietnam: Situation Appraisal as of 9 May 1966," 10 May 1966, LBJL, NSF, VNCF, box 31.

30 American Embassy Saigon, "Report of our Consul in Hue," 3 April 1966, DDRS, document number CK3100429267. Maxwell Taylor contended that "Tri Quang is a clever, treacherous conspirator who, if not a Communist, shares common aims with them." The time had come, Taylor said, to recognize "that Tri Quang is a perpetual menace who will drag down any government which he cannot control for his devious purposes." Taylor, "Comments on the Present Situation in South Viet-Nam," April 4, 1966, DDRS, document number CK3100125703. Tri Quang would admit afterward that Buddhist demands for democracy in 1966 were a ruse that concealed the Buddhists' true objective: a negotiated solution with the Communists. "The

struggle for democracy," he said in 1973, "was the external appearance of the struggle. The real issue was the restoration of peace and negotiation with the NLF." Topmiller, *The Lotus Unleashed*, 56. For additional evidence of the militant Buddhists' desire to ally with the NLF, see Anne Blair, *There to the Bitter End: Ted Serong in Vietnam* (Crows Nest: Allen & Unwin, 2001), 136.

31 Saigon to State, 4 April 1966, *FRUS*, 1964–1968, 4, 110.

32 Saigon to State, 4 April 1966, LBJL, NSF, VNCF, box 46.

33 Saigon to State, 1 June 1966, NA II, RG 59, Central Files, 1964–1966, box 3000.

34 Saigon to State, 6 April 1966, DDRS, document number CK3100125720.

35 Gibbons, *The U.S. Government and the Vietnam War*, 4, 271.

36 Saigon to State, 17 March 1966, DDRS, document number CK3100125776.

37 "U.S. Keeps Silent on Saigon Crisis," *New York Times*, April 3, 1966.

38 Saigon to State, 17 March 1966, DDRS, document number CK3100125676; Saigon to State, 18 March 1966, DDRS, document number CK 3100432948; Saigon to State, 30 May 1966, DDRS, document number CK3100251766.

39 Saigon to State, 30 March 1966, NA II, RG 59, Central Files, box 2986; Gibbons, *The U.S. Government and the Vietnam War*, 4, 275; Charles Mohr, "Ky Moves Up Date for Constitution," *New York Times*, March 26, 1966.

40 Saigon to State, 29 March 1966, LBJL, NSF, VNCF, box 29.

41 Lodge to Rusk, 31 March 1966, LBJL, NSF, VNCF, box 29.

42 State to Saigon, 2 April 1966, LBJL, NSF, VNCF, box 46; Valenti, meeting notes, 2 April 1966, in Barrett, ed., *Lyndon B. Johnson's Papers*, 334.

43 Rusk to Johnson, "Basic Choices in Viet-Nam," 24 April 1966, *FRUS*, 1964–1968, 4, 126. George Kennan noted in February, "In the light of what has recently happened in Indonesia and on the Indian subcontinent, the danger of the so-called domino effect...seems to me considerably less than it was when the main decisions were taken that have led to our present involvement." He added, however, that a rapid U.S. withdrawal from Vietnam "could represent in present circumstances a disservice to our own interests, and even to world peace, greater even than might have been involved by our failure to engage ourselves in the first place." R. B. Smith, *An International History of the Vietnam War*, 3 (New York: St. Martin's Press, 1991), 185, 269. Concerning the distortion of Kennan's congressional testimony in the Vietnam War documentary produced by Ken Burns and Lynn Novick in 2017, see Mark Moyar, "A Warped Mirror," *City Journal*, 20 October 2017.

44 Charles Mohr, "3,000 Troops Lead Vietnam Protest Against Regime," *New York Times*, April 3, 1966.

45 Jerrold Schechter, *The New Face of Buddha: Buddhism and Political Power in Southeast Asia* (New York: Coward-McCann, 1967), 217.

46 Saigon to State, 4 April 1966, *FRUS*, 1964–1968, 4, 110; Westmoreland to Walt, 4 April 1966, LBJL, Westmoreland Papers, box 8.

47 CIA, "The Situation in South Vietnam," 5 April 1966, DDRS, document number CK3100189887; Clarke, *Advice and Support*, 131–132; Gibbons, *The U.S. Government and the Vietnam War*, 4, 281–282.

48 Saigon to State, 6 April 1966, DDRS, document number CK3100429275.

49 Saigon to State, 8 April 1966, NA II, RG 59, Central Files, 1964–1966, box 2935.

50 Saigon to State, 6 April 1966, DDRS, document number CK3100125717; Saigon to State, 7 April 1966, TTU, Larry Berman Collection, box 4.

51 State to Saigon, 8 April 1966, DDRS, document number CK3100125801.

52 Westmoreland to Wheeler, 13 April 1966, DDRS, document number CK3100037866.

53 "Buddhists See Cong Coalition As Possibility," *New York Herald Tribune*, 11 April 1966.

54 Topmiller, *The Lotus Unleashed*, 55.

55 Clarke, *Advice and Support*, 132.

56 USMACV, 1966 Command History, 607; Westmoreland to Wheeler, 15 April 1966, LBJL, NSF, VNCF, box 30.

57 Saigon to State, 14 April 1966, NA II, RG 59, Central Files, 1964–1966, box 2935; State to Certain Posts, 14 April 1966, *FRUS*, 1964–1968, 4, 122.

58 Lodge to Johnson, 20 April 1966, DDRS, document number CK3100235739; Blair, *There to the Bitter End*, 137.

59 Saigon to State, 21 April 1966, DDRS, document number CK3100061462. Negroponte would become the first U.S. Director of National Intelligence thirty-nine years later.

60 CIA to White House Situation Room, "Indications of Deteriorating Situation in I Corps Area," 16 April 1966, LBJL, NSF, VNCF, box 30; Saigon to State, 6 May 1966, LBJL, NSF, VNCF, box 31; Hammond, *Public Affairs: The Military and the Media, 1962–1968*, 258–259.

61 Shulimson, *U.S. Marines in Vietnam: An Expanding War*, 80–81; USMACV, 1966 Command History, 605.

62 Sharp and Westmoreland, *Report on the War in Vietnam*, 115–116; Westmoreland, *A Soldier Reports*, 167–168; Shulimson, *U.S. Marines in Vietnam: An Expanding War*, 139–145.

63 CG III MAF to CG FMFPAC, 20 March 1966, TTU, Virtual Vietnam Archive, Item 1201063064; CG FMFPAC to RUECEM/CMC, 21 March 1966, TTU, U.S. Marine Corps History Division Vietnam War Documents Collection, Folder 063; Warren Wilkins, *Grab Their Belts to Fight Them: The Viet Cong's Big-Unit War Against the U.S., 1965–1966* (Annapolis, Maryland: Naval Institute Press, 2011), 166–171; Ky Binh 2/4, "Chi Doan 2/4 TQV va Cuoc Hanh Quan Operation Texas (tu ngay 21-23 thang 3-1966 tai Quang Ngai)," in *Ky Binh*, No. 3 (May 2005), 94–96; Shulimson, *U.S. Marines in Vietnam: An Expanding War*, 120–127.

64 Birtle, *U.S. Army Counterinsurgency and Contingency Operations Doctrine, 1942–1976*, 378–381.

65 Boyd T. Bashore, "The Name of the Game is 'Search and Destroy,'" *Army*, February 1967, 56–59.

66 Headquarters 2nd Battalion, 7th Marines, Combat Operations After Action Report, Operation Hot Springs, 30 April 1966, Library of the Marine Corps,

Vietnam Command Chronologies, Archives and Special Collections; Headquarters 3rd Battalion, 7th Marines, Combat Operations After Action Report, Operation Hot Springs, 30 April 1966, Library of the Marine Corps, Vietnam Command Chronologies, Archives and Special Collections; Charles Krulak, "The Captain Draude Story," Mike 3/7 Vietnam Association, http://www.mike37.org/ms_66_01.htm.

67 USMACV, 1966 Command History, 118; Clarke, *Advice and Support,* 188–190.

68 Eric M. Bergerud, *The Dynamics of Defeat: The Vietnam War in Hau Nghia Province* (Boulder, Colorado: Westview Press, 1991), 121–125, 148–154; Gregory A. Daddis, *Westmoreland's War: Reassessing American Strategy in Vietnam* (New York: Oxford University Press, 2014), 102–105. The 1st U.S. Army Division likely would have proceeded along similar lines with the 5th ARVN Division had it not been superseded by events. In the spring, the outbreak of heavy fighting north of Saigon compelled Westmoreland to redeploy the 1st Division to the northern part of III Corps. Clarke, *Advice and Support,* 184–186.

69 Charles S. Sykes Jr., *Interim Report of Operations of the 1st Cavalry Division (Airmobile), July 1, 1965 to December 31, 1966* (Albuquerque, New Mexico: 1st Cavalry Division Association, 1967), 37–38; Carland, *Combat Operations,* 239–243.

70 Vance to Johnson, 8 April 1966, *FRUS, 1964–1968,* 4, 117. See also "The Insurrection Inside the War," *Life,* 22 April 1966, 32B.

71 Joint Chiefs of Staff to McNamara, JCSM-189-66, 26 March 1966, *FRUS, 1964–1968,* 4, 101; Taylor to Johnson, 29 March 1966, *FRUS, 1964–1968,* 4, 104; Rostow to Johnson, 21 April 1966, LBJL, NSF, Memos to the President, Walt Rostow, box 7; Tom Wicker, "Senator Russell: 'Win or Get Out,'" *New York Times,* 1 May 1966.

72 Mueller, *War, Presidents and Public Opinion,* 70–71.

73 Drea, *McNamara, Clifford, and the Burdens of Vietnam,* 71; *Pentagon Papers,* 4, 71–74 (quote).

74 Unger to Rusk, "Increased Military Pressures Against North Vietnam," 30 March 1966, LBJL, Gibbons Papers, box 15.

75 *Pentagon Papers,* 4, 79–80.

76 Khoo, *Collateral Damage,* 26–28; Radchenko, *Two Suns in the Heavens,* 160–161.

77 Radio Free Europe Research, "China's Relations with Hanoi Show Gradual Worsening, 27 July 1967, http://catalog.osaarchivum.org/catalog/osa:d0bd9f40-3bfa-4ddd-a3d3-467afd27758f, 3; Lüthi, *The Sino-Soviet Split,* 336–337; Jian, *Mao's China and the Cold War,* 232 (quote). That same month, Mao caused comparable discontent among the North Vietnamese by scuttling a plan organized by the Japanese Communist Party to create an "anti-imperialist international united front" that included both the Soviet Union and China. Yang Kuisong, "Mao Zedong and the Indochina Wars," in Priscilla Roberts, ed., *Behind the Bamboo Curtain: China, Vietnam, and the World Beyond Asia* (Stanford: Stanford University Press 2006), 82–83; Zhai, *China and the Vietnam Wars,* 154.

78 Memcon, Zhou Enlai, Deng Xiaoping, Kang Sheng and Le Duan, Nguyen Duy Trinh, 13 April, 1966, CWIHP. On the size and activities of Chinese troops in North Vietnam, see Li, *The Dragon in the Jungle.*

79 Khoo, *Collateral Damage,* 34.

CHAPTER 6

1 USMACV, 1966 Command History, 39.

2 Lawrence J. Hickey, "Operation Paul Revere/Sam Houston," Project CHECO Report, 27 July 1967, TTU, Sam Johnson Vietnam Archive Collection, box 2; Carland, *Combat Operations,* 289–303.

3 CIA Directorate of Intelligence, "The Communist Build-up in Northern South Vietnam," 22 November 1966, TTU, Larry Berman Collection, box 5.

4 Ban Chi Dao Tong Ket Chien Tranh Truc Thuoc Bo Chinh Tri, *Tong Ket Cuoc Khang Chien Chong My Cuu Nuoc,* 65.

5 Shulimson, *U.S. Marines in Vietnam: An Expanding War,* 145–147.

6 Miller, "Current Political Crisis in Viet-Nam," 19 May 1966, *FRUS,* 1964–1968, 4, 142; USMACV, 1966 Command History, 608, 614; Charles Mohr, "Questions in Vietnam," *New York Times,* 31 May 1966.

7 Schechter, *The New Face of Buddha,* 226 (quote); Associated Press, "Ky Says Military Will Retain Rule 'At Least' A Year," 7 May 1966.

8 Saigon to State, 22 May 1966, NA II RG 59, Central Files, 1964–1966, Box 2935.

9 Nguyen Cao Ky, *Twenty Years and Twenty Days: How and Why the United States Lost its First War with China and the Soviet Union* (New York: Stein and Day, 1976), 93. According to Ky, Lodge told him upon returning to Vietnam, "I'm delighted you took the decision to send in troops. If you hadn't you'd have disappointed me." Ibid., 97. No available American sources have confirmed or refuted Ky's recounting, but it is consistent with Lodge's earlier comments to Ky.

10 Walt to NMCC, 15 May 1966, LBJL, NSF, VNCF, box 32; Charles Mohr, "Seem in Control," *New York Times,* May 15, 1966; Cao Van Vien, *Leadership* (Washington, DC: U.S. Army Center of Military History, 1981), 78–80.

11 State to Saigon, 15 May 1966, *FRUS,* 1964–1968, 4, 138 (first quote); Saigon to State, 15 May 1966, NA II RG 59, Central Files, 1964–1966, Box 2935 (second quote).

12 Ky, *Twenty Years and Twenty Days,* 96. Walt made no mention of either statement in his account of the conversation. Walt to NMCC, 15 May 1966, LBJL, NSF, VNCF, box 32.

13 State to Saigon, 15 May 1966, DDRS, document number CK3100071981.

14 "Reds Back Buddhists; Pagoda Besieged," *Washington Post,* May 20, 1966; Clarke, *Advice and Support,* 138; Shulimson, *U.S. Marines in Vietnam: An Expanding War,* 87.

15 Ward Just, "Civil Crisis Grows in Vietnam," *Washington Post,* 21 May 1966; Schechter, *The New Face of Buddha,* 230. In one instance, Tri Quang claimed that American helicopter crewmen had shot two pro-Struggle soldiers dead

without cause, when in fact those soldiers had first fired at the helicopter. Saigon to State, 17 May 1966, DDRS, document number CK3100065837. Thien Minh, Tri Quang's close confidante, told a rain-soaked crowd in Saigon at the Buddhist Institute for Secular Affairs that in Da Nang "there is a plot to assassinate all Buddhists." Charles Mohr, "Buddhists Appeal for Johnson's Aid to Overrule Ky," *New York Times,* May 17, 1966. On May 20, the Struggle forces sent General Walt a letter through an American correspondent stating that more than one thousand people had been killed or wounded that day, which far exceeded the total casualties of the nine-day period in which the Da Nang street fighting occurred. USMACV, 1966 Command History, 611.

16 CIA, "The Situation in South Vietnam," 25 May 1966, TTU, Central Intelligence Agency Collection, box 10

17 Hammond, *Public Affairs: The Military and the Media, 1962–1968,* 261–262; Leonhart to Johnson, 30 May 1966, *FRUS, 1964–1968,* 4, 149. Westmoreland later commented that the crisis had been "blown out of proportion in the minds of authorities in Washington and by the American people because of press reports from a group of reporters on the scene attempting to make a name for themselves and to play a role." Gibbons, *The U.S. Government and the Vietnam War,* 4, 323.

18 Saigon to State, 1 June 1966, NA II, RG 59, Central Files, 1964–1966, box 3000. These comments may have been inspired in part by the reporting of Stanley Karnow, which included an article on Tri Quang that omitted his more outrageous accusations and demands. Stanley Karnow, "Hue Religious Chief Demands U.S. End Its Support of Ky," *Washington Post,* May 30, 1966.

19 Neil Sheehan, "Forces Loyal to Premier Ky Take Over the City Hall in Danang," *New York Times,* 17 May 1966.

20 R. W. Apple, "Buddhist Monk Proposes a Successor to Ky," *New York Times,* May 20, 1966.

21 "Blow the Whistle on Saigon," *New York Times,* 20 May 1966.

22 Wheeler to Westmoreland, 20 May 1966, LBJL, Westmoreland Papers, box 8.

23 State to Saigon, 21 May 1966, DDRS, document number CK3100065843. The Gallup results are in *The Gallup Poll: Public Opinion 1935–1971,* 3, 2007. From March to May, the percentage of Americans surveyed who said that sending U.S. troops to Vietnam had been a mistake rose from 25 to 36, while the percentage saying it was not a mistake fell from 59 to 49. Mueller, *War, Presidents and Public Opinion,* 54.

24 Reuters, "Ky's Troops Seize a Danang Pagoda," 21 May 1966; Neil Sheehan, "Ky Men Bar Negotiations," *New York Times,* 23 May 1966; Shulimson, *U.S. Marines in Vietnam: An Expanding War,* 88; Westmoreland, *A Soldier Reports,* 175.

25 CIA, "The Situation in South Vietnam," 25 May 1966, TTU, Central Intelligence Agency Collection, box 10; Saigon to State, 1 June 1966, NA II, RG 59, Central Files, 1964–1966, box 3000; USMACV, 1966 Command History, 614.

26 The American news correspondent Richard Critchfield arrived in the city to find shops reopening and citizens streaming into the streets. "If anyone was

disappointed that the Buddhist rebellion was crushed," Critchfield reported, "their happy, relieved faces showed no signs of it." Richard Critchfield, *The Long Charade: Political Subversion in the Vietnam War* (New York: Harcourt, Brace & World, 1968), 258. See also Schechter, *The New Face of Buddha,* 231–232.

27 Saigon to State, 18 May 1966, DDRS, document number CK3100065745.

28 *The Joint Chiefs of Staff and the War in Vietnam,* Chapter 38, 10; USMACV, 1966 Command History, 615.

29 Saigon to State, 27 May 1966, LBJL, NSF, VNCF, box 32; Gibbons, *The U.S. Government and the Vietnam War,* 4, 326; Kahin, *Intervention,* 429.

30 Schechter, *The New Face of Buddha,* 233–234.

31 Charles Mohr, "4 Buddhists Die As Suicides Rise in Anti-Ky Drive," *New York Times,* 30 May 1966.

32 Hammond, *Public Affairs: The Military and the Media, 1962–1968,* 260; Saigon to State, 1 June 1966, NA II, RG 59, Central Files, 1964–1966, box 3000.

33 R. W. Apple, "Nun's Fiery Death in Hue Sets Off Clash in Saigon," *New York Times,* 29 May 1966.

34 USMACV, 1966 Command History, 617; Shulimson, *U.S. Marines in Vietnam: An Expanding War,* 89–90; R. W. Apple Jr., "Ky Orders Hue Mayor to Quell Dissident Forces," *New York Times,* June 2, 1966.

35 R. W. Apple Jr., "Troops Enter Hue but Their Aims Are in Doubt," *New York Times,* 3 June 1966; R. W. Apple Jr., "Politics Thwarts War on Vietcong in Northern Area," *New York Times,* 5 June 1966.

36 Saigon to State, 7 June 1966, LBJL, NSF, VNCF, box 33; R. W. Apple Jr., "Buddhists to Urge Noncooperation," *New York Times,* 8 June 1966; Charles Mohr, "Stricter Curfew is Imposed by Ky," *New York Times,* 17 June 1966 (quote).

37 Critchfield, *The Long Charade,* 260.

38 Saigon to State, 10 June 1966, DDRS, document number CK3100541832; Associated Press, "Ky Troops Guard Tri Quang in Hue," 20 June 1966; Saigon to State, 22 June 1966, *FRUS, 1964–1968,* 4, 160; Saigon to State, 23 June 1966, RG 59, Central Files, 1964–1966, box 3001; Schechter, *The New Face of Buddha,* 241.

39 When asked in June to predict how the war would end, a mere 6 percent of Americans surveyed said the war would end in a complete defeat for the United States and South Vietnam. Seventeen percent anticipated a complete American and South Vietnamese victory, and 54 percent foresaw a compromise peace settlement. George Gallup, "Quit-Vietnam Minority Gains," *Washington Post,* 19 June 1966.

40 "Discussion of Viet Nam by Committee Chairmen or Designees," 28 June 1966, LBJL, NSF, Name File, box 6.

41 Ronald H. Spector, "The Vietnam War and the Army's Self-Image," in John Schlight, ed., *The Second Indochina War: Proceedings of a Symposium Held at Airlie, Virginia* (Washington, DC: U.S. Army Center of Military History, 1986), 169.

42 Kenneth Sams, "Operation Hawthorne," Project CHECO Report, 8 September 1966, https://apps.dtic.mil/dtic/tr/fulltext/u2/a486950.pdf.

43 USMACV, 1966 Command History, 39–40, 377; Kenneth Sams, "Operation Hawthorne," Project CHECO Report, 8 September 1966, https://apps.dtic.mil/dtic/tr/fulltext/u2/a486950.pdf; Carland, *Combat Operations*, 276–288.

44 Henry G. Gole, "Gen. William E. DePuy's Relief of Subordinates in Combat," *Army*, August 2008, 35–47 (quote); Samuel Zaffiri, *Westmoreland: A Biography of William C. Westmoreland* (New York: Morrow, 1994), 164–165.

45 Sorley, *Honorable Warrior*, 256–257.

46 Pham Vinh Phuc et al., ed., *Mot So Tran Danh Trong Khang Chien Chong Phap, Khang Chien Chong My, 1945-1975*, Tap III (Hanoi: Ministry of Defense, 1992), 167.

47 Ibid., 170.

48 Sources on El Paso II include Headquarters, 1st Infantry Division, Combat After Action Report, El Paso II/III, 8 December 1966, NA II, RG 550, Command Reporting Files, 1963–1972, box 12; Headquarters, 1st Infantry Division, "The Battle of Ap Tau O," 5 July 1967, NA II, RG 472, USARV Command Historian, Entry UD42196, box 237; William E. DePuy, "Troop A at Ap Tau O," *Army* 36, No. 11 (November 1986), 50–60; Pham Vinh Phuc et al., eds., *Mot So Tran Danh Trong Khang Chien Chong Phap, Khang Chien Chong My, 1945-1975*, Tap III, 157–171; Nguyen Quoc Dung, *Su Doan 9*, 103–107; Wheeler, *The Big Red One*, 437–438; Tracy L. Derks, "Armor Ambushed at Ap Tau O," *Vietnam*, 17, No. 3 (October 2004), 26–32.

49 Lawrence C. Vetter Jr., *Never Without Heroes: Marine Third Reconnaissance Battalion in Vietnam, 1965-70* (New York, Ivy Books, 1996), 66–75; Bruce H. Norton, ed., *Stingray* (New York: Ballantine, 2000), 98–99; Shulimson, *U.S. Marines in Vietnam: An Expanding War*, 157–158 (quote). The North Vietnamese had just completed a revision of their military regions in South Vietnam by adding the B5 Front in the northernmost section of the country, evidently in anticipation of heightened combat activity there. The B1 Front consisted of the six coastal provinces of central Vietnam; the B2 Front covered the southern half of South Vietnam; the B3 Front encompassed the central highlands; the B4 Front, also called the Tri-Thien or Tri-Thien-Hue Military Region, included Quang Tri Province south of Highway 9 and Thua Thien Province; and the B5 Front, also known as the Route 9 Front, comprised Quang Tri Province north of Highway 9. Bui Vinh Phuong, ed., *Tu Dien Bach Khoa Quan Su Viet Nam* (Hanoi: People's Army Publishing House, 2004), 239.

50 OP Jay, 24 June 1966, TTU, Marine Corps History Division Vietnam War Documents Collection, folder 063; Shulimson, *U.S. Marines in Vietnam: An Expanding War*, 150–156.

51 Smith, NSC meeting notes, 17 June 1966, *FRUS*, 1964–1968, 4, 159.

52 Jacob Van Staaveren, *Gradual Failure: The Air War Over North Vietnam, 1965-1966* (Washington, D.C.: Air Force History and Museums Program, 2002), 288–292; Sharp, *Strategy for Defeat*, 117–118; Drea, *McNamara, Clifford, and the Burdens of Vietnam*, 75–76.

53 Nguyen Chi Thanh, "On the South's Ideological Task," in Patrick J.
McGarvey, ed., *Visions of Victory: Selected Vietnamese Communist Military
Writings* (Stanford: Hoover Institution, 1969), 61–71; Latimer, "Hanoi's
Leaders and Their South Vietnam Policies," 252–266; Nguyen, *Hanoi's War,*
79.

54 Lien-Hang T. Nguyen, "The War Politburo: North Vietnam's Diplomatic and
Political Road to the Tet Offensive," *Journal of Vietnamese Studies* 1, nos. 1, 2
(February-August 2006), 22.

55 Merle Pribbenow, "General Vo Nguyen Giap and the Mysterious Evolution
of the Plan for the 1968 Tet Offensive," *Journal of Vietnamese Studies,* 3, No. 2
(summer 2008), 6.

56 Combat Operations Department of the General Staff, *Lich Su Cuc Tac Chien,*
223–225; Pribbenow, "General Vo Nguyen Giap and the Mysterious Evolution
of the Plan for the 1968 Tet Offensive," 8–9; 324th Infantry Division
Headquarters and Division Party Committee, *Lich Su Su Doan Bo Binh 324*
(Hanoi: People's Army Publishing House, Hanoi, 2005) (quotes).

57 Combat Operations Department of the General Staff, *Lich Su Cuc Tac Chien,*
224.

58 Simulmatics Corporation, "Studies of the Chieu Hoi Program: Interviews
with the Hoi Chanh," interview CH-29.

59 Speech by PAVN General Nguyen Van Vinh, July 1966, TTU, Virtual
Vietnam Archive, Item 2361108113.

CHAPTER 7

1 Ho Si Huu et al., *Lich Su Quan Chung Phong Khong,* Tap II (Hanoi: People's
Army Publishing House, Hanoi, 1993), 103–105.

2 Lewy, *America in Vietnam,* 389–406, 413, 450; Thompson, *To Hanoi and Back,*
45–47, 82–83; Clodfelter, *The Limits of Air Power,* 136–137. The estimate of fifty-
two thousand was produced by American analysts. The North Vietnamese
never released their own figures on civilian casualties.

3 Gerald Coffee, *Beyond Survival: Building on the Hard Times—A POW's
Inspiring Story* (New York: Putnam, 1990), 119.

4 James Stockdale, *A Vietnam Experience: Ten Years of Reflection* (Stanford:
Hoover Institution Press, 1984), 10.

5 Stuart I. Rochester and Frederick Kiley, *Honor Bound: American Prisoners of
War in Southeast Asia, 1961–1973* (Annapolis: Naval Institute Press, 1999), 183.

6 John G. Hubbell, *P.O.W.: A Definitive History of the American Prisoner-of-War
Experience in Vietnam, 1964–1973* (New York: Reader's Digest Press, 1976), 184.

7 Hubbell, *P.O.W.,* 186. Other sources on the Hanoi march are Rochester and
Kiley, *Honor Bound,* 188–200; Alvin Townley, *Defiant: The POWs Who Endured
Vietnam's Most Infamous Prison, the Women Who Fought for Them, and the One
Who Never Returned* (New York: Thomas Dunne, 2014), 98–109. The event
is also described in the memoirs of numerous prisoners. See, for instance,
Everett Alvarez, Jr., and Anthony S. Pitch, *Chained Eagle: The True Heroic Story
of 8-1/2 Years as a POW by the First American Shot Down Over North Vietnam*

(New York: Dutton, 1989); Robinson Risner, *The Passing of the Night: My Seven Years as a Prisoner of the North Vietnamese* (New York: Random House, 1973).

8 Jeremiah A. Denton with Ed Brandt, *When Hell Was in Session* (New York: Reader's Digest Press, 1976), 83.

9 Hubbell, *P.O.W.*, 193.

10 "Scores of U.S. Pilots Paraded, Hanoi Says," *Washington Post*, 7 July 1966.

11 *Congressional Record*, 112, 15851, 15853.

12 William Chapman, "POWs' Nightmarish Ordeal," *Washington Post*, 30 March 1973.

13 P. J. Honey, "North Vietnam and the War; Strategy and the DRV Leaders," in Wesley R. Fishel, ed., *Vietnam: Anatomy of a Conflict* (Itasca, Illinois: F. E. Peacock, 1968), 807; CIA-DIA, "An Appraisal of the Bombing Of North Vietnam Through 11 August 1966," August 1966, *FRUS, 1964–1968*, 4, 224; CIA-DIA, "An Appraisal of the Bombing of North Vietnam through 12 September 1966," *FRUS, 1964–1968*, 4, 268; Van Staaveren, *Gradual Failure*, 290–307; *The Joint Chiefs of Staff and the War in Vietnam*, Chapter 36, 5; Sharp, *Strategy for Defeat*, 118–119. A CIA report issued on November 5 observed that Rolling Thunder had compelled the enemy to divert 70,000 troops to air defense activities and another 220,000 full-time and 100,000 part-time personnel to repair and dispersal programs in North Vietnam and Laos. CIA, "The Effectiveness of the Rolling Thunder Program in North Vietnam, 1 January–30 September 1966," 5 November 1966, *FRUS, 1964–1968*, 4, 292.

14 Mueller, *War, Presidents and Public Opinion*, 70. The American public favored even greater intensification of military actions. Gallup polls taken in August and October found that 55 percent wanted the United States to increase the strength of its attacks on North Vietnam, while 18 percent wanted the country to carry on the war at present levels, and 18 percent wanted to begin withdrawing American troops. *The Gallup Poll: Public Opinion 1935–1971*, 3, 2030.

15 Louis Harris, "President's Over-All Rating of 54 Pct. Reflects Trouble Other Than Viet War," *Washington Post*, 18 July 1966.

16 Westmoreland, *A Soldier Reports*, 181–182.

17 Nguyen Viet Phuong, *Lich Su Bo Doi Truong Son Duong Ho Chi Minh* (Hanoi: People's Army Publishing House, 1994), 139; Dang Phong, *5 Duong Mon Ho Chi Minh* (Hanoi: Nha Xuat Ban Tri Thuc, 2008), 246–248. The Cambodians drove a hard bargain, charging roughly $2 per kilogram for weapons and ammunition and $1 per kilogram for other supplies. Dang Phong, *Kinh Te Mien Nam Viet Nam Thoi Ky 1955–1975* (Hanoi: Nha Xuat Ban Khoa Hoc Xa Hoi, 2004), 572.

18 *Quan Doi Nhan Dan*, 2 March 2011.

19 Moyar, *Triumph Forsaken*, 358.

20 A grand total of 4,379 tons of supplies had moved down the Ho Chi Minh Trail in 1965, of which 2,479 went to combat units in the South, the remainder being used to operate the trail and feed infiltrators. Nguyen Viet

Phuong, *Van Tai Quan Su Chien Luoc Tren Duong Ho Chi Minh Trong Khang Chien Chong My,* 2nd ed., 382.

21 Military History Institute of Vietnam, *Victory in Vietnam,* 193; Sharp and Westmoreland, *Report on the War in Vietnam,* 115; USMACV, 1966 Command History, 51–52.

22 Clarke, *Advice and Support,* 283–284; *The Joint Chiefs of Staff and the War in Vietnam,* Chapter 51, 2, 7; Sorley, *Westmoreland,* 138–139. The allocation of M-16s to American forces before South Vietnamese forces accorded with Westmoreland's policy of pitting American forces against the most formidable enemy units. South Vietnamese forces generally did not need the most advanced firearms to fight the enemy's local force and guerilla units. While better weaponry would have provided some improvement in capability, it would not have been sufficient to compensate for severe leadership deficiencies.

23 CIA Directorate of Intelligence, "The South Vietnamese Army Today," 12 December 1966, DDRS, 1999, 263.

24 Le Kinh Lich, ed., *Tran Danh Ba Muoi Nam: Ky Su Lich Su,* Tap 1 (Hanoi: People's Army Publishing House, 1995), 173. See also Nguyen Viet Phuong, *Truong Son: Duong Ho Chi Minh Huyen Thoai,* Tap II (Ho Chi Minh City: Nha Xuat Ban Tre, 2004), 15–17.

25 Ban Chi Dao Tong Ket Chien Tranh Truc Thuoc Bo Chinh Tri, *Tong Ket Cuoc Khang Chien Chong My Cuu Nuoc,* 318.

26 Saigon to State, 10 August 1968, FRUS, 1964–1968, 4, 208; Westmoreland, *A Soldier Reports,* 181–182.

27 USMACV, 1966 Command History, 40.

28 Nguyen Huu An with Nguyen Tu Duong, *Chien Truong Moi,* 54.

29 Dang Van Nhung et al., *Su Doan 7: Ky Su* (Hanoi: People's Army Publishing House, 1986), 14, 22–30.

30 *Essential Matters: A History of the Cryptographic Branch of the People's Army of Viet-Nam, 1945-1975,* translated by David W. Gaddy (Fort Meade: National Security Agency, 1994), 113–114.

31 Headquarters, 1st Infantry Division, Combat After Action Report, El Paso II/III, 8 December 1966, NA II, RG 550, Command Reporting Files, 1963–1972, box 12; James E. Parker Jr., *Last Man Out: A Personal Account of the Vietnam War* (Camden, South Carolina: John Culler & Sons, 1996), 237–261 (quotes); Nguyen Quoc Dung, *Su Doan 9,* 103–110; Hoang Cam, *Chang Duong Muoi Nghin Ngay,* 191–193; Starry, *Mounted Combat in Vietnam,* 66–72; Carland, *Combat Operations,* 319–325.

32 McNeil, *To Long Tan,* 305–375; Ho Son Dai and Nguyen Van Hung, *Lich Su Doan 5* (Hanoi: Army Publishing House, Hanoi, 1995), 90–93; Harry Smith, "No Time for Fear," *Wartime: Official Magazine of the Australian War Memorial,* issue 35 (2006).

33 Headquarters 1st Cavalry Division, "Combat After Action Report, Operation Paul Revere II," 25 January 1967, NA II, RG 550, Command Reporting Files,

1963–1972, box 1; Lawrence J. Hickey, "Operation Paul Revere/Sam Houston," Project CHECO Report, 27 July 1967, TTU, Sam Johnson Vietnam Archive Collection, box 2; Carland, *Combat Operations*, 293–303.

34 George L. MacGarrigle, *Combat Operations: Taking the Offensive, October 1966 to October 1967* (Washington, DC: U.S. Army Center of Military History, 1998), 77–79; Vietnam Documents and Research Notes, No. 2, "Resolution Adopted During the Regular Conference of An Thai Committee," 16 March 1967, TTU, Pike Collection, Unit 02, box 9 (quote).

35 Alfred M. Gray Jr., foreword to Otto J. Lehrack, *Road of 10,000 Pains: The Destruction of the 2nd NVA Division by the U.S. Marines, 1967* (Minneapolis: Zenith, 2010), xi–xii; Shulimson, *U.S. Marines in Vietnam: An Expanding War*, 213–220; Pham Van Chung et al., eds., *Hai Muoi Mot Nam Chien Tran Cua Binh Chung Thuy Quan Luc Chien Viet Nam (1954–1975)*, Tap II (Santa Ana, CA: Tong Hoi TQLC/VN tai Hoa Ky, 2005), 110–117 (quote).

36 Vu Anh Tai et al., *Su Doan 2*, Tap I, 54.

37 CIA, Directorate of Intelligence, "The Communist Build-up in Northern South Vietnam," 22 November 1966, TTU, Larry Berman Collection, box 5; USMACV, 1966 Command History, 21–22, 25; Shulimson, *U.S. Marines in Vietnam: An Expanding War*, 160; *The Joint Chiefs of Staff and the War in Vietnam*, Chapter 33, 8–9; Willard Pearson, *The War in the Northern Provinces, 1966–1968* (Washington, DC: Department of the Army, 1991), 9.

38 *The Joint Chiefs of Staff and the War in Vietnam*, Chapter 35, 12–15.

39 Shulimson, *U.S. Marines in Vietnam: An Expanding War*, 166.

40 Headquarters, Task Force Delta, After Action Report Operation Hastings, 17 September 1966, TTU, Virtual Vietnam Archive, Item 1201062033; "Operation Hastings/Operation Lam Son 289," n.d. TTU, Virtual Vietnam Archive, Item 1201064001; Jack Butts, "Operation Hastings," *Leatherneck*, 49, No. 10 (October 1966), 52–54; Shulimson, *U.S. Marines in Vietnam: An Expanding War*, 161–176; Robert Shaplen, *The Road From War: Vietnam 1965–1970* (New York: Harper & Row, 1970), 102–111.

41 Shulimson, *U.S. Marines in Vietnam: An Expanding War*, 177–195; CIA, Directorate of Intelligence, "The Communist Build-up in Northern South Vietnam," 22 November 1966, TTU, Larry Berman Collection, box 5; USMACV, 1966 Command History, 368.

42 Saigon to State, 26 July 1966, LBJL, NSF, VNCF, box 34.

43 Thomas L. Ahern Jr., *CIA and the Generals: Covert Support to Military Government in South Vietnam* (Center for the Study of Intelligence, 1998), 45.

44 Allen to Helms, "Comments on Vietnamese Election Results," 14 September 1966, *FRUS, 1964–1968*, 4, 230; Charles Mohr, "Turnout is Heavy in South Vietnam Despite Vietcong," *New York Times*, September 12, 1966.

45 Ward Just, "Saigon Scores Over Reds as 75% Vote," *Washington Post*, September 12, 1966; Critchfield, *The Long Charade*, 307–309; National Intelligence Estimate 53-66, "Problems of Political Development in South Vietnam Over the Next Year or So," 15 December 1966, *FRUS, 1964–1968*, 4, 343.

46 Bui Diem, *In the Jaws of History*, 170.

47 Saigon to State, 14 September 1966, NA II, RG 59, Central Files, 1964–1966, box 3008.

48 National Intelligence Estimate 53-66, "Problems of Political Development in South Vietnam Over the Next Year or So," 15 December 1966, *FRUS*, 1964–1968, 4, 343; Ky, *Buddha's Child*, 229-234.

49 Ton That Thien, "In Love and War," in Fishel, ed., *Vietnam: Anatomy of a Conflict*, 677–678; Uwe Siemon-Netto, *Triumph of the Absurd: A Reporter's Love for the Abandoned People of Vietnam*, 3rd ed. (Corona, California: NRP Books, 2015), 150–151; Nguyen Cong Luan, *Nationalists in the Viet Nam Wars: Memoirs of a Victim Turned Soldier* (Bloomington: Indiana University Press, 2012), 298–299, 358–360; Philippa Schuyler, *Good Men Die* (New York: Twin Circle Publishing, 1969), 162–174; Marr, "Political Attitudes and Activities of Young Urban Intellectuals in South Viet-Nam," 256–258; Bradley, *Vietnam At War*, 119–123.

50 USMACV, 1966 Command History, 641.

51 Stur, *Saigon at War*, 48.

52 Saigon to State, 18 August 1966, DDRS, document number CK3100065779; National Intelligence Estimate 53-66, "Problems of Political Development in South Vietnam Over the Next Year or So," 15 December 1966, *FRUS*, 1964–1968, 4, 343; McNamara to Johnson, "Actions Recommended for Vietnam," 14 October 1966, *FRUS*, 1964–1968, 4, 268; USMACV, 1966 Command History, 19 April 1967, NA II, 464; Cao Van Vien, *Leadership*, 119–122; Dong Van Khuyen, *The RVNAF* (Washington, DC: U.S. Army Center of Military History, 1980), 347–361.

53 Bui Diem, *In the Jaws of History*, 154.

CHAPTER 8

1 McNamara to Johnson, "Actions Recommended for Vietnam," 14 October 1966, *FRUS*, 1964–1968, 4, 268. After listening to conflicting claims from intelligence analysts, McNamara concluded that enemy recruiting in South Vietnam appeared to be much higher than the 42,000 that MACV had estimated, perhaps as high as 96,000. The estimate of 96,000 recruits was derived not from hard intelligence but from a formula that included other estimates, which were themselves of questionable accuracy. One such estimate was the enemy's annual personnel losses, which had been put at 116,000 based upon casualty reports and assumptions about unrecorded enemy losses. By adding the estimated change in enemy strength of 36,000 to the enemy's estimated casualties and subtracting estimated enemy infiltration of 56,000, enemy recruiting in South Vietnam came to 96,000 men. McNamara to Johnson, "Recommended FY67 Southeast Asia Supplemental Appropriation," 17 November 1966, LBJL, Warnke Papers, McNaughton Files, box 3. Later U.S. estimates put infiltration and recruitment for the year as nearly equal, with 80,000 recruited or conscripted and 79,600 infiltrated during 1966. Based upon these revisions, enemy losses for the year were estimated at 92,000. OASD/ISA, "North Vietnamese Infiltration into South

Vietnam," 17 March 1967, LBJL, NSF, VNCF, box 42; Roche to Rostow, 16 March 1967, LBJL, NSF, Name File, box 7; Westmoreland to Sullivan, 1 March 1967, LBJL, Gibbons Papers, box 25. The estimated change in enemy strength of 36,000, derived from estimates of the enemy's current forces, appears to have been too modest; later analysis concluded that North Vietnamese strength grew from approximately 237,000 in January 1966 to 290,000 in December 1966. Combined Intelligence Center Vietnam, Order of Battle Summary, September 1972, 2, Records of the Military Assistance Command Vietnam, Part 2, Classified Studies from the Combined Intelligence Center Vietnam, 1965–1973, reel 18. The limited evidence published later by the Vietnamese Communists suggests that local recruitment was considerably lower than infiltration and that it declined over the course of 1966 as the result of diminishing Communist control of the population. For instance, during 1966, the number of North Vietnamese infiltrators exceeded the number of new local recruits in the Communist forces in the B2 region for the first time as 9,809 infiltrated into the B2 area while only 6,351 were recruited locally. Communist recruiters had been able to recruit 14,918 in the same area during the previous year. General Department of Rear Services, *Tong Ket Cong Tac Hau Can Chien Truong Nam Bo-Cuc Nam Trung Bo Trong Khang Chien Chong My,* (Hanoi: General Department of Rear Services, 1986), 546. A captured report for Viet Cong Military Region IV stated that the recruitment goal for the region in 1966 was 5,000 men but only 600 had been recruited. CIA Directorate of Intelligence, "Viet Cong Manpower Problems," March 1967, NA II, RG 407, Westmoreland vs. CBS Litigation Collection, box 10.

2 Telcon, McNamara and Johnson, 19 September 1966, *FRUS, 1964–1968,* 4, 240. For additional details on McNamara's rationale for the ceiling, see McNamara to Johnson, "Recommended FY67 Southeast Asia Supplemental Appropriation," 17 November 1966, LBJL, Warnke Papers, McNaughton Files, box 3.

3 Gibbons, *The U.S. Government and the Vietnam War,* 456–457.

4 *Pentagon Papers,* 4, 120–123; McNamara to Starbird, "Infiltration Interdiction System for Vietnam," 15 September 1966, *FRUS, 1964–1968,* 4, 233.

5 McNamara to Johnson, "Actions Recommended for Vietnam," 14 October 1966, *FRUS, 1964–1968,* 4, 268.

6 In February 1966, Johnson put Deputy Ambassador William J. Porter in charge of coordinating all U.S. support to rural construction within South Vietnam. Previously, Ambassador Lodge had given the mission of fixing pacification to Edward Lansdale, who had sought to push a variety of crucial measures, foremost among them bringing back the South Vietnamese officials who had been purged for their loyalty to Diem. But Westmoreland and Philip Habib, the State Department's chief political officer and a Lodge favorite, disliked Lansdale's freewheeling ways and prevented Lansdale from wielding authority or influence over the American organizations involved in pacification. Grant, *Facing the Phoenix,* 264–266; Rufus Phillips, *Why Vietnam Matters: An Eyewitness Account of Lessons Not Learned* (Annapolis, Maryland:

Naval Institute Press, 2008), 249–269; Critchfield, *The Long Charade,* 166–170; Gibbons, *The U.S. Government and the Vietnam War,* 4, 182–185.

7   Komer to Johnson, "Second Komer Trip to Vietnam, 23–29 June 1966," 1 July 1966, LBJL, NSF, Files of Robert W. Komer, box 2; Komer, "Giving a New Thrust to Pacification," 7 August 1966, LBJL, NSF, Files of Robert W. Komer, box 7; Komer to McNamara, 29 September 1966, NA II, RG 59, Central Files, 1964–1966, box 3009.

8   R. W. Komer, "Organization and Management of the 'New Model' Pacification Program, 1966–1969," Rand Corporation, 7 May 1970, 20; Mark Moyar, *Phoenix and the Birds of Prey: The CIA's Secret Campaign to Destroy the Viet Cong* (Annapolis, Maryland: Naval Institute Press, 1997), 48–49.

9   One contemporary described Komer as "wily, ambitious, slippery, two-faced" and a "dangerous and devastating bureaucratic adversary." Phillip B. Davidson, *Secrets of the Vietnam War* (Novato, California: Presidio Press, 1990), 7.

10 Unger to Rusk, "Ambassador Porter's Views on Secretary McNamara's Proposal to Place the Viet-Nam Pacification/RD Program Under COMUSMACV," 2 October 1966, DDRS, document number CK3100261161; Gibbons, *The U.S. Government and the Vietnam War,* 4, 470–471.

11 Thomas W. Scoville, *Reorganizing for Pacification Support* (Washington, DC: U.S. Army Center of Military History, 1982), 39–41; Hunt, *Pacification,* 82–83; State to Saigon, 12 November 1966, NA II, RG 59, Central Files, 1964–1966, box 3013 (quote).

12 "General Westmoreland's Historical Briefing," 17 October 1966, LBJL, Westmoreland Papers, box 9.

13 Phillip B. Davidson, *Vietnam At War: The History, 1945–1975* (Novato: Presidio Press, 1988), 392; McNaughton to McNamara, 26 October 1966, *FRUS,* 1964–1968, 4, 284; *The Joint Chiefs of Staff and the War in Vietnam,* Chapter 35, 28.

14 *Pentagon Papers,* 4, 136; CIA, "The Effectiveness of the Rolling Thunder Program in North Vietnam, 1 January–30 September 1966," 5 November 1966, *FRUS,* 1964–1968, 4, 292; Sharp, *Strategy for Defeat,* 122.

15 *The Joint Chiefs of Staff and the War in Vietnam,* Chapter 36, 11.

16 Marshall L. Michel III, *Clashes: Air Combat Over North Vietnam, 1965–1972* (Annapolis, Maryland: Naval Institute Press, 1997), 58–73; Chau Minh Vung et al., *Lich Su Su Doan Khong Quan 371* (Hanoi: People's Army Publishing House, 1997), 70.

17 Merle Pribbenow, "North Korean Pilots in the Skies over Vietnam," 1 December 2011, Woodrow Wilson Center, http://www.wilsoncenter.org/publication/nkidp-e-dossier-no-2-north-korean-pilots-the-skies-over-vietnam.

18 Associated Press, "North Korea: Pilots Fought in Vietnam War," July 7, 2001.

19 The history of the North Vietnamese Air Defense Service lamented that "We still had great difficulty in engaging low-flying, maneuvering aircraft, especially in detecting enemy targets and locking on and tracking low-flying

targets with our surface-to-air missiles. Many times our forces were taken by surprise and missed their opportunities. In many cases, our missiles crashed to earth, causing considerable casualties and property losses among the civilian population." Ho Si Huu et al., *Lich Su Quan Chung Phong Khong,* Tap II, 104.

20 William W. Momyer, *Air Power in Three Wars* (Washington, DC: Government Printing Office, 1978), 136–137; Van Staaveren, *Gradual Failure,* 267–272; Michel, *Clashes,* 32–38; Ho Si Huu et al., *Lich Su Quan Chung Phong Khong,* Tap II, 103–105; Le Nguyen Ba, *Lich Su Su Doan Phong Kong Ha Noi [Luu Hanh Noi Bo],* (Hanoi: Railways and Roadways Traffic University Printing Press, 1985), 55–100.

21 Wheeler to McNamara, "Military Actions against North Vietnam," 8 November 1966, *FRUS,* 1964–1968, 4, 295; Drea, *McNamara, Clifford, and the Burdens of Vietnam,* 78–79.

22 McNamara to Johnson, "JCS Recommendations for Military Actions Against North Vietnam," 9 November 1966, *FRUS,* 1964–1968, 4, 299.

23 Telcon, Johnson, and McNamara, 9 November 1968, *FRUS,* 1964–1968, 4, 298.

24 Harriman, "Personal: Absolutely No One to See," 26 November 1966, in Barrett, ed., *Lyndon B. Johnson's Vietnam Papers,* 375.

25 Headquarters, 1st Cavalry Division, Combat After Action Report, Binh Dinh Pacification Campaign, 13 January 1967, NA II, RG 550, Command Reporting Files, 1963–1972, box 1; Marshall, *The Fields of Bamboo,* 2–4 (quote).

26 USMACV, 1966 Command History, 756–759; Hammond, *Public Affairs: The Military and the Media, 1962–1968,* 266–270. A British journalist from *The Economist* reported in June 1967: "The testimony of most correspondents who have flown on American air strikes is that the pilots take immense pains to pin-point their targets and in particular to avoid hitting civilians. When one is sitting in a slow-moving Forward Air Control reconnaissance plane awaiting 'ground clearance' from a local Vietnamese official—nervously asking the pilot as he circles the Vietcong target what the hell he's hanging around for—one cannot suppress the thought that the vast battalion of well-meaning clergymen, university dons and theatrical luminaries who are falling over themselves to sign full-page denunciations of American 'atrocities' may be, to put it mildly, somewhat misinformed." *The Economist,* June 1967, in Fishel, ed., *Vietnam: Anatomy of a Conflict,* 647.

27 Lewy, *America in Vietnam,* 450–453.

28 Sources on Operation Irving include Headquarters, 1st Cavalry Division, Combat After Action Report, Binh Dinh Pacification Campaign, 13 January 1967, NA II, RG 550, Command Reporting Files, 1963–1972, box 1; Marshall, *The Fields of Bamboo,* 170–215 (quotes); John H. Hay Jr., *Tactical and Materiel Innovations* (Washington, DC: Department of the Army, 1974), 24–41; James T. Root Jr., "1st Battalion, 12th Cavalry in the Battle of Hoa Hoi," *Vietnam,* August 1994; Hymoff, *First Air Cavalry Division in Vietnam,* 114–118; Carland, *Combat Operations,* 262–274.

29 MacGarrigle, *Combat Operations,* 83–87; USMACV, 1966 Command History, 40–41. When two battalions of the 3rd North Vietnamese Army Division

launched an attack in Binh Dinh near the end of the year, each soldier had to march to the battlefield with only a single handful of cooked rice. The troops were told that they would have to collect bananas and other food themselves on the way back. So famished were they before the operation had even begun that when they arrived at their attack positions, the commanders permitted them to search rice fields that had been burned by their adversaries in order to extract whatever grains of rice could be found by sifting through the charred stalks. Nguyen Tri Huan et al., *Su Doan Sao Vang*, 90.

30 Lewy, *America in Vietnam*, 59.

31 Headquarters 4th Infantry Division, "Combat After Action Report, Operation Paul Revere IV," 28 January 1967, TTU, 35th Infantry Regiment Association Collection, box 4.

32 Ibid.; MacGarrigle, *Combat Operations*, 66–76.

33 Nguyen Van Minh et al., *Luc Luong Vu Trang Nhan Dan Tay Nguyen Trong Khang Chien Chong My Cuu Nuoc*, Chapter 3. The history of the 325th North Vietnamese Army Division conceded that "the troop strengths of our units were greatly reduced." Pham Gia Duc, *Su Doan 325*, Tap II, 74–75.

34 Military History Institute of Vietnam, *Victory in Vietnam*, 196.

35 Nguyen Quoc Dung, *Su Doan 9*, 116.

36 Headquarters 25th Infantry Division, Combat Operations After Action Report, Operation Attleboro, 28 April 1967, NA II, RG 472, USARV Command Historian, Entry UD42196, box 237; Headquarters 2nd Brigade, 25th Infantry Division, Combat After Action Report, Attleboro, 1966, TTU, Virtual Vietnam Archive, Item 168300010089; Ho Son Dai and Nguyen Van Hung, *Lich Su Doan 5*, 94–99; MacGarrigle, *Combat Operations*, 31–59; Zaffiri, *Westmoreland*, 225–226; Nguyen Quoc Dung, *Su Doan 9*, 114–117; Nguyen Viet Ta et al., *Mien Dong Nam Bo Khang Chien*, Tap II, 253–260.

37 *The Joint Chiefs of Staff and the War in Vietnam*, Chapter 35, 18–19.

38 CIA, Directorate of Intelligence, "The Communist Build-up in Northern South Vietnam," 22 November 1966, TTU, Larry Berman Collection, box 5; Shulimson, *U.S. Marines in Vietnam: An Expanding War*, 197–198.

39 Westmoreland, *A Soldier Reports*, 199.

40 Shulimson, *U.S. Marines in Vietnam: An Expanding War*, 195–196; Westmoreland, *A Soldier Reports*, 198 (quote).

41 Military Assistance Command Vietnam and Joint General Staff Republic of Vietnam Armed Forces, "Combined Campaign Plan 1967," 7 November 1966, TTU, Larry Berman Collection, box 5; Clarke, *Advice and Support*, 179–180; Birtle, *U.S. Army Counterinsurgency and Contingency Operations Doctrine, 1942–1976*, 390. To help goad South Vietnamese commanders into action, Westmoreland instructed U.S. advisers to stress that in pacification, "the destruction of guerrillas and the VC infrastructure is more important in disrupting the enemy's overall efforts than is destruction of main force units." USMACV, 1966 Command History, 553.

42 Westmoreland to Wheeler, 12 December 1966, *FRUS*, 1964–1968, 4, 339. Although political purging subsided after the 1966 Buddhist crisis, it reared its head again in November with the removal of Lieutenant General Dang

Van Quang as IV Corps commander. Ky removed the general primarily because of rumors that he had been plotting a coup, though Ky told the Americans that corruption was the cause of the dismissal. The U.S. embassy had been pushing for Quang's removal on grounds of corruption, but Westmoreland was sorry to see him go because his leadership had made the South Vietnamese forces in the Mekong Delta more effective than those elsewhere. To the relief of Ky and the Americans, Quang did not resist or seek to foment a coup as General Thi had done in I Corps during the spring. Clarke, *Advice and Support,* 192–193.

43 The few South Vietnamese Army divisions that performed well in independent operations, like the 7th and 9th, owed their successes to strong commanders. The 5th and 25th South Vietnamese divisions showed improvement because they were partnered with American divisions, whose officers provided the technical and motivational skills that the South Vietnamese officers lacked. Because the South Vietnamese leadership was already stretched thin, Westmoreland rejected recommendations to expand the South Vietnamese Army during 1966. CIA Directorate of Intelligence, "The South Vietnamese Army Today," 12 December 1966, DDRS, 1999, 263; Sharp and Westmoreland, *Report on the War in Vietnam,* 119–120; USMACV, 1966 Command History, 469–473.

44 National Intelligence Estimate 53–66, "Problems of Political Development in South Vietnam Over the Next Year or So," 15 December 1966, *FRUS, 1964–1968,* 4, 343. The leadership of many militia units and RD Cadre teams remained unsatisfactory. USMACV, 1966 Command History, 118, 460–463; McNamara to Johnson, "Recommended FY67 Southeast Asia Supplemental Appropriation," 17 November 1966, LBJL, Warnke Papers, McNaughton Files, box 3.

45 CIA Directorate of Intelligence, "Viet Cong Manpower Problems," March 1967, NA II, RG 407, Westmoreland vs. CBS Litigation Collection, box 10; Birtle, *U.S. Army Counterinsurgency and Contingency Operations Doctrine, 1942–1976,* 394–397; Hunt, *Pacification,* 40–41, 45–47. According to U.S. statistics, the total number of refugees and evacuees reached 980,000, up from a total of 510,000 for the previous two years. Louis A. Wiesner, *Victims and Survivors: Displaced Persons and Other War Victims in Viet-Nam, 1954–1975* (New York: Greenwood Press, 1988), 346. The number of new refugees and evacuees is uncertain because it is not known how many of those 510,000 returned to their homes during 1966.

46 *Rand Vietnam Interviews,* ser. AG, No. 545.

47 *Rand Vietnam Interviews,* ser. AG, No. 509.

48 *Rand Vietnam Interviews,* ser. AG, No. 573.

49 Memcon, Zhou Enlai, Chen Yi, Pham Van Dong, and Vo Nguyen Giap, 12 April 1967, CWIHP.

50 Wedeman, *East Wind Subsides,* 209–268; Jung Chang and Jon Halliday, *Mao: The Unknown Story* (New York: Alfred A. Knopf, 2005), 495–513; Taylor, *China and Southeast Asia,* 51–59; Tang Tsou, *The Cultural Revolution and Post-Mao*

Reforms: A Historical Perspective (Chicago: University of Chicago Press, 1986), 52–60.

51 Roderick MacFarquhar and Michael Schoenhals, *Mao's Last Revolution* (Cambridge: Belknap, 2006), 86–131; Alexander V. Pantsov with Steven I. Levine, *Mao: The Real Story* (New York: Simon & Schuster, 2012), 507–530; Ji Chaozhu, *The Man on Mao's Right: From Harvard Yard to Tiananmen Square, My Life Inside China's Foreign Ministry* (New York: Random House, 2008), 221–237; Chin Peng, *My Side of History* (Singapore: Media Masters, 2003), 444–446. Concerning the total number of deaths, see Song Yongyi, "Chronology of Mass Killings during the Chinese Cultural Revolution (1966–1976)," *SciencesPo,* August 25, 2011.

52 Chen Jian, *Mao's China and the Cold War,* 230.

53 Xiaoming Zhang, "China's Involvement in Laos During the Vietnam War, 1963–1975," *Journal of Military History,* 66, Issue 4 (October 2002), 1165.

54 Hoang Van Hoan, "Distortion of Facts About Militant Friendship Between Viet Nam and China is Impermissible," *Beijing Review,* 22, No. 49 (7 December 1979), 18; Gaiduk, *The Soviet Union and the Vietnam War,* 79; Zhai, *China and the Vietnam Wars,* 170.

55 Anatoly Dobrynin, *In Confidence: Moscow's Ambassador to America's Six Cold War Presidents* (New York: Times Books, 1995), 149–150; Zubok, *A Failed Empire,* 199.

56 Phung Duc Thang et al., *Ho Chi Minh: Bien Nien Tieu Su,* Tap IX (Hanoi: Nha Xuat Ban Chinh Tri Quoc Gia, 1996), 486. Nguyen Khac Huynh, a North Vietnamese diplomat who was extensively involved in the negotiations between Hanoi and the United States, said that the North Vietnamese did not seriously consider negotiations in the period 1965–1967 because they thought that "what happened on the battlefield would be the decisive determinant of what would happen at the negotiating table" and during this period they thought they could win militarily. McNamara et al., *Argument Without End,* 259. See also Ibid., 245.

57 Herring, ed., *The Secret Diplomacy of the Vietnam War,* 211–274.

58 James G. Hershberg, "Who Murdered 'Marigold': New Evidence on the Mysterious Failure of Poland's Secret Initiative to Start U.S.-North Vietnamese Peace Talks, 1966," Cold War International History Project, Working Paper No. 27 (Washington, DC: Woodrow Wilson International Center for Scholars, 2000), 50.

59 Hershberg, *Marigold,* 386.

60 State to Warsaw, 23 December 1966, *FRUS,* 1964–1968, 4, 349; Warsaw to State, 24 December 1966, *FRUS,* 1964–1968, 4, 351.

61 Sharp to Wheeler, 24 December 1966, *FRUS,* 1964–1968, 4, 350.

CHAPTER 9

1 Mai Van Bo, *Hanoi-Paris: Hoi Ky Ngoai Giao* (Ho Chi Minh City: Cultural Publishing House, 1993), 86. Mai Van Bo later divulged that the North

Vietnamese leadership wanted to demonstrate an interest in negotiations merely to enhance its military position, not to reach a diplomatic resolution, for "conditions were not yet ripe for negotiations that would be favorable to us." Ibid., 85. A *New York Times* report provided a slightly different translation, stating that Mai Van Bo said, "if the United States comes to halting the bombardment definitively and without conditions, this fact will be examined and studied by the [Hanoi] government." Richard E. Mooney, "Hanoi Envoy Hints End to Bombings Could Spur Talks," *New York Times,* 6 January 1967. Later in the month, Pham Van Dong told a Soviet diplomat that Hanoi was in reality uninterested in diplomacy at the present time as it was focused on military activities that could be used to gain diplomatic advantage: "It is the military struggle which we consider the main at the present time, and the diplomatic struggle must support the military and political ones." Gaiduk, *The Soviet Union and the Vietnam War,* 100. At the 13th Plenum of the Communist Party Central Committee in late January, Party leaders observed that negotiations were not intended to end the conflict right away but to pave the way for a diplomatic settlement once Communist forces had won decisively on the battlefield. Tran Tinh, ed., *Van Kien Dang,* Tap 28, 1967 (Hanoi: Nha Xuat Ban Chinh Tri Quoc Gia, 2003), 174–177; High-Level Military Institute, *Vietnam: The Anti-U.S. Resistance War for National Salvation, 1954–1975, Military Events* (Arlington, Virginia: Foreign Broadcast Information Service, 1982), 93.

2 Karl E. Meyer, "Criticism of U.S. Bombing Mounts in Britain," *Washington Post,* 3 January 1967; Hammond, *Public Affairs: The Military and the Media, 1962–1968,* 276–277.

3 Thompson, *To Hanoi and Back,* 45–47.

4 Phil G. Goulding, *Confirm or Deny: Informing the People on National Security* (New York: Harper & Row, 1970), 52–92; Hammond, *Public Affairs: The Military and the Media, 1962–1968,* 278–279; William V. Kennedy, *The Military and the Media: Why the Press Cannot be Trusted to Cover a War* (Westport, Connecticut: Praeger, 1993), 87–88.

5 Harrison Salisbury, "Hanoi Reiterates Its Stand that Four Points Are Basic," *New York Times,* 8 January 1967; Harrison Salisbury, *Behind the Lines—Hanoi* (New York: Harper & Row, 1967), 192–205; Luu van Loi and Nguyen Anh Vu, *Tiep Xuc Bi Mat Viet Nam-Hoa Ky Truoc Hoi Nghi Pa-Ri,* 167–184. For Salisbury's private messaging on the meeting, see John Colvin, *Twice Around the World: Some Memoirs of Diplomatic Life in North Vietnam and Outer Mongolia* (London: Leo Cooper, 1991), 102; memcon, 13 January 1967, *FRUS, 1964–1968,* 5, 3.

6 "462 on Yale Faculty Urge Halt in Bombing of North Vietnam," *New York Times,* 16 January 1967.

7 Goulding, *Confirm or Deny,* 67.

8 Associated Press, "Goldwater Scores Times on Articles," 13 January 1967. See also Joseph Alsop, "Hanoi's Propaganda Offensive," *Washington Post,* 9 January 1967.

9 Kennedy, *The Military and the Media*, 88.

10 Tran Tinh, ed., *Van Kien Dang*, Tap 28, 84–85. Ho Chi Minh continued the cultivation of sympathetic Westerners later in the month in discussions with William Baggs and Harry S. Ashmore of the Center for the Study of Democratic Institutions. See Luu van Loi and Nguyen Anh Vu, *Tiep Xuc Bi Mat Viet Nam-Hoa Ky Truoc Hoi Nghi Pa-Ri*, 185–194; Harry S. Ashmore and William C. Baggs, *Mission to Hanoi: A Chronicle of Double-Dealing in High Places* (New York: G. P. Putnam's Sons, 1968), 41–51.

11 Taylor to Johnson, 30 January 1967, *FRUS*, *1964–1968*, 5, 30.

12 *American Foreign Policy: Current Documents, 1967*, 841.

13 Nguyen Duy Trinh asserted, "The mission of protecting North Vietnam is of extremely important strategic value and has a major impact on our strategic mission of liberating South Vietnam." Tran Tinh, ed., *Van Kien Dang*, Tap 28, 130.

14 State to Moscow, 7 February 1967, *FRUS*, *1964–1968*, 5, 40.

15 Rostow to Johnson, 15 February 1967, *FRUS*, *1964–1968*, 5, 82.

16 Congressional briefing transcript, 15 February 1967, LBJL, Congressional Briefings on Vietnam, box 1.

17 Gibbons, *The U.S. Government and the Vietnam War*, 4, 555–556; Rostow, meeting notes, 17 February 1967, *FRUS*, *1964–1968*, 5, 84.

18 *The Joint Chiefs of Staff and the War in Vietnam*, Chapter 41, 2–3; Drea, *McNamara, Clifford, and the Burdens of Vietnam*, 205–206; *Pentagon Papers*, 4, 148–149. Foul weather in February and March impeded the unleashing of Rolling Thunder 54; its full weight would not be felt until April. Sharp, "Air Operations: North Vietnam," 22 June 1967, LBJL, NSF, Memos to the President, Walt Rostow, box 18.

19 Jeff Shesol, *Mutual Contempt: Lyndon Johnson, Robert Kennedy, and the Feud That Defined a Decade* (New York: W. W. Norton, 1997), 372.

20 Telcon, Johnson, and Jackson, 3 March 1967, *FRUS*, *1964–1968*, 5, 95.

21 Hammond, *Public Affairs: The Military and the Media, 1962–1968*, 280; Cosmas, *MACV: The Joint Command in the Years of Escalation*, 388 (quotes).

22 CIA Office of National Estimates, "Communist Policy and the Next Phase in Vietnam," 12 April 1967, LBJL, NSF, VNCF, box 42.

23 Dobrynin, *In Confidence*, 161–163.

24 Memcon, Zhou Enlai and Pham Van Dong, 10 April 1967, in Odd Arne Westad, et al., *77 Conversations Between Chinese and Foreign Leaders on the Wars in Indochina, 1964–1977* (Washington, DC: Woodrow Wilson International Center for Scholars, 1998), 101–104.

25 *The Joint Chiefs of Staff and the War in Vietnam*, Chapter 41, 5–6; Drea, *McNamara, Clifford, and the Burdens of Vietnam*, 207.

26 Merle L. Pribbenow, "The -Ology War: Technology and Ideology in the Vietnamese Defense of Hanoi, 1967," *The Journal of Military History*, 67, No. 1. (January 2003), 175–176; Chau Minh Vung et al., *Lich Su Su Doan Khong Quan 371*, 75–77.

27 MACV, 1967 Command History, 326–330.

28 Cosmas, *MACV: The Joint Command in the Years of Escalation*, 421.

29 Bernard W. Rogers, *Cedar Falls–Junction City, A Turning Point* (Washington, DC: Department of the Army, 1989), 36–37.

30 MacGarrigle, *Combat Operations*, 109.

31 Sources on Operation Cedar Falls include Seaman, Combat Operation After Action Report, Cedar Falls, n.d., NA II, RG 472, USARV Command Historian, Entry UD42196, Box 241; Headquarters, 173d Airborne Brigade, Combat Operation After Action Report, Niagara/Cedar Falls, 25 February 1967, NA II, RG 472, USARV Command Historian, Entry UD42196, box 241; Joseph A. McChristian, *The Role of Military Intelligence, 1965-1967* (Washington, DC: Department of the Army, 1994), 116–125; Rogers, *Cedar Falls–Junction City, A Turning Point*, 15–22, 36–39, 67–73, 78, 154; MacGarrigle, *Combat Operations*, 95–112; Weingartner, ed., *Blue Spaders*, 194–202.

32 MacGarrigle, *Combat Operations*, 115–122; Rogers, *Cedar Falls–Junction City*, 97–107; Momyer, *Air Power in Three Wars*, 294–299.

33 Wheeler, *Big Red One*, 458–459; MacGarrigle, *Combat Operations*, 122–123.

34 Rogers, *Cedar Falls–Junction City*, 117–121; Starry, *Mounted Combat in Vietnam*, 96–97.

35 Nguyen Quang Dat and Tran Hanh, eds., *Mot So Tran Danh Trong Khang Chien Chong Phap*, Tap I, 83.

36 Starry, *Mounted Combat in Vietnam*, 97–100; Rogers, *Cedar Falls–Junction City*, 129–135; Wheeler, *Big Red One*, 459–461.

37 Rogers, *Cedar Falls–Junction City*, 135-140; Nguyen Quang Dat and Tran Hanh, eds., *Mot So Tran Danh Trong Khang Chien Chong Phap*, Tap I, 84–93; Nguyen Quoc Dung, *Su Doan 9*, 130–133; Hoang Cam, *Chang Duong Muoi Nghin Ngay*, 240–243; Bergerud, *Red Thunder, Tropic Lightning*, 153-163; Momyer, *Air Power in Three Wars*, 300–301; MacGarrigle, *Combat Operations*, 127–132; Christopher P. Worick, "The Battle of Suoi Tre: Viet Cong Infantry Attack on a Firebase Ends in Slaughter When Armor Arrives," *Armor*, 109, No. 3 (May–June 2000), 23–28; Robert L. Hemphill, "VC Onslaught at Fire Support Base Gold," *Vietnam*, December 1998, 22–28.

38 Weingartner, ed., *Blue Spaders*, 209–224; Wheeler, *Big Red One*, 461–464; Rogers, *Cedar Falls–Junction City*, 140–148, 157; MacGarrigle, *Combat Operations*, 136–139.

39 Rogers, *Cedar Falls–Junction City*, 160.

40 MacGarrigle, *Combat Operations*, 141–143; Rogers, *Cedar Falls–Junction City*, 149–153.

41 Special National Intelligence Estimate 57–67, "Significance of Cambodia to the Vietnamese Communist War Effort," 26 January 1967, *FRUS*, 1964–1968, 27, 199; Denny to Rusk, "SNIE 57–67: Significance of Cambodia to the Vietnamese Communist War Effort," n.d., *FRUS*, 1964–1968, 27, 200.

42 Combat Operations Department of the General Staff, *Lich Su Cuc Tac Chien*, 236–237; General Department of Rear Services, *Tong Ket Cong Tac Hau Can*

Chien Truong Nam Bo-Cuc Nam Trung Bo Trong Khang Chien Chong My, 54–56; Nguyen Van Hoang et al., *Lich Su A101 Doan 962: Ben—Ben Tre 1961–1976* (Hanoi: Nha Xuat Ban Quan Doi Nhan Dan, 2004), 70–75. A smaller shipment arrived in Sihanoukville the next month. After the 1970 incursion into Cambodia, U.S. intelligence concluded that the shipments of December 1966 and February and March 1967 totaled 6,200 tons. MacGarrigle, *Combat Operations*, 327–328. Given the reported tonnage of 3,000 for the December 1966 delivery and the same amount for the February 1967 delivery, the March 1967 shipment would have been approximately 200 tons.

43 Rostow to Johnson, 25 March 1967, LBJL, NSF, International Meetings and Travel File, box 12.

44 Lawrence J. Hickey, "Operation Paul Revere/Sam Houston," Project CHECO Report, 27 July 1967, TTU, Sam Johnson Vietnam Archive Collection, box 2; Warren K. Wilkins, *Nine Days in May: The Battles of the 4th Infantry Division on the Cambodian Border, 1967* (Norman: University of Oklahoma Press, 2017), 14–24; MacGarrigle, *Combat Operations*, 166–177.

45 Headquarters, 3rd Brigade Task Force, "Combat Operations After Action Report for Pershing," 1 May 1967, TTU, 35th Infantry Regiment Association Collection, box 4; *Rand Vietnam Interviews*, ser. Tet-VC, No. 43; MacGarrigle, *Combat Operations*, 180–192, 315–316.

46 Gary Telfer et al., *U.S. Marines in Vietnam: Fighting the North Vietnamese, 1967* (Washington, DC: History and Museums Division, Headquarters, U.S. Marine Corps, 1984), 10–14; MACV, 1967 Command History, 352–353; Gibbons, *The U.S. Government and the Vietnam War*, 4, 568–569.

47 Pearson, *The War in the Northern Provinces*, 21–24; MACV, 1967 Command History, 1090-1092.

48 Telfer et al., *U.S. Marines in Vietnam: Fighting the North Vietnamese*, 95.

49 Greene to JCS, "Principal Observations of CMC Trip to WestPac, 2-12 Jan 1967," 19 January 1967, MCHC, Greene Papers; *The Joint Chiefs of Staff and the War in Vietnam*, Chapter 45, 20–21; Shulimson and Wells, "First In, First Out," 274. For more on North Vietnamese infiltration and logistics, see Westmoreland to Sullivan, 1 March 1967, LBJL, Gibbons Papers, box 25.

50 Pearson, *The War in the Northern Provinces*, 12-15; MACV, 1967 Command History, 73–74, 335-337; Telfer et al., *U.S. Marines in Vietnam: Fighting the North Vietnamese*, 77–79; MacGarrigle, *Combat Operations*, 203–214, 255–257.

51 MACV, 1967 Command History, 337–338.

52 DePuy to Goodpaster, 18 April 1967, *FRUS*, 1964–1968, 5, 135. For the deployment of U.S. forces to the Mekong Delta, see Rostow to Johnson, 25 March 1967, LBJL, NSF, International Meetings and Travel File, box 12.

53 Birtle, *U.S. Army Counterinsurgency and Contingency Operations Doctrine, 1942–1976*, 390.

54 Clarke, *Advice and Support*, 230. See also Ngo Quang Truong, *RVNAF and U.S. Operational Cooperation and Coordination* (Washington, DC: U.S. Army Center of Military History, 1980), 164–166; Bui Diem, *In the Jaws of History*, 209.

55 Raphael Littauer and Norman Uphoff, eds. *Air War in Indochina*, rev. ed. (Boston: Beacon Press, 1972), 267–268.

56 Westmoreland to Sharp, 18 March 1967, *FRUS, 1964–1968*, 5, 110; *Pentagon Papers*, 4, 427–431.

57 *The Joint Chiefs of Staff and the War in Vietnam*, Chapter 43, 2–7. The 568,000 figure was the sum of the prior ceiling of 470,000 and a total of approximately 98,000 new troops.

58 In February, Westmoreland had stated, "Having studied the situation in South Vietnam for some months, I am convinced that the Panhandle in Laos must be cleared of enemy elements and secured before we can expect any stability in Southeast Asia. Little thought has been given to this solution by the State Department, so I have decided to develop a scenario which could be presented and hopefully accepted." Westmoreland, Historical Briefing, 3 February 1967, in Barrett, ed., *Lyndon B. Johnson's Vietnam Papers*, 391. See also Charles F. Brower IV, "Strategic Reassessment in Vietnam: The Westmoreland 'Alternate Strategy' of 1967–1968," *Naval War College Review*, 44, No. 2 (Spring 1991), 20–51; Zaffiri, *Westmoreland*, 183. In recent months, other men of influence, including Ky, General Vien, and Mike Mansfield had made the case to Johnson for ground operations in Laos. David Lilienthal, *The Journals of David Lilienthal*, 6 (New York: Harper & Row, 1976), 417; Carver, "Working Notes on First Day's Session of Guam Conference," 20 March 1967, *FRUS, 1964–1968*, 5, 115; Mansfield to Johnson, 29 April 1967, *FRUS, 1964–1968*, 5, 151.

59 Christian, meeting notes, 27 April 1967, *FRUS, 1964–1968*, 5, 149.

60 Hammond, *Public Affairs: The Military and the Media, 1962–1968*, 287–288; "Gallup Poll Finds Democratic Critics of Johnson on Rise," *New York Times*, 10 April 1967.

61 Douglas Robinson, "Dr. King Proposes a Boycott of War," *New York Times*, 5 April 1967; Leroy F. Aarons, "King Urges Cease-Fire and End of Bombing, Denounces U.S. Role," *Washington Post*, 5 April 1967.

62 David J. Garrow, *Bearing the Cross: Martin Luther King Jr. and the Southern Christian Leadership Conference* (New York: William Morrow, 1986), 553–554.

63 "N.A.A.C.P. Decries Stand of Dr. King on Vietnam," *New York Times*, 11 April 1967.

64 Associated Press, "Text of Gen. Westmoreland's Remarks at AP Meeting," 25 April 1967.

65 Gardner, *Pay Any Price*, 363–364; Zaffiri, *Westmoreland*, 195–196.

66 Hammond, *Public Affairs: The Military and the Media, 1962–1968*, 289.

67 Douglas Brinkley, "The Other Vietnam Generation," *New York Times*, February 28, 1999; "220 Writers Urge Continuing of War," *New York Times*, 24 December 1968.

68 Thomas E. Barden, ed., *Steinbeck in Vietnam: Dispatches from the War* (Charlottesville: University of Virginia Press, 2012), 141–142.

69 CIA Office of National Estimates, "Communist Policy and the Next Phase in Vietnam," 12 April 1967, LBJL, NSF, VNCF, box 42.

70 Combat Operations Department of the General Staff, *Lich Su Cuc Tac Chien,* 230–232.

CHAPTER 10

1 Norton, ed., *Stingray,* 149.

2 Joseph C. Long, *Hill Of Angels: U.S. Marines And The Battle For Con Thien, 1967 To 1968* (Quantico: Marine Corps University Press, 2016), 8.

3 324th Infantry Division Headquarters and Division Party Committee, *Lich Su Su Doan Bo Binh 324;* James P. Coan, *Con Thien: The Hill of Angels* (Tuscaloosa: University of Alabama Press, 2004), 65–72; Francis J. Kelly, *U.S. Army Special Forces: 1961–1971* (Washington, DC: Department of the Army, 1973), 110–113.

4 Mark A. Cauble, *Into the DMZ: A Battle History of Operation Hickory* (Westminster, Maryland: Heritage Books, 2005), 14, 27.

5 Coan, *Con Thien,* 86–100; Cauble, *Into the DMZ;* Telfer et al., *U.S. Marines in Vietnam: Fighting the North Vietnamese,* 23–30; Long, *Hill Of Angels,* 10–15.

6 Combat Operations After Action Report, Operation Malheur, 2 September 1967, https://www.army.mil/e2/downloads/rv7/medalofhonor/kettles/pdf/operation_malheur_AAR.pdf; MacGarrigle, *Combat Operations,* 233–239.

7 Lehrack, *Road of 10,000 Pains,* 86.

8 Operation Union, OP file, 24 April 1967, TTU, Virtual Vietnam Archive, Item 1201064042; Operation Union II, OP file, 26 May 1967, TTU, Virtual Vietnam Archive, Item 1201064050; Telfer et al., *U.S. Marines in Vietnam: Fighting the North Vietnamese,* 63–74.

9 Rod Andrew Jr., *Hill Fights: The First Battle Of Khe Sanh* (Quantico: Marine Corps University Press, 2017); Telfer et al., *U.S. Marines in Vietnam: Fighting the North Vietnamese,* 35–45; Pearson, *The War in the Northern Provinces,* 17–18.

10 Wilkins, *Nine Days in May,* 351.

11 Ibid., 37–353.

12 Edward F. Murphy, *Dak To: The 173d Airborne Brigade in South Vietnam's Central Highlands, June–November 1967* (Novato, California: Presidio Press, 1993), 59–82; Rick Atkinson, *The Long Gray Line* (Boston: Houghton Mifflin, 1989), 232–236; MacGarrigle, *Combat Operations,* 299-302.

13 Littauer and Uphoff, eds., *The Air War in Indochina,* 267–268; Telfer et al., *U.S. Marines in Vietnam: Fighting the North Vietnamese,* 83.

14 Schuyler, *Good Men Die,* 188.

15 Frank L. Jones, *Blowtorch: Robert Komer, Vietnam, and American Cold War Strategy* (Annapolis: Naval Institute Press, 2013), 126–130. Komer had initially sought to become deputy ambassador in charge of all civil operations, reporting only to the ambassador. The president, however, gave Komer the slightly lower position of deputy to Westmoreland for pacification. When Komer learned of the new command structure, he complained to the president, "I feel somewhat disconcerted and confused about the changed role you now have in mind for me. I had thought you intended to send me as No. 2 to run the whole civil side. The change in plans (which I first

read of by accident three days late) seems to downgrade me to No. 3 (or No. 4 coming after Westy), and dealing only with 'pacification.'" Komer to Johnson, 18 March 1967, in Barrett, ed., *Lyndon B. Johnson's Vietnam Papers,* 402–403. As consolation, Komer was able to secure the rank of ambassador and a chauffeured Chrysler Imperial limousine of the sort normally reserved for a four-star general. When Komer demanded that his vehicle bear the license plate of a four-star general, he was told that such plates were reserved for military officers, but after he berated the officer who delivered that message, he received a plate resembling that of the secretary of the Army. Jones, *Blowtorch,* 137. Concerning the resource advantages of putting CORDS under the military, Komer said later, "If I needed men, AID and State and CIA could provide me with men very slowly. Maybe a dozen a month. The military could give me twenty thousand men. If I had to have trucks to move stuff around the country, who had all the trucks? The military." Moyar, *Phoenix and the Birds of Prey,* 49.

16 Scoville, *Reorganizing for Pacification Support,* 43–73; Hunt, *Pacification,* 87–98; William Colby with James McCargar, *Lost Victory: A Firsthand Account of America's Sixteen-Year Involvement in Vietnam* (Chicago: Contemporary Books, 1989), 207–208.

17 Moyar, *Phoenix and the Birds of Prey,* 50–54.

18 *Pentagon Papers,* 2, 502–503; Clarke, *Advice and Support,* 212, 245.

19 The Provincial Reconnaissance Units were the successors of the Counter-Terror Teams that had been created in 1964. For further information, see Moyar, *Phoenix and the Birds of Prey.*

20 Ahern, *CIA and Rural Pacification in South Vietnam,* 253–260, 266–270 (quote on 257).

21 Hunt, *Pacification,* 37; McPherson to Johnson, 13 June 1967, *FRUS, 1964–1968,* 5, 197.

22 Rostow to Vance, Helms, and Bundy, 22 May 1967, LBJL, NSF, VNCF, box 43.

23 Michel, *Clashes,* 95; Sharp, "Air Operations: North Vietnam," 22 June 1967, LBJL, NSF, Memos to the President, Walt Rostow, box 18.

24 Pribbenow, "The -Ology War," 184, 188; Michel, *Clashes,* 60–62, 100–101; Nguyen Xuan Mau with The Ky, *Bao Ve Bau Troi: Hoi Ky* (Hanoi: People's Army Publishing House, 1982), 129–162.

25 CIA Directorate of Intelligence, Intelligence memorandum 0643/67, "Bomb Damage Inflicted on North Vietnam Through April 1967," 12 May 1967, LBJL, Gibbons Papers, box 27; CIA Directorate of Intelligence, intelligence memorandum 0648/67, "The Status of North Vietnam's Electric Power Industry as of 25 May 1967," 26 May 1967 LBJL, NSF, VNCF, box 44. The North Vietnamese had imported an estimated two thousand diesel generators in recent years, but their total generating capacity was believed to be only fifteen thousand to twenty thousand kilowatts. Ibid.

26 The generals advocated reducing the thirty-mile circle around Hanoi to ten miles and the ten-mile circle around Haiphong to four miles; launching heavy attacks on all North Vietnamese airfields, including Phuc Yen and Gia Lam; and mining and bombing North Vietnam's ports. Bundy to Rusk,

"Bombing Policy and Possible Communication with the Soviets," 19 May 1967, *FRUS*, 1964–1968, 5, 175; Wheeler, JCSM-286-67, "Operations Against North Vietnam," 20 May 1967, LBJL, Gibbons Papers, box 27.

27 McNaughton, "Proposed Bombing Program Against North Vietnam," 5 May 1967, LBJL, Warnke Papers, McNaughton Files, box 2; Vance to Johnson, "Proposed Bombing Program Against North Vietnam," 9 May 1967, *FRUS*, 1964–1968, 5, 169 (quote). For the intelligence estimates, see CIA Directorate of Intelligence, Intelligence memorandum 0643/67, "Bomb Damage Inflicted on North Vietnam Through April 1967," 12 May 1967, LBJL, Gibbons Papers, box 27; CIA Directorate of Intelligence, intelligence memorandum 0648/67, "The Effectiveness of the Rolling Thunder Program," 23 May 1967, LBJL, NSF, VNCF, box 43.

28 Concerning the perception of civilian officials as eggheads, see Davidson, *Vietnam At War*, 338.

29 *The Joint Chiefs of Staff and the War in Vietnam*, Chapter 43, 22.

30 Bundy to Rusk, "Bombing Policy and Possible Communication with the Soviets," 19 May 1967, *FRUS*, 1964–1968, 5, 175; Rostow to Johnson, 19 May 1967, *FRUS*, 1964–1968, 5, 176.

31 Helms to Johnson, "North Vietnam Bombing," 22 May 1967, FRUS, 1964–1968, 5, 180.

32 Drea, *McNamara, Clifford, and the Burdens of Vietnam*, 209. Admiral Sharp sent Wheeler an objection to McNamara's decision, asserting, "If we want to get this war over with we ought to keep the pressure on Hanoi and move in on Haiphong as JCS have recommended." *The Joint Chiefs of Staff and the War in Vietnam*, Chapter 41, 12.

33 McNamara to Johnson, "Future Actions in Vietnam," 19 May 1967, *FRUS*, 1964–1968, 5, 177.

34 Robert S. McNamara with Brian VanDeMark, *In Retrospect: The Tragedy and Lessons of Vietnam* (New York: Times Books, 1995), 273.

35 USVNR, book 5, IV.c.6(b), 176; Gibbons, *The U.S. Government and the Vietnam War*, 4, 640.

36 Rostow to Johnson, 20 May 1967, LBJL, Gibbons Papers, box 27 (first quote); Rostow to Johnson, 28 June 1967, LBJL, NSF, Memos to the President, Walt Rostow, box 18 (second quote).

37 William Bundy, "Comments on DOD First Rough Draft of 19 May," 30 May 1967, DDRS, Document Number CK2349143061.

38 For biographical details on Bunker, see Howard B. Schaffer, *Ellsworth Bunker: Global Troubleshooter, Vietnam Hawk* (Chapel Hill: University of North Carolina Press, 2003), 175. Quote is from Richard Eder, "A Quiet American Goes to Vietnam," *New York Times*, 26 March 1967.

39 Bui Diem, *In the Jaws of History*, 188.

40 Saigon to State, 9 February 1967, LBJL, Gibbons Papers, box 24.

41 Saigon to State, 24 May 1967, in Douglas Pike, ed., *The Bunker Papers: Reports to the President from Vietnam, 1967–1973*, 1 (Berkeley: Institute of East Asian Studies, 1990), 24–25.

42 Rostow to Johnson, 30 May 1967, LBJL, NSF, VNCF, box 44; Blaufarb to Bundy, n. d., *FRUS, 1964–1968*, 5, 211n.

43 Lansdale to Bunker, 7 July 1967, *FRUS, 1964–1968*, 5, 232; CIA to State, 19 June 1967, *FRUS, 1964–1968*, 5, 209 (quotes).

44 Bundy to Habib, "Analysis of Ambassador Bunker's Proposal for Political Action in Viet-Nam," 20 June 1967, *FRUS, 1964–1968*, 5, 211; Jorden to Rostow, "Ambassador Bunker's Proposals," 20 June 1967, *FRUS, 1964–1968*, 5, 212; CIA to Saigon, 20 June 1967, *FRUS, 1964–1968*, 5, 213.

45 Saigon to State, 30 June 1967, *FRUS, 1964–1968*, 5, 226; Saigon to State, 1 July 1967, *FRUS, 1964–1968*, 5, 229; Saigon to State, 1 July 1967, *FRUS, 1964–1968*, 5, 230; Wheeler to Sharp, 1 July 1967, in Barrett, ed., *Lyndon B. Johnson's Vietnam Papers*, 440.

46 Ahern, *CIA and the Generals*, 53; CIA, "Agreement Between Chief of State Thieu and Prime Minister Ky," 2 July 1967, CREST, document number 0000447082; Saigon to State, 5 July 1967, in Pike, ed., *The Bunker Papers*, 1, 72–73; Lansdale to Bunker, 7 July 1967, *FRUS, 1964–1968*, 5, 232; Bui Diem, *In the Jaws of History*, 203–204.

47 Saigon to State, 23 August 1967, in Pike, ed., *The Bunker Papers*, 1, 130.

48 *The Joint Chiefs of Staff and the War in Vietnam*, Chapter 45, 1.

49 Keith William Nolan, *Operation Buffalo: USMC Fight for the DMZ* (Novato, California: Presidio Press, 1991), 22–23.

50 Westmoreland, *A Soldier Reports*, 204.

51 Nolan, *Operation Buffalo*, 105.

52 C. J. Chivers, *The Gun* (New York: Simon & Schuster, 2010), 313–316; Andrew Jr., *Hill Fights*, 54–55.

53 Nolan, *Operation Buffalo*, 252.

54 For Operation Buffalo, see "General Westmoreland's Military Assessment For July 1967," 11 August 1967, TTU, Larry Berman Collection, Box 7; "Operations of U.S. Marine Forces, Vietnam," July 1967, TTU, Virtual Vietnam Archive, Item 1201001145; Telfer et al., *U.S. Marines in Vietnam: Fighting the North Vietnamese*, 95–104; Coan, *Hill of Angels*, 109–136; Vetter, *Never Without Heroes*, 163–164; Norton, ed., *Stingray*, 152–156; Long, *Hill of Angels*, 15-22; Nguyen Khac Tinh et al., *Phao Binh Nhan Dan Viet Nam: Nhung Chang Duong Chien Dau*, Tap II (Hanoi: Bo Tu Lenh Phao Binh, 1986), 133–134.

55 MACV, 1967 Command History, 1099-1101; *The Joint Chiefs of Staff and the War in Vietnam*, Chapter 45, 27.

56 MacGarrigle, *Combat Operations*, 339–347; Wheeler, *The Big Red One*, 469–472.

57 Robert C. Taber, Combat Lessons Bulletin, number 18, Headquarters U.S. Army Vietnam, 15 August 1967, http://www.dtic.mil/dtic/tr/fulltext/u2/387328.pdf (quote); Dang Van Nhung et al., *Su Doan 7*, 33–35.

58 Ronnie A. Mendoza, "After Action Report of 165th NVA Regiment Attack on Tong Le Chon," 14 August 1967, TTU, Glenn Helm Collection, box 3; Dang Van Nhung et al., *Su Doan 7*, 36–38.

59 Nguyen Van Minh et al., *Lich Su Khang Chien Chong My Cuu Nuoc, 1954–1975*, Tap V, 29–30.

60 Truong Son, "The Lessons of NFLSV Victories," in McGarvey, ed., *Visions of Victory*, 129 (quote); Latimer, "Hanoi's Leaders and Their South Vietnam Policies," 294–296.

61 Nguyen Van Minh et al., *Lich Su Khang Chien Chong My Cuu Nuoc, 1954–1975*, Tap V, 30-31 (first and second quotes); Le Duan, *Thu Vao Nam*, 161 (third quote). Truong Chinh subsequently elaborated on the concept of attacking the cities: "In our resistance war of national salvation against the Americans, with the balance of forces so heavily weighted against us in terms of troop strength, weapons, mobility, and modernization, it would be very difficult for our forces to annihilate campaign-sized and strategic-sized elements of the U.S. expeditionary army. We had to find a new way, not the traditional way, to defeat the American will to commit aggression by launching a simultaneous general offensive against the enemy's political and military nerve centers in the cities and the provincial capitals. Our attacks against the cities and the provincial capitals would be a major surprise to the enemy, would totally upset the enemy's strategic posture, and would shake the United States to its very foundations." Nguyen Van Minh et al., *Lich Su Khang Chien Chong My Cuu Nuoc, 1954–1975*, Tap V, 41.

62 Combat Operations Department of the General Staff, Lich Su Cuc Tac Chien, 232–236; Pribbenow, "General Vo Nguyen Giap and the Mysterious Evolution of the Plan for the 1968 Tet Offensive," 17.

63 Robert K. Brigham, "Why the South Won the American War in Vietnam," in Marc Jason Gilbert, ed., *Why the North Won the Vietnam War* (New York: Palgrave Macmillan, 2002), 112. For another source confirming the general's presence in Hanoi, see Nguyen Thi Bao, "Nhung Ngay Cuoi Cung Cua Anh Nguyen Chi Thanh," in Ha Huu Khieu, ed., *Dai Tuong Nguyen Chi Thanh: Nha Chinh Tri Quan Su Loi Lac* (Hanoi: People's Army Publishing House, Hanoi, 1997), 351. Early American reports erroneously concluded that Thanh had been killed by an American bomb. Don Oberdorfer, *Tet!* (New York: Doubleday, 1971), 42; Dave R. Palmer, *Summons of the Trumpet: U.S.-Vietnam in Perspective* (Novato, California: Presidio Press, 1978), 121.

64 Van Phac, "General Nguyen Chi Thanh on the Battlefield," in Ha Huu Khieu, ed., *Dai Tuong Nguyen Chi Thanh*, 102–103.

65 Gibbons, *The U.S. Government and the Vietnam War*, 4, 725–726.

66 Sharp, *Strategy for Defeat*, 178–84, 285–292; Thompson, *To Hanoi and Back*, 76.

67 Davidson, *Vietnam At War*, 463–464.

68 Sharp, *Strategy for Defeat*, 184.

69 Gibbons, *The U.S. Government and the Vietnam War*, 4, 728–729; USVNR, book 5, IV.c.6(b), 195–196.

70 Enthoven to McNamara, 4 May 1967, *Pentagon Papers*, 4, 461–462.

71 Enthoven, "Increase of SEA Forces," 1 May 1967, USVNR, book 5, IV.c.6(b), 117–123.

72 Littauer and Uphoff, eds., *The Air War in Indochina*, 267–268.

73 CIA, "The Attrition of Vietnamese Communist Forces, 1968–1969," 30 March 1968, DDRS, Document Number CK2349337572.

74 Saigon to State, 17 June 1967, NA II, RG 59, Lot Files, Entry 5408, East Asia and Pacific, box 10; Westmoreland to McNamara, "Laos," 10 July 1967, LBJL, Gibbons Papers, box 29.

75 Saigon to State, 12 July 1967, *FRUS, 1964–1968*, 5, 237; Johnson, meeting notes, 12 July 1967, *FRUS, 1964–1968*, 5, 238.

76 Sullivan to Bundy, "Limitations on Military Actions in Laos," 1 May 1967, LBJL, Warnke Papers, McNaughton Files, box 2. At the same time, Sullivan was rebuffing a recommendation from the Laotian king for military action to retake Laotian territory from the North Vietnamese. Dommen, *The Indochinese Experience of the French and the Americans*, 608.

77 Vientiane to State, 29 May 1967, *FRUS, 1964–1968*, 28, 289.

78 Vientiane to State, 29 July 1967, *FRUS, 1964–1968*, 28, 302.

79 Vientiane to State, 24 July 1967, NA II, Central Files, 1967-1969, box 2786.

80 Gibbons, *The U.S. Government and the Vietnam War*, 4, 754–759.

81 *Congressional Record*, 113, 21897-21900. Former President Eisenhower himself voiced doubt about the Tonkin Gulf Resolution, telling Republican congressmen that "it is time that Congress decided whether or not to declare a state of war exists with North Vietnam." Eisenhower also spoke in favor of more robust military action. He asserted that to win, "You need all the power you have and you must use it quickly and secretly so as to achieve surprise. You cannot win a war of gradualism." Raymond Lahr, "Gradualism Can't Win in Vietnam, Ike Says," *Washington Post*, 22 July 1967. President Johnson bristled at the measures proposed by Ford, saying, "I am not going to do what Ford says, because we would be in a war with China tonight if we did." Johnson, "Notes of the President's Meeting with Democratic Congressmen," 9 August 1967, LBJL, Tom Johnson's Notes of Meeting, box 1. American allies in the region shared Ford's views on Haiphong. The South Koreans "would close Haiphong and bomb all legitimate military targets," reported Clark Clifford and Maxwell Taylor following a visit to Seoul. "The Koreans are unimpressed with the risks entailed in sinking foreign flag ships. They believe that any country sending supplies to soldiers killing our men is an enemy." Clifford and Taylor, Report to the President, 5 August 1967, TTU, Ronald B. Frankum Jr., Collection, box 1.

82 For Fulbright's earlier support for the war and his leading role in selling the Tonkin Gulf Resolution, see Randall Bennett Woods, *Fulbright: A Biography* (New York: Cambridge University Press, 1995).

83 Johnson, meeting notes, 25 July 1967, LBJL, Tom Johnson's Notes of Meetings, box 1.

84 Lady Bird Johnson, *A White House Diary* (Austin: University of Texas Press, 2007), 556.

85 Scanlon, *The Pro-War Movement*, 57–61; "Thousands to March in Support of Vietnam G.I.'s," *New York Times*, 3 May 1967.

86 Val Adams, "Parade to Back Vietnam G.I.'s Will be Held on 5th Avenue Today," *New York Times,* 13 May 1967.

87 Murray Schumach, "70,000 Turn Out to Back U.S. Men in Vietnam War," *New York Times,* 14 May 1967.

88 Leroy F. Aarons, "Support for War Policy," *Washington Post,* 14 May 1967.

89 "Youth Assaulted by 30 Paraders," *New York Times,* 14 May 1967.

90 Gibbons, *The U.S. Government and the Vietnam War,* 4, 702.

91 Johnson, notes of Tuesday Luncheon, 8 August 1967, LBJL, Tom Johnson's Notes of Meetings, box 1.

92 Thompson, *To Hanoi and Back,* 84–85; *The Joint Chiefs of Staff and the War in Vietnam,* Chapter 44, 2–5.

93 Sharp, *Strategy for Defeat,* 194. The timing of these authorizations, plus McNamara's last-minute refusal to hand over classified military reports on the air campaign, spurred further doubts among congressmen about McNamara's integrity. Drea, *McNamara, Clifford, and the Burdens of Vietnam,* 215-216.

94 U.S. Senate, Preparedness Investigating Subcommittee of the Committee on Armed Services, *Air War Against North Vietnam,* 90th Cong., 1st sess. (Washington, DC: Government Printing Office, 1967), 123–515.

95 U.S. Senate, Preparedness Investigating Subcommittee of the Committee on Armed Services, *Air War Against North Vietnam,* 236.

96 Ibid., 416.

97 Johnson, meeting notes, 17 October 1967, *FRUS, 1964–1968,* 5, 355.

98 Johnson, meeting notes, 16 August 1967, *FRUS, 1964–1968,* 5, 283.

99 Wallace J. Thies, *When Governments Collide: Coercion and Diplomacy in the Vietnam Conflict* (Berkeley: University of California Press, 1980), 180–187; Chester L. Cooper, *The Lost Crusade: America in Vietnam* (New York: Dodd, Mead and Company, 1970), 377–378; Marvin Kalb and Bernard Kalb, *Kissinger* (Boston: Little, Brown and Company, 1974), 70–74; Niall Ferguson, *Kissinger, 1923–1968: The Idealist* (New York: Penguin, 2015), 754–756.

100 Luu van Loi and Nguyen Anh Vu, *Tiep Xuc Bi Mat Viet Nam-Hoa Ky Truoc Hoi Nghi Pa-Ri,* 214–227; Herring, ed., *The Secret Diplomacy of the Vietnam War,* 720–725.

101 Kissinger to Katzenbach, 21 August 1967, *FRUS,* 5, 286; Herring, ed., *The Secret Diplomacy of the Vietnam War,* 727–729; Ferguson, *Kissinger,* 758–759.

102 *The Joint Chiefs of Staff and the War in Vietnam,* Chapter 44, 3; Helms to Johnson, "The Kissinger Project," 7 September 1967, CREST document number CIA-RDP79B01737A001800170001-7.

103 U.S. Senate, Preparedness Investigating Subcommittee of the Committee on Armed Services, *Air War Against North Vietnam,* 305.

104 Ibid., 277, 299, 309 (quote). The CIA, which in April had estimated that the combination of mining the ports and intensifying the strikes on transportation targets in northern Vietnam would "threaten Hanoi's ability to support the war," had more recently stated that those measures could

at best reduce North Vietnam's transport capacity for imports to 3,900 per day. At that level, the CIA concluded, Hanoi could still keep seventy-five tons of supplies moving daily in support of the war in the South. CIA, "Consequences of Mining the Seaports and Water Approaches to North Vietnam and Bombing the Northern Railroads and Roads," 23 May 1967, CREST, document number CIA-RDP78T02095R000800030019-9.

105 Admiral Sharp had made this point in his testimony to the Stennis committee. "We say that they are able to go into combat one day out of thirty," Sharp had said. "I am sure they would like to be able to go into combat fifteen days out of thirty." U.S. Senate, Preparedness Investigating Subcommittee of the Committee on Armed Services, *Air War Against North Vietnam*, 68.

106 U.S. Senate, Preparedness Investigating Subcommittee of the Committee on Armed Services, *Air War Against North Vietnam*, 435 (first quote); Shapley, *Promise and Power*, 432 (second quote).

107 Gibbons, *The U.S. Government and the Vietnam War*, 4, 751.

108 Mark Perry, *Four Stars* (Boston: Houghton Mifflin, 1989), 162–166.

109 Herring, *LBJ and Vietnam*, 56–57; Sorley, *Honorable Warrior*, 285–287.

110 E. W. Kenworthy, "Senate Unit Asks Johnson to Widen Bombing in North," *New York Times*, 1 September 1967.

111 News Conference, 1 Sept 1967, *Congressional Quarterly Almanac*, 1967.

112 "Poll Finds a Drop in Support of War," *New York Times*, 29 August 1967.

113 Connell to Humphrey, "A Strong Party-Line on the Riots and Vietnam," 30 August 1967, TTU, Virtual Vietnam Archive, Item 0240719005.

CHAPTER 11

1 Saigon to State, 6 September 1967, in Pike, ed., *The Bunker Papers*, 1, 148–155; Taylor, *A History of the Vietnamese*, 600–601; Schaffer, *Ellsworth Bunker*, 187–188; Phillips, *Why Vietnam Matters*, 282–283.

2 Sean Fear, "The Ambiguous Legacy of Ngo Dinh Diem in South Vietnam's Second Republic," *Journal of Vietnamese Studies*, 11, No. 1 (Winter 2016), 26–27; Fishel, ed., *Vietnam*, 674–676; Bui Diem, *In the Jaws of History*, 208; Critchfield, *The Long Charade*, 356–361; Shaplen, *The Road From War*, 151–155; Blair, *There to the Bitter End*, 156–157.

3 Coan, *Hill of Angels*, 173–252; Saigon to State, 12 October 1967, in Pike, ed., *The Bunker Papers*, 1, 202.

4 *The Joint Chiefs of Staff and the War in Vietnam*, Chapter 45, 6–7.

5 Telcon, Johnson and Dirksen, 4 October 1967, *FRUS, 1964–1968*, 5, 344.

6 Telfer et al., *U.S. Marines in Vietnam: Fighting the North Vietnamese*, 135; *The Joint Chiefs of Staff and the War in Vietnam*, Chapter 45, 6. The events at Con Thien also caused Westmoreland to lend a more sympathetic ear to ongoing Marine protests that McNamara's barrier project was tying them down in exposed positions for little gain. At the end of September, Westmoreland accepted the recommendation of the Marine leadership to abandon the westward extension of the bulldozed strip beyond the eastern

end of McNamara's barrier. The rest of the area that had been scheduled for bulldozing would instead be seeded with mines, sensors, and barbed wire. Thereafter, the Marines focused on bolstering the strongpoints near Route 9 and conducting mobile anti-infiltration operations. Shulimson and Wells, "First In, First Out," 275; Cosmas, *MACV: The Joint Command in the Years of Escalation,* 426; *The Joint Chiefs of Staff and the War in Vietnam,* Chapter 45, 8–9; Westmoreland, *A Soldier Reports,* 200.

7   Erik B. Villard, *Combat Operations: Staying the Course, October 1967–September 1968* (Washington, DC: U.S. Army Center of Military History, 2017), 226–228; MacGarrigle, *Combat Operations,* 275–283.

8   Peers, Combat Operations After Action Report, Operation Francis Marion, 25 November 1967, https://apps.dtic.mil/dtic/tr/fulltext/u2/387627.pdf; MacGarrigle, *Combat Operations,* 309–314.

9   The Americans reported an enemy death toll of 101, though the actual total might have been considerably higher or lower. That figure was the sum of numbers from several different sources and thus might have included the double counting of some corpses. Another cause for skepticism was the sighting of only two enemy bodies during a later search of the battlefield. Enemy losses during the battle nonetheless were likely high. Subsequent interrogations of prisoners from the 271st Regiment would reveal that the regiment had been crippled while fighting the Americans in this area during October, though at least some of the damage was incurred on other days. The lack of commentary on the October 17 battle in postwar North Vietnamese histories is another indicator that it did not go especially well for the North Vietnamese. Sources on the Battle of Ong Thang Stream are James E. Shelton, *The Beast Was Out There: The 28th Infantry Black Lions and the Battle of Ong Thanh, Vietnam, October 1967* (Chicago: Cantigny First Division Foundation, 2002); MacGarrigle, *Combat Operations,* 353–361; David Maraniss, *They Marched Into Sunlight: War and Peace, Vietnam and America, October 1967* (New York: Simon & Schuster, 2003); Wheeler, *Big Red One,* 474–479.

10 Thies, *When Governments Collide,* 187–189; Herring, ed., *The Secret Diplomacy of the Vietnam War,* 733–738; Ferguson, *Kissinger,* 760–762. On September 29, at the National Legislative Conference in San Antonio, Johnson announced, "The United States is willing to stop all aerial and naval bombardment of North Vietnam when this will lead promptly to productive discussions. We, of course, assume that while discussions proceed, North Vietnam would not take advantage of the bombing cessation or limitation." *Public Papers of the Presidents of the United States: Lyndon B. Johnson, 1967,* Book II, 876–881. This offer had no more effect on the North Vietnamese than the bombing pause.

11 Johnson, meeting notes, 26 September 1967, *FRUS, 1964–1968,* 5, 336.

12 Johnson, meeting notes, 18 October 1967, *FRUS, 1964–1968,* 5, 357.

13 Christian, "Private Meeting in the President's Office," 13 October 1967, LBJL, Meeting Notes File, box 2; JCSM-555-67, "Increased Pressures on North Vietnam," 17 October 1967, NA II, RG 59, Central Files, 1967–1969, box 2792.

14 CIA Directorate of Intelligence, "Rolling Thunder: The 1967 Campaign Against LOC's," September 1967, LBJL, NSF, VNCF, box 84.

15 Rostow to Johnson, 18 October 1967, LBJL, NSF, Files of Walt W. Rostow, box 7.

16 CIA-DIA, "An Appraisal of the Bombing of North Vietnam (Through 31 December 1967)," n.d., LBJL, NSF, VNCF, box 84.

17 Dang Vu Hiep, *Ky Uc Tay Nguyen*, 184, 190.

18 Nguyen Quoc Dung, *Su Doan 9*, 142. See also "PLAF Logistic Problems," January 1968, TTU, Douglas Pike Collection, unit 5, box 11.

19 On the importance of the Doumer Bridge, see Momyer, *Air Power in Three Wars*, 183–186.

20 "Raid Lull Assists Enemy's Harvest," *Agence France-Presse*, 8 December 1967; Carol Cohen McEldowney, *Hanoi Journal*, 1967 (Amherst and Boston: University of Massachusetts Press, 2007), 75.

21 A prime example from this period was Carol Cohen McEldowney, who traveled to Hanoi in September 1967 together with Tom Hayden, Rennie Davis, and several other antiwar activists. An American radical who admired the North Vietnamese regime, McEldowney nonetheless grew frustrated with the restriction of the group's interlocutors to people who recited official propaganda. McEldowney, *Hanoi Journal*, 52.

22 United Press International, "Hungarian Reports Illness Is Keeping Ho Chi Minh in Bed," 26 November 1967.

23 CIA, Intelligence Information Cable, 10 October 1967, TTU, Virtual Vietnam Archive, Item 0010204004.

24 Colvin, *Twice Around the World*, 113–116. No available records indicate that Colvin's observations made it to anyone in the U.S. government in the fall of 1967. The most plausible explanation is that the British government of Prime Minister Harold Wilson purposefully avoided sharing them with Washington. Wilson may still have been miffed at the United States for foiling his personal effort to broker peace in February 1967, and he almost certainly wanted to avoid giving the Americans any encouragement to intensify a bombing program that he viewed as an obstacle to peace. After the collapse of his peace effort in February, Wilson groused that he had "been made a fool of by Washington and that his credibility, which had built up with great effort over the last 20 years, was now badly damaged." Cooper, Memorandum for the Record, 12 February 1967, *FRUS, 1964–1968*, 5, 63. Concerning Wilson's views on the bombing of North Vietnam, see Ray Clinton Barker, "In the Giant's Shadow: Harold Wilson and the Vietnam War, 1964–1968" (PhD dissertation, SUNY at Buffalo, 2003); Nicholas Tarling, *The British and the Vietnam War: Their Way with LBJ* (Singapore: NU.S. Press, 2017). On September 25, British Foreign Secretary George Brown reiterated to Rusk the British government's desire that the United States reconsider the intensity of its bombing of North Vietnam because of "the unfavorable impact it is having on public opinion." Katzenbach to Johnson, "Your Meeting with Foreign Secretary Brown," 26 September 1967, LBJ, NSF, Country File, UK, box 211.

25 Nguyen Quy, ed., *Van Kien Dang*, Tap 30, 1969 (Hanoi: Nha Xuat Ban Chinh Tri Quoc Gia, 2004), 152. Le Duan did not state the time period during which

the nine hundred thousand tons were delivered, but his reference to "several hundreds of thousands" suggests that it spanned multiple years. Nor did he make clear whether he was referring to tons of polished rice or the heavier unpolished rice.

26 The absence is most conspicuous in CIA Directorate of Intelligence, "Rolling Thunder: The 1967 Campaign Against LOC's," September 1967, LBJL, NSF, VNCF, box 84; and CIA-DIA, "An Appraisal of the Bombing of North Vietnam (Through 31 December 1967)," n.d., LBJL, NSF, VNCF, box 84.

27 Another indication of the confidence in this conventional wisdom was the CIA's estimate of September, the peak month of the North Vietnamese supply crisis, which concluded that even with the mining of ports, the United States would "not be able to cut off the flow of essential supplies." CIA Directorate of Intelligence, "Rolling Thunder: The 1967 Campaign Against LOC's," September 1967, LBJL, NSF, VNCF, box 84.

28 Johnson, meeting notes, 26 September 1967, *FRUS, 1964–1968*, 5, 336; Xiaoming Zhang, "The Vietnam War, 1964–1969: A Chinese Perspective," *Journal of Military History*, 60, issue 4 (October 1996), 755; Thompson, *To Hanoi and Back*, 84–86.

29 Johnson, meeting notes, 16 October 1967, *FRUS, 1964–1968*, 5, 353; McNamara to Johnson, 1 November 1967, in Barrett, ed., *Lyndon B. Johnson's Vietnam Papers*, 515–522.

30 CIA Intelligence Memorandum 1391/67, "The Consequences of a Halt in the Bombardment of North Vietnam," 9 October 1967, DDRS, document number CK2349074218. See also Johnson, meeting notes, 16 October 1967, *FRUS, 1964–1968*, 5, 353.

31 Johnson, meeting notes, 18 October 1967, *FRUS, 1964–1968*, 5, 357.

32 Johnson, meeting notes, 23 October 1967, *FRUS, 1964–1968*, 5, 363; Bundy to Rusk, "Implications of RT-58 and General JCS Bombing Strategy," 31 October 1967, *FRUS, 1964–1968*, 5, 372.

33 *The Joint Chiefs of Staff and the War in Vietnam*, Chapter 44, 10; Drea, *McNamara, Clifford, and the Burdens of Vietnam*, 220.

34 Turley, *The Second Indochina War*, 124.

35 Shapley, *Promise and Power*, 427–428, 437; Gardner, *Pay Any Price*, 403–405; McNamara, *In Retrospect*, 311–314.

36 Notes of Cabinet meeting, 4 October 1967, TTU, Larry Berman Collection, Box 8.

37 William L. Shaw, "Selective Service and the 1967 Statute," *Military Law Review*, 40 (April 1968), 33–34.

38 For assessments of the Baby Boom Generation, see Christopher Caldwell, *The Age of Entitlement: America Since the Sixties* (New York: Simon & Schuster, 2020); Tom Brokaw, *Boom! Voices of the Sixties Personal Reflections on the '60s and Today* (New York: Random House, 2007); Peter Collier and David Horowitz, *Destructive Generation: Second Thoughts About the Sixties* (New York: Summit Books, 1989).

39 Roger Rosenblatt, *Coming Apart: A Memoir of the Harvard Wars of 1969* (Boston: Little, Brown, 1997), 48.

40 On the influence of the academic left on the Baby Boom generation, see Roger Kimball, *The Long March: How the Cultural Revolution of the 1960s Changed America* (San Francisco: Encounter Books, 2000); Thomas Wheatland, *The Frankfurt School in Exile* (Minneapolis: University of Minnesota Press, 2009); Paul Berman, *A Tale of Two Utopias: The Political Journey of the Generation of 1968* (New York: W. W. Norton, 1996); Carl R. Trueman, *The Rise and Triumph of the Modern Self: Cultural Amnesia, Expressive Individualism, and the Road to Sexual Revolution* (Wheaton, Illinois: Crossway, 2020); Gitlin, *The Sixties;* Collier and Horowitz, *Destructive Generation.*

41 Maraniss, *They Marched Into Sunlight,* 99.

42 Michael Medved, *Right Turns: Unconventional Lessons from a Controversial Life* (New York: Crown Forum, 2004), 84–86.

43 Steven Kelman, *Push Comes to Shove: Escalation of Student Protest* (Boston: Houghton Mifflin, 1970), 61, 119–120 (quotes); Rosenblatt, *Coming Apart,* 23.

44 Lawrence M. Baskir and William A. Strauss, *Chance and Circumstance: The Draft, the War, and the Vietnam Generation* (New York: Alfred Knopf, 1978), 6–7. See also Stephen E. Ambrose, *Nixon: The Triumph of a Politician, 1962-1972* (New York: Simon & Schuster, 1989), 264-265; Burkett and Whitley, *Stolen Valor,* 53–54.

45 James Fallows, "What Did You Do in the Class War, Daddy?" *Washington Monthly,* 8, No. 12 (February 1977).

46 Anderson, *The Movement and the Sixties.*

47 Arnold Barnett, Timothy Stanley, and Michael Shore, "America's Vietnam Casualties: Victims of a Class War?" *Operations Research* 40, No. 5 (September/October 1992), 859; Lind, *Vietnam: The Necessary War,* 107–126; Burkett and Whitley, *Stolen Valor,* 55–57; Arthur T. Coumbe, *A History of The U.S. Army Officer Corps, 1900-1990* (Carlisle: U.S. Army War College Press, 2014), 89–104.

48 Rebecca E. Klatch, *A Generation Divided: The New Left, the New Right, and the 1960s* (Berkeley: University of California Press, 1999), 18–96; Scanlon, *The Pro-War Movement,* 63–65, 242–288.

49 Barnett, Stanley, and Shore, "America's Vietnam Casualties," 856–866. Barnett, Stanley, and Shore analyzed neighborhood data and other background information of a large sample of the deceased to see whether they were as affluent as the average members of their community or were instead poor individuals living in an affluent community and found that they were in general representative of their communities in terms of family income. See also Milam, *Not A Gentleman's War,* 26–27; Sorley, *A Better War,* 302–303.

50 Martin Binkin and Mark J. Eitelberg, *Blacks and the Military* (Washington: Brookings Institution, 1982), 76–78; Burkett and Whitley, *Stolen Valor,* 56–57, 452–454; DCAS, Active Duty Military Deaths—Race/Ethnicity Summary,

25 July 2009, https://dcas.dmdc.osd.mil/dcas/pages/Documents/RACE-OMB-WC.pdf. Hispanic deaths have been estimated at roughly 5 percent of the total, but most of them appear to have been included in the categories of white or black, for the official tally lists only 0.6 percent of the fatalities in the Hispanic category.

51 William Sloane Coffin Jr., *Once to Every Man: A Memoir* (New York: Atheneum, 1977), 244–251 (quotes); Jim Hoagland, "Anti-Draft Group Leaves 992 Cards at Justice Department," *Washington Post,* 21 October 1967.

52 Gibbons, *The U.S. Government and the Vietnam War,* 4, 861–865 (quotes); Joseph A. Califano, *The Triumph and Tragedy of Lyndon Johnson: The White House Years* (New York: Simon & Schuster, 1991), 195–197.

53 William Chapman, "GIs Repel Pentagon Charge," *Washington Post,* 22 October 1967.

54 Vietnam Documents and Research Notes, No. 9, "Forward under the Glorious Banner of the October Revolution," 4 November 1967, TTU, United States Department of State Collection, box 3.

55 Smith, meeting notes, 8 November 1967, *FRUS, 1964–1968,* 5, 390; Lee Kuan Yew, *From Third World to First,* 456–7. See also Bundy to Rusk, 14 November 1967, NA II, RG 59, Lot Files, Entry 5005, Files of Ambassador-at-Large Averell Harriman, box 4; Bundy, "Comments on DOD First Rough Draft of 19 May," 30 May 1967, LBJL, Warnke Papers, McNaughton Files, box 5; Charles Mohr, "Laos, Thailand and War," *New York Times,* 20 October 1967. In his 1995 book *In Retrospect,* McNamara invoked a highly compartmentalized CIA report dated September 11, 1967, to support his contention that the risks of an American withdrawal from Vietnam were not as high as many thought at the time. McNamara cited a section on the consequences of an "unfavorable outcome" in Vietnam, which stated, "Probably the net effects would not be permanently damaging to this country's capacity to play its part as a world power." McNamara, *In Retrospect,* 292–294. Other sections of the document, however, contravene McNamara's interpretation. The document stated that this "unfavorable outcome" did not mean "the precipitate withdrawal of American forces or sweeping political concessions tantamount to granting Hanoi outright achievement of its aims in the South" but rather a negotiated settlement involving a relatively orderly transition to Communist rule over a period of roughly one year. The authors conceded, "It is possible, however, that events would be precipitated in such a manner that the outcome—the taking of power by the communists—would emerge very rapidly and in conditions of breakdown and disorder on the non-Communist side. There could be a spectacle of panic flight from the country, suicidal resistance by isolated groups, and Communist terror and vengeance. Clearly, if this worst case came about, the discredit the U.S. would earn, which would be seen by many as not merely political, but also as moral discredit, would be far greater." Given the pervasive fear of the Communists in 1967, as well as the panicked flight of South Vietnamese civilians from North Vietnamese forces during the 1972 and 1975 offensives, an orderly selling out of South Vietnam seems far less likely than a mad rush for the exits. The report also

acknowledged that the fate of other Asian nations would hinge on how the Thais responded to pressure from Hanoi and Beijing, and "we have no sound basis for estimating how the Thais would respond to such pressure." CIA, "Implications of an Unfavorable Outcome in Vietnam," 11 September 1967, LBJL, VNCF, box 259. The Thai government was in the process of building its combat troop strength in Vietnam to eleven thousand, up from a pittance at the beginning of the year, despite the fact that they were fighting a growing Communist insurgency within their own borders. Most of the Thai troops were pledged after Clark Clifford and Maxwell Taylor visited Thailand in July 1967. Roland A. Paul, *American Military Commitments Abroad* (New Brunswick, New Jersey: Rutgers University Press, 1973), 114; MACV, 1967 Command History, 273–276. Clifford and Taylor had accurately predicted in their trip report that the Thais would fulfill their pledge. Clifford and Taylor, Report to the President, 5 August 1967, TTU, Ronald B. Frankum Jr., Collection, box 1. This deployment of Thai troops to Vietnam contradicted Clifford's subsequent statement in his memoir that he was appalled to hear in his summer 1967 trip to Southeast Asia that American allies in the region "did not want to contribute any more troops" and, "with the exception of Korea, resented having had to send any soldiers to Vietnam in the first place." Clark Clifford with Richard Holbrooke, *Counsel to the President: A Memoir* (New York: Random House, 1991), 449. According to Taylor's recounting of the trip, "Our Anglo-Saxon friends in Australia and New Zealand seemed to think the strategy of the war being pursued was about right whereas the Asians felt that we were not pressing the enemy hard enough...On the sensitive subject of troop requirements, no one argued against the increased needs set forth in our strategic presentation. But each country had good reasons why little more could be expected from it. The Thais had a growing guerrilla threat in their northeast; the Australians and New Zealanders pointed to new defense problems arising from the planned British withdrawal of troops from Malaysia and Singapore; the Koreans faced an increase of terrorist infiltration from North Korea." Taylor, *Swords and Plowshares*, 376.

56 William Chapman, "GIs Repel Pentagon Charge," *Washington Post*, 22 October 1967; Joseph A. Loftus, "Guards Repulse War Protesters at the Pentagon," *New York Times*, 22 October 1967; Drea, *McNamara, Clifford, and the Burdens of Vietnam*, 282–283.

57 CIA, "International Connections of U.S. Peace Groups," 15 November 1967, LBJL, Gibbons Papers, box 32.

58 On October 25, Ambassador Bunker cabled from Saigon that "Hanoi has been reporting with obvious relish and in great detail the current anti-war demonstrations in the U.S." Saigon to State, 25 October 1967, in Pike, ed., *The Bunker Papers*, 1, 222.

59 James S. Robbins, *This Time We Win: Revisiting the Tet Offensive* (New York: Encounter Books, 2010), 317.

60 Christian, notes of the president's meeting with Robert Manning, 19 October 1967, LBJL, Diary Backup, box 79. Rusk made similar comments earlier that month. "The Administration made a deliberate decision not to create

a war psychology in the United States," he said. "There have been no war bond campaigns, etc. The decision was made because it is too dangerous for this country really to get worked up. Maybe this was a mistake; maybe it would have been better to take steps to build up a sense of a nation at war." Gibbons, *The U.S. Government and the Vietnam War*, 4, 906–907.

61 Westmoreland later recounted that the president had arranged the trip "ostensibly for further consultations, but in reality for public relations purposes." Westmoreland, *A Soldier Reports*, 230-231.

62 Sorley, *Westmoreland*, 128.

63 Eric Wentworth, "Bunker Reports War Gain," *Washington Post*, 14 November 1967; "Westmoreland Optimistic," *Washington Post*, 16 November 1967 (first quote); Peter Grose, "War of Attrition Called Effective by Westmoreland," *New York Times*, November 20, 1967 (second and third quotes). This forecast would later be criticized as Pollyannish, yet American troop withdrawals and the transfer of combat responsibilities to the South Vietnamese would actually begin twenty months after the statement.

64 "Poll Finds Johnson Reverses His Popularity Loss," *New York Times*, 5 December 1967.

65 Louis Harris, "Public Takes Harder Line On Viet War," *Washington Post*, 23 December 1967.

66 Louis Harris, "Tolerance for War Protests Waning," *Washington Post*, 18 December 1967.

67 "Debrief of the Meeting of General Westmoreland with the Joint Chiefs of Staff," 17 November 1967, MCHC, Greene Papers; Westmoreland to JCS, 21 November 1967, *FRUS, 1964–1968*, 5, 418n; JCSM-663-67, 27 November 1967, NA II, RG 59, Lot Files, Entry 5005, Files of Ambassador-at-Large Harriman, box 2.

68 Kerwin, Planning Directive 1-68, 29 January 1968, NA II, RG 472, MACJ03, Historians Background Files, box 181; John M. Collins, "Going to Tchepone: OPLAN El Paso, *Joint Force Quarterly*, No. 17 (Autumn/Winter 1997–98), 118–129; Andrew R. Finlayson, "Operation El Paso," *Vietnam Veterans for Factual History Magazine*, 1, No. 2 (2018), 21–25.

69 Vientiane to State, 27 November 1967, LBJL, NSF, VNCF, box 93. Sullivan's optimism about the aerial interdiction in Laos came under fire from military intelligence analysts. Sullivan to Wheeler, 1 December 1967, LBJL, NSF, VNCF, box 93.

70 Li, *The Dragon of the Jungle*, 234. A senior Communist cadre who was captured in early 1967 attested that six of ten trucks sent down the Ho Chi Minh Trail were lost. *Rand Vietnam Interviews*, ser. AG, No. 573.

71 Jacob Van Staaveren, *Interdiction in Southern Laos*, 1960-1968 (Washington, DC: Center for Air Force History, 1993), 238-239.

72 The North Vietnamese history stated that 25,536 tons of supplies reached the South Vietnamese battlefields and that another 8,416 stayed in Laos for the functioning of the infiltration system, for a total of 33,952. Nguyen Viet Phuong, *Van Tai Quan Su Chien Luoc Tren Duong Ho Chi Minh Trong Khang Chien Chong My*, 2nd ed., 382. The North Vietnamese figures are roughly

consistent with those of contemporary American intelligence estimates. In October 1967, U.S. intelligence estimated North Vietnamese infiltration at 85 tons per day, amounting to 31,025 tons per year. Rostow to Johnson, 18 October 1967, LBJL, NSF, Files of Walt W. Rostow, box 7.

73 "Eisenhower Backs U.S. Land Forays in North Vietnam," *New York Times,* 29 November 1967. The press later speculated that Eisenhower had coordinated his message with the Joint Chiefs, to which Eisenhower responded that he had not spoken with any of the Joint Chiefs since his departure from the White House in January 1961. Felix Belair, "Eisenhower Urges Support for War," *New York Times,* 24 December 1967.

74 "Eisenhower-Bradley Excerpts," *New York Times,* 29 November 1967.

75 Robert J. Hanyok, *Spartans in Darkness: American SIGINT and the Indochina War, 1945–1975* (Fort Meade: National Security Agency, 2002), 317; Lee Lescaze, "Dakto: The Enemy's Choice," *Washington Post,* 25 November 1967.

76 Sources on the Battle of Dak To include C. William Thorndale, "Battle for Dak To," Project CHECO Report, 21 June 1968, TTU, Vietnam Archive Collection, box 4; Headquarters, 4th Infantry Division, "Battle for Dak To," 3 January 1968, TTU, Douglas Pike Collection, Unit 2, box 7; W. R. Peers, "Presentation to MACV Commanders Conference," 3 December 1967, TTU, Veteran Members of the 109th Quartermaster Company Collection, box 1; Nguyen Huu An with Nguyen Tu Duong, *Chien Truong Moi,* 59–78; Chu Huy Man, *Thoi Soi Dong,* 463–467; Nguyen Quang Dat and Tran Hanh, eds., *Mot So Tran Danh Trong Khang Chien Chong Phap,* Tap I, 103–122; Nguyen Van Minh et al., *Luc Luong Vu Trang and Nhan Dan Tay Nguyen Trong Khang Chien Chong My Cuu Nuoc;* Bui Quyen, *The 3rd Airborne Battalion At Ngok Wan (The Kham Zei 180 Campaign),* unpublished manuscript; Lee Lescaze, "Dakto: The Enemy's Choice," *Washington Post,* 25 November 1967; Michael A. Eggleston, *Dak To and the Border Battles of Vietnam, 1967–1968* (Jefferson, North Carolina: McFarland, 2017), 28–98; Murphy, *Dak To,* 128–301; Allan W. Sandstrum, "Three Companies at Dak To," in Cash et al., eds., *Seven Firefights in Vietnam,* 85–108; Atkinson, *Long Gray Line,* 242–253; Villard, *Combat Operations,* 152–178; Leonard B. Scott, "The Battle for Hill 875, Dak To, Vietnam 1967," U.S. Army War College, March 1988; George P. Long, "Battle for Dak To," in Albert N. Garland, ed., *A Distant Challenge: The U.S. Infantryman in Vietnam, 1967–1972* (Nashville: Battery Press, 1983), 45–50.

77 Nguyen Huu An with Nguyen Tu Duong, *Chien Truong Moi,* 59–60.

78 Nguyen Quang Dat and Tran Hanh, eds., *Mot So Tran Danh Trong Khang Chien Chong Phap,* Tap I, 103–122.

79 Murphy, *Dak To,* 235.

80 Ibid., 240.

81 Eggleston, *Dak To and the Border Battles in Vietnam,* 79.

82 Ibid., 84.

83 Nguyen Huu An with Nguyen Tu Duong, *Chien Truong Moi,* 77.

84 Ibid., 81.

85 Wheeler to McNamara, "Operations in the Triborder Area," 16 December 1967, LBJL, NSF, VNCF, box 93.

86 Westmoreland to Wheeler, 10 December 1967, TTU, Veteran Members of the 109th Quartermaster Company Collection, box 1.

87 Wheeler to McNamara, "Operations in the Triborder Area," 16 December 1967, LBJL, NSF, VNCF, box 93; "Operations in the Cambodia/Laos/SVN Tri-Border Area," n.d., LBJL, NSF, VNCF, box 93.

88 Westmoreland to JCS, 5 December 1967, *FRUS, 1964–1968*, 27, 213 (quotes); Sharp to Wheeler, 5 December 1967, LBJL, NSF, VNCF, box 92.

89 Johnson, meeting notes, 5 December 1967, *FRUS, 1964–1968*, 27, 216. At this time, the U.S. intelligence community continued to express doubts about the U.S. military's views that military supplies were moving through Sihanoukville to Communist forces in South Vietnam and that Cambodian rice was especially valuable to the North Vietnamese war effort. Special National Intelligence Estimate 57/1-67, "Significance of Cambodia to the Vietnamese Communist War Effort," 14 December 1967, *FRUS, 1964–1968*, 27, 220.

90 "Meeting of the President with the Australian Cabinet," 21 December 1967, TTU, Ronald B. Frankum Jr., Collection, box 5; CIA, "Cambodia and the Vietnamese Communists," 29 January 1968, CREST, document number CIA-RDP85T00875R001100070006-3.

91 Latimer, "Hanoi's Leaders and Their South Vietnam Policies," 292–294 (quotes); W. R. Smyser, *The Independent Vietnamese: Vietnamese Communism Between Russia and China, 1956–1969* (Athens, Ohio: Ohio University Center for International Studies), 99–100.

92 Barbara Barnouin and Yu Changgen, *Chinese Foreign Policy During the Cultural Revolution* (London: Kegan Paul, 1998), 83–86, 120; Radchenko, *Two Suns in the Heavens*, 166–200; Chen Jian, *Mao's China and the Cold War*, 230–237; Chang and Halliday, *Mao*, 537–546; Li, *The Dragon in the Jungle*, 144–149; Wedeman, *East Wind Subsides*, 269–270; Tsou, *The Cultural Revolution and Post-Mao Reforms*, 60–62. China experienced negative economic growth of 5.7 percent in 1966 and 4.1 percent in 1968. https://data.worldbank.org/indicator/NY.GDP.MKTP.KD.ZG?locations=CN.

93 Vo Chi Cong, *Tren Nhung Chang Duong Cach Mang (Hoi Ky)* (Hanoi: Nha Xuat Ban Chinh Tri Quoc Gia, 2001), 231.

94 Ford, *CIA and the Vietnam Policymakers*, 97–100; Wirtz, *The Tet Offensive*, 158–162; Cubbage II, "Westmoreland vs. CBS," 150–153; Bunker to Rostow, 29 August 1967, *FRUS, 1964–1968*, 5, 297; Abrams to Wheeler, Sharp, and Westmoreland, 20 August 1967, TTU, Larry Berman Collection, box 7; Cosmas, *MACV*, 449–454.

95 Saigon to Director, 13 September 1967, in Directorate of Intelligence, *Fifty Years of Informing Policy: Expanded Edition Containing Declassified Documents* (Washington, DC: Center for the Study of Intelligence, 2002), 178–183; Carver to Bunker, "Agreement on Viet Cong Strength Figures," 15 September 1967, TTU, Sam Johnson Vietnam Archive Collection, box 5. The mutually agreed figures on enemy personnel were incorporated into Special National Intelligence Estimate 14.3-67, "Capabilities of the Vietnamese Communists

for Fighting in South Vietnam," 13 November 1967, LBJL, Gibbons Papers, box 32.

96 CBS News, "The Uncounted Enemy: A Vietnam Deception," 23 January 1982, CREST document number CIA-RDP88-01070R000100040003-8.

97 At the conclusion of the trial, CBS agreed to issue a public statement that the network "never intended to assert, and does not believe, that General Westmoreland was unpatriotic or disloyal in performing his duties as he saw them." For details on the trial, see Renata Adler, *Reckless Disregard: Westmoreland v. CBS, Sharon v. Time* (New York: Knopf, 1986); Bob Brewin and Sydney Shaw, *Vietnam on Trial: Westmoreland vs. CBS* (New York: Atheneum, 1987); Burton Benjamin, *Fair Play: CBS, General Westmoreland, and How a Television Documentary Went Wrong* (New York: Harper & Row, 1988); Cubbage, "Westmoreland vs. CBS," 144–167; Don Kowet, *A Matter of Honor* (New York: Macmillan, 1984); M. Patricia Roth, *The Juror and the General* (New York: William Morrow, 1986).

98 Affidavit of Gains B. Hawkins, 7 September 1983, TTU, Virtual Vietnam Archive, Item 0250204001; Affidavit of David C. Morgan, 18 February 1983, TTU, Virtual Vietnam Archive, Item 0250204001; Carver to Helms, 11 September 1967, TTU, Virtual Vietnam Archive, Item 0250209002.

99 Special National Intelligence Estimate 14.3-67 of November 1967 included the political cadres in roughly the numbers favored by the CIA and put the total of combat forces plus political cadres at between 298,000 and 333,000. The estimate acknowledged the existence of self-defense and secret self-defense forces but did not provide numbers for them because the CIA leadership had accepted Westmoreland's argument that their numbers were too imprecise to include the estimate. Special National Intelligence Estimate 14.3-67, "Capabilities of the Vietnamese Communists for Fighting in South Vietnam," 13 November 1967, LBJL, Gibbons Papers, box 32. See also Carver to Helms, 10 July 1967, TTU, Virtual Vietnam Archive, Item 0240708003; Direct Examination of George Carver, 8 November 1984, TTU, Virtual Vietnam Archive, Item 0250312001.

100 Affidavit of Everette S. Parkins, 3 August 1983, TTU, Virtual Vietnam Archive, Item 0250201001.

101 Affidavit of James Meacham, 3 October 1983, TTU, Virtual Vietnam Archive, Item 0250150001.

102 Burton Benjamin, "An Examination," 8 July 1982, TTU, Larry Berman Collection (Westmoreland vs. CBS), box 11; Affidavit of Walt Rostow, 6 March 1984, TTU, Virtual Vietnam Archive, Item 0250201001. Burton Benjamin, a senior CBS executive whom the network asked to conduct an internal investigation of the production, concluded that "A 'conspiracy,' given the accepted definition of the word, was not proved." He also faulted the producers for ignoring witnesses and evidence that contradicted the claims of Adams and for "the coddling of sympathetic witnesses." Benjamin, "An Examination."

103 Direct examination of John F. Stewart, 5 November 1984, TTU, Virtual Vietnam Archive, Item 0250309001.

104 John Limond Hart, "The Statistics Trap in Vietnam," *Washington Post,* 6 January 1985.

105 Affidavit of James Meacham, 3 October 1983, TTU, Virtual Vietnam Archive, Item 0250150001; Direct examination of John F. Stewart, 5 November 1984, TTU, Virtual Vietnam Archive, Item 0250309001.

106 Hanyok, *Spartans in Darkness,* 110–116; Sorley, *A Better War,* 48–52.

107 Combined Intelligence Center Vietnam, Order of Battle Summary, September 1972, 2, Records of the Military Assistance Command Vietnam, Part 2, Classified Studies from the Combined Intelligence Center Vietnam, 1965–1973, reel 18. The total for the year came to 103,173.

108 MACV, 1967 Command History, 2, 111. Estimates of enemy guerrilla strength had fallen the most because the Communists generally used guerrillas to replace losses in their regular units. Westmoreland to RUEPJ5/NMCC, "Order of Battle," 4 April 1968, TTU, Virtual Vietnam Archive, Item 0250209002; Affidavit of James Meacham, 3 October 1983, TTU, Virtual Vietnam Archive, Item 0250150001. For agreement between the CIA and the military on the strengths of regulars, guerrillas, and support troops, see Carver to Bunker, "Agreement on Viet Cong Strength Figures," 15 September 1967, TTU, Sam Johnson Vietnam Archive Collection, box 5.

109 Combined Intelligence Center Vietnam, Order of Battle Summary, September 1972, 2, Records of the Military Assistance Command Vietnam, Part 2, Classified Studies from the Combined Intelligence Center Vietnam, 1965–1973, reel 18. The North Vietnamese official history claimed that strength increased from 204,000 to 278,000 during the year. Military History Institute of Vietnam, *Victory in Vietnam,* 211. If, however, those figures were accurate and the figures on recruitment and infiltration in the same history were accurate, then Communist losses for the year would have been a mere 14,600, an absurdly low number.

110 Johnson, meeting notes, 15 November 1967, *FRUS, 1964–1968,* 5, 400; Johnson, meeting notes, 21 November 1967, *FRUS, 1964–1968,* 5, 409; Blair, *There to the Bitter End,* 160. The enemy loss figures included individuals who were not part of the enemy's combat forces, such as political cadres and civilians who were carrying supplies or evacuating casualties for the Communists. Figures on enemy killed in action, defections, non-battle casualties, and total losses are listed in MACV, 1967 Command History, 2, 111. The figure on prisoners is taken from Special National Intelligence Estimate 14.3-67, "Capabilities of the Vietnamese Communists for Fighting in South Vietnam," 13 November 1967, LBJL, Gibbons Papers, box 32. The number of enemy permanently lost from wounds was calculated by subtracting the other loss categories from the total losses. The accuracy of casualty figures is analyzed further in Chapter 16.

111 Special National Intelligence Estimate 14.3-67, "Capabilities of the Vietnamese Communists for Fighting in South Vietnam," 13 November 1967, LBJL, Gibbons Papers, box 32.

112 Military History Institute of Vietnam, *Victory in Vietnam,* 466.

113 General Department of Rear Services, *Tong Ket Cong Tac Hau Can Chien Truong Nam Bo-Cuc Nam Trung Bo Trong Khang Chien Chong My,* 546. For

details on the recruiting problems in the Mekong Delta Province of Dinh Tuong, see David W. P. Elliott, *The Vietnamese War: Revolution and Social Change in the Mekong Delta, 1930–1975* (Armonk: M. E. Sharpe, 2003), 2, 984–988.

114 For a detailed description of U.S. involvement in pacification in the last months of 1967, see Villard, *Combat Operations,* 43–255.

115 The number of citizens living in secure areas increased from 10.3 million to 11.5 million. The percentages were calculated based on the assumption that all of the 463,000 newly registered refugees moved from contested or Communist-controlled areas to secure areas. Thomas C. Thayer, *War Without Fronts: The American Experience in Vietnam* (Boulder: Westview Press, 1985), 142-145, 227.

116 General Department of Rear Services, *Tong Ket Cong Tac Hau Can Chien Truong Nam Bo-Cuc Nam Trung Bo Trong Khang Chien Chong My,* 547. In Phu Yen Province, the North Vietnamese reported in mid-1967 that the number of people under Communist control in the province had fallen from a peak of 260,000 to 20,000. Vietnam Documents and Research Notes, No. 3, "Political Task in the Summer 1967 Campaign," 13 May 1967, TTU, Douglas Pike Collection, Unit 1, Box 6. A resolution produced by the Communist headquarters in the South in the middle of 1967 stated that the U.S. and South Vietnamese were "able to seize a number of areas and gain control of a larger portion of the population, thereby emptying a number of our springboard areas and base areas of their civilian population." Tran Tinh, ed., *Van Kien Dang,* Tap 28, 490.

117 Wirtz, *The Tet Offensive,* 181–185; Affidavit of Walt Rostow, 6 March 1984, TTU, Virtual Vietnam Archive, Item 0250201001.

118 United States Mission in Vietnam, "Captured Document Indicates Final Phase of Revolution at Hand," 5 January 1968, TTU, Douglas Pike Collection, unit 2, box 9.

119 CIA, "The Viet Cong/North Vietnamese Winter-Spring Campaign," n. d., *FRUS, 1964-1968,* 5, 440n; Wirtz, *The Tet Offensive,* 172–179; Ford, *Tet 1968,* 179–183.

120 Nguyen Van Minh et al., *Lich Su Khang Chien Chong My Cuu Nuoc, 1954–1975,* Tap V, 33–34. At a meeting in December, the Politburo acknowledged that although the impending offensive would most likely produce a historic victory, it was possible that the offensive's successes would not entirely destroy the enemy and might provoke the United States into expanding the war into North Vietnam, Laos, and Cambodia. Ibid., 37–40.

121 Vu Thu Hien, *Dem Giua Ban Ngay* (Westminster, California: Van Nghe, 1997), translated by T. Lan Tran as *Darkness in Daytime* (unpublished, 2019); Sophie Quinn-Judge, "The Ideological Debate in the DRV and the Significance of the Anti-Party Affair," 1967–68," *Cold War History,* 5, No. 4 (November 2005), 479–500; Pribbenow, "General Vo Nguyen Giap and the Mysterious Evolution of the Plan for the 1968 Tet Offensive," 21–22; Huy Duc, *Ben Thang Cuoc, Tap II: Quyen Binh* (Los Angeles: Osinbook, 2012), 155–160; Nguyen, "The War Politburo," 25–32; Nguyen, *Hanoi's War,* 91–107.

122 MACV, 1968 Command History, 48.

123 Gaiduk, *The Soviet Union and the Vietnam War,* 58, 61, 139–140.

124 Ibid., 142.

CHAPTER 12

1 MacGill, interview with author.

2 Robert L. Tonsetic, *Days of Valor: An Inside Account of the Bloodiest Six Months of the Vietnam War* (Philadelphia: Casemate, 2007), 157, 161.

3 Ibid., 165.

4 Headquarters, 199th Infantry Brigade, Combat Operations After Action Report, 14 January–19 February 1968, NA II, RG 472, 199th Infantry Brigade, After Action Reports, Box 1; Tonsetic, *Days of Valor,* 156–165; Nolan, *Battle for Saigon,* 142–148; Albin F. Irzyk, *Unsung Heroes: Saving Saigon* (Raleigh: Ivy House, 2008), 153–161; John C. McManus, *The 7th Infantry Regiment: Combat in an Age of Terror, The Korean War Through the Present* (New York: Forge, 2008), 123–126; Gibler, interview with author; MacGill, interview with author; Johnson, interview with author.

5 Maclear, *The Ten Thousand Day War,* 204–205; Wirtz, *The Tet Offensive,* 201–207; Ford, *Tet 1968,* 103–104; Palmer, *Summons of the Trumpet,* 183.

6 Ford, *CIA and the Vietnam Policymakers,* 112–118; Wirtz, *The Tet Offensive,* 200–223; Cosmas, *MACV: The Joint Command in the Years of Withdrawal,* 48–49; Davidson, *Vietnam at War,* 479–481. Further evidence supporting a northern focus came from Communist radio traffic, which spoke mainly of offensive operations in the northernmost provinces and the highland provinces of Pleiku and Kontum and made scant mention of South Vietnamese towns and cities. Hanyok, *Spartans in Darkness,* 330–331. At least some of this radio traffic represented a deliberate deception effort by the North Vietnamese, for Pleiku and Kontum saw little North Vietnamese military activity during the ensuing period.

7 "Intelligence Warning of the Tet Offensive in South Vietnam," April 8, 1968, http://www.foia.cia.gov/sites/default/files/document_conversions/89801/ DOC_0000097712.pdf; Sharp and Westmoreland, *Report on the War in Vietnam,* 135; Ford, *Tet 1968,* 183–184; Villard, *Combat Operations,* 274–277; Daniel O. Graham, Oral History, LBJL; Westmoreland, *A Soldier Reports,* 321 (quote).

8 Jack Shulimson et al., *U.S. Marines in Vietnam: The Defining Year, 1968* (Washington: U.S. Marine Corps History and Museums Division, 1997), 108; Sharp and Westmoreland, *Report on the War in Vietnam,* 174; Combined Intelligence Center Vietnam, Order of Battle Summary, September 1972, 2, Records of the Military Assistance Command Vietnam, Part 2, Classified Studies from the Combined Intelligence Center Vietnam, 1965–1973, reel 18.

9 Nguyen Khac Tinh et al., *Phao Binh Nhan Dan Viet Nam,* 140–145.

10 Tran Quy Hai, *Ban Ve Nghe Thuat Chien Dich Quan Su* (Hanoi: People's Army Publishing House, 1976), 94–96.

11 Kieu Tam Nguyen, ed, *Chien Truong Tri-Thien-Hue Trong Cuoc Chien Tranh Chong My Cuu Nuoc Toan Thang*, 151. A history commissioned by the Politburo explained that large attacks commenced at Khe Sanh in January because the assault on Khe Sanh was central to the "general offensive," which comprised military attacks in the rural countryside and mountain jungles in combination with the "general uprising." Ban Chi Dao Tong Ket Chien Tranh Truc Thuoc Bo Chinh Tri, *Tong Ket Cuoc Khang Chien Chong My Cuu Nuoc*, 69–70.

12 The North Vietnamese could have moved a large fraction of the forty thousand troops at Khe Sanh to Hue as soon as fighting broke out there but did not do so. They waited until February 10 to move troops and then sent just five battalions. When it became clear that the allies could amass enough forces to retake Hue, the North Vietnamese decided to keep their forces in Hue rather than withdraw them to safety in order to tie down allied troops that otherwise could have gone to Khe Sanh. Col. Gen. Tran Van Quang, who commanded the Communist forces in Hue's military region, later stated that his region was designated "only a minor theater of operations" in early 1968. By contrast, he asserted, the high command chose as its major northern theater in I Corps the B5 Front, within which Khe Sanh was the principal area of operations. Because of orders issued from the high command on February 18, General Quang recounted, "we had to continue to hold Hue in order to support the efforts of the B5 Front" at Khe Sanh. Ho Ban, ed., *Huong Tien Cong va Noi Day Tet Mau Than o Tri-Thien-Hue (nam 1968)* (Hanoi: Military History Institute, 1986), 94–111. The official history of the 325th NVA Division also attested to the preeminence of Khe Sanh and the B5 Front. Pham Gia Duc, *Su Doan 325*, Tap II, 95–96. In the summer of 1968, General Creighton Abrams observed that if the North Vietnamese had not been so obsessed with Khe Sanh, they could have moved a division or two from Khe Sanh to Hue, which would have created enormous problems for U.S. forces. He believed that the North Vietnamese could have held Hue for three months had such a reinforcement taken place. Lewis Sorley, ed., *Vietnam Chronicles: The Abrams Tapes, 1968–1972* (Lubbock: Texas Tech University Press, 2004), 33–34.

13 CIA, "The Enemy Threat to Khe Sanh," 2 February 1968, CREST, document number 02547967; Robert Pisor, *End of the Line: The Siege of Khe Sanh* (New York: W. W. Norton, 1982), 118–120; Zaffiri, *Westmoreland*, 272–275.

14 Westmoreland to Wheeler, 12 January 1968, LBJL, Westmoreland Papers, box 15 (quote); Westmoreland to Wheeler, 22 January 1968, DDRS, 1986, 95; *The Joint Chiefs of Staff and the War in Vietnam*, Chapter 48, 22.

15 Westmoreland, *A Soldier Reports*, 338.

16 Wheeler to Johnson, 3 February 1968, LBJL, NSF, VNCF, box 66; JCS to CINCPAC, 11 February 1968, *FRUS, 1964–1968*, 6, 51n; *Public Papers of the Presidents, 1968–69*, 234; Cosmas, *MACV: The Joint Command in the Years of Withdrawal*, 73; Thompson, *To Hanoi and Back*, 125.

17 Dao Trong Cang, ed., *Van Kien Dang*, Tap 29, 1968 (Hanoi: Nha Xuat Ban Chinh Tri Quoc Gia, 2004), 1–40. See also Luan, *Nationalists in the Viet*

Nam Wars, 331–332. Le Duan and the Central Committee did leave open the possibility that the offensive would not achieve this full measure of success. The United States might respond by sending more forces to Vietnam, they acknowledged. Even in that case, however, the offensive would certainly strengthen Hanoi's hand in the South. Ibid., 55–57; Le Duan, *Letters to the South,* 96–97. Once the military victory had been won, Hanoi planned to mobilize a front organization in the South called the Alliance for National Democratic and Peace Forces, which presumably was intended to play a leading role in the transition of power to the Communist Party. MACV, 1968 Command History, 75. Whether or not the North Vietnamese leadership actually wanted the offensive to succeed has been the subject of dispute. Certain evidence suggests that Hanoi believed the offensive was doomed to failure and launched it as a means of destroying the Southern-born Communists, thus solidifying Northern control over the South after the war. The plans for the offensive were daring to the point of recklessness and were conceived with little regard for reports from Southern Communists that cast doubt on the willingness of the civilian population to engage in uprisings. The Communists dispersed their forces to such an extent that achieving victory in most areas was virtually impossible. Most of the attackers who perished were Southerners, and conflicts between Northern and Southern Communists would later intensify, in some part because of the Southern decimation at Tet. Less than twenty-four hours after most of the attacks began, COSVN appears to have issued a circular in which it described accurately the shortcomings and setbacks of the offensive and stated that the offensive would not achieve a quick and decisive victory. Bay Hong, circular, 1 February 1968, in McGarvey, ed., *Visions of Victory,* 252–256. Within such a short period of time, COSVN most likely would not have known the status of the fighting in most areas. The evidence against the existence of a North Vietnamese conspiracy is, however, stronger. At many other times during the war, both before and after, the Communists suffered heavy losses simply because of poor judgment. Hanoi quite possibly allocated few Northerners to the offensive because the town and city populations would view the Southerners more favorably than they would Northerners. Some high-ranking Communists of Southern origin advocated launching the offensive, believing that victory was likely. North Vietnam's ruling circle, moreover, probably possessed enough confidence in its own power that it did not fear the prospect of squelching Southern aspirations for autonomy after defeating the Saigon government.

18 Ward and Burns, *The Vietnam War,* 206–207. A Party directive, read to all troops on the eve of battle, proclaimed, "It will be the greatest battle ever fought throughout the history of our country. It will bring forth world-wide change but will also require many sacrifices." The attackers would "resolutely move forward to completely defeat the American aggressors" and "completely liberate the 14,000,000 people of South Vietnam." Oberdorfer, *Tet!,* 75.

19 "Intelligence Warning of the Tet Offensive in South Vietnam," April 8, 1968, http://www.foia.cia.gov/sites/default/files/document_conversions/89801/DOC_0000097712.pdf;Hoang Ngoc Lung, *The General Offensives of 1968–69*

(Washington, DC: U.S. Army Center of Military History, 1981), 28–29; MACV, 1968 Command History, 130; James H. Willbanks, *The Tet Offensive: A Concise History* (New York: Columbia University Press, 2008), 26. According to a Communist account, "Many pagodas in the areas temporarily under enemy control became secret facilities where Liberation Army cadre and soldiers were able to hide and where they could cache their weapons, thereby making a not insignificant contribution to the victory achieved by the Tet 1968 General Offensive and Uprising by the soldiers and civilians of South Vietnam. Many Buddhist monks and nuns provided logistical support, supplying food and ammunition to our troops, tending to our wounded soldiers, burying Liberation Army soldiers who had been killed, and concealing soldiers who had become trapped inside the cities before they were able to withdraw back into the liberated zone." Nguyen Phuc Khanh et al., ed., *Chung Mot Bong Co*, 221.

20 Moïse, *The Myths of Tet*, 125–127.

21 Hoang Ngoc Lung, *The General Offensives of 1968-69*, 21–23; Hoang Ngoc Lung, *Intelligence* (Washington, DC: U.S. Army Center of Military History, 1982), 147–148; Ford, *Tet 1968*, 184–185; Wirtz, *The Tet Offensive*, 79, 217. It is conceivable that Thieu actually knew that the attacks were coming. His intelligence organizations had some sources within the Vietnamese Communist Party as well as the garrulous Colonel Nam Dong, the Qui Nhon prisoners, and a variety of valuable captured documents. If Thieu did know, he may have chosen to play ignorant to let the Communists carry through what looked like a self-destructive offensive. It is much more likely, however, that Thieu dismissed evidence of impending attacks for the same reasons that the Americans did. His departure from Saigon during Tet strongly supports that conclusion.

22 Frederick C. Weyand, "Tet Offensive After Action Report," n.d., TTU, Virtual Vietnam Archive, Item 168300010351; Harry Summers Jr., "Troops to Equal Any," *Vietnam*, 1, No. 1 (Summer 1988), 20–25.

23 MACV, 1968 Command History, 881; Sharp and Westmoreland, *Report on the War in Vietnam*, 158–159; Hoang Ngoc Lung, *Intelligence*, 145–146; Villard, *Combat Operations*, 271–272; Cosmas, *MACV: The Joint Command in the Years of Withdrawal*, 50–51; Hammond, *Public Affairs: The Military and the Media, 1962-1968*, 343.

24 *Bao Cong An T.P. Ho Chi Minh*, 26 January 2003; Luan, *Nationalists in the Viet Nam Wars*, 333–334.

25 Irzyk, *Unsung Heroes*, 57–67; *The Joint Chiefs of Staff and the War in Vietnam*, Chapter 51, 3; Cosmas, *MACV: The Joint Command in the Years of Withdrawal*, 54–56; Wirtz, *The Tet Offensive*, 219–222.

26 For difficulties encountered by Communist forces at the start of the offensive, see Ho Son Dai and Tran Phan Chan, *Lich Su Saigon-Cho Lon-Gia Dinh Khang Chien (1945-1975)* (Ho Chi Minh City: Ho Chi Minh City Publishing House, 1994), 481–496; Cao Minh et al., *Quan Khu 8: Ba Muoi Nam Khang Chien (1945-1975)* (Hanoi: People's Army Publishing House, 1998), 618–646; Truong Minh Hoach and Nguyen Minh Phung, *Quan Khu 9*, 423–444;

Cao Hung et al., *Quang Nam-Da Nang*, Tap II, 153; Nguyen Huu Nguyen, *Long An: Lich Su Khang Chien Chong My Cuu Nuoc (1954–1975)* (Hanoi: People's Army Publishing House, Hanoi, 1994), 224; Mai Chi Tho, *Hoi Uc Mai Chi Tho, Tap II: Theo Buoc Chan Lich Su* (Ho Chi Minh City: Nha Xuat Ban Tre, 2001), 164–167.

27 Tran Bach Dang, *Tran Bach Dang: Cuoc Doi va Ky Uc* (Ho Chi Minh City: Nha Xuat Ban Tre, 2006), 168.

28 Joseph L. Dees, "The Viet Cong Attack That Failed," *Department of State News Letter, No.* 85 (May 1968), 22.

29 Saigon to State, 19 April 1968, NA II, RG 59, Central Files, 1967–1969, box 2808; Robert J. O'Brien, "The Attack on The American Embassy During Tet, 1968: Factors That Turned A Tactical Victory Into A Political Defeat," Master's Thesis, U.S. Army Command and General Staff College, 2009; Dees, "The Viet Cong Attack That Failed," 22–30; Irzyk, *Unsung Heroes*, 77–107; Mai Chi Tho, *Hoi Uc Mai Chi Tho*, 165–166; Robbins, *This Time We Win*, 125–133; Villard, *Combat Operations*, 328–330; Oberdorfer, *Tet!*, 2–34; Ho Son Dai and Tran Phan Chan, *Lich Su Saigon-Cho Lon-Gia Dinh Khang Chien*, 485–486.

30 Peter Braestrup, *Big Story: How the American Press and Television Reported and Interpreted the Crisis of Tet 1968 in Vietnam and* Washington (Boulder, Colo.: Westview Press, 1977), 1, 93–104; Don North, "VC Assault on the U.S. Embassy," *Vietnam*, 12, No. 5 (February 2000), 38–47, 72; Hammond, *Public Affairs: The Military and the Media, 1962–1968*, 344–345.

31 CIA, "Initial Assessment of Popular Reactions in the Provinces to the Viet Cong Tet Offensive," 7 February 1968, CREST, document number 00011917; CIA, "Situation Appraisal: Analysis of Attitudes of Saigon Residents in Wake of the Viet Cong Attack," 11 February 1968, LBJL, NSF, VNCF, box 70; CIA, Vietnam Situation Report No. 7/68, 12 February 1968, LBJL, NSF, VNCF, box 70; Saigon to State, 15 February 1968, LBJL, NSF, National Security Council Histories, March 31 Speech, box 48; *Rand Vietnam Interviews*, ser. Tet-VC, No. 2; Martin G. Clemis, *The Control War: The Struggle for South Vietnam, 1968–1975* (Norman: University of Oklahoma Press, 2018), 166–168; Dommen, *The Indochinese Experience of the French and the Americans*, 668–669; Nguyen-Marshall, "Student Activism in Time of War: Youth in the Republic of Vietnam, 1960s–1970s," 56–57.

32 Douglas Pike, "Giap Offensive Aims at War's End by Midyear: Dissension in Hanoi," *Washington Post*, February 25, 1968.

33 *Rand Vietnam Interviews*, ser. Tet-VC, No. 00. For American accounts of the fighting near Tan Son Nhut, see Starry, *Mounted Combat in Vietnam*, 118–123; Villard, *Combat Operations*, 332–343. One of the officers who led Communist forces into Saigon at Tet, Major General Huynh Cong Than, recounted, "We had to conduct a purely military struggle. We were not playing a supporting role for an uprising of the masses as we had thought." Huynh Cong Than, *O Chien Truong Long An: Hoi Uc* (Hanoi: People's Army Publishing House, 1994), 133.

34 Hanoi had evidently anticipated this problem, as it tried to pin the blame on the South Vietnamese and Americans. A Radio Hanoi broadcast claimed that

South Vietnamese and American forces had breached the ceasefire to carry out attacks on the civilian population. CIA, Central Intelligence Bulletin, 30 January 1968, CREST, document number 00809273.

35 Saigon to State, 8 February 1968, LBJL, NSF, National Security Council Histories, March 31st Speech, box 48; CIA, "RVNAF Performance During the Tet Offensive," 10 February 1968, *FRUS, 1964–1968*, 6, 56n; Keeny, notes of 584th meeting of the National Security Council, 4 April 1968, *FRUS, 1964–1968*, 6, 160. The impressive performance of the South Vietnamese forces relieved U.S. forces of the need to rush troops to numerous district and provincial capitals and thus allowed them to keep hounding the North Vietnamese Army in more remote areas. DePuy to Rostow, "Impact of Recent Enemy Operations on the Pacification Program," 7 February 1968, LBJL, NSF, VNCF, box 60.

36 Huynh Cong Than, *O Chien Truong Long An*, 133.

37 Mackubin T. Owens, "Saddam's Secret Weapon," *National Review*, 31 March 2003; Burkett and Whitley, *Stolen Valor*, 120–121; Peter Arnett, "This War is not Working," *Daily Mirror*, 1 April 2003; Ellen C. Cousins, "Peter Arnett: A Few Examples," 19 October 2004, Primos Research.

38 Correspondent Michael Herr, who covered Tet for *Esquire* magazine and subsequently published his observations in the best-selling book *Dispatches*, wrote of the Tet Offensive: "'We had to destroy Ben Tre in order to save it.' That's how most of the country came back under what we called control, and how it remained essentially occupied by the Viet Cong and the North until the day years later when there were none of us left there." Michael Herr, *Dispatches* (New York: Alfred A. Knopf, 1977), 74.

39 Glenn E. Helm, "The Tet 1968 Offensive: A Failure of Allied Intelligence," MA thesis, Arizona State University, 1989, 174.

40 Pearson, *The War in the Northern Provinces*, 30; MACV, 1968 Command History, 131; Momyer, *Air Power in Three Wars*, 318; Vetter, *Never Without Heroes*, 167–174.

41 General sources on the battle for Hue include Erik Villard, *The 1968 Tet Offensive Battles of Quang Tri City and Hue* (Washington, DC: U.S. Army Center of Military History, 2008); George W. Smith, *The Siege at Hue* (Boulder, Colorado: Lynne Rienner, 1999); Nicholas Warr, *Phase Line Green: The Battle for Hue, 1968* (Annapolis: Naval Institute Press, 1997); Dang Kinh, *Vi Tuong Du Kich Lung Danh* (Hanoi: Lao Dong Publishing House, 2013); Le Minh Hoang et al., *Trung Doan 6 (Doan Phu Xuan) 1965–2005* (Hanoi : National Political Publishing House, 2005); Nguyen Van Minh et al., *Lich Su Khang Chien Chong My Cuu Nuoc, 1954–1975, Tap V: Tong Tien Cong Va Noi Day Nam 1968* (Hanoi: National Political Publishing House, Hanoi, 2001); Pham Van Son, *The Viet Cong Tet Offensive 1968* (Saigon: RVNAF Printing and Publications Center, 1969); Andrew Wiest, *Vietnam's Forgotten Army: Heroism and Betrayal in the ARVN* (New York: New York University Press, 2008); Mark Bowden, *Hue 1968: A Turning Point of the American War in Vietnam* (New York: Atlantic Monthly Press, 2017); Shulimson et al., *U.S. Marines in Vietnam: The Defining Year*; Eric Hammel, *Fire in the Streets: The Battle for Hue, Tet 1968* (Pacifica, California: Pacifica Military History, 1991); Oberdorfer, *Tet!*;

Keith William Nolan, *Battle for Hue: Tet, 1968* (Novato, California: Presidio Press, 1983).

42 Smith, *The Siege at Hue,* 170.

43 One North Vietnamese history recounted that the inability of the attackers "to overrun and capture this key, decisive target" allowed their opponents to "use Mang Ca as a springboard from which to launch fierce counterattacks." Le Minh Hoang et al., *Trung Doan 6,* 110. According to another Communist account, the North Vietnamese wanted Mang Ca so badly that they sent low-flying aircraft from North Vietnam to bomb the stronghold. Four of the planes never returned to North Vietnam. *Quan Doi Nhan Dan,* 6 May 1995.

44 Tran Thi Tu Van, *Mourning Headband for Hue: An Account of the Battle for Hue, Vietnam 1968,* translated by Olga Dror (Bloomington: Indiana University Press, 2014); Oriana Fallaci, *Nothing, and So Be It,* translated by Isabel Quigly (Garden City: Doubleday, 1972), 168–169; Bowden, *Hué 1968,* 99, 167, 174–175, 299–312; Langguth, *Our Vietnam,* 475–477; Douglas Pike, *The Viet-Cong Strategy of Terror* (Saigon: United States Mission, 1970), 54–60; Pham Van Son, *The Viet Cong Tet Offensive 1968,* 271–284; Lewy, *America in Vietnam,* 274–275.

45 Nguyen Van Minh et al., *Lich Su Khang Chien Chong My Cuu Nuoc, 1954–1975,* Tap V, 40; Kieu Tam Nguyen, ed, *Chien Truong Tri-Thien-Hue Trong Cuoc Chien Tranh Chong My Cuu Nuoc Toan Thang,* 151–152 (quote); Vu Bach et al., *Tran Danh Ba Muoi Nam,* Tap II (Hanoi: People's Army Publishing House, 1995), 333–335; Nguyen Huy Toan and Pham Quang Dinh, *Su Doan 304,* Tap II, 61–71.

46 CIA, "The Enemy Threat to Khe Sanh," 2 February 1968, CREST, document number 02547967; Davidson, *Vietnam At War,* 563; Hoang Dan et al., *Chien Dich Tien Cong Duong So 9-Khe Sanh Xuan He 1968* (Hanoi: Ministry of Defense, 1987), 70; MACV, 1968 Command History, 420; Westmoreland, *A Soldier Reports,* 317.

47 *Rand Vietnam Interviews,* ser. Tet-VC, No. 59.

CHAPTER 13

1 Alyssa Adams, ed., *Eddie Adams: Vietnam* (Brooklyn: Umbrage Editions, 2008), 144.

2 Braestrup, *Big Story,* 1, 644.

3 Al Santoli, *To Bear Any Burden: The Vietnam War and Its Aftermath in the Words of Americans and Southeast Asians* (New York: Ballantine Books, 1985), 184–185. In 1998, on the day Loan died, Adams declared, "The guy was a hero. America should be crying." Dale Hopper, "Nguyen Ngoc Loan Dies at 67," *Washington Times,* 16 July 1998. See also Tran Minh Cong, "Public Security and the National Police," in Tuong Vu and Sean Fear, eds., *The Republic of Vietnam, 1955–1975: Vietnamese Perspectives on Nation Building* (Ithaca: Southeast Asia Program Publications, 2019), 78–79.

4 Ho Son Dai and Nguyen Van Hung, *Lich Su Doan 5,* 128–133.

5 Huynh Cong Than, *O Chien Truong Long An,* 133–136.

6 Daddis, *Westmoreland's War,* 141. The *New York Times* editorialized on February 4, "Swept away in last week's hurricane of fire were the rising

piles of glowing reports of progress in pacification, retraining of the South Vietnamese Army, and destruction of the enemy's political and military forces." "The Vietcong Launch Their 'Revolution,'" *New York Times,* 4 February 1968. When American and South Vietnamese spokesmen announced that the offensive had resulted in catastrophic military defeat for the Communists, journalists dismissed them as out of touch. Murray Marder, "U.S. Experts Concede Gain by VC," *Washington Post,* 3 February 1968; Braestrup, *Big Story,* 1, 155–157. As days and weeks passed, and more and more evidence surfaced that the Communist offensive had failed to achieve its military and political objectives, correspondents speculated that the countryside had been lost to the Communists because many of South Vietnam's pacification forces had left the countryside at the beginning of the offensive to extinguish the urban attacks. A *Newsweek* article on February 19 announced that pacification "had been dealt a blow from which it would recover only slowly—if ever." "Man on the Spot," *Newsweek,* 19 February 1968, 33.

7 Stanley Karnow, "Thieu Lost Prestige in VC Thrusts," *Washington Post,* 18 February 1968.

8 *Reporting Vietnam: Part One: American Journalism 1959–1969* (New York: Library of America, 1998), 581–582.

9 "Disillusioned with Journalism," *Time,* 1 March 1968, 42.

10 Braestrup, *Big Story,* 1, 705.

11 Robert Elegant, "How to Lose A War: The Press and Viet Nam," *Encounter,* LVII, No. 2 (August 1981), 73–90.

12 Oberdorfer, *Tet!,* 229.

13 Ibid., 206, 214.

14 Alje Vennema, *The Viet Cong Massacre at Hue* (New York: Vantage, 1976), 99; Thomas Taylor, *Where the Orange Blooms: One Man's War and Escape in Vietnam* (New York: McGraw Hill, 1989), 142–144; Pike, *The Viet-Cong Strategy of Terror,* 49–51.

15 Nguyen Ngoc Bich, "The Battle of Hue 1968 as Seen From the Perspective of its NVA Commander," paper presented at the Texas Tech University Vietnam Center Sixth Triennial Symposium, March 14, 2008.

16 CIA, "Alleged Assessment of VC Failure during Tet Offensive in Danang by Representatives from Hanoi and New Plan for Attack of Danang," 17 February 1968, CREST, document number 02797882.

17 CDEC doc log no. 05-1131-68, 29 May 1968, NA II, RG 472, MACV J2, IIRS, Box 34.

18 Shulimson et al., *U.S. Marines in Vietnam: The Defining Year,* 179–180.

19 Richard D. Camp Jr., *Death In The Imperial City: U.S. Marines In The Battle For Hue, 31 January To 2 March 1968* (Quantico: Marine Corps University Press, 2018), 38.

20 Gene Roberts, "U.S. Marines in Hue Drive Wedge Into Enemy Units," *New York Times,* 6 February 1968.

21 William Tuohy, *Dangerous Company: Inside the World's Hottest Trouble Spots with a Pulitzer Prize-Winning War Correspondent* (New York: Morrow, 1987), 119.

22 Kaczmarek, interview with author.

23 Hammel, *Fire in the Streets*, 238.

24 Ho Ban, ed., *Huong Tien Cong va Noi Day Tet Mau Than o Tri-Thien-Hue*, 94–111.

25 Shulimson et al., *U.S. Marines in Vietnam: The Defining Year*, 213; Villard, *The 1968 Tet Offensive Battles of Quang Tri City and Hue*, 78–81; Department of the Army, "Combat After Action Report—Op Hue," 16 August 1968, NA II, RG 407, Westmoreland vs CBS Litigation Collection, box 3.

26 Sources on the Battle of Khe Sanh include Gregg Jones, *Last Stand at Khe Sanh: The U.S. Marines' Finest Hour in Vietnam* (Boston: Da Capo, 2014); John Prados and Ray Stubbe, *Valley of Decision: The Siege of Khe Sanh* (Boston: Houghton Mifflin, 1991); Eric Hammel, *Khe Sanh: Siege in the Clouds* (New York: Crown, 1989); Pisor, *The End of the Line*; Shulimson et al., *U.S. Marines in Vietnam: The Defining Year*; Momyer, *Air Power in Three Wars*.

27 Braestrup, *Big Story*, 1, 426.

28 Ibid., 386. See also MACV, 1968 Command History, 958–959.

29 Larry Berman, *Lyndon Johnson's War* (New York: W. W. Norton, 1989), 167–170; Gardner, *Pay Any Price*, 416–418.

30 Charles R. Smith, *U.S. Marines in Vietnam: High Mobility and Standdown, 1969* (Washington, DC: History and Museums Division, Headquarters, U.S. Marine Corps, 1988), 258-259; Van Staaveren, *Interdiction in Southern Laos*, 290–292; MACV, 1968 Command History, 922–923.

31 Jones, *Last Stand at Khe Sanh*, 100–101.

32 Comments of PFC Newton D. Lyle, April 1968, USMC Oral History Tape #1775.

33 Ray W. Stubbe, *Battalion of Kings: A Tribute to Our Fallen Brothers Who Died Because of the Battlefield of Khe Sanh* (Wauwatosa, Wisconsin: Khe Sanh Veterans, 2005), 152–153.

34 Prados and Stubbe, *Valley of Decision*, 350.

35 Comments of PFC Newton D. Lyle, April 1968, USMC Oral History Tape #1775.

36 Stubbe, *Battalion of Kings*, 153.

37 Comments of LCPL Lance E. Tibbet, USMC Oral History Tape #2572.

38 Breeding, interview with author.

39 Sources on the Battle of Lang Vei are Department of the Army, "After Action Report: Battle of Lang Vei," 22 February 1968, NA II, RG 572, 5th Special Forces Group, Records of A Detachments, box 146; William R. Phillips, *Night of the Silver Stars: The Battle of Lang Vei* (Annapolis: Naval Institute Press, 1997); Jones, *Last Stand at Khe Sanh*, 118–138; John A. Cash, "Battle of Lang Vei," in Cash et al., eds., *Seven Firefights in Vietnam*, 109–138; Edwards, "Unit

Activities," 9 May 1968, NA II, RG 472, 5th Special Forces Group, Records of A Detachments, box 146; Prados and Stubbe, *Valley of Decision*, 352–389; Shulimson et al., *U.S. Marines in Vietnam: The Defining Year*, 273–276; Pham Gia Duc, *Su Doan 325*, Tap II, 100–103.

40 Davidson, *Vietnam At War*, 554–557; Cosmas, *MACV: The Joint Command in the Years of Withdrawal*, 44–48; Sorley, *Westmoreland*, 174–176.

41 Westmoreland, *A Soldier Reports*, 342; Shulimson et al., *U.S. Marines in Vietnam: The Defining Year*, 161–162; Pisor, *End of the Line*, 175–176.

42 Prados and Stubbe, *Valley of Decision*, 466.

43 John Edmund Delezen, *Red Plateau: Memoir of a North Vietnamese Soldier* (Los Angeles: Corps Productions, 2005), 106–107.

44 David Lownds Oral History, USMCHC.

45 Le Kinh Lich, *The 30-Year War: 1945–1975*, vol. 2 (Hanoi: The Gioi Publishers, 2001), 177.

46 Nguyen Huy Toan and Pham Quang Dinh, *Su Doan 304*, Tap II, 121–122.

47 Rostow, Memo for the Record, 29 February 1968, LBJL, NSC Histories, March 31st Speech, box 49; Saigon to State, March 1, 1968, NA II, RG 59, Central Files, 1967–1969, box 2804; Joint Staff, "Analysis of COMUSMACV Force Requirements and Alternatives," March 1, 1968, *FRUS, 1964–1968*, 6, 96; Schaffer, *Ellsworth Bunker*, 197–199.

48 Burns W. Roper, "What Public Opinion Polls Said," in Braestrup, *Big Story*, 1, 686–687; "Thin Green Line," *Time*, 23 February 1968, 16.

49 Johnson, "Notes of The President's Tuesday Luncheon Meeting," 6 February 1968, LBJL, Tom Johnson's Notes of Meetings, box 2; Johnson, "Notes of the President's Meeting with the National Security Council," 7 February 1968, LBJL, Tom Johnson's Notes of Meetings, box 2.

50 Wheeler to Johnson, 3 February 1968, LBJL, NSF, VNCF, box 66; Wheeler to Westmoreland, 8 February 1968, DDRS, document number CK2349001245; CBS News, "The Johnson Years," 25–26 September 1969, LBJL, Special File, CBS interviews, "Why I Chose Not to Run," box 1.

51 Westmoreland to Sharp and Wheeler, "Assessment of Situation and Requirements," 12 February 1968, MHI, Harold K. Johnson Papers, box 143.

52 Johnson, "Notes of the President's Meeting with the Senior Foreign Affairs Advisory Council," 10 February 1968, LBJL, Tom Johnson's Notes of Meetings, Box 2; Schandler, *The Unmaking of the President*, 135.

53 Schandler, *The Unmaking of a President*, 107–111; Perry, *Four Stars*, 187–188; Cosmas, *MACV: The Joint Command in the Years of Withdrawal*, 94–95.

54 Wheeler, "Report of Chairman, JCS on Situation in Vietnam and MACV Force Requirements," 27 February 1968, DDRS, 1979, 383A.

55 Westmoreland, *A Soldier Reports*, 357. See also Kim Willenson, *The Bad War: An Oral History of the Vietnam War* (New York: New American Library, 1987), 96–97.

56 Johnson, meeting notes, 28 February 1968, *FRUS, 1964–1968*, 6, 91.

57 Berman, *Lyndon Johnson's War*, 171.

CHAPTER 14

1 At a meeting on March 4, Clifford remarked, "For a while, we thought and had the feeling that we understood the strength of the Viet Cong and the North Vietnamese. You will remember the rather optimistic reports of General Westmoreland and Ambassador Bunker last year. Frankly, it came as a shock that the Vietcong–North Vietnamese had the strength of force and skill to mount the Tet offensive—as they did. They struck 34 cities, made strong inroads in Saigon and in Hue. There have been very definite effects felt in the countryside.... There are grave doubts that we have made the type of progress we had hoped to have made by this time." Johnson, meeting notes, 4 March 1968, *FRUS, 1964–1968,* 6, 104. See also John Acacia, *Clark Clifford: The Wise Man of Washington* (Lexington: University Press of Kentucky, 2009), 256–265. One CIA report that almost certainly influenced Clifford, given its publication date of 1 March, expressed deep pessimism about the South Vietnamese government's prospects and predicted that the Communists would raise their troop strength enough to offset the impact of American troop increases. CIA, "Questions Concerning the Situation in Vietnam," 1 March 1968, CREST, document number 03398256. Another CIA assessment stated that the North Vietnamese "will probably be able to recoup their recent losses," while the South Vietnamese government was most unlikely to regain its pre-Tet position or make further gains. CIA, "The Outlook in Vietnam," 26 February 1968, LBJL, NSF, National Security Council Histories, March 31 Speech, box 47. See also CIA Directorate of Intelligence, "Pacification in the Wake of the Tet Offensive in South Vietnam," 19 March 1968, LBJL, NSF, VNCF box 60. The Systems Analysis division of the Office of the Secretary of Defense, which was predisposed toward the doves, stated that "the enemy's current offensive appears to have killed the [pacification] program once and for all." *Pentagon Papers,* IV, 556. With respect to the influence of the media, Harry McPherson, another influential dove, acknowledged later, "I put aside my own interior access to confidential information and was more persuaded by what I saw on the tube and in the newspapers." Schandler, *Unmaking of a President,* 82.

2 Clifford, "A Viet Nam Reappraisal," *Foreign Affairs,* July 1969, 609–610.

3 Clifford, *Counsel to the President,* 493.

4 Hoopes, *Limits of Intervention,* 146.

5 Hoopes to Clifford, "The Infeasibility of Military Victory in Vietnam," 14 March 1968, *FRUS, 1964–1968,* 6, 126; McPherson to Johnson, 18 March 1968, in Barrett, ed., *Lyndon B. Johnson's Vietnam Papers,* 680–683; Alain C. Enthoven and K. Wayne Smith, *How Much is Enough? Shaping the Defense Program, 1961–1969* (New York: Harper & Row, 1971), 298–299; *Pentagon Papers,* IV, 556–569; Edward J. Drea, *McNamara, Clifford, and the Burdens of Vietnam, 1965–1969* (Washington, DC: Office of the Secretary of Defense Historical Office, 2011), 223–225.

6 Draft Memorandum for the President, Alternative, "Alternative Strategies in Vietnam," 1 March 1968, LBJL, NSF, National Security Council Histories, March 31st Speech, box 49.

7 *USVNR*, book 5, IV.c.6(c), 42.

8 Clifford, *Counsel to the President*, 494.

9 Draft Memorandum to the President, 4 March 1968, DDRS, 1979, 371A.

10 Gene Roberts, "U.S. Command Sees Hue, Not Khe Sanh, as Foe's Main Goal," *New York Times*, March 7, 1968.

11 Westmoreland to Wheeler, 8 March 1968, LBJL, Westmoreland Papers, box 16. Upon reading the article, Wheeler chided Westmoreland for downplaying the enemy threat, although he couched it in terms of Clifford's concern about raising false hopes in the American public rather than his own concern about convincing Johnson to authorize more troops. "Do not denigrate the enemy," Wheeler notified Westmoreland. "Do not indulge in forecasting enemy plans or our plans. Do not make predictions of victory. Do express the view that there is tough fighting and that the enemy has residual capabilities not yet committed." Wheeler to Westmoreland and Sharp, 8 March 1968, *FRUS, 1964–1968*, 6, 112.

12 Wheeler to Westmoreland, 9 March 1968, LBJL, Westmoreland Papers, box 39.

13 "Poll of Democrats Finds Many Hawks Backed McCarthy," *New York Times*, 15 March 1968; Peter Braestrup, "A Comment on the Vietnam Crisis in America: Tet 1968," in James Titus, ed., *The Home Front and War in the Twentieth Century: The American Experience In Comparative Perspective* (Washington, DC: Government Printing Office, 1984), 200; Oberdorfer, *Tet!*, 276–77.

14 Clifford, memorandum of conference with Senator Robert Kennedy and Theodore C. Sorenson, 14 March 1968, in Barrett, ed., *Lyndon B. Johnson's Vietnam Papers*, 671–674; Arthur M. Schlesinger Jr., *Robert Kennedy and His Times*, 2 (Boston: Houghton Mifflin, 1978), 888-891; Shesol, *Mutual Contempt*, 418–421.

15 Shulimson et al., *U.S. Marines in Vietnam: The Defining Year*, 283; Prados and Stubbe, *Valley of Decision*, 513.

16 Combined Intelligence Center Vietnam, Order of Battle Summary, September 1972, 2, Records of the Military Assistance Command Vietnam, Part 2, Classified Studies from the Combined Intelligence Center Vietnam, 1965–1973, reel 18.

17 Villard, *Combat Operations*, 459–505; *Joint Chiefs of Staff and the War in Vietnam*, Chapter 52, 2–3; Littauer and Uphoff, eds. *Air War in Indochina*, 269.

18 Saigon to State, 28 March 1968, in Pike, ed., *The Bunker Papers*, 2, 393–402; Clarke, *Advice and Support*, 308–311; Villard, *Combat Operations*, 442–443; MACV, 1968 Command History, 561–562.

19 Littauer and Uphoff, eds. *Air War in Indochina*, 269.

20 For a valuable analysis of the uniqueness of William Calley, see Milam, *Not a Gentleman's War*, 126–138, 162–165.

21 William Peers, *Report of the Department of the Army Review of the Preliminary Investigations into the My Lai Incident* (Washington D.C.: Department of the Army, 1974); Howard Jones, *My Lai: Vietnam, 1968, and the Descent into*

Darkness (New York: Oxford University Press, 2017); Michael Bilton and Kevin Sim, *Four Hours in My Lai* (New York: Viking, 1992); William Thomas Allison, *My Lai: An American Atrocity in the Vietnam War* (Baltimore: Johns Hopkins University Press, 2012); Trent Angers, *The Forgotten Hero of My Lai: The Hugh Thompson Story* (Lafayette, Louisiana: Acadian House, 1999); Michael R. Belknap, *The Vietnam War on Trial: The My Lai Massacre and the Court-Martial of Lieutenant Calley* (Lawrence: University Press of Kansas, 2002).

22 Moïse, *The Myths of Tet*, 165.

23 According to the official MACV history, an estimated 37,000 enemy were killed by the end of February, and 17,371 were killed in March. One chart within the history, however, gives a higher figure of 39,667 for February 1967. The history provides no explanation for the discrepancy between that figure and the 37,000 total. MACV, 1968 Command History, 199, 906. General Tran Van Tra, the North Vietnamese commander of the Tet attacks on Saigon, would later speak of the catastrophic losses with unblinking candor and remorse. "There were units that went into battle from which not a single soldier returned," he lamented. Tran Van Tra, "Tet: The 1968 General Offensive and General Uprising," in Jayne S. Werner and Luu Doan Huynh, eds., *The Vietnam War: Vietnamese and American Perspectives* (Armonk: M.E. Sharpe, 1993), 62.

24 Mai Chi Tho, a senior party secretary who was serving near Saigon at the time, recounted, "When the Tet 68 attacks were launched, a number of our cadre and soldiers mistakenly believed that we would be able to quickly liberate Saigon and then the rest of South Vietnam. Then, when the enemy launched savage counterattacks, these individuals became frightened, wavered, and began to defect to the enemy." Mai Chi Tho, *Hoi Uc Mai Chi Tho*, 171. See also Turley, *The Second Indochina War*, 154–156.

25 Tran Van Tra, *Vietnam: History Of The Bulwark B2 Theatre, Vol 5: Concluding The 30-Years War*, translated by Foreign Broadcast Information Service (Arlington, Virginia: Joint Publications Research Service, 1983), 35; MACV, 1968 Command History, 73; Karnow, *Vietnam*, 547; Ahern, *CIA and Rural Pacification in Vietnam*, 313; *Rand Vietnam Interviews*, ser. Tet-VC, No. 43. According to one American estimate, 20 percent of the enemy killed were not soldiers or guerrillas but either civilian cadres or civilians who had been convinced or coerced to take part in the offensive. Villard, *Combat Operations*, 436. The tabulation was further complicated by the fact that a significant number of soldiers and guerrillas served simultaneously as cadres.

26 Hunt, *Pacification*, 138–140; *The Joint Chiefs of Staff and the War in Vietnam*, Chapter 52, 45–46; Cosmas, *MACV: The Joint Command in the Years of Withdrawal*, 69–71.

27 *FRUS, 1964–1968*, 6, 146.

28 Walter Isaacson and Evan Thomas, *The Wise Men* (New York: Simon & Schuster, 1986), 698–700; Clifford, *Counsel to the President*, 513–514 (quote).

29 Saigon to State, 20 March 1968, NA II, RG 59, Central Files, 1967–1969, box 2805.

30 In November 1967, the White House had begun discussing the shift of Westmoreland to the position of Army chief of staff in early 1968. Cosmas, *MACV: The Joint Command in the Years of Withdrawal*, 3–4. Westmoreland wanted to leave because his four-year tenure was longer than he had anticipated and longer than most wartime tours of duty. Telcon, Johnson and Russell, 22 March 1968, *FRUS, 1964–1968*, 6, 150.

31 Johnson, "Notes of the President's Meeting with General Earle Wheeler, JCS, and General Creighton Abrams," 26 March 1968, LBJL, Tom Johnson's Notes of Meetings, box 2.

32 Johnson, "Notes of the President's Meeting with His Foreign Policy Advisers," 26 March 1968, LBJL, Tom Johnson's Notes of Meetings, box 2.

33 Johnson, "Notes of Meeting," 26 March 1968, LBJL, Tom Johnson's Notes of Meetings, box 2. The six included Dean Acheson, George Ball, Arthur Dean, Cyrus Vance, Douglas Dillon, and McGeorge Bundy. The four hawks were Omar Bradley, Abe Fortas, Robert Murphy, and Maxwell Taylor. Those in the middle were Henry Cabot Lodge and Matthew Ridgway. The meeting notes do not indicate the position taken by the other "Wise Man," Averell Harriman. Within the group of six, some advocated withdrawal of U.S. forces over an unspecified period, but others favored only a change in military strategy. Clifford and a number of his supporters later spread a narrative of this period in which Johnson resented Clifford and the Wise Men for opposing escalation and advocating a bombing halt. The meetings of late March, it was said, pressured Johnson into accepting their dovish position at a time when he was of a more hawkish mind. Schandler, *Unmaking of a President*, 264; Harry McPherson, *A Political Education* (Boston: Little, Brown, 1972), 436–443; Roger Morris, *Uncertain Greatness: Henry Kissinger and American Foreign Policy* (New York: Harper & Row, 1977), 44–45; Clifford, *Counsel to the President*, 511–521; Isaacson and Thomas, *Wise Men*, 700–705. In actuality, Johnson had already decided against sending more troops, and the bombing halt was consistent with the plan for a "peace fist" that Johnson had outlined in his phone call with Clifford on March 20.

34 *Public Papers of the Presidents of the United States: Lyndon B. Johnson, 1968–69*, Book I, 469–476.

35 Lyndon Baines Johnson, *Vantage Point: Perspectives of the Presidency, 1963–1969* (New York: Holt, Rinehart and Winston, 1971), 425–431. See also Gittinger, ed., *The Johnson Years*, 77.

36 "Johnson Rating in Poll Hits Low," *New York Times*, 31 March 1968.

37 "Kennedy Leads 44% Against 41% for LBJ," *Washington Post*, 24 March 1968.

38 Louis Harris, "Support for LBJ's War Policy Slips to 54%," *Washington Post*, 25 March 1968.

39 For the tendency of Americans to rally around the flag when crises erupt, see Mueller, *War, Presidents, and Public Opinion;* Russett, *Controlling the Sword;* Gelpi, Feaver, and Reifler, *Paying the Human Costs of War*.

40 George Gallup, "What Combat Does to Our Men," *Reader's Digest*, June 1968, 64. In an early repudiation of what would become a negative stereotype of

Vietnam veterans as social misfits, Gallup stated, "What kind of citizens will they be? Judging by the cross-section we talked to, the answer is: superior."

41 State to Saigon, 29 March 1968, NA II, RG 59, Central Files, 1967–1969, box 2808. Clifford noted this same day that the suspension "could lead to a cessation of bombing" if it were "followed by reciprocal action on the other side." Nitze, Memorandum for Record, March 29, 1968, *FRUS, 1964–1968*, 6, 166.

CHAPTER 15

1 Dallek, *Flawed Giant,* 530.

2 John W. Finney, "Fulbright, in Debate, Calls Curb on Raids Misleading," *New York Times,* 3 April 1968. Senator Mike Mansfield came to the President's defense. The bombing had been halted over the territory where 90 percent of the North Vietnamese population lived, he pointed out. "The more we question the President's veracity," Mansfield pronounced, "the more we weaken his hand and our position in trying to reach a settlement to this barbarous war."

3 Edward J. Drea, *McNamara, Clifford, and the Burdens of Vietnam, 1965–1969* (Washington, DC: Office of the Secretary of Defense Historical Office, 2011), 225; Johnson, *Vantage Point,* 493–495; Dallek, *Flawed Giant,* 537.

4 MACV, 1968 Command History, 414–415. Before Johnson's announcement of March 31, Americans had supported the bombing of the North by a 70 to 16 margin. After the pause, 64 percent of Americans approved of Johnson's bombing halt, with just 26 percent opposed. Mueller, *War, Presidents, and Public Opinion,* 72–73.

5 Gene Roberts, "Saigon Bitterness at Peace Bid Worries U.S. Officials There," *New York Times,* 5 April 1968; Bernard Weinraub, "Saigonese Fear U.S. Withdrawal," *New York Times,* 7 April 1968.

6 CIA to White House Situation Room, "President Thieu's Comments on President Johnson's Vietnam Speech," 4 April 1968, LBJL, NSF, Memos to the President, Walt Rostow, box 32; Saigon to State, 6 April 1968, LBJL, NSF, Memos to the President, Walt Rostow, box 32 (quote); Habib to Katzenbach, "Vietnamese Reaction to Peace Moves," 8 April 1968, NA II, RG 59, Central Files, 1967–1969, box 2717.

7 Johnson to Thieu, 2 April 1968, LBJL, NSF, Head of State Correspondence File, box 12.

8 Saigon to State, 6 April 1968, LBJL, NSF, Memos to the President, Walt Rostow, box 32.

9 Schaffer, *Ellsworth Bunker,* 200–201.

10 For the surprise among the North Vietnamese at Johnson's announcement, see Vo Van Sung, "Cau Chuyen Ngoai Giao 40 Nam Truoc Bay Gio Moi Ke," *Vietnam Net,* 27 January 2008, http://www.vietnamnet.vn/chinhtri/2008/01/766176/.

11 Bui Tin, *From Enemy to Friend: A North Vietnamese Perspective on the War,* translated by Nguyen Ngoc Bich (Annapolis: Naval Institute Press, 2002), 65. See also Truong Nhu Tang, *A Viet Cong Memoir,* 143.

12 Saigon to State, 29 May 1968, NA II, RG 59, Central Files, 1967–1969, box 2743.

13 Hoang Van Hoan, *A Drop in the Ocean: Hoang Van Hoan's Revolutionary Reminiscences* (Beijing: Foreign Languages Press, 1988), 332–334.

14 Hoang Van Hoan, "Distortion of Facts About Militant Friendship Between Viet Nam and China is Impermissible," *Beijing Review*, 22, No. 49 (7 December 1979), 18.

15 Memcon, Zhou Enlai and Pham Van Dong, 13 April 1968, CWIHP.

16 Memcon, Zhou Enlai and Pham Van Dong, 19 April 1968, CWIHP.

17 Johnson, *Vantage Point*, 497.

18 Vientiane to State, 11 April 1968, *FRUS, 1964–1968*, 6, 190n; Johnson, *Vantage Point*, 497–503; *The Joint Chiefs of Staff and the War in Vietnam*, Chapter 50, 9–12.

19 Telcon, Johnson and Harriman, 11 April 1968, *FRUS, 1964–1968*, 6, 191.

20 Meeting notes, 11 April 1968, *FRUS, 1964–1968*, 6, 193.

21 Headquarters 101st Airborne Division, "Operational Report of the 101st Airborne Division for the period ending 30 April 1968," 24 May 1968, TTU, Richard Detra Collection, box 4; Sharp and Westmoreland, *Report on the War in Vietnam*, 166–167; MACV, 1968 Command History, 159, 380; Cosmas, *MACV: The Joint Command in the Years of Withdrawal*, 110–111.

22 "To Khe Sanh and Back," *The Air Cavalry Division*, 1, No. 2 (July 1968), 7–8, 32; Pearson, *The War in the Northern Provinces*, 81–89; Villard, *Combat Operations*, 507–519; Spector, *After Tet*, 123–141.

23 Villard, *Combat Operations*, 520.

24 Yarborough, *A Shau Valor*, 120.

25 Le Minh Hoang et al., *Trung Doan 6*, 131–133; Tran Trong Trung, *Tong Tu Lenh Vo Nguyen Giap Trong Nhung Nam De Quoc My Leo Thang Chien Tranh (1965–1969)* (Hanoi: Nha Xuat Ban Chinh Tri Quoc Gia Su That, 2015), 285–286 (quote).

26 None of the available North Vietnamese histories address the decision to withdraw from the A Shau Valley. Considering the relative ineffectiveness of the initial American aerial bombardment and the prevalence of terrain that was favorable to the defenders, the North Vietnamese most likely could have exacted a high toll in American casualties had they stayed in the valley. Although many North Vietnamese units were suffering from supply problems at this time, the A Shau was a supply hub and thus presumably was not as deficient as others. The most plausible explanation is that the arrival of large American and South Vietnamese units from multiple directions caused the North Vietnamese to fear an encirclement from which they could not escape.

27 James M. Sprayberry, Medal of Honor Award Recommendation, 11 December 1969, NA II, RG 472, Medal of Honor Award Case File.

28 1st Cavalry Division, Operation Delaware After Action Report, 11 July 1968, TTU, Richard Detra Collection, box 4; Wiest, *Vietnam's Forgotten Army*, 138–143; Yarborough, *A Shau Valor*, 118–132; Villard, *Combat Operations*, 520–527; Pearson, *The War in the Northern Provinces*, 89–92; Spector, *After Tet*, 138–140.

29 Thomas A. Johnson, "The U.S. Negro in Vietnam," 29 April 1968; "Negro Expatriates Finding Wide Opportunity in Asia," 30 April 1968; "Negro in Vietnam Uneasy About U.S.," 1 May 1968, all in *New York Times.*

30 High-Level Military Institute, *Vietnam: The Anti-U.S. Resistance War for National Salvation*, 106–107; Nguyen Van Minh et al., *Lich Su Khang Chien Chong My Cuu Nuoc, 1954–1975*, Tap V, 159–162; Tran Trong Trung, *Tong Tu Lenh Vo Nguyen Giap Trong Nhung Nam De Quoc My Leo Thang Chien Tranh*, 284.

31 An additional fifteen thousand North Vietnamese troops arrived in May. Combined Intelligence Center Vietnam, Order of Battle Summary, September 1972, 2, Records of the Military Assistance Command Vietnam, Part 2, Classified Studies from the Combined Intelligence Center Vietnam, 1965–1973, reel 18.

32 Sharp and Westmoreland, *Report on the War in Vietnam*, 162; Saigon to State, 4 July 1968, in Pike, ed., *The Bunker Papers*, 2, 496; Pham Vinh Phuc, "Tran Phuc Kich Da Hang-Ven Ven Cua Trung Doan 88/Quan Khu Mien Dong, Ngay 25 Thang 8 Nam 1968," in Tran Hanh, ed., *Mot So Tran Danh Trong Khang Chien Chong Phap, Khang Chien Chong My, 1945–1975*, Tap II (Hanoi: Military History Institute of Vietnam, 1991), 210.

33 Huynh Cong Than, *O Chien Truong Long An*, 137–139. A North Vietnamese analysis from 1973 delivered this verdict on the 1968 offensives: "We committed a number of errors and were subjective in our assessment of the situation, as a result of which we set goals that were not realistic in light of the actual situation at the time, and in particular after the Tet 1968 wave of attacks we did not review the attacks and derive lessons learned in a timely fashion in order to reassess the situation and make timely decisions to change directions." Nguyen Van Minh et al., *Lich Su Khang Chien Chong My Cuu Nuoc, 1954–1975*, Tap V, 263. See also Nguyen Viet Ta et al., *Mien Dong Nam Bo Khang Chien*, Tap II, 363–364; Ho Ban, ed., *Huong Tien Cong va Noi Day Tet Mau Than o Tri-Thien-Hue*, 94–111.

34 Ho Son Dai and Tran Phan Chan, *Lich Su Saigon-Cho Lon-Gia Dinh Khang Chien*, 507; Moïse, *The Myths of Tet*, 203.

35 Chen Jian, "China, the Vietnam War, and the Sino-American Rapprochement, 1968–1973," in Odd Arne Westad and Sophie Quinn-Judge, eds., *The Third Indochina War: Conflict Between China, Vietnam and Cambodia, 1972–1979* (London: Routledge, 2006), 38; Taylor, *China and Southeast Asia*, 61.

36 Memcon, Zhou Enlai, Chen Yi, and Xuan Thuy, 7 May 1968, CWIHP. See also Memcon, Zhou Enlai and Pham Hung, 29 June 1968, CWIHP.

37 *The Joint Chiefs of Staff and the War in Vietnam*, Chapter 52, 6–7; Villard, *Combat Operations*, 561–564; Tonsetic, *Days of Valor*, 221.

38 Tran Bach Dang, "Mau Than: Cuoc Tong Dien Tap Chien Luoc," *Tap Chi Lich Su Quan Su*, 26, No. 2 (1988), 62; Huynh Cong Than, *O Chien Truong Long An*, 139–142; Ho Son Dai and Tran Phan Chan, *Lich Su Saigon-Cho Lon-Gia Dinh Khang Chien*, 507, 517–519; Villard, *Combat Operations*, 563–590; Pham Van Son, *The Viet Cong Tet Offensive 1968*, 154–247; *The Joint Chiefs of Staff and the War in Vietnam*, Chapter 52, 7. The Communists attacked in Saigon again on May 25 in lesser strength and with similarly one-sided results. Nguyen

Van Minh et al., *Lich Su Khang Chien Chong My Cuu Nuoc, 1954-1975*, Tap V, 175–178.

39 Nguyen Thanh, *Vuot Chet* (Saigon: Cuc Tam Ly Chien, 1972), 23.

40 Cao Minh et al., *Quan Khu 8*, 650–652; Kieu Tam Nguyen, ed., *Chien Truong Tri-Thien-Hue Trong Cuoc Chien Tranh Chong My Cuu Nuoc Toan Thang*, 156–159; Ho Ban, ed., *Huong Tien Cong va Noi Day Tet Mau Than o Tri-Thien-Hue*, 94–111; Nguyen Van Minh et al., *Lich Su Khang Chien Chong My Cuu Nuoc, 1954–1975*, Tap V, 189–195; Le Quoc San, *Cuoc Do Suc Than Ky* (Hanoi: People's Army Publishing House, 1991), 538; Ho Son Dai and Tran Phan Chan, *Lich Su Saigon-Cho Lon-Gia Dinh Khang Chien*, 521–523.

41 Nguyen Van Minh et al., *Lich Su Khang Chien Chong My Cuu Nuoc, 1954–1975*, Tap V, 207.

42 Richard D. Camp, "Taking Command: A Lesson in Leadership," *Marine Corps Gazette*, 83, No. 6 (June 1999), 76–84; Shulimson et al., *Marines in Vietnam: The Defining Year*, 291–311; Spector, *After Tet*, 148–156, 225–226.

43 Alan L. Gropman, *Airpower and the Airlift Evacuation of Kham Duc* (Maxwell Air Force Base, Alabama: Airpower Research Institute, 1979); James D. McLeroy and Gregory W. Sanders, *Bait: The Battle of Kham Duc Special Forces Camp* (Ashland, Oregon: Hellgate, 2018); Bruce Davies, *The Battle at Ngok Tavak: Allied Valor and Defeat in Vietnam* (Lubbock: Texas Tech University Press, 2009); Villard, *Combat Operations*, 539–547; Le Anh Dung, ed., *Nhung Chang Duong Chien Dau: Thuong Tuong, Anh Hung Nguyen Chon* (Hanoi: People's Army Publishing House, Hanoi, 2008), 83–87; "Events & Witnesses," People's Army Newspaper Monthly Supplement, 15 January 2018, http://sknc.qdnd.vn/theo-dong-su-kien/phao-binh-vao-tran-500855; Vu Anh Tai et al., *Su Doan 2*, Tap I, 100–107; Chu Huy Man, *Thoi Soi Dong*, 482.

44 Littauer and Uphoff, eds., *The Air War in Indochina*, 269.

45 Saigon to State, 8 June 1968, in Pike, ed., *The Bunker Papers*, 2, 466.

46 Perry, *Four Stars*, 196. See also Sorley, *A Better War*, 39–40. On another occasion, Harriman said that domestic politics dictated that the United States seek a quick settlement of the war even if it damaged U.S. interests. Rostow to Johnson, 4 May 1968, LBJL, NSF, Memos to the President, Walt Rostow, box 33. Goodpaster would stay in Paris only until July, so Johnson soon sent two other trusted agents, William Jorden and Cyrus Vance, to Paris to keep an eye on Harriman. Herring, *LBJ and Vietnam*, 166–167.

47 Smith, "Summary Notes of 586th NSC Meeting," 22 May 1968, LBJL, NSF, NSC Meetings File, box 2 (quote); Pierre Asselin, "'We Don't Want a Munich': Hanoi's Diplomatic Strategy, 1965–1968," *Diplomatic History*, 36, No. 3 (June 2012), 578; Luu Van Loi and Nguyen Anh Vu, *Le Duc Tho-Kissinger Negotiations in Paris* (Hanoi: The Gioi, 1996), 16–26.

48 MACV, 1968 Command History, 49; *The Joint Chiefs of Staff and the War in Vietnam*, Chapter 50, 12–13; Sharp, *Strategy of Defeat*, 234–236; Momyer, *Air Power in Three Wars*, 215–217; Drea, *McNamara, Clifford, and the Burdens of Vietnam*, 225–226.

49 Tom Johnson, "Notes of the Tuesday Lunch Meeting with Foreign Policy Advisers," 21 May 1968, LBJL, Tom Johnson Notes of Meetings, box 3.

50 Smith, "Summary Notes of 586th NSC Meeting," 22 May 1968, LBJL, NSF, NSC Meetings File, box 2.

51 Christian, meeting notes, 25 May 1968, *FRUS, 1964–1968*, 6, 249.

52 Saigon to State, 29 May 1968, NA II, RG 59, Central Files, 1967–1969, box 2743.

53 John Donnell, "Vietnam's Youth Associations—Social Commitment and Political Promise," TTU, John Donnell Collection, box 10.

54 Saigon to State, 29 May 1968, NA II, RG 59, Central Files, 1967–1969, box 2743.

55 Saigon to State, 11 July 1968, in Pike, ed., *The Bunker Papers*, 2, 500–513; Gene Roberts, "Saigon Is Building More Vital Regime," *New York Times*, 25 July 1968; Ahern, *CIA and Rural Pacification in South Vietnam*, 327. By the end of the year, Thieu had removed twenty province chiefs and ninety-one district chiefs for corruption or ineffectiveness. Saigon to State, 16 January 1969, in Pike, ed., *The Bunker Papers*, 3, 648.

56 Nguyen Ngo Rao, "Thieu Relaxing Curbs on Politicians, Press," *Washington Post*, 2 July 1968; Saigon to State, 4 July 1968, in Pike, ed., *The Bunker Papers*, 2, 495.

57 Saigon to State, 30 May 1968, NA II, RG 59, Central Files, 1967–1969, box 2765.

58 On June 4, Wheeler informed Johnson, "South Vietnam called for chopper support. One rocket of flight of three went erratic. It landed in the command post area and killed the men who directed the operation. This was an accident. It was unfortunate." Johnson, meeting notes, 4 June 1968, *FRUS, 1964–1968*, 6, 261.

59 Joseph B. Treaster, "Investigators Confirm U.S. Rocket Killed Six Saigon Officials," *New York Times*, 5 June 1968; Clarke, *Advice and Support*, 312–313.

60 Saigon to State, 13 June 1968, in Pike, ed., *The Bunker Papers*, 2, 468–475; Bernard Weinraub, "Ousters in Saigon a Setback for Ky," *New York Times*, 9 June 1968. At this time, Thieu also replaced Major General Nguyen Ngoc Loan, the pro-Ky national police chief, who had been wounded a month earlier in combat and was still hospitalized.

61 Carver to Helms, "The Lien Minh," 12 September 1968, *FRUS, 1964–1968*, 7, 11; Saigon to State, 4 July 1968, in Pike, ed., *The Bunker Papers*, 2, 493–495.

62 "Minutes of the Meeting of the 303 Committee," 5 September 1968, LBJL, NSF, Files of Walt W. Rostow, box 2; *FRUS, 1964–1968*, 6, 343.

63 Saigon to State, 20 June 1968, in Pike, ed., *The Bunker Papers*, 2, 480; Saigon to State, 15 August 1968, in Pike, ed., *The Bunker Papers*, 2, 533; Clarke, *Advice and Support*, 314; Bui Quyen, "Reflections of a Frontline Soldier," in Tuong Vu and Sean Fear, eds., *The Republic of Vietnam, 1955–1975: Vietnamese Perspectives on Nation Building* (Ithaca: Southeast Asia Program Publications, 2019), 85.

64 Truong Chinh, "Let us Be Grateful to Karl Marx and Follow the Path Traced by Him," May 1968, TTU, Viet-Nam Documents and Research Notes Collection, box 1.

65 Lewis Sorley, *Thunderbolt: From the Battle of the Bulge to Vietnam and Beyond: General Creighton Abrams and the Army of His Times* (New York: Simon & Schuster, 1992).

66 Saigon to State, 8 June 1968, in Pike, ed., *The Bunker Papers*, 2, 461–467.

67 CIA, "The Impact of Communist Military Pressure on Saigon," 5 July 1968, TTU, Sam Johnson Vietnam Archive Collection, box 6; Sorley, *A Better War*, 25–27; Sorley, ed., *Vietnam Chronicles*, 4; Villard, *Combat Operations*, 626.

68 Villard, *Combat Operations*, 641. Zhou Enlai subsequently warned the North Vietnamese against attacking the cities, a tactic he attributed to malign Soviet influence. If the North Vietnamese continued to assault the cities, Zhou said, "the U.S. will be happy as they can concentrate their forces for counterattack, thus causing greater destruction for you. The losses that you would suffer will lead to defeatism on your side." Memcon, Zhou Enlai and Pham Hung, 29 June 1968, CWIHP.

CHAPTER 16

1 Villard, *Combat Operations*, 597.

2 Cosmas, *MACV: The Joint Command in the Years of Withdrawal*, 132. See also Ibid., 115–116, 129–130; Villard, *Combat Operations*, 592; *The Joint Chiefs of Staff and the War in Vietnam*, Chapter 52, 22.

3 Cosmas, *MACV: The Joint Command in the Years of Withdrawal*, 110.

4 Sorley, ed., *Vietnam Chronicles*, 12.

5 COMUSMACV, "Feasibility Study Supporting OPLAN El Paso," 7 June 1968, NA II, RG 472, MACJ03, Historians Background File, box 181; MACV, 1968 Command History, 781.

6 MACV, 1968 Command History, 916–917; Cosmas, *MACV: The Joint Command in the Years of Withdrawal*, 129–130; Sorley, *Westmoreland*, 172–173. Abrams also discontinued construction of some of the strongpoints of the McNamara barrier near the DMZ. *The Joint Chiefs of Staff and the War in Vietnam*, Chapter 52, 15–17; MACV, 1968 Command History, 916–917; Shulimson et al., *Marines in Vietnam: The Defining Year*, 324–327; Cosmas, *MACV: The Joint Command in the Years of Withdrawal*, 116–118.

7 CIA, "Road Construction in the Laotian Panhandle and Adjacent Areas of South Vietnam, 1967–68," May 1968, *FRUS, 1964–1968*, 28, 363; CIA, "Road Construction and Wet Weather Logistics in the Laotian Panhandle," *FRUS, 1964–1968*, 28, 370.

8 Vientiane to State, 24 April 1968, NA II, RG 59, Central Files, 1967–1969, box 2297.

9 Combined Intelligence Center Vietnam, Order of Battle Summary, September 1972, 2, Records of the Military Assistance Command Vietnam, Part 2, Classified Studies from the Combined Intelligence Center Vietnam, 1965–1973, reel 18.

10 *The Joint Chiefs of Staff and the War in Vietnam*, Chapter 52, 28.

11 Paris to State, 29 July 1968, *FRUS, 1964–1968*, 6, 312. Clifford backed Harriman and Vance, stressing that the bombing could not seriously impede infiltration

of men or supplies. Dallek, *Flawed Giant*, 568. On August 30, Warnke stated, "Our bombing does not, and probably cannot, limit the enemy's operations in South Vietnam." Bombing "does not significantly reduce the flow of supplies and men reaching South Vietnam." Warnke, "Questions on the Air War in North Vietnam," 30 August 1968, LBJL, Papers of Alan Enthoven, box 24.

12 State to Paris, 30 July 1968, *FRUS, 1964–1968*, 6, 313.

13 Telcon, Johnson and Rusk, 30 July 1968, *FRUS, 1964–1968*, 6, 314. In the late summer, Johnson's displeasure with Clifford's views on bombing caused him to deny Clifford and everyone else in the Defense Department access to telegrams pertaining to the Paris talks. Cooper, *The Lost Crusade*, 415.

14 Telcon, Johnson and Hughes, 30 July 1968, *FRUS, 1964–1968*, 6, 315n.

15 Abrams to Rostow, 23 August 1968, *FRUS, 1964–1968*, 6, 337; Abrams to Rostow, 28 September 1968, LBJL, NSF, Memos to the President, Walt Rostow, box 40; *The Joint Chiefs of Staff and the War in Vietnam*, Chapter 54, 1–2.

16 Ho Si Huu et al., *Lich Su Quan Chung Phong Khong*, Tap II, 241, 263–264.

17 Ta Hong, Vu Ngoc, and Nguyen Quoc Dung, *Lich Su Khong Quan Nhan Dan Viet Nam (1955–1977)* (Hanoi: People's Army Publishing House, Hanoi, 1993), 190–199; Ho Si Huu et al., *Lich Su Quan Chung Phong Khong,* Tap II, 254–255, 264–286.

18 Thompson, *To Hanoi and Back*, 143.

19 Ho Si Huu et al., *Lich Su Quan Chung Phong Khong*, Tap II, 257. U.S. intelligence sources observed a precipitous drop in the number of North Vietnamese trucks reaching Laos from July through September. Sorley, ed., *Vietnam Chronicles*, 58, 73. During August, the North Vietnamese were able to move some shipments through the choke points by ferry or by trickery at night, but the arrival of the rainy season in September turned the roads to mud, and the truck traffic slowed to a trickle. Ho Si Huu et al., *Lich Su Quan Chung Phong Khong*, Tap II, 285–292.

20 Nguyen Viet Phuong, *Van Tai Quan Su Chien Luoc Tren Duong Ho Chi Minh Trong Khang Chien Chong My*, 2nd ed., 77–79. During the fall, the North Vietnamese devoted great effort to the construction of a new POL pipeline in southern North Vietnam to reduce reliance upon trucks for the movement of POL. Sorley, ed., *Vietnam Chronicles*, 85; Nguyen Viet Phuong, *Van Tai Quan Su Chien Luoc Tren Duong Ho Chi Minh Trong Khang Chien Chong My*, 2nd ed., 79.

21 Concerning food shortages at this time, see Vu Anh Tai et al., *Su Doan 2*, Tap I, 116; Le Minh Hoang et al., *Trung Doan 6*, 140; MACV, 1968 Command History, 87–88.

22 Le Quoc San, *Cuoc Do Suc Than Ky*, 277; Truong Minh Hoach and Nguyen Minh Phung, *Quan Khu 9*, 453. The fears were validated when top military officers who had voiced doubts about the plan at a meeting in Tay Ninh were placed under surveillance. Nguyen Thanh, *Vuot Chet*, 23–25.

23 Mai Chi Tho, *Hoi Uc Mai Chi Tho*, 173; Ho Son Dai, ed., *Lich Su Bo Chi Huy Mien (1961–1976)* (Hanoi: Nha Xuat Ban Chinh Tri Quoc Gia, 2004), 338–340.

24 Nguyen Van Minh et al., *Lich Su Khang Chien Chong My Cuu Nuoc, 1954–1975*, Tap V, 208–210; Nguyen Viet Ta et al., *Mien Dong Nam Bo Khang Chien*, Tap II, 364.

25 The strongest available evidence of Hanoi's intent to influence the Democratic National Convention by means of the third wave offensive is this comment from Soviet Ambassador Dobrynin on September 9: "Now that the Democratic Convention is over, the offensive may subside." Rostow to Johnson, 10 September 1968, *FRUS, 1964–1968*, 14, 295.

26 Dao Trong Cang, ed., *Van Kien Dang*, Tap 29, 1968, 468–470; Rostow to Johnson, 21 September 1968, *FRUS, 1964–1968*, 7, 25.

27 Dobrynin, *In Confidence*, 179–181.

28 Richard M. Nixon, "Asia After Viet Nam," *Foreign Affairs* 46, No. 1 (October 1967), 111–112.

29 "Nixon Sees Vietnam as 'Cork in Bottle,'" *New York Times*, 13 February 1968.

30 "No Alternative, Nixon Says, U.S. Must Continue the War," *New York Times*, 18 June 1968.

31 Aitken, *Nixon*, 352; Johns, *Vietnam's Second Front*, 197–198.

32 UPI, "Nixon Urges Rise in Allied Soldiers," *New York Times*, 15 March 1968; "Text of Nixon Statement to G.O.P. Platform Panel on the War," *New York Times* 2 August 1968; *FRUS, 1969–1975*, 1, 7.

33 Richard J. Whalen, *Catch the Falling Flag: A Republican's Challenge to His Party* (Boston: Houghton Mifflin, 1972), 136–141; William Safire, *Before the Fall: An Inside View of the Pre-Watergate White House* (New York: Belmont Tower, 1975), 48; Black, *Richard M. Nixon*, 516–517, 534–535; William Burr and Jeffrey P. Kimball, *Nixon's Nuclear Specter: The Secret Alert of 1969, Madman Diplomacy, and the Vietnam War* (Lawrence: University Press of Kansas, 2016), 50–52.

34 H. R. Haldeman, *The Ends of Power* (New York: Times Books, 1978), 82–83. For evidence that Haldeman's account accurately reflected Nixon's views, see Leonard Garment, *Crazy Rhythm: From Brooklyn and Jazz to Nixon's White House, Watergate, and Beyond...* (New York: Times Books, 1997), 174; Kimball, *Nixon's Vietnam War*, 76–86; Melvin Small, *The Presidency of Richard Nixon* (Lawrence: University Press of Kansas, 1999), 60–62.

35 Andrew L. Johns, *Vietnam's Second Front: Domestic Politics, the Republican Party, and the War* (Lexington: University Press of Kentucky, 2010), 159–199; David F. Schmitz, *Richard Nixon and the Vietnam War: The End of the American Century* (Lanham: Rowman & Littlefield, 2014), 23–37; Dueck, *Hard Line*, 144–151; Kimball, *Nixon's Vietnam War*, 40–56; Scanlon, *The Pro-War Movement*, 72–124; Dallek, *Nixon and Kissinger*, 62–64; Stephen Ambrose, *Nixon: The Triumph of a Politician, 1962–1972* (New York: Simon & Schuster, 1989), 140–169.

36 Complete Text of Nixon's Acceptance Speech, 8 August 1968, *Congressional Quarterly Almanac*, 90th Congress, 2nd Session.

37 MACV, 1968 Command History, 134–135; Sorley, ed., *Vietnam Chronicles*, 31; Nguyen Viet Ta et al., *Mien Dong Nam Bo Khang Chien*, Tap II, 364–367; Pham

Vinh Phuc, "Tran Phuc Kich Da Hang-Ven Ven Cua Trung Doan 88/Quan Khu Mien Dong," 210–213.

38 Pham Vinh Phuc, "Tran Phuc Kich Da Hang-Ven Ven Cua Trung Doan 88/ Quan Khu Mien Dong," 227.

39 Ellis W. Williamson, "Combat After Action Report of the Battle of Tay Ninh," 7 February 1969, TTU, Vietnam Helicopter Pilots Association Collection, box 2; Duquesne A. Wolfe, "Tactical Situation, Estimate of Situation and Operations," 10 February 1969, TTU, Vietnam Helicopter Pilots Association Collection, box 2; *The Joint Chiefs of Staff and the War in Vietnam*, Chapter 52, 24–25; Villard, *Combat Operations*, 646-655; Bergerud, *Red Thunder, Tropic Lightning*, 179–180; Starry, *Armored Combat in Vietnam*, 131–133.

40 Nguyen Van Minh et al., *Lich Su Khang Chien Chong My Cuu Nuoc, 1954-1975*, Tap V, 211–213; Huynh Cong Than, *O Chien Truong Long An*, 148–149; Nguyen Huu Nguyen, *Long An*, 263–265.

41 Cao Minh et al., *Quan Khu 8*, 659. A senior Communist commander in the region stated, "Our casualties grew day by day, until finally when they did not have enough troops left to hold their ground the units had to withdraw without authorization. It was during the period we tried to cling to the outskirts of the enemy's urban areas that our forces suffered tremendous losses." Le Quoc San, *Cuoc Do Suc Than Ky*, 275.

42 *The Joint Chiefs of Staff and the War in Vietnam*, Chapter 52, 25–26. For the month of August, enemy killed in action totaled 15,478. Littauer and Uphoff, eds., *The Air War in Indochina*, 269.

43 Saigon to State, 29 August 1968, in Pike, ed., *The Bunker Papers*, 2, 547–549; Saigon to State, 4 September 1968, in Pike, ed., *The Bunker Papers*, 2, 556–559.

44 Chris Connolly, "The American Factor: Sino-American Rapprochement and Chinese Attitudes to the Vietnam War, 1968–72," *Cold War History*, 5, No. 4 (November 2005), 502–503; Linda D. Dillon, Bruce Burton, and Walter C. Soderlund, "Who Was the Principal Enemy?: Shifts in Official Chinese Perceptions of the Two Superpowers, 1968–1969," *Asian Survey*, 17, No. 5 (May 1977), 466; Khoo, *Collateral Damage*, 45–54.

45 Turner, *Vietnamese Communism*, 288–290. See also Smyser, *Independent Vietnamese*, 103; Khoo, *Collateral Damage*, 49–51; Gaiduk, *The Soviet Union and the Vietnam War*, 177. Nguyen Thanh Le, the spokesman of the North Vietnamese delegation to the Paris talks, hailed the Soviet action as a measure aimed at "the strengthening of the unity of the socialist camp" and protecting socialist countries "against reactionary elements." "Nguyen Thanh Le Holds Press Meeting in Paris," AFP, TTU, Douglas Pike Collection, Unit 04, box 7.

46 Turner, *Vietnamese Communism*, 287.

47 Tom Wicker, "Politicians Puzzled by Impact of the Czech Crisis," *New York Times*, 22 August 1968 (first quote); James Reston, "Soviets Turn Back Clock," *New York Times*, 21 August 1968 (second quote); Richard Harwood, "Czech Invasion," *Washington Post*, 22 August 1968.

48 John W. Finney, "The Vietnam Plank Weighs Heavy on the Platform," *New York Times*, 25 August 1968.

49 "Doves' Plank Lists Peace Steps," *Washington Post*, 25 August 1968; Theodore
    H. White, *The Making of the President—1968* (New York: Atheneum, 1969),
    276.

50 Phillips, *Why Vietnam Matters*, 294–295.

51 Walter Pincus, "Panel Votes Pro-LBJ Viet Plan," *Washington Post*, 27 August
    1968; John W. Finney, "Vietnam Plank Supports Johnson on War Policies,"
    New York Times, 27 August 1968.

52 John Connally with Mickey Herskowitz, *In History's Shadow: An American
    Odyssey* (New York: Hyperion, 1993), 203, 214; W. Marvin Watson with
    Sherwin Markman, *Chief of Staff: Lyndon Johnson and His Presidency* (New
    York: Thomas Dunne, 2004), 295–299; Kyle Longley, *LBJ's 1968: Power, Politics,
    and the Presidency in America's Year of Upheaval* (Cambridge: Cambridge
    University Press, 2018), 205–214; Johns, *The Price of Loyalty*, 27–96; Califano,
    The Triumph and Tragedy of Lyndon Johnson, 321–323.

53 Alan J. Matusow, *The Unraveling of America: A History of Liberalism in the 1960s*
    (New York: Harper & Row, 1984), 418–419; Watson, *Chief of Staff*, 299–300;
    Longley, *LBJ's 1968*, 223–225; Dallek, *Flawed Giant*, 575.

54 White, *The Making of the President—1968*, 287; Amity Shlaes, *Great Society: A
    New History* (New York: Harper, 2019), 294–296.

55 Wells, *The War Within*, 279.

56 Peter Collier and David Horowitz, "Lefties for Reagan," *Washington Post
    Magazine*, March 17, 1985.

57 Kuhn, *The Hardhat Riot*, 25.

58 J. Anthony Lukas, "Police Battle Demonstrators in the Streets," *New York
    Times*, 29 August 1968; Carl Solberg, *Hubert Humphrey: A Biography* (New
    York: W. W. Norton, 1984), 362–365; White, *The Making of the President—1968*,
    295–301; Matusow, *The Unraveling of America*, 419–420.

59 Todd Gitlin, *The Sixties: Years of Hope, Days of Rage* (New York: Bantam, 1987),
    335. For polling data concerning the Democratic National Convention, see
    Louis Harris, "Conventions: Nixon Gained, HHH Was Hurt," *Washington
    Post*, 3 October 1968; Philip E. Converse, Warren E. Miller, Jerrold G. Rusk
    and Arthur C. Wolfe, "Continuity and Change in American Politics: Parties
    and Issues in the 1968 Election," *The American Political Science Review*, 63, No.
    4 (December 1969), 1087–1088. Disgust with the antiwar movement may have
    helped sustain support for the war among the general population at this time.
    For polling data demonstrating continued support in September, see Mueller,
    War, Presidents, and Public Opinion, 91.

60 Paris to State, 3 September 1968, *FRUS, 1964–1968*, 7, 2; Rostow to Johnson,
    10 September 1968, *FRUS, 1964–1968*, 14, 295. At this same time, Harriman
    was telling Johnson that the North Vietnamese delegation in Paris sincerely
    desired a negotiated peace and would be mindful of avoiding provocations
    in the demilitarized zone or on South Vietnamese cities in the event of a
    bombing halt. When Johnson said that Harriman would need to "to lead the
    government in demanding a resumption of bombing if they violate these
    understandings," Harriman promised that he would advocate a bombing

resumption "with enthusiasm." Johnson, *Vantage Point*, 514–515. Harriman separately informed Ball, "We here all agree that if NVN 'takes advantage' President would have wide support for bombing again. I would certainly recommend it." Harriman to Ball, n.d., *FRUS, 1964–1968*, 7, 49n.

61 Nguyen Viet Ta et al., *Mien Dong Nam Bo Khang Chien*, Tap II, 369; Shulimson et al., *Marines in Vietnam: The Defining Year*, 392–393; Villard, *Combat Operations*, 666–672; Littauer and Uphoff, eds., *The Air War in Indochina*, 269.

62 CIA, "The Coming Political Struggle for South Vietnam," 16 September 1968, CREST, document number CIA-RDP79R00904A001400020004-3.

63 Luu Van Loi and Nguyen Anh Vu, *Le Duc Tho-Kissinger Negotiations in Paris*, 43, 66. Tran Do observed that "during the general offensive we committed all our forces. . . . No theater of operations held back a campaign reserve force." Tran Do, "Tet Mau Than: Tran Tap Kich Chien Luoc," *Tap Chi Lich Su Quan Su*, 26, No. 2 (1988), 47. See also Tran Bach Dang, "Mau Than," 62; Ho Son Dai and Tran Phan Chan, *Lich Su Saigon-Cho Lon-Gia Dinh Khang Chien*, 523.

64 Le Minh Hoang et al., *Trung Doan 6*, 144–145; Tran Quoc Tuan et al., eds., *Lich su Bo Tong tham muu trong Khang chien Chong My, cuu nuoc* (1954–1975), Tap IV (Hanoi: People's Army Publishing House, 2010), 18.

65 Combined Intelligence Center Vietnam, Order of Battle Summary, September 1972, 2, Records of the Military Assistance Command Vietnam, Part 2, Classified Studies from the Combined Intelligence Center Vietnam, 1965–1973, reel 18.

66 Tran Bach Dang, "Mau Than," 58. See also Combat Operations Department, *Lich Su Cuc Tac Chien*, 265; Military History Institute of Vietnam, *Victory in Vietnam*, 231.

67 Tran Quoc Tuan et al., eds., *Lich su Bo Tong tham muu trong Khang chien Chong My*, Tap IV, 18.

68 *The Gallup Poll: Public Opinion 1935–1971*, 3, 2162.

69 Johns, *The Price of Loyalty*, 115.

70 In a private letter to Ball, Harriman had stated that he was "convinced that we can work out a situation" that would lead to a bombing halt, which "will be our last chance before the election and I feel action now is essential to give Hubert a fighting chance." Harriman to Ball, n.d., *FRUS, 1964–1968*, 7, 49n. See also Johns, *The Price of Loyalty*, 114–115.

71 Lyndon Johnson and Hubert Humphrey, telcon, 30 September 1968, *Presidential Recordings Digital Edition* [Chasing Shadows, ed. Ken Hughes] (Charlottesville: University of Virginia Press, 2014); David L. DiLeo, *George Ball, Vietnam, and the Rethinking of Containment* (Chapel Hill: University of North Carolina Press, 1991), 174.

72 R. W. Apple Jr., "Humphrey Vows Halt in Bombing if Hanoi Reacts," *New York Times*, 1 October 1968; Joseph Kraft, "Televised Speech on Vietnam Gets Humphrey Off Ground," *Washington Post*, 3 October 1968.

73 Democratic National Committee, "Vice President Hubert H. Humphrey's Address to the Nation on Vietnam and American Foreign Policy," 30

September 1968, Minnesota Historical Society, http://www2.mnhs.org/library/findaids/00442/pdfa/00442-02747.pdf.

CHAPTER 17

1 E. W. Kenworthy, "Nixon Asks Clarification Lest Foe Be Misled," *New York Times,* 2 October 1968.

2 Hedrick Smith, "Harriman Denies Nixon Charge that Humphrey Harmed Talks," *New York Times,* 3 October 1968.

3 Harriman, "General Review of Last Six Months," *FRUS, 1964–1968,* 7, 255.

4 Joseph Kraft, "Televised Speech on Vietnam Gets Humphrey Off Ground," *Washington Post,* 3 October 1968. On the same day, the *Washington Post* printed a piece by Rowland Evans and Robert Novak in which Ball promoted Humphrey's Salt Lake City position by dismissing as unrealistic the Johnson administration's aversion to an unconditional bombing halt. Ball also was reported to believe that Johnson had made secret agreements with the South Vietnamese that had "convinced the Communists in Hanoi that the United States was not bargaining in good faith." As a consequence, the article stated, "the careful diplomatic initiative then being nurtured by Harriman and his aides in Paris was pulled up by the roots." Rowland Evans and Robert Nowak, "George Ball's Resignation is Linked to Hidden Concern Over Paris Talks," *Washington Post,* 3 October 1968.

5 "Humphrey for President," *New York Times,* 6 October 1968.

6 "Gallup Poll Shows A Humphrey Gain," *New York Times,* 22 October 1968.

7 Lyndon Johnson and Dean Rusk, telcon, 3 October 1968, *Presidential Recordings Digital Edition.*

8 Telcon, Johnson and Rusk, 6 October 1968, *FRUS, 1964–1968,* 7, 51.

9 Davidson, "October 11 Private Meeting," 11 October 1968, NA II, RG 59, Lot Files, Entry 5005, Files of Ambassador at Large Averell Harriman, box 7; Paris to State, 11 October 1968, *FRUS, 1964–1968,* 7, 58; Luu Van Loi and Nguyen Anh Vu, *Le Duc Tho-Kissinger Negotiations in Paris,* 45–46.

10 William Bundy, *A Tangled Web: The Making of Foreign Policy in the Nixon Presidency* (New York: Hill and Wang, 1998), 30; Clifford, *Counsel to the President,* 574–576.

11 State to Paris, 14 October 1968, *FRUS, 1964–1968,* 7, 66.

12 Johnson, meeting notes, 29 October 1968, *FRUS, 1964–1968,* 7, 140.

13 Spector, *After Tet,* 298; Rostow, meeting notes, 14 October 1968, *FRUS, 1964–1968,* 7, 67.

14 Drew Pearson and Jack Anderson, "Ball Feared for Policy Under Nixon," *Washington Post,* 12 October 1968.

15 "Excerpts from the Address by Bundy on the Direction of U.S. Policy in Vietnam," *New York Times,* 13 October 1968.

16 Rostow to Johnson, 16 October 1968, *FRUS, 1964–1968,* 7, 76.

17 Instructions sent from Hanoi on October 13 directed Le Duc Tho to insist that "the U.S. should consent to talk to the NLF, and the Saigon

administration should change its policies" before negotiations could begin. Luu Van Loi and Nguyen Anh Vu, *Le Duc Tho-Kissinger Negotiations in Paris*, 47. Hanoi had issued similar instructions before Bundy's speech on October 10, but Johnson may have been unaware of them or may have concluded that they had been superseded by the October 11 discussion. Dao Trong Cang, ed., *Van Kien Dang*, Tap 29, 1968, 468–474.

18 For Johnson's suspicion about Bundy, see telcon, Johnson and Mansfield, 16 October 1968, *FRUS, 1964-1968*, 7, 77. The quote is from Elsey, meeting notes, 17 October 1968, *FRUS, 1964-1968*, 7, 83.

19 Luu Van Loi and Nguyen Anh Vu, *Le Duc Tho-Kissinger Negotiations in Paris*, 47–48, 52–53; Dao Trong Cang, ed., *Van Kien Dang*, Tap 29, 1968, 475–477 (quote).

20 Memcon, Chen Yi and Le Duc Tho, 17 October 1968, in Westad, et al., *77 Conversations Between Chinese and Foreign Leaders on the Wars in Indochina*, 138–140. See also Asselin, "'We Don't Want a Munich,'" 576.

21 Zhai, *China and the Vietnam Wars*, 179; Khoo, *Collateral Damage*, 56; Li, *The Dragon in the Jungle*, 209. At its peak, the Chinese force in North Vietnam totaled 170,000 troops. Khoo, *Collateral Damage*, 31.

22 CIA, "President Thieu's Views Regarding the Issues Involved in Agreeing to a Bombing Halt," 26 October 1968, LBJL, Reference File, Chennault; DIRNSA to White House, 30 October 1968, LBJL, NSF, Memos to the President, Walt Rostow, box 41; Bui Diem, *In the Jaws of History*, 239. The North Vietnamese Politburo came to the same conclusion about Johnson's intentions in stopping the bombing. In an October 20 message to COSVN, it stated that Johnson intended to halt the bombing and negotiate "to win the support of American voters in order to win victory for Humphrey in the elections and to extol Johnson's role in the 'road to peace.'" Dao Trong Cang, ed., *Van Kien Dang*, Tap 29, 1968, 484–487.

23 Saigon to State, 21 October 1968, LBJL, NSF, VNCF, box 124; Saigon to State, 21 October 1968, *FRUS, 1964-1968*, 7, 96 (quote); Nguyen Phu Duc, *The Viet-Nam Peace Negotiations: Saigon's Side of the Story* (Christiansburg, VA: Dalley Book Service, 2005), 106–109.

24 Read, situation report, 22 October 1968, *FRUS, 1964-1968*, 7, 101; Rostow to Johnson, 24 October 1968, *FRUS, 1964-1968*, 7, 116; Gaiduk, *The Soviet Union and the Vietnam War*, 184–185.

25 Richard Nixon, *RN: The Memoirs of Richard Nixon* (New York: Grosset & Dunlap, 1975), 326–327.

26 William Safire, *Before the Fall: An Inside View of the Pre-Watergate White House* (New York: Belmont Tower, 1975), 85.

27 "Nixon: '… Reports Are True,'" *Washington Post*, 26 October 1968.

28 Johnson, meeting notes, 27 October 1968, *FRUS, 1964-1968*, 7, 129.

29 Cartha DeLoach, *Hoover's FBI: The Inside Story by Hoover's Trusted Lieutenant* (Washington: Regnery, 1995), 396–399; Richard Powers, *The Man Who Kept the Secrets: Richard Helms and the CIA* (New York: Knopf, 1979), 252.

30 Anna Chennault, *The Education of Anna* (New York: Times Books, 1980), 176–186; Black, *Richard M. Nixon*, 551–552; Solberg, *Hubert Humphrey*, 394.

31 Bui Diem, *In the Jaws of History*, 235–238.

32 Safire, *Before the Fall*, 90.

33 Jules Witcover, *The Year the Dream Died: Revisiting 1968 in America* (New York: Warner Books, 1997), 442–443. Only once during the final months of the race, on October 22, was Nixon known to have been present at a discussion on Chennault. According to fragmentary meeting notes, one of the participants said, "Keep Anna Chennault working on South Vietnam." https://assets. documentcloud.org/documents/3248783/H-R-Haldeman-s-Notes-from-Oct-22-1968.pdf. John Farrell cited this document as proof that Nixon was using Chennault to convince Thieu to sabotage the Paris peace negotiations. Farrell, *Richard Nixon*, 342, 638. But it is not clear who made the statement, nor is it clear whether the statement referred to a conspiracy to sabotage the peace talks, to the monitoring of developments in South Vietnam, or to something else.

34 Powers, *The Man Who Kept the Secrets*, 252. See also James Bowman, "A Wilderness of Mirrors," *New Criterion*, May 2017; Nixon Foundation, "Misunderstanding A Monkey Wrench," June 2, 2017, https://www. nixonfoundation.org/2017/06/misunderstanding-a-monkey-wrench.

35 DIRNSA to White House," 23 October 1968, LBJL, Reference File, Chennault; CIA, "Interior Minister Khiem's Claim that Prime Minister Huong is Cause of Government of Vietnam's Hard Stand on Question of Attendance at Paris Talks," 14 November 1968, TTU, Central Intelligence Agency Collection, box 5.

36 Karamessines to Rostow and Rusk, 28 October 1968, *FRUS, 1964–1968*, 7, 148n.

37 Hung and Schecter, *The Palace File*, 21. For American accounts that corroborate this depiction of Thieu's views on Humphrey and Nixon, see Rostow to Johnson, "The Bombing Halt and U.S. Politics," 29 October 1968, LBJL, NSF, Memos to the President, Walt Rostow, box 41; Elsey, meeting notes, 2 November 1968, *FRUS, 1964–1968*, 7, 180. For the views of others in South Vietnam, the United States, and North Vietnam, see Saigon to State, 15 August 1968, in Pike, ed., *The Bunker Papers*, 2, 534; Rostow to Johnson, 21 September 1968, *FRUS, 1964–1968*, 7, 25; Telcon, Johnson and Rusk, 3 October 1968, *FRUS, 1964–1968*, 7, 50; Johnson, meeting notes, 29 October 1968, *FRUS, 1964–1968*, 7, 150; Dao Trong Cang, ed., *Van Kien Dang*, Tap 29, 1968, 469–470; Bui Diem, *In the Jaws of History*, 238.

38 Rostow to Johnson, "The Bombing Halt and U.S. Politics," 29 October 1968, LBJL, NSF, Memos to the President, Walt Rostow, box 41; Nguyen Phu Duc, *The Viet-Nam Peace Negotiations*, 126–131.

39 Johnson, meeting notes, 14 October 1968, *FRUS, 1964–1968*, 7, 69; Rostow, "Meeting with the President," 23 October 1968, *FRUS, 1964–1968*, 7, 110.

40 Johnson, meeting notes, 29 October 1968, *FRUS, 1964–1968*, 7, 140.

41 Sorley, *Thunderbolt*, 253.

42 Nguyen Phu Duc, *The Viet-Nam Peace Negotiations*, 131–133; Tom Johnson, "Additional Notes on Meeting in the Cabinet Room," 29 October 1968, in Barrett, ed., *Lyndon B. Johnson's Vietnam Papers*, 820–823.

43 Telcon, Johnson and Rusk, 29 October 1968, *FRUS, 1964–1968*, 7, 147; Johnson, meeting notes, 29 October 1968, *FRUS, 1964–1968*, 7, 150.

44 State to Saigon, 30 October 1968, *FRUS, 1964–1968*, 7, 151. The document does not indicate who drafted it, but the content and tone suggest that Clifford played a large role in its production.

45 CIA, "President Thieu's Comments on Peace Talks Impasse at Private Dinner Parties on 11 and 12 November 1968," 18 November 1968, LBJL, Reference File, Chennault.

46 Bunker to Rusk, 30 October 1968, in Barrett, ed., *Lyndon B. Johnson's Vietnam Papers*, 839–841.

47 Read, situation report, 31 October 1968, *FRUS, 1964–1968*, 7, 165 (first quote); Nguyen Phu Duc, *The Viet-Nam Peace Negotiations*, 146–153 (second and third quotes).

48 Ginsburgh to Johnson, 31 October 1968, NSF, VNCF, box 137.

49 Saigon to State, 1 November 1968, *FRUS, 1964–1968*, 7, 170.

50 Lyndon B. Johnson, "The President's Address to the Nation Upon Announcing His Decision To Halt the Bombing of North Vietnam," 31 October 1968, American Presidency Project, https://www.presidency.ucsb.edu/node/236813.

51 White, *The Making of the President—1968*, 382.

52 *FRUS, 1964–1968*, 7, 171n.

53 Gene Roberts, "Thieu Says Saigon Cannot Join Paris Talks Under Present Plan," *New York Times*, 2 November 1968. See also Saigon to State, 3 November 1968, NA II, RG 59, Central Files, 1967–69, box 2725; "S. Vietnam Leaders Back Thieu Stand," *Washington Post*, 3 November 1968.

54 Saigon to State, 6 November 1968, *FRUS, 1964–1968*, 7, 200.

55 White, *The Making of the President—1968*, 379–383.

56 High-Level Military Institute, *Vietnam: The Anti-U.S. Resistance War for National Salvation*, 112–113; Luu Van Loi, *Fifty Years of Vietnamese Diplomacy, 1945–1995*, 1 (Hanoi: The Gioi, 2000), 198.

57 Rostow to Johnson, 2 November 1968, LBJL, Reference File, Chennault; Witcover, *The Year the Dream Died*, 421.

58 Lyndon Johnson and Everett Dirksen, telcon, 2 November 1968, *Presidential Recordings Digital Edition*.

59 Lyndon Johnson and Richard Nixon, telcon, 3 November 1968, *Presidential Recordings Digital Edition*.

60 DeLoach, *Hoover's FBI*, 404–406.

61 Catherine Forslund, *Anna Chennault: Informal Diplomacy and Asian Relations* (Lanham, Maryland: Rowman & Littlefield, 2002), 70–71. In her memoirs, Chennault recounted that Mitchell phoned her shortly before the election and asked her to make sure the South Vietnamese understood Nixon's position, though she made no mention of a request to inform the South Vietnamese ambassador of the need to "hold on." Chennault, *The Education of Anna*, 190–191.

62 Telcon, Johnson, Clifford, Rusk, and Rostow, 4 November 1968, *FRUS, 1964–1968*, 7, 192.

63 Telcon, Johnson and Smathers, 23 November 1968, *FRUS, 1964–1968*, 7, 232.

64 Solberg, *Hubert Humphrey*, 398.

65 Michael Nelson, *Resilient America: Electing Nixon in 1968, Channeling Dissent, and Dividing Government* (Lawrence: University Press of Kansas, 2014); Converse et al., "Continuity and Change in American Politics," 1083–1090; Louis Harris, *The Anguish of Change* (New York: W. W. Norton, 1973), 195–197; Johns, *Vietnam's Second Front*, 230–236.

66 Hung and Schecter, *The Palace File*, 29.

67 Bui Diem, *In the Jaws of History*, 248.

68 High-Level Military Institute, *Vietnam: The Anti-U.S. Resistance War for National Salvation*, 121.

69 Burr and Kimball, *Nixon's Nuclear Specter*, 256.

70 Truong Nhu Tang, *A Viet Cong Memoir*, 143–144.

71 Combat Operations Department, *Lich Su Cuc Tac Chien*, 268–269.

72 Khoo, *Collateral Damage*, 60.

73 Rostow to Johnson, 16 November 1968, LBJL, NSF, Memos to the President, Walt Rostow, box 42; Rostow to Johnson, 12 December 1968, *FRUS, 1964–1968*, 7, 252; MACV, 1968 Command History, 39, 382–383; Shulimson et al., *Marines in Vietnam: The Defining Year*, 443–450.

74 In mid-November, for instance, after American intelligence located a large concentration of North Vietnamese soldiers in Quang Nam Province, seven U.S. Marine battalions chased after them in what was termed Operation Meade River. The Marines killed an estimated 1,023 North Vietnamese and captured 123, at a cost of 108 Marines killed and 510 wounded. James Hubert Embrey, "Reorienting Pacification: The Accelerated Pacification Campaign of 1968" (PhD dissertation, University of Kentucky, 1997), 124; Spector, *After Tet*, 306–310; Shulimson et al., *Marines in Vietnam: The Defining Year*, 425–437.

75 Stanley Robert Larsen and James Lawton Collins Jr., *Allied Participation in Vietnam* (Washington, DC: Department of the Army, 1985), 153.

76 MACV, 1968 Command History, 525.

77 Hunt, *Pacification*, 156–159; Saigon to State, 2 October 1968, in Pike, ed., *The Bunker Papers*, 2, 588.

78 Saigon to State, 30 October 1968, in Pike, ed., *The Bunker Papers*, 2, 614–618; Colby, *Lost Victory*, 254–263; Hunt, *Pacification*, 172–192. During 1968, the number of Regional Force and Popular Force troops increased by 91,000. The Regional Forces and Popular Forces took on greater responsibilities, while the RD Cadre units were downsized and their members integrated into the territorial forces. Sorley, *A Better War*, 72–73; Blaufarb, *The Counterinsurgency Era*, 264, 273–274.

79 On November 5, the administration announced that the discussions would not begin on November 6 and that the United States would simply "continue to consult with the Government of the Republic of Viet-Nam on this matter."

Department of State Bulletin, 25 November 1968, 538. See also Saigon to State, 30 November 1968, in Pike, ed., *The Bunker Papers*, 2, 622–625.

80 Saigon to State, 12 November 1968, *FRUS, 1964–1968*, 7, 214. For the views of Rusk and Rostow, see Rostow, meeting notes, 14 October 1968, *FRUS, 1964–1968*, 7, 67; Johnson, meeting notes, 14 October 1968, *FRUS, 1964–1968*, 7, 68; State to Moscow, 26 November 1968, *FRUS, 1964–1968*, 14, 325.

81 Harriman, "General Review of Last Six Months," *FRUS, 1964–1968*, 7, 255.

82 Elsey, meeting notes, 5 November 1968, *FRUS, 1964–1968*, 7, 195. At this meeting, Clifford claimed that Thieu "wants the war to go on forever" because his government "is getting richer and richer." How Clifford came to this interpretation of Thieu's motives remains a mystery as it was not an interpretation shared by U.S. intelligence agencies or other U.S. officials. Concerning the inclusion of Communists in the South Vietnamese government, see Harriman, "General Review Of Last Six Months," 14 December 1968, *FRUS, 1964–1968*, 7, 255.

83 Harriman, "General Review Of Last Six Months," 14 December 1968, *FRUS, 1964–1968*, 7, 255.

84 *Department of State Bulletin*, 2 December 1968, 568–573. For the lack of White House clearance, see Rostow, "Sec. Clifford's Press Conference of November 12, 1968," 23 November 1968, LBJL, NSF, VNCF, box 138.

85 CIA, "President Thieu's Remarks on U.S./South Vietnamese Relations and His Justification for His Initial Negative Reaction to President Johnson's Announcement," 19 November 1968, *FRUS, 1964–1968*, 7, 225.

86 Clifford, *Counsel to the President*, 601.

87 Saigon to State, 15 November 1968, *FRUS, 1964–1968*, 7, 222.

88 *Department of State Bulletin*, 16 December 1968, 621–622.

89 Saigon to State, 21 October 1968, LBJL, NSF, VNCF, box 124; FBI to White House, 21 December 1968, LBJL, Reference File, Chennault; Saigon to State, 23 December 1968, NA II, RG 59, Central Files, 1967–1969, box 2727; Luu Van Loi and Nguyen Anh Vu, *Le Duc Tho-Kissinger Negotiations in Paris*, 52–53.

90 Nguyen Phu Duc, *The Viet-Nam Peace Negotiations*, 171–173; Holbrooke, memcon, 11 December 1968, *FRUS, 1964–1968*, 7, 250; Rostow to Johnson, 12 December 1968, *FRUS, 1964–1968*, 7, 252. North Vietnamese and South Vietnamese diplomats also wrangled over the order of speaking. Hanoi wanted the order to be determined by drawing four names at random from a hat. Saigon wanted only two names to be drawn.

91 For a summation of their arguments, see Saigon to State, 19 December 1968, in Pike, ed., *The Bunker Papers*, 3, 629–630.

92 CBS News, transcript of Face the Nation, 15 December 1968, LBJL, Clifford Papers, box 16. See also Robert G. Kaiser, "Clifford Sees Limited U.S. Role in Talks," *Washington Post*, 16 December 1968; Drea, *McNamara, Clifford, and the Burdens of Vietnam*, 200–201.

93 Paul Hofmann, "Clifford Assailed by Ky for Stand on Lag in Parley," *New York Times*, 17 December 1968.

94 CIA, "President Thieu's Angry Reaction to Statements Made by U.S. Secretary of Defense Clifford," 21 December 1968, CREST, document number 0000880869. To a group of reporters at Vung Tau, Thieu remarked that statements like Clifford's encouraged Hanoi to become more rigid in its negotiating position, making diplomatic progress harder. Saigon to State, 23 December 1968, NA II, RG 59, Central Files, 1967–1969, box 2727.

95 State to Moscow, 26 November 1968, *FRUS, 1964–1968*, 14, 325.

96 *The Joint Chiefs of Staff and the War in Vietnam*, Chapter 52, 37–38. A few days before Clifford's speech, Abrams had remarked bitterly about the North Vietnamese, "I am fully aware of all the 'conversations' about 'good will and serious intent.' There has been no evidence of either." Abrams to Wheeler, 11 December 1968, LBJL, NSF, Memos to the President, Walt Rostow, box 43.

97 James Webb, "The Price of Duty," *Parade*, 27 May 2001.

98 Vo Tran Nha, ed., *Lich Su Dong Thap Muoi: Gui Nguoi Dang Song* (Ho Chi Minh City: Ho Chi Minh City Publishing House, 1993), 347.

99 Nguyen Huu Nguyen, *Long An*, 269–270.

100 Hunt, *Pacification*, 173, 182.

101 *The Joint Chiefs of Staff and the War in Vietnam*, Chapter 52, 50.

102 In addition to the sources in the preceding section and following section, see Dang Van Nhung et al., *Su Doan 7*, 85–86.

103 Hunt, *Pacification*, 188–192; Lewy, *America in Vietnam*, 141–144; Hammond, *Public Affairs: The Military and the Media, 1968–1973*, 238–242.

104 Vo Tran Nha, ed., *Lich Su Dong Thap Muoi*, 345 (quote); Le Quoc San, *Cuoc Do Suc Than Ky*, 363.

105 One North Vietnamese account stated, "We were able to recruit only a small number of replacements from the local population, because we were gradually losing our liberated zones that had a civilian population." Nguyen Viet Ta et al., *Mien Dong Nam Bo Khang Chien*, Tap II, 372.

106 Embrey, "Reorienting Pacification," 153–154; *The Joint Chiefs of Staff and the War in Vietnam*, Chapter 52, 47.

107 Bernard C. Nalty, *The War against Trucks: Aerial Interdiction in Southern Laos, 1968–1972* (Washington, D.C.: Air Force History and Museums Program, 2005), 98–106.

108 Pham Te, *Nhung Nam Thang Soi Dong Nhat Tren Duong Ho Chi Minh* (Ho Chi Minh City: Ho Chi Minh City Publishing House, 1994), 10.

109 Nguyen The Ky and Nguyen Si, *Cu Truong Son–Duong khat vong* (Hanoi: Nha Xuat Ban Chinh Tri Quoc Gia, 2009), 146–147 (quote); Pham Te, *Nhung Nam Thang Soi Dong Nhat Tren Duong Ho Chi Minh*, 11–15; Luu Van Loi, *Le Duc Tho-Kissinger Negotiations in Paris*, 66.

110 Vietnam Documents and Research Notes, No. 59, "To Urgently Produce Secondary Crops and Food During the Winter-Spring and the 1968–1969 Rice Crop," 29 November 1968, TTU, Viet-Nam Documents and Research Notes Collection, box 1.

111   Johnson, meeting notes, 29 October 1968, *FRUS, 1964–1968*, 7, 140. The CIA continued to take issue with the military's view that Cambodia was a vital source of supply for the enemy. CIA analyst Jim Graham played down the importance of infiltration of arms and ammunition from Cambodia to South Vietnam, claiming that most came from the Ho Chi Minh Trail. Thomas L. Ahern Jr., *Good Questions, Wrong Answers: CIA Estimates of Arms Traffic Through Sihanoukville, Cambodia, During the Vietnam War* (Washington, DC: Center for the Study of Intelligence, 2004), 15–16. This stance would be decisively discredited following the overthrow of Sihanouk in 1970, which gave the United States access to overwhelming evidence of North Vietnamese movement of supplies through Cambodia. Ibid., xi–xii.

112   Sorley, ed., *Vietnam Chronicles*, 77.

113   Spector, *After Tet*, 240–241; Shulimson et al., *Marines in Vietnam: The Defining Year*, 411.

114   Dorland, *Legacy of Discord*, 157–158.

115   Joseph L. Galloway and Marvin J. Wolf, *They Were Soldiers: The Sacrifices and Contributions of our Vietnam Veterans* (Nashville: Nelson Books, 2020), 214–215.

116   Littauer and Uphoff, eds. *Air War in Indochina*, 269.

117   Ibid. Official North Vietnamese accounts provide much lower figures, listing Communist casualties for the year at 113,295. Tran Bach Dang, *Lich su Nam Bo Khang Chien*, Tap II (Hanoi: National Political Publishing House, 2010), 673.

118   For infiltration, see Combined Intelligence Center Vietnam, Order of Battle Summary, September 1972, 2, Records of the Military Assistance Command Vietnam, Part 2, Classified Studies from the Combined Intelligence Center Vietnam, 1965–1973, reel 18. The annual total is not far off the figure of 140,000 provided in a North Vietnamese history. Tran Van Quang et al., *Tong Ket Cuoc Khang Chien Chong My Cuu Nuoc*, 314. For the estimate of recruitment and impressment, which was based upon less reliable information, see MACV, 1968 Command History, 88–89. The change in North Vietnamese strength comes from Combined Intelligence Center Vietnam, Order of Battle Summary, September 1972, 2, Records of the Military Assistance Command Vietnam, Part 2, Classified Studies from the Combined Intelligence Center Vietnam, 1965–1973, reel 18. Precise figures on captures are not available; the 14,000 figure is an estimate based on the ratio of killed to captured of 13 to 1 in 1967. Special National Intelligence Estimate 14.3-67, "Capabilities of the Vietnamese Communists for Fighting in South Vietnam," 13 November 1967, LBJL, Gibbons Papers, box 32.

119   Hoang Van Thai, "May Van De Ve Chien Luoc Trong Cuoc Tien Cong Va Noi Day Xuan 1968," *Tap Chi Lich Su Quan Su*, 26, No. 2 (1988), 24.

120   The figure of 480,000 is the sum of 435,000 for the period from the beginning of the war to the end of 1968 and roughly 45,000 in the first three months of 1969. Thayer, *War Without Fronts*, 102; Littauer and Uphoff, eds. *Air War in Indochina*, 270.

121 Oriana Fallaci, "'Americans Will Lose,' Says Gen. Giap," *Washington Post*, 6 April 1969. Vietnamese Communist leaders were known for using inaccurate statistics in public statements in the interest of making their side appear more successful. At the end of 1968, Ho Chi Minh had declared that in a year of "glorious victories," Communist forces had killed 165,555 enemy troops, which was nearly four times the actual number of allied fatalities. MACV, 1968 Command History, 2. The Vietnamese Communists provided further corroboration of the proximity of their casualty figures to American figures in a postwar disclosure of total losses from 1960 to 1975. During that period, they stated, they lost 849,018 killed plus approximately 232,000 missing and 463,000 wounded. Casualties fluctuated considerably from year to year, but a degree of accuracy can be inferred from the fact that 500,000 was 59 percent of the 849,018 total and that 59 percent of the war's days had passed by the time of Fallaci's conversation with Giap. The killed in action figure comes from "Special Subject 4: The Work Of Locating And Recovering The Remains Of Martyrs From Now Until 2020 And Later Years," downloaded on 1 December 2017 from the Vietnamese government website datafile. chinhsachquandoi.gov.vn/Quản%20lý%20chỉ%20đạo/Chuyên%20đề%204. doc. The above figures on missing and wounded were calculated using Hanoi's declared casualty ratios for the period from 1945 to 1979, during which time the Communists incurred 1.1 million killed, 300,000 missing, and 600,000 wounded. Ho Khang, ed., *Lich Su Khang Chien Chong My, Cuu Nuoc 1954–1975, Tap VIII: Toan Thang* (Hanoi: Nha Xuat Ban Chinh Tri Quoc Gia, 2008), 463.

122 In December, the North Vietnamese did come up with one new idea for hastening victory, although it is not clear how likely they believed it to succeed. Inspired by memories of the overthrow of Ngo Dinh Diem, the Politburo directed COSVN to foment a coup in Saigon by manipulating pro-French elements in the South Vietnamese government. Hanoi could then launch an aggressive military campaign that would force Nixon to remove all American troops in rapid fashion. Instigating a coup would be far more difficult than in prior years, though, because Hanoi's underground in Saigon lay in ruins. Dao Trong Cang, ed., *Van Kien Dang*, Tap 29, 1968, 549–551.

123 Saigon to State, 19 December 1968, in Pike, ed., *The Bunker Papers*, 3, 630.

124 Saigon to State, 28 December 1968, *FRUS, 1964–1968*, 7, 265.

125 MACV, 1968 Command History, 303–304.

126 Saigon to State, 19 October 1968, in Pike, ed., *The Bunker Papers*, 2, 608; Saigon to State, 6 May 1969, in Pike, ed., *The Bunker Papers*, 3, 680.

127 Saigon to State, 19 October 1968, in Pike, ed., *The Bunker Papers*, 2, 608.

128 Littauer and Uphoff, eds. *Air War in Indochina*, 268–269.

129 Saigon to State, 19 December 1968, in Pike, ed., *The Bunker Papers*, 3, 635.

130 CIA, National Intelligence Estimate 50-68, "Southeast Asia After Vietnam," 14 November 1968, CREST, document number 0001166458.

131 Army veteran Gil Dorland captured the Zeitgeist of the intelligentsia in describing an event he attended at Vanderbilt University during this period.

In an auditorium packed with enthralled faculty and students, William
Sloane Coffin, the chaplain of Yale University, railed against the war. When a
young veteran spoke up to say that he was proud to have served his country
in Vietnam, Coffin "verbally dismembered" him, in Dorland's description.
"The audience of intelligent Americans was on its feet, hooting and jeering
the soldier," Dorland recounted. "I thought they were going to lynch him.
Then, I saw his legs. They were cut off at the thighs—blown off by a VC land
mine. I was sick and angry; I ran outside and vomited." Dorland, *Legacy of
Discord*, xi.

132 Mueller, *War, Presidents, and Public Opinion*, 52–57.

133 Louis Harris, "De-Escalation of War Gains Public Favor," *Washington Post*, 7
October 1968.

134 Mueller, *War, Presidents and Public Opinion*, 92; Lunch and Peter W. Sperlich,
"American Public Opinion and the War in Vietnam," 27. The raw data are
available on the website of the Inter-university Consortium for Political
and Social Research. The 1966 and 1968 data were erroneously reversed in
Gibbons, *The U.S. Government and the Vietnam War*, 3, 143.

135 Moyar, *Triumph Forsaken*, 414.

136 Several political scientists have concluded, based upon the experiences
of Vietnam and other wars, that wartime public opinion in the United
States has generally been based upon rational assessment of the war and
its relationship to U.S. interests. Bruce Russett, *Controlling the Sword: The
Democratic Governance of National Security* (Cambridge: Harvard University
Press, 1990); Eric V. Larson, *Casualties and Consensus: The Historical Role of
Casualties in Domestic Support for U.S. Military Operations* (Santa Monica:
Rand, 1996); Christopher Gelpi, Peter D. Feaver, and Jason Reifler, *Paying
the Human Costs of War: American Public Opinion and Casualties in Military
Conflicts* (Princeton: Princeton University Press, 2009).

137 See, for instance, Louis Harris, "Raids on N. Viet-Nam Strongly Supported,"
Washington Post, 22 February 1965; Louis Harris, "Viet Policy Supported, But
With Misgivings," 28 June 1965.

INDEX

II Corps, 40, 110, 114, 144, 149, 190, 251, 314, 378

III Corps, 106, 114, 149, 161, 189, 241, 288, 379, 455, 478, 544

IV Corps, 78, 79, 149, 224

COSVN. *See* Central Office for South Vietnam

Cronkite, Walter, 398–99, 440

Cultural Revolution (China). *See* Great Proletarian Cultural Revolution

Cushman, Robert E., 423–24

Cuu, Pham Cong, 56

Czech Communist Party, 494

Dac, Tran Van, 464

Dak To, 271, 316, 337, 339, 340, 343

Da Nang, 126, 127, 130, 133, 149, 150, 155, 311, 493

Dang, Tran Bach, 503

Dang Van Quang. *See* Quang, Dang Van

Dang Vu Hiep. *See* Hiep, Dang Vu

Daniel, Charles L., 381

Darlac Province, 224

Davidson, Phillip B., 371

Davis, Angela, 324

Davis, Raymond, 467

Davis, Rennie, 498, 499

Dellinger, David, 498–99

De Man, Paul, 324

Democratic National Convention, 499

Deng Xiaoping, 146

Denton, Jeremiah, 175, 177

Denver Post, 261

DePuy, William, 219, 442; arrival of, 160; background on, 161; "fighting positions," 249; intensive attrition of North Vietnamese forces, 22;

officers relieved by, 162; speech to troops, 185–86

Derrida, Jacques, 324

De Saussure, Edward H., 218, 220

Diem, Bui, 518, 529, 533

Diem, Ngo Dinh: assassination of, 19, 199; Can Lao Party of, 128; Chennault and, 519

Dien Bien Phu, 266, 373–74, 413, 415, 436

Dirksen, Everett, 98, 322, 530

DMZ: American and South Vietnamese battalions crossing into, 268; clearing for barrier near, 287; Communist units sitting idle in hideouts within, 221, 266; lack of preparedness among the Marine units near, 424; network of strongpoints built near, 222; North Vietnamese activity near, 542; Operation Hickory and, 268, 284; permission received to fire artillery into, 253; request for authorization of B-52 strikes in, 192; unleashing of new array of firepower on, 313

Dobrynin, Anatoly, 89, 239, 487

Don, Tran Van, 126

Dong, Nam, 378

Dong, Pham Van: demands of, 96, 228, 232; meeting of Marcovich and Aubrac with, 305; meeting of Zhou Enlai with, 452; objection to reciprocity, 234

Dong, Truong Cong, 318

Dong Ha, 222

Dong Xoai, 77

Dos Passos, John, 261

draft, 325–29

Draude, Thomas, 140